INTERNATIONAL
POLITICAL
ECONOMY

INTERNATIONAL POLITICAL ECONOMY

A Reader

Kendall W. Stiles
Bowling Green State University

Tsuneo Akaha
Monterey Institute of International Studies

HarperCollins*Publishers*

Sponsoring Editor: Catherine Woods
Project Editor: Diane Rowell
Art Direction: Teri Delgado
Cover Illustration: Ben Arrington
Production: Willie Lane/Sunaina Sehwani
Compositor: ComCom Division of Haddon Craftsmen, Inc.
Printer and Binder: R. R. Donnelley & Sons Company
Cover Printer: Lynn Art Offset Corporation

INTERNATIONAL POLITICAL ECONOMY: A Reader

Library of Congress Cataloging-in-Publication Data

International political economy : a reader   /   [edited by] Tsuneo Akaha,
   Kendall Stiles.
      p.   cm.
   Includes index.
   ISBN 0-673-46382-6
   1. International economic relations.   I. Akaha, Tsuneo, 1949–
II. Stiles, Kendall W.
HF1359.I586   1991   90-19363
337—dc20   CIP

94 9 8 7 6 5 4

Contents

Part Four   The Politics of International Investment 205

Part Five   Aid For the Poor 267

Part Six   Political Economy of Security 331

Part Seven   Southern Choices 383

Preface

For the past twenty years, traditional Western conceptions of global order have been dispelled one by one. The collapse of the Bretton Woods system of fixed exchange rates in 1971 was hardly noticed by the American public, but its effects are as far reaching as "stagflation" in the 1970s and the U.S. budget and trade deficits of the 1980s. The emergence of the Asian "tigers" (South Korea, Taiwan, Singapore, and Hong Kong) as well as the near superiority of Japan over Atlantic industries have led to an agonizing reappraisal of fundamental economic and social values, including the American work ethic and the European welfare state. The Third World emerged in this period as a force with which to be reckoned. The OPEC-engineered oil price hikes have permanently changed Western energy politics, and the call for a "New International Economic Order" by an at least superficially united Third World coalition dominates the agenda of major international public institutions. The dawning of the "Information Age" and the resulting global network have linked together individuals and businesses far beyond what governments can manage or control. Nations of the world are more and more permeable—susceptible to outside influence—to the point that the classic "domestic versus foreign" dichotomy has lost much of its relevance. Finally, the astonishing changes in the political economy of Europe have left traditionalists with few answers and many questions—Is Gorbachev for real? Will Eastern Europe join Western Europe in a continental economic compact? Will the European Community's plans for complete market unification in 1992 result in a "fortress Europe," suspicious of outside business?

These major changes all fall under the general heading of "international political economy" (IPE), and their dominance of recent news headlines helps explain scholars' attraction to their study. Perhaps even more important than intellectual curiosity is the urgency of identifying central ordering principles and providing some possible solutions to some of the world's most pressing problems—environmental decay, Third World debt, chaos and uncertainty in international trading and financial circles, global poverty and hunger, and the business of global violence. IPE is far from a purely academic endeavor—its research agenda is closely tied to the fast changing real world around us. For all of these reasons, the study of IPE is expanding dramatically in academic and governmental circles. Furthermore, for these reasons, IPE is of great importance to the advanced undergraduate and graduate student of international affairs. It is to this end that this reader has been compiled.

This book is aimed at offering the student and scholar alike the best of what IPE has to offer in the way of insights and findings. In addition to providing selections from well-known experts in the field, the book also offers a broad range of perspectives and viewpoints—the stuff of lively intellectual debate. The three dominant perspectives of IPE—realist, liberal, and radical—are well represented, and writings by authors with differing approaches are often juxtaposed to facilitate and invite comparison and contrast. In addition to the dominant theories of IPE—*hegemonic stability, regimes, world-system theory*—the responses of critics and a few notable mavericks in the field are included.

The book first presents discussions of economic policy issues most frequently addressed by IPE analysts and policy makers: trade, finance, investment, and aid. These policy concerns need to be understood against the backdrop of broad global trends such as changing international leadership patterns, structural changes in the world economy, increasingly crucial relationships between economics and national and international security, and international order. Therefore, these broad trends and debates about them are also presented in subsequent sections, again from different and conflicting perspectives. It is anticipated that a reasonable mix of conceptual work and policy-oriented studies will help the student to relate ideas to action, perspectives to policy.

The authors of these selections differ in terms of backgrounds and characteristics. While most are traditional academics, some authors are also engaged in policy dialogue with public officials (see the selections by Sewell & Contee, Huntington, Morse), some operate in purely research capacities (Galtung), and some are best-selling authors (Kennedy). A significant number of women (six) and non-Americans (seven) authored these selections, which provides a much broader coverage of the field than is typical for a text. Finally, although political scientists dominate the table of contents, roughly half of the authors are either economists, sociologists, or historians. What these differences of background and opinion should demonstrate to the reader is the very interdisciplinary nature of IPE and the high tolerance for diversity on the part of many IPE scholars—a tolerance that is shared by the editors of this volume. The one significant bias present in the work is the consistent selection of English-language articles and book excerpts, which places some limit on the potential range of perspectives.

What follows is a brief history of the field of IPE, including a more precise specification of the substance and scope of IPE research.

What is IPE? In answering this question, it may be useful to indicate what IPE is not. IPE is not a *policy* sub-field of international economics. While many economists contribute to IPE, they typically do so by moving against the current of their deductively oriented discipline. IPE is likewise not merely a sub-field of political science, even though some IPE sociologists have wondered whether this is the case. Political scientists who focus on IPE questions have had to develop new concepts—often borrowing insights from other disciplines—and take a much broader and comprehensive approach than either area studies specialists or scholars of security issues such as arms races and terrorism. Finally, IPE is not a theory. As already emphasized, the field of IPE pulls together a variety of concepts, assumptions, and approaches, as well as a variety of methods and epistemic schemes, which undermine attempts at a single *paradigm* of IPE.

IPE is, however, the study of those international and global phenomena that have an inherently economic, political, and social dimension. IPE scholars are often concerned with the intersection of economics and politics: more fundamentally, they look for developments in a world in which economics and politics—wealth and power—are intertwined at the most basic level. IPE emphasizes the symbiosis of wealth and power on the global stage, and does not attempt to separate them. Attention to and tolerance of complex and interactive dynamics is characteristic of IPE research. It is perhaps due to the recognition that economic and political forces are frequently enmeshed with each other that the field has chosen to use the nineteenth century term *political economy.*

Examples of these types of "political economy" phenomena would include the market for oil, the global division of labor resulting from multinational corporate structures, economic integration, the organization of Third World debt, and the economic costs of military investments and commitments to gain international political influence and enhance national security. IPE scholars not only focus on *political economy* phenomena, but they also tend to adopt a much larger temporal scope. Specifically, many IPE scholars approach current problems of debt and trade from very long-term perspectives.

The typical study of contemporary trade and finance begins with the establishment of the Bretton Woods in 1944. Studies of American *hegemony* (political and economic dominance over the free world) looks at the nineteenth century as a frame of reference. Some studies of global economic cycles adopt a 500-year time frame. Paul Kennedy's major work begins with empires that emerged shortly after the time of Christ! The more comprehensive historical perspectives provide many unusual and important insights not attainable by focusing on the current or near future. For example, Immanuel Wallerstein sees parallels in the way the Latin American colonies served their Spanish motherland in the sixteenth century and how American corporations intertwined Third World subsidiaries and the *home office*. Robert Gilpin and Robert Keohane have pointed out that American efforts to create and perpetuate a free trade system in the West are similar to how Great Britain dominated the world in the late-nineteenth century. Attention to how history repeats itself in cycles or patterns has almost always yielded valuable insights for those devoted to avoiding the mistakes of the past.

Finally, IPE scholars are sensitive to the domestic/foreign policy nexus and the intricate and often variable relationships between governments and the societies in which they are found. Traditional concepts of comparative politics are often discarded by IPE scholars who appreciate symbiotic and dynamic causal relationships. Just as IPE scholars discard the politics vs. economics dichotomy, they tend to deemphasize the domestic vs. foreign and state vs. society conceptions of other disciplines (political science in particular). The recognition of the interplay between these actors, and even their periodic merger and blending, has had a liberating effect on the theoretical constructs that IPE scholars can develop.

Lest the reader assume that IPE is a purely modern invention, it is important to emphasize the links between the field and social science literature. Because IPE is rich and diverse, the intellectual heritage is likewise varied. (The reader is encouraged to read carefully the first selection by Robert Gilpin.) The realist, liberal, and radical traditions that are preserved in IPE have their roots in centuries-old debates over theory and values.

Perhaps the oldest tradition in IPE is the realist approach, since its roots are contained in the practices of such ancient political actors as the Greek city-states. Primarily during the Renaissance period, it was widely assumed that a realist approach was more useful for explaining international political economy phenomena. During the sixteenth and seventeenth centuries, it was generally believed that a principal purpose of statesmanship was the enrichment of the state itself. The classic empires of Spain and Portugal were largely tribute and wealth generating machines which brought untold millions of gold and silver specie into the European economy. This activity was assumed to be both legitimate and prudent, since the result was the dominance of the Iberian peninsula on nearly four continents. Until a stormy day in the English Channel decimated the Spanish Armada, the realist emphasis on state enrichment and power was unchallenged.

During the latter part of the eighteenth century, writers such as Adam Smith and David Ricardo began questioning the merits of a state-centric conception of political economy. They developed theories of economic life based on the vitality of autonomous investment and unregulated commerce. While far from being "supply siders," these early liberals helped to lay the conceptual groundwork for the "laissez-faire" regime of the Industrial Revolution of the nineteenth century. By this time, the state was expected to play a secondary role in economic life: the provider and enforcer of basic property and contract law. While it is now well known that the capitalist system was anything but politically neutral, the conceptual dichotomization of economics and politics began during this period.

It took such writers as Marx and Engels, Kautsky and Lenin, to challenge the capitalist bourgeois paradigm. These radical authors assumed the interplay between state and society, power and wealth, and developed a theoretical and political model that not only explained such capitalist *externalities* as unemployment and pollution in terms of profit maximization and elite collusion, but also assisted in developing a plan to bring these social ills to an end through revolutionary change. First Soviet and then Chinese scholars of the twentieth century adapted the central radical concepts that explained domestic class warfare into a theory of global imperialism and worldwide division of labor. In the postwar period, these ideas gave birth to the *dependency* school, which argued that even if the imperialist institutions of colonizing armies and slavery were removed, the Third World was still dependent on the industrialized "First" world for its future economic and social progress. What is interesting from a theoretical perspective, is that this dependency theory actually led to the implicit adoption of the most traditional form of state-centric realism on the part of many developing nations and their governments.

It is interesting to see the connections between these philosophical and theoretical traditions. At the center of the debate are the age old questions of causal primacy—Does the state dominate international life, or is it simply tossed about by global economic interests? Which is more important: growth and technological progress or equity and social justice? Can international order and stability be maintained without sacrificing freedom and national identity?

Each section begins with some introductory comments by the editors about the central themes and issues of concern to IPE students and policymakers and how the substantive selections address them. The introductory comments also raise some key questions to guide the reader's adventure into the theoretical and policy debates.

What follows are additional, broader questions that are suggested for further discussion and research in IPE courses.

• Which IPE approaches offer the most compelling explanation of overall global dynamics? Are there logical or empirical inconsistencies that undermine the theory? Which approach offers the most useful policy suggestions for addressing pressing current problems? Are there ideas in these selections that you would hope the current leaders of the world are aware of and are taking into account when making policy?

• How have the central debates changed over time? Are some debates of a purely conceptual nature? Do they matter, or are they pertinent to understanding causal dynamics in real-world situations?

• What are the views on how the world ought to be organized and led? What is the proper and/or necessary role for the U.S. today? Has U.S. leadership since 1945 been beneficial to the people and nations of the world? Does the world economy require the type of leadership America provided? Would a consortium of several powerful nations do the job better? How do the weak take part in planning and managing the global system?

• What does the future hold? Will the Third World continue to slip further and further toward the precipice of total economic chaos? Will Eastern Europe and the Soviet Union follow them? Will the U.S. choose confrontation as a way out of its growing pressures? Will Tokyo be the global "hegemon" in the next century? How do I, as an individual, fit in?

Acknowledgments

Many individuals have contributed to this book, the most significant group being those authors whose work has been reprinted here. To them we extend our heartfelt thanks for allowing us to combine in one volume their collective wisdom and scholarly achievements. We firmly believe that the result is a helpful and significant contribution to IPE curriculum. In particular, we appreciate the candid and helpful comments of Robert Keohane, Teresa Hayter, David Law and Stephen Gill. We also would like to thank Vincent Ferraro (Mount Holyoke College), Vincent A. Mahler (Loyola University), and Chung-in Moon (University of Kentucky) for their valuable recommendations as reviewers of the final draft manuscript. We would especially like to thank those many authors who accepted minimal or no financial reward for reprinting their articles in order to do their part to contain the ever-rising costs of higher education.

We would like to thank those editors and project heads from both Scott Foresman/Little, Brown—where this project had its early genesis—and HarperCollins, for shepherding this book through the tortuous path of academic publishing and corporate merger. In particular, we thank Bruce Nichols, Richard Welna, Lauren Silverman, and Catherine Woods.

Finally, we thank those close to us for their support and encouragement. Specifically, we thank our respective institutions, Bowling Green State University and the Monterey Institute of International Studies, for providing essential logistical support. Also, we thank our colleagues in the International Political Economy section of the International Studies Association for their comments and promotional assistance. And, lastly, we thank our spouses without whose active interest this project would have been a lonely and tedious endeavor. Although we cannot claim sole responsibility for this book's strengths, we do accept ownership of its weaknesses.

Kendall Stiles
Tsuneo Akaha

Part
One

PERSPECTIVES OF IPE

*P*art One introduces a few of the most important perspectives and arguably the most influential world views in IPE: liberalism, nationalism, Marxism, world-systems approach, and dependency theory. Each perspective represents a distinct intellectual tradition within the field. We do not contend that these are the only perspectives that qualify as such, nor do we presume that every IPE scholar accepts the characterization of each perspective offered by the three articles included in this section. We do maintain, however, that the three works represent some of the best discussions available on the basic premises, theoretical foci, and normative concerns of the perspectives they introduce. The reader is invited to return to the brief overview of IPE theory presented in the introduction.

In "Three Ideologies of Political Economy," Robert Gilpin introduces liberalism, nationalism, and Marxism as ideologies representing conflicting moral and intellectual models regarding the role and significance of the market in the organization of society and economic affairs. Liberalism, which emerged from the Enlightenment in the writings of Adam Smith and others, assumes that politics and economics are separate spheres of human society and that markets should be kept free from political influence. Economic nationalism, or "mercantilism," has developed from the practices of statesmen in the early modern times and assumes and advocates the subordination of economics to politics. Marxism, which appeared in the mid-nineteenth century as a radical reaction to liberalism and economic nationalism, asserts that economic relationships in society define and give rise to class conflict and determine the distribution of wealth.

Chase-Dunn and Rubinson introduce the reader to a structuralist approach to international political economy known as the "world-system" approach. Originally formulated by Fernand Braudel, Immanuel Wallerstein, and others, the approach assumes the international economic and political system is dominated by a capitalist international division of labor. More specifically, the authors argue that since the sixteenth century, the world has been divided into "core" states and "periphery" states. In the core is found the most dynamic of all global activities at any given point in history: The most advanced production techniques, the most sophisticated communication and transportation devices, the leading financial institutions. The world-system approach assumes that this dynamic core derives its power and vitality from its dominant position over the periphery of the system, which serves to function as provider of labor, raw materials, investment opportunities, and markets. A "semiperiphery" acts as a conduit for core influence and is made up of moderately developed nations (either in ascendance or in decline).

Caporaso introduces yet another tradition: dependency theory. Initially conceived as a critical response to liberal theories of economic development, dependency theory has challenged the basic tenets of liberalism. The author outlines the nature of the challenge through a review of two works on the history of Latin American economic development. According to Caporaso, dependency theory offers an explanation for "dependent development" (see the Evans selection in Part IV) by focusing on both domestic and external factors and their interactions, and on the interests and behavior of the nation-states, corporate entities, and social classes. Dependency theorists attempt not only to explain reality but also to use theory ideas to change reality, and to promote development in developing countries. Finally, according to Caporaso, dependency theorists reject the mainstream assumption that all societies follow the same developmental path.

A careful reader may find some direction in these articles in answering the following fundamental questions: What role does government have in economic development within and among nations? If government has some role, what legitimate means can it employ to influence the character of economic development? If government influence is to be minimized, what private sector institutions should be nurtured and promoted to meet the nation's developmental needs? Is it inevitable that nations which hold to conflicting perspectives on the proper economic role of government will conflict with each other? Have global circumstances changed so much in the past generation that no developing country can be guided by the past experiences of now industrialized nations? Moreover, if economic development in today's developing countries is conditioned by external factors and past developments, is the pursuit of autonomous economic development—a professed goal of many governments in the Third World—nothing more than an unrealizable dream or empty rhetoric?

Three Ideologies of Political Economy

Robert Gilpin

Over the past century and a half, the ideologies of liberalism, nationalism, and Marxism have divided humanity. This book uses "ideology" to refer to "systems of thought and belief by which (individuals and groups) explain . . . how their social system operates and what principles it exemplifies" (Heilbroner, 1985, p. 107.) The conflict among these three moral and intellectual positions has revolved around the role and significance of the market in the organization of society and economic affairs.

Through an evaluation of the strengths and weaknesses of these three ideologies it is possible to illuminate the study of the field of international political economy. The strengths of each perspective set forth here will be applied to subsequent discussions of specific issues, such as those of trade, investment, and development. Although my values are those of liberalism, the world in which we live is one best described by the ideas of economic nationalism and occasionally by those of Marxism as well. Eclecticism may not be the route to theoretical precision, but sometimes it is the only route available.

The three ideologies differ on a broad range of questions such as: What is the significance of the market for economic growth and the distribution of wealth among groups and societies? What ought to be the role of markets in the organization of domestic and international society? What is the effect of the market system on issues of war or peace? These and similar questions are central to discussions of international political economy.

These three ideologies are fundamentally different in their conceptions of the relationships among society, state, and market, and it may not be an exaggeration to say that every controversy in the field of international political economy is ultimately reducible to differing conceptions of these relationships. The intellectual clash is not merely of historical inter-

Robert Gilpin, *Political Economy of International Relations.* Copyright © 1987 Princeton University Press. Excerpt, pp. 25–41, 43–54, reprinted with permission of Princeton University Press.

est. Economic liberalism, Marxism, and economic nationalism are all very much alive at the end of the twentieth century; they define the conflicting perspectives that individuals have with regard to the implications of the market system for domestic and international society. Many of the issues that were controversial in the eighteenth and nineteenth centuries are once again being intensely debated.

It is important to understand the nature and content of these contrasting "ideologies" of political economy. The term *ideology* is used rather than *theory* because each position entails a total belief system concerning the nature of human beings and society and is thus akin to what Thomas Kuhn has called a paradigm (Kuhn, 1962). As Kuhn demonstrates, intellectual commitments are held tenaciously and can seldom be dislodged by logic or by contrary evidence. This is due to the fact that these commitments or ideologies allege to provide scientific descriptions of how the world *does* work while they also constitute normative positions regarding how the world *should* work.

Although scholars have produced a number of "theories" to explain the relationship of economics and politics, these three stand out and have had a profound influence on scholarship and political affairs. In highly oversimplified terms, economic nationalism (or, as it was originally called, mercantilism), which developed from the practice of statesmen in the early modern period, assumes and advocates the primacy of politics over economics. It is essentially a doctrine of statebuilding and asserts that the market should be subordinate to the pursuit of state interests. It argues that political factors do, or at least should, determine economic relations. Liberalism, which emerged from the Enlightenment in the writings of Adam Smith and others, was a reaction to mercantilism and has become embodied in orthodox economics. It assumes that politics and economics exist, at least ideally, in separate spheres; it argues that markets—in the interest of efficiency, growth, and consumer choice—should be free from political interference. Marxism, which appeared in the mid-nineteenth century as a reaction against liberalism and classical economics, holds that economics drives politics. Political conflict arises from struggle among classes over the distribution of wealth. Hence, political conflict will cease with the elimination of the market and of a society of classes. Since both nationalism and Marxism in the modern era have developed largely in reaction to the tenets of liberal economics, my discussion and evaluation of these ideologies will begin with economic liberalism.

THE LIBERAL PERSPECTIVE

Some scholars assert that there is no such thing as a liberal theory of political economy because liberalism separates economics and politics from one another and assumes that each sphere operates according to particular rules and a logic of its own.[1] This view is itself, however, an ideological position and liberal theorists do in fact concern themselves with both political and economic affairs. Whether it is made explicit in their writings or is merely implicit, one can speak of a liberal theory of political economy.

There is a set of values from which liberal theories of economics and of politics arise; in the modern world these political and economic values have tended to appear together (Lindblom, 1977). Liberal economic theory is committed to free markets and minimal state intervention although, as will be pointed out below, the relative emphasis on one or the other may differ. Liberal political theory is committed to individual equality and liberty, although again the emphasis may differ. We are primarily concerned here with the economic component of liberal theory.

The liberal perspective on political economy is embodied in the discipline of economics as it has developed in Great Britain, the United States, and Western Europe. From Adam Smith to its contemporary proponents, liberal thinkers have shared a coherent set of assumptions and beliefs about the nature of human beings, society, and economic activities. Liberalism has assumed many forms—classical, neo-classical, Keynesian, monetarist, Austrian, rational expectation, etc. These variants range from those giving priority to equality and tending toward social democracy and state interventionism to achieve this objective, to those stressing liberty and noninterventionism at the expense of social equality. All forms of economic liberalism, however, are committed to the market and the price mechanism as the most efficacious means for organizing domestic and international economic relations. Liberalism may, in fact, be defined as a doctrine and set of principles for organizing and managing a market economy in order to achieve maximum efficiency, economic growth, and individual welfare.

Economic liberalism assumes that a market arises spontaneously in order to satisfy human needs and that, once it is in operation, it functions in accordance with its own internal logic. Human beings are by nature economic animals, and therefore markets evolve naturally without central direction. As Adam Smith put it, it is inherent in mankind to "truck, barter and exchange." To facilitate exchange and improve their well-being, people create markets, money, and economic institutions. Thus, in his "The Economic Organization of a P.O.W. Camp," R. A. Radford (1945) shows how a complex and sophisticated market arose spontaneously in order to satisfy human wants, but his tale also demonstrates how a form of government was necessary to police and maintain this primitive market system.[2]

The rationale for a market system is that it increases economic efficiency, maximizes economic growth, and thereby improves human welfare. Although liberals believe that economic activity also enhances the power and security of the state, they argue that the primary objective of economic activity is to benefit individual consumers. Their ultimate defense of free trade and open markets is that they increase the range of goods and services available to the consumer.

The fundamental premise of liberalism is that the individual consumer, firm, or household is the basis of society. Individuals behave rationally and attempt to maximize or satisfy certain values at the lowest possible cost to themselves. Rationality applies only to endeavor, not to outcome. Thus, failure to achieve an objective due to ignorance or some other cause does not, according to liberals, invalidate their premise that individuals act on the basis of a cost/benefit or means/ends calculus. Finally, liberalism argues that an individual will seek to acquire an objective until a market equilibrium is reached, that is, until the costs associated with achieving the objective are equal to the benefits. Liberal economists attempt to explain economic and, in some cases, all human behavior on the basis of these individualistic and rationalistic assumptions (Rogowski, 1978).

Liberalism also assumes that a market exists in which individuals have complete information and are thus enabled to select the most beneficial course of action. Individual producers and consumers will be highly responsive to price signals, and this will create a flexible economy in which any change in relative prices will elicit a corresponding change in patterns of production, consumption, and economic institutions; the latter are conceived ultimately to be the product rather than the cause of economic behavior (Davis and North, 1971). Further, in a truly competitive market, the terms of exchange are determined solely by considerations of supply and demand rather than by the exercise of power and coercion. If exchange is voluntary, both parties benefit. In colloquial terms, a "free exchange is no robbery."

Economics, or rather the economics taught in most American universities (what Marxists call orthodox or bourgeois economics), is assumed to be an empirical science of maximizing behavior. Behavior is believed to be governed by a set of economic *laws* that are impersonal and politically neutral; therefore, economics and politics should and can be separated into distinct spheres. Governments should not intervene in the market except where a "market failure" exists (Baumol, 1965) or in order to provide a so-called public or collective good (Olson, 1965).

A market economy is governed principally by the law of demand (Becker, 1976, p. 6). This "law" (or, if one prefers, assumption) holds that people will buy more of a good if the relative price falls and less if it rises; people will also tend to buy more of a good as their relative income rises and less as it falls. Any development that changes the relative price of a good or the relative income of an actor will create an incentive or disincentive to acquire (or produce) more or less of the good; this law in turn has profound ramifications throughout the society. Although certain exceptions to this simple concept exist, it is fundamental to the operation and success of a market system of economic exchange.

On the supply side of the economy, liberal economics assumes that individuals pursue their interests in a world of scarcity and resource constraints. This is a fundamental and inescapable condition of human existence. Every decision involves an opportunity cost, a tradeoff among alternative uses of available resources (Samuelson, 1980, p. 27). The basic lesson of liberal economics is that "there is no such thing as a free lunch"; to get something one must be willing to give up something else.

Liberalism also assumes that a market economy exhibits a powerful tendency toward equilibrium and inherent stability, at least over the long term. This "concept of a self-operating and self-correcting equilibrium achieved by a balance of forces in a rational universe" is a crucial one for the economists' belief in the operation of markets and the laws that are believed to govern them (Condliffe, 1950, p. 112). If a market is thrown into a state of disequilibrium due to some external (exogenous) factor such as a change in consumer tastes or productive technology, the operation of the price mechanism will eventually return it to a new state of equilibrium. Prices and quantities will once again balance one another. Thus, a change in either the supply or the demand for a good will elicit corresponding changes in the price of the good. The principal technique of modern economic analysis, comparative statics, is based on this assumption of a tendency toward systemic equilibrium.[3]

An additional liberal assumption is that a basic long-term harmony of interests underlies the market competition of producers and consumers, a harmony that will supercede any temporary conflict of interest. Individual pursuit of self-interest in the market increases social well-being because it leads to the maximization of efficiency, and the resulting economic growth eventually benefits all. Consequently, everyone will gain in accordance with his or her contribution to the whole, but, it should be added, not everyone will gain equally because individual productivities differ. Under free exchange, society as a whole will be more wealthy, but individuals will be rewarded in terms of their marginal productivity and relative contribution to the overall social product.

Finally, most present-day liberal economists believe in progress, defined most frequently as an increase in wealth per capita. They assert that the growth of a properly functioning economy is linear, gradual, and continuous (Meier and Baldwin, 1963, p. 70). It proceeds along what an economist colleague has called "the MIT standard equilibrium growth curve." Although political or other events—wars, revolution, or natural disasters—can dramatically disrupt this growth path, the economy will return eventually to a stable pattern of growth that is determined principally by increases in population, resources, and productivity. Moreover, liberals see no necessary connection between the process of economic growth and political developments such as war and imperialism; these political evils affect and may be affected by economic activities, but they are essentially caused by political and not by economic factors. For example, liberals do not believe that any causal relationship existed between the advance of capitalism in the late nineteenth century and the upheavals of imperialism after 1870 and the outbreak of the First World War. Liberals believe economics is progressive and politics is retrogressive. Thus they conceive of progress as divorced from politics and based on the evolution of the market.

On the basis of these assumptions and commitments, modern economists have constructed the empirical science of economics. Over the past two centuries, they have deduced the "laws" of maximizing behavior, such as those of the theory of comparative advantage, the theory of marginal utility, and the quantity theory of money. As Arthur Lewis has commented to me, economists discover new laws at the rate of about one per quarter century. These "laws" are both contingent and normative. They assume the existence of economic man—a rational, maximizing creature—a variant of the species homo sapiens that has been relatively rare in human history and has existed only during peculiar periods of favorable conditions. Further, these laws are normative in that they prescribe how a society must organize itself and how people must behave if they are to maximize the growth of wealth. Both individuals and societies may violate these laws, but they do so at the cost of productive efficiency. Today, the conditions necessary for the operation of a market economy exist, and the normative commitment to the market has spread from its birthplace in Western civilization to embrace an increasingly large portion of the globe. Despite setbacks, the modern world has moved in the direction of the market economy and of increasing global economic interdependence precisely because markets *are* more efficient than other forms of economic organization (Hicks, 1969).

In essence, liberals believe that trade and economic intercourse are a source of peaceful relations among nations because the mutual benefits of trade and expanding interdependence among national economies will tend to foster cooperative relations. Whereas politics tends to divide, economics tends to unite peoples. A liberal international economy will have a moderating influence on international politics as it creates bonds of mutual interests and a commitment to the status quo. However, it is important to emphasize again that although everyone will, or at least can, be better off in *absolute* terms under free exchange, the *relative* gains will differ. It is precisely this issue of relative gains and the distribution of the wealth generated by the market system that has given rise to economic nationalism and Marxism as rival doctrines.

THE NATIONALIST PERSPECTIVE

Economic nationalism, like economic liberalism, has undergone several metamorphoses over the past several centuries. Its labels have also changed: mercantilism, statism, protectionism, the German Historical School, and, recently, New Protectionism. Throughout all these manifestations, however, runs a set of themes or attitudes rather than a coherent and systematic body of economic or political theory. Its central idea is that economic activities are and should be subordinate to the goal of state building and the interests of the state. All nationalists ascribe to the primacy of the state, of national security, and of military power in the organization and functioning of the international system. Within this general commitment two basic positions can be discerned. Some nationalists consider the safeguarding of national economic interests as the minimum essential to the security and survival of the state. For lack of a better term, this generally defensive position may be called *benign* mercantilism.[4] On the other hand, there are those nationalists who regard the international economy as an arena for imperialist expansion and national aggrandizement. This aggressive form may be termed *malevolent* mercantilism. The economic policies of Nazi economic minister Hjalmar Schacht toward eastern Europe in the 1930s were of this type (Hirschman, 1969).

Although economic nationalism should be viewed as a general commitment to state building, the precise objectives pursued and the policies advocated have differed in different times and in different places. Yet, as Jacob Viner has cogently argued in an often-quoted passage, economic nationalist (or what he calls mercantilist) writers share convictions concerning the relationship of wealth and power:

> I believe that practically all mercantilists, whatever the period, country, or status of the particular individual, would have subscribed to all of the following propositions: (1) wealth is an absolutely essential means to power, whether for security or for aggression; (2) power is essential or valuable as a means to the acquisition or retention of wealth; (3) wealth and power are each proper ultimate ends of national policy; (4) there is long-run harmony between these ends, although in particular circumstances it may be necessary for a time to make economic sacrifices in the interest of military security and therefore also of long-run prosperity (Viner, 1958, p. 286).

Whereas liberal writers generally view the pursuit of power and wealth, that is, the choice between "guns and butter," as involving a tradeoff, nationalists tend to regard the two goals as being complementary (Knorr, 1944, p. 10).

Economic nationalists stress the role of economic factors in international relations and view the struggle among states—capitalist, socialist, or whatever—for economic resources as pervasive and indeed inherent in the nature of the international system itself. As one writer has put it, since economic resources are necessary for national power, every conflict is at once both economic and political (Hawtrey, 1952). States, at least over the long run, simultaneously pursue wealth and national power.

As it evolved in the early modern era, economic nationalism responded to and reflected the political, economic, and military developments of the sixteenth, seventeenth, and eighteenth centuries: the emergence of strong national states in constant competition, the rise of a middle class devoted at first to commerce and increasingly to manufacturing, and the quickening pace of economic activities due to changes within Europe and the discovery of the New World and its resources. The evolution of a monetarized market economy and the wide range of changes in the nature of warfare that have been characterized as the *Military Revolution* were also critically important (Roberts, 1956). Nationalists (or "mercantilists," as they were then called) had good cause to identify a favorable balance of trade with national security.

For several reasons, the foremost objective of nationalists is industrialization (Sen, 1984). In the first place, nationalists believe that industry has spillover effects (externalities) throughout the economy and leads to its overall development. Second, they associate the possession of industry with economic self-sufficiency and political autonomy. Third, and most important, industry is prized because it is the basis of military power and central to national security in the modern world. In almost every society, including liberal ones, governments pursue policies favorable to industrial development. As the mercantilist theorist of American economic development, Alexander Hamilton, wrote: "not only the wealth but the independence and security of a country appear to be materially connected to the prosperity of manufactures" (quoted in Rostow, 1971, p. 189); no contemporary dependency theorist has put it better. This nationalist objective of industrialization is itself a major source of economic conflict.

Economic nationalism, both in the early modern era and today, arises in part from the tendency of markets to concentrate wealth and to establish dependency or power relations between the strong and the weak economies. In its more benign or defensive form it attempts to protect the economy against untoward external economic and political forces. Defensive economic nationalism frequently exists in less developed economies or in those advanced economies that have begun to decline; such governments pursue protectionist and related policies to protect their nascent or declining industries and to safeguard domestic interests. In its more malevolent form, economic nationalism is the conduct of economic warfare. This type is most prevalent in expanding powers. The classic example is Nazi Germany.

In a world of competing states, the nationalist considers relative gain to be more important than mutual gain. Thus nations continually try to change the rules or regimes governing international economic relations in order to benefit themselves disproportionately with respect to other economic powers. As Adam Smith shrewdly pointed out, everyone wants to be a monopolist and will attempt to be one unless prevented by competitors. Therefore, a liberal international economy cannot develop unless it is supported by the dominant economic states whose own interests are consistent with its preservation.

Whereas liberals stress the mutual benefits of international commerce, nationalists as well as Marxists regard these relations as basically conflictual. Although this does not rule out international economic cooperation and the pursuit of liberal policies, economic interdependence is never symmetrical; indeed, it constitutes a source of continuous conflict and insecurity. Nationalist writers from Alexander Hamilton to contemporary dependency theorists thus emphasize national self-sufficiency rather than economic interdependence.

Economic nationalism has taken several different forms in the modern world. Responding to the Commercial Revolution and the expansion of international trade throughout the early period, classical or financial mercantilism emphasized the promotion of trade and a balance of payments surplus. Following the Industrial Revolution, industrial mercantilists like Hamilton and List stressed the supremacy of industry and manufacturing over agriculture. Following the First and Second World Wars these earlier concerns have been joined by a powerful commitment to the primacy of domestic welfare and the welfare state. In the last decades of this century, the increasing importance of advanced technology, the desire for national control over the *commanding heights* of the modern economy, and the advent of what might best be called *policy competitiveness* have become the distinctive features of contemporary mercantilism. In all ages, however, the desire for power and independence have been the overriding concern of economic nationalists.

Whatever its relative strengths and weaknesses as an ideology or theory of international political economy, the nationalist emphasis on the geographic location and the distribution of economic activities provide it with powerful appeal. Throughout modern history, states have pursued policies promoting the development of industry, advanced technology, and those economic activities with the highest profitability and generation of employment within their own borders. As far as they can, states try to create an international division of labor favorable to their political and economic interests. Indeed, economic nationalism is likely to be a significant influence in international relations as long as the state system exists.

THE MARXIST PERSPECTIVE

Like liberalism and nationalism, Marxism has evolved in significant ways since its basic ideas were set forth by Karl Marx and Friedrich Engels in the middle of the nineteenth century.[5] Marx's own thinking changed during his lifetime, and his theories have always been subject to conflicting interpretations. Although Marx viewed capitalism as a global economy, he did not develop a systematic set of ideas on international relations; this responsibility fell upon the succeeding generation of Marxist writers. The Soviet Union and China, furthermore, having adopted Marxism as their official ideology, have reshaped it when necessary to serve their own national interests.

As in liberalism and nationalism, two basic strands can be discerned in modern Marxism. The first is the evolutionary Marxism of social democracy associated with Eduard Bernstein and Karl Kautsky; in the contemporary world it has tapered off and is hardly distinguishable from the egalitarian form of liberalism. At the other extreme is the revolutionary Marxism of Lenin and, in theory at least, of the Soviet Union. Because of its triumph as the ruling ideology in one of the world's two superpowers, this variation is the more important and will be stressed here.

As Robert Heilbroner (1980) has argued, despite the existence of these different Marxisms, four essential elements can be found in the overall corpus of Marxist writings. The first element is the dialectical approach to knowledge and society that defines the nature of reality as dynamic and conflictual; social disequilibria and consequent change are due to the class struggle and the working out of contradictions inherent in social and political phenomena. There is, according to Marxists, no inherent social harmony or return to equilibrium as liberals believe. The second element is a materialist approach to history; the development of productive forces and economic activities is central to historical change and operates through the class struggle over distribution of the social product. The third is a general view of capitalist development; the capitalist mode of production and its destiny are governed by a set of "economic laws of motion of modern society." The fourth is a normative commitment to socialism; all Marxists believe that a socialist society is both the necessary and desirable end of historical development (Heilbroner, 1980, pp. 20–21). It is only the third of these beliefs that is of interest here.

Marxism characterizes capitalism as the private ownership of the means of production and the existence of wage labor. It believes that capitalism is driven by capitalists striving for profits and capital accumulation in a competitive market economy. Labor has been dispossessed and has become a commodity that is subject to the price mechanism. In Marx's view these two key characteristics of capitalism are responsible for its dynamic nature and make it the most productive economic mechanism yet. Although its historic mission is to develop and unify the globe, the very success of capitalism will hasten its passing. The origin, evolution, and eventual demise of the capitalist mode of production are, according to Marx, governed by three inevitable economic laws.

The first law, the law of disproportionality, entails a denial of Say's law, which (in oversimplified terms) holds that supply creates its own demand so that supply and demand will always be, except for brief moments, in balance (see Sowell, 1972). Say's law maintains that an equilibrating process makes overproduction impossible in a capitalist or market economy. Marx, like John Maynard Keynes, denied that this tendency toward equilibrium existed and argued that capitalist economies tend to overproduce particular types of goods. There is, Marx argued, an inherent contradiction in capitalism between its capacity to produce goods and the capacity of consumers (wage earners) to purchase those goods, so that the constantly recurring disproportionality between production and consumption due to the *anarchy* of the market causes periodic depressions and economic fluctuations. He predicted that these recurring economic crises would become increasingly severe and in time would impel the suffering proletariat to rebel against the system.

The second law propelling the development of a capitalist system, according to Marxism, is the law of the concentration (or accumulation) of capital. The motive force of capitalism is the drive for profits and the consequent necessity for the individual capitalist to accumulate and in-vest. Competition forces the capitalists to increase their efficiency and capital investment or risk extinction. As a result, the evolution of capitalism is toward increasing concentrations of wealth in the hands of the efficient few and the growing impoverishment of the many. With the petite bourgeoisie being pushed down into the swelling ranks of the impoverished proletariat, the reserve army of the unemployed increases, labor's wages decline, and the capitalist society becomes ripe for social revolution.

The third law of capitalism is that of the falling rate of profit. As capital accumulates and becomes more abundant, the rate of return declines, thereby decreasing the incentive to invest. Although classical liberal economists had recognized this possibility, they believed that a solution could be found through such countervailing devices as the export of capital and manufactured goods and the import of cheap food (Mill, 1970 [1848], pp. 97–104). Marx, on the other hand, believed that the tendency for profits to decline was inescapable. As the pressure of competition forces capitalists to increase efficiency and productivity through investment in new labor-saving and more productive technology, the level of unemployment will increase and the rate of profit or surplus value will decrease. Capitalists will thereby lose their incentive to invest in productive ventures and to create employment. This will result in economic stagnation, increasing unemployment, and the *immiserization* of the proletariat. In time, the ever-increasing intensity and depth of the business cycle will cause the workers to rebel and destroy the capitalist economic system.

The core of the Marxist critique of capitalism is that although the individual capitalist is rational (as liberals assume), the capitalist system itself is irrational. The competitive market necessitates that the individual capitalist must save, invest, and accumulate. If the desire for profits is the fuel of capitalism, then investment is the motor and accumulation is the result. In the aggregate, however, this accumulating capital of individual capitalists leads to the periodic overproduction of goods, surplus capital, and the disappearance of investment incentives. In time, the increasing severity of the downturns in the business cycle and the long-term trend toward economic stagnation will cause the proletariat to overthrow the system through revolutionary violence. Thus, the inherent contradiction of capitalism is that, with capital accumulation, capitalism sows the seeds of its own destruction and is replaced by the socialist economic system.[6]

Marx believed that in the mid-nineteenth century, the maturing of capitalism in Europe and the drawing of the global periphery into the market economy had set the stage for the proletarian revolution and the end of the capitalist economy. When this did not happen, Marx's followers, such as Rudolf Hilferding and Rosa Luxemburg, became concerned over the continuing vitality of capitalism and its refusal to disappear. The strength of nationalism, the economic successes of capitalism, and the advent of imperialism led to a metamorphosis of Marxist thought that culminated in Lenin's *Imperialism* (1939), first published in 1917. Written against the backdrop of the First World War and drawing heavily upon the writings of other Marxists, *Imperialism* was both a polemic against his ideological enemies and a synthesis of Marxist critiques of a capitalist world economy. In staking out his own position, Lenin in effect converted Marxism from essentially a theory of domestic economy to a theory of international political relations among capitalist states.

Lenin set himself the task of accounting for the fact that nationalism had triumphed over proletarian internationalism at the outbreak of the First World War and thereby sought to provide the intellectual foundations for a reunification of the international communist movement under his leadership. He wanted to show why the socialist parties of the several European powers, especially the German Social Democrats under Karl Kautsky, had supported their respective bourgeoisies. He also tried to explain why the impoverishment of the proletariat had not taken place as Marx had predicted, and instead wages were rising and workers were becoming trade unionists.

In the years between Marx and Lenin, capitalism had experienced a profound transformation. Marx had written about a capitalism largely confined to western Europe, a closed economy in which the growth impulse would one day cease as it collided with various constraints. Between 1870 and 1914, however, capitalism had become a vibrant, technological, and increasingly global and open system. In Marx's day, the primary nexus of the slowly developing world economy was trade. After 1870, however, the massive export of capital by Great Britain and subsequently by other developed economies had significantly changed the world economy; foreign investment and international finance had profoundly altered the economic and political relations among societies. Furthermore, Marx's capitalism had been composed mainly of small, competitive, industrial firms. By the time of Lenin, however, capitalist economies were dominated by immense industrial combines that in turn, according to Lenin, were controlled by the great banking houses *(haut finance)*. For Lenin, the control of capital by capital, that is, of industrial capital by financial capital, represented the pristine and highest stage of capitalist development.

Capitalism, he argued, had escaped its three laws of motion through overseas imperialism. The acquisition of colonies had enabled the capitalist economies to dispose of their unconsumed goods, to acquire cheap resources, and to vent their surplus capital. The exploitation of these colonies further provided an economic surplus with which the capitalists could buy off the leadership *(labor aristocracy)* of their own proletariat. Colonial imperialism, he argued, had become a necessary feature of advanced capitalism. As its productive forces developed and matured, a capitalist economy had to expand abroad, capture colonies, or else suffer economic stagnation and internal revolution. Lenin identified this necessary expansion as the cause of the eventual destruction of the international capitalist system.

The essence of Lenin's argument is that a capitalist international economy does develop the world, but does not develop it evenly. Individual capitalist economies grow at different rates and this differential growth of national power is ultimately responsible for imperialism, war, and international political change. Responding to Kautsky's argument that capitalists were too rational to fight over colonies and would ally themselves in the joint exploitation of colonial peoples (the doctrine of *ultra-imperialism*), Lenin stated that this was impossible because of what has become known as the "law of uneven development":

> This question [of the possibility of capitalist alliances to be more than temporary and free from conflict] need only be stated clearly enough to make it impossible for any other reply to be given than that in the negative; for there can be *no* other conceivable basis under capitalism for the division of spheres of influence . . . than a calculation of the *strength* of the participants in the division, their general economic, financial, military strength, etc. And the strength of these participants in the division does not change to an equal degree, for under capitalism the development of different undertakings, trusts, branches of industry, or countries cannot be *even*. Half a century ago, Germany was a miserable, insignificant country, as far as its capitalist strength was concerned, compared with the strength of England at that time. Japan was similarly insignificant compared with Russia. Is it "conceivable" that in ten or twenty years' time the relative strength of the imperialist powers will have remained *un*changed? Absolutely inconceivable (Lenin, 1939 [1917], p. 119).

In effect, in this passage and in his overall attempt to prove that an international capitalist system was inherently unstable, Lenin added a fourth law to the original three Marxist laws of capitalism. The law is that, as capitalist economies mature, as capital accumulates, and as profit rates fall, the capitalist economies are compelled to seize colonies and create dependencies to serve as markets, investment outlets, and sources of food and raw materials. In competition with one another, they divide up the colonial world in accordance with their relative strengths. Thus, the most advanced capitalist economy, namely Great Britain, had appropriated the largest share of colonies. As other capitalist economies advanced, however, they sought a redivision of colonies. This imperialist conflict inevitably led to armed conflict among the rising and declining imperial powers. The First World War, according to this analysis, was a war of territorial redivision between a declining Great Britain and other rising capitalist powers. Such wars of colonial division and redivision would continue, he argued, until the industrializing colonies and the proletariat of the capitalist countries revolted against the system.

In more general terms, Lenin reasoned that because capitalist economies grow and accumulate capital at differential rates, a capitalist international system can never be stable for longer than very short periods of time. In opposition to Kautsky's doctrine of ultra-imperialism, Lenin argued that all capitalist alliances were temporary and reflected momentary balances of power among the capitalist states that would inevitably be undermined by the process of uneven development. As this occurred, it would lead to intracapitalist conflicts over colonial territories.

The law of uneven development, with its fateful consequences, had become operative in his own age because the world had suddenly become finite; the globe itself had become a closed system. For decades the European capitalist powers had expanded, gobbling up overseas territory, but the imperialist powers increasingly came into contact and therefore into conflict with one another as the lands suitable for colonization diminished. Lenin believed that the final drama would be the imperial division of China and that, with the closing of the global undeveloped frontier, imperialist clashes would intensify. In time, conflicts among the imperialist powers would produce revolts among their own colonies and weaken Western capitalism's hold on the colonialized races of the globe.

Lenin's internationalization of Marxist theory represented a subtle but significant reformulation. In Marx's critique of capitalism, the causes of its downfall were economic; capitalism would fail for economic reasons as the proletariat revolted against its impoverishment. Furthermore, Marx had defined the actors in this drama as social classes. Lenin, however, substituted a political critique of capitalism in which the principal actors in effect became competing mercantilistic nation-states driven by economic necessity. Although international capitalism was economically successful, Lenin argued that it was politically unstable and constituted a war-system. The workers or the labor aristocracy in the developed capitalist countries temporarily shared in the exploitation of colonial peoples but ultimately would pay for these economic gains on the battlefield. Lenin believed that the inherent contradiction of capitalism resided in the consequent struggle of nations rather than in the class struggle. Capitalism would end due to a revolt against its inherent bellicosity and political consequences.

In summary, Lenin argued that the inherent contradiction of capitalism is that it develops the world and plants the political seeds of its own destruction as it diffuses technology, industry, and military power. It creates foreign competitors with lower wages and standards of living who can outcompete the previously dominant economy on the battlefield of world markets. Intensification of economic and political competition between declining and rising capitalist powers leads to economic conflicts, imperial rivalries, and eventually war. He asserted that this had been the fate of the British-centered liberal world economy of the nineteenth century. Today he would undoubtedly argue that, as the U.S. economy declines, a similar fate threatens the twentieth-century liberal world economy, centered in the United States.

With the triumph of Bolshevism in the Soviet Union, Lenin's theory of capitalist imperialism became the orthodox Marxist theory of international political economy; yet other heirs of the Marxist tradition have continued to challenge this orthodoxy. It has also been modified by subsequent changes in the nature of capitalism and other historical developments. Welfare-state capitalism has carried out many of the reforms that Lenin believed to be impossible, the political control of colonies is no longer regarded by Marxists as a necessary feature of imperialism, the finance capitalist of Lenin's era has been partially displaced by the multinational corporation of our own, the view that capitalist imperialism develops the less developed countries has been changed to the argument that it underdevelops them, and some Marxists have been so bold as to apply Marxist theory to Lenin's own political creation, the Soviet Union. Thus modified, at the end of the twentieth century Marxism in its various manifestations continues to exercise a powerful influence as one of the three dominant perspectives on political economy.

. . .

Critique of Economic Liberalism

Liberalism embodies a set of analytical tools and policy prescriptions that enable a society to maximize its return from scarce resources; its commitment to efficiency and the maximization of total wealth provides much of its strength. The market constitutes the most effective means for organizing economic relations, and the price mechanism operates to ensure that mutual gain and hence aggregate social benefit tend to result from economic exchange. In effect, liberal economics says to a society, whether domestic or international, "if you wish to be wealthy, this is what you must do."

From Adam Smith to the present, liberals have tried to discover the laws governing the wealth of nations. Although most liberals consider the laws of economics to be inviolable laws of nature, these laws may best be viewed as prescriptive guides for decision makers. If the laws are violated, there will be costs; the pursuit of objectives other than efficiency will necessarily involve an opportunity cost in terms of lost efficiency. Liberalism emphasizes the fact that such tradeoffs always exist in national policy. An emphasis on equity and redistribution, for example, is doomed to failure in the long run if it neglects considerations of efficiency. For a society to be efficient, as socialist economies have discovered, it cannot totally disregard the pertinent economic *laws.*

The foremost defense of liberalism is perhaps a negative one. Although it may be true, as Marxists and some nationalists argue, that the alternative to a liberal system could be one in which all gain equally, it is also possible that the alternative could be one in which all *lose* in absolute terms. Much can be said for the liberal harmony of interest doctrine; yet, as E. H. Carr has pointed out, evidence to support this doctrine has generally been drawn from historical periods in which there was "unparalleled expansion of production, population and prosperity" (Carr, 1951 [1939],

p. 44). When sustaining conditions break down (as happened in the 1930s and threatens to occur again in the closing decades of the century), disharmony displaces harmony and, I shall argue, the consequent breakdown of liberal regimes tends to lead to economic conflict wherein everyone loses.

The major criticism leveled against economic liberalism is that its basic assumptions, such as the existence of rational economic actors, a competitive market, and the like, are unrealistic. In part, this attack is unfair in that liberals knowingly make these simplifying assumptions in order to facilitate scientific research; no science is possible without them. What is more important, as defenders correctly point out, is that they should be judged by their results and ability to predict rather than by their alleged reality (Posner, 1977, ch. I). From this perspective and within its own sphere, economics has proven to be a powerful analytical tool.

By the same token, however, liberal economics can be criticized in several important respects. As a means to understand society and especially its dynamics, economics is limited; it cannot serve as a comprehensive approach to political economy. Yet liberal economists have tended to forget this inherent limitation, to regard economics as the master social science, and to permit economics to become imperialistic. When this occurs, the nature and basic assumptions of the discipline can lead the economist astray and limit its utility as a theory of political economy.

The first of these limitations is that economics artificially separates the economy from other aspects of society and accepts the existing sociopolitical framework as a given, including the distribution of power and property rights; the resource and other endowments of individuals, groups, and national societies; and the framework of social, political, and cultural institutions. The liberal world is viewed as one of homogeneous, rational, and equal individuals living in a world free from political boundaries and social constraints. Its *laws* prescribe a set of maximizing rules for economic actors regardless of where and with what they start; yet in real life, one's starting point most frequently determines where one finishes (Dahrendorf, 1979).

Another limitation of liberal economics as a theory is a tendency to disregard the justice or equity of the outcome of economic activities. Despite heroic efforts to fashion an *objective* welfare economics, the distribution of wealth within and among societies lies outside the primary concern of liberal economics. There is some truth in the Marxist criticism that liberal economics is a tool kit for managing a capitalist or market economy. Bourgeois economics is, in the Marxist view, a discipline of engineering rather than a holistic science of society. It tells one how to achieve particular objectives at the least cost under a given set of constraints; it does not purport to answer questions regarding the future and destiny of man, questions dear to the hearts of Marxists and economic nationalists.

Liberalism is also limited by its assumption that exchange is always free and occurs in a competitive market between equals who possess full information and are thus enabled to gain mutually if they choose to exchange one value for another. Unfortunately, as Charles Lindblom has argued, exchange is seldom free and equal (Lindblom, 1977, pp. 40–50). Instead, the terms of an exchange can be profoundly affected by coercion, differences in bargaining power (monopoly or monopsony), and other essentially political factors. In effect, because it neglects both the effects of noneconomic factors on exchange and the effects of exchange on politics, liberalism lacks a *true* political economy.

A further limitation of liberal economics is that its analysis tends to be static. At least in the short run, the array of consumer demands, the institutional framework, and the technological environment are accepted as constants. They are regarded as a set of constraints and opportunities within which economic decisions and tradeoffs are made. Questions about the origins of, or the directions taken by, economic institutions and the technological apparatus are, for the liberal, a secondary matter. Liberal economists are incrementalists who believe that social structures tend to change slowly in response to price signals. Although liberal economists have attempted to develop theories of economic and technological change, the crucial social, political, and technological variables affecting change are considered to be exogenous and beyond the realm of economic analysis. As Marxists charge, liberalism lacks a theory of the dynamics of international political economy and tends to assume the stability and the virtues of the economic status quo.

Liberal economics, with its laws for maximizing behavior, is based on a set of highly restrictive assumptions. No society has ever or could ever be composed of the true *economic man* of liberal theory. A functioning society requires affective ties and the subordination of individual self-interest to larger social values; if this were not the case the society would fly apart (Polanyi, 1957). Yet Western society has gone far in harnessing for social and economic betterment a basic tendency in human beings toward self-aggrandizement (Baechler, 1971). Through release of the market mechanism from social and political constraints, Western civilization has reached a level of unprecedented affluence and has set an example that other civilizations wish to emulate. It has done so, however, at the cost of other values. As liberal economics teaches, nothing is ever achieved without a cost.

Critique of Economic Nationalism

The foremost strength of economic nationalism is its focus on the state as the predominant actor in international relations and as an instrument of economic development. Although many have argued that modern economic and technological developments have made the nation-state an anachronism, at the end of the twentieth century the system of nation-states is actually expanding; societies throughout the world are seeking to create strong states capable of organizing and managing national economies, and the number of states in the world is increasing. Even in older states, the spirit of nationalist sentiments can easily be inflamed, as happened in the Falkland War of 1982. Although other actors such as transnational and international organizations do exist and do influence international relations, the economic and military efficiency of the state makes it preeminent over all these other actors.

The second strength of nationalism is its stress on the importance of security and political interests in the organization and conduct of international economic relations. One need not accept the nationalist emphasis on the primacy of security considerations to appreciate that the security of the state is a necessary precondition for its economic and political well-being in an anarchic and competitive state system. A state that fails to provide for its own security ceases to be independent. Whatever the objectives of the society, the effects of economic activities upon political independence and domestic welfare always rank high among its concerns (Strange, 1985c, p. 234).

The third strength of nationalism is its emphasis on the political framework of economic activities, its recognition that markets must function in a world of competitive groups and states. The political relations among these political actors affect the operation of markets just as markets affect the political relations. In fact, the international political system constitutes one of the most important constraints on and determinants of markets. Since states seek to influence markets to their own individual advantage, the role of power is crucial in the creation and sustaining of market relations; even Ricardo's classic example of the exchange of British woolens for Portuguese wine was not free from the exercise of state power (Choucri, 1980, p. 111). Indeed, as Carr has argued, every economic system must rest on a secure political base (Carr, 1951 [1939]).

One weakness of nationalism is its tendency to believe that international economic relations constitute solely and at all times a zero-sum game, that is, that one state's gain must of necessity be another's loss. Trade, investment, and all other economic relations are viewed by the nationalist primarily in conflictual and distributive terms. Yet, if cooperation occurs, markets *can* bring mutual (albeit not necessarily equal) gain, as the liberal insists. The possibility of benefit for all is the basis of the international market economy. Another weakness of nationalism is due to the fact that the pursuit of power and the pursuit of wealth usually do conflict, at least in the short run. The amassing and exercising of military and other forms of power entail costs to the society, costs that can undercut its economic efficiency. Thus, as Adam Smith argued, the mercantilist policies of eighteenth-century states that identified money with wealth were detrimental to the growth of the real wealth created by productivity increases; he demonstrated that the wealth of nations would have been better served by policies of free trade. Similarly, the tendency today to identify industry with power can weaken the economy of a state. Development of industries without regard to market considerations or comparative advantage can weaken a society economically. Although states in a situation of conflict must on occasion pursue mercantilistic goals and policies, over the long term, pursuit of these policies can be self-defeating.

In addition, nationalism lacks a satisfactory theory of domestic society, the state, and foreign policy. It tends to assume that society and state form a unitary entity and that foreign policy is determined by an objective national interest. Yet, as liberals correctly stress, society is pluralistic and consists of individuals and groups (coalitions of individuals) that try to capture the apparatus of the state and make it serve their own political and economic interests. Although states possess varying degrees of social autonomy and independence in the making of policy, foreign policy (including foreign economic policy) is in large measure the outcome of the conflicts among dominant groups within each society. Trade protectionism and most other nationalist policies result from attempts by one factor of production or another (capital, labor, or land) to acquire a monopoly position and thereby to increase its share of the economic rents. Nationalist policies are most frequently designed to redistribute income from consumers and society as a whole to producer interests.[7]

Nationalism can thus be interpreted as either a theory of state building or a cloak for the interests of particular producer groups that are in a position to influence national policy. In their failure to appreciate fully or distinguish between the two possible meanings of economic nationalism, nationalists can be faulted for not applying, both to the domestic level and to the determination of foreign policy, their assumption that the political framework influences economic outcomes. They fail to take sufficient account of the fact that domestic political groups frequently use a nationalist rationale, especially that of national security, to promote their own interests.

Whereas in the past, land and capital were the primary carriers of nationalist sentiments, in advanced economies labor has become the most nationalistic and protectionist of the three factors of production. In a world of highly mobile capital and resources, labor seeks to use the state to advance its threatened interests. The increased power of labor in the contemporary welfare state, as I shall argue below, has become a major force for economic nationalism.

The validity of nationalists' emphasis on protectionism and industrialization is more difficult to ascertain. It is true that all great industrial powers have had strong states that protected and promoted their industries in the early stages of industrialization and that without such protectionism, the "infant" industries of developing economies probably would not have survived the competition of powerful firms in more advanced economies. Yet it is also the case that high levels of protectionism in many countries have led to the establishment of inefficient industries and even retarded economic development (Kindleberger, 1978b, pp. 19–38). In the final quarter of the twentieth century, economies like those of Taiwan and South Korea, which have limited protectionism while favoring competitive export industries, have performed better than those less developed countries that have attempted to industrialize behind high tariff walls while pursuing a strategy of import substitution.

The nationalist's bias toward industry over agriculture also must get a mixed review. It is true that industry can have certain advantages over agriculture and that the introduction of industrial technology into a society has spillover effects that tend to transform and modernize all aspects of the economy as it upgrades the quality of the labor force and increases the profitability of capital.[8] Yet one must remember that few societies have developed without a prior agricultural revolution and a high level of agricultural productivity (Lewis, 1978a). In fact, certain of the most prosperous economies of the world, for example, Denmark, the American farm belt, and western Canada, are based on efficient agriculture (Viner, 1952). In all these societies, moreover, the state has promoted agricultural development.

One may conclude that the nationalists are essentially correct in their belief that the state must play an important role in economic development. A strong state is required to promote and, in some cases, to protect industry as well as to foster an efficient agriculture. Yet this active role of the state, though a necessary condition, is not a sufficient condition. A strong and interventionist state does not guarantee economic development; indeed, it might retard it. The sufficient condition for economic development is an efficient economic organization of agriculture and industry, and in most cases this is achieved through the operation of the market. Both of these political and economic conditions have characterized the developed economies and the rapidly industrializing countries of the contemporary international system.

It is important to realize that, whatever its relative merits or deficiencies, economic nationalism has a persistent appeal. Throughout modern history, the international location of economic activities has been a leading concern of states. From the seventeenth century on states have pursued conscious policies of industrial and technological development. Both to achieve stable military power and in the belief that industry provides a higher "value added" than agriculture, the modern nation-state has had as one of its major objectives the establishment and protection of industrial power. As long as a conflictual international system exists, economic nationalism will retain its strong attraction.

Critique of Marxist Theory

Marxism correctly places the economic problem—the production and distribution of material wealth—where it belongs, at or near the center of political life. Whereas liberals tend to ignore the issue of distribution and nationalists are concerned primarily with the *international* distribution of wealth, Marxists focus on both the domestic and the international effects of a market economy on the distribution of wealth. They call attention to the ways in which the rules or regimes governing trade, investment, and other international economic relations affect the distribution of wealth among groups and states (Cohen, 1977, p. 49).[9] However, it is not necessary to subscribe to the materialist interpretation of history or the primacy of class struggle in order to appreciate that the ways in which individuals earn their living and distribute wealth are a critical determinant of social structure and political behavior.

Another contribution of Marxism is its emphasis on the nature and structure of the division of labor at both the domestic and international levels. As Marx and Engels correctly pointed out in *The German Ideology,* every division of labor implies dependence and therefore a political relationship (Marx and Engels, 1947 [1846]). In a market economy the economic nexus among groups and states becomes of critical importance in determining their welfare and their political relations. The Marxist analysis, however, is too limited, because economic interdependence is not the only or even the most important set of interstate relations. The political and strategic relations among political actors are of equal or greater significance and cannot be reduced to merely economic considerations, at least not as Marxists define economics.

The Marxist theory of international political economy is also valuable in its focus on international political change. Whereas neither liberalism nor nationalism has a comprehensive theory of social change, Marxism emphasizes the role of economic and technological developments in explaining the dynamics of the international system. As embodied in Lenin's law of uneven development, the differential growth of power among states constitutes an underlying cause of international political change. Lenin was at least partially correct in attributing the First World War to the uneven economic growth of power among industrial states and to conflict over the division of territory. There can be little doubt that the uneven growth of the several European powers and the consequent effects on the balance of power contributed to their collective insecurity. Competition for markets and empires did aggravate interstate relations. Furthermore, the average person's growing awareness of the effects on personal welfare and security of the vicissitudes of the world market and the economic behavior of other states also became a significant element in the arousal of nationalistic antagonisms. For nations and citizens alike, the growth of economic interdependence brought with it a new sense of insecurity, vulnerability, and resentment against foreign political and economic rivals.

Marxists are no doubt also correct in attributing to capitalist economies, at least as we have known them historically, a powerful impulse to expand through trade and especially through the export of capital. The classical liberal economists themselves observed that economic growth and the accumulation of capital create a tendency for the rate of return (profit) on capital to decline. These economists, however, also noted that the decline could be arrested through international trade, foreign investment, and other means. Whereas trade absorbs surplus capital in the manufacture of exports, foreign investment siphons off capital. Thus, classical liberals join Marxists in asserting that capitalist economies have an inherent tendency to export goods and surplus capital.

This tendency has led to the conclusion that the nature of capitalism is international and that its internal dynamics encourage outward expansionism. In a closed capitalist economy and in the absence of technological advance, underconsumption, surplus capital, and the resulting decline in the rate of profit would eventually lead to what John Stuart Mill called *the stationary state* (Mill, 1970 [1848], p. 111). Yet, in an open world economy characterized by expanding capitalism, population growth, and continuing improvement in productivity through technological advance, there is no inherent economic reason for economic stagnation to take place.

On the other hand, a communist or socialist economy has no inherent *economic* tendency to expand internationally. In a communist economy, investment and consumption are primarily determined by the national plan and, moreover, the state has a monopoly of all foreign exchange.[10] A communist economy may of course have a political or strategic motive for exporting capital, or it may need to invest abroad in order to obtain vital sources of raw materials. A Marxist regime may also find it profitable to invest abroad or to engage in other commercial transactions. Certainly the Soviet Union has been rightly credited on occasion with being a shrewd trader, and Ralph Hawtrey's point that the advent of a communist or socialist government does not eliminate the profit motive but merely transfers it to the state has some merit (Hawtrey, 1952). Nevertheless, the incentive structure of a communist society with its stress on prestige, power, and ideology is unlikely to encourage the economy's expansion abroad. The tendency is rather for economics to be subordinated to politics and the nationalistic goals of the state (Viner, 1951).

Marxists are certainly correct that capitalism needs an open world economy. Capitalists desire access to foreign economies for export of goods and capital; exports have a Keynesian demand effect in stimulating economic activity in capitalist economies, and capital exports serve to raise the overall rate of profit. Closure of foreign markets and capital outlets would be detrimental to capitalism, and a closed capitalist economy would probably result in a dramatic decline in economic growth. There is reason to believe that the capitalist system (certainly as we have known it) could not survive in the absence of an open world economy. The essential character of capitalism, as Marx pointed out, is cosmopolitan; the capitalist's ideology is international. Capitalism in just one state would undoubtedly be an impossibility.

In the nineteenth and twentieth centuries the dominant capitalist states, Great Britain and the United States, employed their power to promote and maintain an open world economy. They used their influence to remove the barriers to the free flow of goods and capital. Where necessary, in the words of Simon Kuznets, "the greater power of the developed nations imposed upon the reluctant partners the opportunities of international trade and division of labor" (Kuznets, 1966, p. 335). In pursuit of their own interests, they created international law to protect the property rights of private traders and investors (Lipson, 1985). And when the great trading nations became unable or unwilling to enforce the rules of free trade, the liberal system began its steady retreat. Up to this point, therefore, the Marxists are correct in their identification of capitalism and modern imperialism.

The principal weakness of Marxism as a theory of international political economy results from its failure to appreciate the role of political and strategic factors in international relations. Although one can appreciate the insights of Marxism, it is not necessary to accept the Marxist theory that the dynamic of modern international relations is caused by the needs of capitalist economies to export goods and surplus capital. For example, to the extent that the uneven growth of national economies leads to war, this is due to national rivalries, which can occur regardless of the nature of domestic economies—witness the conflict between China and the Soviet Union. Although competition for markets and for capital outlets can certainly be a cause of tension and one factor causing imperialism and war, this does not provide an adequate explanation for the foreign policy behavior of capitalist states.

The historical evidence, for example, does not support Lenin's attribution of the First World War to the logic of capitalism and the market system. The most important territorial disputes among the European powers, which precipitated the war, were not those about overseas colonies, as Lenin argued, but lay within Europe itself. The principal conflict leading to the war involved redistribution of the Balkan territories of the decaying Ottoman Empire. And insofar as the source of this conflict was economic, it lay in the desire of the Russian state for access to the Mediterranean (Hawtrey, 1952, pp. 117). Marxism cannot explain the fact that the three major imperial rivals—Great Britain, France, and Russia—were in fact on the same side in the ensuing conflict and that they fought against a Germany that had few foreign policy interests outside Europe itself.

In addition, Lenin was wrong in tracing the basic motive force of imperialism to the internal workings of the capitalist system. As Benjamin J. Cohen has pointed out in his analysis of the Marxist theory of imperialism, the political and strategic conflicts of the European powers were more important; it was at least in part the stalemate on the Continent among the Great Powers that forced their interstate competition into the colonial world (Cohen, 1973). Every one of these colonial conflicts (if one excludes the Boer War) was in fact settled through diplomatic means. And, finally, the overseas colonies of the European powers were simply of little economic consequence. As Lenin's own data show, almost all European overseas investment was directed to the "lands of recent settlement" (the United States, Canada, Australia, South Africa, Argentina, etc.) rather than to the dependent colonies in what today we call the Third World (Lenin, 1939 [1917], p. 64). In fact, contrary to Lenin's view that politics follows investment, international finance during this period was largely a servant of foreign policy, as was also the case with French loans to Czarist Russia.[11] Thus, despite its proper focus on political change, Marxism is seriously flawed as a theory of political economy.

NOTES

1. The term *liberal* is used in this book in its European connotation, that is, a commitment to individualism, free market, and private property. This is the dominant perspective of most American economists and of economics as taught in American universities. Thus, both Paul Samuelson and Milton Friedman, despite important differences between their political and theoretical views, are regarded here as representatives of the American liberal tradition.
2. I would like to thank Michael Doyle for bringing this interesting article to my attention.
3. The method of comparative states was invented by David Ricardo. It consists of a model of a market in a state of equilibrium, the introduction of an exogenous variable into the system, and a calculation of the new equilibrium state. Because this mode of analysis is generally unconcerned with the origins of the exogenous variable itself, it is limited as a means of examining the problem of economic change.
4. One can identify Friedrich List with the benign mercantilist position. List believed that true cosmopolitanism could only be possible when all states had been developed. For a discussion of benign and malevolent mercantilism, see Gilpin 1975, pp. 234–237.
5. Although there were important differences between the views of Engels and Marx, I shall refer to Marx throughout this discussion as standing for the combined contribution of both men.
6. In effect, the Marxists are accusing the defenders of capitalism with employing the fallacy of composition. This is "a fallacy in which what is true of a part is, on that account alone, alleged to be also *necessarily* true of the whole" (Samuelson, 1980, p. 11). Similarly, Keynes argued that although individual saving is a virtue, if everyone saved it would be a calamity.
7. The literature on the political economy of tariffs and other forms of trade protectionism as rent-seeking is extensive. As noted earlier, the subject of economic policy making falls outside the scope of this book. Frey (1984b) is an excellent discussion of this approach to tariff policy and related topics.
8. Cornwall (1977) provides a representative argument of the benefits of industry over agriculture in economic development.
9. The volume edited by Krasner (1982c) contains a wide-ranging discussion of the concept of international regimes.
10. Wiles (1968) presents a valuable analysis of the contrasting behavior of capitalist and communist economies.
11. Herbert Feis (1964 [1930]) and Eugene Stanley (1953) have effectively made this argument.

Toward a Structural Perspective on the World-System

Christopher Chase-Dunn
Richard Rubinson

Recent work on development and modernization has turned away from the assumption of independently evolving national societies. There is instead a growing emphasis on interdependence between nations. Discussion of the development gap between *advanced* and *underdeveloped* areas has been recast in terms of the power relationships between them, and work on the emergence of *interdependence* between nations has focused on the recent growth of multinational corporations and the rates of exchange across national boundaries.[1] None of these analyses, however, has systematically elaborated the structural characteristics of the larger system within which national societies operate. This paper will attempt to isolate the basic structural elements that make up the world-system and to use those elements to formulate a preliminary descriptive schema of the world-system based on the work of Immanuel Wallerstein.

The first section of the paper summarizes Wallerstein's description of the emergence of the world-system and some of the main concepts used to describe its structure. The second section contains our preliminary formulation of the descriptive schema. The final section describes the processes that reproduce one of the crucial structural characteristics of the world-system: the division of labor between the core and the periphery.

Christopher Chase-Dunn and Richard Rubinson, "Toward a Structural Perspective on the World System," *Politics and Society*, 7:4 (1977): pp. 453–473. Reproduced with the permission of the copyright holder, Butterworth and Heinemann.

WALLERSTEIN'S ACCOUNT OF THE MODERN WORLD-SYSTEM

Wallerstein describes the creation of the main structural features of the modern world-system in sixteenth-century Europe. He distinguished two types of world-systems. The first is a territorial division of labor encompassing a set of political entities, which Wallerstein calls a *world economy.* The second is a territorial division of labor encompassed by a single political structure, which he terms a *world empire.* Historically, world economies have tended to disintegrate or to become world empires. The uniqueness of the European world economy of the sixteenth century was its flexibility and its resistance to becoming a world empire.[2]

Commercial capitalism grew out of and substantially developed a territorial system of exchange of fundamental commodities. The division of labor in this exchange network was not only functional but also geographic, involving the exchange of relatively processed and differentiated goods for raw materials. The main structural feature of this world-system came to be this division of labor between the emerging core areas producing manufactured goods and the emerging peripheral areas producing raw materials. The boundaries of the system were determined by the extent and intensity of economic production and exchange. All areas within the system were engaged in production of fundamental commodities for exchange on the world market in a way that radically altered their structure of production and class relations. Changes in the larger system of production and exchange had significant effects on the internal structure of the areas that came to be integrated into this world-system.[3]

At the end of the sixteenth century, the European world economy included northwestern Europe as the core, eastern Europe and Latin America as the periphery, and the Mediterranean Europe, including Portugal and Spain, as a *semiperiphery* intermediate between the core and periphery. Wallerstein discusses the boundaries of the system and the more limited interactions that the European world economy had with external arenas, such as the long distance trade in luxuries with empires and other areas of the geographical world. The integration of this system was not normative but functional, based on capitalist commodity production organized by a world market in which both purely *economic competitive advantage* and *political interference by states* play an interactive role. Wallerstein argues that in the modern world-system there is only one mode of production, commodity production for profit on the world market, that articulates different forms of labor exploitation and encompasses a system of differentially powerful states and peripheral areas.[4]

The uniqueness of such a system is that the market is an important determinant of the organization of production and the decisions of economic actors. Polanyi describes two central features of this type of system.[5] First, under a market system, greater profit accrues to those economic actors that possess larger amounts of resources. Consequently, there is a continual pressure in the market system toward monopolization and the creation of privileged access to resources. Second, the market system is dynamic and creates risks and uncertainties for any specific economic actors, since new areas of demand and new profit opportunities continually arise and often undercut and disadvantage previous centers of profit. Consequently, there is a continual pressure for economic actors to attempt to stabilize uncertainties in order both to protect and to increase their advantages. These two features of markets lead to continuing attempts for "actors in the market to avoid the normal operation of the market whenever it does not maximize their profit. The attempts of these actors to use non-market devices to ensure short-run profits makes them turn to the political entities which have power to affect the market—the nation states."[6] Since states, which are the political units of the world system, are organizations with considerable power, economic actors orient their actions toward these political structures to secure privileged access to resources and protection from the risks of the market. Under this production system the power and autonomy of states continue to grow as different economic actors find it necessary to support the state and to increase its authority. As Wallerstein says, "the functioning of a capitalist world-economy requires that groups pursue their economic interests within a single world-market while seeking to distort this market for their benefit by organizing to exert influences on states, some of which are more powerful than others but none of which controls the market in its entirety.[7]

The differences in strength of state structures is partially a result of the division of labor being geographic as well as functional in the world system. Different areas of the world, and the states within those areas, tend to specialize in different economic roles (suppliers of raw materials vs. suppliers of manufactured goods, for example) and consequently occupy different positions in the overall system. This geographic division of labor is itself a consequence of the different times at which areas were incorporated into the world-system, the type of resources in those areas, and the form and strength of the political structures in those areas at the time of their incorporation into this system. This geographic division of labor has two consequences. First, coalitions of economic interest often form among actors located within different states. For example, in many states the producers of raw materials become aligned with those groups in other states that use those materials in manufacturing. Second, economic actors in some states attempt to directly control and influence the economic and political process in other states. These two tendencies, in turn, result in international differences in strength of various states and uneven economic development across the system as a whole.[8]

Core areas are characterized by a diversified internal structure resembling in some ways the structure of the world-system as a whole. They have a relatively well integrated home economy, an infrastructure that interconnects a large part of the internal market, a complex division of labor, and a high level of productivity in both manufacturing and agriculture.[9] The major mode of labor exploitation is wage labor (the process of proletarianization is relatively advanced), and medium-sized farms that are owner occupied and worked predominate in agriculture.[10]

The internal structure of periphery areas is typically dualistic, that is, there is a *modern* sector (mines, plantations, ports) and a *traditional* sector (villages, tribal reserves, the bush, the mountains, etc.), with the latter serving as a labor reserve for the former. The modern sector is usually specialized in the production of one or two raw materials for export. This results in an infrastructure that is externally oriented and that does not link different areas with one another but rather with the larger world economy. The home market is relatively underdeveloped and dependent on imports from the core. During the era of mercantile capitalism, the class structure of the periphery was composed of capitalist landowners and commercial capitalists (often nonindigenous) and *low wage* coerced labor of either slaves or serfs producing raw materials for export. The state was relatively weak (or nonexistent as in the case of colonies) and tended to exclude the interests of domestic manufacturers producing for the home market in competition with imports from the core. A manufacturing bourgeoisie did not develop and the towns declined, except for ports of exchange with the world economy.

Intermediate in terms of internal structure and functional location in the world-system is the semiperiphery.[11] In the sixteenth century the semiperiphery was composed of the Christian Mediterranean, including Portugal and Spain. Wallerstein describes semiperipheral Venice as a declining core state of an earlier Mediterranean world economy. The semiperiphery trades with both the core and the periphery and has an internal class structure composed of mixed modes of labor exploitation that differ depending on whether the core state is upwardly or downwardly mobile in the larger system. Downwardly mobile semiperipheral areas have large amounts of fixed capital invested in less competitive industry, political constraints on new investment, and high and rigid wage levels. Venice was a producer of expensive luxury goods by skilled craftsmen organized in guilds that had attained high wages relative to productivity. In agriculture the form of labor control in semiperipheral Venice (sharecropping) was "intermediate between the freedom of the lease system and the coercion of slavery and serfdom."[12] Upwardly mobile semiperipheral areas have a wage bill that is relatively low compared to levels of productivity and may engage in mercantile protection of domestic economic activity and political mobilization of economic development by the state.

The basic structure of the modern world-system is reproduced as the system moves through a series of geographical expansions to encompass the whole globe. Wallerstein suggests that there have been four epochs since the birth of the system: its emergence from 1450 to 1640, its consolidation between 1640 and 1815, its expansion to the whole globe between 1815 and 1917, and its consolidation and "revolutionary" tensions from 1917 to the present.[13]

A DESCRIPTIVE STRUCTURAL SCHEMA OF THE MODERN WORLD-SYSTEM

We wish to put forth a tentative analytic schema of the world-system in order to stimulate theoretical work and to suggest directions for research. This schema will not attempt to provide a comprehensive causal model of the development and transformation of the world-system. Rather, the intention is much more limited: to isolate and define the decisive structural elements that constitute the world-system as a whole and to suggest some of the important linkages between these various elements. Such an effort at conceptual clarification is a necessary step in any process of theory construction, but it must not be confused with the actual development of a causal theory of the world-system itself.

The basic elements of this structural schema can be classified under three broad headings: structural constants, structural variables that cycle from one form to another, and trend variables that increase at varying rates (the variations of which tend to correspond with the cyclical variables). Under these headings, we will analyze a total of nine basic elements.

Structural Constants

The three main structural constants, the core-periphery division of labor, the state system, and capitalist commodity production for the world market, have been described above. Here we will discuss the way in which these structural constants can be seen as reproducing themselves over time and point out the analytic dimensions underlying those structural constants.

The Core-Periphery Division of Labor   The division of labor and the resulting exchange between core and periphery is reproduced even though the particular commodities and the absolute levels of productivity change over time and even though the specific areas in the core and periphery may change. The relative differences in productivity, capital intensity, and differentiation of national economies are maintained between the core and the periphery through the processes of unequal exchange and state formation. (These processes are discussed below.) The sixteenth-century exchange of core textiles for peripheral wheat and other raw materials has been replaced, for example, by the exchange of core computers for peripheral textiles, but the differences in terms of levels of productivity and processing have not diminished and may have increased with the concentration of capital in the core. Raw materials produced at a high level of productivity (such as industrial wheat in the U.S.) may be exported from the core to the periphery. This raises the question of the underlying economic dimension of the core-periphery division of labor.[14]

It is not the type of commodity itself that constitutes the difference between core and periphery production but rather the way labor, technology, raw materials, and fixed capital are combined. Aside from differences in production relations (forms of control over labor), the main differences between core and periphery production are the productivity of labor and capital and the wage level holding constant productivity.

Productivity varies according to the ratio of constant capital (plant, raw materials, and machinery) to variable capital (the amount of labor power) incorporated into production, according to the capacity of machinery to transform raw materials, and according to the skill levels of labor. In core countries the ratio of constant to variable capital is higher (production is capital intensive) and the machinery employed and the average labor employed are more productive than in peripheral countries. In peripheral countries production is labor intensive, and average capacity of machinery and skill of labor is lower. This means that if the same product were produced in both the core and the periphery (e.g., wheat), it would have much more labor per unit incorporated into it in the periphery.[15]

The second dimension of the core-periphery division of labor is the wage level holding constant differences in productivity and skill. In the periphery workers at the same level of skill and using the same methods of production are paid much less than similar workers in the core. This wage differential holding constant productivity is related both to the differences in production relations (including relations with the state) between the core and periphery and the differences in the political power of workers' organizations.

It might be asked why lower wages in the periphery do not allow the periphery to increase its own rate of accumulation (by having a higher rate of exploitation), and thus gradually cease to be peripheral. This apparent paradox—higher rates of exploitation and lower rates of accumulation in the periphery—is solved by the theory of "unequal exchange," which argues that the world-market prices at which core and periphery products exchange conceal a transfer of labor value from the periphery to the core (see below). The surplus value produced in the periphery, therefore, is accumulated in the core.

We refer to the core-periphery division of labor as a structural constant of the world-system in the sense that, although the level of productivity may go up in both the core and the periphery, the relative difference is reproduced. And though the level of wages may change, the gap tends to remain. The magnitude of these differences may vary in some regular way with the structural variables described below. For instance, it is possible that differential levels of productivity and wages vary with the expansion and contraction of production and with the changes in core-periphery control structures described below. However, over the long run the differentials are reproduced rather than eliminated. It is in this sense that the core-periphery division of labor is a structural constant.

The State System   The political structure of the world-system is a multiplicity of *sovereign* nation-states, encompassed by a single economic division of labor. These states are of unequal power, and they align themselves in a shifting set of alliances that has so far prevented the takeover of the whole system by any single state. The world economy has not become a world empire. The state system is a constant structural feature of the world-system, although the number of states has periodically increased as peripheral areas become "independent" states and larger states are broken up into smaller ones. Core states are strong vis à vis their own populations and vis à vis other states, while peripheral areas are either colonized (have no independent states) or have a relatively weak state, internally and externally. A *strong* state is a state that has the capacity to mobilize resources—human and financial. The strength of the state, therefore, cannot be equated with the size of the state apparatus or the degree of repression by the state. Large, statewide civil and military bureaucracies are often a result of greater opposition, rather than strength. The British state of the nineteenth century or the Dutch state of the seventeenth century were relatively nonrepressive, relatively small compared to other states of the period, but they were clearly strong states in the sense of being able to mobilize vast resources during an emergency.

Political integration between nation-states, except by conquest, is very difficult. State strength vis à vis internal population tends everywhere to increase, although the relative differences between core and peripheral states remain. Another characteristic of the state system is the tendency for individual core states to politically dominate particular peripheral areas. The class coalitions, of which the regimes of states in the system are composed, often are based on class interests that cut across national boundaries. This is especially true of peripheral states. (See the discussion of power block formation below.) The colonial empires and the bilateral neocolonial relationships between core states and peripheral areas are discussed below as a structural variable of the world-system.

Capitalist Commodity Production   In commodity production, production is undertaken "for sale in a market in which the object is to realize the maximum profit." *Capitalist* commodity production adds to this a differentiated set of production relations with free wage-labor in the core and various forms of coerced labor in the periphery.[16] The different forms of labor exploitation—wage labor, capitalist slavery and serfdom, small commodity producers, and state socialist labor control—are articulated into a single international system of production relations. This capitalist commodity production for the world market, in which competitive states alternatively interfere with or encourage the price-setting operation of the market, is the dominant mode of production in the modern world-system, and it incorporates precapitalist modes into itself as the system expands.

Production relations (controls over production) involve the relationship between laborer and capitalist, as well as the relationship of both to the state. The state backs up by force the juridical relationship between free labor and capital as well as the more apparent and direct coercion of slave and serf labor. In addition the state mediates between capitals in different sectors (i.e., industry and agriculture). Individual states, and the competitive state system, enforce or reorganize production relations between the core and the periphery. The market system integrates different types of labor control into a differentiated but articulated system of production relations.[17]

Attempts to explain the dynamics of the world-system from Marx's accumulation model usually start with the dominance of industrial capital and the full proletarianization of labor that occurred in the core in the nineteenth century.[18] Wallerstein's argument that the essential structural characteristics and dynamics of the world-system have been in operation since the sixteenth century implies that these structural features are a function of differentiated capitalist commodity production (both agricultural and industrial), rather than of fully developed industrial capitalism. Industrial capitalism and the expanded accumulation process increase intensity of world-system processes, but the institutional bases of capitalism predate the nineteenth-century Industrial Revolution.

Structural Cycles at the System Level

Core-Periphery Control Structures The structure of power between the core and the periphery alternates between direct political control by individual core states over peripheral areas and less direct economic control through unequal exchange and through the operation of *private* transnational economic actors. During periods when average economic production in the system as a whole is expanding, the structure of control is less direct and political domination by core states over peripheral areas is relaxed. During periods when average economic production is contracting and competition among core states is increasing, political domination is increased over older colonies and new areas are brought under the colonial domination of individual core states. This alternating between political and economic modes of control corresponds, to some extent, with changes in the structure of exchange between core states and peripheral areas. The colonial empires tend to monopolize trade with their own colonies, and so the structure of exchange becomes relatively bilateral, with little exchange between core states and peripheral areas not associated politically. During periods in which direct colonial domination is relaxed or obstructed, exchange between the core and the periphery is relatively more multilateral, although previous exchange patterns have a certain momentum. A good part of the shift away from purely bilateral colonial exchange patterns may be due to the increased share of exchange between an emerging hegemonic core state (see below) and the colonial empires of other core states. Emerging core powers are *free trade* advocates (since they have a competitive advantage in the world market) and they interfere with the colonial ties between other core states and their empires. Also, independence movements in peripheral areas that establish new states tend to occur during periods of conflict between core states, and this also may make the exchange network more multilateral between core and periphery.[19]

Distribution of Power Among Core States   The distribution of power among core states varies from unicentric in which there is a single hegemonic core state, to multicentric in which the power is more evenly distributed among core states. A shift from one to the other is produced by the tendency for economic competitive advantage to become concentrated in a single state causing its rise to hegemonic power and to a central position in the world economy. Its power advantage gradually changes from one based on production to one based on the state's financial position in the world monetary system and on its centrality in the maintenance of world political stability (through military and political means).[20] This shift from productive to financial and political hegemony allows other core states to incorporate new productive technology and to avoid the overhead costs of maintaining stability in the system.[21] They grow rapidly and overtake the original hegemonic power in productivity, and a period of competition between core states ensues (multicentric distribution of power in the core). Britain and the United States are the two most recent hegemonic powers, but the Dutch played this role to a certain extent in the mid-seventeenth century. The multicentric periods are characterized by intense economic competition and military conflict between core states and by competition for access to peripheral areas. Unicentric periods are characterized by relatively peaceful economic competition in a relatively integrated world economy supported by the institutional framework based on the hegemonic core state in international agreements.

Krasner has shown that the distribution of power among core states is related to the structure of trade between core and peripheral states as is suggested above.[22] A unicentric distribution of power in the core, in which a hegemonic core power is clearly dominant, is correlated with an open structure of international trade and less trade monopoly between core states and their colonial areas. It is suggested by the argument above that these changes in the structure of exchange are due to changes in the structure of power between the core and the periphery. A more equal distribution of competitive advantage in the core leads to greater competition between core states and a more formal and monopolistic structure of control between core states and peripheral areas.[23]

Expansion and Contraction of Production: The Long Wave   Periods of expansion and contraction of economic production in the capitalist world economy have followed one another in waves since the origin of this system in the sixteenth century. In periods of rising economic activity, new lands were cultivated, manufacturing increased, and trade expanded integrating local, regional, and national markets. In periods of contraction, production fell and trade diminished, although rarely below the level of earlier *troughs* in this wavelike upward trend of economic growth and capital accumulation.[24]

Wallerstein focuses on the way in which the influx of bullion from Spanish *primitive accumulation* in the New World and the inflation of prices across Europe in the sixteenth century affected different producers and created the conditions for economic expansion on a new basis. As capitalist commodity production grew and markets became more and more integrated over a larger and larger area, these cycles of expansion and contraction, which had previously occurred at different times in different areas, tended to come into phase across the system.

The process of the concentration and centralization of capital and the dominance of *monopoly capital* in core states has not suppressed these long cycles of expansion and contraction, although individual state policies may have flattened out the shorter-term cycles to some extent.[25] But state action, especially in a period of general economic contraction in the world economy, is itself competitive, and there are no overarching international mechanisms (or only weak ones) to prevent the intensification of competition and conflict between states. The nation-states attempt to interfere with the operation of the world market and this competition adds to the intensity of the cycles of expansion and contraction of production. In periods of contraction, when the surplus available is shrinking, states tighten up their controls over trade and peripheral areas in order to protect revenues and the incomes of their dominant classes. This creates a mercantilist world economy of trade wars and military conflict between core powers, the intensity of which depends on the distribution (unicentric or multicentric) of power in the core.

Upward Trends at the System Level

Accumulation of Capital   As economic development takes place in both the core and the periphery the total productive capacity of the system increases, albeit at different rates in different places. This increase occurs in waves, but production in the system as a whole does not drop below its low point in the previous contraction. The organization of production on an increasing scale by states and transnational corporations (the centralization of capital) is also an upward trend that corresponds to expansions and contractions of production. It is this trend that causes national economies to be described as *monopoly capitalist* or *state socialist* rather than any major decrease in competition at the level of the system as a whole. The scale of the organization of production has increased relative to the size of national markets.

The Number of States in the System   Another secular trend, although one that increases in abrupt jumps, is the total number of states in the system. Waves of decolonization have periodically brought peripheral areas into the state system.[26] These new states, while weaker than core states, nevertheless represent a relative increase in autonomy for the peripheral areas in which they are formed, although this varies depending on the class coalitions composing the new regimes and the opportunities for internal mobilization for independent development.[27] For most peripheral nations these opportunities are extremely limited.[28]

Expansion of the System to New Territories and Populations
There has been a periodic expansion of the system to new territory and to new populations brought about by the waves of colonial expansion by core states. This ceased at the end of the nineteenth century when the system became global. The *ceiling effect* of having no new populations or territory to conquer had two consequences. It increased the level of competition among core states for access to resources and surplus value of the periphery, thus bettering the bargaining position of the periphery and increasing the costs of exploitation. And it caused capitalist expansion to increase its *internal* intensity, that is, to make into commodities the aspects of life within the system that had not previously been brought into the sphere of capitalist relations.

MECHANISMS OF CORE-PERIPHERY REPRODUCTION

The most fundamental structural characteristic of the world-system is the differentiation of areas into the core-periphery division of labor. The organization and reproduction of this division of labor occurs through the operation of four basic processes: the formation of power blocks within the state, state-formation, unequal exchange, and the contradiction between the economic and political bases of class formation. This section analyzes how these processes operate to determine this division of labor. Thus, from a world-system approach, development and underdevelopment are part of the same set of processes.

Power-Block Formation

Power-block formation is the process by which the interests of a political-economic coalition are institutionalized within the state apparatus.[29] Political means are necessary to secure permanent economic advantages, and thus economic groups constantly attempt to convert their economic power into political power. Consequently, a struggle over state power develops. Historically, in those areas where economic groups producing primary products for export controlled the political center, this type of production became dominant and the position of indigenous manufacturing and merchant classes declined. In those areas where the manufacturing and commercial classes dominated the political center, those economic interests became dominant and the position of those classes was strengthened. This is because the possession of political authority is the crucial mechanism for controlling the type of production within areas of the capitalist world-system. Which type of power block develops is itself a consequence of the initial vectors of economic interest formed in the process of the production and trading of commodities. The crucial point is that once a set of economic interests becomes dominant within a state apparatus—the process of power-block formation—those types of production become relatively secure in those areas. And the political victory of some types of economic interests in core areas is matched by the political victory of complementary types of economic interests in peripheral areas. Consequently, the economic division of labor becomes also structured into a geographic division of labor. This organization of economic production into a territorial structure is a permanent feature of the capitalist world-system.

In peripheral countries within the world-system there has developed a power block based on an economic elite whose predominant interests have been tied to the needs of core capital. Initially this economic and political alliance centered around the production and export of food and raw materials required by the core countries. More recently, this alliance has also centered around the development of foreign-controlled manufacturing for both domestic and foreign consumption. This shift to dependent industrialization has occurred as a means for manufacturing firms located in the core to enter the highly protected markets of many peripheral countries and to take advantage of the lower wage rates which are found there. These elites, in turn, have suppressed or limited the development of national groups which have attempted to develop indigenous manufacturing and industrial production.

In core countries within the world-system there has developed a power block based on an alliance between manufacturing and commercial interests. These elites have supported the development of indigenous manufacturing and industrialization and have placed limitations on the development of economic groups engaged in raw-material production for export. This has occurred for exactly the same reasons as in the peripheral countries in the world-system: the interests of indigenous manufacturing, and consequently the political requirements, are in opposition to the interests of economic production of raw materials for export. Historically this conflict formed part of the background to the English and French Revolutions and the American Civil War and in each instance the forces of indigenous manufacturing and commerce were victorious.

State Formation

State formation is the process by which states increase or decrease their strength, both in relation to their own populations and in relation to foreign actors. The processes of power-block formation and state formation are closely related. Core areas within the world-system have strong states, states in which political authority is quite extensive and stable. Peripheral areas within the world-system have relatively weak states, in which political authority is less extensive and stable. Here again it is important to emphasize that a strong state has the ability to mobilize resources whenever it needs to. State strength, in this sense, tends to be a function of the extent to which the support of a country's dominant classes is institutionalized within the machinery of the state and the economic roles of these classes are institutionalized in the world economy.[30] The relationship between power-block formation and state formation arises from the political demands and requirements of the different kinds of economic interests institutionalized within the political center.

Before explaining why different types of power blocks produce different types of state formation, it is necessary to explain why state strength is so important to economic production in the world-system. There are three reasons. First, strong states are effective mechanisms for protecting economic actors from the risks and uncertainties generated by the world market. They accomplish this task through the regulation of the economic production that occurs within their borders. For example, many of the poorest areas in Latin America today were at one time highly active centers of raw material production in the world-system. But when the demand for these materials declined, the capital and organization that exploited these resources were withdrawn. Strong states, however, are relatively effective mechanisms for preventing such occurrences. They can erect barriers to prevent external control of production by forcing ownership into the hands of indigenous groups. They can regulate the flow of capital and profit to ensure that the gains of production are not withdrawn from the country but are channeled into other economic activities within the national economy. And through trade and tariff policies they can stimulate a diversification of production. Thus, strong states typically have elaborate rules and regulations controlling the production within their boundaries, and much political activity is directed toward controlling and managing economic activity.

Second, states are effective mechanisms for securing privileged access to resources and markets, including their own national markets. Economic actors engaged in producing consumption goods, for example, often attempt to influence the state to secure foreign markets as outlets for their goods and to secure a steady supply of the materials needed for production. Most of the trade and commercial policies of states are directed toward these two ends. Third, states are effective mechanisms for organizing economic actors to work in concert in the world market. States provide a means for pooling the resources of economic actors and achieving the benefits that large-scale economic activity has under a market system. These benefits can be achieved either through advantage in direct competition or through control over prices. The ability of states to function in these ways is a function of the strength of the state in relation to its own population and of the strength of the state in relation to other states.

Because of the importance of the state to economic production, economic actors all attempt to use the state for regulating the market to their own advantage. Thus, dominant economic groups attempt to institutionalize their interests within the state. But the type of state formation is dependent on the *nature* of the power block. The industrial-commercial block in core states produces strong states, while the export-oriented block in peripheral states produces weaker states. This difference comes from the different political requirements and demands of these types of production.

The effects of the nature of the power block on the degree of state formation can be separated into external and internal causes. There are two external mechanisms. First, where the interests in a state are composed primarily of manufacturing and commerce, those economic actors put great demands on the state to create an aggressive foreign policy. This is because such economic production requires access to foreign markets both for raw materials and for the selling of both capital and consumption goods. Economic actors engaged in this type of production will be competing for access to such markets. One of the most effective means to compete is to employ an aggressive foreign commercial and military policy. Thus, we can expect that the demands for such policy will lead to an increase in the authority and strength of the state, as economic actors support increasing its strength in order to pursue such policies. Countries in which the dominant economic interests are in producing primary products for export will experience much fewer demands on foreign policy. Economic actors in control of export production are likely to want a less extensive foreign policy because their gains rest merely with finding an importing country to buy their raw materials. It is almost impossible to affect the demand for such primary goods directly. Thus, there will be fewer vectors of economic interest pushing the state toward an aggressive foreign policy, and consequently the authority and strength of the state will be less.

The second external consideration affecting the strength of states arises from strong states actively attempting to weaken peripheral states. Thus, for example, there is the Dutch intrusion into Poland and the British and later United States intrusions into Latin America. Core states employ this process because weakening peripheral states is one way to further monopolize markets and to insure a steady supply of raw materials.

Among the *internal* reasons, strong states arise in the core because extensive political regulation is needed to foster and protect manufacturing and commercial production. For example, a highly sophisticated trade and commercial policy is required both to protect home manufacturing and to provide the infrastructure needed for industrial production. Since production in the core is much more extensive and diversified, there will be many more political demands placed on the state, and consequently a greater degree of state formation. Consequently, this explains why the political structure of the core is more "pluralistic": there is a far greater range of economic interests, all of which make political demands on the state. The periphery is less "pluralistic" for exactly the opposite reasons. Similarly, this explains not only why the core is pluralistic but why states in the core are the strongest states in the system.

The importance of a strong state for development has been pointed out previously. Here we need to repeat that once strong states develop, they become a central mechanism for reproducing the core-periphery division of labor through their ability to influence and protect production. This analysis also helps to explain why the form of government in the core tends to be more democratic and pluralistic. And further, there are distinct economic advantages to such a political structure, since this makes for much greater political flexibility. As the world market changes, and new areas of profit are created, a strong state, which has incorporated a large variety of interests into it, is in a position both to feel the pressures for shifting political advantage to some rising new area of profit and to have the ability—because of its greater authority—to effect such a shift of political advantage to new types of production.

Power-block formation and state formation, then, are two of the basic processes that reproduce the core-periphery division of labor. It is important to emphasize that these processes create differentiation in the world-system. This necessary structuring of the system into core and peripheral areas follows from the interdependent nature of the process of power-block and state formation: the type of alliances and the nature of power-block formation in the core are possible because of the creation of the complementary and opposite type of power-block formation in the periphery.

What of the semiperiphery in this analysis? The territorial organization of the world-system into core and periphery areas is not a pure differentiation. Within core areas there are located some periphery types of economic activities, but these are relatively unimportant. And in periphery areas there are likewise some core activities, but again these are few. Core activities combine very productive technology with highly skilled paid labor. Peripheral activities use relatively unproductive technology and cheap unskilled labor.

The semiperiphery areas are those in which there is a relatively equal mix of core and periphery activities. This mix may be due to upward or downward mobility of the area within the larger system. Some semiperiphery areas have previously been core areas (e.g., the Italian city-states, Spain, and Portugal). Others are periphery areas that have obtained an advantage due to changing conditions of competition in the system (e.g., twentieth-century Brazil, Mexico, and India). Other areas enter the system as semiperipheries in the sense that at the time of their incorporation into the larger system they have advantages, such as size, natural resources, relatively complex social structures, and so on, that enable them to rapidly develop core activities (e.g., nineteenth-century United States, Russia, and Japan, or twentieth-century China).

Political coalitions between classes and state formation may take on distinctive forms in the semiperiphery. Because of the mix of core and periphery activities, dominant classes tend to have very opposing interests. Some have alliances with core powers based on their control of peripheral activities, while others favor more independent policies which would expand core-type activities. Thus it is often the case that the state apparatus itself becomes the dominant element in forming the power block and is able to shape the political coalitions among economic groups. In semiperipheral countries with potential for upward mobility in the larger system state mobilization of development is often an important feature. This may take either a leftist or a rightist political form. Those upwardly mobile countries that rely on alliances with core powers tend to develop rightist political regimes (e.g., Brazil since 1964) while those that attempt autonomous development move toward the left (e.g., China and the Soviet Union). Whether leftist or rightist, upwardly mobile semiperipheral countries tend to employ more state-directed and state-mobilized development policies than do core countries.

Peripheral countries tend to have high levels of political instability and either right-wing regimes backed by core powers or left-wing anticore regimes. But in the periphery the opportunities for real upward mobility in the system (the expansion of core activities) are much more limited,[31] and so the class forces backing autonomous development tend to be weak. Anti-imperialist movements may take state power and try to mobilize for development (e.g., Angola, Cuba, Vietnam, Mozambique, Cambodia, etc.), but the development of core-type activities requires resources that small periphery countries most often do not have. Internal market size, state strength, natural resources, and sufficient political will to isolate the country from core powers, are necessary if such anti-imperialist mobilization is not to become either an isolationist backwater or a CIA countercoup. Those areas that escape the system but do not economically develop are soon reconquered (e.g., Haiti, Ghana, Chile). However, these constraints on successful development in opposition to the system are reduced the more it becomes possible to make alliances with other, more developed, socialist states.

Unequal Exchange

The third process that maintains the core-periphery division of labor is unequal exchange, or the economic transfer of surplus from the periphery to the core.[32] The embedding of this transfer in formal market transactions has come to replace the plunder of the peripheral areas by core powers that were instrumental in the formation of the system.[33] While, as Amin argues, direct political coercion is still essential to maintaining the conditions for unequal exchange between the core and the periphery, the actual transfer of surplus value to the core nevertheless occurs through relatively noncoercive market transactions.[34]

A variety of different conceptions of unequal exchange have developed in recent years.[35] These conceptions differ somewhat, but what is common to them all is the thesis that the process of exchanging commodities between core and peripheral countries operates in an asymmetrical fashion to advantage core countries and to disadvantage peripheral countries. Since good accounts of these theories of unequal exchange are readily available, we will not review them here. The critical issue in the present context is to examine how unequal exchange operates to reproduce the core-periphery division. This occurs in two ways.

First, its direct effect is to increase the economic gain of the core, and this extra increment of gain will have expansive effects on the national economy due to multiplier effects. Second, the added gain to the core can be used to further increase investment in technology and research and development, thus operating to maintain the difference in productivity levels between the core and the periphery. This effect may be quite important. Theories that emphasize the independent effect of technology on development often never ask the question of why new technologies and productivity increases almost always occur in the core. The perspective afforded by unequal exchange tends to make technology itself a function of the development of the system. This occurs for two reasons. First, the gains from unequal exchange provide the core countries with extra capital, part of which can be used to develop new technologies. Second, because of the greater political and economic power of the work force in core countries, which is used to keep wages high, there is an impetus to create new technology, since this is the only way to increase profits. That is, if the political power of the work force is employed to keep wages rising along with productivity, then there is a constant vector of interest exerted for capitalists to increase technology and save on labor costs.

Class Struggle

The fourth mechanism by which the core-periphery division of labor is reproduced is the operation of class conflict on a world scale. Classes are conventionally understood in terms of their operation within national societies, and class struggle is therefore seen as taking place primarily within countries. But Marx argued that classes must be understood in their relationship to the mode of production that, if Wallerstein is right, is a characteristic of the capitalist world-system as a whole. Objective economic classes cut across national boundaries to form a structure that can only be understood in terms of the world-system. Amin begins this type of analysis in his discussion of the world proletariat and the world bourgeoisie, and others have elaborated the notion of world classes.[36]

Since the major political units in the world economy are nation-states, class struggles tend to be oriented toward state structures. Hence there is a contradiction between the economic basis of class formation and the political basis of class struggle. Class struggle takes the form of competition for the seizure of state structures, and this fractionalizes objective classes and stabilizes the system. Proletarian internationalism has not yet been an effective force even between core workers of different states, let alone between core and peripheral workers. The state system tends to confine class struggle within nation-states. This has the effect of reproducing the core-periphery division of labor by producing class alliances that politically stabilize the mode of production.

Exploitation takes place along two dimensions: between capital and labor and between core and periphery. The exploitation of the periphery by the core enables core capital to coopt core labor into a national alliance. Similarly, opposition to core exploitation may produce alliances between domestic capital and labor in the periphery. In the semiperiphery, on the other hand, class alliances of this type are more difficult precisely because the core-periphery dimension of exploitation presents contradictory alternatives. There are real simultaneous possibilities in some semiperipheral countries for either an alliance with core powers or a mobilization for autocentric development. The state is the key organization and its control is hotly contested between groups with widely opposed interests. This results either in authoritarian regimes that strongly suppress class struggle or in class struggles that result in leftist movements taking state power. The contradictions between capital and labor are muted in both the core and the periphery by the operation of the core-periphery contradiction, but in the semiperiphery the struggle between capital and labor is not so muted. This is part of the explanation for the emergence of social democratic class alliances in the core. It also partly explains why socialist movements based on the power of workers and peasants have first come to state power in the semiperiphery (Russia and China).[37] The coming to power of socialist movements in the periphery does not contradict this analysis. These have most often been anti-imperialist struggles that have taken state power on the basis of anticore class alliances. Of course, nationalist class alliances have been important in the semiperiphery also, but the level of domestic class struggle involved in the creation of socialist regimes has been greater in the semiperiphery than in the periphery. The point here is not to explain the class basis of all states but to point out that one consequence of core-periphery exploitation is to stabilize class alliances in the core and in the periphery. This reinforces the state system and helps reproduce the core-periphery division of labor. The political function of the semiperiphery, according to Wallerstein, is to stabilize the system by concentrating deviant political forms in an intermediate position. This also tends to depolarize and stabilize the core-periphery dimension of exploitation.

CONCLUSIONS

Our focus in this paper has been on the factors that tend to stabilize and reproduce the capitalist world-system. This is only one side of the coin, and we are greatly interested in the limits of this system and its transformation. But the understanding of the transition requires that we be able to distinguish old cycles from new departures. What does it mean that the whole globe is now in the system, that the state system has spread to the entire periphery, that state socialist production relations have expanded greatly since 1917, or that transnational corporations plan production on a global scale? These developments can only be interpreted when we have an adequate theory of the normal functioning and growth of the capitalist world-system.

NOTES

1. Richard Rosecrance and Arthur Stein, "Interdependence: Myth or Reality," *World Politics* 26 (October 1973): 1–27.
2. Immanuel Wallerstein, "Three Paths of National Development in Sixteenth Century Europe," *Studies in Comparative International Development* 7 (Summer 1972): 95–101.
3. Immanuel Wallerstein, "The Rise and Future Demise of the World Capitalist System: Concepts for Comparative Analysis," *Comparative Studies in Society and History* 16 (1972): 387–415.
4. Immanuel Wallerstein, *The Modern World-System: Capitalist Agriculture and the Origins of the European World-Economy in the Sixteenth Century* (New York: Academic Press, 1974), pp. 126–127. This definition of capitalism differs from that of Marx in that wage labor is understood to be only one of the forms of labor exploitation occurring within the mode of production.
5. Karl Polanyi, *The Great Transformation* (Boston: Beacon, 1944).
6. Wallerstein, "World Capitalist System," p. 403.
7. Ibid., p. 404.
8. Wallerstein, "Three Paths of National Development," p. 96.
9. Uneven development on a regional basis also occurs *within* core nations, but the size of the high wage, high productivity sector within core nations is much greater than in periphery areas. See Michael Hechter, *Internal Colonialism: The Celtic Fringe in British National Development, 1536–1966* (Berkeley and Los Angeles: University of California, 1975).

10. Wallerstein, "Three Paths to National Development," pp. 95–96.

11. Wallerstein's fullest discussion of the contemporary semiperiphery is in "Semi-Peripheral Countries and the Contemporary World Crisis," *Theory and Society* 3 (Fall 1976): 461–483. He compares Brazil, Mexico, India, the Soviet Union, China, and Mediterranean Europe, all of which are seen as upwardly mobile semiperipheral countries or recently arrived members of the core.

12. Wallerstein, "Three Paths to National Development," p. 96.

13. Wallerstein, *The Modern World-System,* p. 10.

14. Johan Galtung argues that the "level of processing" is the key underlying dimension of the core-periphery division of labor. "A Structural Theory of Imperialism," *Journal of Peace Research* 8 (1971): 81-117. He focuses on the raw material-manufactured goods dimension, ignoring the different ways in which labor and constant capital are combined to transform commodities and the question of wages holding constant productivity.

15. Wallerstein, "World Capitalist System," p. 398.

16. Again, this understanding of the capitalist mode of production differs from Marx. For Marx the payment of a wage is crucial to the commodity nature of labor power. The notion of the social relations of production has been interpreted by M. Dobb (*Studies in the Development of Capitalism* [New York: International Publishers, 1963]) and others as referring only to the relationship between the direct producer and his or her immediate exploiter. This well intentioned attempt to simplify the study of class relations unfortunately does not allow for an understanding of multitiered systems of exploitation such as the tributary mode of production or the capitalist world system. The assertion that capitalism only exists where labor is exploited by a wage system ignores the extent to which labor can be made into a commodity and subjected to capitalist production using other juridical types of production relations. It is not the juridical form of labor control that is crucial to capitalist production relations but rather the ability of capital to bend labor to the purpose of profitable production, whether this be done by the wage system or by the use of more openly coercive institutions such as slavery or serfdom. The Wallersteinian heresy asserts that it is the *articulation* of relatively less coerced labor in the core with relatively more coerced labor in the periphery that is constitutive of capitalist production relations. This articulation is not only accomplished through the world market but is built into the state system itself in the form of colonial empires and neocolonial types of domination. Clearly, so-called *precapitalist* forms of labor control such as slavery involve much more transparent political coercion than does wage labor. But the trend to proletarianization of the world work force that has eliminated serfdom and slavery has not eliminated the differential degree of coercion between core and periphery labor. Wallerstein's prophetic sentence, "when labor is everywhere free we shall have socialism," must not be taken literally. Sufficiently different levels of coercion are possible between sectors of wage labor (i.e., split labor markets) to maintain a core-periphery dimension even if the entire world world work force were composed of wage labor.

17. This understanding of capitalism has been criticized for placing too much emphasis on market-mediated relations. See Robert Brenner, "The Origins of Capitalist Development: A Critique of Neo-Smithian Marxism," *New Left Review,* vol. 104 (July-August 1977).

18. Cf. Ernest Mandel, *Late Capitalism* (London: NLB, 1975), chap. 2.

19. Gayl D. Ness and Jeannine R. Ness, "Metropolitan Power and the Demise of the Overseas Empires" (Paper presented at the Annual Meeting of the American Sociological Association, New Orleans, 1972).

20. E.g., Dutch, British, and U.S. centrality in world finance and their importance for the maintenance of international stability during the later part of their respective hegemonies.

21. Albert Szymanski, "Military Spending and Economic Stagnation," *American Journal of Sociology* 79 (July 1973): 1–14.

22. Stephen D. Krasner, "State Power and the Structure of International Trade," *World Politics* 28 (April 1976): 317–347.

23. A causal model of this relationship is proposed in Christopher Chase-Dunn, "Core-Periphery Relations: The Effects of Core Competition," in *Social Change in the Capitalist World Economy,* ed. Barbara Kaplan (Beverly Hills: Sage, 1978).

24. For a causal explanation of the Kondratiev, or fifty-year business cycle, see Ernest Mandel, *Late Capitalism,* chap. 4. A general discussion of "cyclical rhythms" in the growth of the world economy is included in a recent article by Immanuel Wallerstein and Terence K. Hopkins, "Patterns of Development of the Modern World-System," *Review 1,* no. 2 (Fall 1977): 122–123.

25. Samir Amin, *Unequal Development* (New York: Monthly Review, 1976).

26. Ness and Ness, "Metropolitan Power."

27. Ellen Kay Trimberger, *Revolution from Above* (New Brunswick, NJ: Transaction, 1978).

28. See Immanuel Wallerstein, "Dependence in an Interdependent World: The Limited Possibilities for Transformation within the Capitalist World Economy," *African Studies Review* 17:1–26.

29. Nicos Poulantzas, following Gramsci, has used the expression "power block" to describe the coalition of classes and class fractions that occupy a dominant position within political relations of the capitalist state. See especially his discussion in *Political Power and Social Classes* (London: New Left Books, 1973). The same notion is termed a "center coalition" by Barrington Moore, *Social Origins of Democracy and Dictatorship* (Boston: Beacon Press, 1966).

30. For a thorough discussion of the concept of state power see Richard Tardanico, "A Structural Perspective on State Power in the Capitalist World-System" (Paper presented at the Annual Meeting of the American Sociological Association, San Francisco, 1978). For an analysis of power-block formation and its link to state power, see Richard Rubinson, "Political Transformation in Germany and the United States," in *Social Change in the Capitalist World-Economy,* ed. Barbara Kaplan.

31. Wallerstein, "Dependence in an Interdependent World."

32. Charles Bettelheim has correctly argued that the greater part of the surplus value accumulated in the core has been produced there by core workers. See the appendix of Arghiri Emmanuel's *Unequal Exchange.* Contrary to Robert Brenner's critique in "Origins of Capitalist Development," the world-system perspective does not need to argue that core accumulation is entirely based on exploitation of the periphery. Rather, the periphery provides an important alternative source of surplus and an opportunity for capital to escape the demands of core labor. This political function has allowed the accumulation process to adapt to its own contradictions.

33. K. Marx, *Capital* (New York: International Publishers, 1967), 1: 751.

34. Samir Amin, *Accumulation on a World Scale* (New York: Monthly Review Press, 1974).
35. See Emmanuel, *Unequal Exchange,* Hans Singer, "The Distribution of Gains between Investing and Borrowing Countries," *American Economic Review* 40 (May 1950): 473–485; Galtung, "Structural Theory of Imperialism"; Mandel, *Late Capitalism,* chap. 11; and Raul Prebisch, *El desarrollo Economico de Latino-America y sus Principales Problems* (U.N., ECLA, 1950).
36. Amin, *Unequal Development,* pp. 351–364. See also Sidney Mintz, "Was the Plantation Slave a Proletarian?" (Working Seminar Paper, Fernand Braudel Center, SUNY, Binghamton, 1977).
37. It has been argued that China was not in the semiperiphery at the time of its revolution. China was an external arena to the capitalist world-system (a world empire in its own right) until the nineteenth century when the core powers began to make colonial inroads. But China was never completely colonized nor deeply penetrated by the process of peripheralization. Thus when China became part of the world-system in the twentieth century it brought with it strengths that enabled it to quickly develop core-type activities and to become intermediate in the capitalist world-system.

Dependency Theory: Continuities and Discontinuities in Development Studies

James A. Caporaso

INTRODUCTION

Currently, the field of development is in disarray. One of its most important sub-fields, development economics, has run into difficulties because of both empirical and normative difficulties: empirical difficulties due to the failure to correctly predict which countries would develop and which would not, normative difficulties because the emphasis of economic development studies expanded from an exclusive focus on growth to include questions of distribution and equity.

Theories developed in political science and sociology suffered too, but here the reason lay not so much in explanatory defects of the theories as in the simple failure to agree upon what was important—e.g., mass participation, democracy, capacity of the government to direct social change, structural differentiation, equilibrium, etc. Only anthropology, possibly because of its suspicion of grand theory on the one hand, and its relative distance from governmental forces on the other, was able to maintain any appearance of continuity.

These intellectual changes, of course, had a material base. The decline of the cold war made talk of a *third world* less politically pressing. The rise of oil-rich countries, along with a substantial group of newly industrializing countries competing with the advanced countries, pointed to important differentiations among less developed countries. Thus, although development and underdevelopment were clearly major problems in the late

James A. Caporaso, "Dependency Theory: Continuities and Discontinuities in Development Studies." Reprinted from *International Organization,* 34:4 (Autumn 1980) by permission of The MIT Press, Cambridge, MA.

seventies, they were problems that had dropped a peg or two on the political agenda.

To all of this we should perhaps concur with Wallerstein's "Modernization: Requiescat in Pace."[1] Nevertheless, in this paper, I shall review two recent books which attempt to make sense of the processes of development and underdevelopment. In so doing, I shall try to raise some general issues related to development theory, and to probe the possibilities for progress in what has become a stagnant field.

It is a sad irony that recent interest in dependency theory in the United States and in the English-speaking world in general has taken place without access to most of the important Latin American works. This had two unfortunate consequences. First, because it eliminated much of the complex material on the domestic structure of dependency, it had the effect of exaggerating the importance of the external forces driving development and underdevelopment. Inevitably the forces focused upon were those describing the phase characteristics of international capitalism: mercantile, industrial, commercial, corporate, etc. The operation of the local society (i.e., national and subnational units) was simply derivative of these great laws of global change. Second (a logical corollary to the first point), this focus on the external forces affecting dependent societies led to a neglect of the complex, and often very influential, internal anatomy of dependency. This has left the impression with many English-speaking scholars that dependency reflects nothing more than a bad case of external reliance—a condition which holds when a country depends on another for some crucial inputs needed to complete its economic cycle. To show that this interpretation of dependency theory is still very much alive, one has only to read the recent article by Tony Smith in *World Politics*.[2] Smith's major criticism of dependency theory is that it subordinates an analysis of parts to the whole and, in so doing "... deprive[s] local histories of their integrity and specificity, thereby making local actors little more than the pawn of outside forces."[3] While this may be an adequate characterization of Wallerstein's world systems analysis or Andre Gunder Frank's[4] stark version of dependency theory, it is certainly not a fair representation of the work of other theorists of dependent development.

The recent publication in English of *Dependency and Development in Latin America*[5] by Fernando Henrique Cardoso and Enzo Faletto, and translated by Marjory Mattingly Urquidi, will go a long way toward placing in proper perspective this "externalization" of the forces behind the dependency situation. This is not to say that external forces are unimportant in their analysis but rather that there is a parallel set of domestic configurations that must be taken into account. These latter forces must not be seen simply as competing for influence with the external ones but rather as criss-crossing and fusing with them in complicated though not mysterious ways. The authors see as one of their central tasks the unravelling of the forces which cause a uniform global capitalism to be associated with such vastly different results in various socio-political settings.

The nearly simultaneous publication of Peter Evans' *Dependent De-*

velopment: The Alliance of Multinational, State and Local Capital in Brazil offers an important case study, within the Brazilian context, with enlightening similarities and contrasts to the Cardoso and Faletto book. The book provides us with the fruit of ten years of research by a sensitive observer of the Brazilian scene and it admirably combines a closeness to subject matter with a broadly insightful comparative eye. Indeed, there is a kind of Schumpeterian quality surrounding the book, relying as it does on a mix of historical insights, comparative contrasts, and statistical data (though not statistical testing). Both books are important and reading them will deepen and broaden our understanding of the literature on dependent development.

BRIEF OVERVIEW OF THE TWO BOOKS

The Cardoso-Faletto book, *Dependency and Development in Latin America,* is broadly focused, both in terms of the number of countries examined and its historical reach. The book draws on material from Argentina, Brazil, Colombia, Chile, Peru, Mexico, Bolivia, Uruguay, and Venezuela, and more selectively, from other countries. The book is also a chronological *tour d'horizon,* attempting to explain processes of development in Latin America from colonial times to the present. The cohesiveness of the analysis is provided by the historical spread of capitalism and its interactions with domestic society and politics.

The authors have provided a very thoughtful special preface to the English edition of the book, a careful reading of which is important for a full understanding of the balance of the book. In it they carefully describe their methodological approach, which is more or less implicit in the bulk of the text, and explain in some detail how they attempt to use an analysis which is simultaneously historical, structural, and dialectical. For those interested primarily in the approach of dependency theory (Cardoso and Faletto do not generally use the word theory), rather than a rich, historical interpretation resting on that approach, this chapter may be the most important one in the book.

The substantive portion of the book begins with Chapter 3, "The Period of Outward Expansion," then moves to a detailed examination of the social and political changes accompanying development, how insertion of the dependent economy into the global capitalist system involved the participation of limited groups, such as commercial classes tied to the export sector at first, then how this gradually broadened to include participation of the urban middle classes and the industrial bourgeoisie. Finally, they document how the period of import-substitution, which grew up in the aftermath of the 1929 depression, gave way to a "new" period which saw the internationalization of productive forces occurring in Latin America. In all of this, the book succeeds in keeping domestic, societal forces as clearly in focus as the global dynamics of capitalism. Indeed, the book is primarily about Latin American society, its differentiation into social groups, and how these groups figure into the interplay of national and international interests.

Dependent Development, by Peter Evans, is a more focused book both in terms of the countries examined and the breadth of the processes explained. Evans focuses on just one country, Brazil, and within Brazil, on the internal structure of its elite, primarily the business elite but also the top segments of the state apparatus. This should not mislead us since the book is anything but a technical report on interviews with corporate managers and owners. Evans' analysis and interpretation are admirably comprehensive, and the presentation of his fascinating interview findings are always sensitively positioned within a context in which Brazil's social, political, and economic composition figure prominently.

The methodology relied upon is diverse and incorporates elite interviews along with objective information, statistical data, and a careful reading of the historical record. The use of business journals, not as the last word, but as a way of incorporating fragmented pieces of information into a more comprehensive picture, is illuminating. In general, the plurality of methodological angles used to approach the problem provides a stimulating example of *convergent operationalism*—a methodological virtue often praised but seldom followed.

Why was Brazil chosen for study? Evans did not want a country which had been only superficially touched by the logic of dependent development, or one in which this logic had not reached an advanced form—e.g., one in which trade relations primarily characterized dependency. If dependency is defined "as a situation in which the rate and direction of accumulation are externally conditioned" (p. 27), then one is interested in "cases where capital accumulation and diversified industrialization of a more than superficial sort are not only occurring in a peripheral country, but are dominating the transformation of its economy and social structure" (p. 32).

Obviously, not all less developed countries are in this category. On the contrary, only a select few have entered this stage of development. Into this stage, which is characterized by an alliance between domestic and international capital, we might place Brazil, Mexico, Hong Kong, South Korea, Taiwan, perhaps Nigeria (though there could be strenuous objections here) and, from the periphery of Europe—Spain, Portugal, and Yugoslavia.[6] Whatever the differences among these countries, and there are many, the common elements are the dynamic patterns of industrial growth and their close integration with the international capitalist system. To the academic left, these countries form a *semiperiphery* between the rich and poor, while to many analysts in the developed world, they are "newly industrializing countries," held up as the success stories of the 1960s and 1970s. But, by whatever label, these countries provide a fertile laboratory in which to study the successes and failures, opportunities and limits, harmonies and contradictions of dependent, capitalist development.

DEPENDENCY AND MAINSTREAM DEVELOPMENT THEORIES

The reception by the English-speaking world of these two books is likely to be heavily influenced by its perception of what I will call *mainstream development theories*, for want of a better term. Of course mainstream theory does not constitute a cohesive intellectual statement; it itself has several roots and expressions. Modern development theory in the United States was a reaction to the institutionalists, whose intellectual categories were supplied by the roster of important Western institutions: courts, executives, bureaucracies, legislatures, political parties, etc.[7] Needless to say, few of these categories had much utility when one shifted the analysis to less developed countries. For this reason alone, the functionalist movement stimulated by Gabriel Almond was a major step forward.[8]

There were also political roots to the rise of development theory. Academic interest in theories of development did not emerge on a significant scale until after World War II, and in particular, until after European economies were rebuilt and West Germany reintegrated into the Western Alliance system. Of course, the rapid decolonization of the British, French, and Dutch empires was important too. Now the world had many *new nations,* a term almost a synonym for less developed countries, and with the form, if not the content, of statehood, they became legitimate objects of development programs by metropolitan and non-metropolitan countries alike. Under the influence of cold war thinking, the idea of a *third world* sprung up, next to the communist world and the western world.

Given the proliferation of development studies during the last twenty-five to thirty years, we must remind ourself of the novelty of this field. One respected development economist tells us that "until 1950 there had been little serious thinking on the growth prospects of 'backward areas.' "[9]

Development theory, once it emerged, took many different forms. There were the functional requisites of Almond and Coleman, tasks that all political systems had to perform if they were to survive; there were Parsonian evolutionary universals, and a further specified list of requisites provided by Marion Levy.[10] Whether these functional requisites described powerful theoretical generalizations about societies or whether they simply stipulated the definitional criteria for identifying societies is not clear; nevertheless, the impact of structural-functional analysis was powerful.

At the same time, and partly influenced by the functional approach, a number of scholars writing in connection with the Social Science Research Council came out with an influential set of books which demonstrated the continued centrality of political institutions: *Political Parties and Political Development,*[11] *Bureaucracy and Political Development,*[12] and *Communications and Political Development.*[13] The *crises* approach, too, was influential.[14] According to this development school, all societies faced basically the same set of environmental challenges, which had to be met and overcome—penetration, legitimacy, identity, participation, and distribution. The path of political development was one of encouraging the growth of institutions, cultural beliefs and attitudes, and patterns of political behavior conducive to a successful management of these crises. Despite the natural affinities between the crisis approach and the functional requisites approach (a function is merely the name for a pattern of activity that solves some problem; since crises are problems *in extremis,* successful resolution of crises can be viewed in functional terms), the two rarely came together.[15]

There is another body of development literature which centers on a syndrome of cultural and psychological traits associated with development.[16] It shifts from the macro to the micro level and refers to *modern man* or *the modern personality.* What is the modern personality and does it make sense to speak of it as a distinct personality type? In answering this question, a list of traits is invoked: mental flexibility, willingness to take risks, psychic mobility, ability to defer gratifications, and above all, pragmatism—a willingness to compromise and to stand not too firmly on principle. One imagines a fluid, almost protean person, not too rooted in tradition, alive to the desirability and possibility of change.

Finally, there are the sociological theories of development—theories that have a grounding in nineteenth century sociology in the works of Maine, Spencer, Comte, and Durkheim.[17] Along with Marxian interpretations of history, this branch of historical sociology can be called *progressive* in the sense that it sees forces as moving historical change in a consistent and desirable direction. These scholars did not provide a theory of development per se, but instead deduced a theory of development from a general theory about society. The polarities defining the end points between which societies move are feudal society, based on heroic-military values and industrial society, based on commercial-bourgeois values. Since historical forces were pushing inexorably in the direction of industrialism, these sociologists drew optimistic conclusions.

Alejandro Portes is quite right in arguing that social evolutionism did not die out in the twentieth century; rather the continuity of evolutionary theory was maintained by compressing many dualities into a single bipolar theme: Durkheim's mechanical-organic, Toennies' Gemeinschaft-Gesellschaft, Redfield's folk-urban, and Parson's five pattern variables—each one a bipolar type.[18]

THE DEPENDENCY APPROACH

What is remarkable about all of the above approaches to development is how little they contribute to constructing explanations of change based on factors residing in the external environment.[19] As such, at the outset there is very little similarity between mainstream theories and dependency theory. True, some broad points of contact exist (trade-led models of growth come to mind), but by and large dependency theory represents a distinct approach to development. At the most general level, it may provide a critique of other development theories, but it is the kind of critique that one draws out by implication rather than by explicit argument.

Latin American dependency theory is a native construction. In terms of its intellectual genealogy, evolutionary coherence, working assumptions, research programs, and policy goals it stands on its own. While other studies focus primarily on domestic causes of development, dependency focuses on internal and external forces (including their interactions). While others take the nation-state as the exclusive unit of analysis (indeed development is almost synonymous with nation-building and state-building), dependency theorists introduce corporate actors and social classes as important additional units. While others see their theories as intellectual constructions which attempt to explain reality, dependency theorists attempt to use their ideas to change reality. Finally, while mainstream theories of development see countries presently on the way to development following the same historical path as the early modernizers of the eighteenth and nineteenth centuries, dependency theorists see today's historical path as altered by the very modernization of the earlier modernizers.

In all of these senses, dependency theory is not a reconstruction of traditional development theory but a qualitatively new departure. If anything, it is closer in spirit to the work of Gerschenkron (because of the importance of timing considerations) and to Barrington Moore (because of the methodology of contextual historical analysis).[20]

THE IMPORTANCE OF THE TWO BOOKS

Dependency and Development in Latin America and *Dependent Development* are important contributions to the literature on development both in terms of their intrinsic merits as well as for their timely appearance in filling a huge gap in the contemporary literature. If these books are to stimulate our interest, reorient our thinking, and direct our research, they will have to be read sympathetically, which is not to say uncritically. However, given the misgivings with which prior dependency studies have been received, at least in the United States, it may be useful to highlight several points about the books. I will address five areas in which I feel the books have an important contribution to make.

Definitions

The starting point for an appreciation of the two books is their definitions of development, which are profoundly different from those of conventional development theory. First, a word on what development is not. It is not economic productivity, increases in GNP or GNP per capita, the spread of urbanization, literacy, and transportation, or improvement in quality of life indicators, such as reduced infant mortality, increased longevity, or better medical care. Neither is development necessarily the movement away from a dominant primary sector toward greater diversification of production and decreased reliance on external inputs. As Cardoso and Faletto put it:

> . . . we do not mean by the notion of *development* the achievement of a more egalitarian or more just society. These are not consequences expected from capitalist development, especially in peripheral economies. . . . Development, in this context, means the progress in productive forces, mainly through the import of technology, capital accumulation, penetration of local economies by foreign enterprises, increasing numbers of wage-earning groups, and intensification of social division [of] labor (pp. 23–24).

The definition offered by Evans is similar to Cardoso and Faletto's. In fact, it is clear that Evans is much influenced by the latter two. Perhaps more than Cardoso and Faletto, Evans emphasizes the accumulation of capital and industrialization on the periphery as the core phenomena of development:

> dependent development implies both the accumulation of capital and some degree of industrialization on the periphery. Dependent development is a special instance of dependency, characterized by the association or alliance of international and local capital (p.32).

Development, for both books, implies progress of the productive forces. Progress here does not have its usual normative implication of being desirable. It may entail improvement in material conditions or it may involve regress in these.

Causes of Development

Despite the fact that the reception of dependency literature in the United States has taken the relationship between dependency and development as the centerpiece of analysis, I think it is fair to say that Cardoso and Faletto are not substantially concerned with this question. They are more concerned with development (i.e., development of the productive forces of capitalism) and how this affects the social and political struggles inside countries. Their primary task is to show how foreign capital interacts with domestic society to produce different alliances of social groups and, in turn, how these alliances attempt to use the state to further their own interests.

Cardoso and Faletto are also anxious to demonstrate how different modes of peripheral incorporation into the global system (e.g., enclave economies versus one dominated by local bourgeoisies), affect the entire process by which capital is created, employed, valorized, and realized. It is worthwhile to quote these authors:

In enclave economies foreign invested capital *originates in the exterior,* is incorporated into local productive processes, and transforms part of itself into wages and taxes. Its value is increased by the exploitation of local labor forces, which transform nature and produce goods that *realize* again the life of this capital when staples (oil, copper, bananas, etc.) are sold in the *external markets.*

In economies controlled by local bourgeoisie, the circuit of capital is formally just the opposite. Accumulation is the result of the appropriation of natural resources by local entrepreneurs and the exploitation of the labor force by this same local group. The starting point for capital accumulation is thus *internal.* The process of capital valorization also takes place in the local productive process, but insofar as merchandise consists of staples and food products, the *international market* is required to realize the final steps of the capital circuit (p. xix).

A society is dependent then when it requires an outside complement to make possible the full circle of capital creation, expansion, and accumulation. Forms of dependency may vary widely so that the concrete expression which economic processes take will be different, but there is an underlying structural similarity beneath these various expressions.

The account of the different forms which capital accumulation can take, together with the social and political consequences of these, is a legitimate project, of course. Still, I am disappointed at the reluctance of Cardoso and Faletto to explicitly develop their theory. Indeed, as they suggest on several occasions, they are somewhat suspicious of the entire enterprise of theory-building and indeed can bring themselves to use the term only when putting it in quotes (pp. xii and xxiii).

I find this position troubling for the following reasons. Theory is after all only a preferred explanation; it is neither more nor less complicated than that. If we do not develop theories, we, by definition, do not offer explanations. In addition (and this is not a minor point) if the structure of an explanation is not developed, there is little we can do to falsify, and inversely to corroborate, the argument. Despite disfavor within dependencia circles of the criteria of falsifiability and verification, the scientific process cannot proceed without them. Outside of a scholastic preoccupation with logical canons such as consistency and deduction, which play a central role in formal modelling, there is simply no substitute for attempting to fit evidence into the explanatory structure of an argument.

While nearly everyone would agree, when put this way, I have difficulty imagining how a non-circular process of fit can take place without a theory—i.e., without an explanatory structure that is not merely a redundant restatement of historical observations. To put this another way, a theory must offer more than a summary of, or even exhaustive restatement of, the facts used to develop it. Cardoso and Faletto's approach to historical analysis seems so close to the data that there is little room for testing ideas.

After having said this, it is necessary to add that the authors provide us with a subtle description of the narrative of dependent development, a narrative that never fails to show the complex interactions between various phase characteristics of international capitalism and the prevailing social, economic, and political conditions in dependent societies. The subtlety of the analysis is important, for it allows us to see the essential condition of domination existing across a variety of forms of organizational expression. This is a helpful antidote to overly simplistic rejections of *political causes* as explanations for underdevelopment.

From the beginning, Evans' *Dependent Development* is more satisfactory on the relationship between dependency and development. Indeed, I suspect that the book is self-consciously titled *Dependent Development*[21] in order to suggest a category of development problems, rather than *Dependency and Development* which suggests two separate variables related to one another. Both terms really modify and limit the scope of the other. Thus, Evans is interested in countries that are simultaneously dependent and developing.

Though Brazil has been singled out, the most inclusive set of units suggested by Evans' theoretical focus is all of the peripheral capitalist countries which are industrializing. They are countries which are showing some movement; the object of Evans' analysis is to explain why. The key to this movement lies in the needs of capital accumulation. Evans shows how classic dependence in Brazil generated opposing forces which gradually undermined it. In this dialectical analysis, Evans concretizes for us that elusive "surplus" of which we so often hear. He brings this concept to life and provides it with some operational content by detailing how part of the excess value created from primary production and export went to the Brazilian elite, rather than foreign economic and political actors. In addition, he shows how the diversification of the origins of foreign investment, as well as imports and exports, gave the Brazilian state more room for maneuver. All in all, the book provides us with an impressive account of the long-term, structural, hegemonic forces as well as those countervailing forces which make change possible.

Interplay Between Internal and External Factors

As the previous discussion has tried to show, much of traditional development theory has had a tendency to offer one-sided interpretations of the sources of development—showing a blind spot to either internal or external factors. Dependency theory was originally received in the United States in such a way as to highlight the external components of the theory so that soon dependency came to mean high trade reliance, necessity for outside markets, foreign technology, etc. Rarely was a serious internal analysis undertaken. This external interpretation was partly due to dependency writings, some of which oversimplified the forces involved. It was also due in part to an overzealous interpretation of the dependency literature in some academic circles, as well as to a confusion of dependency theory with the world systems approach. For example, Tony Smith writes that:

> The chief feature of the dependency school is its insistence that it is not internal characteristics of particular countries so much as the structure of the international system—particularly in its economic aspects—that is the key variable to be studied in order to understand the form that development has taken in non-communist industrializing countries.[22]

Smith develops his argument further and argues that dependency theory *globalizes* national development and hence deprives local histories of their integrity.[23] This interpretation of dependency, which reduces it to a set of external explanatory factors, is simply not based on an accurate reading of the dependency literature.

Cardoso and Faletto do not make the mistake of overemphasizing the global system and treating domestic society and politics as derivative. They take great pains to point out, in both the preface (xiv–xvi) and in the bulk of the book (chapters 3 to 5), that the interweaving of the internal and external is complicated and, in terms of influencing outcomes, the former is at least as important as the latter.

Although Cardoso and Faletto are strongly critical of writing which, in stressing global interpretations, treats domestic societies as derivative, they are also quick to point out that broad changes in the international economy (from mercantilism to monopoly capitalism to industrial capitalism), set important structural limits on the scope of actions domestically. But constraints, while they set limits, do not churn out specific behavioral outcomes. This is why a close detailed analysis of the social, economic, and political conditions within each country is necessary.

For Evans also the nodal point for analysis is the complex intersection among three major groups of actors: domestic capital interests, foreign capital, and the state in the dependent society. In providing the details of this three-way alliance, an alliance that sometimes resembles a tug-of-war, Evans does an excellent job of showing us how local capital and the Brazilian state have reacted to the development of foreign capital and industry. Foreign capital did not simply replace domestic capital; it built on top of it in many cases, added to it, and reinforced its existing structures. This is not to say that foreign capital "benignly complemented" (page 102) local capital, but it just as clearly is not a simple matter of denationalization by foreign interests.

Some of the dependency literature offers bland charges about the harmful effects of foreign capital penetration on development and leaves it at that. Evans goes well beyond that and offers us some specific case materials as well as some refined conclusions about the links among the state, foreign capital, and private capital. For example, he makes a serious effort to assess the characteristics of industries where local or foreign interests predominate. Local capital is strongest in small industries with low rates of growth while successful large Brazilian corporations are those which emphasize commercial and marketing strategies—not product development, innovation, research, etc. This process has two effects. The first is to reduce the role of local Brazilian industry in the high-technology, high-profit, oligopolistic parts of industrial activity. The second effect is a variation on the first. Even if Brazilian firms enter the oligopolistic industries, the functions within them relating to product innovation and high profits will remain under the control of firms in the center countries.

The Role of the State

Though the state is the centerpiece of the discipline of political science, its position in relation to other social structures and to the economy has not been adequately developed. This is true whether the state is dealt with in Deutschian terms as a steering mechanism for the pursuit of societal goals, as a pluralist regulator of various group positions, or as a Marxian agent of class domination. There have been excellent studies of the operation of selected parts of the state—e.g., studies of legislatures, executives, foreign offices, as well as research on the relationship between parts of the private sector, for example, interest groups, and how they interact with the state bureaucracy.

However, what is needed for purposes of development studies is more than this. What is needed is a theory of the state[24], not only in its internal workings nor just in relation to organized pressure groups, but in relation to society as a whole. We need to know how the state, and by that I mean the institutions, roles, norms and behavioral patterns responsible for setting policies and non-policies at the highest level, respond to, activate, and combine with various parts of the private sector in the pursuit of group goals.

For Cardoso and Faletto, as well as for Evans, the state forms a crucial component of their analysis. Although the state definitely plays a role in the goals of dominant classes, it partly takes on an independent existence and develops its own social base—i.e., it explicitly cultivates the constellation of economic and social interests that support it. As Cardoso and Faletto point out, in some countries the state is used to build an industrial class (p. 128). In doing this, the state acts out its own version of primitive accumulation and must extract the necessary capital from taxes and duties while later that capital reproduces itself and expands, due to the profits accumulated by the state enterprises (p. 203).

It is interesting to note, in an analysis that owes much to Marxism, that the state is involved in the very process of class formation, rather than passively executing an already formed class interest. In carrying out this project, the state forges an alliance among the internationalized sector, the public bureaucracies, and the local bourgeoisie.

Much the same line of analysis is pursued by Evans. Evans is at pains to stress that the state enters the alliance with local and foreign capital not as a *third partner* but as a motivator of local capital (pp. 39–43). Consistent with the general approach, Evans treats the role of the state in historical terms, from the earliest periods when the state limited itself to ". . . counter the reluctance of international capital to invest in the development of Brazil" (p. 84), to the period of the late 1950s where the ideology of "desenvolvimentiso" held sway and the state's share of investment in the economy increased (p. 93), to the period of multinational expansion where the state enterprises kept pace with the growth of foreign investment (p. 222).

Finally, the role of the state in dependent development is not without important macro effects. To single out one of the most important of these effects, one has only to recall Evans' point about the way state enterprises affect the balance between local and foreign capital. If one looks only to the distribution of private local and foreign shares in Brazil, one soon comes to the conclusion that the multinationals are gaining ground. However, once state enterprises are taken into account, this unfavorable distribution is reversed. In other words, the state is more than a broker between foreign and domestic interests. It also performs an independent entrepreneurial role, and by this latter function, acts as a regulator of the distribution of foreign and local capital in Brazil.

. . .

STRUCTURAL ANALYSIS

Coupled with the historical approach, dependency analysis is structural (i.e., it focuses on stable, persistent, though not unchanging patterns). These structural factors may have to do with the links between the peripheral economy and the global system, the forms of foreign penetration, etc. Although these links are not fluid and do not provide the raw material for a behavioral analysis, they are subject to change. This is where the authors, particularly Cardoso and Faletto, find the link between historical and structural analysis.

The implications of this methodology are significant. First of all, behavioral changes—i.e., those transpiring within structural contexts which themselves change infrequently—become less important. Second, since Cardoso and Faletto are interested in these structural changes, they are severely limited in the number of independent cases to be examined. This degrees-of-freedom problem is further aggravated by the fact that in each society the domestic conditions surrounding the insertion of that society into the global system are likely to be different. In formal terms, dependency theorists are likely to be handicapped by inadequate degrees of freedom to unravel the historical puzzles.[25]

Nevertheless, there is a structure to dependency theory, and if it experiences difficulties in the testing stage, this is due to insufficient variability of cases in the world. The form of the theory includes a set of general factors describing the changes in the global capitalist system, and a set of specific or contextual factors relevant to individual cases (whether countries or time periods). These act together to produce outcomes that may vary from country to country. They are outcomes that are explainable by reference to a theory incorporating statements about both the international system and domestic societies.

In short, what we mean when we say *historical* is that generalizations may be temporally limited, that cases for analysis may not always be drawn from any historical time period, and that indicators and strategies of measurement may change across periods.

These discontinuities are not often appreciated by people who do research. In both of the books under review, there are important historical discontinuities; in particular, there is a real sense in which the history of the advanced, capitalist countries has "preempted" a possible, even probable, history of the currently developing countries. Part of the reason that the early industrializers succeeded in developing is that they consolidated their economies at the same time that the world market offered large opportunities for expansion, and with no *superior* countries to interfere. Thus, we should not expect to see the less developed countries today remake themselves in the same image as the European societies during the eighteenth century. History should still be studied not primarily because it provides a crystal ball enabling us to forecast the future image of the less developed countries, but rather because it allows presently developed countries to catch a glimpse of their historical *alter ego.*

NOTES

1. Immanuel Wallerstein, "Modernization: Requiescat in Pace," in *The Uses of Controversy in Sociology,* Lewis A. Coser and Otto N. Larsen, eds. (New York: The Free Press, 1976), pp. 131–135.
2. Tony Smith, "The Underdevelopment of Development Literature: The Case of Dependency Theory," *World Politics,* XXXI, 2 (January 1979): 247–288.
3. Ibid., p. 257.
4. Andre Gunder Frank, "Sociology of Development and Underdevelopment of Sociology," in *Latin America: Underdevelopment or Revolution?* (New York: Monthly Review Press, 1969), pp. 21–94; and Andre Gunder Frank, *Capitalism and Underdevelopment in Latin America: Historical Studies of Chile and Brazil* (New York: Monthly Review Press, 1967).
5. This book is not new and the 1978 date applies only to the English translation. The book was written between 1965 and the first months of 1967. It was published in 1971 under the title, *Dependencia y desarrollo en Americana Latina* (Siglo Veintiuno Editors, SA, 1971). The English version is an expanded and amended version of the Spanish edition. Obviously, Peter Evans has read and profited from the writings of Cardoso and Faletto.
6. . . . From the Organization for Economic Cooperation and Development (OECD), two works are notable: *The Impact of the Newly Industrializing*

Countries on Production and Trade in Manufactures, Report by the Secretary-
General (Paris: OECD, 1979), and *Facing the Future: Mastering the Probable
and Managing the Unpredictable,* prepared by Intcrfutures Group, (Paris:
OECD, 1979), see especially part IV on the "Advanced Industrial Societies and
the Third World." The World Bank has published some relevant papers also.
See "The Changing International Division of Labor in Manufactured Goods,"
World Bank Staff Working Paper, prepared by Bela Balassa (Washington, D.C.:
World Bank, 1979) and Donald B. Keesing, "World Trade and Output of
Manufactures: Structural Trends and Developing Countries' Exports," (Wash-
ington, D.C.: World Bank, 1978). From a very different perspective, that of an
evolving division of labor serving the needs of the capitalist center, see Kirsten
Worm, ed., *Industrialization, Development and the Demands for a New Inter-
national Economic Order* (Copenhagen, Denmark: Samfundsvidenskabeligt
Forlag, 1978); and Folker Fröbel, Jürgen Heinrichs and Otto Kreye, *Die Neue
Internationale Arbeitsteilung* (Hamburg: Rororo Aktuell, 1977).

7. For an excellent book of this genre, see Carl J. Friedrich, *Constitutional Government and Democracy* (Boston: Ginn and Co., 1950, revised ed.).

8. Gabriel A. Almond and James S. Coleman, eds., *The Politics of the Developing
Areas* (Princeton, N.J.: Princeton University Press, 1960); and Gabriel Almond
and G. Bingham Powell, *Comparative Politics: A Developmental Approach*
(Boston, Mass.: Little, Brown and Co., 1966).

9. David Morawetz, *Twenty Five Years of Economic Development, 1950 to 1975.*
(Baltimore, Maryland: Johns Hopkins University Press, 1977), p. 11.

10. Talcott Parsons, *The Social System* (New York: Free Press, 1951) and Talcott
Parsons, "Evolutionary Universals in Society," in *Sociological Theory and
Modern Society,* Talcott Parsons, ed. (New York: Free Press, 1967), pp. 490–
520. Marion J. Levy, *The Structure of Society* and Levy, *Modernization and
the Structure of Society* (Princeton, N.J.: Princeton University Press, 1966).

11. Joseph LaPalombara and Myron Weiner, eds., *Political Parties and Political
Development* (Princeton, N.J.: Princeton University Press, 1966).

12. Joseph LaPalombara, ed., *Bureaucracy and Political Development* (Princeton,
N.J.: Princeton University Press, 1963).

13. Lucien W. Pye, ed., *Communications and Political Development* (Princeton,
N.J.: Princeton University Press, 1967).

14. For a statement of the crisis approach, along with its relationship to historical
sequences, see Leonard Binder, James S. Coleman et al., *Crises and Sequences
in Political Development* (Princeton, N.J.: Princeton University Press, 1971).

15. The primary exception to this generalization is the book by Gabriel A. Almond,
Scott C. Flanagan, and Robert J. Mundt, *Crisis, Choice, and Change: Historical
Studies of Political Development* (Boston, Mass.: Little, Brown and Co., 1973).
In the introductory essay in this volume, Professor Almond outlines five phases
of a system's development and suggests a distinct conceptual approach for
each. He suggests the systems-functional approach for the first phase while
later phases, characterized by crises, call for a choice or decision-theoretic
perspective (pp. 24–25). While this formulation does not establish a theoretical
integration between the concepts of crisis and function, it does promote a
broad historical sequencing of them.

16. Relevant literature includes Daniel Lerner, *The Passing of Traditional Society: Modernizing the Middle East* (Glencoe, Ill.: Free Press, 1963), David
McClelland, *The Achieving Society* (Princeton, N.J.: Van Nostrand, 1961); and

Alex Inkeles and Davis A. Smith, *Becoming Modern: Individual Change in Six Developing Countries* (Cambridge, Mass.: Harvard University Press, 1974).

17. Henry Maine, *Ancient Law: Its Connection with the Early History of Society and Its Relation to Modern Ideas* (N.Y.: Dutton, 1965); Herbert Spencer, *Social Statics, or the Conditions Essential to Human Happiness* (New York: Appleton, 1893); August Comte, *The Positive Philosophy of History* (London: George Bell and Sons, 1894); and Emile Durkheim, *The Division of Labor in Society* (N.Y.: Free Press, 1964).

18. For a review of some of this literature see Alejandro Portes, "On the Sociology of National Development: Theories and Issues," *American Journal of Sociology*, 82, 1 (1977): 61–62.

19. My colleague Peter Van Ness has pointed out to me that perhaps this state of affairs is not so curious, given that the cluster of variables under the label imperialism did not exist for many of these authors.

20. Alexander Gerschenkron, *Economic Development in Historical Perspective* (Cambridge, Mass.: Belknap Press of Harvard University Press, 1962); Barrington Moore, Jr., *Social Origins of Dictatorship and Democracy: Lord and Peasant in the Making of the Modern World* (Boston, Mass.: Beacon Press, 1966).

21. Cardoso had by this time written an important essay with a similar title—see Fernando H. Cardoso, "Associated-Dependent Development: Theoretical and Practical Implications," in *Authoritarian Brazil: Origins, Policies, Future*, Alfred Stepan, ed. (New Haven, Connecticut: Yale University Press, 1973).

22. Tony Smith, "The Underdevelopment of Development Literature: The Case of Dependency Theory," *World Politics*, XXXI, 2 (January 1979): 248.

23. Ibid., p. 257.

24. I do not mean to imply that no fruitful work on the theory of the state has been done. Some excellent analyses have been provided. See Ralph Miliband, *The State in Capitalist Society* (N.Y.: Basic Books, 1969); Erik Olin Wright, *Class, Crisis, and the State* (London: New Left Books, 1978); James O'Connor, *The Fiscal Crisis of the State* (N.Y.: St. Martin's Press, 1973); Leon N. Lindberg, Robert Alford et al., *Stress and Contradiction in Modern Capitalism: Public Policy and the Theory of the State* (Lexington, Mass.: D.C. Heath and Co., 1975); Nicos Poulantzas, *Political Power and Social Classes* (London: New Left Books, 1973); and Nicos Poulantzas, *Classes in Contemporary Capitalism* (London: New Left Books, 1975).

25. The degrees of freedom problem is not just a statistical concern but one that is rooted in all inductive inferences. The general problem arises when there are several explanations to account for an observed phenomenon but where the set of observations (cases or time points) is inadequate to discriminate among competing interpretations. This problem is likely to be especially severe in the social sciences where, in addition to the predominance of multicausal explanations, social phenomenan are likely to be affected by rare conjunctions of variables in an interactive rather than additive way. For example, in an additive world, if there are five variables thought to affect a phenomenon of interest, there are only five competing explanations. In an interactive world, there are 120 separate explanations (5 factorial). The data base necessary to discriminate among these would have to be quite large.

Part
Two

THE POLITICS OF MONEY

*S*ince World War II, the global financial system has been largely centered on the ready availability of U.S. dollars. The lack of dollars outside the U.S. in the 1940s was a major factor in the creation of the Marshall Plan, through which some $13 billion was provided to Western European nations to allow them to rebuild their war-ravaged economies. The U.S. continued to run a *capital account* deficit as American multinational firms and banks invested and lent heavily to overseas markets and producers. It was not until the 1960s that this high dollar liquidity began to have the negative effect of stimulating global inflation and depreciating the worth of the currency. When the Nixon administration abandoned the Bretton Woods system of fixed exchange rates and took the dollar off the gold standard in August 1971, marking the end of the Bretton Woods system, it was simply adjusting to an unsustainable situation.

Since 1971, several important developments—made possible by the collapse of Bretton Woods—have dominated the international financial agenda. In a series of economic summit meetings and conferences, the most wealthy industrialized nations—members of the Organization for Economic Cooperation and Development (OECD)—have essentially agreed to disagree on the subject of recreating the gold standard of fixed exchange rates. What has evolved is a sort of managed float of the major currencies, known as hard currencies for their international prestige. Europeans have gone the farthest in coordinating their currency values, while the U.S. has found it difficult to have a consistent approach which reconciles the dual requirements of credibility and trade-stimulation.

International financial managers have asked whether a new currency could be used to replace the fickle dollar. The answer to this question, as explained by Calleo, van Cleveland, and Silk, is mixed. Ultimately, they argue, the fate of the dollar is inextricably intertwined with the fate of the Western political/military alliance. The presence of United States troops (spending millions of U.S. dollars) exacerbates the already voluminous stockpile of *Eurodollars*—American currency in use overseas. To withdraw these troops might relieve the problem of dollar *overhang* (excessive liquidity creating inflationary pressures), but it could undermine the more general role of the U.S. as guarantor of Western security. These dilemmas are discussed in great detail in this piece.

A symptom of the dollar overhang was the difficulty in recirculating the profits of the oil producers. The newly-rich oil sheikdoms had difficulty putting their money in profitable and safe investments. They turned to U.S. banks. This, in turn, put the bankers in a difficult position, since they were forced to quickly find sound lending outlets in the midst of a global recession. The answer came with lending to Latin American and Eastern European governments and government-controlled corporations. According to Kahler, this was facilitated by the intervention of U.S. and other industrialized nations' governments on the bankers' behalf. The debacle of the debt crisis of the mid-1980s, which has yet to be resolved, brought political actors to the forefront of international financial decisions. According to Kahler, the present outcome of cooperation without reform (or muddling through) is best explained by domestic political forces in wealthy countries. For example, lending by U.S. banks was shaped by U.S. regulatory policies requiring reporting of loan viability. Domestic political pressures in debtor nations directly influenced their bargaining relationships to the North. To ignore these political forces in the debt crisis would be to grossly distort the nature of the problem and its dynamics.

Finally, the proliferation of speculative currency trisections and the emergence of round-the-clock securities trading have led to what Susan Strange calls a *casino* mentality among the highrollers of the international financial community. Where a 1 percent shift in the value of the yen relative to the dollar can either make or break an exchange house, the tension and drama of this fast-paced game has dramatically altered the character of international finance and portfolio investment.

While reading these selections, students would do well to ask themselves a few of those questions posed in the introduction: What role should the United States have in the international financial system? Has U.S. leadership been healthy for the world thus far? What is the current trend with regard to the basic problems of international finance—liquidity, confidence, and stability?

In addition, the world of international finance, while far from ethereal and incomprehensible, carries with it problems that reach into the day-to-day lives of nearly every individual on the globe. Should Third World nations still be expected to pay out double-digit interest rates on loans taken out nearly twenty years ago? Is there another solution to the debt crisis, such as debt forgiveness? And is it possible for the international financial markets to be redirected to actually producing long-term wealth, rather than merely short-term profits (or is this what the business of Wall Street has always been)?

Finally, should the stability of international finance depend on one major currency when the nation in charge of that currency is not really "in charge"? If multicurrency arrangements are to replace a single currency's dominant position, what would such arrangements look like? Who should participate in the development of such arrangements?

The Dollar and the Defense of the West

David P. Calleo
Harold van B. Cleveland
Leonard Silk

The world economic system is in deep trouble. The threat to the international economic system has been a long time in the making: the growth of the world economy has depended overwhelmingly on the strength of the U.S. economy and the dollar. Paradoxically, many have thought growth depends on continuous dollar deficits, the source of growing monetary reserves believed essential to expanding world trade. But others have long feared that this dependence on the dollar points toward eventual disaster. Three decades ago Robert Triffin warned that a strong dollar and chronic U.S. payments deficits could not indefinitely coexist. Either the dollar would weaken and the system would break down, or the American payments deficit would end, the supply of monetary reserves would contract and economic expansion of the system would cease.

But no purely economic explanation for today's gathering crisis is adequate. All along, U.S. deficits have been in large measure a consequence of America's willingness to carry the heaviest share of the defense burdens of the noncommunist world. An end to the American deficits suggests an end to the American burdens. This gives the present financial crisis a geopolitical and historical dimension. It appears a crisis, not only of the dollar, but of American *hegemony* and of the global political economy which that hegemony has built. This creates the grim possibility that the United States, the country that created the postwar global economy, is now on a course fated to destroy it. As Professor Paul Kennedy's recent [sic] book reminds us, history is full of examples of hegemonic powers that brought themselves down because they were unable to sustain a viable relationship between geopolitical pretensions and economic resources.[1] His is an ancient and recurrent lesson among historical moralists: a country with too-great power grows overextended and then self-destructive.

If this course is to be averted, it must be understood that the solution to America's dollar problem is not purely economic but also geopolitical. Furthermore, the adjustments needed cannot be made by the United States alone, but must also involve its major allies. There are few alternatives: the current method of financing the Pax Americana makes a weak and fluctuating dollar inevitable and has increasingly destructive consequences for the world economy.

II

The Bretton Woods fixed exchange rate system broke down in 1971–73. But with the switch to a system of floating exchange rates, something closely resembling the old system of open international trade relations survived. The floating rate system has made it possible to believe that the essentials of a liberal international order could be preserved. While the United States remained in balance-of-payments deficit—which the widening budget deficit of the Reagan years worsened seriously—the dollar remained the world's principal currency, and the United States the chief provider of military protection for the noncommunist world. The monetary system survived, at least in a semi-stable state, because the American payments deficit was covered by capital inflow from abroad. Even though the American national debt grew by more than $1.5 trillion over the Reagan years, foreign governments were eager to prevent both a collapse of the dollar and a withdrawal of the United States from its defense commitments. Nor did the United States want to give up the dollar's role or America's political-military hegemony, despite the heavy costs.

Yet events in 1987, culminating in the stock market crash that began in New York and swiftly ran around the world, again raised fears that the American-led economic and security system would end with a bang. Those fears were eased by actions taken in 1987 and early 1988 by the United States and its major allies to arrest a further fall of the dollar, which had plummeted to an all-time low. Profound and volatile anxiety nevertheless remains. Unfortunately, it seems well founded.

The year 1988 opened inauspiciously for the American economy. With a heavy hangover of inventories from the final months of 1987, a recession appeared to threaten as consumers began to react to the October crash by cutting spending. Fear of a recession in an election year now dominates thinking about economic policy in Washington. The Administration is giving top priority to keeping the economy growing and would doubtless, in a crisis, use monetary and fiscal policy actively to that end. But excessive stimulus would weaken the dollar, causing Wall Street and the financial community to worry about renewed downward pressure on U.S. securities markets. Part of the country, however, welcomes the dollar's slide as providing an opportunity for American farmers and manufacturers to recapture markets lost to foreigners. Unlike Europeans, most Americans have never learned to see the value of their money on the foreign exchanges as a measure of the nation's economic health.

The Reagan Administration has blown hot and cold on the dollar, depending on the pressures of the moment. When concerns about the trade deficit mount, the Administration threatens to let the dollar fall further; when worries about the securities markets or a slowing of foreign capital inflow rise, it seeks to stabilize the dollar. Actually, the U.S. authorities seem quite prepared to see the dollar fall wherever markets and foreign central banks will allow. Europe and Japan, the Administration assumes, are anxious enough about the effect of the dollar's decline on their exports to support it indefinitely.

The expectation underlying this latter-day Republican version of *benign neglect,* akin to the earlier Carter and Nixon versions, is that the dollar's fall will narrow the U.S. trade deficit and restore confidence in the dollar once it has fallen far enough. Foreign investors will again be willing to finance a persistent but diminishing trade deficit by buying U.S. securities and other dollar assets on a large scale, as they did before they dropped that responsibility in the lap of the central banks over a year ago. All this will happen, some optimists assume, regardless of the posture of U.S. fiscal and monetary policy. Hence, the theory goes, the Administration and the Federal Reserve are free to use expansive monetary and fiscal policy to forestall a possible recession without having to give more than lip service to the problem of the dollar.

But less cheerful analysts warn that *benign neglect* of the dollar contains, in present circumstances, the threat of a financial crisis or series of crises that could drive the dollar into a free-fall, which would drive interest rates up and bring on a severe recession throughout the Western world. According to this view, there is no clear bottom for the dollar if U.S. domestic policy remains stimulative: if fiscal and monetary policy are used to spur domestic demand, imports will stay high and the trade balance will scarcely improve in real terms and could even worsen, due to the constantly renewed effect of a falling dollar in raising U.S. import prices. Foreign private investors' confidence would then not be restored, and they would stay away from dollar investments. Sooner or later, the willingness of foreign central banks to support the dollar would falter, as it did in 1979, and for the same reason.

Any prudent policy avoids placing all its bets on one scenario. Yet in a serious crisis, wavering can be disastrous. So great are the present dangers that we believe the United States should abandon its gamble on *benign neglect* and resolutely adopt a strategy that gives a high priority to preventing undue deterioration of the dollar. The reasons seem clear from a closer analysis of how the crisis has been unfolding.

III

The critical difference between the two possible approaches—benign neglect based on belief in a self-stabilizing dollar and defense of the dollar to prevent a major crisis of confidence—lies in the assumption made about the connection between the foreign exchange market and the financial markets. In the first, more sanguine view, the dollar's fall will be self-limiting as it restores trade equilibrium. There will, therefore, be no untoward consequences for interest rates and securities prices. In the second view, however, a falling dollar would eventually trigger a collapse in the U.S. credit and securities markets, with grave consequences for the real economy.

Which view is more likely to prove correct? The experience of the last couple of years throws light on this question. In early 1986 the dollar unexpectedly lost 11 percent of its value against the West German mark in only six weeks. Although the U.S. currency had been declining irregularly for nearly a year, there had not previously been so steep a plunge or an adverse reaction in the U.S. bond market. This time, however, the U.S. bond market nose-dived; in late April 1986 it lost more than seven points. At the time, it was the largest one-week fall in memory.

Until then, foreign investors had been willing to buy U.S. bonds and other dollar assets despite the falling dollar. Why? Because the advantage in U.S. interest rates or the expected capital gains on dollar investments compared to other currencies offset the exchange risk. Then, in January 1986, as the dollar plunged, foreign investors' assessment of the exchange risk changed, with two consequences. One was that many investors, unwilling to buy more dollar securities or even hold all those they already owned without hedging the exchange risk, hedged by borrowing dollars from banks in the United States or abroad and then selling the borrowed dollars for hard foreign currencies such as the Japanese yen, the German mark, or the Swiss franc. The surge of demand for dollar credit drove up short-term interest rates in the United States and the Eurodollar market, and the selling of the borrowed dollars drove the dollar down.

The second effect was on the U.S. bond market; the new perception of increased exchange risk knocked bond prices down and raised U.S. long-term interest rates. Fears of rising U.S. import prices and inflation due to the falling dollar further lifted long-term rates.

The dollar's plunge in January-March 1986 had been precipitated by the decisions of the Federal Reserve, which was under heavy pressure from the Administration and manufacturing and farm interests to try to remedy the situation by opening the money tap wider. The money supply took off, with M1 accelerating from 11.5 percent in 1985 to nearly 17 percent in 1986. In this expansive monetary environment the dollar was bound to go on falling. By the spring of 1987 there was a full-fledged crisis. Treasury bond prices declined, and net private foreign purchases of dollars fell to zero and below; purchases of U.S. securities were offset by short-term bank outflows reflecting borrowing to hedge against dollar exposures. To finance the trade deficit and slow the dollar's fall, foreign central banks had to step into the breach and absorb $70 billion in five months (January-May 1987). Since then, the financing of the U.S. trade deficit and the support of the dollar have been in the hands of the central banks, particularly the Bank of Japan.

For the year 1987 as a whole, foreign central banks bought a total of $140 billion to underpin the dollar but succeeded only in slowing its fall. Quite evidently, something more than central bank intervention will eventually be needed to avoid a hard landing, for intervention on this scale cannot continue indefinitely. To close the external deficit there must be enough excess domestic production to take advantage of the lower relative prices of domestic versus foreign goods caused by the devaluation.

In our view, the notion that there can be a painless correction of a large trade deficit is an illusion, though a convenient one for a party or government facing an election. It minimizes the costs and dangers that lie ahead, and rationalizes a policy of trying to put onto foreign governments the main responsibility for the fate of the dollar and the U.S. economy.

This is not to suggest that U.S. economic policy is solely responsible for the present difficulties and their solution. The present dangerous imbalance of trade and capital flows between the United States and the two main surplus countries, West Germany and Japan, is after all the joint product of the opposite macroeconomic strategies the debtor and surplus countries have followed over the last few years. In the United States huge fiscal deficits, along with monetary expansion, have encouraged consumption at the expense of saving; in Germany and Japan fiscal consolidation and monetary restraint have held down consumption and made a large surplus of savings available for investment or loans in the United States.

IV

Purely economic analysis cannot explain why the United States has followed policies so different from the Germans and Japanese. Nor can purely economic analysis cope with the broader geopolitical consequences that might be expected if the United States were to change its economic policies.

America's large geopolitical role bears a heavy responsibility for its fiscal deficit, which compels, in turn, its monetary instability. As America's relative economic strength has diminished, its geopolitical burdens have grown harder to carry.

What should American policymakers do to reduce the imbalance between America's public resources and commitments? How much of the remedy lies with a reallocation of domestic resources and how much with a readjustment of international role? There is as yet no national consensus on that critical question. It raises political issues well beyond the bounds of economic analysis. The search for an answer should begin with examining the causes of the fiscal deficit. What does our political system demand that causes us regularly to exceed our fiscal resources?

Some blame America's budget deficit on an excessive level of public welfare and *entitlements.* But others respond that claims that the share is excessive cannot be supported by comparing such American spending with that of other advanced Western countries. Compared to West European countries that have similar ratios of wealth to population, the American level of public benefits and civilian spending is remarkably low. Public spending in France and West Germany is, in proportion to their economies, much higher than in the United States. But so is their taxation.

From a European perspective—and that of many Americans as well—the U.S. fiscal imbalance arises not from spending too much but from taxing too little. Yet American resistance to paying higher taxes seems deeply rooted—and the landslide defeat of Walter F. Mondale on the tax issue in 1984 makes politicians wary of proposing it too boldly or openly.

Why are European countries able to raise so much more in taxes, proportionately, than the United States? Judging from Europe's experience, America's fiscal problem may be that it spends too little on civilian benefits rather than too much. It seems difficult to separate the greater tolerance for higher taxes among French and German citizens from the substantially higher level of benefits those citizens—particularly middle-class taxpayers—receive from the state. Higher pensions, heavily graduated according to working incomes, free medical care, excellent free secondary schools, superior public transport, better police protection and superior public amenities in general—above all in the big cities—make Europeans' willingness to pay higher taxes not so difficult to understand. But to expect Americans to pay a European level of taxes in return for an American level of civilian expenditures is politically unrealistic.

Equally unrealistic, in our view, is the strategy that would eliminate the deficit by heavy cuts in our country's comparatively underdeveloped welfare spending, as the Reagan Administration has always advocated rhetorically, or by huge cuts in America's comparatively low level of *middle-class entitlements,* as advocated by many of the Administration's critics. Despite its rhetorical enthusiasm for cutting civilian spending, the Reagan Administration has been unable to do more than slow its growth somewhat. The already comparatively low level of such expenditures, plus the widespread complaints about the insufficiencies of education, public housing, health services, pollution control, and public infrastructure, all point to more rapid growth of civilian spending in the future. America's fiscal profile—its particular mix of taxation and civilian and military spending—seems unable to achieve equilibrium.

V

If a combination of lower civilian spending and higher taxes is un-likely, what then are the prospects for cutting military spending?

Although American public spending and taxation are substantially lower than in France and Germany, American military spending is very much higher—over twice the proportion of national income in the United States as in the Federal Republic. While military spending has powerful support in the United States, the American defense constituency evidently cannot generate support for European levels of taxation. Despite the insistence of advocates of high military spending that the public can and must be *educated* to pay the necessary taxes, postwar experience does not suggest that the experiment can succeed. Congress and the American electorate do not generally disapprove of the country's geopolitical role, but have been reluctant to raise enough taxes to pay for it.

How can military spending be cut and with what consequences? Roughly speaking, there are three strategies for reducing the military budget substantially. The first is what might be called managerial efficiency; the second, hegemony on the cheap; and the third, geopolitical efficiency.

Every new administration vows to make the Pentagon more efficient. International comparisons suggest great possibilities. European states, France in particular, are thought to be far more efficient in the management of their military resources. Why cannot the United States similarly cut its costs without impairing its power? Present circumstances, after all, seem particularly promising. After the buildup during the Weinberger period, it would be surprising if there were not substantial room for managerial improvement. Recent changes in the structure of the Joint Chiefs of Staff, moreover, promise more efficient coordination of operations and weapons procurement.

The fundamental problem remains, however: America's federal budgetary process is such that no president or secretary of defense has the power to maintain the same tight control over spending that is characteristic of the more centralized political structures of Western Europe. While the struggle to improve the efficiency of American military spending is indispensable, without fundamental and perhaps undesirable changes in our constitutional processes it may not succeed sufficiently to have a profound effect on our present fiscal imbalances.

Furthermore, many experts predict that ballooning costs are built into maintaining our present force posture and will not be easy to reverse. Costs for our increasingly sophisticated weapons technology seem to rise inexorably. Many weapons systems already being developed show sharp projected increases once the systems are ready for deployment. Thus, if the Pentagon wants to keep its present force structure, it will be hard put to keep its present budget from shooting upward.

Savings in the Pentagon budget mean, therefore, deciding which weapons systems and forces are essential and which are not. Reducing forces and weapons systems, however, logically implies reducing our capacity for certain geopolitical roles and commitments. Reduced spending without reduced burdens constitutes the familiar strategy of hegemony on the cheap, the consequences of which will be taken up presently.

Some experts, however, believe that very substantial savings can be made in our military budget without changing America's military commitments or even troop levels. For example, in an analysis for the authors, Professor William W. Kaufmann, a defense specialist at Harvard University, proposes specific five-year cuts in a long array of military programs that he argues would save $367.2 billion from the last projected Weinberger five-year defense outlay of $1,577.4 billion (in constant fiscal year 1988 dollars).

In terms of reduction by mission, Kaufmann's approach would break down into savings over five years in the categories and amounts set out in Table 1. The "other" category includes savings on military personnel ($17.5 billion), national guard and reserve ($8.5 billion), civil service ($9.5 billion), retirement pay ($0.5 billion), military construction ($20 billion), other research, development, testing and equipment ($31.2 billion), and burden-sharing ($30 billion—$15 billion with the Federal Republic of Germany and $15 billion with Japan.)

The cuts in weapons programs would break down into savings of $6.5 billion for the Army, $75.3 billion for the Navy, and $168.2 billion for the Air Force.

Kaufmann is hardly alone in believing that very substantial savings in the defense budget can and must be made. Secretary of Defense Frank Carlucci has submitted a new five-year plan involving one percent real annual growth from the fiscal year 1988 total outlays and 1.7 percent annual real growth in budget authority; in 1989 dollars this growth

Table 1   REDUCTION BY MISSION
(In Billions of 1988 Dollars)

Mission	Savings
Strategic nuclear retaliation	$ 120.8
Land warfare	6.5
Amphibious warfare	22.8
Carrier battle groups	33.2
Antisubmarine warfare	6.1
Air superiority/interdiction	28.3
Intercontinental mobility	32.3
Other	117.2
Total	$ 367.2

amounts to $122.7 billion in outlays and $188.4 billion in budget authority. Such a plan could yield savings, over five years, of about $140 billion in defense outlays and $190 billion in budget authority from the Weinberger baseline, which projected three percent annual real growth.

Some downward adjustment, provoked by economic pressures, is now clearly in process. How durable and efficacious will these defense cuts prove to be? Is it true that they can or should be made without any corresponding geopolitical adjustment—that is, without any change in American commitments? Defense spending has, of course, been severely pruned in the past. But cuts have never proved durable.

Postwar American military spending has always tended to be a cyclical process, with the United States regularly trying to sustain traditional commitments with cheaper forces. Thus, after the buildup that accompanied the Korean War, the Eisenhower Administration cut military force levels substantially while relying on nuclear weapons to sustain our geopolitical commitments. Realization that the Soviets were developing serious nuclear capabilities of their own in turn prompted the Kennedy-Johnson military buildup of the 1960s. By Nixon's time, with Congress refusing to sustain military spending and eliminating conscription, the American global position relied on MIRV (multiple independently targetable reentry vehicles), détente, arms control, the *China card* and hyperactive diplomacy in general. By the mid-1970s a dangerous gap between American global commitments and the military forces able to back them up began to be perceived widely throughout America and Europe. Carter's buildup was succeeded by Reagan's more massive buildup. Today, with the United States already into a new period of retrenchment, arms control, détente and *smart* weapons are again in favor.

What are the prospects for a retrenchment more durable than Nixon's or Eisenhower's? Are the 1990s fated to discover a new *missile gap* or *window of vulnerability,* to be followed by another hectic buildup in response? The Reagan rearmament has been highly wasteful, and therefore offers ample opportunities for greater management efficiency, but has it been any more so than the Korean or Vietnam Wars?

The durability of defense cutbacks depends on whether what results represent some reasonable fit between forces, military doctrines, and geopolitical commitments. To cut forces and weapons systems without corresponding coherent alterations in military doctrines or geopolitical commitments obviously runs the risk of merely perpetuating the old cyclical pattern of defense spending, itself a major cause not only of military inefficiency but also of fiscal waste.

VI

Since the Eisenhower presidency, nuclear weapons have allowed the United States to maintain its military protectorate for Western Europe without having to match Soviet conventional forces on the Eurasian continent. In effect, the United States has threatened to initiate a nuclear war rather than see Europe overrun by Soviet conventional forces. A nuclear defense of this kind has always been much cheaper than conventional defense—a differential grown still greater with the years. NATO's reliance on U.S. nuclear deterrence has, of course, continued long after the Soviets developed intercontinental ballistic missiles. An enormous American superiority in missiles and bombers persisted through the 1960s and continued to lend credence to the nuclear protectorate. A lead in MIRV technology prolonged the American superiority still longer. By the later 1970s, however, strategic parity had clearly come about, and it had become widely perceived that the U.S. nuclear commitment to Europe could suddenly expose the United States to a high degree of risk.

A number of trends have followed. Europeans have demanded further reassurance of American *coupling*. Hence the dual-track decision in 1979 to deploy new American missiles in Europe capable of reaching the Soviet Union. The United States, in turn, has grown more fearful of the nuclear risk. Hence the Strategic Defense Initiative, the Intermediate-range Nuclear Forces Treaty and the new American emphasis on conventional as opposed to nuclear defense for Europe.

The prospect of having to maintain a European military balance with less reliance on nuclear weapons has already started to cause severe strains within the Atlantic alliance. Some American military experts see the solution in a transformation of military weaponry in order to give NATO a more powerful conventional defense. One school, for example, argues for a revolutionary new form of conventional defense based on technologically advanced *smart* weapons. Another group sees a radical transformation of American ground tactics, weapons, and formations away from reliance on static positions and overwhelming firepower. But neither solution, whatever its intrinsic military merits, seems a promising way to reconcile the traditional American position in European defense with an urgent need to shrink budgetary deficits. If the past is any guide, high-tech conventional weapons will not save money. Nor is the American military likely itself to develop, let alone lead its allies through, a revolutionary transformation of forces and tactics that will bring large budgetary savings.

This situation explains the revival of interest in a greater *Europeanization* of NATO. This is a solution that would hope to cut American military spending through geopolitical efficiency rather than hegemony on the cheap. Since the European allies are much stronger economically in relation to the United States and the Soviet Union than in 1950, when NATO's hegemonic pattern was established, the United States ought to be able to devolve to those allies some of the geopolitical responsibilities for sustaining the Pax Americana from which all have profited so handsomely. In particular, the time has come for the European states to take the primary role in organizing their own territorial defense. Current strategic trends suggest that a Europeanized NATO could be more efficient militarily.

By the Pentagon's own calculations the U.S. commitment to NATO is responsible for roughly half of the American defense budget. Why the NATO portion of the U.S. defense budget is so large is easy to understand. Of America's 18 standing divisions, for example, ten are devoted to NATO—five deployed in Europe and five more in the United States ready to arrive in Europe within a few days, where they are to find large quantities of stored equipment and supplies. Unlike air and naval forces assigned to NATO, these very expensive and heavily armored land divisions are not easily adaptable to purposes beyond the NATO theater. Hence the particular attractiveness, military as well as fiscal, of a substantial reduction in these ground forces—particularly those deployed in the United States.

Obviously, Europeans have a very substantial comparative advantage over the United States when it comes to providing land forces for European territorial defense. And certainly, if European defense is to depend increasingly on conventional forces, U.S. fiscal conditions preclude an increased American contribution to those forces. On the contrary, with severe cuts in military spending likely, these forces are a logical target.

Even if no U.S. troops were withdrawn from Europe, some analysts estimate that gradually eliminating the five U.S.-based NATO divisions could, in the long run, save as much as $50 billion annually in the U.S. defense budget. While exact calculations are inevitably contentious and elusive, common sense suggests that cutting five of our 18 divisions would eventually have major fiscal consequences, even if the cuts took several years to reach their full extent.

The argument for devolution in NATO is, of course, military as well as fiscal. Replacing NATO forces that are based an ocean away from Europe with, for example, an enlarged and firmly committed French force could be more effective militarily as well as substantially cheaper. Indeed, it is not easy to imagine a serious conventional defense for Western Europe without the wholehearted participation of the French. Military arguments for Europeanization can also be made in the realm of nuclear forces. Strategic parity has inevitably undermined the effectiveness of America's extended deterrence. To the extent that Europeans wish to continue relying on nuclear deterrence, the future does not lie with more American coupling but with a larger role for indigenous European nuclear forces. The United States can perhaps help sustain those European nuclear forces, but it cannot expect that it would have dominance over them.

Europeanization of NATO is hardly a new idea, but it means different things to different people. Traditionally, American administrations have called for greater *burden-sharing,* by which is meant a desire for Europeans to contribute more money and forces to the American-run NATO defense. The past forty years have made clear the limits of such an approach. Present military and fiscal trends suggest more radical alternatives. Among these are not only *devolution*—a reduced American participation under a European-run NATO command—but also *disengagement,* an outright American withdrawal from NATO.

Complete American disengagement from Europe would constitute a diplomatic revolution difficult to justify in terms of American interest. While other parts of the world have gained in importance since the 1950s, the American-European connection is as vital to the postwar system as ever. Western Europe is still an agglomeration of industrial, commercial, and financial power rivaled in scale only by the United States itself. Culturally and politically, Western Europe is the other part of the world where political and economic liberty is deeply implanted and reliably practiced. Western Europe also has three of the world's half-dozen major modern military powers, two of them nuclear. Thanks principally to the alliance between the United States and the major states of Western Europe, the Soviet Union has been contained in Eurasia and the United States has been given the margin of superior power to shape the global system. If, instead, Western Europe and the Soviet Union were allies, we would be living in a very different world.

The very strength of Europe is, however, what makes the radical alternative of devolution seem feasible. Not only do West European states have great economic and military resources, but they also have had extensive postwar experience in intimate confederal cooperation. The European Community is by far the most impressive experiment in intergovernmental cooperation in modern history. The cooperation required to coordinate Europe's economies reaches intimately into the domestic interest-group politics of every member state. Compared to the difficulties of an economic confederation, managing a military coalition against the Soviet Union should be relatively simple, once the necessity of replacing part of the American military forces committed to NATO is clear.

Proponents of devolution, moreover, see it not as a policy reflecting American weakness or failure but as an overdue adjustment to the consequences of America's successful earlier policies. Building a liberal global order that has rejuvenated Western Europe and Japan, developed at least parts of the Third World and contained the Soviets has also inevitably eroded the overwhelming American global predominance that characterized the earlier postwar decades.

Devolution is the logical policy of adjustment. While managing it undeniably carries risks, to its proponents those risks are preferable to the almost certain deterioration that would follow from trying either to sustain the old predominance or to withdraw from the global order.

The attractiveness of devolution, to be sure, is greater to Americans than to many Europeans, who have grown comfortable in a military dependence that has exacted a very low political and economic price. Those who hunt through the present European scene for illustrations of the risks and limits will have no trouble finding them. There is no way to prove that Europe will rise to the occasion of an American devolution. Most European leaders have little interest in precipitating such a move by affirming their capacity to cope with it. Publicly, they take every opportunity to profess their own weakness. Privately, some are more sanguine. Few

European politicians, of course, care to be blamed for giving the Americans a pretext to reduce their NATO forces.

Nevertheless, the major European states—France, Germany, and to some extent Britain—have clearly been intensifying their own military cooperation, at least partly in anticipation of American pressures for a greater European role in the alliance. Progress so far suggests hope, but no easy assurance. Military and political differences remain that make the familiar American leadership seem a more comfortable alternative. But given the urgent need to bring America's budget under control, those comforts are very precarious. Those in this country who genuinely want to save NATO should get on with reforming it. And those Europeans who want an Atlantic alliance would be well advised to get to work on its European pillar.

VII

American policy in recent years has been more and more addicted to wishful thinking. Economically, as we have suggested, the era of comfortable self-indulgence appears near its close. Today the United States is on a collision course with history. The American fiscal dilemma must be resolved, and the perpetual instability of the dollar that is its consequence must cease. This will require a radical and resolute policy to stop the United States from perpetually living beyond its means. Austerity will have to include the federal government and there will be no quick fix by either an abrupt rise in taxes or a sharp cut in civilian spending. Taxes will have to be raised from their Reagan levels, but so will civilian expenditures. Major and durable military cuts are essential and these logically require a readjustment of America's geopolitical role and alliance commitments. Needless to say, none of this will be easy. Under normal circumstances, political leaders here and in Europe would certainly prefer to patch up the status quo one more time.

Present trends are not likely to present them with the opportunity to succeed, however. In the next decade the world's most critical problems are likely to be in the economic sphere. The prospect of a breakdown of world monetary and trading arrangements now constitutes so grave a danger that no responsible American government can ignore our own heavy responsibility for the present disarray. American policymakers can no longer give military commitments automatic priority over fiscal balance. The United States needs a long-term geopolitical posture that is compatible with a durable fiscal and monetary balance. European and Japanese governments, too, are faced with a compelling self-interest in seeing the United States regain its political and economic equilibrium.

But while reality is finally closing in on the economic fantasies of the past, there is the danger of a new explosion of wishful thinking in the geopolitical sphere. This is fed by the marked change in Soviet internal policies and external tactics. While the Soviet shifts may offer new opportunities to sustain a military balance at a lower cost and with less tension, they also pose the danger that both Americans and Europeans will find a new pretext for putting off the long needed reform of the Western alliance itself. As in the early 1970s, détente and arms control once more seem to offer promising prospects for fiscal retrenchment without geopolitical adjustment. The Soviet Union now shows an interest in reducing its own military spending, and therefore in pursuing arms control agreements and perhaps in finding solutions to the political tensions that make armaments seem so necessary.

Skeptics note, however, how limited and transitory periods of détente have proved in the past. Even if Gorbachev should be taken seriously as a domestic reformer or diplomatic conciliator, his internal and alliance problems are formidable and his own capacity to control or even survive them is questionable. In any event, however Gorbachev fares, the Soviet Union will remain a great Eurasian military power, its very existence weighing on the independence of the neighboring countries of Europe, Asia, and the Middle East. The need for a powerful military counterweight will remain, even if the level of the balance can be somewhat reduced and stabilized.

Under the circumstances, it is imperative that the United States not become so preoccupied with Soviet relations that it fails to make the fundamental changes in the West that are the precondition for future stability within the global system. No imaginable arms control agreement is going to eliminate the urgent necessity for the United States to reduce its highly destabilizing budget deficits by, among other steps, very substantial cuts in current military outlays. If arms control agreements with the Soviets may offer an intelligent way to reduce some part of the cost and danger of sustaining a military balance in Europe, they will not eliminate either the need for such a balance or the need for the Europeans to bear a greater responsibility for sustaining it.

To argue for the priority of Western needs over U.S.-Soviet détente is not to denigrate détente's opportunities. It may be that the Soviets now feel constrained to accept a more modest agenda of global ambitions in return for urgently needed progress at home. If so, it will confirm with success the long-standing Western policy of containment. But the victory will be Pyrrhic, and highly transitory, if meanwhile there is a breakdown of the global economy. The swarm of troubles that a Western economic breakdown would generate would soon reconvert the Soviets to Leninism. In any event, an economic crash will set many other demons loose in the world besides Soviet ambition.

NOTES

1. *The Rise and Fall of the Great Powers,* New York: Random House, 1987.

Politics and International Debt: Explaining the Crisis

Miles Kahler

Since mid-1982 the existence of a "debt crisis" has been almost universally acknowledged; many would argue that the crisis had existed unrecognized for much longer, despite alarms sounded regularly over the preceding decade. The definition of the crisis in the Northern industrial countries was remarkably uniform: the onset of widespread difficulties in servicing the mountain of developing country debt threatened the stability of the international financial system. The nightmare in the North was an episode of onrushing financial collapse in the mold of those described so vividly by Charles Kindleberger—a default by a major debtor country (or domino defaults by debtors large and small), followed by the failure of a major bank or banks, a collapse of confidence in the financial system, and ultimately a sharp contraction of economic activity and international trade.[1] The model was that of a panic; the fear, that the financial system, which had appeared so robust in dealing with successive shocks in the 1970s, might prove less so in the harsher circumstances of the 1980s.

From the South—and the Southern view was heard in this crisis as it had not been heard in the past—the debt crisis was a crisis of development, one element of the deepest economic downturn since the Great Depression, which had begun for some developing countries after the first oil shock. The link between debt and economic distress varied among the regions of the Third World, however. In Latin America, which held the lion's share of private debt (and posed the greatest threat to system stability), and in Eastern Europe the sudden collapse in international lending led to sharp curbs on imports and severe economic retrenchment, complicated in the case of Eastern Europe by worsening East-West relations. Africa's disastrous economic decline had begun in the early 1970s, but the roots of its economic malaise seemed to lie in a sharp worsening of its

Miles Kahler, "Politics and International Debt: Explaining the Crisis." Reprinted from *International Organization*, 39:3 (Summer 1985) by permission of The MIT Press, Cambridge, MA.

terms of trade, a decline in official development assistance, and damaging national policies; the bulk of its debt was owed to governments, not commercial banks. Asia, with the exception of the Philippines, stood outside the crisis: growth rates held up remarkably well, and the region had never entered the private financial markets with the gusto shown by the Latin Americans. Although some developing countries made clear their own interest in avoiding further weakening of the international financial system, the costs to national development objectives were paramount in Southern eyes.

Each of these competing views of the debt crisis implies a need for political intervention to resolve the crisis, even though the level and kind of political intervention espoused, North and South, differ sharply. The competing views also imply differing explanations for the crisis itself. Most analyses, however, while mentioning a political dimension to the debt crisis *sotto voce*, emphasize economic explanations for the crisis and economic paths out of it. At the risk of simplification one can discern three principal economic arguments, which, though often combined, point to quite different sources of and solutions to the crisis. These models can be labeled "macroeconomic shock," "failure to adjust," and "market imperfections."

The first is a conjunctural argument: the debt crisis was caused by surprising shifts in macroeconomic policy on the part of the major industrial countries, particularly the United States, after the second oil shock. The United States embarked in late 1979 on a turn in policy that took both the developing countries and the commercial banks by surprise. Rather than a brief recession, continuing high levels of inflation, and low or negative real interest rates, this policy shift produced the unprecedented combination of disinflation in the industrial countries, high real interest rates, and a collapse both in the terms of trade and in the volume of exports of developing countries as the industrialized economies entered a deep recession. The debtors and the banks had gambled on an economic environment that resembled the 1976–79 period; they lost. The conclusions drawn by those who take this view are that, given the present financial system, the debt crisis is manageable if the macroeconomic environment shifts toward higher growth rates in the OECD countries and lower real interest rates.[2]

Needless to say, this explanation of the debt crisis is favored by the commercial banks and the debtor countries, principal actors in the system that developed in the 1970s and early 1980s. It awards primary responsibility to economic policy shifts beyond their control, not to their own actions or to imperfections in financial markets. Equally clear is the discomfort that this reading of the debt crisis causes for Northern elites. Though they (and the international organizations that tend to reflect their point of view) may accept that the change in economic conditions was swift, they also emphasize that the disinflationary change was essential to longer-term growth and that the new environment is permanent; hence adjustment, however painful, is required.

Some spokesmen for the North go further, however, shifting responsibility for the debt crisis to inadequate policies in the debtor countries. Observing the pattern of developing country experience during the 1980s—the regional divergence in economic performance noted above—they conclude that the economic environment cannot be a principal explanation for economic decline in the major Latin American debtors.[3] Even if a shift to higher growth rates in the North were desirable, the "short leash" of IMF conditionality and frequent renegotiation would have been necessary to ensure that policies in the South were set aright. The balance between financing and adjustment should shift sharply toward the latter, since one assumption of the "failure to adjust" view (an assumption held also by many of those who endorse the "macroeconomic shock" explanation) is that the limits to financing are relatively fixed (though how they are fixed remains obscure); the limits to adjustment on the part of the developing countries are far more flexible. As one International Monetary Fund (IMF) publication blandly notes,

> although a program of adjustment may involve austerity by comparison with some earlier period of policy, it cannot be considered to represent austerity by comparison with any feasible alternative. . . . An adjustment program involving a slower restoration of external viability, while attractive in theory, would in practice have placed in doubt the willingness of creditors to play an adequate role in the financing process, or else would have permitted a potentially threatening further increase in the external debt burden borne by the indebted countries themselves.[4]

Despite criticisms of the short-term adjustment programs urged on debtor countries, it is clear that some in the North are aiming at even more: a fundamental reorientation of the pattern of development undertaken by the major debtors during the period of easy finance. The outward orientation pushed by the IMF and the World Bank in the 1980s will now be implemented on a fast track under the pressures of adjustment.

A third set of economic explanations for the debt crisis does not exclude those given above, but awards a larger role to imperfections in financial markets. These observers see not the efficient system of intermediation portrayed by the banks but a system prone to crisis and with no obvious lender of last resort, a system in which collective action problems within bank syndicates can threaten system stability.[5] Contagion effects and herd behavior produce "feast or famine" cycles of lending; confidence is easily undermined.[6] Some of these observers do not champion the virtues of lower regulation in international lending but prefer to point to the inadequacy of existing regulation in countering the risks of sovereign lending—risks that the banks, suffering from "disaster myopia," choose to ignore.[7] Finally, these microlevel analyses factor in the behavior of *borrowers.* Replacing the smooth allocation of lending toward economies with high growth rates and high rates of return and the easy assumption that "countries never go bankrupt" is the threat of default or repudiation, which acts as a barrier to optimal levels and distribution of lending.[8]

Such critical views of the system of commercial bank lending for balance-of-payments financing as it had developed in the 1970s were popular with none of the principal actors in the crisis. They implied that the banks acting collectively could produce perverse outcomes in the absence of external intervention. Those who viewed the threat of repudiation as a serious obstacle to the continuation of adequate lending proposed additional sanctions directed toward the developing countries or restraints on their policies, changes that borrowers hardly welcomed. Moreover, the presumption that political intervention by international organizations or national governments might be required to redress these imperfections was unlikely to win the support of Northern finance ministers and politicians increasingly inclined against regulation of or intervention in financial markets and unwilling to increase public sources of financing. These arguments at the microlevel about the existing system of international finance, however, do more than point to a possible need for political intervention in a *solution* to the debt crisis. They also raise, however obliquely, the question of a political dimension in the development of the crisis itself.

This third set of economic arguments, focused on market imperfections in the smooth-running financial system of the 1970s, calls into question the depoliticized view of international lending widely held before 1982 and helps to explain the more overt political dimension—the higher level of intervention by states and international organizations—to the debt crisis since that time. The market imperfections model also suggests a means of organizing the analysis of state intervention in international financial systems, past and present.

The means by which the world financial system has integrated economies with large capital needs, underdeveloped financial institutions, and high political risk have varied from era to era. But whenever private financial intermediaries have been central and the market imperfections described above likely to appear, governments are potentially involved in three political tasks that set boundaries for the private actors and influenced their behavior.

The first is to *ensure the stability* of the international financial system. Governments have interpreted their responsibilities for maintaining system stability in two ways. One is the classic role of lender of last resort: a willingness to lend directly to financial institutions during a threatened panic, adding liquidity at higer risk than a private actor would be willing to assume.[9] The role of state intervention here is to maintain confidence in *lenders.* Underlying the need for a lender of last resort is a belief that financial markets, and particularly international ones, are subject to instability as the result of their structure (collective action problems of large numbers of lenders), the fragility of confidence in highly leveraged institutions, and the threat of contagion.[10]

States have also undertaken a second stabilizing role, one that reinforces confidence in the system indirectly by assuring the ability and the willingness of *borrowers* to pay. At times enforcement action taken by the dominant states has underpinned stability (though the importance of such public enforcement in the past has been overstated). Kindleberger has expanded the notion of lender of last resort to imply a more general responsibility for system stability that may include additional, counter-cyclical lending to borrowing governments as well as maintaining open markets for exports.[11]

Linked to the role of lender of last resort is the second political task that governments have assumed: *regulation.* This concept should also be interpreted broadly, for regulation may mean supervision of financial intermediaries in the interest of "outsiders," particularly depositors, thereby ensuring the safety and soundness of the financial system (hence the link to the lender-of-last-resort function). Governments can also attempt to divert financial flows from their market-determined course to further other national interests, such as foreign policy goals.

Finally, governments in the borrowing economies are responsible for *adjustment* to assure scheduled repayment of debts and to guarantee continued inflows of capital necessary for development. Willingness to adjust may be influenced by the enforcement mechanisms in the system (sanctions available to private lenders) and by perceptions of the economic benefits of staying inside the system, but elites on the periphery also enter into their calculus the *political* costs that they are likely to suffer in imposing those policy changes which external financial obligations require.

POLITICAL INTERVENTION AND SYSTEMS OF INTERNATIONAL FINANCE

If politics, defined as state intervention, is potentially important in defining international financial outcomes, *how* important is it? Before 1945, four patterns of international lending produced different outcomes. The pre-1914 system of lending based in London and its counterpart in Paris and Berlin, as Albert Fishlow notes, seemed to provide financial system stability and an impressive flow of private capital to (richer) countries on the periphery. The New York-based system of the 1920s and its less important counterpart in London provided less capital and ended with massive defaults during the Great Depression (though the London-based system proved more resilient under strain).

These different outcomes resulted, at least in part, from different patterns of state intervention. The London-based system of international lending before 1914 was characterized by little government interference in the relations between lenders and borrowers. Fishlow's account of that era suggests that the absence of intervention to ensure system stability was not due solely to an ideological commitment to laissez-faire but to the peculiar private organization of the marketplace: merchant banks mediated between the mass of bondholders (organized in the Corporation of Foreign Bondholders) and borrowers on the periphery. Because lending in this system was based on bonds, debt-servicing difficulties did not have immediate implications for the domestic financial system, and hence the stabilizing role of the British Treasury and the Bank of England was limited. (The principal exception was the Baring Crisis of 1890, and then, through organizing a system of guarantees though not through direct lending, the Bank of England did serve as system stabilizer to preserve confidence in the City of London and stave off a panic.)[12]

The absence of a direct link between international lending and the domestic financial system also reinforced the lack of governmental supervision or regulation, though the Paris and Berlin patterns displayed stronger government efforts to manipulate financial flows to serve foreign policy ends (perhaps best considered a form of protomilitary assistance).[13] Adjustment on the periphery was seldom hindered by governments, many of them within the British formal and informal empires, committed to integrating their countries into the international economy, a stance that also assured that the burden of adjustment to financial crisis would fall squarely on them.[14] Not only did elites on the periphery fail to perceive any alternative to financial dependence on London, they also faced populations not yet mobilized to resist the harshness of adjustment.

If the pre-1914, London-based system suggests the stability of a market (organized in a particular fashion) within a set of nearly invisible political parameters, the interwar financial system offers a portrait of destabilizing political intervention in certain spheres and inadequate political intervention in others. The financial system, as Kindleberger and others have emphasized, was in transition between its old London focus and its new center in New York. Although New York became the source of new capital ouflows, as Fishlow notes, the United States as a creditor had "neither [the] trade policy nor [the] foreign perspective . . . compatible with the role."[15] When financial crisis broke in 1929–31, the American authorities were unwilling to play even the passive stabilizing role that their counterparts in London had undertaken earlier. In the absence of a governmental stabilizer the private markets proved incapable of meeting the crisis, which overwhelmed them. The shift to New York had placed the financial system in inexperienced hands: replacing merchant banks linked to their country clients through a web of financial and trade relations were New York banks that floated foreign bonds as a simple variation on the placement of domestic bonds.[16] Not only did private stabilization fail to substitute for a passive government in the New York market, self-regulation on the London model did not fill the gap left by an absence of government supervision. When the boom came to an end, the pattern of defaults divided countries in the British orbit (particularly those with an export surplus with Britain) and those in the U.S. orbit.[17] As David Felix describes, the British carved out a sterling area in which London still exercised the stabilizing function that it used to offer to the world economy as a whole: its export market and promise of future capital induced some governments, such as Argentina, to undergo the risks of adjustment in order to honor their sterling debts. The United States, maintaining its nationalist stance, declined even such a "ministabilizing" role in its financial sphere.

The cascade of defaults in the early 1930s signaled more than the failure of any hope for reestablishing an open system for trade and capital exports; elites on the periphery also faced a different calculus of adjustment at home. Two critical features set the breakdown of the 1930s apart from the earlier period, and both spurred default. First, the political resistance to stabilization, particularly from a partially mobilized working class, was greater, and the political risks to any elite undertaking stabilization correspondingly elevated. Second, and equally important, economic alternatives to those imposed by the plummeting international economy were haltingly discovered. Policy experiments with import substitution and delinking from international capital markets soon expanded into acceptance of more unorthodox and state-led strategies of structural change.[18]

The financial crisis and widespread defaults of the 1930s could be explained in the purely economic terms of the macroeconomic shock model: deteriorating economic conditions for the exporters of primary products (beginning before the Great Depression) followed by a drying up of capital flows. But such a model neglects the political failure that accompanied financial failure: no clear stabilizer at the international level, an absence of regulation or self-regulation in the financial markets, and increasing political resistance to adjustment on the periphery.

POLITICS AND INTERNATIONAL FINANCE AFTER 1945: TO THE MEXICAN RESCUE

The financial and monetary disorder of the 1930s produced a political legacy that would persist into the financial crisis management of the 1980s. After the Great Depression the principal candidate for a system stabilizer would be the United States, a continental economy whose stabilizing role would be shaped by the strong pull of domestic policy goals. The level of government regulatory involvement in the financial system took a quantum jump upward during the Great Depression; motivations, particularly in the United States, were principally domestic, but they would later prove to have international implications. And finally, as noted above, governments on the periphery took on much greater responsibility for economic development, beginning with the delinking of the 1930s that persisted into the postwar period. In the balance between domestic and international, incentives were skewed toward domestic economic objectives.

These shifts meant that future state intervention in international finance would be embedded in *domestic* politics, but they were easily overshadowed by the fact that private financial flows were far less significant in the years immediately after 1945. For the first time, public international institutions—the International Monetary Fund and the multilateral development banks—played a role in the international financial system; the attitude of the founders of the postwar order toward private capital flows, which were viewed as inadequate for the capital needs of reconstruction and potentially destabilizing, was at best ambiguous. It was not capital flows on the prewar model but development assistance and foreign direct investment that assumed a more prominent role. Such supply-side limitations on private finance coincided with the adoption of inward-looking, import-substitution development strategies in many of the developing countries, which reduced their demand for foreign capital.

What might have happened had New York continued its development, interrupted in 1929, as an international financial center, and developing countries had "graduated" to it, is an interesting question. What actually happened was that in the 1960s private financial intermediation between North and South found a new "technology," one born in part of regulatory changes in the United States: the Euromarkets. Refinements in the technology of bank lending through the Euromarkets—waivers of sovereign immunity in loans, syndication, and the institution of floating-rate credits—lowered risks for any individual bank participating and opened the way for a new era of sovereign lending.[19]

With the new intermediaries in place, a shift toward more outward-oriented policies by some of the larger, newly industrializing economies—Brazil, South Korea, Yugoslavia—made these new, relatively unregulated financial markets attractive. The political and economic strings of the IMF and bilateral aid donors could be avoided; Euromarket loans fitted better than did foreign direct investment with state-led industrialization and the growth of a parastatal sector.

The pattern and the intermediaries for North-South capital flows were thus established before the first oil shock, though demand for financing from this source shot up to meet the current account deficits that oil price increases produced. For seven years private financial markets reassumed a major role in financing the deficits of developing countries and their economic growth, which continued, for many middle-income countries, during a time of recession among the OECD countries. Developing country debt—highly concentrated in a relatively small number of newly industrializing countries—increased at an annual rate of 10 percent in real terms during these years; the share of that debt owed to private financial institutions grew from 25 to 41 percent during the same period.[20]

At first glance, and in many of the early analyses of this system of North-South financial intermediation, the absence of political intervention by governments or by international organizations seemed its most striking feature.[21] But the new system of bank lending to developing countries, despite its appearance of being managed by banks and dominated by market criteria, was (like previous systems) influenced by state actions and state choices in system stabilization, regulation, and adjustment. Kindleberger's questions—"Is there a lender of last resort in case of trouble? Who is it? Does he or it know it?"—suggest the anxiety that surrounded the role of system stabilizer. Apart from a vague statement issued by Group of 10 central bank governors in 1974, concrete governmental assurances to the banks were lacking.[22] International organizations also seemed to decline in importance as guarantors of system stability in the broader sense. Just before the onset of widespread debt-servicing difficulties, the *Economist* characterized the International Monetary Fund's role in the 1970s as "helpful, steadying—and very marginal," financing only 4 percent of all current account deficits in 1978.[23] Although some observers argue that the IMF continued to play a central role in awarding its "seal of approval" to national economic policies, the Fund was only sporadically involved. The number of rescheduling cases before 1982 was relatively small (though rising), and the countries in question were not of system-threatening size: they were most often smaller, nonoil developing countries that were barely eligible for commercial bank lending in any case.

Although no obvious stabilizer was waiting in the wings, it is clear from bank behavior that many lenders assumed that such a lender of last resort existed. In Eastern Europe a belief in the "Soviet umbrella" persisted—perhaps the first Communist lender of last resort! At least part of the regional bias in bank lending—with American banks taking the preponderant role in Latin America and West German banks in Eastern Europe—must be attributed to beliefs that strategic interests would force government intervention on behalf of troubled borrowers. In sum, Eurobanks could feel reasonably secure—perhaps too secure—in their lending, at least to large borrowers in the regional spheres of interest of their home governments.

The stabilizing function is linked to the regulatory: a lender of last resort must know whether the financial institution or country to which it is lending is solvent or not. Obstacles to extending regulation of Eurobanks were greater than in earlier systems since the banks and their lending had moved offshore precisely to avoid regulation, and some national governments resisted a collective tightening of regulatory oversight. Commercial bank lending to the developing countries did pose risks to domestic banking systems (in contrast to the pre-1930s reliance on bond markets), making all the more striking the apparent lack of regulatory concern during the 1970s.

Part of the apparent lack of effect of national regulation is simply an illusion, however. Banks, as Philip Wellons argues forcefully, though they tried to take refuge from home country regulation in the Euromarkets, were tugged back into dependence on their home governments and home economies by cost advantages and by the direct support their governments offered through market protection and lender-of-last-resort assistance. Not only did the regulatory climate of home countries affect the behavior of banks despite the development of transnational syndicates, as Wellons suggests, the relations between governments and banks also varied *across* the industrialized countries, with implications for bank behavior.[24] Although governments were hardly as blatant in using bank lending to further their strategic interests as the French government had been before 1914, regulation, broadly defined, could go beyond government intervention to further strategic goals.[25]

Most accounts of the heyday of the Euromarkets during the 1970s also omit the third political boundary imposed by states: the politics of adjustment was only a minor theme of the period because so little adjustment seemed to take place. Stephan Haggard notes the effect that "temptation" had in undermining the willingness of elites to undertake adjustment programs; financing for current account deficits was available with few strings attached, whether in the form of economic and military assistance (Egypt, the Philippines) or in the form of commercial bank lending. The inability of banks alone to impose adjustment was demonstrated definitively in the case of Peru in 1976–77.[26]

Warning signals were apparent for those willing to see, however. Jamaica, a case of what Haggard terms democratic stalemate, clearly illustrated the continuing political hazards of adjustment. The government of Michael Manley, whose populist program rode the bauxite boom of the early 1970s, confronted vigorous political opposition and finally defeat when lending from the commercial banks declined. In Mexico the burst of oil revenues reinforced a pattern of state-led industrialization but did not quell political opposition to the course that had been chosen. That stalemate in the context of financial plenty produced the drift in Mexican policy that led directly to the crisis of 1982. Most of the major debtor states, however, were not pluralist: in the rest of Latin America the pattern of public-sector-led industrialization continued under "soft" authoritarian regimes, which used easy external finance to temper social divisions and lower the level of repression. Unlike Mexico, they did not face the question of stalemate in a pluralist context, but Robert Kaufman suggests that "authoritarian stalemate" had nonetheless set in by the late 1970s. Easy finance had enabled elites to postpone both political and economic choices; the development trajectory would demonstrate the shortcomings of the policy in the adverse external circumstances that were soon to arrive.[27]

In the pre-1914 London model governmental functions of system stabilization were undertaken by private actors and adjustment was viewed not as a political choice but as an inevitable element of economic life. The system of commercial bank lending to the developing countries during the 1970s, it could be argued, resembled as closely in its political outlines the unstable interwar system based on New York. In the New York system private actors could not stabilize the system and governments would not, underregulation was more characteristic than self-regulation, and the national choices of adjustment strategy were perilous for political elites. Only the threat of financial crisis would produce novel forms of political intervention that did not parallel any of the historical models. They have to date managed to stave off financial breakdown.

PATTERNS OF COOPERATION IN THE CRISIS

Each of the economic models described earlier can find some evidence for its interpretation of the debt crisis in events following the second oil shock. The harsh new environment after 1979, of a different order from the recession of 1974–75, lends weight to the notion of macroeconomic shock: an even steeper recession was coupled this time with high real interest rates and a strong dollar. Terms of trade shifted dramatically against first the nonoil developing countries and then, with the emergence of an oil glut, the oil producers. Yet a new burst of bank lending was soon under way, and developing countries received mixed signals on the need for adjustment with an apparent easing of IMF conditionality in 1979, increases in Fund resources through quota increases and borrowing, and adoption of enlarged access. The new wave of lending was characterized by several disturbing features that suggested growing weaknesses in the financial markets. Short-term debt expanded twice as rapidly as medium- and long-term debt from 1979, although this shift in composition was hardly clear at the time.[28] In addition, European and Japanese banks entered the competition more aggressively, reducing spreads and encouraging overlending. Their entrance hinted at a herd logic that the first sign of crisis could quickly reverse.

Strains in a system in which political intervention remained sporadic and even destabilizing also became clear in two reschedulings that surpassed in scale those of earlier years: first Turkey, then Poland. Poland in particular provided a critical link to the 1982 crisis in the scale of debt and its demonstration of the weakness of a wholly bank-managed rescheduling (though government urging and intervention were added). The Polish plight also laid to rest any hope of a Soviet "umbrella," and rising East-West tensions after the imposition of martial law produced the first clear signs of regional contagion in the lending patterns of the banks, affecting Romania (already in arrears), Hungary, and Yugoslavia. By early 1982 syndicated bank lending to Eastern Europe had virtually ended. The Falklands/Malvinas War and the freeze instituted by Britain on Argentinian assets directed attention to yet another heavily indebted region and increased perceptions of risk; an international redlining of Latin America threatened. At the same time several financial institutions failed with wide publicity, notably Drysdale Securities, Penn Square Bank, and Banco Ambrosiano, heightening fears of a generalized weakening of the international financial system. Adverse economic conditions led to an accumulation of arrears by many developing country borrowers, and the shift toward short-term (and thus more unstable) debt structures continued.

The precipitant of the crisis came in August 1982 when Mexico, the largest single borrower from the international financial markets, requested a 120-day moratorium (later extended 90 days) on its debt payments. That request spurred the rapid construction of an innovative "template" for providing immediate liquidity to debtor countries while a refinancing of their debt was negotiated, a template used (with variations) in other cases in the following months. The most striking change, however, was the activist role assumed by both governments and international organizations, which now recognized the potential for dangerous instability in the international financial system. The stabilizing task, which protected the financial system by preventing an even sharper contraction of bank lending, was performed in a surprising display of cooperative behavior by industrial country governments led by the United States, commercial banks, international financial organizations, and Mexico itself.

Central banks, led by the U.S. Federal Reserve, were key players in short-term crisis management, providing their first extra-European bridge loan to Mexico (to be followed by similar loans to Argentina and Brazil). Central bank cooperation, in contrast to the financial crises of the 1930s, was effective, and the bankers' transnational network, centered on the Bank for International Settlements, proved resilient. Central banks were effective stabilizers in the early stages of the crisis for two reasons: as their governments' eyes and ears in the financial markets they often had some warning of developing difficulties on the part of borrowers (quite apart from their ties to the central banks of the borrowers); their resources, though inadequate for more than bridging purposes, and sometimes not even for that, could be mobilized quickly and without political complications. Later in the crisis, as described below, their regulatory role in national banking systems became crucial.

The *national governments of the Group of 5* (G-5) were effective in supplying the remainder of the emergency finance—cobbled together in the American case from accelerated oil purchases, credits from the Commodity Credit Corporation, and, eventually, export credits. In other instances bilateral assistance was increased or accelerated. Official debt was rescheduled under the auspices of the Paris Club.

The *International Monetary Fund,* as Kindleberger noted well before the debt crisis, moved too slowly to serve as a crisis manager, but its stabilizer role was perhaps the central and most expanded one in the period after the Mexican operation. Fund conditionality became the linchpin of the system: a Fund program or negotiations for one became a condition for rescheduling or refinancing official and private debt; even other forms of bilateral assistance were linked to adjustment programs. As a result, borrowing countries faced a much tighter system of cross-conditionality. The Fund had long been an active observer in Paris Club reschedulings; it now became much more intimately involved in the rescheduling of commercial bank debt.[29] A more radical innovation was introduced when the Fund used its new position to leverage the banks into new, involuntary lending. For the first time, in effect, a public entity was playing a direct role in credit allocation, even if only in certain cases. A less drastic change, though one derived from precrisis lessons, was greater Fund activity in information gathering, particularly on the debt structure of member countries.

The *World Bank,* with development lending responsibilities, was not an important player in the initial crisis management, but its actions ran parallel with these actors. Its structural adjustment loans added another element of conditionality directed to longer-term economic policy changes, and, through accelerated disbursements and cofinancing arrangements, it could contribute modestly to the financing needs of the imperiled borrowers.

The *commercial banks* undertook debt refinancing at a new order of complexity after Mexico; the organization of large numbers of lending institutions by an advisory committee became the normal procedure, and the hierarchical and multinational organization of the lenders tightened. As Joseph Kraft said of the Mexican case, "A communications network has been created through a series of regional subcommittees. Each American member of the advisory committee took responsibility for ten different regional banks. Each regional bank took responsibility for ten smaller banks in its area and so on down the line."[30] Information sharing also became a prominent concern for the banks, and in 1983 they established the Institute of International Finance as a clearinghouse for information among lenders. The Japanese had in the meantime established their own, similar institute.

Finally, the *debtor countries* themselves undertook severe adjustment programs, under IMF standby agreements or extended arrangements, and renegotiated a means by which to continue servicing of their debts. Mexico was the first of the large, system-threatening borrowers to seek a rescheduling; others soon followed. From a relatively rare occurrence, usually requested by smaller and poorer developing countries, rescheduling became the norm: from six debt restructurings in 1981 (only one, Turkey, a significant borrower) to over twenty in 1983, including the largest borrowing countries—Argentina, Brazil, Nigeria, and Yugoslavia. Though bargaining was tough, the system established in the Mexican case held until renewed pressures in early 1984 threatened to derail it and forced modifications, managed by the same key actors.

EXPLAINING COOPERATION WITHOUT REFORM

This outcome was hardly predictable: state intervention may have been necessary to correct shortcomings in the financial markets, but overt political intervention might not have produced system stability. Two features of the debt crisis in this new, politicized phase are both striking and puzzling. First, despite the large number of state and private actors that participated in the case-by-case management of the debt crisis and their potentially conflicting interests, the level of cooperative behavior in managing the crisis—among industrialized countries, between banks and their home governments, and between industrialized and developing countries—has remained high.

The North-South division provides the second puzzle. The apparent threat to the financial systems of the North gave leverage to the borrowers. The Northern definition of the debt crisis and creditor solutions to the crisis nonetheless prevailed, and in the Mexican case and after the "case-by-case, on a short leash" approach remained in place. Southern complaints had not shaped Northern economic management (particularly the policy mix of the United States or the anti-Keynesian bent of the European governments), the terms of debt restructuring in the first rounds were not generous, conditionality remained orthodox in its prescriptions. The scale of the reschedulings had not shaken a template that fitted the interests of the commercial banks and Northern finance ministries far more than those of the debtors. Southern efforts to redefine the crisis and change the existing system had, it seemed, utterly failed.

"Cooperation without reform" best describes the outcome to date in the management of the debt crisis. One can attempt to explain that outcome exclusively at the international level, but I shall argue here, tracing again the political tasks of stabilization, regulation, and adjustment, that even an explanation at the level of the international financial system depends at crucial points on domestic political processes. Those processes—in particular, regulation in the industrialized countries and adjustment in the South—are essential to any effort at piecing together solutions to the two puzzles.

One superficially appealing explanation of the first puzzle is that existing sets of conventions or rules were readily transferred to the new situation, and those structures shaped national incentives and behavior in a cooperative direction.[31] Such a "regime autonomy" explanation is inadequate, not least because the existence of a coherent regime, rather than fragments of a regime, is doubtful earlier than 1982. Certainly a "case law" had been established by that time, but to posit an existing regime is to understate the level of innovation in 1982–83. Participants in the events after mid-1982 emphasize dramatic changes in ordinary procedures: as Mexico's finance minister Silva Herzog remarked, "The world was different after that. . . . The blueprints for dealing with this situation quite simply did not exist; we had to draw them up."[32] What had previously been regime fragments were linked; what had previously been a relatively leisurely means of dealing with small debtors became a crisis management mechanism for dealing with threats to the entire financial system. And perhaps most important, governments emerged as critical actors in instituting these changes.

Inclusion of the largest debtors also weakens a regime explanation. As Robert Keohane has noted, explanations of this sort are strongest in situations of shared interests, which may exclude this and other aspects of North-South relations.[33] Certainly the legitimacy of the existing regime fragments had not been tested against the interests of the larger debtors— both Turkey and Poland had been special cases. Nor was it only Southern actors that resisted the rules of the game as they emerged in 1982–83. Bankers were also, oddly enough, resistant to the formation of a regime, in the sense of a clear-cut body of rules applied across cases: in Paul Mentré's words, "many bankers fear that precise guidelines could confer respectability and normality to a process which, in their view, should be regarded as exceptional and penalizing."[34] Thus an effort at regime consolidation faced potential resistance from lenders who preferred to maximize their bargaining power in a case-by-case approach and from borrowers who might resist the extension of existing conventions and benefit from individual treatment.

An alternative or a supplement to an explanation of cooperative and stable patterns of behavior based on regimes focuses on the renewed energy displayed by the United States in managing the crisis. Hegemonic stability arguments have been challenged both for their inability to demonstrate a close association between international power distribution and particular outcomes and for their inability to predict when and how the hegemon-designate will act.[35] Certainly, any variant of the theory would have had difficulty predicting the activism of the United States in managing this crisis "after hegemony." Yet closer examination offers reasons from *domestic* politics not only for the definition of American interests in the crisis but also for both American equivocation in the months preceding the crisis and the abrupt turnaround in the American position once the crisis had broken.

A parsimonious explanation of American actions in 1982 would revolve around the threat to a domestic financial system already under strain and the fact that it was the Mexican case that came first and provided a model for others that followed. The first set of concerns activated the Federal Reserve, and dense connections in trade and energy, as well as the strategic importance of Mexico, provided a potent glue in the often fragmented American executive. Nevertheless, as Benjamin Cohen's account of Reagan administration attitudes toward the International Monetary Fund suggests, what is most marked until the outbreak of crisis is how *little* concerned the United States appeared to be with system stability.[36] Resistance to a more active role came from two sources: the profoundly domestic orientation of American economic management and an ideological distrust of government intervention in what were regarded as efficient financial markets.

The first obstacle to American leadership has been well documented in Joanne Gowa's account of the American decision to close the gold window in August 1971: when regime maintenance or system stabilization conflicted with the autonomy of domestic economic policy making or strategic interests, regime maintenance was consistently regarded as the subordinate interest.[37] The same pattern was apparent in 1981 and 1982: the behavior of the U.S. government (and particularly its visible internal debate) on the question of declaring Polish official debt "in default" in 1982 made clear to the worried Europeans that threats to the international financial system were not an unquestioned priority in Reagan administration policy on East-West relations. At the time of the Mexican rescue the Treasury, still dominant in international financial policy making, was run by men with little experience in international monetary affairs. They remained blinded to the onrushing crisis. Even the Federal Reserve, one of the more internationally oriented actors in the U.S. government, did not determine its monetary targets with international financial consequences as a primary concern. (One informant offered 20 percent as an estimate of its weighting.)[38]

A second obstacle to intervention by the American government was the Reagan administration's deep-seated faith in the stability and flexibility of markets and its hostility to government tampering with private transactions. Stephen Marris has captured the sea change in international attitudes toward institutions of international economic cooperation, no longer regarded as "the brightest of man's creations" but, "at best, as clearinghouses for the exchange of information or, at worst, as having a negative influence on world economic welfare."[39] The early Reagan administration shared that same revolution of declining expectations.

It is because the American government resisted acting as a stabilizer of the system for these essentially domestic reasons that the peculiarities of the situation that triggered U.S. action should be emphasized. Intervention would probably not have been so swift had Mexico not been the first of the large debtors to encounter servicing difficulties. The costs of crisis management in terms of resources and domestic political risks, despite congressional and public resistance to the IMF quota increase in 1983, were relatively small. Moreover, the United States defined the limits of intervention very narrowly. Its actions help to explain not only the stability but the conservatism of the crisis outcome: only the IMF's crisis management role was expanded; there was virtually no concession to complaints that the American economic policy mix was producing interest rates burdensome to debtors; and all of the innovations were regarded as ad hoc and temporary, unfortunate way stations on the return to the market.

THE DOMESTIC DILEMMAS OF BARGAINING STRATEGIES

The special, and largely domestic, circumstances of American action in the debt crisis go some distance toward explaining innovations in procedures of crisis management, as well as the limits to those innovations. Nevertheless, the United States was intervening in a setting that on its own it could neither control nor even predictably influence. It required the cooperation of a host of actors, governmental and private, and it could expect resistance to its preferred solutions from at least some of the actors, particularly the debtors.

The complexities of the debt crisis after mid-1982 are difficult to simplify into a bargaining framework, but the dynamics can be viewed as bargaining between and within two coalitions, one more loosely organized than the other. The Northern coalition of the banks, the G-5 governments, and the International Monetary Fund shared an interest not only in avoiding disruption of the international financial system but also in the rough outlines of a rescheduling and adjustment regime for debtors. The coalition displayed potential fissures in the ordering of interests among its members—G-5 governments and the Fund ranked international financial stability higher than autonomy of decision making for the banks or adherence to particular payments schedules—and in the collective action problem of organizing such a large army of actors, particularly the commercial banks. Other incipient divisions among the industrialized countries depended upon regional biases in their national interests and bank lending patterns, as well as their differing attitudes toward reform—the French, for example, were relatively conciliatory toward the debtors. The Southern coalition was barely a coalition. There was little apparent coordination among the debtors until new strains in 1984 raised the possibility of a debtors' club. Much of Northern policy was directed to deepening the divergent interests among large debtors and between large debtors and those countries that could not on their own threaten the system.

Bargaining between the two coalitions most closely resembled a game of chicken: both shared an interest in avoiding financial collapse, but the Southern side was tempted to exploit the vulnerability of the North to obtain concessions in the rules of the rescheduling game or even wider reforms. The North pursued a complex strategy, offering incentives and also threatening sanctions to prevent cooperative action by Latin American debtors that could be transformed into a system-threatening moratorium on debt servicing. One incentive that the North could offer—given involuntary lending by the banks—was immediate financing on a scale unavailable outside the existing rules of the game. The sanctions were those which had always served as the principal means of enforcement in private bank lending: exclusion from private financial markets for an indefinite period and disruption of trade finance. In the longer term the promised rewards were markets for exports in the industrialized countries, renewed growth, and eventual eligibility for renewed voluntary financing from financial markets.

In pursuing this strategy the North faced several dilemmas, each of them rooted in domestic political constraints. First, it had to ease strains on the financial system that gave the debtors their principal bargaining threat. One tool for doing so—easing monetary policy and lowering interest rates—would also provide additional incentives for the debtors to accept the preferred G-5/IMF solution. It could, however, also conflict with other domestic economic policy goals, particularly the restraining of inflation. This conflict was not serious as the United States recovered from deep recession in 1983, but as the economy raced ahead in 1984 the Federal Reserve opted to tighten monetary policy. Interest rates drifted upward in early 1984 with predictable effects: a renewed burst of activity to organize the Latin American debtor countries and signs of strain on the financial system (particularly the failure of Continental Illinois). As a former vice-chairman of the Federal Reserve Board commented, "There are times when your lender-of-last-resort responsibilities and your monetary-policy responsibilities are somewhat in conflict, and this is one of those periods."[40]

REGULATION AND SYSTEM STABILITY: DOMESTIC POLITICS INTRUDES

The maintenance of coalition unity, and particularly maintaining the cooperation of the banks, was yet another obstacle-ridden path that governments, central banks, and the IMF had to negotiate. The strategy of the G-5 governments and the IMF depended on bank cooperation in two respects. In the first and purely crisis management phase the banks had to be kept in the game: the rational response of each individual bank to reduce its exposure as quickly as possible had to be curbed in order to prevent general collapse. The innovation of involuntary lending added to this burden: the banks had to be convinced not only to maintain but to increase their exposure. Without such an increase the harsh conditions asked of the debtors would probably have been unacceptable: as the IMF knows too well from experience, adjustment programs are likely to fail if the amount of financing offered to sustain them is inadequate.

The intrabank hierarchy described above was crucial to maintaining bank cooperation, but it seems unlikely that it would have held without the intervention of public authorities, wielding both pressure and regulatory dispensations. As Wellons notes, the level of "administrative guidance" varied from case to case and depended in part on the wishes of the bargaining parties—the banks and the debtor country—but pressure from regulators was important in establishing the innovation of involuntary lending. As one banker said, "It's peer-group type pressure. . . . And if that peer-group pressure does not work, they'll get a call from some public-sector person."[41] Regulators could also offer the incentive of relief from regulatory scrutiny. The most prominent example was Paul Volcker's speech to the New England Council on 16 November 1982, in which he suggested that because of unprecedented conditions, no one would question new lending to countries that had agreed an adjustment program with the IMF.[42]

The regulatory carrot offered by the Federal Reserve ran headlong into the peculiarities of the American political system. Banking supervision in most industrialized countries is, as Wellons indicates, a fairly cozy process involving the central bank and a banking sector far more concentrated than that in America. The United States, however, is host to a "crazy quilt of banking regulation," including state regulatory authorities as well as three regulatory authorities at the federal level—the Federal Reserve, the comptroller of the currency, and the Federal Deposit Insurance Corporation.[43] As the most internationally minded of the regulatory agencies, the Federal Reserve was willing to relax scrutiny in the interests of further lending as the debt crisis deepened, whatever the shortcomings of previous bank practice. Other regulators, with fewer international concerns, had different priorities. As Volcker waved his regulatory concession in November 1982 in an effort to make involuntary lending easier, the Securities and Exchange Commission was requiring banks to publish the extent of their exposure in individual "problem countries" if loans grew to more than 1 percent of the total outstanding.

Using regulation to ensure bank cooperation and system stability became even more difficult in 1983 because of the deepening politicization of regulatory questions during the debate over an increased U.S. quota in the International Monetary Fund. The quota increase was held hostage to any number of congressional concerns—efforts to target particular countries, new housing legislation—but perhaps most serious in their implications for the debt crisis were congressional demands for regulatory tightening. The American political system had once again set elements of an international strategy for stabilizing the system one against another, a necessary increase in IMF resources versus the need for U.S. banks to continue lending.

BARGAINING AND THE POLITICS OF ADJUSTMENT

In mixing sanctions and rewards to keep the debtor states in the game, the G-5 governments and the IMF had to contend with one final domestic constraint, one far more difficult than the use of regulatory instruments to influence bank behavior. They had even less control over the politics of adjustment inside the debtor countries, yet that politics was critical in determining the bargaining behavior of debtor states. For not only did elites in debtor countries have to weigh the carrots and sticks waved by international actors and the economic costs of severe adjustment programs, they also had to look over their shoulder at the consequences for their domestic political position. The gains and losses implied in internal competition with their rivals formed an element essential to their calculus.

That domestic political calculus also supplies an element needed to explain the puzzles of continuing cooperation between creditor and debtor and failure of debtors to coordinate their bargaining with the banks and the industrialized countries. It is clear that, while each of the major debtors in Latin America—Mexico, Brazil, and Argentina—might threaten system stability on its own, the smaller debtors were unlikely to be able to act collectively without leadership from one or more of those three. That possibility—a coalition of the great and the small debtors in a debtors' club—was what the North regarded as most threatening of all, a prospect that their strategy of rewarding those who remained within orthodox adjustment programs was designed to thwart.

The pattern of debtor collaboration that emerged did not, in fact, involve large countries leading a program of defiance. Rather, it was the smaller economies, hardest hit by collapsing commodity prices and unlikely to regain their creditworthiness in the near term, that first began efforts at debtor organization. At meetings in Panama in March 1983 and in Caracas (under OAS auspices) in September 1983 the big debtors indicated their lack of interest. The first sign of change came at the Latin American Economic Conference at Quito in January 1984: the new Argentinian government under Raúl Alfonsín took a more prominent and activist role.

The next debtors' meeting, at Cartagena in June 1984, was the high water mark of debtor collaboration, founded on deteriorating economic circumstances and in particular on rising interest rates. The meeting had been designed to send a signal to the London summit of industrialized countries, and the new line subsequently taken by the Federal Reserve and the IMF on better terms for rescheduling signified that they, if not industrial country leaders, may have received the signal. The Cartagena group had reached a modest consensus, but it had also been carefully managed to avoid any militant proposals despite agreement on a consultative mechanism. The chief managers of the meeting had been Mexico, Brazil, Venezuela, and the host, Colombia, arrayed against Argentina and several smaller countries. These same four countries had participated in the March 1984 "rescue" of Argentina as it approached its deadline for payment of interest to American banks. In the deal devised by Mexico the four Latin American countries and a consortium of banks contributed enough to make the necessary payments; the United States guaranteed the Latin American contributions if Argentina reached an agreement with the IMF. (Apparently, the bank contributions were also guaranteed by the Argentinian government.) Many had argued at the same time that the March action demonstrated an unwillingness by debtors to break with the system. Mexico's active role at Cartagena a few months later, however, suggested that it was playing a different strategy: keeping the other Latin Americans from actions that would, through contagion, affect its own standing with the banks, at the same time demonstrating that its leadership could be used for other purposes if a better bargain were not struck.

The reasons that Mexico and the other largest debtors did not organize a debtors' club are fairly clear: given their own bargaining power, the smaller debtors were pure free riders, unnecessary except perhaps for purposes of legitimation. Yet the contrasting courses that Mexico and Argentina followed are still puzzling: why did one become the model debtor of the IMF and the banks while the other engaged in repeated displays of brinksmanship (tied to U.S. regulatory deadlines) and foot-dragging in an effort to force a change in the rules of the game? Part of the explanation surely lies in their differing economic situations. Mexico was deeply embedded in a web of economic ties with the international economy and particularly the United States: trade disruption, particularly the disruption of food imports, would have been costly. (Brazil faced the same constraint with energy imports.) Argentina, in contrast, was not linked closely to any single industrialized country, and its economic self-sufficiency was greater.

Beneath the economic divergence, however, lay an equally important political divergence. As both Kaufman and Haggard indicate, Mexico was far better situated to undertake adjustment: the domestic political costs for its elite were lower. With the transition to the de la Madrid presidency, technocrats who were essentially in agreement with Fund prescriptions held the levers of economic policy. Alternative economic programs were advanced, but no organized group pushed hard for a coherent economic alternative; orthodox prescriptions, though hardly popular, had not been discredited by recent national experience. Most important, the corporatist or authoritarian structure of Mexico, based on a powerful presidency and a well-institutionalized political party (the PRI), provided a basis for containing resistance to stabilization, particularly from labor.

In Argentina, following the election of Alfonsín, the political landscape contrasted starkly with that of Mexico. Technocrats were hardly in control; rather, the new political leadership saw orthodox economic policies as thoroughly discredited by their association with the old regime and particularly with the government of Martínez de Hoz. Alfonsín and his cabinet repeatedly pledged themselves to no reduction in real wages and no recession. The Argentinian president, who was also institutionally powerful, acted not with the solid and centralized base of a PRI but in a setting of political flux in which the old verities had been erased by his victory. In their scramble to consolidate that surprising triumph, the Radicals had to confront a labor movement under the control of their adversaries, the Peronists. In such circumstances, given the risks of an effort to stabilize and the potential gains to be made in working-class support by resisting the IMF, the new Argentinian leaders challenged the existing rules again and again, externalizing their weakness in an effort to reduce the political burdens of adjustment.

The pattern of bargaining by Latin American states and the weakness of their collaboration reflected divergence in their domestic capabilities for adjustment. The divisions were less between democratic and authoritarian regimes than, adapting the arguments of Kaufman and Haggard, between "hard" and "soft" ones. "Hard" regimes—democratic or authoritarian—had two characteristics: they were able to curb the state sector itself in the interests of stabilization, and they were able to pursue Kaufman's containment option toward resistance to stabilization programs by labor and other groups. Although the military authoritarian regimes that took power in Latin America in the 1960s and 1970s may have begun as hard regimes—hostile in many cases to expansion of the state sector and willing to repress opposition to conservative economic policies—by the end of the 1970s (with the exception of Chile) they had softened, presiding over burgeoning public sectors and lower levels of resistance to demands from labor and other groups in civil society. The onset of economic crisis in the 1980s brought a hardening in the cases of Chile and the nonmilitary PRI government of Mexico, but it also brought great difficulties for the other, soft authoritarian regimes in pursing an adjustment program, difficulties that spurred the transition to civilian rule. In either case there was little incentive to take a tough bargaining line with the creditors. In the case of soft authoritarian regimes, such brinksmanship would risk loss of already waning middle-class support with few prospective gains in legitimation; in those regimes that could pursue adjustment programs with fewer political risks, tougher external bargaining was unnecessary. As the Argentinian case suggests, it was the "soft democratic" regime that seemed most tempted to toughen its bargaining stance and seek debtor collaboration. Such regimes were at the apogee of risk taking—not solidly grounded enough to pursue orthodox adjustment yet perceiving gains rather than losses to their domestic political base from a more resistant position toward creditors.

AN END TO THE DEBT CRISIS?

By early 1985 each of the three biggest Latin American debtors had elected governments that enjoyed a longer time horizon than any since the beginnings of the debt crisis in 1982. Each had reached agreement with the IMF (though disbursements were soon suspended for Argentina and Brazil); each had negotiated or was nearing agreement on a multiyear rescheduling arrangement with the commercial banks. The financial system no longer looked so shaky; year-end reports of the major banks suggested no overall weakness because of international lending. Was the debt crisis "all but over"?[44]

The answer from the South was clearly "no." The latest report of the Economic Commission for Latin America painted a picture that seemed promising only because of the bleakness of recent years. The favored, larger debtors had made some gains in economic growth, but even they were hardly successful by past standards: Mexico's per capita gross domestic product (GDP) declined in 1984; Brazil's overall increase of 3.5 percent only offset the decline in 1983. Among the smaller countries the record was catastrophic: declines in per capita GDP from 1981–84 of 25 percent in Bolivia, 16 percent in Uruguay, 11 percent in Chile.[45]

Northern countries saw a much brighter picture. The evolving bargain, which remained highly favorable to the creditors, looked as though it would hold. Certainly the evolution of economic parameters—interest rates, commodity prices, OECD growth rates—provides a major element in any prediction. My argument suggests, however, that the structure of international finance is now far more politicized and that political unknowns, *domestic* political unknowns, are equally important in predicting the outcome of the debt crisis. System stabilization continues to rest on cooperation among the industrialized countries and on continuing engagement by the United States. Despite its activism in crisis management since 1982, the United States is an unstable stabilizer, constantly tugged toward domestic policy goals that may conflict with its systemic role and seduced by a faith in the virtues of the unleashed market.

The domestic regulatory environment in all of the industrialized countries and particularly in the United States is likely to continue to influence the management of the debt crisis. On the one hand, the crisis itself induced a tightening of the regulatory environment for international lending. Some observers contend this new strictness could have a chilling effect on any new lending to Third World borrowers, but it could also, paradoxically, strengthen the hand of the debtors in their bargaining with the banks.[46] On the other hand, an opposite trend—hardly interrupted by the debt crisis—is also likely to have contradictory effects on bank behavior, and that is the continuing *deregulation* of financial institutions in the United States and elsewhere. Deregulation offers incentives for money center banks in the United States to turn away from their riskier international business, but it could also, as a by-product of the financial supermarkets of tomorrow, produce new financial technologies to sustain capital flows to the developing countries. Commercial banks, in this last view, may be the dinosaurs of international finance; the needs of developing country borrowers, like those of domestic consumers, may be better served by new, diversified institutions.[47]

Perhaps most unpredictable, however, is the course of politics and economic policy in the debtor countries. As soft authoritarian regimes give way to democratic regimes, whether hard or soft, the historical record is not encouraging: both authoritarian and democratic regimes in Latin America have been weighed in the stabilization balance and found wanting. Conservative, dependency, and neodependency models of Latin American development also seem wanting as the region (and other indebted countries) grope toward a new model that will fit the changed international economic circumstances. As in the 1930s, so it is in the 1980s: the gambles that political elites on the periphery take or decline to take—weighing both their economic and their domestic political prospects as well as their hunches about the international economy—will set the final political boundary to the future of the debt crisis.

NOTES

1. Charles Kindleberger, *Manias, Panics, and Crashes* (London: Macmillan, 1978), especially pp. 201–209.
2. William R. Cline, *International Debt and the Stability of the World Economy* (Washington, D.C.: Institute for International Economics, 1983), and *International Debt: Systemic Risk and Policy Response* (Washington, D.C.: Institute for International Economics, 1984); Carlos Diaz-Alejandro, "Latin American Debt: I Don't Think We Are in Kansas Anymore," *Brookings Papers on Economic Activity* 2 (1984), especially pp. 351–355.
3. Of course, proponents of the first or third models can reply that *within* Latin America widely divergent policy stances seemed to fail, indicating a common external cause for failure. See Diaz-Alejandro, "Latin American Debt," p. 336.
4. *World Economic Outlook* (Washington, D.C.: IMF, April 1984), p. 25.
5. Kindleberger, *Manias, Panics, and Crashes,* especially chaps. 10 and 11; Jeffrey Sachs, *Theoretical Issues in International Borrowing* (Princeton, N.J.: International Finance Section, Princeton University, July 1984), pp. 29–32.
6. Diaz-Alejandro attributes the financial shock that reinforced an external real shock to the gap between the "private and [the] collective rationality" of banks ("Latin American Debt," p. 355).
7. Jack Guttentag and Richard Herring, "The Current Crisis in International Banking," mimeo (Wharton School, University of Pennsylvania, October 1983), pp. 1–3, and their *The Lender-of-Last-Resort Function in an International Context* (Princeton, N.J.: International Finance Section, Princeton University, May 1983), pp. 2–4.
8. Jonathan Eaton and Mark Gersovitz, *Poor-Country Borrowing in Private Financial Markets and the Repudiation Issue* (Princeton, N.J.: International Finance Section, Princeton University, June 1981), chap. 2; Sachs, *Theoretical Issues,* chap. 4.
9. Kindleberger, *Manias, Panics, and Crashes,* p. 161; Guttentag and Herring, *Lender-of-Last-Resort Function,* p. 4.
10. Sachs, *Theoretical Issues,* chap. 5; Guttentag and Herring, *Lender-of-Last-Resort Function,* pp. 6–7.
11. Charles Kindleberger, *The World in Depression, 1929–1939* (Berkeley: University of California Press, 1975), p. 28.
12. Albert Fishlow, "Lessons from the Past," *International Organization* 39 (Summer 1985); Kindleberger, *Manias, Panics, and Crashes,* pp. 153–156.
13. Fishlow's contrast of London with the far more politically direct Paris and Berlin financial centers holds, though on occasion the British government could make its foreign-policy wishes known to the City; see Herbert Feis, *Europe, the World's Banker, 1870–1914* (New York: Norton, 1965), p. 89.
14. David Felix, "The Baring Crisis of the 1890s and the International Bond Defaults of the 1930s: Delphic Prophecies on the Outcome of the Current Latin American Debt Crises," mimeo (Dept. of Economics, Washington University, St. Louis, Mo., November 1984), pp. 20–25; also L. S. Pressnell, "The Sterling System and Financial Crises before 1914," in Charles Kindleberger and Jean-Pierre Laffargue, eds., *Financial Crises: Theory, History and Policy* (New York: Cambridge University Press, 1982), pp. 148–164.
15. "Lessons from the Past."

16. Marcello de Cecco, "The International Debt Problem in the Interwar Period" (paper presented at the Lehrman Institute series on Politics and International Debt, New York, May 1984), pp. 15–18.

17. Carlos Diaz-Alejandro, "Stories of the 1930s for the 1980s," in Pedro Aspe Armella et al., eds., *Financial Policies and the World Capital Markets: The Place of Latin American Countries* (Chicago: University of Chicago Press, 1983), pp. 5–35; Felix, "Baring Crisis of the 1890s," pp. 46–50.

18. Carlos Diaz-Alejandro, "Latin America in the 1930s," in Rosemary Thorpe, ed., *Latin America in the 1930s: The Role of the Periphery in World Crises* (London: Macmillan, 1984), pp. 17–50.

19. Charles Lipson, "The International Organization of Third World Debt," *International Organization* 35 (Autumn 1981), pp. 609–610. The concept of a financial technology is from Marcello de Cecco. Among the many studies of the Euromarkets and sovereign lending by commercial banks, see Ronald I. McKinnon, *The Eurocurrency Market* (Princeton, N.J.: International Finance Section, Princeton University, December 1977), and Stefan Mendelsohn, *Money on the Move: The Modern International Capital Market* (New York: McGraw-Hill, 1980).

20. E. Brau and R. C. Williams, *Recent Multilateral Debt Restructurings with Official and Bank Creditors* (Washington, D.C.: IMF, December 1983), p. 25.

21. For example, Lipson, "International Organization of Third World Debt."

22. G. G. Johnson, *Aspects of the International Banking Safety Net* (Washington, D.C.: IMF, March 1983), p. 23.

23. "Survey: IMF—Ministry without Portfolio," *Economist,* 26 September 1981, p. 16.

24. Philip Wellons, "International Debt: The Behavior of Banks in a Politicized Environment," *International Organization* 39 (Summer 1985); also Andrew Spindler, *The Politics of International Credit* (Washington, D.C.: Brookings, 1984).

25. See the examples given by Benjamin J. Cohen, "International Debt and Linkage Strategies: Some Foreign-Policy Implications for the United States," *International Organization* 39 (Autumn 1985).

26. Stephan Haggard, "The Politics of Adjustment: Lessons from the IMF's Extended Fund Facility," *International Organization* 39 (Summer 1985); William Cline and Sidney Weintraub, eds., *Economic Stabilization in Developing Countries* (Washington, D.C.; Brookings, 1981), p. 300.

27. Robert Kaufman, "Democratic and Authoritarian Responses to the Debt Issue: Argentina, Brazil, Mexico," *International Organization* 39 (Summer 1985).

28. Brau and Williams, *Recent Multilateral Debt Restructurings,* p. 3.

29. Paul Mentré, *The Fund, Commercial Banks, and Member Countries* (Washington, D.C.: IMF, April 1984), p. 31.

30. Joseph Kraft, *The Mexican Rescue* (New York: Group of Thirty, 1984), pp. 26–27.

31. Stephen Krasner, "Regimes and the Limits of Realism: Regimes as Autonomous Variables," *International Organization* 36 (Spring 1982), pp. 497–510.

32. Kraft, *The Mexican Rescue,* p. 3.

33. Robert O. Keohane, *After Hegemony* (Princeton: Princeton University Press, 1984), p. 7.

34. Mentré, *The Fund, Commercial Banks, and Member Countries,* p. 30.

35. Keohane, *After Hegemony,* chap. 3.

36. Cohen, "International Debt and Linkage Strategies," sec. 5.

37. Joanne Gowa, *Closing the Gold Window: Domestic Politics and the End of Bretton Woods* (Ithaca: Cornell University Press, 1983), pp. 24–27.

38. Kraft, *The Mexican Rescue,* p. 8.

39. Stephen Marris, *Managing the World Economy: Will We Ever Learn?* (Princeton, N.J.: International Finance Section, Princeton University, 1984), p. 8.

40. Quoted in *Wall Street Journal,* 7 June 1984, p. 1.

41. Quoted in *New York Times,* 12 December 1982, p. D3; also Kraft, *The Mexican Rescue,* p. 53.

42. Mentré, *The Fund, Commercial Banks, and Member Countries,* p. 10; Kraft, *The Mexican Rescue,* p. 49.

43. Martin Mayer, *The Money Bazaars* (New York: Dutton, 1984), p. 335; Richard Dale, *Bank Supervision around the World* (New York: Group of Thirty, 1982), p. 62; David Lascelles, "U.S. Bank Regulation after the Debt 'Crisis,' " *Banker,* January 1983, p. 21.

44. *New York Times,* 4 February 1985, p. D1.

45. Economic Commission for Latin America and the Caribbean, "Preliminary Overview of the Latin American Economy during 1984," LC/G. 1336 (Santiago, 17 January 1985).

46. Robert A. Bennett, "Bankers Fear Effects of Regulators' Moves," *New York Times,* 17 November 1984, pp. 31, 33; Karin Lissakers, "Bank Regulation and International Debt," in Richard E. Feinberg and Valeriana Kallab, eds., *Uncertain Future: Commercial Banks and the Third World* (New Brunswick, N.J.: Transaction, 1984), pp. 66–67.

47. The future of the commercial banks is considered by Mayer, *The Money Bazaars,* especially chap. 2.

Casino Capitalism

Susan Strange

The Western financial system is rapidly coming to resemble nothing as much as a vast casino. Every day games are played in this casino that involve sums of money so large that they cannot be imagined. At night the games go on at the other side of the world. In the towering office blocks that dominate all the great cities of the world, rooms are full of chain-smoking young men all playing these games. Their eyes are fixed on computer screens flickering with changing prices. They play by intercontinental telephone or by tapping electronic machines. They are just like the gamblers in casinos watching the clicking spin of a silver ball on a roulette wheel and putting their chips on red or black, odd numbers or even ones.

As in a casino, the world of high finance today offers the players a choice of games. Instead of roulette, blackjack, or poker, there is dealing to be done—the foreign exchange market and all its variations; or in bonds, government securities or shares. In all these markets you may place bets on the future by dealing forward and by buying or selling options and all sorts of other recondite financial inventions. Some of the players—banks especially—play with very large stakes. These are also many quite small operators. There are tipsters, too, selling advice, and peddlers of systems to the gullible. And the croupiers in this global financial casino are the big bankers and brokers. They play, as it were, *for the house.* It is they, in the long run, who make the best living.

These bankers and dealers seem to be a very different kind of men working in a very different kind of world from the world of finance and the typical bankers that older people remember. Bankers used to be thought of as staid and sober men, grave-faced and dressed in conservative black pinstripe suits, jealous of their reputation for caution and for the careful guardianship of their customers' money. Something rather radical and serious has happened to the international financial system to make it

Susan Strange, "Casino Capitalism," in Strange, *Casino Capitalism,* New York: Basil Blackwell, 1986.

so much like a gambling hall. What that change has been, and how it has come about, are not clear.

What is certain is that it has affected everyone. For the great difference between an ordinary casino which you can go into or stay away from, and the global casino of high finance, is that in the latter all of us are involuntarily engaged in the day's play. A currency change can halve the value of a farmer's crop before he harvests it, or drive an exporter out of business. A rise in interest rates can fatally inflate the cost of holding stocks for the shopkeeper. A takeover dictated by financial considerations can rob the factory worker of his job. From school leavers to pensioners, what goes on in the casino in the office blocks of the big financial centers is apt to have sudden, unpredictable, and unavoidable consequences for individual lives. The financial casino has everyone playing the game of Snakes and Ladders. Whether the fall of the dice lands you on the bottom of a ladder, whisking you up to fortune, or on the head of a snake, precipitating you to misfortune, is a matter of luck.

This cannot help but have grave consequences. For when sheer luck begins to take over and to determine more and more of what happens to people, and skill, effort, initiative, determination, and hard work count for less and less, then inevitably faith and confidence in the social and political system quickly fades. Respect for ethical values—on which in the end a free democratic society relies—suffers a dangerous decline. It is when bad luck can strike a person not only from directions where luck has always ruled: health, love, natural catastrophes, or genetic chance, but from new and unexpected directions as well, that a psychological change takes place. Luck, now, as well as idleness or inadequacy, can lose you a job. Luck can wipe out a lifetime's savings, can double or halve the cost of a holiday abroad, can bankrupt a business because of some unpredictable change in interest rates or commodity prices or some other factor that used to be regarded as more or less stable and reliable. There seems less and less point in trying to make the right decision, when it is so difficult to know how the wheel of chance will turn and where it will come to rest. Betting on red and on black has equally uncertain results. That is why I think the increase in uncertainty has made inveterate, and largely involuntary, gamblers of us all.

Moreover, the vulnerability to bad luck in a system which is already somewhat inequitable is itself far from equal. Some can find ways to cushion or protect themselves, while others cannot. And inequities that were originally due to a variety of factors become suddenly much more acutely felt and more bitterly resented. Frustration and anger become sharper and are apt to be more violently expressed when the realm of luck becomes too large and when the arbitrariness of the system seems to operate so very unequally.

If this is true for individuals, it is also true for large enterprises and for the governments of countries. Political leaders, and their opponents, like to pretend that they are still in control of their national economies, that their policies have the power to relieve unemployment, revive economic growth, restore prosperity, and encourage investment in the future. But recent years have shown again and again how the politicians' plans have been upset by changes that they could not have foreseen in the world outside the state. The dollar has weakened—or become too strong. Interest rates have made the burden of servicing a foreign debt too heavy to sustain. The banks have suddenly decided to lend the country no more money. Oil prices have suddenly risen—or fallen. Other commodity prices, on which export earnings may depend, fall, because the major economies of major consuming countries are going through a recession. The uncertainty that rules in the financial world spills over not only into individual lives but into the fortunes of governments and of countries—and sooner or later into the relations between states. That spillover happened 50 odd years ago, after the Great Crash of 1929, and whether this time the uncertainty leads to a dramatic crisis or—as seems far more likely—to a stubbornly continuing malaise in the world market economy, this must be of general concern not just to economists.

THE MESS IN PERSPECTIVE

If we stand back from the headlines and concerns of the immediate present we might observe two things. One is that the changes leading to the present mess have happened very fast, in the short space of about 15 years. The other is that in that space of time, change has affected coincidentally some of the key prices which order the functioning of the world economy. They have all become increasingly unstable in the same period—the price of currencies in the foreign exchange market which connects all the national economic systems with each other; the rising price of goods in general in terms of money, otherwise known as the inflation rate; the price of credit, otherwise called the rate of interest, which is a major factor in the production of all goods and services; and the price of oil, which is the other major input on which all mechanical production and the transport of goods depend. Uncertainty in each has fed the uncertainty and the volatility of the others. And the common factor linking them all to each other has been the international financial system. That is the rootstock, from whose disorders stem the various problems which afflict the international political economy, just as blight, disease, or mildew attack the different branches of a plant.

Everyone is familiar with these problems, thanks to newspapers, television, and a spate of books and pamphlets. Best known and understood is the debt problem of the developing countries: the fact that too many were lent too much on terms which laid them open to the risk that if the loans ever stopped, they would be in trouble with the creditors. That is related to the second problem, which is the slow growth of the whole world economy in the late 1970s and the recession of the 1980s. The instability of the banking system is the third problem. But it is not limited to the debtor countries; the extent of corporate debt to the banks is equally great and, if slow growth continues, could be equally menacing, in the absence of a credible lender of last resort. Fourth might be added the uncertainty over oil prices, of consequence to producers and to consumers and, thus, a decisive factor in many countries' balance of payments not least of the major producers in the Middle East, an area doubly afflicted by economic and political instability, both domestic in some cases and international. All these problems are mainly economic in character. But as big as any is the fifth problem: the precariousness of the international political situation—notably the unstable Soviet-American balance and the uneasy American-European alliance. Even these have some roots in the financial disorder and uncertainty. Both are affected by—as they in turn affect—the strength or weakness of the dollar on those flickering computer screens in the foreign exchange rooms of banks around the world.

If, as I shall argue, all these problems are interconnected, and in all of them there is the common factor of financial uncertainty and therefore vulnerability to the play at the tables of the great financial casino, then it must follow that some attention to the common denominator would certainly make the solution of any one of them much easier. It might not be a sufficient condition, but almost certainly it is a necessary one. Any help that restoring financial certainty and stability would give to each one of the problems would also make the solutions of the others a less formidable task.

Before we consider solutions, though, we must ask when and how the rot in the old system set in. When did this rapid change with its many political and economic repercussions really begin? How did it start? It is only by looking back and reviewing how the multiple mess developed that we shall ever be able to work out a solution to it.

HOW DID IT START?

The year of 1973 stands out as a benchmark, a turning point when the snowball of change from the leisurely 1960s to the hectic yo-yo years of the 1970s and 1980s began to gather momentum. It stands out as a year when several big changes coincided—an effective devaluation of the dollar and the accompanying decision to leave the determination of exchange rates to the markets. This is known as the move to floating rates—not a very apt description because some sink while others rise. It was also the year of the first major rise in oil prices, to be followed by much increased dependence on the banking system to find the finance for the current consumption bills and the economic development of the poorer countries (and some developed ones). Each of these changes was to add in a different way to the uncertainty of the system.

It may help to recall a little of the history of international monetary relations to see how this came about. It will also explain why the choice of 1973, or any other precise date, is bound to be somewhat arbitrary. All that can be said is that it seemed to mark a sort of change of gear, as the system moved from a more stable period into a much more unstable one.

Cracks and weak spots in the system had been detected a full 15 years before, when it became clear that the monetary rules and arrangements agreed by the United States and other countries at Bretton Woods during the war were not working out quite as planned. Instead of an evenhanded system in which the same rules applied to all, a highly asymmetric one had developed in which continuing deficits on the U.S. balance of payments were matched by increasing dollar holdings by America's trading partners. These dollar reserves allayed other countries' anxieties that they might run out of money to import, as Britain had in 1945. Trade revived, but the accumulated dollars, though they also helped to finance investment, especially in Europe, were sooner or later going to exceed even the very large gold reserves of the United States. For it was an essential part of the system that the dollars were held as IOUs by the Europeans and others, partly because the United States offered to exchange them for gold at a fixed prewar price. The inherent dangers of this *dollar overhang* were pointed out as early as 1958 by Professor Robert Triffin (Triffin, 1958) in America and by Professor Jacques Rueff in France (Rueff, 1971). This analysis was taken up by the French and other European governments who (somewhat ambivalently) wished to enjoy both growing prosperity and the right to complain about the injustice of a system which allowed the Americans (and to some extent the British) to enjoy the special privileges that came from other countries holding their currency as a reserve of IOUs. This was what General de Gaulle called *the exorbitant privilege,* meaning that the Americans could pay their bills—for defense spending among other things—with IOUs instead of exports of goods and services.

As the 1960s progressed, the cracks widened and the system began to creak under the combined pressure of growing international financial and capital markets, moving more and more money across the exchanges, and of political disagreement among governments about what was wrong with the system. The cracks were patched with such palliative measures as the Gold Pool, and the General Arrangements to Borrow augmenting the resources of the International Monetary Fund set up at Bretton Woods to lend its member countries foreign currency in an emergency. To prevent their payments deficits from being made worse by foreign borrowers coming to New York for loans, the Americans taxed such loans—but in doing so forced their own banks abroad, fostering the nascent London market for the Eurodollar credits. The disagreements continued but some compromises were reached—as for example the agreement at Stockholm in 1968 to allow the IMF to issue Special Drawing Rights (SDRs) which would supplement but not supplant the dollar as an asset which governments could hold in their reserves.

The strains in the system, even late in the 1960s, seemed to afflict mainly the strong European currencies, like the German mark (revalued in 1969), and the weak European currencies like sterling (devalued in 1967) and the French franc (devalued in 1969). Eventually, however, they also affected the U.S. economy. Holding the dollar's exchange rate, while spending heavily on the Vietnam War, had led President Johnson to resort to a deflationary tight money policy at home and to high interest rates which helped somewhat to mitigate the worsening trade balance.

But while Johnson saw the foreign exchange markets as enemies putting the dollar under speculative pressure, Nixon, Kissinger, and Connally were well advised and saw that the markets could also be used as allies, helping the United States to engineer a devaluation of the dollar which other countries could neither resist nor match. The unilateral abrogation by Nixon of the Bretton Woods system in August 1971 closed the gold window (i.e., he refused to exchange any more dollar IOUs for U.S. gold reserves) and allowed the dollar to come down off its fixed exchange rate with other countries.

That was the first step toward the decision in 1973 to abandon fixed exchange rates for good. In the interval there had been the Smithsonian Agreement of December 1971, a negotiated realignment of dollar rates with the Japanese yen and the German mark. But continued inflation, and a commodity boom, partly set off by uncertainty about the future of the dollar, first took the pound sterling out of the fixed rate arrangements and then tore apart the Europeans' *snake in the tunnel*, their first attempt to hold their currency rates steady with each other. Turbulence in the currency markets finally led the United States to take the plunge and let the markets, not governments, decide how many pounds, yen, or marks should be exchanged for a dollar.

THE EFFECTS OF FLOATING RATES

The record, however abbreviated, of the events leading up to this point is chiefly important because of the yawning discrepancy between the promise and the performance of floating exchange rates. The great majority of economists, led by the Americans, had promised that the change would bring the alarming and disturbing currency crises of the previous five years to an end: "The strain," they assured us, "can be taken on the rate instead of the reserves—so governments will not need to worry. The markets will only reflect step by step the proper relation of costs and prices (and inflation rates) in each country with those of its trading partners. There need be no more violent shifts in exchange rates."

That was the theory and the promise. But practice proved very different. Instead of reducing the volatility of the markets, floating rates—or to put it another way, the abstinence of governments from intervening in the markets—seemed to increase the volatility.

After only five years' trial, it was already clear that both the surpluses and the deficits on the major countries' balance of payments were getting larger, not smaller. The invisible hand of a free currency market somehow was not working. In 1978, the countries that had had the largest surpluses under fixed rates—Japan, West Germany, Switzerland, the Netherlands, and Belgium—now had surpluses twice as large, a combined total of $9 billion on average in 1972–1973 and of $18 billion in 1977. The deficit countries—the United States, Britain, France, Italy, and Canada—had deficits more than three times as large as before, even though the market had devalued their currencies (Triffin, 1979). Thus, instead of needing smaller reserves under a floating rate system, everyone needed still larger reserves in order to cope with the possibility of larger deficits.

This, of course, did not apply to the United States. As the chief reserve currency country in what was now, in effect, a paper-dollar system instead of the gold-dollar system that functioned in the 1960s, its reserves of dollars were unlimited. Its economy was also far less vulnerable to exchange rate changes than those of the Europeans. Not only did the Europeans trade much more than the Americans, much of their trade was with their fellow Europeans. They found that the floating rates tended to push their currencies to extremes, polarizing them into the weak and the strong. Especially as the dollar weakened after 1976, footloose funds fled into D-marks or Swiss francs, pulling those currencies further than ever from those of the deficit countries, Britain, France, and Italy (Fabra, 1978). In year-to-year exchange rates, changes were almost twice as large in the 1970s as in the 1960s (Vaubel, 1980).

Moreover, while the need to hold reserves increased because of the added uncertainty of future rates, there remained the question of what to hold in the reserves—dollars, gold, D-marks, or some other asset. To defend the dollar, the Americans had conducted an anti-gold campaign in the mid-1970s, holding its price for official sales or purchases by central banks first to the original $35 and then to $42 an ounce, until as late as 1979, when, in response to dollar weakness, the private gold price took off, and some governments decided to revalue their gold holdings.[1] The campaign had meant that the chances of acquiring larger gold reserves were limited. The bulk of the increased reserves therefore—all but $29 billion out of over $250 billion added by 1978 to the level of reserves 20 years before—were in foreign exchange. And the possibility that governments, as well as the private operators, might change their preferences only added to the instability of the foreign exchange markets.

Nor, it must be added, was the increased movement of financial managers, public and private, in and out of currencies on the foreign exchange markets a once-for-all phenomenon marking the change to floating rates. It was cumulative. The more players joined the game, the greater the volatility of the markets; and the greater the volatility, the more new players were drawn into it and the harder it was for anyone affected by variations in exchange rates to stay out of it. By 1977, the Federal Reserve Bank of New York estimated the *daily* turnover on the New York foreign

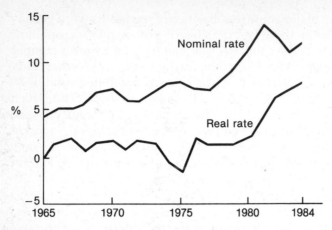

Figure 1 Long-term Interest Rates in the United States, 1965–1984. (*Source: World Development Report*, 1985, p.5. All data are averages of quarterly data.)

exchange market alone at somewhere between $10 billion and $12 billion. Three years later, their estimate was somewhere around $25 billion, nine-tenths of the dealing being done by banks. Over the same period, 1977–80, forward exchange trading in New York rose from a daily $3.5 billion to a daily $10.8 billion (Blin, 1981). Some estimates by the Group of Thirty suggest that the figure for daily turnover in the foreign exchange market in London in 1980 may have been twice as much and by 1985 had doubled to an estimated $45 billion. Worldwide, the Group of Thirty thought that *daily* foreign exchange transactions in 1985 amounted to some $150 billion.

The reasons for this truly revolutionary expansion in daily dealing in foreign exchange—an expansion far, far greater than could possibly be accounted for by the expansion in international trade—are clear enough. They can explain the hyperactivity of the chain-smoking young men in the city center tower blocks.

Under the fixed exchange rate system, corporation finance managers would use the forward market in foreign exchange to protect themselves against possible changes in the interest rate differential between financial assets or commitments incurred in different currencies. Occasionally, when a change was anticipated in any particular exchange rate there was some incentive for companies to join the speculators by buying or selling it according to the direction of the expected change (or more commonly, to indulge in *leads and lags* in payments across the exchanges). But for the most part the acknowledged responsibility of the central banks for holding the rates fixed relieved corporate finance managers of the need to worry about day-to-day changes.

Under the floating or flexible exchange rate system, however, the

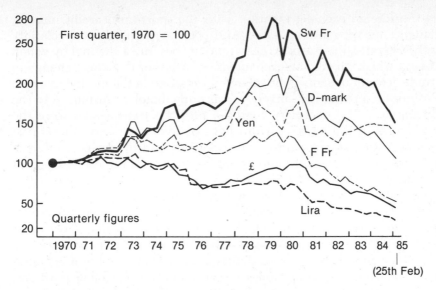

Figure 2 Exchange Rates Against the Dollar 1970–1985. (*Source: The Economist,* 16 March 1985: from IMF/OECD data.)

company had to cope with the day-to-day shifts in the dollar's rate of exchange with other currencies. It is arguable that the costs to the central banks of intervening with their reserves to check exchange rate changes would have been in total far less than the costs of currency hedging now borne by corporations in the private sector. This increased the profits of the banks and caused attention to the financial side of businesses to grow in importance compared to attention to the directly productive side.

What was certain was that the cost had shifted, from the public sector to the private and then, in the end, to the consumers. For under flexible rates, because of the inevitable mismatch of money in different currencies coming in and going out of corporate bank accounts, the finance manager, in order to budget ahead, either had to cover or to safeguard his accounts against the expected receipts being less than they would be at today's exchange rate, and the anticipated payments being more for the same reason. He could do this by buying a currency forward and investing the equivalent in the short-term money market, or by investing in the Eurocurrency market. Every such order given to the corporation's bank would be offset by another contrary transaction because the banks were usually unwilling to have *open*—that is, unbalanced—positions in currencies overnight. The need to swap deposits in different currencies in order to match corporate hedging transactions and to square the books is largely responsible for the growth and size of the interbank market referred to above. And the consequent price of the forward cover (i.e., the premium or discount on a currency's spot value) has tended to be set by these interbank market operations according to the differences between interest rates offered for Eurocurrency deposits in different currencies. This is the link that connects the foreign exchange market with the short-term credit market, exchange rates with interest rates. And because of the greater volatility of exchange rates, the Eurocurrency markets became a channel by which any event which affected an exchange rate, whether that was a change in the trade account or some political event regarded in the market as a plus or a minus for a particular currency, was immediately transmitted to the credit markets. The necessary conditions for this transmission were the unwillingness of the banks—in the light of their own and others' past experience—to take risks in foreign exchange, and the need of international business and exporters and importers to protect themselves against such risks (cf. Moffitt, 1982; Mendelson, 1980; Lever and Huhne, 1985; Sampson, 1981; Versluysen, 1980; and many others).

That need arose from the growth in international trade and from the internationalization of production by so-called *multinational* or, more accurately, transnational corporations. But there is a circularity here too. For, as companies have discovered, forward markets gave them only limited protection. Corporations suffer variations in their cash flow positions, in profits and losses, investments and sales in different countries and currencies. Yet a company's stock exchange rating and the composite company balance sheet at the end of its financial year has to be calculated in one currency. There is therefore a long-term incentive to the finance managers to find additional ways of dealing with this other kind of risk and of protecting themselves against criticism if the balance sheet should show a loss which was not a *real* loss but due entirely to the valuations of certain operations in another currency. Managers have therefore tended first to diversify the company's capital assets and liabilities as much as possible— financing locally or borrowing from local banks or better still, financing in convertible Eurobonds, for instance, and they have often sought to acquire local shareholders who will assume some of the risks. Indeed, geographical diversification of the firm's operations would be a rational long-run hedging strategy. In short, floating and volatile exchange rates, by increasing risks for multinationals, have made them still more *multinational* in response. But this resulting long-run strategy will tend, in turn, to increase their short-term needs for hedging against exchange rate risks, thus adding still further to the volume of transactions in the financial casino.

It goes almost without saying that the volatility of exchange rates, especially between the dollar and other leading currencies, has also increased risks for developing countries even more than for the mobile transnational companies. The latter at least have a variety of products, a variety of countries to operate in and an army of highly paid and well-equipped tax advisers and financial managers to work on the problem. The developing countries are not so well served. In addition to all their other problems, since 1971 they have had to choose between a number of exchange rate strategies for their currencies. They could decide, like Mexico, to peg to the dollar, or like Senegal to the franc, or to the SDR or some other basket of currencies; or they could leave it to the market to decide.[2] But as rates between the pegs changed, some who had pegged had clearly chosen wrongly. Furthermore, the value of their export earnings from primary products was apt to be substantially affected by changes in the dollar, or sometimes even by the sterling rate (Stewart, 1981). For example, one developing country's financial fortunes might be magically enhanced in a year when the dollar appreciates and the D-mark weakens if its currency is pegged to the dollar and its exports are primary products quoted in dollars, while its imports come from Germany, its debts are mostly to German banks, and it is able to borrow in D-marks. But equally, opposite changes in exchange rates could have precisely the opposite effects.

THE VOLATILITY OF INTEREST RATES

From the mid-1970s onward, the instability of the currency markets was compounded by a marked increase in the volatility of the price of borrowing money.

From the 1930s until the mid-1960s, the level of interest rates in industrialized countries remained remarkably low, considering that in that time there was a world war, rapidly succeeded by a long cold war. Defense budgets were heavy, even for neutral states like Sweden, and when superimposed (as in Europe) on social welfare programs, they caused the share of national income taken by government to rise. The first breach in the dyke is conventionally blamed on President Johnson and the Vietnam War. His Administration was reluctant to finance both the war and social reforms by taxation and so resorted to increased government borrowing to meet the increased federal budget. But as Calleo has pointed out, this version is too simple (Calleo, 1982). The increase in U.S. defense costs was not enough to account for so pronounced a worldwide phenomenon as took place in the period 1971–84. In 1963, commercial bills in New York were still paying less than 4 percent, U.S. Treasury Bills just over 3 percent. By 1966 the commercial bill rate was over 6 percent and the rate in the Eurocurrency market, known as LIBOR, or London Inter Bank Offer Rate, was over 7 percent. By 1969 the respective rates were up to 8 and near 11 percent. Thereafter both show a marked increased in the yo-yo tendency, with the New York rate always moving in less extreme fashion.

The Eurocurrency market undoubtedly contributed substantially first to the rise and then to the volatility of interest rates. Mainly located in London, the market's growth owed a great deal not only to the permissiveness of the British authorities but also to their active participation. Through the 1960s, Britain not only had a comparatively large national debt—other countries, having been defeated in the war, were fortunate enough to have been allowed by that fact to default on their creditors both at home and abroad—but suffered a persistent loss of market confidence in sterling. Successive governments responded (in effect) by bribing holders of sterling reserves not to run away. They were offered high interest rates on British Government Treasury bills and gilts (gilt-edged government stock), and by the late 1960s, both high rates and a dollar guarantee. As the Eurocurrency business grew, it first of all allowed people to arbitrage between currencies, so that funds could be attracted on a covered basis into weak currencies by relatively high interest rates while strong currencies could keep interest rates low and still attract foreign funds. Secondly, it allowed funds to move and people to arbitrage between the domestic market and the Eurocurrency ones.[3]

But the choice was inevitably affected by two politically determined factors: the extra risk involved in dealing in a *foreign* currency and the regulations imposed domestically on almost all national bank operations compared with the freedom from control of similar operations conducted in the Euromarkets. The point of this is that the Eurocurrency markets allowed the U.S. banks (which dominated the market) to offer higher deposit rates because the former were free of the reserve requirements asked of banks in the Federal Reserve system. So, as the growth of the Euromarkets exceeded the growth of the domestic credit markets, so their competition tended to push interest rates upwards, though never in a steady or regular fashion. Yet another unpredictable factor was then added to compounded uncertainty.

From the late 1960s onward, as markets became increasingly aware not only of accelerating inflation, especially in the United States, but also of the anticipated inflation differentials, divergence naturally widened between the nominal interest rate and the real interest rate. In other words, the anticipation of the inflation component in interest rates on bank loans became more important as compared with the "price of money" component. It probably cannot be proven, but it seems likely that the nominal interest rates of those economies that were largest and whose banking and credit system was most developed and extensive have had a greater influence than others on the Euromarket rates of interest. By the same two-way transmission system they will also have had a stronger influence on the domestic markets of others than will the policy decisions taken within the smaller national credit systems. Big markets always do sway little ones and there seems no reason to suppose that this does not happen with the market for credit once an easy, cheap, and efficient transmission system like the Eurocurrency market is placed between them. At any rate, the observable and observed fact is that during the 1970s, interest rates generally tended to follow (at different distances given inflation differentials), the lead of the U.S. market.

This phenomenon was apparent even before the major turning point in U.S. domestic monetary management strategy took place in 1979. And of course the U.S. influence on others became far more pronounced when, having arrested the slide in the value of the dollar by the Carter measures

Table 1 LIBOR AND LDC DEBT AT FLOATING RATES 1973–1983[a]

	1973 (%)	1975 (%)	1977 (%)	1979 (%)	1980 (%)	1981 (%)	1982 (%)	1983 (%)
Proportion of developing countries' debt at floating rates	6.4	9.4	11.8	15.5	17.3	19.0	20.2	21.6
LIBOR[b]	9.2	11.0	5.6	8.7	14.4	16.5	13.1	9.6

[a]The overall figures conceal wide differences between countries. In 1983, for instance, Argentina, Mexico, and Brazil had more than 75 percent of their debt at floating rates, compared with 25 percent for Turkey and 9 percent for Kenya.

[b]London Inter Bank Offer Rate, the base for bank loan interest rates.

Source: World Development Report. 1985. p. 79.

Table 2   REAL LONG-TERM INTEREST RATES (9)[a]

	United States	Japan	Britain	West Germany	Switzerland
1965–1969	1.8	2.1	3.1	4.7	1.0
1970–1974	0.7	−3.4	1.0	3.2	−1.3
1975–1979	0.3	0.5	−2.2	3.0	1.6
1980–1984	4.9	4.1	2.9	4.2	0.3
1983	8.1	5.6	6.2	4.6	1.2
1984	8.2	4.5	5.8	5.4	1.6

[a]The real interest rate is the amount charged to borrowers taking account of the rate of inflation. A minus sign therefore denotes that borrowers are lent money at a price less than the rate of inflation.

Source: Bank for International Settlements.

of October 1978, the Reagan Administration appeared to go into reverse gear with the adoption of so-called monetarist methods.

The adjective *so-called* is necessary because of the inability of the Reagan Administration (like others before it) to keep the Government's budget deficit under control. This inability was largely due to the escalating cost of defense. It is fair comment, therefore, that in such circumstances *monetary theory*, which implies a real control of the money supply, could not possibly work. It has therefore never been properly tried out in practice. For even if the monetary authority both restricts and closely monitors the monetary base for credit but at the same time preempts a rather large share of that credit for itself, the natural result will be a restriction of supply of credit and consequently an increase in the price, that is, the rate of interest.

It was not surprising, therefore, that some of the volatility that has been so marked in the foreign exchange market for dollars shifted in the late 1970s and early 1980s to the market for borrowing dollars. Of course there were other factors too—not least the Soviet invasion of Afghanistan[4]—that at least for a time stabilized the dollar exchange rate. Through the mechanism explained earlier, this gave the European Monetary System an easier birth and infancy than recent historical experience might have led anyone to expect. The price of that easier birth, though, was a new vulnerability to any event or decision that altered the level of U.S. interest rates.

THE OIL PRICE

Compounding the volatility of currency and interest rates have been the fluctuations in real oil prices throughout the 1970s and 1980s. When the era of accelerating change began in 1973, the general expectation was that, once the price had been raised by the combination of OPEC solidarity, booming demand, and panic buying as a result of the October War between Israel and her neighbors, the oil price would stay up. It could hardly have been predicted that it would jump again, in 1979 by over 50 percent or that in real terms it would fall twice in the decade, in 1977 by nearly 9 percent (following an increase in 1976 of 20 percent) and again in 1983–84 by an average of over 30 percent.

The first oil price rise not only produced the $80 billion surpluses of *petrodollars* for the banks to recycle, thus swelling the importance of the financial markets and the institutions operating in them, but it also introduced a new, sometimes decisive and usually quite unpredictable factor affecting the balance of payment positions of both the consumer, and eventually the producing, countries.

In Germany's case, for example, a high dependence on imports and the first oil price rise brought the D-mark down on a tradeweighted currency-basket basis from 121 in mid-1973 to 116 at the end of 1975. But Germany reacted with tough enough financial policies to bring the rate back up again—only to suffer another check in 1981 after the second oil price rise. Japanese susceptibility and responses, especially in exporting more to pay for costlier oil, were even more pronounced. Between 1972 and 1981 the yen yo-yoed from three "highs" in July 1973, October 1978, and September 1981, to two "lows" (following oil price rises) in 1974 and 1980. At these points, both the dollar and sterling had exactly opposite reactions from the foreign exchange markets.

The differential effect of oil price changes on the OECD countries individually was important for the general stability of the world economy mainly because it was they [OECD countries] who traded most heavily with each other. They account for most world trade. It is they, too, who invest most heavily in each other's economies and who account for most international capital flows. It is also they who therefore provide most business to the international markets for foreign exchange and for credit. In the face of the historical record it is hard to disagree with the conclusions (1) that the oil price has contributed to instability in exchange rates; and (2) that these rates cannot easily be stable until oil prices are steadier or until oil becomes less important in world trade and payments. This could happen by states either becoming more self-sufficient in oil or developing alternative energy resources that have less impact on their balance of payments and the external value of their currencies.

Although it may be true that it is the disparities between OECD exchange rates that caused most disruption to the international monetary system, it seems that the consequences of this uneven pattern of oil prices were most sharply felt by the oil-importing developing countries. Although other LDC commodity prices were ahead of oil on a 1972 base in 1973, none of them ever again caught up; and by 1981, food prices, agricultural raw materials, and mineral prices in more or less real terms were all less than a sixth of the price of oil. The oil price index, in short, had outdistanced all the other price indexes—for food, agricultural raw materials, and minerals—by a factor of six or more. Though the recycling of the OPEC surpluses in the mid-1970s allowed the non-oil producing developing countries, or NOPECs, to borrow enough to pay for dearer [more expensive] oil, their development strategies immediately became vulnerable to further rises, *or* to increases in interest rates, *or* to periods of dollar strength, *or* to any combination of these factors. For a country such as Brazil, for example, the country's balance of payments may benefit to the tune of millions of dollars from a 1 percent fall in the price of oil—but equally would lose as much as $1 billion from a 1 percent increase in bank lending rates. While for Mexico, another debtor in trouble but an exporter of oil, both changes would be disastrous.

Like many other countries and corporations, the NOPECs suddenly found themselves playing Snakes and Ladders. And for them, while some of the ladders became longer, the snakes became more numerous and some also became longer. Decision-making on long-term choices—in energy or food production particularly—became an elaborate gamble. A case in point was Brazil's vast hydroelectric project, in which Paraguay is a minor partner, at Itaipu on the Parana River. In the long run, the turbines on this dam will produce 12.6 billion kilowatts, more than any hydroelectric project anywhere in the world. But the calculations on the economics of its construction were made in the early 1970s. They have looked better, then worse, then better and worse again as time has passed.

In the long run, an independent supply of cheap electricity must be the right policy for Brazil in terms of cost as well as for the economic security of the state. But meanwhile, the price of credit to finance the construction of this and other expensive projects brought Brazil reluctantly to seek help from the IMF and the banks—a humiliating experience for a country which, only a few months earlier, had been proud of having so far avoided involvement with the Fund.

As with interest rates, the problem with oil prices is not so much that they have been high, but rather that they have also been so unpredictable and so unstable. Again the instability has engendered a new game in the great financial casino—oil futures. This evolved in the following way. In the 1980s as OPEC's command over the oil market weakened, with some producers desperate for foreign exchange ready to undercut the agreed price with secret, under-the-counter deals, more and more oil cargoes came to be traded on what is rather misleadingly called the Rotterdam spot market. But this is not a market in the ordinary sense in which buyers and sellers are identifiable and prices known to everyone. It is just a network of about a hundred oil traders and brokers, connected with each other by long distance intercontinental telephone and telex. Like other brokers in grain or porkbellies or frozen orange juice, they are often tempted to increase their profits by talking the market price up or down. As late as 1978, the spot market deals still accounted for only 5 percent of all trade in oil. They now account for 40 percent or more. Inevitably, because of the close connection between oil prices, generally denominated in dollars, and the price of the dollar in foreign exchange markets, there has grown up in London and New York a futures market in *paper barrels* to match the forward and futures market in dollars and dollar assets. These *paper barrel* contracts can change hands as many as 50 times, and do not need to be based on barrels of real oil. Future contracts on the British Brent blend of North Sea oil are thought to add up to as much as eight times the total annual output of the Brent field (Hooper, 1985).

In short, while there is little doubt that the instability of exchange rates has helped to destabilize the oil market, the oil market is now adding its own gambling game to all the others.

STRONGER MARKETS OR WEAKER STATES?

The picture so far is one of an international financial system in which the gamblers in the casino have got out of hand, almost beyond, it sometimes seems, the control of governments. The question has occurred already to a good many people whether it is the governments that have got weaker over the past 15 years, or whether it is a fortuitous coincidence of economic forces that have combined to make the markets more powerful. It is an important question, for the answer will dictate what has to be done to control, to moderate, or to close down the great financial gambling game.

That question is linked with a second one: have all states weakened in relation to markets, or only one, or perhaps just a few of the more important governments? Those who think that all governments have weakened tend to find rather broad general explanations of how this has come about. If they offer solutions they are apt to be of the most vague and general kind. In contrast, those who think the explanation lies with the few, or even just with the U.S.A. as the dominant power in the international financial system—as all the figures show it to be—tend to be much more specific both in the explanations they put forward and in the solutions they suggest.

Curiously, these explanations come from both the political Left and the Right, each having grasped a part of the answer. From the Left, there has come the appreciation of the part played by the U.S.A. ever since the Second World War in bringing about a more *open* world economy: open, that is, to investment and international production as well as to international trade (Block, 1977; Wallerstein, 1979; Magdoff and Sweezy, 1969; Parboni, 1980). Instead of competing for territory and command over people and resources, they say, the advanced industrial states have begun increasingly to compete on behalf of their producers for shares of the world market.

It is a perception which accords with some analyses of state policies coming from academic writers on the American Right (Gilpin, Krasner,

Katzenstein, and others). The state in an open, interconnected world economy needs not only a military strategy, but also a scientific and industrial strategy, if it is to hold its own in economic growth and market shares. Japan has seemed more successful than the United States at this new game; and the United States, this argument goes, has been undermining its own power and wealth by following the British example and letting its financial institutions build up the wealth and power of others, especially through investment.

Through the 1970s, this notion of the self-defeating behavior of a hegemonic power in the world economy took such a hold that whole journals and research projects in the United States have been devoted to what became known as "hegemonic stability theory". This was the idea that the stability of the world economy had to be sustained by a dominant state or hegemon. But it followed that there was a *hegemon's dilemma,* which was that in sustaining the world economy, the hegemonic power (i.e., the United States) destroyed itself. Therefore, if the world economy appeared less stable than it used to, this must be because the United States had lost power, partly because it had borne the burden of acting as hegemon (Krasner, 1983; Keohane, 1984).

To most people outside the United States, this argument sounded very much like an elaborate but unconvincing excuse. It seemed hard to reconcile this whining complaint with the magnitude of American military power and, so far as the financial system was concerned, with the size and influence of the American banks (Sampson 1981). It was inconsistent with the universal use and acceptability of the U.S. dollar which, as explained earlier, had made the United States less vulnerable than others to the volatility of exchange rates and other prices than the other advanced industrial countries. Many Americans were not as acutely aware as other people that when U.S. domestic monetary policy changed direction, and when interest rates in the United States responded to changes of policy, other states had no choice but to adjust their own interest rates and their domestic policies to such changes, whereas it never happened the other way around.

Far more convincing was the observation, sometimes made by the same writers, that the United States was, and for a long time had been, a *weak state* in the rather special sense that its government was permeated by pressure groups and pushed around by special interests, each possessing a "black ball" to veto positive policies so that there was no strong or consistent pursuit of the general national interest. This situation was contrasted with that of post-revolutionary China or the Soviet Union which looked like *strong states.* The reason for the weakness of the American state could be ascribed partly to its Constitution, and the principle of the separation of powers between the executive, legislature, and judiciary which it contained; and partly to the liberal ideology of market-oriented economy in which the freedom of economic enterprise to function free of government interference was enshrined as a political principle.

What was less often mentioned, either because it was less evident to people living in such a large continental country or because it implied an unwelcome acknowledgement of American responsibility for the growing instability of the whole international financial system on which the market or capitalist system depended, was that American banks had taken very large profits from that financial system but had been saved from the consequences of very risky operations by the financial power of the U.S. government. There was, and still is, a conflict of interest within American society between the banks and large corporations on the one side, who can profit by and survive—for the most part—in this unstable, uncertain environment, and the farmers, workers, and small businesses who find it far more difficult. So long as life in the United States can, by various short-term measures, be made to look better than life in other parts of the world, there are not many politicians who find that it pays to draw attention to the asymmetry of the system, both outside and inside the United States.

Political horizons are notoriously limited, in the United States as elsewhere. But the limited perceptions and foreshortened political horizons of American politicians matter far more to the system than do those of other countries. The record of the last 15 years suggests that in making certain key decisions affecting the international financial system, successive U.S. governments have been far more swayed by short-term domestic considerations than by any awareness of the long-term national interest in building a healthy, well-ordered, and stable financial system capable of sustaining a healthy, stable, and prosperous world economy.

NOTES

1. The market price—overshooting as usual—rose to around $800 an ounce, before eventually falling back below $400.
2. A few countries in 1971 chose to peg to sterling but have since thought better of it. Three peg to the South African rand and one to the Spanish peseta (see Strange 1972, 1976, ch. 11). Forty-two countries, mainly in Latin America and the Middle East, peg to the dollar. The risks of pegging to one particular currency can be somewhat modified by pegging to a collection or *basket* of major currencies weighted according to their importance. The SDR (see above, p. 7) is one such basket. The European Currency Unit (ECU) is another which does not include the U.S. dollar.
3. To *arbitrage* means to shift money (assets or liabilities) from one market to another so as to make a profit, or avoid a loss.
4. The Soviet invasion increased fears of an escalation of the cold war between Russia and America. Many people then calculated that if this happened their money would be safer in America than in Europe or the Middle East.

Part
Three

THE POLITICAL
ECONOMY OF
TRADE

*I*nternational trade, along with international currency and finance, represents the core of the international economic system. Since its inception in 1947, the General Agreement on Tariffs and Trade (GATT) has promoted the establishment of a liberal trade system. It has done so by encouraging governments to negotiate substantially reduced tariffs and other trade barriers in accordance with the principle of nondiscrimination. Many observers warn, however, that the most recent round of negotiations (the *Uruguay Round*), scheduled for completion in late 1990, is the "make-or-break" round. The international trade system today is critically strained under the pressure of growing protectionism in industrialized countries struggling with mounting competition from other developed nations and increasingly from developing countries as well. A failure of the Uruguay Round could spell the end of the vitality of the international trading system, according to many analysts.

Two simultaneous phenomena have alarmed many liberals who favor open trade. First is the consolidation of the European Community (EC). By December 31, 1992, the EC hopes to integrate its market for goods, services, money, and labor, whereas now it is only a free market for goods. Such a unified European economy would have roughly 350 million people and production levels on a par with the U.S. If current overtures to a newly democratic Eastern Europe bear fruit, the European economic system could sustain itself largely without external trade. Many Americans fear a *fortress Europe* with which it will be difficult to trade and compete.

Second, the U.S. Congress continues to react defensively to what are perceived as unfair trading practices overseas, particularly among Pacific Rim countries (South Korea, Taiwan, Hong Kong, Singapore, Japan, Australia, and New Zealand). The 1988 Omnibus Trade and Competitiveness Act provided the President, through its "Super 301" provisions, to carry out retaliatory measures against trading partners guilty of unfair practices, as defined by the Department of Commerce and other U.S. agencies. According to liberals, this gun-to-the-head approach has greatly increased tensions while showing little substantive improvement in international trading practices. From a realist perspective, U.S. policy is a natural outgrowth of a desire to defend the national interest in industrial competitiveness.

Susan Strange, an optimist when it comes to the future of free trade, proclaims that the fear of this so-called new protectionism is not based on an accurate understanding of facts. According to the author, the phenomenon in question is erroneously believed to present a major obstacle to Third World development, world economic recovery, and good international relations. The British political economist maintains that protectionism, while responsible for the depression of the 1930s, was not the cause of the recession of the early 1980s. According to Strange, the recent depression was largely a result of financial uncertainty and the resulting diminution of credit. She concludes that current bilateral trade agreements are sustaining growth in trade despite financial difficulties.

Beth and Robert Yarbrough address another important question regarding international trade: Is it possible to sustain international trade cooperation after the demise of the postwar global hegemon—i.e., the United States? (See Part IX). The authors maintain that both the scope and form of successful trade liberalization are determined most importantly by the extent of transaction-specific investment—i.e., the costs incurred in developing and maintaining cooperative procedures—and by the inability (or unwillingness) of the hegemon to bear these transaction costs. The authors attempt to explain historical variations in the form of trade liberalization by examining the nineteenth-century experience under British dominance, the postwar multilateral trading regime under the United States hegemonic leadership, and the more recent, selective *minilateral* trading practices involving small groups of countries.

Benjamin Cohen finds a glaring gap between the liberal economic theory of international trade and the reality of international trade. On the one hand, the theory says that nations will behave in ways that will maximize the benefits of open markets based on underlying differences of comparative advantage. On the other hand, mercantilism and protectionism are rampant in the trading practices of nations. Cohen also finds current economic theories quite inadequate in explaining this incongruity. In his article Cohen looks to political scientists for help and finds much value in the five recent books that he reviews. The economist, argues Cohen, must (1) broaden his/her research focus and understand the role of power and state interests—traditionally a focus of political analysis; (2) address the question of how sovereign states "collectively manage to cope with their own potentially conflictual mercantilist impulses"; and (3) develop a model of interaction between market and politics, which necessarily encompasses all levels of analysis—i.e., the international system, states, and domestic processes.

Some of the questions the student should be asking when reading these works are: What are the necessary and sufficient conditions for development of a liberal international trade system, and what is the role of the developed countries? What is the relationship between international trade in goods and services, and domestic finance and international currency transactions? Who should decide which country is engaged in unfair trading practices? What will be the impact of bilateral or minilateral trade agreements on the multilateral system? What is and what determines the actual mix of economic and political motives and goals in nations' behavior? How do state actors manage or fail to manage their conflicts? To the extent that governments cooperate, what determines the degree and manner of the cooperation?

Protectionism and World Politics

Susan Strange

Much public debate and speculation in many Western countries today—in political parties and government circles, in the business community, and among academics—is about international trade. It concerns both the prospects for the future and the policies that governments should, or should not, adopt in their own interest or for the general welfare of world society.

In this debate it is high time students of international relations and international political economy finally threw off the intellectual bondage of liberal economics and began to think for themselves about international trade and its part in the international system. This cultural dependence has led them to accept too easily the liberal assumption that the connection between international trade and international relations works both ways, that not only do better trade relations result from better political relations but that better political relations result from better trade relations. Historical experience does indeed sustain the contention that more and freer trade improves political relations. However, the second, Cobdenite assertion, that restricted trade damages political relations, is much more doubtful.

Yet its wide acceptance has led to a further assumption. Positive corrective measures have to be consciously taken, its proponents hold, to secure international trade against the shortsighted tendency of states to interfere with it—to the detriment not only of efficiency and wealth in the economic system but of peace in the political system. These measures, it has been widely supposed, must be either imposed by the power of a hegemonial strong trader with a self-interest in freer trade or else engineered on the basis of negotiated rules strong enough to restrain the perverse and misguided nationalist impulses of states to obstruct commerce.

Susan Strange, "Protectionism and World Politics." Reprinted from *International Organization* 39:2 (Spring 1985): pp. 233–260 by permission of The MIT Press, Cambridge, MA.

The gloom and despondency of liberal economics notwithstanding, trade experience in the early 1980s tells us that protectionism in fact poses no great threat to the world's trade system. On the contrary, the only really serious disorders in the system result from ten years' mismanagement of money and credit and to some extent from an interrelated instability in the world oil market.

The explanation for this gulf between theory and experience, I shall argue, is to be found in a changing world production structure and its effects both on the decisions of governments and on the decisions of corporations. Because national wealth, and eventually power, depend on success in a world market, the argument goes, governments have a natural resistance, widespread and growing, to protectionist pressures from special interests. And because a corporation's survival also depends on success in a world market, trade between countries in goods and services will be, and is being, sustained by a complex network or web of transnational, bilateral bargains—bargains between corporations and other corporations, between corporations and governments, and between governments. The interest of both parties to these bilateral exchanges is (and will continue to be) a far more powerful influence on the level, the direction, and the content of international trade than the puny efforts of states to interfere with market forces.

It follows that the collapse of the system of rules which people (still, alas) refer to as a regime is of little moment—except to those with a vested professional or ideological interest in it. The alleged decline of the hegemonial power is also irrelevant to this particular issue, except insofar as it may lead to war or civil disorder.

The argument has both policy implications and intellectual implications. Politicians and officials need to know what the real choices are in trade matters; yet they are still apt, as Keynes remarked, to be the mental prisoners of defunct economists. And some academics, at least, seek a better understanding regardless of ideology of what is going on. The analytic implications of the argument are clear: trade in the international system has to be seen as a *secondary* structure. It is subsidiary to four primary structures of the international political economy: the security structure; the production structure; the money and credit structure; and the knowledge structure. The security structure includes both external security and internal security; it determines whether there is war or peace in the international political system of states and whether and how governments within states are able to maintain domestic order. Trade is obviously highly vulnerable to both. It is also responsive to the production structure, which together with the knowledge structure decides what is to be produced, how (i.e., with what technology), where, by whom, and for whom; and it is vulnerable to the money and credit structure, which decides who can pay for traded goods or services and how.

It follows that if war and civil disorder can be avoided in the security structure and *if* (a big if) the money and credit structure can be even

moderately well managed, the production and knowledge structures, between them, will take care of the future of world trade. If we abandon
both the hegemonial and the multilateral regime model as inadequate
approximations to reality in trade matters, and if we adopt instead a
web-of-contracts model, we may begin to hope that trade will satisfy more
basic values of political economy than either of the other two models leads
us to expect. Trade, we might realize, is more stable and durable than we
had thought because it is better able to sustain growth in the face of
technical and economic change. It may be more equitable because it may
redress some of the asymmetry between North and South. And it may ease
the coexistence of a unified world economy with a political system of
divided authority, allowing states more leeway to choose freer trade or
protection—or both at the same time for different sectors—without risking damage either to world peace or to world prosperity.

A first step in the argument must be to rehearse, for the benefit of
those still in bondage to them, the myths of liberal economics and the
reasons, derived from a study of international history, why they need no
longer be taken too seriously.

THE MYTHS OF LIBERAL DOCTRINE

The main tenet of liberal economics regarding international trade is that
the less governments intervene to obstruct the flow of trade, the better.
The more generally liberal policies are adopted toward foreign competition, the better the national welfare and global welfare will be served.
Free trade, it is held, allows the most effective allocation of resources to
the production of goods and services and thus maximizes the production
of wealth for the community. Protection, conversely, encourages inefficiency and impoverishes both individual consumers and the society as a
whole.

Much conventional liberal opinion goes on to argue that protectionism
adopted by one country provokes retaliatory protectionism in others, setting off a vicious spiral. To avoid this vicious spiral, it is held essential to
maintain the momentum of multilateral diplomacy aimed at the reduction
of trade barriers. The more protectionist policies multiply, the more imperative for world order it becomes that the states that have signed the
General Agreement on Tariffs and Trade (GATT) should make a "new
joint initiative," in the words of the 1983 GATT report, to stop the rot.[1]
Moreover, it is sometimes argued, the economic effects are apt to spill over
into politics, poisoning international relations and contributing if not actually leading to conflict between allies and to war between states that might
otherwise have been content to coexist.

Like most other simple doctrines, liberal economics is held with enormous passion but with rather less than unassailable logic or strict regard
for historical facts. The chief fallacies, false premises, and historical mis-

representations that sustain the liberal doctrine can be fairly briefly stated, since most of them have already been perceived and identified.[2]

The basic premise that state policy should, or even can, be based on the single criterion of maximizing efficiency in the production of goods and services for the market is demonstrably false. Efficiency never has been, *and never can be,* the sole consideration in the choice of state policies. Given an international political system in which the world is divided territorially among states over whom there is no reliable higher authority to prevent conflict among them, security from external attack and the maintenance of internal order are, and always have been, the first concern of government in each state. Efficiency can be given priority only if the provision of security, internally and externally, is taken for granted— as indeed it is by many if not most liberal economists.

Some, it is true, have acknowledged that guns must sometimes take priority over butter. Adam Smith himself saw that the defense of the realm and security from invasion had to be an objective of political economy for the state. Some modern liberal economists will admit that military production can count as part of the national product, even though it is not exactly consumable or productive in the usual sense. They may even concede, if reluctantly, that it is rational for the state in the interests of national security to adopt a *second-best* strategy, maintaining a less than fully efficient agriculture or coal mining or textile industry to make the country less vulnerable in wartime to the cutting off of imports of food, fuel, or clothes.

Where liberal economists are reluctant to follow the logic of the admission that security is a basic value is where internal order and the security of government are concerned, for it is no more irrational to sacrifice efficiency in the allocation of resources to the need for social cohesion than it is to do so to the need for national security. An inefficient group of producers might constitute a potential group of revolutionary dissidents. It would be cheaper and quicker to pay the price of keeping them in business than to pay the police to quell their rioting.[3] To maintain the loyalty of its citizens—a necessary condition of political security—the state in wealthier societies is also called on to provide economic security. Economic security may mean setting up a welfare or social security system for all. It may also mean making special provisions for groups considered to be disadvantaged, whether the physically handicapped or those like steelworkers most acutely afflicted by the rapid rate of change in the international division of labor. From a politician's point of view there is no essential difference between the two. Both are claiming a measure of justice as the price of their continued support of and loyalty to the politician at the polls or even to the state itself. A political order within the state cannot be stable without the consent and support of major groups in society.

Efficiency, in short, is only one of four basic values that any politically organized society seeks to achieve for its members. Wealth, order, justice, and freedom; these are the basic elements of political compounds just as hydrogen, oxygen, and carbon are the essential elements of some chemical compounds. And just as chemical elements can be combined differently to produce oil, wood, or potatoes, so basic values will be combined differently in all politically organized societies to produce, for example, fast-growing authoritarian states or slow-growing democracies, or conversely, fast-growing democracies or slow-growing police states. Wealth and efficiency in the production of wealth will seem the most important objective of government only if the safety of the state and civil order within it can be taken for granted, either because consent is freely given because the existing order is thought to be just or because potential dissidents are coerced and frightened into silent compliance. It is no coincidence that the two strongest champions of free trade—19th-century Britain and mid-20th-century America—were both states secure and confident in the basic justice of the social order. They did not normally need to fear revolution from within or invasion from without. Both were so strong that they could afford to have relatively limited government. Others whose societies were actually less secure, both internally and externally, paradoxically required strong central government in order to protect their society from internal division, external attack, or both.

Freedom, too, is a basic value, and one that market economies enshrine and liberal economists extol. But it is precisely the freedom to choose to be governed differently from others, to be governed by those with whom people identify as *us* rather than *them,* that is the sustaining reason for the continued existence of a society of states as prone as is the present international political system to destructive and debilitating internecine conflict and war. If history has not shown that men and women do from time to time choose freedom and justice rather than the most efficient allocation of resources, it has shown nothing. Individuals the world over, for all the superficial concessions they may make to internationalism, do tend to identify themselves with a particular national group and do give their loyalty to one particular nation-state.

Government, consequently, is a matter of finding an appropriate tradeoff between these four basic values—security (or order), wealth, justice, and freedom—when it comes to making state policy. On occasion it may be necessary to sacrifice some freedom and accept binding rules (as under the GATT), if it is thought the rules are just and that greater wealth through faster economic growth will thus be attained. At other times it may be necessary to assert independence over efficiency in order to preserve the order of national unity. The French did so in the 1880s, as Alan Milward has argued, when the National Assembly voted to protect peasant farmers against cheap imported grain. That decision he characterizes as a de facto extension of democracy, "a set of stages in the widening participation of different groups in that body politic." In this sense, "the transition from mid-nineteenth century liberalisation of trade to late nineteenth century protectionism was not a regressive atavistic response by conservative agrarian pressure but a progression in political participation."[4] After the peasants have come the steelworkers, the textile workers, and the shipbuilders, and to the needs of each important social group the policy-making process has—in order to maintain national unity in a democratic society—become more attentive.

So much for the first myth, the pursuit of economic efficiency. It raises all sorts of enticing questions of political philosophy, but exploring them is not my present purpose.

The second myth is almost a rider to the first. Liberal economists believe that the individual pursuit of private gain is consistent with the general welfare of the society, since the hidden hand of the market ensures that the producer will make what the consumer wants and at the lowest price, or else he will go out of business. Transposing the coincidence of individual and collective interest from the national to the international level produces a corollary myth. It holds that the pursuit of national interests by individual or states is consistent with the general welfare of international society—or, in short, that the world economy will be well served if each individual government or state observes the laws of comparative costs and sells on the world market what it produces best.

The fallacy here is that the political or economic security of the state may *not* in fact be best served by observing the law of comparative costs. The supposed coincidence of national and global welfare objectives, moreover, assumes the absence or unimportance of adjustment costs and risks. In theory, states can freely adapt either to the changing prices of factors of production or to the changing demands and conditions of the world market. In reality, the political as well as material costs of having to chop and change from one production sector to another are by no means inconsiderable, especially for poor countries or ones that do not share the high degree of conformism, respect for authority, and adaptability of, for instance, Japanese society. These costs, moreover, are probably higher now than they used to be as the pace of technical change accelerates and the cost of capital investment in the latest technology appreciates. Prompt adjustment may be in the collective interest, but it will not always be in the interest of the individual state. The law of comparative costs is an essentially static concept, ever more open to question as the world economy becomes more dynamic.

All this is not to say that political choices are always rational and always made in the best general interest. The point is simply that the choices involve a difficult trade-off among different values and value-laden objectives; and the discounting of time—that is, the weighing of certain present discomforts against uncertain future benefits—is not an easy and certainly not a scientific business. Economists are apt to complain that politicians are irrational because they make *political* choices, but what is politically rational, how one takes political values into account, is not that simple to define and cannot be assessed by quantitative methods.

The next three myths of liberal economics all concern the interpretation of 20th-century economic history. Everyone knows that two different bystanders may give totally conflicting accounts of a road accident. Similarly, two quite unbiased witnesses of a world depression may give entirely different versions of the sequence of cause and effect. But when, as I believe is the case with protectionism in the last great world depression in the 1930s, almost all those who have spent most time studying the evidence have come up with one conclusion while those liberals who have a political axe to grind have come up with a quite different one, the latter conclusion must be doubted even though it may be widely accepted as the *true* version of what happened.

Regarding the world depression of the interwar years, the conventional wisdom of liberal economics is that, though it may have started with financial crisis, a main cause of shrinking markets was the raising of trade barriers. The major problem was protectionism; the system was trapped in a vicious spiral of beggar-thy-neighbor policies, in which each country retaliated against the others for barriers raised against its own products. The result was that all suffered and no one benefited.

But this is not what the economic historians say—or rather, what they said when, a few years later, they finally got around to sifting the evidence and looking at the figures. Unfortunately, that was just the time when all over the world people's attention was already turning to the impending outbreak of another world war, or when that war had actually started, threatening the very survival of states and political systems. The result was that the economic historians' verdict on the Depression was little heeded and soon forgotten. What they said was that tariffs, though substantially raised, had made surprisingly little difference either to the volume of world trade or to its direction. (Even Frank Taussig concurred with this view.) Nor had retaliation been the significant motive. There was not much tit for tat. It was just that as markets shrank, politicians were everywhere under pressure to handicap foreign producers against domestic ones, to keep jobs open at home if it could be done. Yet the handicaps actually did little to alter the pattern of trade flows. Instead, as Arthur Lewis concluded, "The decline of trade in manufactures was due neither to tariffs nor to the industrialisation of new countries. The trade in manufactures was low and only because the industrialised countries were buying too little of primary products and paying so low a price for what they bought."[5] They were buying too little not only because commodity prices had tumbled long before tariffs had been raised but also because credit had dried up in London and New York, especially credit for foreign borrowers. By comparison, the effects of tariffs (and that other bogey of the historical imagination, competitive devaluation of currencies) were minimal.[6]

Why, then, did the myth gain such popularity that it persists to this day? The answer is simple. Americans correctly perceived themselves as the strong traders of the postwar world, both because they were technologically more advanced and because American corporations were better organized to produce for and to sell to a mass market of consumers.[7] They also regarded British and other Europeans' sheltered colonial markets as obstructing their conquest of the world market after the war, and the destruction of preferential barriers against American exports was the first target of U.S. commercial policy. The myth that protectionism had been the main cause of the prewar Depression, propagated by economists led by Clair Wilcox, was echoed by U.S. policy makers.[8] The Europeans, including the British, accepted the argument, recognizing that whether or not trade barriers had done much harm, they certainly had done little good, and that a fresh start at the end of the war would probably be in everyone's interest.

Another historical myth holds that the postwar recovery of Europe and the unprecedented growth of all industrialized countries' economies in the 1960s was primarily the result of multilateral tariff reduction conducted under the aegis of the GATT—and perhaps of the earlier cuts in quotas and quantitative restrictions which the Americans demanded of the Europeans as a condition of Marshall Plan aid. That these tariff-bargaining rounds were an important innovation in economic diplomacy and that they helped make business more confident about expanding markets for most capital and consumer goods is not in doubt. But were tariff reductions the *main* cause of postwar prosperity? No one can ever prove conclusively which of two factors was the more decisive. Correlation can be demonstrated, but causation in either direction can only be implied, never proven.

In this case it seems to me far more probable that prosperity permitted liberalization. Trade revived after the war, and continued to grow, because the United States injected large doses of purchasing power into the system at a rate that pretty well matched the physical ability of enterprises to increase production. Impelled by a perceived national interest in holding the line against Soviet expansion, in Europe and elsewhere, the United States came up first with UNRRA aid and the British Loan, then with the European Recovery Program, and finally with military aid to NATO and other allies (which even financed British wheat imports) and with dollars to pay for the stationing of U.S. troops abroad. By that time the U.S. private sector was able to take over from the government a share of the task of maintaining an outflow of dollars to the rest of the world. Americans bought up foreign companies or invested in new plants for foreign affiliates, allowing their allies and associates to rebuild their monetary reserves (composed largely of dollar IOUs) to the point where most of them— Britain excepted—no longer needed to fear the political consequence of a temporary deficit on their balance of trade. Eventually, of course, and especially after the mid-1960s, the injection of dollar purchasing power became increasingly inflationary as the U.S. government also took on the financing of social welfare. But that it was instrumental for a generation in spreading purchasing power more widely throughout the whole economy is hardly in doubt.

When it comes to more recent history and the present state of the world economy, one must be careful not to overstate what the liberals say. There are, of course, substantial differences of emphasis both in their analyses of past events and in their prescriptions for future policy. But three general observations crop up again and again, observations that do not always accord well with the analysis that precedes them. One is that the main problem afflicting the world economy is the deterioration in the trade system. Sometimes this is explicitly stated, sometimes it is implicit in recommendations for governments.

Another is that if the drift toward protectionism is not arrested, things will get a lot worse. We might call it the *bicycle theory,* since it says that if you do not keep up the momentum of trade liberalization, disaster will follow. For instance, Miriam Camps and William Diebold wrote recently for the Council on Foreign Relations in New York that "Doing nothing will lead to trouble." *Hanging on*—by which they mean protesting devotion in principle to the GATT and its rules while in practice giving in to protectionist pressures—is a "prescription for deterioration."[9] Similarly, a recent experts' report written for the Commonwealth Secretariat in London stated flatly, and apparently without any supporting evidence, that recent expansionary trends in the exports of developing countries "cannot continue even if world expansion is soon resumed unless the drift toward protectionism is arrested and reversed."[10]

The final historical myth is the unwarranted but very widespread assumption that the only hope lies in multilateral agreement, negotiated through international organization. This assumption rests, of course, on that biased interpretation of postwar history which ascribes so much importance to multilaterally negotiated reductions in trade barriers and so little to other factors. It greatly underrates the importance of some key bilateral relationships within the American alliance, specifically those of the United States with Britain, with Canada, with Germany, and with Japan. Each of the four had its own reasons for complying with American policy objectives. It also underrates the steady creation of credit first by the U.S. government, then through the investment of dollars abroad by U.S. corporations, and finally, after the first oil price rise of 1973, by international bank lending through the Eurodollar and other Eurocurrency markets.

By contrast with these rather dogmatic assertions, the analysis that leads up to them often gives far more importance to the disorder of the monetary and financial system than it does to the state of trade. (World trade fell only in 1982, after nearly a decade of mounting protectionism, and by 1 percent, a trivial amount compared with the 28 percent fall in world trade in 1926–35. The inflation-adjusted increase in world trade in 1973–83 has been of the order of 6 or 7 percent.) Camps and Diebold, for example, begin by describing the financial problems of the world economy before going on to assert that a *solution* of trade problems is a necessary condition of economic recovery. And it is even more true of the analysis made by Jan Tumlir, the research director of the GATT, in a British bank review. He begins his analysis with the statement that "the key issue of the moment is the precariousness of all financial structures." Neither debtors nor creditors, Tumlir thinks, "would go along indefinitely with patchwork rescheduling arrangements." The overloading of the financial system with bad debts—loans for which creditors claim an inflated book value far above their marketable value—calls for a comprehensive plan for the stabilization of the world economy.[11]

Several economists point to the slower growth of the great industrialized countries as the major problem and the proximate cause of the trend toward protectionism. Perhaps prematurely, Max Corden has written that "the developed world has just emerged from a major recession created essentially by tight monetary policies designed to squeeze inflation out of the system. During this period there has been a great increase in protectionist pressures and also some increase in actual protection."[12] Corden is careful, however, to note that there is no unambiguous evidence that this new protectionism has had a significant effect on trade. Yet he hesitates to conclude that it does not much matter, saying that the effects may come later, *or* the distortion will work through exchange rates and an overvalued dollar to handicap exports, *or* trade would have expanded faster had it not been for these restrictive measures.

These three afterthoughts, or riders, indicate a reluctance to admit that protectionism has not, after all, had very much effect. They tally with an apparent disinclination to look beyond tighter U.S. monetary policies to the deeper causes of the recession of the early 1980s. Such inhibitions are fairly common among liberal economists, for example, and are to be found in British explanations of the slower economic growth of recent years.[13] Except for a few academic economists particularly interested in international finance and for people engaged with financial markets whether as central or commercial bankers, there is a curious distaste for acknowledging the tremendous structural changes that have taken place in financial markets and thus the reason why tighter monetary policies in the United States should have had such enormous worldwide consequences. The relation between monetary disorders and either the commodity boom of the early 1970s or the commodity slump of the early 1980s (the worst in 15 years according to the World Bank) is thus glossed over. And so is the coincidence of the slackened demand that accompanied recession with the major structural changes in the international division of labor, which have in fact buoyed up the exports of manufacturers from developing countries even in the face of mounting protection.

Why should there be this widespread reluctance to face up to the financial and monetary factors contributing to present difficulties or to the structural changes in production resulting from the internationalization of business? There are several possible explanations. At the lowest possible level there is the institutional interest of international bureaucracies in preserving their role and their importance. Ever since the fiasco of the trade ministers' meeting at Geneva in November 1982, the GATT secretariat, for instance, has had to face the uncomfortable fact that the road to further progress in trade liberalization was firmly closed by yawning gulfs of disagreement between the Americans and the Europeans, between the Europeans and the Japanese, and between all the industrialized countries and the Group of 77 developing countries. No wonder the GATT reports sound so full of doom and gloom. The truth is that if the whole organization were wound up, and its tax-exempt officials made redundant with a golden handshake, the world's trade would be remarkably little affected. At a somewhat higher level, there is a natural preference among many academic economists for an interpretation of economic change that allows them both to ignore politics and to be rather self-righteous about it. They can thus condemn politicians for their lack of moral fiber while telling their students that all would have been well if only their priestly advice had been heeded. That is much easier and a lot more fun than trying to come to grips with the complexities of a monetary and financial conundrum to which no one has a sure or simple answer.

At the political level there is, I think, an ideological explanation. The ideology of free trade, private enterprise, and competition unimpeded by the interference of government still has a strong appeal for the business community in most cities of the world. It is an ideology that tends to persist long after the material interest reflected in government policy and in business behavior has turned from open competition to protection, cartelization, and restrictive practices. Well into the 1940s and 1950s, British government officials continued to believe and advocate the ideology of free trade even though by that time only a few in British industry were still able to win in open competition with Americans, Germans, or Japanese. I suspect the same thing is now true of the United States, where the rhetoric of free, nondiscriminatory trade still strongly persists in Washington long after the reality of U.S. policy in some sectors is pointed in quite an opposite direction.[14]

So strong is this ideological hangover that the quite unwarranted belief still also persists among a few economists and politicians that protectionism jeopardizes peace and that world order at the political level may be directly threatened if the multilateral trade order is allowed to crumble. The Commonwealth Secretariat, for example, commenting on the wider effects of protectionism, declares that "resentments may build up and issue in aggressive exchanges and a breakdown of peaceful relations when opportunities of fruitful efforts are cut off by arbitrary and discriminatory acts on the part of foreign powers."[15] Historical examples of deliberate trade wars being pursued by countries engaged in commerce with each other or even competing for shares of third markets are extremely hard to find, but the difficulty does not stop the myth persisting. Nor does the fact that political and military conflicts have seldom if ever grown out of commercial rivalry. The competitors in pre-1914 Britain most feared, curiously enough, were Japan—then a newly industrializing country undercutting Britain with cheap manufactures of china and tex-

tiles—and the United States, already beginning to buy up British companies and set up affiliates across the Atlantic. But it was Germany that
Britain fought. And of all the many international conflicts either since
1914 or before, it is hard to think of one that was provoked or exacerbated
by the protectionist policies of one or both contestants. How much has
protectionism had to do with the Cold War, with the recurrent Arab-
Israeli conflicts, the tensions between Indian and Pakistan, the Iraq-Iran
war, or the battle of the Falklands?

RECENT TRENDS IN TRADE

Even the most cursory examination of recent trends in world trade shows
that while world trade, as pointed out earlier, declined only a trivial 1
percent, growth rates, output, and employment suffered a much more
severe setback. In the early 1980s the world passed through quite a severe
recession, and indeed it may not yet have fully emerged from it. Yet
recession did not have nearly so violent an effect on the volume of international trade as the Depression of the 1930s. The reasons for this paradox
are not at all well understood, but one plausible explanation implicates the
growth of what Judd Polk first described as *international production*—
that is to say, production for a world market by large corporations that
operate with a global strategy and not only sell abroad but actually produce in more than one country.[16] Charles-Albert Michalet has made a
further useful distinction between two kinds of international production.
One takes place in a *relay affiliate,* which merely reproduces abroad the
production process developed at home—a practice that fits with product-
cycle theory. The other takes place in *workshop affiliates,* where one stage
of a production process is farmed out, as it were, to another country where
labor is cheaper or more docile or taxes are lower.[17]

Whatever the reason, trade in manufacturers has grown much faster
than trade in primary products. Moreover, there is far more trade between industrialized countries than trade between them and the developing countries. The conventional notion holds that trade is determined by
differences in resource endowment. But, as Fred Meyer has argued, technology and the accelerating rate of technical change has a lot more to do
with the drive to produce for the world market. For, as technology becomes more complex, and expensive, each new plant or process a company installs is costlier and is destined to more rapid obsolescence than the
one it replaces.[18] In most industries it becomes impossible to recoup the
investment fast enough by selling on only a local or national market. One
result is that trade in semimanufactures—half-finished goods—has also
grown faster than the average rate of growth. Thus a totally Swedish Volvo
car or a totally American Boeing aircraft, even a totally South Korean ship,
no longer exists. Components are put together from all over, and the
figures on trade collected by international organizations tell only half-

truths inasmuch as they allow us to continue to think in these obsolete terms of trade as an international exchange of national products.

A second point is that developing countries' penetration of industrialized countries' markets has been faster in manufactured goods in the 1970s than ever before and faster than the general rise in trade in manufactures. . . . Though textiles, shoes, and electrical goods are the sectors were Third World exports are best known, they are by no means the only ones. Exports of paper, paper products, and printed matter, for instance, increased by 26 percent in the 1970s, those of chemicals, petroleum, coal, rubber, and plastic products by 25 percent, and those of all fabricated metal products, machinery, and equipment by nearly 33 percent.

It is clear from these figures that protectionism does not work as a check on the industrial development of developing countries. Very precise arrangements, bilaterally negotiated between industrialized countries such as Japan and the United States, for well-defined products, do apparently check market penetration. Quota restrictions and tariffs, and even voluntary export agreements reached with the developing countries, apparently do not. The only export markets where LDC manufactures did take a knock in 1982 (and probably in 1983 too) were the OPEC countries, then suffering from the falling oil price and the other LDCs, then suffering from the falling commodity prices (and therefore earnings of foreign exchange) and the shrinkage of credit associated with debt problems. But no one has suggested that the drift toward protectionism has been most marked in either of these groups of countries. They may perhaps have been protectionist, but it is the developed countries that have become markedly more protectionist in the last decade.

Throughout the period of the so-called new protectionism the developed countries have continued to lose their share of total markets and of other countries' markets. In an analysis conducted for the World Bank, H. Hughes and A. Krueger concluded that "the rate of increase of LDC market shares was sufficiently great that it is difficult to imagine that rates would have been significantly higher in the absence of any protectionist measures."[19] Welfare losses, presumably therefore, fell not on the developing but on the developed countries.

The new international division of labor appears to be unstoppable. The move of manufacturing industry to the Third World is structural, not cyclical. Though more visible in the export-oriented economies of South Korea and Taiwan, it is also happening in India and Brazil where an expanding mass market—for clothes, radios, even computers—is increasingly satisfied by domestic production rather than by imports from the old industrialized countries. (No one would deny that this is so, though statistics on consumption in such countries are sometimes so scanty that it is hard to find statistical evidence.)

The progress of the newly industrialized countries that are the main targets of protectionism is indicated by . . . figures . . . on South Korea . . . and . . . Taiwan—a country arbitrarily excluded from most UN statistics because of its anomalous legal status. Though the value of Korean exports to the United States of primary products (fruit, vegetables, and tobacco) took something of a knock between 1981 and 1983, Korean exports of most manufactures continued to grow rather substantially. In the space of two supposedly bad recession years Korean exports of textiles to America grew by 60 percent, of machinery and transport equipment by 140 percent, of steel by 20 percent, of rubber by 24 percent, and of clothing and shoes by 27 percent. Overall, the growth in U.S. imports from Korea was 43 percent.

Korean exports to Japan, though on a smaller scale, show equally striking growth rates. Over four years clothing textile exports more than quadrupled, iron and steel exports increased seven times, and machinery and transport equipment increased by more than five times. Exports of textile fiber and manufactures were up in some years and down in others, but they were in any case not as important as any of the other categories of manufactures.

. . . [A] similarly strong upward trend can be seen in Taiwan's exports of manufactures until 1982, the last year for which figures are available. Here, the only hiccup is from 1981 to 1982 (and from 1974 to 1975, when slack demand interrupted the upward trend) except in transportation equipment—mainly container ships, of which Taiwan is now the second most important producer in the world.

The conclusion is surely clear: protectionism is far less important to LDCs than the rate of growth in the world economy as a whole. Although it may well be, as Corden has suggested, that these exports would have been greater still had it not been for the barriers they encountered, the rate of growth remains astonishing. It is far beyond anything anticipated by economic forecasts made in the 1960s. The record of the four leading East Asian NICs (South Korea, Taiwan, Hong Kong, and Singapore) is of course streets ahead of the ASEAN group and still further ahead of the Latin American countries. Nevertheless, the point is still valid that if protectionism has not effectively held back the leaders (those whose products pose the greatest threat to the domestic industries of the developed countries), then protectionism cannot be the main problem.

Such at least is the conclusion of Bela Belassa. He has pointed out that despite the industrialized countries' protection of their domestic textile producers against Third World imports, the latter rose from 7.3 percent of domestic consumption in 1973 to 17.4 percent in 1981. Despite U.S. protection of American steel producers, imported carbon steel took 26 percent of the American market in 1982 against 5 percent in the 1960s. The 1 percent decline in the volume of world trade in manufactured goods in 1982, he concluded, was attributable to a 2 percent fall in production rather than to increased protection in the developed countries. "Quantitative restrictions have not substantially limited the expansion of the imports of manufactured goods into the developed countries."[20]

All the evidence, in fact, points to volatility in the availability of credit as the dominant factor. Here, the Latin American experience differs vastly from the East Asian, and mainly because it was the Latin Americans who borrowed most heavily in the Eurocurrency markets, led to do so by the big U.S. banks. (South Korea was also a big borrower but mostly from Japanese banks. The same sort of difficulties that brought Brazil, Mexico, Venezuela, Indonesia, and the Philippines to the door of the IMF were resolved for Korea by a quietly negotiated bilateral agreement with Japan, extending by $4 billion the credit line linked to a long-standing postwar reparations agreement.) When credit ran out and the mounting burden of interest rates made it necessary to reschedule Latin American debts under IMF surveillance, an immediate consequence of what the Fund refers to primly as *good housekeeping* was a drastic cut in imports. The GATT noted that in 1982 the total deficit in LDCs fell from $74 billion in 1981 to just over $60 billion in 1982—an "improvement" of $14 billion and one achieved largely by *not buying abroad*. Argentina, Mexico, and Chile all cut their imports by half, according to the GATT.[21] And, as a recent study for the Federal Reserve Bank of New York observed, "The initial effect of the Latin American debt crisis has been felt most severely in the United States by exporters." Between 1978 and 1981, U.S. exports to Latin America had grown over 50 percent faster than U.S. exports to the rest of the world, presumably as a result of loans. But as the loans dried up, so did U.S. exports, reversing the trend and accounting for as much as 40 percent of the total decline of U.S. exports in 1982 over 1981. By the first half of 1983, U.S. exports were less than two-thirds of what they had been a year earlier.[22] As Lewis observed about the 1930s, trade declined primarily because of a lack of purchasing power.

Significantly, this lack has affected LDC trade with the industrialized countries more than it has their trade with each other. More than one-third of their exports of manufactures now go to other LDCs, and in some cases even more than that. Over half of South Korea's growing exports of cars and trucks—now nudging the half-million mark—go to other LDCs, even though ten years ago the industry did not exist. The explanation for this expanding trade in manufactures within the Third World may lie in the growing number of regional and bilateral trade arrangements between the countries concerned.

Finally, there is no doubt that other domestic factors have heavily affected the divergent experience of trade which marks the Third World scene in the 1970s and early 1980s. World Bank studies have shown, for example, that though wages in Colombia were no higher than in East Asia, labor productivity was much lower. Because of government policies, moreover, imported raw materials were often dearer and management less prompt in executing orders and making deliveries. It was neither quotas nor tariffs that was holding Colombia back.[23] Mexico, which in its border zones long enjoyed preferential treatment from the United States over other developing countries, was yet unable to compete with less favored LDCs, mainly because its own import-substituting, protectionist policies kept its prices high and the quality of its products low.[24]

By about the mid-1980s, however, in Mexico and in several other previously protectionist countries, a change was beginning. It was due less to the exhortations of liberal economists or the urging of international organizations than to the urgent need to earn foreign exchange. Governments of all political kinds began to perceive the handicap that protection imposed on national competitiveness in world markets and to extol the advantages of opening the home market to more competition. The South Koreans, for example, declared that they would learn by Japan's mistakes and allow in many more foreign firms to compete with local enterprise in the home market. Bob Hawke, a Labor prime minister of Australia who might have been expected to be under pressure from unions to protect jobs, not only liberalized restrictions on foreign banks but declared his government's intention of dismantling the defensive barriers surrounding (and, he argued, choking) the Australian car industry. In these and other instances governments were responding to the imperative need to be competitive in at least some sectors in a world market.

Their need is one very strong reason why protectionism is not such a great threat, why the bicycle theory is unconvincing, and why the fear of retaliatory trade wars has even less foundation today than in the past. It is even possible that governments in some industrialized countries—the United States, for instance—are shadowboxing with their protectionist lobbies. Ostentatiously appearing to respond with quotas or other barriers to foreign competition, they succeed in quelling the clamor of protest. But at the same time they are well aware that the barriers (e.g., against LDC clothing or shoes) will soon be breached. They may even think that the broad national interest will be better served if they are.

Another reason is that the developing countries are getting much better at finding ways to wriggle around the barriers raised against them. In the well-known case of Hong Kong, quotas on low-cost textiles and clothes forced exporters to go up-market, where barriers were fewer, thus actually increasing the total value of exports. Provenance and final destination in trade are always tricky matters, as those running blockades or strategic embargoes soon find out. There are always third party go-betweens ready and willing to pass on consignments above the producers' quota as their own exports.

Most important of all in explaining why protectionism is not working to keep out LDC manufactures is the connivance of the transnational corporations. Between them and the governments of developing countries there is a strong symbiotic relationship that accelerates the shift of manufacturing industry from North to South. It is this symbiosis that leads TNCs to negotiate complex bargains with other corporations and with state enterprises and governments around the world. Some estimates of the proportion of world trade which is actually trade between different sections of transnational corporations suggest that intrafirm transfers account for as much as half of some countries' total imports.

Many developing countries, in consequence, recognize that the bargaining which the government conducts with the private sector—foreign banks and foreign corporations—is a good deal more important than ordinary diplomacy with other states. Ecuador's negotiations with Gulf Oil in recent years, for example, have probably been more important to the country than its diplomatic relations with its neighbors. In this new form of diplomacy the state's control of territory gives it control over access to its markets as well as to its natural resources, its work force, and its financial resources and borrowing capacity. The corporation, on its side, can be taxed for revenue and often has new technology based on its R&D capacity; it has managerial experience and the capacity to market products in other countries, all of which it can exchange for the access that the state alone can give or withhold. A mutuality of interest exists which both parties acknowledge when they bargain with each other but which both often deny in public.[25]

Yet the extent of these trade-creating agreements between states and corporations is unknown. No one has a vested interest in collecting the figures comparable to the interest that governments have always had (originally for tax and revenue reasons) in collecting statistics about the volume of goods entering or leaving their territory. Though most government-corporation agreements are probably with developing countries, there are quite a few well-publicized ones with the developing countries. Both Britain and the United States, for instance, have concluded agreements with Japanese car companies to invest in new plants. Moreover, it is probable that most Western trade with Soviet bloc countries and China has been negotiated by companies rather than governments. Under a 1984 Franco-Soviet commercial agreement, French exports of capital goods to the Soviet Union will rise from Fr. 2 billion to Fr. 10 billion in the first year alone, and French exports of steel will triple; but the most important negotiations will be those with the French companies. Most of the Soviet-West European gas-pipeline arrangements were negotiated over a long period between the Soviet government, the oil companies (notably Shell), and major engineering firms (such as John Brown). Although in their commercial relations with Saudi Arabia the South Koreans have negotiated with the government (arranging, for instance, first to build hospitals and later to staff them with doctors, nurses, and technicians), in other bilateral relationships negotiations with governments are often only a preliminary to more detailed bargaining with foreign companies.

Such spotty and uncoordinated evidence as we have, chiefly from the financial press, strongly suggests that this bilateral network of contracts is not only sustaining—despite the financial disorder—the continued expansion of world trade but is actually doing a great deal more than debates in the United Nations to achieve the much-discussed New International Economic Order. This quiet commercial diplomacy produces more tangible results in the shape of new investments, new jobs, and new production in the South than all the resolutions, codes of conduct, guidelines, and declarations on which so much official time has been spent. Meanwhile the

GATT reports on international trade make a great deal of those bilateral arrangements which restrict trade, notably the market-sharing arrangements for steel between the United States, Japan, and the European Community. They are, however, curiously reticent about trade-creating agreements, even those between governments, such as the Australian-New Zealand Closer Economic Relations agreement of 1983, let alone those between governments and corporations or corporations and other corporations.

One partial indicator of how important these agreements are is the rapid growth in recent years of countertrade, a new elaborate form of barter in which exchange takes place without the use of money. Sometimes the goods concerned are part of the output of a plant in which a foreign corporation has made the initial investment. They can also be goods that are totally different from those which the receiving corporation normally markets. Countertrade by one estimate now accounts for $500 billion a year, about one-quarter of world trade and ten times as much as existed ten years ago. Quite recently the United States decided that countertrade was important enough to warrant changing the law so that U.S. banks could finance countertrade deals.

That such energetic attempts should be made by firms and governments to overcome the economic uncertainty that has characterized the past decade should not surprise us. In the 1930s the first reaction of governments to economic depression and the shrinkage of trade that followed was to seek trading partners with whom special deals could be done, to restore confidence and reopen markets for exporters. The Roosevelt administration, armed with the Reciprocal Trade Agreements Act of 1934, signed sixteen bilateral agreements covering one-third of American trade before concluding the 1938 agreement with Britain. The Latin Americans were particularly active in building a continental cobweb of bilateral arrangements, abandoning them only reluctantly after the war under pressure from Washington. Though Hjalmar Schacht's bilateral arrangements with Germany's southeastern neighbors are the best documented set of commercial arrangements of that time, and are notorious for their *exploitation* of primary producers they were, in most respects, not at all unusual.

From an international relations perspective, moreover, it does not seem strange that a commercial system should be made up of an interlocking network of bilateral arrangements and relationships. All the talk of an *international system* notwithstanding, that is what most international relations actually consist of—relations between particular pairs of states. The Western alliance, for instance, boils down to a set of bilateral relationships between the United States and certain key countries, first Britain, latterly Germany and Japan, but also Canada, Australia, and other minor allies. The biggest issue of world politics—nuclear arms control—is generally acknowledged to be a matter of bilateral relations by the superpowers. And when the future of Hong Kong has to be settled, no one finds it surprising that it should be negotiated bilaterally between the British and the Chinese.

What has happened between the 1930s and the 1980s is that international corporations have taken over in large part from governments in arranging trade deals across frontiers. This bilateralism is regarded with disdain in international organization circles and by liberal economists, but their attitudes are more than a little biased, by self-interest in the first case and by ideology in the second. It seems at the least arguable that the model of a web of bilateral contracts is capable of producing a more durable and generally satisfactory tradeoff among the basic values of political economy than any other. It would appear capable—always given the necessary monetary management—of sustaining growth and efficiency in the production of wealth. By aiding the changing international division of labor to benefit the NICs, it is also bringing about some more just and equitable distribution of the benefits of economic integration. And it is certainly giving greater freedom to states to be openly inconsistent (instead of covertly, as before) in their trade policies. For political security reasons they may choose to be protectionist in one sector (German shipbuilding) while open and competitive in others (German automobiles). The choice is theirs, and there is no reason why governments should not change their mind in either direction.

In any case, the next few years will show whether world trade can continue to survive despite the deadlock in the GATT and despite a certain amount of increased protectionism. My contention is that a combination of political and economic interests, reinforced by structural change in the international division of labor brought about by the mobility of capital and technology, is preventing a world depression from seriously arresting or reversing the steady growth in world trade.

THEORETICAL IMPLICATIONS

If this conclusion is correct, it undermines some of the basic assumptions of liberal economic doctrine about the political economy of trade. Liberal doctrine assumes that there is something inherent in the nature of the state which biases its decisions toward protectionism and other interventions in the market, and that this bias ought somehow to be corrected. It needs to be corrected, so the argument goes, for economic reasons, so that wealth will be maximized through international specialization. It needs to be corrected for political reasons, so that beggar-thy-neighbor trade policies will not start a vicious spiral of retaliation ending in open violence.

Liberal doctrine leads in two directions, to the hegemonial model and to the multilateralist model. The first says that the best way to correct this regrettable tendency is to depend on the coercive and persuasive power of a dominant economic and military power, a hegemon, to restrain the other states in the system. The second says that if all major trading countries can agree on a binding set of rules, the benefits reaped by each of them from expanding trade will far outweigh the inconvenience of obedience to the rules.

It was Charles Kindleberger who first argued that the integrated world economy of our times requires a hegemon at its center to function in an orderly and productive way. He also defined the basic requirements of such a hegemonial system.[26] A capitalist or market system is apt, as experience has shown, to suffer cylical booms and slumps and to fail periodically to match its demands and supply. The hegemon thus has to function in three ways in order to preserve order in the system. Whenever necessary it must offer a vent or outlet for surplus production; it must act as a lender of last resort to maintain monetary liquidity; and it must generate an outflow of capital or credit to keep the system expanding. Kindleberger argued (and many people have accepted his argument) that Britain played this role more or less successfully in the three or four decades before World War I, and the United States played it in the two decades following World War II. Between the wars, however, Britain was unable and the United States was unwilling to do so. The result was that the world suffered the worst depression in its history.

Most Americans believe that the United States today, like Britain 50 years ago, has suffered a decline in power that no longer permits it to play this hegemonial role. Most non-Americans are highly skeptical about this decline in U.S. power and would agree with Hedley Bull that "The problem America presents for us is not, as so many Americans appear to think, the relative decline of its power, but the decline of its capacity for sound judgment and leadership."[27] Bull was referring more to matters of security and defense, but the observation applies equally to money and trade. In these matters it is not so much that the United States is unable as that it is unwilling. It is not so much that it has lost power to Japan, Germany, or any other state as that the private sector has grown so large that its regulation has been allowed to go (or seems to have gone) beyond the power of any government.

In the version of the hegemonic model developed by Robert Gilpin and later Stephen Krasner, the political and economic decline of the hegemon inevitably brought about the collapse of the liberal trade order.[28] Arthur Stein recently went on to argue that this decline was itself inevitable, inherent in what he called the "hegemon's dilemma."[29] Both Britain in the 19th century and the United States in the 20th century adopted economic policies that undercut their own dominant position. The hegemon's dilemma was to reconcile the national interest with maintenance of the system. The crucial question, according to Stein, was "whether the hegemon, now facing economic collapse, will be able to forgo retaliation" when others act illiberally.

The point Stein misses is that the trade system is secondary to the security system and the monetary and credit system. Therefore it is not what the hegemon does or does not do in trade that matters, but what it does or fails to do to maintain the peace and what it does or fails to do to keep the monetary system stable and credit flowing in a steady fashion. Kindleberger was right to emphasize that the basic hegemonic tasks in the interwar period were all monetary—that is, stabilizing the flow of purchasing power through the issue of credit, stabilizing the price of goods in terms of money, and keeping the exchange rates of the major currencies in some sort of rough equilibrium. Neither of the alternative trade policies that Stein suggests might have allowed the hegemon to keep its dominance, and thus save the system (according to his argument) from collapse, was ever feasible. Britain could never have kept a monopoly of the secrets of the Industrial Revolution, and the United States could not have prevented the eventual recovery of the major industrial powers. Rather, it was the failure to maintain peace in 1914 and the failure to maintain monetary order in 1929 and 1979 that caused the decline in trade in each case. At no significant point, as Stein's own narrative makes clear, was the system threatened by the hegemon resorting to retaliation.

Hegemonic leadership may have been useful in accelerating and maximizing the dismantling of trade barriers. Given the structural changes outlined above, however, it is not essential now even if it was in the past. It is worth remembering that trade liberalization in the 1950s, the 1960s, and the 1970s continued just as long as the credit system was expanding. It stopped when credit and purchasing power ran out. At no point did it depend on a clear, consistent, and uncompromising lead from the United States. Trade liberalization continues despite all the contradictions of U.S. trade policy, such as the waiver for agricultural trade in the 1950s, Buy American and tied-aid policies, subsidized shipping, and featherbedded defense industries. The contradictions and inconsistencies (in favor of freer trade in services and of managed trade in manufactures) have changed, but they are hardly new. Perhaps the reason that the hegemonic model has been so appealing, however, is that it claims the status of a law of nature. In the fact of such *force majeure,* failure to be consistent or to deal with the underlying monetary problems can be more easily excused.

The same can be said of the second, multilateralist model in which all the major participants in the trading system accept a standard body of rules and neither cheat nor change the rules too frequently. It is the model preached by the GATT and championed by liberal economists. Both are apt to confuse correlation and cause and to make exaggerated claims for trade liberalization as the major cause of trade expansion and growth in the world economy. It is very likely that the agreement on rules boosted confidence. Confidence probably assisted other factors—political alliance and peace between the Western allies, credit expansion and the internationalization of production through the TNCs—which were powerfully contributing to the growth of trade.

But to say that standard rules are an *essential* prerequisite for expanding trade goes too far. In the first place, standard trade rules mean little if combined with an asymmetric monetary system. The GATT was originally designed to work in tandem with a system of fixed exchange rates between currencies, one in which the rules would apply to all. But the Bretton Woods system diverged from the model from the very start. The development of the dollar-gold exchange system allowed the United States, by exercising its *exorbitant privilege* of paying its debts with IOUs, to escape the discipline imposed on other deficit countries. Since 1973 floating rates have created what Robert Triffin called a *paper dollar standard,* imposing even less discipline than ever on the United States. Thus it has been free to restore a weak trade balance by allowing the dollar to depreciate—a more effective method of boosting exports and repelling commercial invaders than any tariff policy. At other times, when domestic pressures called for a strong dollar, it could compensate for any handicap this put on American industry by insisting on voluntary export restrictions or by borrowing heavily abroad to make up on the financial side what it lost on the trade balance.

And in the second place, there is no correlation between rules and growth. World trade in food has grown substantially without rules to restrain agricultural protection. So has world trade in services, from tourism and shipping to banking and insurance. By now, moreover, the deviations from the standard achieved through nontariff barriers, subsidies, quota agreements, and preferential purchasing are so great that the overnight disappearance of the GATT beneath the waters of Lac Leman would hardly be noticed in the world of commerce.

As with the hegemonic model, the multilateral *regime* (as it is inaccurately still referred to) appeals to academics in search of tidy models and general rules. The reality of hegemonic domination and multilateral surveillance was far messier and more full of contradictions than the intellectual bystanders appreciated.[30] The degree of order achieved in the system, whether by Britain as hegemon in the 19th century and America in the postwar decades or thanks to the GATT and its rule making, was always very relative. Only in ideal form is either model inherently truer to life than the complex web of contracts and bilateral deals on which we now depend.

NOTES

1. GATT, *International Trade 1982–1983* (Geneva, 1983).
2. R. Cox, "Social Forces, States and World Orders: Beyond IR Theory," *Millennium,* Summer 1981, pp. 126–155; G. Sen, *Military Origins of Industrialization and International Trade Rivalry* (New York: St. Martin's, 1983); J. Finalyson and M. Zacher, "The GATT and the Regulation of Trade Barriers: Regime Dynamics and Functions," *International Organization* 35 (Autumn 1981), pp. 561–602; F. Block, *The Origins of International Economic Disorder* (Berkeley: University of California Press, 1977); and R. Tooze, "In Search of International Political Economy, *Political Studies* 32 (1984).

3. This is what the Mitterrand government in France decided when it took no action against Breton farmers incensed by imports of British meat. A contrary decision in 1984 by the Thatcher government in Britain to resist the miners' refusal to accept pit closures has proved immensely costly—according to one estimate it was running after six months into £4 billion.

4. A. Milward, "Tariffs as Constitutions," in S. Strange and R. Tooze, eds., *The Management of International Surplus Capacity* (London: Allen & Unwin, 1981), p. 63.

5. W. A. Lewis, *Economic Survey, 1919–1939* (1949; rpt. London: Allen & Unwin, 1970).

6. C. Kindleberger, *The World in Depression, 1919–1939* (London: Allen Lane, 1973); W. Ashworth, *A Short History of the International Economy since 1850,* 2d ed. (London: Longman, 1962). For an interesting account of the predicament and policies of a debtor country at that time, see Arturo O'Connell, "Argentina under the Depression: Problems of an Open Economy," mimeo (Instituto Torcuato Di Tella, Buenos Aires, December 1983).

7. A. Chandler, *The Visible Hand* (Cambridge: Harvard University Press, 1977); S. Melman, *Pentagon Capitalism: The Political Economy of War* (New York: McGraw-Hill, 1970).

8. G. Patterson, *Discrimination in International Trade: The Policy Issues* (Princeton: Princeton University Press, 1966); R. Gardner, *Sterling Dollar Diplomacy in Current Perspective: The Origins and Prospects of Our International Economic Order,* new ed. (New York: Columbia University Press, 1981); and A. S. Milward, *The Reconstruction of Western Europe, 1945–1951* (London: Methuen, 1984). C. Wilcox, *A Charter for World Trade* (New York: Macmillan, 1949); S. Harris, *The European Recovery Program* (Cambridge: Harvard University Press, 1948).

9. Miriam Camps and William Diebold, Jr., *The New Multilateralism: Can the World Trading System Be Saved?* (New York: Council on Foreign Relations, 1983).

10. Commonwealth Secretariat, *Protectionism: Threat to International Order. The Impact on Developing Countries,* report by a Group of Experts (London, 1982), para. 1.29, p. 5.

11. Jan Tumlir, "The World Economy Today: Crisis or New Beginning?" *National Westminster Bank Quarterly Review,* August 1983, pp. 26–44.

12. W. M. Corden, *The Revival of Protectionism,* Group of Thirty Occasional Paper 14 (New York, 1984).

13. R. C. O. Matthews, ed., *Slower Growth in the Western World* (London: Heinemann, 1982).

14. R. S. Walters, "America's Declining Industrial Competitiveness: Protectionism, the Marketplace and the State," *Political Studies,* Winter 1983, pp. 25–33. See also I. M. Destler, *The Textile Wrangle: Conflict in US-Japanese Relations, 1969–1971* (Ithaca: Cornell University Press, 1979); M. Hudson, *Global Fracture* (New York: Harper & Row, 1977), chap. 16; and Commonwealth Secretariat, *Protectionism.* The assertion is also made that "protectionism . . . can have repercussions on all aspects of policy and affect international relations profoundly" (p. 89).

15. Commonwealth Secretariat, *Protectionism.* Arthur Dunkel is also admiringly quoted as saying (p. 105): "There is no salvation outside a generally applied system of multilateral rules, and every departure from the rules, however

temporary or exceptional it is intended to be, helps to create the system and to destroy the confidence which governments and businessmen should be able to repose in it."

16. Judd Polk, "U.S. Production Abroad and the Balance of Payments: A Survey of Corporate Investment Experience," mimeo (National Industrial Conference Board, New York, May 1966).
17. C. A. Michalet, *Le capitalisme mondiale* (Paris: PUF, 1976).
18. F. V. Meyer, *International Trade Policy* (New York: St. Martin's, 1978).
19. H. Hughes and A. Krueger, "Effects of Protection on Developing Countries' Exports of Manufactures," mimeo, January 1983, p. 37.
20. B. Belassa, "The End of a Liberal Era?" *SAIS Review,* Summer-Fall 1983, pp. 133–142. Belassa, nevertheless, still subscribes to the bicycle theory of multilateral negotiation on trade policies. See also C. F. Bergsten and W. Cline, "Trade Policy in the 1980s: An Overview of the Problem," in Cline, ed., *Trade Policy in the 1980s* (Washington, D.C.: Institute for International Economics, 1983).
21. GATT, *International Trade 1982-83,* p. 5.
22. Sanjay Dhar, "United States Trade with Latin America: Consequences of Financing Constraints," Federal Reserve Bank of New York, *Quarterly Review,* Autumn 1983.
23. D. Morawetz, *Why the Emperor's New Clothes Are Not Made in Colombia: A Case Study in Latin American and East Asian Manufactured Exports* (New York: Oxford University Press for the World Bank, 1981), first published as a World Bank staff working paper.
24. World Bank country study. See also Hughes and Krueger, "Effects of Protection"; W. Cline, *Exports of Manufactures from Developing Countries: Performance and Prospects for Market Access.* (Washington, D.C.: Brookings, 1983); and John Odell, "Growing Conflict and Growing Cooperation in Trade between Latin America and the United States," in K. Middlebrook and C. Rico, *U.S.-Latin American Relations in the 1980s* (1984).
25. An extreme instance of practice diverging from (socialist) theory is the agreement of China to allow the 3M Corporation to set up a 100 percent wholly owned subsidiary in Shanghai.
26. Kindleberger, *World in Depression.*
27. H. Bull, "The International Anarchy in the 1980s," *Australian Outlook* 37 (December 1983), pp. 127–131.
28. R. Gilpin, *U.S. Power and the Multinational Corporation* (New York: Basic Books, 1975). See also R. O. Keohane and J. Nye, *Power and Interdependence: World Politics in Transition* (Boston: Little, Brown, 1977); S. Krasner, *Defending the National Interest* (Princeton: Princeton University Press, 1978). For a contrary view that finds Keohane's hegemonic stability theory less persuasive than my own explanation of "surplus capacity," see P. Cowhey and E. Long, "Testing Theories of Regime Change: Hegemonic Decline or Surplus Capacity?" *International Organization* 37 (Spring 1983), pp. 157–188.
29. A. Stein, "The Hegemon's Dilemma: Great Britain, the United States and International Economic Order," *International Organization* 38 (Spring 1984), pp. 355–386. See also T. McKeown, "Hegemonic Stability and Nineteenth Century Tariff Levels in Europe," *International Organization* 37 (Winter 1983), pp. 73–91.
30. For a good, realistic summary see L. Rangarajan, "The Politics of International Trade," in S. Strange, ed., *Paths to International Political Economy* (London: Allen & Unwin, 1984), pp. 126–163.

Cooperation in the Liberalization of International Trade: After Hegemony, What?

Beth V. Yarbrough
Robert M. Yarbrough

Nations dwell in perpetual anarchy, for no central authority imposes
limits on the pursuits of sovereign interests. . . . Because as states, they
cannot cede ultimate control over their conduct to a supranational
sovereign, they cannot guarantee that they will adhere to their promises.
The possibility of a breach of promise can impede cooperation even
when cooperation would leave all better off. Yet, at other times, states
do realize common goals through cooperation under anarchy.

K. A. Oye, Cooperation under Anarchy, p. 1.

Contracts are agreements that are legally enforceable by the state. Each
nation's contract law specifies the conditions under which nonperformance under a contract may be met with state enforcement and the punishments that may be imposed (e.g., monetary damages or specific performance). The enforcement institutions embodied in a state's contract law are
obviously valuable in facilitating transactions, economic and otherwise.
The transactions facilitated by contracts are mutually beneficial to the
parties involved since the contractual relationship must, by definition, be
voluntary.[1] Despite the mutuality of benefits under a contract, breach is
sometimes advantageous to a party; and the complex institution of contract law is designed to prevent and compensate for breach. Were it not

Beth and Robert Yarbrough, "Cooperation in the Liberalization of International Trade: After
Hegemony, What?" Reprinted from *International Organization,* 41:1 (Winter 1987): pp.
13–26 by permission of The MIT Press, Cambridge, MA.

for the enforcement and remedy available in contract law, many potentially mutually beneficial transactions would not be undertaken.

It can be argued that it is the absence of this enforcement mechanism of the state which makes international economic relations more insecure and more obviously discordant than economic relations confined within a single nation. The relationship of states to international law is quite different from the relationship of citizens to the law of a single state: "A higher propensity to deny the rule of law . . . and to resort to coercion is a characteristic distinguishing international from domestic politics. . . . Organs of state are, international lawyers remind us, immune from international law."[2] The same concept of sovereignty (i.e., authority over citizens with no recourse to higher law) which contributes to domestic stability and order also contributes to international *anarchy,* for states have little recourse to higher law in their dealings with one another.[3]

Prognosticators of the future of international trade appear to split into two groups according to their perception of this international anarchy.[4] One group, concerned with the rise of pressures for protectionism and aware of the lack of an efficacious worldwide policymaking and enforcement structure, foresees at best the stagnation of trade liberalization and at worst the return to protectionism at levels reminiscent of the 1930s. Of particular concern to a subset of this group is the decline in the willingness and/or ability of the United States to perform a leadership or hegemonic role in the world trading system.[5] Proposed solutions range from the creation of a single worldwide government to more modest proposals for supranational institutions to handle certain issues of worldwide concern, including international trade policy. The current outlook from this perspective is rather pessimistic: the mechanisms that it sees as prerequisites for cooperation do not appear to be forthcoming, despite recognition of the mutual gains from cooperation. A second group, on the other hand, also aware of increased protectionist pressures and decreased leadership potential by the United States, foresees either persistence of the liberalizing force from the period of U.S. hegemony or evolution of viable alternative institutions to maintain the openness of the world trading system.[6] For this group, international anarchy is more apparent than real, a misnomer for subtle patterns of cooperation which are poorly understood.

Informed by the second tradition, this article asks: Given the potential of liberal international trade to be mutually beneficial for all participants, what types of institutional arrangements can facilitate liberalization (i.e., cooperation) under different conditions in the world economy? We focus less on *whether* or *when* trade liberalization will occur,[7] or *where*—that is, in which industries,[8] than on *how* and *in what form* trade liberalization will occur.[9] Liberalization can be unilateral, multilateral, or minilateral[10] and can be accompanied by varying degrees of bargaining, threats, harmony, discord, and explicit coordination. Why has trade liberalization historically taken different forms? To answer this question, we construct a theory to connect the various forms of observed liberalization with the economic and political environments in which they occur. The framework we adopt emphasizes the role of transaction costs[11] and the resulting hazards of opportunism in determining the forms of successful trade liberalization.[12] Rather than prescribing trade policies, we highlight the potential costs of prohibiting some trade practices, the complete role of which in facilitating cooperation may yet be imperfectly understood.[13]

We view the extent of transaction-specific investment and the viability of hegemonic cooperation as determinants of the scope of opportunistic protectionism and, therefore, as determinants of the *form* of successful liberalization. When there is little investment in transaction-specific assets for trade, then opportunistic protectionism is unlikely and unilateral liberalization is viable, regardless of whether or not the world economy is dominated by a hegemonic country. Arguably, such a situation characterized the position of nineteenth-century Britain, which did indeed pursue unilateral liberalization. When substantial investment in trade-related transaction-specific assets does occur, then trade liberalization takes on characteristics of a Prisoner's Dilemma and unilateral liberalization is not viable. Under the Prisoner's Dilemma, cooperation or liberalization can still emerge. A hegemonic country can facilitate cooperation, for example, the United States' support of the multilateral GATT (General Agreements on Tariffs and Trade) system following World War II. Or, in the absence of a hegemon, minilateral cooperation can arise through the use of issue linkage, hostages, and repeated play. This last case, minilateral cooperation, can be argued to approximate the situation of recent years.

TRANSACTION COSTS, ADJUSTMENT COSTS, AND OPPORTUNISM: THE NEED FOR COOPERATION

Traditional economic trade theory provides a powerful demonstration of the potential gains from international specialization and trade according to comparative advantage. Given a few basic assumptions,[14] unrestricted international trade maximizes total world income and welfare from a fixed quantity of available resources and technology. Even if one or more of these assumptions are violated, restrictions on international trade are generally a second-best remedy. By ignoring transaction and adjustment costs associated with international trade liberalization, this traditional view posits trade as a situation of near-perfect harmony (excepting the nationalistic *optimal* tariff), a positive-sum game with little role for strategy, negotiation, or disagreement. Implicit in the near-perfect harmony of the orthodox economic view of trade is the absence of a role for cooperation in Keohane's sense of the word.[15] Each country, acting in its individual self-interest, chooses unilaterally to liberalize trade; and total world income is maximized as an (unintended) result.

We maintain the traditional assumption that unrestricted international trade maximizes total world income by facilitating specialization according to comparative advantage.[16] By contributing to a more efficient use of the world's resources, liberalization by any country (e.g., elimination of a tariff or loosening of a quantitative restriction) contributes to the gains from trade. Despite this positive effect of a country's liberalization on the total gains from trade, a more liberal policy may impose a number of costs on an individual country, especially interindustry resource dislocations and (undesired) redistributions of domestic income.

These costs, typically referred to as *adjustment costs,* constitute an effective barrier to liberalization only in the presence of substantial transaction costs. With zero transaction costs, *winners* from liberalization could compensate *losers* without cost; tax-subsidy schemes could effect any desired sectoral realignments; the future benefits of improved resource allocation could be borrowed against to cover current adjustment costs; and the barrier to liberalization which adjustment costs represent would disappear. Even the optimal tariff argument for a welfare-enhancing tariff by a large country relies on transaction costs insofar as the harm that such a tariff imposes on trading partners exceeds the benefit to the tariff-raising country. With no transaction costs, the trading partners could pay the large country to forgo the tariff, and world welfare would rise. Therefore, it is transaction costs that turn adjustment costs into a potent source of discord.

The explicit consideration of transaction and adjustment costs introduces two bases of protectionism or of failure to liberalize trade. The first, well-known source is the internal distributional effect of liberalization. By blocking costless compensation of losers (e.g., owners of resources employed in import-competing sectors)[17] by gainers (e.g., domestic consumers and owners of resources in export-oriented sectors), transaction costs may bring about an outcome in which domestic interest groups are able to effect governmental trade policies that do not maximize national, much less world, welfare. A larger-scale reflection of the same phenomenon is the *free-riding* problem where small states pursue protectionist policies in the belief that those policies do not significantly influence the openness of the world trading system. In each case, self-interest on the part of each individual interest group causes a less than socially optimal amount of liberalization. This problem has been widely studied in both its domestic and international versions. Proposed solutions range from domestic trade adjustment assistance programs to special efforts to convince small (particularly developing) countries of the advantages to all of trade liberalization.

A second source of protectionism as a result of transaction costs is more subtle and less studied. Not only may a country choose policies that are less liberal than the socially optimal policies, but a country may renege on negotiated commitments to liberalization. A trade liberalization agreement consists merely of policy commitments by the signatory countries. One country, by choosing to ignore or cheat on its commitment to liberalization while other countries abide by theirs, may gain by avoiding re-source reallocation costs, redistributions of domestic income, or other adjustment costs. Such a policy (protection in violation of a negotiated commitment to liberalization) can be referred to as *opportunistic protectionism*. By definition, opportunism is possible only in the presence of transaction costs; otherwise agreements could be designed and enforced without cost in such a way as to make opportunistic violations impossible. So transaction costs not only block efforts to deal with the intracountry distributional impact of liberalization; they also introduce the potential hazard of opportunistic violations of commitments to liberalization.

A transaction that would be mutually beneficial if all parties abided by their commitments may not be mutually beneficial if one or more parties reneges. When opportunistic nonperformance in a transaction is a hazard, then obtaining the mutual benefits from the transaction requires designing a governance structure to control nonperformance. In everyday economic transactions, these governance structures include such common arrangements as collateral to prevent opportunistic nonrepayment of loans, the use of brand names to convey information about quality, better business bureaus to provide information about the reliability of firms, automobile *lemon* laws to protect car buyers from opportunistic dealers, and product guarantees or free samples to compensate for or prevent dissatisfaction with a product's quality. By making transactions more secure, each of these arrangements facilitates mutually beneficial transactions that otherwise might not be undertaken.[18] Each of the arrangements is an example of cooperation; and the cooperation is needed because the possibility of opportunism introduces an element of conflict among the commonality of interests.

The same problem arises in international trade liberalization. After arriving at a mutual agreement to liberalize trade policies, one country may find it advantageous to renege on its commitments. Other parties to the agreement may be harmed if such opportunism occurs. Under these circumstances, a need for cooperation replaces harmony. But the orthodox neoclassical framework has little to say about the possible mechanisms for cooperative organization and governance of international trading relations because the neoclassical viewpoint is basically apolitical and ahistorical. Such a theory cannot adequately address the particular forms that trade agreements have historically taken (e.g., unilateral by nineteenth-century Britain, multilateral by the postwar United States, or minilateral recently). These organizational distinctions in the form of cooperation are assumed away in neoclassical theory, where international trade occurs in an idealized, harmonious world of zero transaction costs.

When a country behaves opportunistically by imposing protection proscribed under a trade agreement, the total gains from trade are reduced. So long as liberalization involves adjustment costs and cheating cannot be easily detected and traced to the guilty country, incentives exist to behave opportunistically. That liberalization does indeed impose adjustment costs on a country hardly needs documentation. The anarchic nature of international economic relations prevents effective detection and punishment of opportunistic states; even if detection were easy (which we shall argue is not the case), punishment would be problematic.

At first glance, the problem of detecting opportunistic violations of trade agreements may appear trivial. After all, governments and international organizations collect mountain of trade statistics; tariff lists are publicly available; and it is possible to trace goods through customs. However, several factors make this observation misleading. First, there is no uniform international consensus about whether or not a trade agreement automatically becomes domestic law in signatory countries. In most cases, international agreements have no direct effects but must be converted into domestic law and enforced domestically.[19] The U.S. Congress, for example, has periodically altered the domestic status of agreements reached through GATT negotiations.[20] This additional step introduces the opportunity for individual states to alter the terms of an agreement through definitional changes as well as by stating explicit reservations to specific terms. The result of this process can be a signed agreement embodying substantial differences among the signatory parties over the behaviors that are or are not acceptable under the (now multiple) terms. Detecting violations under such conditions is not a trivial problem.

Second, trade agreements, like domestic contracts, are not intended to be binding under all circumstances. It is a well-established principle of contract law that situations arise in which, as a result of unforeseen changes in circumstance, it is impossible or in no one's interest to honor the contract.[21] Failure to perform in such situations (e.g., if an entertainer dies prior to a contractually scheduled concert or if a transportation strike makes timely delivery of promised goods impossible) is termed *discharge* rather than *breach*. But parties may disagree over whether performing is in fact impossible (in which case discharge may be permitted) or whether one party is opportunistically making such a claim in order to breach the contract without punishment. A country that had promised to permit unrestricted access for imports of an agricultural product might, for example, claim to have discovered a dangerous chemical, pesticide, or disease in the product and close its market to imports. In a rather colorful episode during the spring of 1985 (a period of depressed prices for most agricultural products in the United States), three northern states halted imports of hogs from Canada, claiming that the hogs had been treated with the unapproved antibiotic chloramphenicol. Canadian producers denied use of the antibiotic, calling the states' action (opportunistic) protectionism. U.S. producers had, in fact, been pressing for relief from the effects of Canadian exports. Detecting whether or not a country is acting opportunistically or in good faith in such circumstances may be difficult, costly, or even impossible. Japan often explicitly uses the doctrine of *rebus sic stantibus* (so long as principal circumstances remain unchanged) in its commercial treaties.[22] This doctrine, as its name suggests, permits agreements to be broken should unexpected changes make honoring the commitments undesirable. The use of this *escape clause* is not popular with Japan's trading partners for obvious reasons; and the status of the clause vis-à-vis international law is murky.

A third factor hampering the detection of opportunistic protection under trade agreements is more obvious: the inability to define precisely the behaviors that are or are not permissible. A brief list of recent trade disputes should suffice to illustrate this point. The United States and the EC (European Community) have a long-standing argument over which *domestic* policies constitute subsidies to exports and are therefore proscribed under the GATT. Are controlled natural gas prices in the United States a subsidy to exported goods that use gas as an input? What about export credits at low interest rates? At what levels do interest rates become *artificially low?* Is government subsidized or insured research and development an export subsidy for the commercial products that result? Within the EC itself, the use of different exchange rates to finance different activities, particularly agricultural trade at so-called *green rates*, has been a source of disagreement because an artificial exchange rate can have essentially the same impact as an export subsidy. In trade between the developed and developing countries, transshipment under quantitative restrictions (i.e., clandestine rerouting through unrestricted third countries) provides a classic case of an opportunistic violation that may be exceedingly difficult to detect or prove. For example, Britain has claimed that Japan circumvented its voluntary restraint on automobile exports to Britain by shipping from Australia.[23] Even after an opportunistic violation of an agreement *is* established to have occurred, the problem of forcing termination of the practice or of imposing punishment in the face of national sovereignty still exists. The problems of detection and enforcement make opportunism a real threat to cooperation.

The goal of opportunistic protectionism is not generally to halt trade. Rather, a threat is made to halt trade in order to force a renegotiation leading to more favorable terms for the opportunistic country (in the same sense that the goal of blackmail is not to reveal the secret but to transfer resources from the victim to the blackmailer). Of course, the threat may be successful or unsuccessful depending upon the opportunistic country's ability to judge the scope of its power. Italy in 1887 imposed a new tariff averaging 60 percent which abrogated treaties with Austria-Hungary, Switzerland, Spain, and France. Renegotiation with more favorable terms for Italy rather than a radical reduction in trade was presumably the goal since speedy renegotiations did occur with Austria-Hungary, Switzerland, and Spain. With France, however, Italy apparently miscalculated. Efforts at renegotiation were unsuccessful; and a decade-long trade war of retaliation and counterretaliation ensued. Interestingly, Italy did not abrogate its existing treaty with (more powerful) Germany at the same time.[24]

Recognition of the problem of opportunism in international trade relations has important implications for the expected structure of international trade agreements. In considering any agreement, each party must evaluate not only the effect on the country as a whole and the domestic distributional consequences should the agreement be reached and honored, but the likelihood and impact of opportunism as well. As a result, the form of cooperation should reflect the extent of the threat of breach.

In analyzing different forms of trade liberalization, it is possible to combine what have been viewed as two major competing theories of international trade policy: hegemonic cooperation and surplus capacity, each a key element in defining the politico-economic environment within which trade relations take place. It has been argued elsewhere that a synthesis of the two perspectives may prove more useful than either taken in isolation.[25] The hazard of opportunism under an international trade agreement depends, first, upon the extent of assets that are specific to international trade (a consideration closely related to the existence of surplus capacity) and, second, upon whether or not the agreement is reached in a hegemonic or nonhegemonic environment (as in the hegemonic cooperation hypothesis).

TRANSACTION-SPECIFICITY AND SURPLUS CAPACITY: THE BARS IN THE PRISONER'S DILEMMA

The crux of the Prisoner's Dilemma game typically used to describe international trade problems lies in one aspect of the payoff structure: a defection harms a cooperating party more than it does a defecting party. It is this vulnerability to opportunism, or cost of naiveté, which renders defection the dominant strategy regardless of the other player's strategy. This issue arises within the context of international trade as the question of whether or not a country that is cooperating by complying with a liberalization agreement is made worse off by a trading partner's opportunistic protectionism than had the countries never agreed to cooperate in liberalization. The answer to this question, and therefore the extent to which the Prisoner's Dilemma accurately characterizes the situation, depends upon the extent of transaction-specific investment in trade.

By definition, transaction-specific investment is undertaken to be used in specific transactions; and the value of such assets in alternative uses is low.[26] Transaction-specificity is related to but usefully distinguished from what are usually referred to as *specialized* assets. The distinction has important implications for the vulnerability to opportunism. A few examples will illustrate the relationship between transaction-specificity and the hazard of opportunistic protectionism. Consider the Soviet-European gas pipeline. European technology helped build the pipeline in exchange for the promise of Soviet natural gas exports. Once completed, the pipeline is susceptible to Soviet opportunism since, if the Soviets reduce the amount of gas they are willing to export to Europe (i.e., by placing a quota on exports), the pipeline loses part of its value to the Europeans. The lack of good alternative uses for the pipeline (a transaction-specific asset) from the point of view of the Europeans implies that they could be forced to settle for less than the promised amount of natural gas. If European technology and personnel are required on a continuing basis to maintain the pipeline, then the hazard of European opportunism may also exist. It may be possible for Europeans to demand more than the agreed-upon quantity of natural gas exports in exchange for continued maintenance of the asset. The hazard of opportunism is not a result of a traditional monopoly nor of the specialized purpose of the pipeline (to carry natural gas) but, rather, of the pipeline's specificity to one particular transaction, namely, Soviet-European trade in gas. The European countries do not have a monopoly in the supply of pipeline technology, nor the Soviets in the supply of natural gas. Prior to the construction of the pipeline, a number of possible buyers and sellers existed. However, once the transaction-specific investment in the pipeline is undertaken, the Soviets and Europeans find themselves in a bilateral monopoly. The Soviets cannot use the pipeline to provide non-European buyers with natural gas; and the Europeans cannot use the pipeline to obtain gas from non-Soviet suppliers. As a result of a breakdown of the unique relationship, the value of the asset depreciates.

A different example of transaction-specific assets is presented by the refusal (for political or security reasons) of the United States to provide replacement parts for military equipment sold to a number of countries. The assets are specific in the sense that continued trade with the United States is necessary to retain their usefulness. The United States then has the option of exploiting its position by charging high prices for replacement parts or by providing the parts only in exchange for some concession. Of course, the United States may also refuse to provide the parts on any terms, using its power in the transaction to keep the equipment out of commission. The purchasers of that equipment could have bought similar non-U.S. equipment and the U.S. firms could have sold their equipment elsewhere; the initial relationship was not a monopoly. But once the U.S. equipment is purchased, then a monopoly results. As a third example, the U.S. computer industry made a substantial transaction-specific investment in its development of computer hardware and software capable of using Japanese kanji characters. The market for such a capability outside of Japan is quite limited, making Japan's ability to close its market to the technology a substantial threat. Japan, on the other hand, has invested in the capital equipment and skills necessary to produce automobiles meeting the safety and pollution standards set by the United States. A complete closure of the U.S. automobile market to Japan could impose losses up to the value of those trade-specific assets. In each case, by threatening to withdraw from the relationship, one country can extract from the other an amount up to the difference between the value of the current transaction and the best available alternative. The alternative involves a loss of at least part of the asset's value since the asset is specific to a transaction between two particular parties. The lack of an alternative use with approximately equal value is the source of the potential for opportunism in each case. A transaction-specific asset renders the trading relationship irreversible (or reversible only at a cost equal to the value of the specific asset).

International trade tends to give rise to transaction-specific investment by altering the pattern of production and investment in the participating economies. Transaction-specific assets can take a number of forms; but for present purposes the most important are *dedicated assets,* which are specialized to a particular relationship the loss of which would result in significant excess capacity and associated losses.[27] Dedicated assets are common in international trade. The process of specialization according to comparative advantage involves investing in increased productive capacity designed to service export markets. In the absence of transaction and adjustment costs and specific assets, these structural effects of liberalization do not block cooperation; if two states agree to liberalize trade and one country invests in capacity for servicing the other's market, that investment can be easily dismantled or redirected in the event that the agreement breaks down. But once transaction-specific assets are introduced, one party can "hold up" the other for an amount equal to the excess of the value of the current trading relationship over the value of the best alternative. The greater is the potential return from such opportunism, the stronger the safeguards (i.e., the assurances against opportunism) that will be required in order for countries to enter into liberalization agreements.

As noted earlier, the primary form of transaction-specific investment in international trade consists of dedicated assets, or productive capacity designed for trade so that the loss of markets results in losses through surplus capacity. Susan Strange and others have put forward the existence of surplus capacity as an explanation for increased pressures for protectionism and decreased momentum in trade liberalization.[28] They argue that when productive capacity in an industry substantially exceeds the level of demand at remunerative prices for a sustained period (i.e., not merely at a stage of the business cycle), then antiliberalization pressure rises. Surplus capacity is argued to have increased recently as a result of a rise in the capital intensity of production in many sectors, a rise in the number of industrialized or industrializing countries competing in world markets, and an accelerated pattern of change in the demands for manufactured products owing to shocks such as changes in petroleum prices.[29]

Surplus capacity is similar to the presence of dedicated assets in that both imply a loss of asset value owing to a loss of markets. The existing literature on surplus capacity emphasizes the tendency of industries that find themselves in a situation of surplus capacity to exert pressure for governmental assistance in the form of trade barriers. Because we are interested primarily in the perceived hazard of opportunism and its effect on the form of trade liberalization, our focus is somewhat different. The possibility of losing markets which would result in surplus capacity becomes important since the possibility itself (whether or not it actually materializes) lessens willingness to enter into trade-liberalizing agreements.

The existence of dedicated assets and potential surplus capacity results in a Prisoner's Dilemma payoff structure since a country that agrees to liberalize trade and undertakes associated specific investment stands to lose the value of that investment should its partners impose opportunistic protectionism, leaving the country worse off than had the agreement never been reached. When transaction-specific assets result in a Prisoner's Dilemma, then the success of trade liberalization depends upon an institutional arrangement for breaking the dilemma. One possibility is suggested by a theory of hegemonic cooperation.

HEGEMONIC STABILITY VERSUS HEGEMONIC COOPERATION

A hegemon is a state that is dominant in its leadership in the world economy.[30] Among other attributes of leadership, such a country is willing and able to act as an arbitrator in disputes and to support international cooperative institutions such as the GATT but is not omnipotent or able to impose its leadership without regard to the positions of other countries. If it is to lead, the hegemon must do so on terms that convince other states to follow or defer to its leadership. The precise role of the hegemon has been viewed by various writers as the provision of international stability, international security, rules of behavior, stability of expectations, and enforcement of rules.

The most common version of the hegemonic stability hypothesis views trade liberalization as a public good that must be provided by a hegemonic country. Nonhegemonic countries are free-riders that have inadequate incentives to contribute to the maintenance of a liberal trading system. The main source of disagreement among analysts in the hegemonic-stability tradition concerns the extent of benevolence or exploitation on the part of the hegemon. In the view of some, the hegemon is benevolent, overcoming the tendency of other countries to free-ride by carrying the burden of system maintenance on its own shoulders with little or no reward for its efforts. For others, the hegemon is exploitative and coercive, forcing other countries into openness that serves primarily if not exclusively the interests of the hegemon itself.[31]

The traditional version of the hegemonic stability hypothesis predicts that the presence of a hegemonic country is both necessary and sufficient for an open trading system and, further, that the hegemon is instrumental in bringing about that system. Full historical support for the hypothesis would find Britain and the United States, during their respective periods of hegemony, actively and successfully promoting a cooperative, open trading system and would also find movements away from such a cooperative, open system at all other times. The actual empirical evidence is mixed.[32] Although the periods of hegemony were relatively open by historical standards, Britain did not pursue worldwide liberalization very actively; and nonhegemonic periods have not been uniformly characterized by a lack of cooperation or openness.

The view of hegemonic cooperation taken here involves a related but slightly different role for the hegemon in trade liberalization.[33] This alternative view avoids several theoretical criticisms of the hegemonic stability hypothesis[34] and appears to be consistent with the (admittedly limited and sometimes ambiguous) empirical evidence. We focus on two issues that Keohane suggests have been inadequately addressed by the literature on hegemonic stability: the incentives facing the hegemon and the incentives facing other countries to defer or defect.[35] The hypothesis of hegemonic cooperation also helps resolve the scientific problem of evaluating a theory that applies to only two cases (Britain and the United States). By attempting to say something about the particular form that trade liberalization would take under different conditions, this perspective puts forth additional potentially refutable implications for evaluation.

To avoid reneging on liberalization agreements and to avoid the costs of the associated protectionism, the rewards to individual countries for participating in the world trading system must discourage such opportunism. As noted above, problems of both detection and enforcement arise. The gains to a country from opportunistic protectionism come at the expense of the country's trading partners; and hegemonic cooperation focuses on the hegemon's role as provider of a reward structure intended to discourage beggar-thy-neighbor opportunism.

Two aspects of the hegemon's role facilitate cooperation. *Ex ante,* an acceptable allocation among countries of the costs and benefits of liberalization must be achieved if an agreement is to be reached. This negotiation stage aligns the incentives of the participating countries and forms the "carrot" aspect of the hegemon's role. *Ex post,* the hegemon must be willing and able to monitor countries for compliance with their commitments and to apply agreed-upon punishments in the case of opportunism. This monitoring stage forms the "stick" of the enforcement mechanism. Under a system of hegemonic cooperation, the "stick" should be applied rarely since an effective hegemon can persuade other countries to follow rather than relying on force. This is consistent with John Gannett's observation in a military context that the actual use of force is evidence of the breakdown of power, of impotence rather than strength.[36]

The reward to each country for compliance under hegemonic cooperation must be sufficient to compensate it for forgoing opportunistic protectionism; that is, the reward must at least cover the adjustment costs that the country incurs as a result of its compliance with liberalization. The hegemon must absorb these costs and pay each country an additional side-payment to ensure compliance. The larger the side-payments, the stronger are the incentives provided (but the higher the costs to the hegemon). The size of the side-payments is determined through bargaining between the hegemon and other countries. The constraints on that bargaining are that the side-payments must be positive and that the residual from the gains from trade (which is the reward to the hegemon for its efforts) must be positive. The threat to each country is that, should it act opportunistically, then the hegemon will alter its trade policy in such a way as to punish defection. The enforcement power of the hegemon depends on its ability to influence a large share of world trade through its own policies, including retaliation and control of access to its market. It has been estimated, for example, that protectionism by the United States can immediately and directly affect one-half of the world's trade.[37] The hegemon's trade policy is therefore a response to the policies of other countries; and a hegemon would not necessarily be expected to pursue pure free trade.

It will be in the hegemon's interest to act as a cooperative mechanism so long as opportunistic protection in the absence of the hegemon's enforcement reduces the total gains from trade sufficiently to make the residual the hegemon's most favored outcome. The hegemon shares the gains from openness with other countries to achieve their cooperation; but net gains remain for the hegemon. Should this cease to be the case, then the hegemon ceases to perform its role in the world trading system.[38]

The argument over whether the hegemon is benevolent or exploitative becomes more subtle in this view. Hegemonic cooperation is mutually beneficial to all participants; however, there is no reason to expect the gains to be distributed evenly. The hegemon is breaking the Prisoner's Dilemma that results from the inability of various countries to make binding precommitments to avoid opportunistic protectionism. Consider the classic Prisoner's Dilemma with two alleged criminals each facing a sentence of thirty days in jail if both confess, twenty days in jail if neither confesses, or ten days (for the confessor) and forty days (for the nonconfessor) in jail if only one confesses. Assume also that each individual values a day in jail at one dollar, that is, each would be willing to pay one dollar to reduce the time spent in jail by one day. Then the two together would be willing to pay up to twenty dollars for some sort of institution that would allow them to cooperate. They might, for example, each pay a five-dollar bribe to the police officer to interrogate them in the same room at the same time. If their pleas could be entered simultaneously and in one another's presence, then the incentive to defect would be eliminated. Each prisoner would be better off by five dollars; and the police officer would be better off by the amount of the bribe ($10), ignoring any societal costs of releasing the individuals as well as the risk that the officer might be discovered accepting the bribe and fired. Cooperation is valued by the prisoners; and the police officer is able to facilitate the cooperation by changing the rules of the game.[39] Is the officer self-interested, altruistic, benevolent, or exploitative? Each term has an element of truth; the important point is that all have been made better off. Similarly, a hegemon able to alter the nature of the Prisoner's Dilemma facing participants in the international trading system can establish an environment for mutually beneficial cooperation.

The theory of hegemonic cooperation in the presence of transaction costs views a hegemon as facilitating cooperation in a Prisoner's Dilemma situation. However, the extent to which the Prisoner's Dilemma accurately characterizes payoffs in international trade and, therefore, the role of a hegemon, depends upon the character of investment undertaken for trade-related purposes. This causes the implications of hegemonic cooperation to differ somewhat from those of the traditional hegemonic stability hypothesis. The hypothesis of hegemonic stability implies that the presence of a hegemonic state is *both necessary and sufficient* for a liberal trading system. The hypothesis of hegemonic cooperation, on the other hand, implies that the presence of a hegemon is *one possible way* of breaking a Prisoner's Dilemma in trade policy, a dilemma that exists *only* in the presence of substantial transaction-specific investment for trade. Before turning to a brief examination of the history of trade liberalization, a word of comparison is in order between our analysis of transaction-specificity and opportunism in international trade and Albert Hirschman's well-known argument that the potential to stop trade is an important source of national power.[40]

OPPORTUNISTIC PROTECTION VERSUS NATIONAL-POWER TRADE POLICY

Hirschman examined the pursuit of national power as a goal of international trade policy, a goal that implied the importance to each state of gains relative to those of other states. The primary tool of such a power policy, according to Hirschman, was fostering a monopoly position in one's exports (implying a vulnerability of one's trading partners to trade stoppages) and avoiding a monopoly position in one's import suppliers (implying a lack of vulnerability to stoppages). The ability to monopolize trade in certain products was viewed as largely technologically determined, with market size also an important consideration.

There are three major differences between our analysis and that of Hirschman. First and foremost, the assumed purpose of international trade differs. Hirschman explored the possibility of a power-oriented policy in international trade which could imply steps inconsistent with a wealth- or income-maximizing policy. We do not wish to argue here over the pros and cons of the wealth-maximization goal versus the power goal. Nonetheless, the distinction is important to a comparison of our argument with that of Hirschman. According to our perspective, international trade liberalization increases total world income, implying that in a world of zero transaction costs all countries could agree to eliminate trade barriers. But, of course, transaction costs are positive, which introduces the hazard of opportunistic protectionism. When such opportunism occurs, the *victimized* country may be worse off than had no liberalization agreement been reached. This will be true if the country invested in substantial transaction-specific assets for trade which provide the partner country with the basis for a hold-up.

The problem is, therefore, a Prisoner's Dilemma: neither country can credibly promise *ex ante* not to behave opportunistically; and this barrier can prevent a mutually beneficial transaction (i.e., trade liberalization) from occurring. The goal, then, is to arrive at some sort of institutional arrangement to facilitate credible commitments to compliance, thereby removing the block to completion of the mutually beneficial transaction. The vulnerability to opportunism is inherently associated with the desired activity (liberalization), and the goal is to *break* the link. Hirschman's perspective is quite different. The goal of the power policy is to *foster* vulnerability to opportunism in order to act opportunistically. In fact, the trade involved in such a power policy might not be beneficial but might serve merely to create a dependency that could then be exploited. If the goal of trade is solely to foster exploitable dependency, then the trade presumably imposes costs on the opportunistic country during the *set-up* period; and the expected power gains during subsequent periods would have to offset these costs. This limitation may be important since any power gains are inherently short-lived since they are based on the victim's inability to find alternative sources of trade, a condition that does not usually last forever.

This point suggests the second distinction between our argument and that of Hirschman. The deliberate fostering of dependence which can then be exploited seems to require an asymmetry of information about the relationship between the parties. Either the intended victim must be for some reason so desperate to trade with the opportunistic country that the potential danger is ignored; or the intended victim must be unaware of the danger being plotted. The framework we develop, on the other hand, does not rely on this asymmetry of information. Both parties are assumed to be aware of any potential opportunism that might result from a particular trade agreement. The point is that when the potential for opportunism exists and is known *ex ante,* the agreement will take a form that can secure against the opportunism. In a mutually beneficial transaction, both parties have an incentive to arrive at some arrangement that will facilitate the agreement, just as lenders and borrowers have an incentive to arrive at an arrangement (e.g., collateral) to prevent the risk of opportunistic non-repayment that could otherwise prevent a mutually beneficial loan from being made.

A third, more subtle difference is in the assumed source of asset specificity. For Hirschman, a country wants to be a monopolist in its export markets and a competitor in its import markets; and these market structures are largely determined by technology along with the relative sizes of markets. Transaction-specific investment is a much broader category than technologically based monopoly. As noted earlier in the example of the gas pipeline, transaction-specific investment can transform *any* relationship into a bilateral monopoly. Because the transaction-specific investment transforms a previously competitive situation into a monopoly subject to opportunism, the importance of these issues is much larger than it would appear based on the few technological monopolies of strategic minerals, unique patents, and such.

THE POLITICO-ECONOMIC ENVIRONMENT AND THE FORM OF INTERNATIONAL COOPERATION

When the hazard of opportunistic protectionism is high, and a Prisoner's Dilemma results, there are incentives for parties to an international trade agreement to renege on the agreement's commitments. To the extent that parties to a potential agreement are aware of the scope for *ex post* opportunism, that awareness will be reflected in the form of the agreement. This can happen in three ways. First, if it is obvious to all parties that no agreement could be enforced in the face of the incentives for opportunistic protectionism, then no agreement may be reached despite the existence of mutual gains from trade. This outcome is the trade analogy to the school of arms-control thought which holds that meaningful arms control is impossible, despite the mutual gains from arms control, because no agreement can be mutually verifiable and enforceable. The dilemma defeats the prisoners; and cooperation does not emerge. The second possible outcome is that efforts may be channeled into negotiation of naive agreements that ignore the possibility of opportunism. Such agreements will be difficult to reach and short-lived, so the implications of this second possibility are not unlike those of the first: gains from trade are eventually lost because of bargaining problems that transaction costs and opportunism pose. The arms-control analogy would be a simple mutual promise to eliminate weapons with no monitoring or enforcement mechanism. An example of this behavior in international trade is provided by the Anglo-Hanse trade wars (1300–1700). The two sides repeatedly negotiated agreements to provide for relatively free trade; but the agreements repeatedly broke down, starting successive rounds of the trade wars.[41] The third possibility is to use an understanding of the incentives for opportunism to construct enforceable agreements. This is a costly process; but in a world of transaction costs and opportunism, the choice is not between protectionism and ideal trade agreements enforced without costs. Similarly, the arms-control choice is not between an uncontrolled arms race and a costlessly enforced ideal arms-control agreement. Rather, the relevant choice is between forgoing the benefits of trade (or arms control) and designing effective governance structures to facilitate trade (or arms-control) agreements. This link between the degree of hazard of opportunistic protectionism and the benefits to particular institutional arrangements implies that we may expect different forms of international trade liberalization to be successful under various conditions. Historically, the major forms of trade liberalization have been unilateral, multilateral, and minilateral; we shall now examine each briefly.

UNILATERALISM: NINETEENTH-CENTURY BRITAIN

We expect unilateral trade liberalization only from countries facing little or no threat of opportunism; for example, whenever the country had little investment in trade-specific assets that could be held up by an opportunistic trading partner. The most commonly cited historical example of extensive unilateral trade liberalization is the case of mid-nineteenth-century Britain.[42] Although Britain was (at least by most definitions) a hegemonic power, its hegemony alone cannot explain the unilateral policy since the later hegemon, the United States, did not pursue unilateral liberalization.

Further, Timothy McKeown has argued that the actions of nineteenth-century Britain provide evidence against the traditional version of hegemonic stability theory.[43] That theory, according to McKeown, predicts that Britain would conduct an active, persuasive policy for lowering tariffs, use its bargaining strength in other areas to coerce other nations into lowering tariffs, and be successful in these efforts. The empirical evidence suggests that none of these predictions held and that both France and the Zollverein, the other major industrialized areas of the period, followed liberal policies despite a general lack of pressure to do so from Britain. In addition, Britain maintained a number of restrictive measures dictated by domestic interests. The smaller powers maintained their trade barriers in the face of substantial reductions by Britain, France, and the Zollverein. All of these observations are consistent with the view of hegemonic cooperation which sees a crucial role for the hegemon in systemwide liberalization only in the presence of transaction-specific investment that turns international trade liberalization into a Prisoner's Dilemma. This condition was not met during the period of British hegemony; and we predict that Britain would follow a unilateral trade policy: liberal but maintaining barriers demanded by domestic interest groups and not pressuring for systemwide liberalization.

Unilateral liberalization was feasible for Britain because of its industrial strength, high rate of capacity utilization, and need for raw material and export markets. Purchasers of manufactured goods from Britain faced limited alternative suppliers, while in most cases export markets and raw material sources were highly substitutable. Britain would have been vulnerable, of course, to a simultaneous stoppage of trade by a sizable group of its trading partners, but such a group was unlikely to form since defection from the group and continued trade with Britain would have been beneficial for each country. Those British investments that were highly vulnerable to opportunism were protected through the links of empire. Surplus capacity was not a problem for Britain; and the industrializing British labor force was becoming relatively mobile for the time.[44] Most smaller countries maintained trade barriers; but Britain liberalized unilaterally, capturing gains from trade and incurring low bargaining and enforcement costs. Britain was a hegemon as defined by most measures of status relative to other countries, but hegemony cannot be the explanation for the unilateral form of its trade liberalization.

MULTILATERALISM: POSTWAR AMERICA AND THE EARLY GATT YEARS

By the end of World War II, transportation and communication costs had declined precipitously from their levels during the period of British hegemony a century earlier. Manufacturing technology had made large-scale production efficient; and the number of industrialized economies had expanded substantially, although several were in ruins from the war. Another major change in the nature of trade was a move away from intersectoral trade (e.g., the exchange of agricultural products for manufactured goods) to intra-industry or even intrafirm trade in manufactures. Much of this trade, by its nature, gives rise to trade-specific assets and to a vulnerability to opportunism. This runs counter to the common argument that dependence on imported food is the ultimate vulnerability. Food, however, is not transaction-specific; if one food supplier halts trade, a large number of alternative suppliers are typically available. Of course, if all suppliers halted trade simultaneously, then the problem would be much more serious; but such concerted action has been rare historically (and for good economic reasons). On the other hand, a manufacturing industry that imports a unique component for use in its manufacturing process may be unable to locate an alternative supplier quickly. Or the producer of a unique component may be unable to sell the product should the original buyer threaten to end the relationship. Therefore, the rise of trade in manufactures and especially of intra-industry trade is associated with an increase in trade-specific assets. Firms can protect these assets from opportunism through internalization in the form of intracorporate trade. However, this still leaves a vulnerability to governmental trade policies. Trade-specific assets imply a vulnerability to opportunistic protectionism, imparting a Prisoners' Dilemma payoff structure to the trade-liberalization game. Hegemonic cooperation implies that in the presence of substantial trade-specific assets, a hegemonic country can facilitate cooperation and liberalization by breaking the Prisoners' Dilemma in which individual countries find themselves.

The GATT framework supported by U.S. hegemony appears to fit the model of hegemonic cooperation well. The GATT consists of a set of continuously negotiated rules for trade policies and a set of arbitration or dispute-settlement procedures for members. The goal of the GATT framework is an open, cooperative trading system; but the emphasis has always been on negotiation and arbitration rather than on *free trade* as a dogmatic ideology. GATT contracting parties never committed themselves to follow free trade; protectionist policies to aid domestic industries were always permitted on a number of grounds. In turn, the framework provides for punishment of protectionism (primarily in the form of withdrawn concessions or countervailing duties), but only protectionism that violates specific GATT commitments.

Hegemonic cooperation based upon U.S. leadership implies that the United States should have actively provided "carrots" to other countries to ensure their support for liberalization under the GATT. In fact, the United States not only initiated and *marketed* the entire GATT system but in exchange for support continued to tolerate a number of practices that it would have liked to see terminated. These included preference systems such as that between Britain and the Commonwealth countries, the use of quotas for balance-of-payments problems, and the continuation of both tariffs and quotas by LDCs for *development* reasons. Each of these practices clearly violated the central GATT norm of nondiscriminatory liberalization. The United States also permitted continued discrimination against its own exports during the early years of the GATT by not demanding reciprocity in liberalization from either Europe or the developing countries. At the same time, the United States provided substantial aid for the reconstruction of Europe, primarily in the form of grants rather than loans. Each of these items represents a "carrot," or a concession made by the United States to achieve the support of other countries. Developing countries continue to be generally excused from demands for reciprocity within the GATT framework, a side-payment that was (and is) clearly necessary to bring about even lukewarm support for the system.

The enforcement or "stick" role of U.S. trade policies was also clear during the early postwar years. The United States never threatened to retaliate against all protectionism on the part of its trading partners; and it rarely claimed seriously to follow free trade policies itself. As noted above, continued discrimination in a number of forms against U.S. exports was tolerated in the early years of the GATT. The United States also excluded several sectors from liberalization (most notably, agriculture and later textiles) for its own domestic reasons. U.S. policy was designed to promote an open trading system, especially in manufactures; and retaliation was reserved for protectionism in violation of commitments within the GATT. The same principles of nondiscriminatory liberalization which formed the norms of GATT liberalization also applied for the most part to punishment under the GATT.[45]

The United States pushed other countries toward liberalization, though only at a mutually acceptable pace. For example, the U.S. battle to gain entry for Japan into the GATT was a long one. The battle was finally won gradually over a number of years. First, Japan was allowed to send an observer to the GATT. Next, after a four-year push by the United States, Japan was admitted as a signatory country, but other countries were allowed to continue to discriminate against Japan in their trade policies. Finally, over the next four years, the discriminatory trade practices were gradually dropped.

The success of the GATT in its early years was crucially dependent upon U.S. hegemony in the world trading system. The enforcement powers of the GATT or any other body against a sovereign state are, in a legal sense, almost nonexistent. In the absence of strong legal enforcement, a strong arbitrator is necessary to ensure cooperation. The arbitration that successful multilateral agreements contain is unlikely in the absence of a hegemon to act as an enforcer and supporter of international institutions such as the GATT.

MINILATERALISM: COOPERATION IN THE 1980S

When international trade involves large-scale trade-specific assets, the international trade liberalization game takes on a Prisoner's Dilemma payoff structure. A hegemonic country can alter the rules of the game to facilitate cooperation, which is to the advantage of all. When the world trading system is not dominated by a hegemonic country, then cooperation requires alternative institutional arrangements to break the Prisoner's Dilemma. Each party compares the discounted present value of the expected benefits from cooperation against the discounted present value of the expected benefits from opportunism; and cooperation occurs only when its expected benefits outweigh those of opportunism.

Liberalization agreements among small groups of countries (i.e., bilateralism or minilateralism as opposed to multilateralism) are more likely to be successful under such circumstances for two reasons. First, the benefits and costs of liberalization must be carefully allocated among participating countries to arrive at a mutually acceptable agreement. Such allocations become more difficult as the number of parties rises, so small groups enjoy an advantage at the bargaining or negotiation stage. Second, an agreement once reached must somehow be enforced; and overcoming the difficulties of detecting opportunism requires effort. Monitoring within a small group is less costly and more effective than monitoring within a large group, so small groups also enjoy an advantage over larger ones at the enforcement stage. Multilateralism, nondiscrimination, and most-favored-nation status were the most important norms within the GATT during the early years when cooperation was based upon U.S. hegemony. More recently, the outstanding examples of successful trade liberalization have been bilateral or minilateral. Automobile trade between the United States and Canada has been relatively free for the last twenty years even though the industry worldwide has been subject to a growing web involving almost every conceivable form of trade barrier. In current negotiations, the United States and Canada are seeking to extend the liberalization beyond the automobile industry to a free-trade pact eliminating all barriers to trade. Israel has completed bilateral free-trade pacts with both the EC and the United States. The agreement between Israel and the United States (although obviously supported by a special political relationship) has generated particular interest as a model for future liberalization because of its successful handling of several previously troublesome areas of trade. Even within the GATT itself, with its strong organizational commitment to multilateralism, agreements among small groups (at least in comparison with the ninety contracting parties) have become more common. Most of the progress made in sticky areas at the Tokyo Round (e.g., the codes on subsidies, government procurement, and other nontariff barriers) occurred in a minilateral framework. Those successes earned some temporary and grudging support for a less than completely multilateral approach even from those who believe that the hope for long-term liberalization continues to lie in multilateralism.[46]

Beyond the use of minilateralism to alleviate bargaining and monitoring problems, the main tools for promoting cooperation under a Prisoner's Dilemma with no hegemon include issue linkage, the use of self-enforcing agreements or the threat of cancellation for noncompliance, and the provision and taking of economic *hostages.*[47] Examples of each can easily be found in recent international trade relations.

Issue linkage has a long and interesting history in international trade negotiations. Linkage can occur in two forms. The first and most obvious is linkage of several goods on which trade is to be liberalized in a single agreement. One stage of the U.S.-Israeli free-trade pact, for example, covers aluminum, gold jewelry, radio-navigational equipment, refrigerators, cut roses, and tomatoes. These are goods that proved to be especially sensitive in the negotiations and are included in the final stage of the pact to take effect (in 1995). A second, more extensive means of linkage is the formation of long-standing groups such as customs unions within which a range of decisions are made collectively. Linkages can be forged not only across issue areas at a point in time but across time as well. By creating an iterated game situation, such groups make a contribution toward cooperation along the lines Robert Axelrod suggests.[48]

Continuity is important for two reasons. First, the essence of the transaction-specificity of assets is that it places a premium on continuity of trading relationships. Otherwise, the value of the assets is lost since they are, by definition, less valuable in alternative relationships. Second, because of the possibility of continuity, intertemporal linkages become incentives for cooperation. Ironically, these two roles imply that continuity is both an inhibitor and a facilitator of cooperation. The need for continuity (or its mirror image, the vulnerability to opportunistic protectionism) that arises in the presence of transaction-specific assets is the source of the Prisoner's Dilemma payoff structure that blocks cooperation. But continuity in the sense of ability to make future cooperation contingent on current cooperation can prevent opportunism.

Agreements that explicitly use future benefits from a relationship as a carrot for current cooperation are called *self-enforcing agreements.*[49] Cancellation is the only possible punishment for opportunistic violations in a self-enforcing agreement; so if a party behaves opportunistically, then the other party automatically terminates the agreement. As a principle of self-help, self-enforcing agreements are used in areas where effective third-party enforcement is lacking; and international trade is obviously one such area. The need for self-enforcing agreements automatically to impose punishment on an opportunistic party provides a nonprotectionist argument for reciprocity. The increased emphasis in recent years on reciprocity has been interpreted as a move toward a less open trading system. It has been argued that the meaning of the term *reciprocity* has been changed from a positive concept involving mutual liberalization to a negative concept involving threats and retaliation similar to *tit-for-tat.* Even threats to withdraw from future cooperation may induce cooperation, however, in an international system where agreements need strong elements of self-enforcement.[50]

Voluntary provision of a hostage or bond by a party to a trade agreement serves two purposes. First, the hostage raises the cost of opportunism by the value (to the provider) of the hostage. Second, the willingness to provide a hostage signals to the recipient the provider's intention not to behave opportunistically. During the fifteenth-century trade wars between England and the Hanseatic League, English merchants in Prussia were required to post direct bonds against the levying of British taxes on traders from the League. Unfortunately for the prospects for cooperation, the use of the hostages violated a cardinal rule: punishment was not reliably directed at those responsible for opportunism. Retaliation was sanctioned against any citizen of the other side, so the true enforcement power of the hostages was lost.[51] In a more modern context, some forms of technical trade standards such as safety, pollution, and health regulations may serve as a form of hostage taking. Exporting countries must invest in the (transaction-specific) assets necessary to meet the standards; and a loss of the market means losing the value of the assets.

CONCLUSION

Given the potential of international trade to be mutually beneficial and the existence of transaction costs and associated enforcement problems, a variety of forms of trade liberalization agreements should be expected. In particular, the alternative to unilateral liberalization or to multilateral nondiscriminatory liberalization is not necessarily protectionism. We have focused on the politico-economic environment (hegemonic or nonhege-monic) and on the extent of transaction-specific investment as the deter-minants of the scope for opportunism and, therefore, as the determinants of the form of successful trade agreements.

When investment is generic or footloose, the discipline of the market-place provides an adequate governance structure for trade; and unilateral liberalization is viable as in the case of nineteenth-century Britain. When investment is transaction-specific, the discipline of the marketplace must be bolstered or replaced. A hegemonic country may act as an arbitrator and supporter of international institutions, thereby facilitating multilat-eral liberalization conducted at least cost under institutions such as the GATT during the period of U.S. hegemony. In a nonhegemonic politico-economic environment, agreements must become more self-contained. Minilateral, reciprocal agreements embodying binding precommitments to compliance are most likely to be successful under such circumstances; and such agreements have, in fact, become prevalent during the decline of U.S. hegemony.

NOTES

1. For example, contractual promises extracted through duress, fraud, or undue influence may be exempt from enforcement.
2. J. A. C. Conybeare, "International Organization and the Theory of Property Rights," *International Organization* 34 (Summer 1980), pp. 325–326.
3. J. Stoessinger, "The Anatomy of the Nation-State and the Nature of Power," in M. Smith, R. Little, and M. Shackleton, eds., *Perspectives on World Politics* (London: Croom Helm, 1981), p. 26.
4. The members of the two groups discussed here accept to a greater or lesser extent the desirability of a liberal international trading system. A third group could be added, including many Marxist analysts, who do not accept the basic premise of mutual gains from liberal world trade.
5. A variety of perspectives can be found in R. Gilpin, *U.S. Power and the Multi-national Corporation* (New York: Basic, 1975); C. P. Kindleberger, *The World in Depression* (Berkeley: University of California Press, 1973), and "Domi-nance and Leadership in the International Economy," *International Studies Quarterly* 25 (June 1981), pp. 242–254; R. Keohane, "The Theory of Hege-monic Stability and Changes in Inernational Ecnonomic Regimes," in O. R. Holsti, R. M. Siverson, and A. L. George, eds., *Change in the International System* (Boulder: Westview, 1980); S. D. Krasner, "State Power and the Struc-ture of International Trade," *World Politics* 38 (April 1976), pp. 317–343; and D. Snidal, "The Limits of Hegemonic Stability Theory," *International Organi-zation* 39 (Autumn 1985), pp. 579–614.
6. See Conybeare, "International Organization"; R. Keohane, *After Hegemony: Cooperation and Discord in the World Political Economy* (Princeton: Prince-ton University Press, 1984); S. Strange, "Protectionism and World Politics," *International Organization* 39 (Spring 1985), pp. 233–260; and B. V. Yar-brough and R. M. Yarbrough, "Free Trade, Hegemony, and the Theory of

Agency," *Kyklos* 38, fasc. 3 (1985), pp. 348–364, "Reciprocity, Bilateralism, and Economic 'Hostages': Self-Enforcing Agreements in International Trade," *International Studies Quarterly* 30 (March 1986), pp. 7–21, and "Opportunism and Governance in International Trade: After Hegemony, What?" (Paper read at the National Bureau of Economic Research Conference on the Political Economy of Trade Policy, MIT Endicott House, Dedham, Mass., 10–11 January 1986).

7. These questions are the focus of the traditional hegemonic stability literature as well as of business-cycle theories of trade policy.

8. This question is emphasized in political economy, public choice, and pressure-group theories of trade policy.

9. The other questions mentioned can also be addressed using the framework developed in this article. However, we chose to limit our focus to the single question of the various possible forms of international trade liberalization. Understanding the historical variation in the structure of international trade liberalization is essential to progress toward a general structural or systemwide theory of trade policy. Some theories that have been suggested (e.g., hegemonic stability) may be able to explain this historical variation; others (e.g., business-cycle theories or domestic pressure-group theories) seem by their nature less likely to be able to address this question, although they certainly play a role in the actual determination of trade policy.

10. J. D. Richardson has suggested the term *minilateralism* for agreements among small numbers of like-minded participants; see, for example, his "Trade-Policy Implications of 'Strategic' Economic Models" (Paper read at the NBER Conference on the Political Economy of Trade Policy, MIT Endicott House, Dedham, Mass. (10–11 January 1986).

11. Transaction costs include information, negotiation, contracting, and inspection or enforcement costs. See R. Coase, "The Problem of Social Cost," *Journal of Law and Economics* 3 (October 1960), pp. 1–44.

12. This general approach to problems has come to be known by various names, including transaction-costs economics and the economics of organization. See O. E. Williamson, *The Economic Institutions of Capitalism* (New York: Free, 1985); B. V. Yarbrough and R. M. Yarbrough, "Institutions for the Governance of Opportunism in International Trade," *Journal of Law, Economics, and Organization* (forthcoming).

13. For a similar caution in a business-regulation context, see B. Klein, "Transaction Cost Determinants of 'Unfair' Contractual Relations," *American Economic Review* 70 (1980), pp. 356–362.

14. The primary assumptions include competitive output and factor markets, the absence of external effects in production or consumption, and the absence of economies of scale.

15. Keohane, *After Hegemony,* especially pp. 51–55.

16. Factors such as monopoly power, economies of scale, and externalities in production and consumption are ignored or, alternatively, are assumed to be dealt with using policies other than restrictions on trade.

17. The division of gainers and losers refers to the short run. In the long run, the owners of resources used intensively in production of the country's goods of comparative advantage gain from liberalization, while the owners of resources used intensively in production of the country's goods of comparative disadvantage lose according to the Stolper-Samuelson Theorem.

18. This is a functional view of institutions, holding that the existence of institutions can be understood through the functions that those institutions serve. For a discussion in terms of international issues, see Keohane, *After Hegemony,* especially chaps. 5 and 6.

19. S. Piccioto, "Political Economy and International Law," in S. Strange, ed., *Paths to International Political Economy* (London: Allen & Unwin, 1984), p. 172.

20. R. E. Baldwin, "The Changing Nature of U.S. Trade Policy since World War II," in Baldwin and A. O. Krueger, eds., *The Structure and Evolution of Recent U.S. Trade Policy* (Chicago: University of Chicago Press, 1984), pp. 5–27.

21. See, for example, A. T. Kronman, "Mistake, Disclosure, Information, and the Law of Contracts," *Journal of Legal Studies* 7 (January 1978), pp. 1–34.

22. T. B. Millar, ed., *Current International Treaties* (New York: New York University Press, 1984), p. 2.

23. P. F. Cowhey and E. Long, "Testing Theories of Regime Change: Hegemonic Decline or Surplus Capacity?" *International Organization* 37 (Spring 1983), p. 178.

24. J. A. C. Conybeare, "Trade Wars: A Comparative Study of Anglo-Hanse, Franco-Italian, and Hawley-Smoot Conflicts," in K. A. Oye, ed., *Cooperation under Anarchy* (Princeton: Princeton University Press, 1986), p. 159.

25. Cowhey and Long, "Testing Theories."

26. Williamson, *Economic Institutions.* Transaction-specific investment can occur in any durable asset, including human skills. The term *capital* is used to denote durability.

27. Williamson, *Economic Institutions,* especially pp. 194–195.

28. S. Strange, "The Management of Surplus Capacity: or, How Does Theory Stand up to Protectionism 1970s Style?" *International Organization* 33 (Summer 1979), pp. 303–334; S. Strange and R. Tooze, eds., *The International Politics of Surplus Capacity* (London: Butterworth, 1980); L. Tsoukalis and A. da Silva Ferreira, "Management of Industrial Surplus Capacity in the European Community," *International Organization* 34 (Summer 1980), pp. 355–376; Cowhey and Long, "Testing Theories."

29. Cowhey and Long, "Testing Theories," p. 163.

30. For more extensive discussion of the concept of hegemony, see the works mentioned in nn. 5 and 6.

31. This line of reasoning, if carried further, leads to the Marxist view of hegemony as represented in the work of Stephen Hymer, e.g., "The Efficiency (Contradictions) of Multinational Corporations," *American Economic Review* 60 (1970), pp. 441–448.

32. See, for example, T. J. McKeown, "Hegemonic Stability Theory and 19th-Century Tariff Levels in Europe," *International Organization* 37 (Winter 1983), pp. 73–91; Cowhey and Long, "Testing Theories"; Keohane, *After Hegemony;* Snidal, "Limits."

33. For a detailed explanation, see Yarbrough and Yarbrough, "Free Trade, Hegemony." The terminology *hegemonic cooperation* is from Keohane, *After Hegemony,* p. 55.

34. See J. A. C. Conybeare, "Public Goods, Prisoners' Dilemmas and the International Political Economy," *International Studies Quarterly* 28 (1984), pp. 5–22.

35. Keohane, *After Hegemony,* p. 39.

36. J. Gannett, "The Role of Military Power," in Smith et al., *Perspectives,* p. 71.
37. A. I. MacBean and P. N. Snowden, *International Institutions in Trade and Finance* (London: Allen & Unwin, 1981), p. 79.
38. For a more detailed examination of the incentives facing the hegemon in its bargaining with other countries, see B. V. Yarbrough and R. M. Yarbrough, "Side-payments and Holdouts in a Principal-Agent Model" (Working paper, Department of Economics, Amherst College, 1985).
39. See E. D. Elliott, B. A. Ackerman, and J. C. Millian, "Toward a Theory of Statutory Evolution: The Federalization of Environmental Law," *Journal of Law, Economics, and Organization* 1 (Fall 1985), p. 325.
40. A. O. Hirschman, *National Power and the Structure of Foreign Trade* (Berkeley: University of California Press, 1945).
41. Conybeare, "Trade Wars," especially pages 152–158.
42. See J. T. Cuddington and R. I. McKinnon, "Free Trade versus Protectionism: A Perspective," in *Tariffs, Quotas and Trade: The Politics of Protectionism* (San Francisco: Institute for Contemporary Studies, 1979). The bilateral Cobden-Chevalier treaty was an exception to the basic unilateralism of Britain's trade policy, but noneconomic considerations were prominent in the negotiation of the treaty.
43. McKeown, "Hegemonic Stability."
44. Cuddington and McKinnon, "Free Trade," p. 12.
45. See Yarbrough and Yarbrough, "Reciprocity, Bilateralism," p. 12.
46. For example, R. Vernon, "International Trade Policy in the 1980s," *International Studies Quarterly* 26 (December 1982), pp. 504–505.
47. O. E. Williamson, "Credible Commitments: Using Hostages to Support Exchange," *American Economic Review* 73 (1983), pp. 519–540.
48. R. Axelrod, *The Evolution of Cooperation* (New York: Basic, 1984).
49. For development of the general theory of self-enforcing agreements, see L. Telser, "A Theory of Self-enforcing Agreements," *Journal of Business* 27 (1980), pp. 27–44; for international applications, see Yarbrough and Yarbrough, "Reciprocity, Bilateralism."
50. J. L. Goldstein and S. D. Krasner, "Unfair Trade Practices: The Case for a Differential Response," *American Economic Review* 74 (1984), pp. 282–287; Axelrod, *Evolution.*
51. Conybeare, "Trade Wars," pp. 153–157.

The Political Economy of International Trade

Benjamin J. Cohen

John A. C. Conybeare. *Trade Wars: The Theory and Practice of International Commercial Rivalry.* New York: Columbia University Press, 1987.

Robert Gilpin. *The Political Economy of International Relations.* Princeton, N.J.: Princeton University Press, 1987.

David A. Lake. *Power, Protection, and Free Trade: International Sources of U.S. Commercial Strategy, 1887–1939.* Ithaca, N.Y.: Cornell University Press, 1988.

Helen V. Milner. *Resisting Protectionism: Global Industries and the Politics of International Trade.* Princeton, N.J.: Princeton University Press, 1988.

Richard Rosecrance. *The Rise of the Trading State: Commerce and Conquest in the Modern World.* New York: Basic Books, 1986.

For economists trained in the conventional neoclassical tradition, the subject of international trade is inherently frustrating. On the one hand, we have our theory, descended from Adam Smith and David Ricardo, which stresses all the benefits of open markets and unrestricted exchange between nations based on underlying differences of comparative advantage. On the other hand, we have the real world, where forces of mercantilism and protection always seem rampant if not wholly dominant. Rarely in the economics profession do we encounter greater dissonance between what we are taught in principle and what we observe in practice. And try as we might to find logical reasons for all this in the tenets of our own discipline, ultimately we are tempted simply to throw up our hands and proclaim: "It's all politics!"

Benjamin J. Cohen. "The Political Economy of International Trade," *International Organization,* 44:2 (Spring 1990): pp. 261–281 by permission of The MIT Press, Cambridge, MA.

Enter the political scientists. Scholars trained in the study of international relations or comparative politics find it far less difficult to locate logical reasons for behavior and outcomes that traditional economic theory would regard as irrational. In their discipline, politics *is* all—or nearly so. The mercantilist element of trade is not an aberrant exogenous variable to be deplored but, rather, a central and systematic endogenous factor to be explained. In recent years, a veritable flood of literature has been produced by political scientists exploring the political economy of international trade.

What can economists learn from all this writing? That is the question addressed by this article, which reviews a sample of five reasonably representative contributions to the field published since the mid-1980s.[1] Two of the authors under consideration, Robert Gilpin and Richard Rosecrance, are senior scholars already well known and widely respected for their professional accomplishments. While Gilpin's book, a comprehensive treatise touching on much more than international trade alone, is intended mainly for a scholarly audience, Rosecrance's is written in a more popular vein and aims more for the general literate reader. The three remaining authors—John Conybeare, David Lake, and Helen Milner—are by contrast all at comparatively earlier stages of their careers and have written works primarily directed to specialists. Two of their three books, in fact, began life as doctoral dissertations.

My review will begin by setting the five contributions in their overall scholarly context. Studies of the politics of trade form an integral part of the broader field of international political economy (IPE); and like other work currently being done in the IPE field on other aspects of economic relations between states, writings on the political economy of trade tend to focus on either or both of two central sets of questions concerning actor behavior and system management. The logic of that research agenda will be followed here. The first of the two central sections of this essay will look at what the five authors have to say about the question of actor behavior, focusing in particular on the issue of levels of analysis and on the appropriate definition of sovereign state interests, while the second will address these scholars' responses to the question of how the international system is or could be managed, if at all, to contain conflict or promote cooperation in trade relations. The review will conclude with a brief summary of my main comments and conclusions.

THE RESEARCH AGENDA OF INTERNATIONAL POLITICAL ECONOMY

The emergence of IPE as a standard field of scholarly inquiry is a relatively recent phenomenon in the English-speaking world. As recently as two decades ago, economists and political scientists in the United States and similar nations barely talked to each other about their overlapping interests in the area of international relations, displaying instead what Susan Strange called a kind of *academic astigmatism.*[2] According to Joan Spero, the deep divide between the two disciplines could be attributed in part to the philosophical heritage of nineteenth-century liberalism, with its emphasis on the duality of the economic and political orders, and in part to the professional imperatives of modern academia, which tend to prize disciplinary specialization over cross-disciplinary adventurism.[3] Exceptions could always be found, of course, but mostly among Marxist commentators or others outside the mainstream of conventional Western scholarship. Within the intellectual mainstream, few challenged or even questioned the *disciplinary tunnel-vision*[4] that tended to characterize the social sciences.

Only toward the end of the 1960s were there serious efforts to bridge the divide between the specialties of international economics and world politics, efforts coinciding with the thawing of the Cold War and the first signs of decay in the monetary and trade regimes established at the end of World War II. From the economics side came such pioneering studies as Richard Cooper's *The Economics of Interdependence* and Charles Kindleberger's *Power and Money,* as well as Albert Hirschman's rediscovered classic, *National Power and the Structure of Foreign Trade.*[5] From the political science side came the innovative and imaginative work of Robert Keohane and Joseph Nye, Robert Gilpin, Stephen Krasner, and Peter Katzenstein, among others.[6] Within one decade, IPE came to be recognized as an exciting, emergent area of scholarship. After two decades, IPE is now firmly established in Western academic circles, especially among political scientists, as a legitimate research specialty in its own right, emphasizing formal integration of market and political analyses in the study of international affairs.

The research agenda of IPE focuses largely on two broad sets of questions. One set has to do with *actor behavior*—meaning, in particular, government behavior, since the fundamental unit of authority in the international system still remains the sovereign nation-state. What motivates government behavior in foreign economic relations, and how is it best explained and analyzed? The other has to do with *system management*—coping with the consequences of economic interdependence. How do state actors manage (or fail to manage) their conflicts, and what determines whether they cooperate or fail to cooperate to achieve common objectives? Methodologies used to seek answers to these questions vary, depending both on the disciplinary training of the individual scholar and on the nature of the specific issue-area under consideration. International trade, of course, is one of the most central of the issue-areas explored in the IPE literature.

Political scientists are not alone in studying the political economy of trade. Some economists have also been stimulated by recent intellectual developments to pay more attention to the political dimensions of trade.

But for the most part, scholars trained in the discipline of economics have chosen to focus on two rather narrowly drawn questions, both related to actor behavior. One question, reflecting an international extension of domestic public choice theory, has to do with the interindustry structure of protection in individual countries. In this area, work on what is sometimes called *endogenous* trade policy has been mostly empirical and quantitative, seeking to explain the marked differences that we observe across sectors in either the level of import protection provided or the extent of trade liberalization negotiated by governments.[7] The other question, reflecting an international extension of industrial organization theory, goes under the heading of *strategic* trade policy. In this area, work has primarily taken the form of more abstract theorizing focused on the implications that monopolistic elements in international markets (such as economies of scale, product differentiation, and rent seeking) have for the traditional case for free trade based largely on models of perfect competition.[8] Developments in the literature on strategic trade policy have been reviewed recently in this journal in an article by J. David Richardson.[9]

The contributions of political scientists, by contrast, tend to be rather more diverse, covering a broader range of questions of both actor behavior and system management. As indicated, the sample of works under review here is representative. While two of the books, those by Lake and Milner, are primarily concerned with the formulation of commercial policy by individual governments, the remaining three all concentrate more on systemic issues of conflict and cooperation. Each of the five has its own distinct analytic focus.

Rosecrance offers perhaps the broadest focus: an analysis of nothing less than the entire system of international relations. In Rosecrance's view, the world is presently poised "between two fundamentally different modes of organizing international relations: a territorial system . . . and an oceanic or trading system."[10] The territorial system is composed of states preoccupied with the accumulation of power, defined in terms of land mass: "the more territory, the more power."[11] The trading system is composed of states preoccupied instead with economic development, defined in terms of improvements in consumption standards and in the allocation of productive resources: "progress sustained by the medium of international trade."[12] The main thesis of the book, taking a long historical perspective, is that a triumph of the trading system in international relations today would be the best possible guarantee of sustained world peace in the future.

Gilpin, too, offers a broad focus. His analysis of the "evolution of the international political economy over the next several decades"[13] encompasses all dimensions of economic relations between states, albeit set in a more formal theoretical context than is Rosecrance's treatment. For Gilpin, the central issue is the decline of American economic leadership of the postwar order: "The United States and its conception of a liberal order have dominated the postwar era, [but] with the relative decline of Ameri-

can power and the rise of economic powers that have different conceptions of legitimacy, the future of the liberal world economy has become
severely threatened."[14] In trading relations, this has meant the emergence of a *mixed* regime combining multilateralism with elements of
economic nationalism and regionalism which "may or may not prove
stable over the long run."[15]

Conybeare's aim is "to provide a perspective on trade wars"[16] through
development of a theoretical model based on a small number of game
structures. A variety of hypotheses about negotiating processes and outcomes are developed and then applied to a sample of six historical cases,
ranging from the Anglo-Hanse trade wars of the late Middle Ages to the
U.S.-European "chicken war" of the 1960s. The core theme of the book
is the need for an integrated analytic framework that would help explain
"why trade conflicts (including trade wars) occur, how they escalate, and
the types of bargaining behavior that one may expect to observe during
them."[17]

Lake also aims to provide an integrated analytic framework, though
in his case the object of explanation is the determination of policy within
states rather than the evolution of relations between states. A "theory of
trade strategy," in which protection and free trade are both conceived as
"legitimate and effective instruments of national policy," is developed and
then used to illuminate the evolution of U.S. commercial policy between
1887 and 1939.[18] In Lake's view, national trade interests and political
choices ultimately are shaped and influenced by the constraints and opportunities of the international economic structure. "Protection and free
trade . . . are not simply the result of domestic political pressures but the
considered response of self-seeking nation-states to varying international
structures."[19]

Finally, like Lake, Milner focuses specifically on trade policy formulation in individual states, but with emphasis more on the domestic political
pressures that are discounted in Lake's analysis. In particular, Milner
stresses the role of corporate trade preferences as influenced by changing
degrees of international economic integration over time, and she compares preference formation and policymaking among a number of different industries in the United States during the 1920s and 1970s and in
France during the 1970s. For Milner, "The consequences of interdependence are *internal* to states: they affect *domestic* social actors' policy
preferences, not states' policy instruments."[20]

Within such a diverse body of literature, it is hardly surprising to find
numerous points of controversy as well as areas of shared agreement. But
for economists unaccustomed to the terms of debate among political scientists, it can all be quite confusing. How do we know what is accepted by
consensus among political scientists, since (as in any discipline) this is often
left unstated? How do we judge among alternative viewpoints, since (as
in all the social sciences) the empirical evidence is often indeterminate?
And, above all, how much do we actually learn, since a certain amount of

insight into the political economy of trade is already available in the work of fellow economists? A closer look at key analytic issues common across the breadth of this literature is required before answers to these questions can be essayed.

THE QUESTION OF ACTOR BEHAVIOR

Two issues related to actor behavior permeate the writing of political scientists: the issue of how best to explain or analyze the foreign economic policy behavior of governments and the issue of what it is that fundamentally motivates states in their international economic relations. The first of these is a methodological issue involving the familiar problem of choosing among applicable levels of analysis. The second is more conceptual and involves an appropriate definition of sovereign state interests. Both issues involve crucial intellectual judgments that can significantly influence the outcome of analysis.

The Choice of Level of Analysis

In trying to understand the foreign economic policy behavior of governments, political scientists variously espouse three alternative *levels* of analysis, each corresponding to one of Kenneth Waltz's well-known *images* of international relations.[21] Perhaps most popular is the *system level* (or structural level) of analysis, analogous to Waltz's "third" image, which focuses on the sovereign state itself, treated as a rational and unitary actor, as the basic unit of study. The methodological value of the systemic type of approach is that it makes state preferences constants (exogenous) rather than variables (endogenous) for purposes of analysis. Since conceptions of self-interest may thus be assumed to be given and unchanging, discussion is able to concentrate exclusively on constraints and incentives for government behavior that derive from the broader structure of interstate relations. Behavior, as Waltz has described it more recently, is studied from the *outside-in.*[22]

But, of course, behavior may also be studied from the *inside-out,* concentrating on the internal characteristics of states rather than solely on their external environment. That is the purpose of both the remaining types of approach to be found in the IPE literature. Better known is the *unit level* of analysis, analogous to Waltz's *second* image, which focuses attention on the strategic interactions among all domestic actors, inside or outside the government, with actual or potential influence on a state's foreign actions—in short, the political and institutional basis at home for economic policy preferences abroad. Less familiar, though not necessarily less important, is the *cognitive level* of analysis, analogous to Waltz's *first* image, encompassing the base of consensual knowledge or *economic culture* that legitimates policymaking at the unit level.[23]

For most purposes, both the unit and cognitive approaches can be subsumed under the single heading of *domestic-level analysis,* which is in contrast to *system-level analysis.* The attractions of either domestic-level or system-level analysis from a methodological point of view are clear. But it is equally clear that neither type of analysis is likely to prove sufficient per se to explain all of state behavior in the international political economy. Even while favoring one level or the other, most political scientists acknowledge that each is partial at best as a formal framework of analysis.

Both Conybeare and Lake, for example, clearly prefer system-level analysis for the development of their theoretical models. Yet both explicitly incorporate internal political and cognitive factors as additional influences on behavior. Milner, conversely, stresses the central role of political pressures at the domestic level in the formulation of foreign trade policy but formally admits systemic influences too through the role she assigns to changes in the degree of economic interdependence in her analysis, in a manner analogous to Peter Gourevitch's *second image reversed.* [24] The real issue in this context is not whether one level of analysis or the other might be complete on its own; clearly, neither is. Rather, the issue concerns the relative importance to be attached to variables at either the domestic or system level and the manner in which these variables can be presumed to relate and interact. On this issue, little consensus prevails for the guidance of economists or others.

For Gilpin and Rosecrance, indeed, the issue barely seems to exist. Although both make occasional references to the presumed importance of domestic politics or *ideology,* each quite clearly feels most comfortable simply treating states as unitary actors for purposes of exposition. For the three other authors, the issue exists but is treated in a relatively nonformal and unstructured fashion. Both Conybeare and Lake merely assert the primacy of system-level analysis, principally on the grounds of its parsimony, without convincingly demonstrating why internal political and cognitive factors must necessarily be relegated to a status of secondary importance in explaining state behavior. Each brings in domestic-level variables, such as rent seeking (Conybeare) or intragovernmental bargaining (Lake), to help account for deviations from expectations derived from their respective structural models. But neither explains why it could not also be done the other way around (as many political scientists do), starting first with an exclusively domestic model and then adding system-level variables as needed.[25] Milner, in reverse, argues for the centrality of domestic analysis but fails to formalize the links between internal and external influences on policy. The relationship between the two levels of analysis in her approach is specified in a manner that is not much more than ad hoc.

What is needed is a methodology that considers domestic- and system-level variables simultaneously, rather than sequentially, and specifies whatever interactions there may be among all relevant variables in a rigorous manner. In practical terms, this would mean not only more systematic efforts at abstract model building but also greater use of appropriate empirical tests—either carefully structured case study comparisons or else more formal statistical procedures—to evaluate alternative hypotheses concerning the foreign economic policy behavior of governments. Certainly more use could be made of standard multiple regression techniques, extending the sort of work that has been done on questions of endogenous trade policy in recent years by economists as well as by the occasional political scientist.[26] Or in cases in which the applicability of regression techniques is limited by problems inherent in a linear probability model, it might be possible to employ other, more complex tools such as discriminant analysis, probit or logit analysis, or even experimental simulations. Although these methodologies have not typically been applied to questions of commercial policy,[27] some of them have been used with some success to explain choices of exchange rate arrangements by different governments.[28] In principle, the procedures would permit effective testing of hypotheses that simultaneously incorporate factors at both the domestic and system levels of analysis, including, for example, interest group pressures of the sort stressed by Milner as well as national strategic concerns like those emphasized by Lake.

Admittedly, there are considerable practical difficulties in applying empirical tests—particularly formal econometric techniques—to questions of this kind. Especially problematic, as past work on endogenous trade policy has demonstrated, is the struggle to operationalize satisfactorily many of the key variables identified by deductive theory. In the absence of adequately refined or disaggregated statistics, analysts must use proxy measures that can often be interpreted to support more than one competing hypothesis. Still, there seems little alternative to further efforts along this line if analysts are to be able to achieve more systematic specification of the relative roles of factors at each level and the nature of the relationships among them. More powerful explanations of state behavior could eventually result.

The Definition of State Interests

Closely related to the issue of the level of analysis is the issue of an appropriate definition of state interests. What is it that fundamentally motivates governments in their international economic relations? What are they trying to achieve? In formal language, what is a state's preference ordering? What are the arguments of its utility function?

These questions are obviously related to the level-of-analysis issue in the sense that the choice of analytic approach at least partly predetermines the range of goals that governments can be presumed to regard as relevant. A state assumed to be responsive to domestic political pressures could logically have a preference ordering quite different from that of a state conceived as a unitary actor. But the two issues are not identical. Even states conceived exclusively as unitary actors may potentially respond to quite different notions of utility. The issue of defining state interests is more than methodological; it goes to the very basics of what governments *care about*.

On this more conceptual issue, political scientists clearly do have something to teach economists. Economists, after all, tend to be rather narrow-minded when it comes to the question of interests, reflecting the traditional biases of their profession. For anyone trained in neoclassical orthodoxy, utility is instinctively defined simply in terms of real economic welfare—a term synonymous with the amount of goods and services available for final use—to the exclusion of all other possible values or goals.[29] While consumers seek to maximize their consumption, producers seek to maximize their net income in order to gain the greatest possible command over goods and services. By extension, therefore, it seems only logical to assume that governments, too, seek to maximize real economic welfare, in this case for the nation as a whole. The sole interest of a state is or should be to gain the greatest possible income for its society. All else, in the eyes of the economist, is irrational.[30]

Is it any surprise, then, that economists find the subject of international trade so inherently frustrating? A variety of routes have been followed in attempts to resolve the apparent dissonance between inherited principle and observed practice in nations' trade policies. Some economic theorists have looked for arguments for protection that could be regarded as logically compatible with global income maximization, such as the traditional infant-industry argument, which advocates temporary trade restriction as a means to promote new additions to the world's efficient productive capacity. Others have focused on arguments compatible with income maximization at the national level, such as the well-known optimum tariff argument, which suggests that a country with monopolistic or monopsonistic power in international markets can shift the terms of trade to its advantage and thereby capture a greater share of the total gains from trade. Contemporary theorizing about strategic trade policy takes the same route, contending that in the presence of imperfectly competitive markets, governments might be able to use trade policy to shift profits (monopoly rents) from foreign to domestic corporations and thereby improve the competitive position of their national industries. And yet others have sought explanations framed in terms of income maximization for particular groups within the nation-state, as in studies of endogenous trade policy. But none of these routes, it is evident, have proved especially satisfactory. As Lake remarks dryly, "Economists have struggled to make the real world of trade policy conform to their model, with limited success."[31]

Political scientists, on the other hand, have long recognized that governments care about more than merely maximizing income. At a minimum, states also care about the preservation of their political sovereignty and territorial integrity—in short, their *national security*. At a maximum, there may be a whole range of additional values that they pursue, covering everything from domestic distributional objectives to the international prestige of their national language and culture. Economists have struggled precisely because their standard models exclude all such *noneconomic* motivations. As Harry Johnson, known in his generation as the quintessential economists' economist, lamented a quarter of a century ago, this exclusion left economists "without a theory capable of explaining a variety of important and observable phenomena, such as the nature of tariff bargaining, the commercial policies adopted by various countries, the conditions under which countries are willing to embark on customs unions, and the arguments and considerations that have weight in persuading countries to change their commercial policies."[32] If economists would take a cue from political scientists and open up the analysis of state motivations to include equally relevant noneconomic interests, this certainly would help to make the real world conform more to theory.

There is a problem, however. The longer the list of interests, obviously, the more unwieldy is the analysis. Realism is gained, but at the sacrifice of parsimony and probably rigor. The conventional response of political scientists to this problem is to subsume most or all noneconomic motivations under the convenient catch-all heading of *power,* conceived as a single means to a variety of ends. Power, the ability to influence outcomes, becomes what governments care about along with *wealth,* the shorthand term used for income maximization. This is precisely what Gilpin had in mind a decade and a half ago when he defined IPE as "the reciprocal and dynamic interaction in international relations of the pursuit of wealth and the pursuit of power."[33] It is this interest in power, inherently a political matter, that economists have for too long tended to ignore.

But how important is the interest in power, relative to the state's interest in wealth, and precisely how do the two motivations relate and interact? Here again, little consensus prevails among political scientists for the guidance of economists or others. Opinions vary widely about the weights implicitly to be attached to each of these motivations in the utility functions of states. The relationship between the two goals tends for the most part to be treated in a manner that is nonformal at best and ad hoc at worst. Economists can certainly benefit from being reminded that power matters. But beyond that, it is not at all clear what more they actually learn about this issue from the comments of political scientists, who follow a variety of approaches.

One approach, exemplified by Conybeare, simply mimics economists by specifying income maximization as the sole objective of government policy. In Conybeare's theoretical model, power is purely instrumental and is not a goal in itself. States are treated as unitary actors effectively equivalent to the atomistic profit-seeking firms of familiar microeconomic analysis. In this respect, his system-level model differs not at all from the models of strategic trade policy developed by economists.

A second approach, exemplified by Rosecrance, simplifies the problem by in effect assigning each of the two goals, power and wealth, to separate types of states: territorial states, which seek power, and trading states, which seek wealth. The dichotomy is not absolute, he concedes. While "defense and territory are not the only concerns of states," he argues, "no nation entirely neglects its territorial defense and stakes its livelihood solely on trade" and "every state procures some defense and participates in some trade."[34] But the distinction between states is in fact drawn so sharply that Rosecrance's gesture of qualification is effectively nullified: "Nations at all times and places have had to decide to emphasize one method or the other. . . . The difference between states is that some rely primarily on military force and only incidentally engage in trade; others make their livelihood in trade and use defense only against the most remote contingencies. . . . Some states are primarily trading states, [while] others are maximizers of power and territory."[35] Such an approach is an improvement over models that emphasize the pursuit of wealth alone and ignore the goal of power, but it is still remote from the real world in which every state can be legitimately assumed to have a keen interest in both.

The solution, of course, is to explicitly incorporate both goals into the presumed utility functions of individual governments and to treat them as inextricably linked. That is the most typical approach among political scientists, exemplified by Gilpin and Lake, each of whom stresses the simultaneous concern of states with wealth and power alike.[36] Few students of trade politics today seem inclined to join Conybeare in solely emphasizing income maximization in the definition of state interests, a perspective most consistent with the traditional liberalism of neoclassical economics. But neither do many now subscribe completely to the exclusive preoccupation with power accumulation characteristic of the realist school of international relations theory. Liberalism implies that all states are like Rosecrance's trading states, caring only about the *absolute gains* from trade and indifferent to the gains achieved by others. Realism, by contrast, suggests that every state is like Rosecrance's territorial state, valuing *relative gains* (positional advantage) above all. In practice, clearly, both perspectives are needed, as Gilpin and Lake each properly insist. Liberalism and realism—absolute gains versus relative gains—can be assumed to be in constant competition for the minds and hearts of policy-makers.

But the solution is not only to acknowledge the importance and linkage of these two pivotal perspectives but also to spell out and formalize their relationship—to provide clear, systematic insight into how they fit together functionally in the preference orderings of different governments. How much does any given state care about absolute versus relative gains, to what extent are these interests regarded as substitutes rather than as complementary, what are the trade-offs between them, and how and why do these trade-offs change over time? Here again, more systematic effort at abstract model building as well as greater use of carefully structured case study comparisons or more formal statistical procedures could aid in the formulation and evaluation of alternative hypotheses. It may never be possible to settle definitively the contentious debate between liberalism and realism, which encompasses issues far broader than just the political economy of trade and, indeed, is as old as the study of international relations itself. But it is surely incumbent on scholars in this area to build as much formal structure as possible into their discussions if they really wish to add significantly to our understanding of the motivations behind trade policy.

THE QUESTION OF SYSTEM MANAGEMENT

Beyond the question of the behavior of individual actors is the question of system management, the manner in which states act collectively to preserve the mutual benefits of their trade relations. Economists have much to learn on this question, since they themselves devote so little time to formal study of the governance of international economic structures. For most economists of neoclassical persuasion, the economic interdependence of nations is simply a given, the natural consequence of market-driven specialization within a global division of labor. It is left largely to students of world politics to explore systematically how that interdependence can be maintained and protected—how conflict can be suppressed and cooperation promoted—in the absence of some de jure substitute for the *magistracy* role (to use Adam Smith's word) played by government within nations.[37] As the flood of recent literature on the political economy of trade testifies, political scientists have not hesitated to rise to the intellectual challenge.

Typically, one of two directions is taken by political scientists to address the question of system management: *upward-looking* analysis, which examines the consequences for the system as a whole of the policy choices made by individual actors, or *downward-looking* analysis, which looks at the implications for individual actors of the way the system as a whole is organized.[38] Examples of the former are provided by Conybeare and Lake, each of whom employs tools of game theory to consider the processes and outcomes of strategic interactions among trading states. One example of the latter is provided by Gilpin, who makes use of elements of regime theory to focus attention directly on the normative and institutional context in which the ongoing commercial interactions among states are conducted. Economists have much to learn from both types of approach, though here too limits are set by a lack of consensus on crucial analytic points.

Upward-looking Analysis

The logic of game theory, as Duncan Snidal has pointed out, can be applied to the analysis of international relations in at least four different ways: as metaphor, analogy, model, or theory.[39] Most ubiquitous are uses of game structures as metaphor and analogy, intended mainly to highlight similarities or differences between various types of entities or interactions. Such applications are undoubtedly of heuristic value, helping to provide insight or provoke thought, but they are also inherently limited by their susceptibility to misunderstanding or misuse. More ambitious are uses of game structures as models or theory, intended to develop systematic and generalizable propositions about actor behavior in alternative circumstances. These are the sorts of uses pursued by Conybeare and Lake.

For both Conybeare and Lake, game models offer a concise means to define and distinguish among different strategic settings. Each setting is characterized in the usual terms by its own configuration or matrix of payoffs, understood to stand for the preference orderings of all players among available alternative combinations of strategies. Each payoff matrix, in turn, leads to a different set of incentives and disincentives for the central decision-makers in individual countries. In Conybeare's approach, direct use is made of the familiar noncooperative games of prisoners' dilemma, stag hunt, and chicken. In Lake's approach, four rather less familiar structures derived from standard variable-sum models are identified and labeled *hegemony, bilateral opportunism, multilateral opportunism,* and *unilateral opportunism.* In both approaches, the nature of the strategic setting at the international level becomes the ultimate determinant of policy choices at the national level.

Obviously, there is much that can be learned from applications of this sort about the conditions or *circumstantial dimensions*[40] that will promote either conflict or cooperation in trade relations. One key insight of both approaches, for example, is the central role that an actor's relative size plays in determining bargaining strategies and outcomes. But inherent in these applications are distinct limitations that must be noted as well. Parsimonious and rigorous game-based analytic frameworks like those constructed by Conybeare and Lake are certainly capable of yielding relatively *strong* and precise hypotheses about actor behavior. They are not, however, likely to be as generalized as these authors would have us believe.

The limitations, as every serious game theorist knows, lie in the methodology of game theory itself. Two problems, in particular, stand out. One is the likelihood of multiple equilibriums in game models set in the iterated format favored by both Conybeare and Lake. It is surely not inappropriate to treat trade relations as a continuing, rather than a single-play, interaction. But because of the ever-present possibility that there could be significant changes in key variables over time—such as in the number of players, the magnitude of payoffs, the availability of information, or the size of different players' discount rates—repeated games are widely recognized to be poor tools for predictive purposes. For this reason, neither author's policy interpretations can be regarded as anything like definitive.

Even more critical is the familiar problem of specifying player motivations. Game models as such are only as good as the assumptions on which they are built. They provide insights into the strategic choices that can be expected of individual players once the orderings of all the actors' preferences are fully detailed. However, as Milner correctly notes, there is nothing in the essential logic of game theory that tells us how the configurations of payoffs get to be determined in the first place.[41] By their very nature, game models are silent on the subject of what initially motivates players. Preference orderings at the outset are simply assumed to be exogenously—that is, arbitrarily—determined. And it is clear that the more arbitrary the specification, the less generalizable is the result.[42] The point is well illustrated by Conybeare's and Lake's contrasting views on what role, if any, broader systemic considerations play in the trade strategies of *large* countries. While Conybeare, reasoning from the old optimum tariff argument, contends that large countries would selfishly and single-mindedly prefer trade restriction, even at the risk of destructive trade wars,[43] Lake asserts to the contrary that such states would also "possess incentives voluntarily to provide the infrastructure necessary for a liberal international economy."[44] Where the inputs are so different, is it any surprise that there could be profound disagreements about the outcomes?

Game theory's inherent silence on motivation would be a handicap in almost any analytic context. It is especially so in the context of international trade relations, where there is so little consensus about how governments define their own interests. The partiality shown by both Conybeare and Lake for system-level analysis is understandable, given game theory's fundamental premises and, in particular, its simplifying premise that all actors are purely unitary and rational and have invariant utility functions. It is a partiality also shared by most economists who write about strategic interactions between governments in the world economy.[45] But we know how unrealistic and potentially misleading that type of *black box* approach can be: helpful as a first approximation, perhaps, but certainly not the last word. In addressing the question of system management, there is no escaping the logically antecedent question of actor behavior stressed above, the question of why states order their preferences as they do. The limitation of even the most ambitious applications of game theory lies in the tendency to concentrate on what comes out of state conceptions of self-interest rather than what goes into them.

Downward-looking Analysis

An alternative to game theory is regime theory, characterized by Krasner as the study of the "implicit or explicit principles, norms, rules, and decision-making procedures around which actors' expectations converge in a given area of international relations."[46] Regime theory assumes that despite the absence of formal world government, interactions between sovereign states are not conducted in an environment of total anarchy. Rather, de facto substitutes tend to develop in many issue-areas, to a greater or lesser extent, to help contain conflict and promote cooperation.

Regimes exist because even the most power-oriented nations recognize the advantages that can potentially accrue from mutual restraint in the common interest. This is certainly evident in the area of trade relations, where quite explicit efforts have been made since World War II to maintain a formal regime under the auspices of the General Agreement on Tariffs and Trade (GATT).

The problem with the GATT regime, however, is that it appears to be losing its effectiveness as a constraint on the mercantilist impulses of individual states. Gilpin is hardly alone in suggesting that the future of the liberal world economy is threatened. All the authors under review agree that the postwar multilateral trading system is at something of a crossroads, "poised" (as Rosecrance says) between different modes of organization. And all agree as well that the problem is closely related to the decline of American economic leadership that Gilpin deplores. This brings us back to the issue of relative actor size highlighted by both Conybeare and Lake. GATT was established at a time of unquestioned U.S. dominance in commercial affairs and embodied principles largely drawn from America's own trade legislation; the apparent decay of the GATT regime has clearly coincided with a waning of America's overall economic *hegemony*. The issue is whether the openness of the trading system can be preserved now that the United States is manifestly no longer at the top of the heap—*after hegemony*, in Keohane's pithy phrase.[47] Can some alternative form of governance be found to enforce the "rules of the game," or is the GATT regime destined to wither away under the pressure of intensifying trade conflicts? This is, of course, the central question posed by the celebrated theory of hegemonic stability, which was developed more than a decade ago by Kindleberger, Gilpin, and Krasner[48] and which plainly continues to be central to debates among students of the political economy of trade.

The theory of hegemonic stability, in its original strong form, contended that hegemony was both a necessary and a sufficient condition for the maintenance of order in international economic relations. As Kindleberger stressed in his early formulation, "For the world economy to be stabilized, there has to be a stabilizer, one stabilizer."[49] Only the hegemonic power with the biggest stake in the system could be expected to take a firm interest in the responsibility for regime management, even if this also entailed bearing a disproportionate share of the cost. Others might be tempted into mercantilist *free riding*, risking a collective *market failure* of systemic breakdown. Only the hegemonic power could be counted on to be willing to pay the price of providing the *public good* of stability. Following its introduction, the theory initially enjoyed a considerable vogue in political science circles. In such strong form, it also had an obvious appeal to economists, not only because of the clarity of its central hypothesis but also because of the familiarity of the concepts borrowed from economic theory.

More recently, however, a substantial reaction has set in among political scientists, who are increasingly inclined to challenge both the premises and the conclusions of the theory.[50] And this in turn has plainly diminished the theory's appeal to economists, who once again find little consensus to provide them with guidance. Lake, for example, even while accepting the basic logic of the theory, questions whether hegemony is really a necessary condition for stability. That proposition, he correctly points out, "has no grounding in collective goods theory." Since "privileged groups need not be limited to one actor," there is "no a priori reason to conclude that international cooperation under a nonhegemonic system is impossible."[51] Conybeare, meanwhile, questions whether hegemony is even sufficient, since it may well be—again on optimum tariff grounds—that "the purely economic interest of hegemons is better served by restricting, rather than maintaining, the freedom of international economic transactions."[52] And Milner's whole analysis is based on empirical observations that appear to contradict the presumed correlation between hegemonic decline and rising protectionism.[53]

Even Gilpin now seems less deterministic about the theory. While he once attributed past periods of trade liberalism exclusively to the presence of hegemonic leadership (referring specifically to the Pax Britannica of the late nineteenth century and the Pax Americana of the first decades after World War II),[54] he now concedes that "the mere existence of a hegemonic power . . . is not sufficient to ensure the development of a liberal international economy."[55] Nor apparently is hegemony any longer even necessary in his view, since he now admits the possibility of alternative organizing principles to preserve an open trading regime, such as "an agreed-upon set of rules binding all" or "continuous policy coordination among the reigning economic powers."[56] America's economic leadership may be in decline today. But the potential consequences for the GATT regime are by no means as certain as the early strong form of the theory implied. In Gilpin's words, "No particular outcome is inevitable."[57]

Not surprisingly, therefore, opinions vary widely about where we are likely to go from here. Gilpin himself remains essentially pessimistic in forecasting a *mixed* regime of indeterminate stability. Rosecrance, at the other extreme, seems basically optimistic—primarily on cognitive grounds—that the "current equipoise in international relations" will ultimately be resolved intelligently in favor of the trading system.[58] In between, Milner cautiously suggests that "the persistence of interdependence, itself a legacy of U.S. hegemony, may promote the maintenance of an open trading system, even after hegemony has passed,"[59] while Lake expresses restrained confidence that "the international economy will remain relatively open and liberal, despite the decline of American hegemony, [because] considerable potential for international economic cooperation presently exists."[60] Conybeare, meanwhile, emphasizes the positive role that institutions such as GATT can play in limiting conflict or preventing trade wars.[61]

Diversity of opinion is no sin, of course. It is undoubtedly true that no particular outcome is inevitable. Nonetheless, can anyone blame economists for finding it all a bit confusing? In order to judge effectively among alternative scenarios of this kind, we would need more formal specification and modeling of all the key variables on which each alternative outcome depends as well as far more extensive and rigorous empirical studies. Otherwise, it all seems merely a game of idle speculation or casual empiricism. There is no reason why serious analysts should constrain their studies to the extremely small standard sample of past global hegemonies represented by the Pax Britannica and Pax Americana. They could also study regional trading systems that have been more or less openly hegemonic, including some of the formal imperial arrangements of the late nineteenth century, Nazi Germany's trade relations with southeastern Europe in the 1930s,[62] and the Soviet Union's relations with eastern Europe since World War II. Historical analysis is not limited to just two data points. The *bottom line* message therefore remains the same. Whether looking downward or upward, scholars have a responsibility to be as systematic and comprehensive as possible. The question of system management is surely too important to be left with so few definitive answers.

CONCLUSION

So what do economists learn from the works reviewed here? Mainly, they learn how much they need to broaden their horizons if they truly want to understand the real world of trade policy. They need to pay closer attention to the question of interests and, in particular, to the role that power plays in motivating actor behavior. They also need to focus more on the question of governance in the international trading system, the question of how sovereign states collectively manage to cope with their own potentially conflictual mercantilist impulses. Political scientists make a vital contribution by *endogenizing* questions of this kind. They sensitize us all to issues and variables that conventional economic analysis tends to ignore. They improve our conceptual frameworks by compelling us to reconsider what is really worth explaining.

But sensitization and conceptualization are only half the battle. It is also necessary to build a formal structure to the interactions between market and politics that appear to be most pivotal in the trade area. Factors at each level of analysis must be clearly and systematically specified; their relative roles and the nature of their functional relationships must be modeled in ways that are theoretically robust and empirically generalizable. The lack of consensus on key analytic issues among the authors under review does not detract from the importance of the insights they provide. But it does suggest that in the study of the political economy of trade, much work yet remains to be done by scholars on both sides of the traditional disciplinary divide between economics and political science.

NOTES

1. By focusing this review on just these five books, I of course do not mean to imply that this sample is adequate to capture the full richness and diversity of recent political science writings on the politics of trade. No limited sample could possibly do that. But it can be reasonably claimed that these five selections all fall sufficiently within the mainstream of the current literature to provide a useful basis for a critical evaluation of some of the main themes and questions currently being addressed by scholars working in the field.

2. See Susan Strange, *Sterling and British Policy: A Political Study of an International Currency in Decline* (London: Oxford University Press, 1971), p. 3. See also her classic article, "International Economics and International Relations: A Case of Mutual Neglect," *International Affairs* 46 (April 1970), pp. 304–315.

3. Joan Edelman Spero, *The Politics of International Economic Relations*, 3d ed. (New York: St. Martin's Press, 1985).

4. Robert O. Keohane and Joseph S. Nye, "World Politics and the International Economic System," in C. Fred Bergsten et al., eds., *The Future of the International Economic Order: An Agenda for Research* (Lexington, Mass.: D. C. Heath, 1973), p. 115.

5. See Richard N. Cooper, *The Economics of Interdependence: Economic Policy in the Atlantic Community* (New York: McGraw-Hill, 1968); Charles P. Kindleberger, *Power and Money: The Politics of International Economics and the Economics of International Politics* (New York: Basic Books, 1970); and Albert O. Hirschman, *National Power and the Structure of Foreign Trade* (Berkeley: University of California Press, 1945).

6. See Robert O. Keohane and Joseph S. Nye, eds., *Transnational Relations and World Politics* (Cambridge, Mass.: Harvard University Press, 1972); Robert O. Keohane and Joseph S. Nye, *Power and Interdependence: World Politics in Transition* (Boston: Little, Brown, 1977); Robert Gilpin, "Three Models of the Future," in C. Fred Bergsten and Lawrence B. Krause, eds., *World Politics and International Economics* (Washington, D.C.: Brookings Institution, 1975), pp. 37–60; Robert Gilpin, *U.S. Power and the Multinational Corporation: The Political Economy of Foreign Direct Investment* (New York: Basic Books, 1975); Stephen D. Krasner, "State Power and the Structure of International Trade," *World Politics* 28 (April 1976), pp. 317–347; Stephen D. Krasner, *Defending the National Interest: Raw Materials Investments and U.S. Foreign Policy* (Princeton, N.J.: Princeton University Press, 1978); and Peter J. Katzenstein, ed., *Between Power and Plenty: Foreign Economic Policies of Advanced Industrial States* (Madison: University of Wisconsin Press, 1978).

7. See, for example, J. J. Pincus, "Pressure Groups and the Pattern of Tariffs," *Journal of Political Economy* 83 (August 1975), pp. 757–778; Richard E. Caves, "Economic Models of Political Choice: Canada's Tariff Structure," *Canadian Journal of Economics* 9 (May 1976), pp. 278–300; Robert E. Baldwin, *The Political Economy of U.S. Postwar Trade Policy* (New York: New York University Graduate School of Business Administration, 1976); E. J. Ray, "Tariff and Nontariff Barriers in the United States and Abroad," *Review of Economics and Statistics* 63 (May 1981), pp. 161–168; R. P. Lavergne, *The Political Economy of U.S. Tariffs: An Empirical Analysis* (New York: Academic Press, 1983); and Robert E. Baldwin, *The Political Economy of U.S. Import Policy* (Cambridge,

Mass.: MIT Press, 1985). For a comprehensive, albeit brief, survey of this literature, see Robert E. Baldwin, "Trade Policies in Developed Countries," in Ronald W. Jones, ed., *International Trade: Surveys of Theory and Policy* (Amsterdam: North-Holland, 1986), pp. 184–194.

8. For an early survey of this literature, see Gene M. Grossman and J. David Richardson, *Strategic Trade Policy: A Survey of Issues and Early Analysis* (Princeton, N.J.: International Finance Section, 1985). For useful synopses, see the following works of Elhanan Helpman and Paul R. Krugman: *Market Structure and Foreign Trade* (Cambridge, Mass.: MIT Press, 1985), and *Trade Policy and Market Structure* (Cambridge, Mass.: MIT Press, 1989). For instructive collections of essays, see Paul R. Krugman, ed., *Strategic Trade Policy and the New International Economics* (Cambridge, Mass.: MIT Press, 1986); and Robert M. Stern, ed., *U.S. Trade Policies in a Changing World Economy* (Cambridge, Mass.: MIT Press, 1987).

9. See J. David Richardson, "The Political Economy of Strategic Trade Policy," *International Organization* 44 (Winter 1990), pp. 107–135. For an alternative perspective, see Klaus Stegemann, "Policy Rivalry Among Industrial States: What Can We Learn from Models of Strategic Trade Policy?" *International Organization* 43 (Winter 1989), pp. 73–100.

10. Rosecrance, *The Rise of the Trading State*, p. 16.

11. Ibid.

12. Ibid., p. 13.

13. Gilpin, *The Political Economy of International Relations*, p. 5.

14. Ibid., p. 228.

15. Ibid., p. 408.

16. Conybeare, *Trade Wars*, p. ix.

17. Ibid., p. 265.

18. Lake, *Power, Protection, and Free Trade*, p. 2.

19. Ibid., p. 3.

20. Milner, *Resisting Protectionism*, p. 292; emphasis added.

21. Kenneth N. Waltz, *Man, the State and War* (New York: Columbia University Press, 1959).

22. Kenneth N. Waltz, *Theory of World Politics* (Reading, Mass.: Addison-Wesley, 1979), p. 63.

23. For more on the cognitive approach, see Paul Egon Rorhlich, "Economic Culture and Foreign Policy: The Cognitive Analysis of Economic Policy Making," *International Organization* 41 (Winter 1987), pp. 61–92.

24. Peter A. Gourevitch, "The Second Image Reversed," *International Organization* 32 (Autumn 1978), pp. 881–912.

25. The relative merits of the two modes of analysis are, of course, a hotly debated topic among political scientists. See, for example, the contrasting comments of Katzenstein in *Between Power and Plenty*, pp. 12–15, and Robert O. Keohane in *After Hegemony: Cooperation and Discord in the World Political Economy* (Princeton, N.J.: Princeton University Press, 1984), pp. 25–26.

26. See, for example, John A. C. Conybeare, "Tariff Protection in Developed and Developing Countries: A Cross-Sectional and Longitudinal Analysis," *International Organization* 37 (Summer 1983), pp. 441–467.

27. One exception is Baldwin's *The Political Economy of U.S. Postwar Trade Policy*, which makes use of multivariate probit analysis.

28. See, for example, H. Robert Heller, "Choosing an Exchange Rate System,"

Finance and Development 14 (June 1977), pp. 23–26; H. Robert Heller, "Determinants of Exchange Rate Practices," *Journal of Money, Credit and Banking* 10 (August 1978), pp. 308–321; Jacob Dreyer, "Determinants of Exchange Rate Regimes for Currencies of Developing Countries: Some Preliminary Results," *World Development* 6 (April 1978), pp. 437–445; and Gordon Weil, *Exchange-Rate Regime Selection in Theory and Practice* (New York: New York University Graduate School of Business Administration, 1983).

29. The key word here is *instinctively.* It is not that economists are unaware of the potential for extending their traditional apparatus of utility analysis to incorporate other possible interests or goals; it is just that, typically, they are not inclined to do so. One frequently cited excuse is the difficulty of formally quantifying any values other than real income.

30. There are exceptions, of course. For an early (and unfortunately neglected) example, see Harry G. Johnson, "An Economic Theory of Protectionism, Tariff Bargaining, and the Formation of Customs Unions," *Journal of Political Economy* 73 (June 1965), pp. 256–283.

31. Lake, *Power, Protection, and Free Trade,* pp. 20–21.

32. Johnson, "An Economic Theory of Protectionism," p. 257.

33. Gilpin, *U.S. Power and the Multinational Corporation,* p. 43.

34. Rosecrance, *The Rise of the Trading State,* pp. 8, 17, and 30.

35. Ibid., pp. 17, 30, and 62.

36. See Gilpin, *The Political Economy of International Relations,* p. 32; and Lake, *Power, Protection, and Free Trade,* p. 22. The *locus classicus* on this subject is Jacob Viner's "Power Versus Plenty as Objectives of Foreign Policy in the Seventeenth and Eighteenth Centuries," *World Politics* 1 (October 1948), pp. 1–29.

37. A major exception is the economist Charles Kindleberger. See, for example, his *Government and International Trade* (Princeton, N.J.: International Finance Section, 1978).

38. Robert Axelrod and Robert O. Keohane, "Achieving Cooperation Under Anarchy: Strategies and Institutions," in Kenneth A. Oye, ed., *Cooperation Under Anarchy* (Princeton, N.J.: Princeton University Press, 1986), p. 252.

39. Duncan Snidal, "The Game *Theory* of International Politics," in Oye, *Cooperation Under Anarchy,* pp. 25–57.

40. Kenneth A. Oye, "Explaining Cooperation Under Anarchy: Hypotheses and Strategies," in Oye, *Cooperation Under Anarchy,* pp. 1–24.

41. Milner, *Resisting Protectionism,* p. 299.

42. The same criticism, of course, can also be made of standard theoretical models of economic behavior developed in the neoclassical tradition, which also by convention simply take preferences as given. Economists have no claim to superiority on this issue.

43. See Conybeare, *Trade Wars,* pp. 22–28. The optimum tariff argument was already fully developed by economic theorists more than three decades ago, with intellectual roots going as far back as the early nineteenth century. For some recent discussion, see W. M. Corden, "The Normative Theory of International Trade," in Jones, *International Trade,* pp. 82–86.

44. Lake, *Power, Protection, and Free Trade,* p. 38.

45. This is certainly true of the literature on strategic trade policy. It is also characteristic of most of the recent writing by economists on issues relating to international macroeconomic interdependence and policy coordination. For

useful surveys of the latter, see Richard N. Cooper, "Economic Interdependence and Coordination of Economic Policies," in Ronald W. Jones and Peter B. Kenen, eds., *Handbook of International Economics,* vol. 2 (Amsterdam: North-Holland, 1985), pp. 1195–1234; and Jocelyn Horne and Paul R. Masson, "Scope and Limits of International Economic Cooperation and Policy Coordination," *International Monetary Fund Staff Papers* 35 (June 1988), pp. 259–296.

46. Stephen D. Krasner, "Structural Causes and Regime Consequences: Regimes as Intervening Variables," in Stephen D. Krasner, ed., *International Regimes* (Ithaca, N.Y.: Cornell University Press, 1983), p. 2.

47. Keohane, *After Hegemony.*

48. See Charles P. Kindleberger, *The World in Depression, 1929–1939* (Berkeley: University of California Press, 1973); Gilpin, *U.S. Power and the Multinational Corporation;* and Krasner, "State Power and the Structure of International Trade." The conventional appellation for the theory is attributed to Robert O. Keohane, "The Theory of Hegemonic Stability and Changes in International Economic Regimes," in Ole R. Holsti, Randolph M. Siverson, and Alexander L. George, eds., *Change in the International System* (Boulder, Colo.: Westview Press, 1980), pp. 131–162.

49. Kindleberger, *The World in Depression,* p. 305.

50. See, for example, Keohane, *After Hegemony,* pp. 31–46; and Duncan Snidal, "The Limits of Hegemonic Stability Theory," *International Organization* 39 (Autumn 1985), pp. 579–614.

51. Lake, *Power, Protection, and Free Trade,* p. 36.

52. Conybeare, *Trade Wars,* p. xi.

53. Milner, *Resisting Protectionism,* pp. 4–12.

54. See, for example, Robert Gilpin, *War and Change in World Politics* (New York: Cambridge University Press, 1981), p. 145.

55. Gilpin, *The Political Economy of International Relations,* p. 72.

56. Ibid., p. 78.

57. Ibid.

58. Rosecrance, *The Rise of the Trading State,* p. 165.

59. Milner, *Resisting Protectionism,* p. 298.

60. Lake, *Power, Protection, and Free Trade,* p. 229.

61. Conybeare, *Trade Wars,* pp. 278–281.

62. The analytic relevance of the German experience was, of course, well demonstrated by Hirschman in his classic work, *National Power and the Structure of Foreign Trade.*

Part
Four

THE POLITICS OF INTERNATIONAL INVESTMENT

S ince 1950, the multinational corporation (MNC) has grown to be more significant than most governments in shaping international and domestic social and economic structures. By *multinational corporation*, IPE scholars typically refer to private businesses whose major investments (production and assembly, raw material collection, and marketing facilities) are located in nations other than where the headquarters are located. This does not include businesses that sell their products to foreign markets (these are called *exporters*), nor does it include business whose investment portfolio includes some stock in foreign enterprises. Rather, the multinational (also called *transnational*) is a firm which is committed to a direct international presence. In many cases, the overseas investments of the corporation have outpaced domestic activities so that, for a few firms, the headquarters are merely office buildings where accountants, lawyers, and executives direct operations from a distance.

The explosive growth of MNCs has caused alarm, especially to radicals and realists, for different reasons. Radicals fear the intervention of MNCs in the affairs of weak Third World nations has the direct effect of creating higher levels of poverty among the already poorest segments of society, as well as distorting the domestic social and economic structures that in the past allowed the vast majority to survive. Examples of trends criticized by radicals include: Food prices are subsidized for the benefit of the working class and those who employ it at the expense of the farmers, government investment is concentrated in infrastructural projects most useful to foreign industry rather than for rural development and social programs, and the best land is devoted to cash crop production for export rather than local food production.

Realists fear the loss of control by the government over national economic planning. Radicals and realists both deplore the tendency for Third World nations, where investments are located, to continually lose in bargaining and trade talks. Realists also worry about the exposure of OECD countries to the political instability of Third World countries where investments have been made (the case of the collapse of the Shah in Iran and the subsequent nationalization of foreign assets by the Ayatollah is often cited). The articles in the section further explore these perspectives.

The activities of foreign subsidiaries present many opportunities and problems for the governments and societies of both the home country (where the headquarters is located) and the host (where the investments have been made). Peter Evans goes into some detail to describe how the presence of multinationals in Brazil has shaped the domestic society, to the point that Brazil is governed and dominated by an unholy alliance of local, government-owned, and foreign businesses. According to Evans, the interests of the masses are secondary to the goals of these dominant actors. Kudrle asks a more general question when he addresses the effects of multinationals on both the receiving (often Third World) country and the home country. He points out that just as host nations often find themselves overwhelmed by the wealth and political weight of multinationals, the home country is also poorly adapted to control their activities outside their territory. Problems of job loss, transfer pricing, and tax evasion are explained, although the reader is asked to come up with solutions. Here is a case in which political control clashes with economic autonomy. Is it possible that government regulation of multinational activity could stifle economic incentives and growth? Or are the interests of the people too important to leave unprotected when multinationals cause damage?

Mytelka's piece opens the image of the multinational beyond the stereotypical oil company or banana plantation models to include companies of the information age. She addresses the question of how modern firms adapt to the changing requirements of the rapid global pulse of information and data. In particular, she points out that there exists a certain amount of uncertainty regarding the emergence of new and pressing problems. Can patent and copyright laws protecting intellectual property be made global? How does one secure electronically stored information? Does dominance in the computer industry by American and Japanese firms prohibit other countries from entering the market? When measuring the impact of multinationals on the global economy, can we continue to rely on nationally attributed indexes of wealth and production, such as GNP statistics, which do not capture the massive transnational economic activities carried on by multinationals?

Multinational Strategies and Dependent Development

Peter Evans

Nylon was the centerpiece of Dupont's corporate growth in the fifties, but they decided that Brazil was not one of the places they would develop nylon manufacture. By the seventies that decision looked lamentable from Dupont's point of view. Rhone Poulenc, starting with a license from Dupont, developed the nylon business in Brazil into something approaching $100 million dollars a year. By this time Dupont was making more adventurous choices, but the nylon industry was definitely lost. Dupont's decision not to develop nylon in Brazil had little effect on the country's industrialization. To Brazil it made little difference whether Dupont or Rhone Poulenc controlled nylon manufacture. But, if Dupont, Celanese, Rhone Poulenc, Hoechst, and ICI had all decided not to make nylon in Brazil, then Brazilian industrialization would have suffered and not just Dupont's profits.

If one multinational fails to engage in entrepreneurial behavior for idiosyncratic reasons, then its competitors will fill the gap. But if there are systematic similarities among the multinationals, then their common logic has consequences for dependent development. The argument has already been made in general terms in the first chapter. Multinational managers are expected to make decisions that differ systematically from those which would be made by local capitalists.

It has already been suggested that foreign capitalists were unwilling to undertake the kind of entrepreneurial initiatives that were required for the transition from classic dependence to dependent development until they were prodded and enticed by the state. This chapter will try to show that dependent development has not eliminated the conflict between the global rationality of the multinational and a nationalist logic that places a primary emphasis on local accumulation. The issue of whether the multinationals are willing to engage in manufacturing operations has been replaced by other issues, but the tension persists.

One of the chief areas of tension in the context of dependent development is, not surprisingly, technology. Technology is what the multinationals have and what the countries of the periphery, especially dependent developing countries of the *semiperiphery,* want. On the surface nationalists and the multinationals appear to be in agreement. The multinationals want to bring their technology to Brazil and the Brazilians want it implanted in their country. But underlying this apparent common interest are two quite contradictory interests. Both sides recognize that proprietary control over knowledge creates the potential for extracting monopoly rents. The multinationals want to be able to exercise that potential over the widest possible range. They are happy to bring their technology to Brazil as long as making it available does not jeopardize their monopoly. The Brazilians want just the opposite. They want to see the local utilization of the multinationals' technology precisely because they see local utilization as the first step toward local control. Ultimately, nationalists would like to be able to reap their own monopoly rents from locally generated knowledge.

In the initial discussion of the triple alliance, I tried to emphasize the continued existence of contradictions between the strategies of the multinationals and the priorities of local accumulation. Negative effects of multinational strategies on local capacities to generate new knowledge would be a good indication of these contradictions. This chapter employs a detailed examination of local product innovation in the pharmaceutical industry to get at the ways in which the centripetal logic of the multinational runs counter to the nationalist logic of local accumulation. The argument has two steps. First, the relative failure of multinationals to engage in local product innovation is described. Then rationales that might explain this behavior in *neutral* efficiency terms are examined and rejected, leaving the conclusion that failure to engage in local product innovation may be a *correct* decision in terms of the logic of a global corporation without being correct in terms of any geographically neutral economic logic.

If the argument stopped at the point of demonstrating a contradiction between global strategies and local accumulation, it would hardly support the idea of a triple alliance. Rather it would lead to a conclusion that conflicting interests separate the local bourgeoisie and foreign capital. So, having pointed out the tension, I then try to show how nationalist pressures have been able to modify the behavior of the multinationals, making it more compatible with the requirements of local accumulation.

Throughout the discussion it is important to keep in mind that *nationalist* logic is being narrowly defined. Nationalists in the broader sense (those whose concerns lie with the welfare of the entire citizenry) are likely to find the kind of local product innovation that the multinationals can be persuaded to do irrelevant or even pernicious. In the eyes of cultural radicals like Ivan Illich, for example, "the plows of the rich can do more harm than their swords" (1969:24). Questioning the substantive content of local innovation raises the issue of contradictions between the needs of the mass of the peripheral population and product innovation aimed at profitability. That issue is not discussed here. The nationalist is defined here simply as one with a primary interest in local accumulation, which in the context of dependent development means maximizing long-run rates of profit and investment within the local economy.

The crux of the argument is that there is tension between the multinationals and the nationalist even when nationalism is defined in terms of local profits. Once one has accepted the view (Boulding, 1964:431) that rates of return on new knowledge are "substantially above the rates of return on investment in material capital," then multinationals and the nationalists must disagree on the issue of where innovative activities should take place, even when *nationalist* is defined simply as an interest in local capital accumulation.

As long as contradictory interests separate the multinationals and the nationalists, the issue of control will be central to the progress of dependent development. As long as the multinationals can maintain control over their enterprises and investments within Brazil, decisions will be made according to their own global rationality, and considerations of local accumulation will take second place. Raising the issue of control means evaluating the possibility that the multinationals can be constrained to place a higher priority on local accumulation even at some sacrifice of their own global strategies.

The degree of divergence between global strategies and local accumulation, as well as the chance of modifying the former in favor of the latter, depends on the context. The less well endowed the peripheral country in question and the less favorable an *investment climate* it offers, the greater the contradiction between the global rationality of the multinationals and local nationalist logic. The tension is obviously much less severe for the countries undergoing dependent development than for other peripheral countries. Among such countries, Brazil has been something of a limiting case, especially in the late sixties and early seventies when most of the decisions discussed in this chapter were made.

BRAZIL AS AN INVESTMENT CLIMATE

The fact that Brazil's "economic miracle" made it "the Latin American darling of the international business community" (*Business Latin America,* 1972:196) is well known and does not need to be reiterated with barrages of quotations. The impressive economic figures of this period are also well known. GNP growth rates of over 10 percent per year were characteristic, with growth rates for industry even higher, particularly in certain key areas such as automobiles. Table 1 and Table 2 provide a statistical overview of the growth of investments, sales, and profits, which puts Brazil into perspective as a potential location for investment.

Gross sales statistics of American manufacturers abroad confirm the importance of the Brazilian boom to the expansion of the multinationals.

Table 1   SALES OF U.S. MAJORITY OWNED MANUFACTURING AFFILIATES IN BRAZIL AND OTHER SELECTED MARKETS, 1966–1973 (Millions of Current $US)

	1966		1973		Growth as a % of 1966 sales
	Amount	(%)	Amount	(%)	
Total	47,374	100.0	140,878	100.0	197
Europe	21,738	45.1	75,254	53.4	246
U.K.	8,275	17.4	19,559	13.9	136
France	3,114	6.6	11,774	8.4	278
Germany	4,795	10.1	19,347	13.7	303
Latin America	5,861	12.3	16,220	11.6	185
Argentina	1,302	2.7	2,246	1.6	72
Mexico	1,543	3.3	3,945	2.8	154
Brazil	1,283	2.7	5,738	4.1	347

Source: Survey of Current Business, vol. 55, no. 8 (August 1975): 22–37.

Table 2   GROWTH OF U.S. ASSETS IN BRAZIL AND OTHER SELECTED MARKETS, 1966–1973 (Direct Investments in Manufacturing in Millions of Current $US)

	1966		1973		Growth as a % of 1966 assets
	Amount	(%)	Amount	(%)	
Total	22,058	100.0	44,370	100.0	101
Europe	8,876	40.2	20,777	46.8	134
U.K.	3,716	16.8	6,611	14.9	78
France	1,201	5.4	2,946	6.6	145
Germany	1,839	8.7	4,449	10.0	142
Latin America	3,081	14.0	6,456	14.5	109
Argentina	656	3.0	781	1.8	19
Mexico	802	3.6	1,798	4.1	124
Brazil	846	3.8	2,033	4.6	146

Sources: Survey of Current Business, vol. 48, no. 10 (October 1968): 19–31; vol. 55, no. 10 (October 1975): 43–63.

Brazil during this period grew much more rapidly than any other major Latin American market. Even the European markets of American overseas manufacturers, which generally grew faster than their Latin American counterparts, did not match the growth in Brazilian consumption. By 1973 the Brazilian market was the sixth largest in the world for American manufacturing affiliates. Sales in Brazil in 1973 were as large as combined sales to all of the original six members of the European Economic Community the year before the EEC was formed (1962).

When comparing the growth of the United States manufacturing affiliates' sales in Brazil to the growth of their sales elsewhere, it should be kept in mind that the growth of foreign manufacturing in general was much more rapid than the growth of the domestic economy during this period. Foreign sales as a proportion of all sales of American manufactures doubled in the sixties, reaching 13 percent of the total. The share of foreign expenditures on plant and equipment rose even faster, reaching 25 percent of total expenditures by 1970. Most important, it has been estimated that by the mid-seventies 30 percent of all United States profits came from overseas (Müller, 1975). Overseas manufacturing was a dynamic area of expansion for American corporations and Brazil was the most rapidly growing of the major overseas markets of American manufacturers.

Growth in itself is attractive, but new investment must get a satisfactory rate of return. In international terms this means a rate approximating that available in other countries. As Table 3 indicates, Brazil has provided

Table 3   RATES OF RETURN FOR U.S. MANUFACTURING AFFILIATES,[a] 1967–1974 (Selected Years)

	1967 (%)	1969 (%)	1972 (%)	1973 (%)	1974 (%)
Total	8.5	10.8	13.0	15.0	12.8
Europe	8.7	11.9	15.0	16.8	12.6
U.K.	8.8	9.3	12.4	11.8	6.2
France	5.4	10.0	13.0	17.5	8.9
Germany	11.1	17.7	19.8	22.5	16.0
Latin America	7.4	10.1	11.8	12.0	11.1
Argentina	4.0	11.5	4.4	4.5	loss
Mexico	8.7	9.4	10.9	11.9	12.0
Brazil	7.7	11.1	14.5	14.9	11.0

[a]"Rates of return" are based on figures reported to the U.S. Department of Commerce. They represent the ratio of "earnings" (not "adjusted earnings") to "assets" of "book value."

Sources: Survey of Current Business, vol. 48, no. 10 (October 1968):19–31; vol. 50, no. 10 (October 1970):21–37; vol. 54, no. 8 (August 1974):10–24; vol. 55, no. 10 (October 1975):43–63.

good rates of return as well as opportunities for rapid growth.[1] While official rates of return for American manufacturers in Latin America have generally been lower than those available in Europe, Brazil provided, at least during the late sixties and early seventies, among the best such rates available; only Germany provided better.

Gross averages convey the general situation and also are a way of describing the context in which the individual manager is working. Within the Brazilian context, however, it is important to distinguish long-established firms from newcomers. For the latter, the prospect of getting in on a fast-growing market is probably the paramount motivation. Newcomers may have to sacrifice short-term profits in order to get started. As Connor and Mueller (1977:50) put it, "Many firms with large start-up costs or other transient conditions distort the true profit picture." They corrected for this in their report by eliminating unprofitable firms and came up with an average return on equity of 21.4 percent for the rest of the sample. This may represent an overcorrection, but it is true that established firms have higher rates of profit than newcomers. McDonough's (1974) analysis of company profitability in 1970 indicates that one of the strongest predictors of the profitability of multinationals in Brazil was the date of their establishment. Long-established multinationals made significantly higher profits than newer ones. The profit rates of longer-established firms are the best gauge of what multinationals can expect to make in Brazil over the long run.

The individual rates of return for large, established companies is a good complement to the aggregate statistics on United States manufacturing affiliates. The rates of return shown in Table 4 are based on local accounting procedures and are not equivalent to the U.S. Department of Commerce data, but they do suggest that there is a foundation for the enthusiasm of the multinational managers. Seven of the ten companies received better than 15 percent on capital and reserves. Even in the early part of the period (1967, 1968) when the economy was still recovering, the average returns for all companies never dropped below 10 percent. In addition, almost all of the companies experienced these rates of return in conjunction with substantial growth of assets. Finally, it should be noted that these figures underestimate real returns to the parent corporation since they do not include items that appear as costs at the level of the subsidiary but profits at the level of the parent. Official rates of return do not include royalties and fees, or payments for technical assistance, to say nothing of profits on transfer prices (see Vaitsos, 1974).

If ever there was an economic environment in the periphery in which the multinationals should have been willing to take risks and engage in entrepreneurial behavior, it was Brazil in the late sixties and early seventies. Given the rates of growth and the rates of return available there, the contradictions between global rationality and local accumulation ought to have been minimal or nonexistent. The fact that such contradictions re-

Table 4 GROWTH AND RETURN FOR TEN SELECTED MULTINATIONALS 1967–1973

	1967[a] assets	1973 assets	Growth of assets 1967–1973 (%)	Rate of return[b]							Average rate of return 1967–1973 (%)
				1967 (%)	1968 (%)	1969 (%)	1970 (%)	1971 (%)	1972 (%)	1973 (%)	
Volkswagen	107.7	338.3	214	6.5	11.6	7.6	1.6	21.1	18.2	17.7	12.0
Cia. Cigarros Souza Cruz (Brit. Amer. Tob.)	115.2	226.3	96	16.6	19.5	21.9	23.4	31.9	36.7	35.8	26.5
General Motors	83.0	163.5	97	3.3	8.4	12.1	24.7	31.5	22.4	9.5	16.0
Rhodia (Rhone Poulenc)	100.0	160.0	60	4.8	2.8	8.9	7.9	11.2	11.2	18.5	9.3
Pirelli	86.1	139.8	62	3.2	12.6	6.4	7.2	19.0	60.1	28.7	19.6
Shell	54.9	114.7	107	31.3	24.0	16.3	10.9	17.3	3.8	12.2	16.5
Esso	43.5	81.0	86	25.8	3.5	8.5	14.5	13.5	19.2	30.9	16.6
General Electric	62.5	80.4	29	16.2	12.8	11.3	6.8	10.9	44.8	20.4	17.6
Alcan	32.4	71.2	120	3.0	1.7	1.1	1.9	15.2	24.2	25.6	10.4
Nestle	39.9	66.5	68	4.6	5.3	8.4	11.1	26.4	23.5	27.2	15.2
Average Rate of Return by Year:				11.5	10.2	10.3	11.0	19.8	26.4	22.6	16.0 (overall average)

[a]Assets are in millions of current $US.

[b]Rate of return is as calculated by *Business Latin America* and refers to ratio of net profit to capital and reserves.

Source: *Business Latin America,* "Major Brazilian Firms and How They Fared" (yearly feature 1967–1973).

mained, even in Brazil during the boom, suggests that they can never be reduced beyond a certain point.

MULTINATIONAL STRATEGY AND LOCAL PRODUCT INNOVATION

The behavior of multinationals with respect to local research and development in the pharmaceutical industry can provide only one illustration of the kinds of contradictions that separate global and nationalist rationality, not a proof of their pervasiveness. The development of local capacity for technological innovation is only one of the demands the nationalist perspective would make on multinationals. Investments in forward integration in the case of extractive industry or backwards integration in the case of consumer products, or commitments to local purchase or production of capital goods are others. Nonetheless, research and development in the drug industry provides an excellent illustrative case, one well worth developing in some detail.

. . . Exclusive new products are the *sine qua non* of profitable operations for an international pharmaceutical corporation. The question is whether the capacity to develop these new products should be moved to the periphery along with manufacturing operations or kept in the center despite the decentralization of the manufacturing function. This can be put less abstractly: Does it make sense to attempt to develop new drugs in Brazil? Research done in the late sixties indicated that there were two answers, one offered by local capital and one offered by the multinationals.

In 1969 when I began working on this question few multinationals claimed to have developed any products locally. In a sample of 17 American subsidiaries that included all of the largest subsidiaries, only 5 claimed to have developed any products locally within the last five years (Evans, 1971:126). Given the degree of denationalization in the industry, it was impossible to find a sample of local firms whose scale was comparable to that of the subsidiaries, even if only sales within Brazil were taken into account. The majority of the American subsidiaries had annual local sales of over $5 million while only one of the local firms was in this league. Nonetheless, all local firms with sales of over $2.5 million could claim locally developed products. The majority of local firms with sales over $1 million could also make this claim. Only the smallest local firms did not try to develop products of their own.

Data from other investigations generally support these findings. A survey of 183 firms in the state of São Paulo done by the Instituto de Estuodos para o Desenvolvimento Social e Econômico (INED) surveyed 13 pharmaceutical firms, 5 locally owned and 8 foreign-owned.[2] All 5 locally owned were coded as doing research while only 3 of the foreign-owned were credited with having local research activities.[3]

Carlos Bertero, who interviewed 29 pharmaceutical firms, including both subsidiaries and locally owned drug companies, found that 6 out of 24 subsidiaries claimed to do formulations locally, and one other did toxicological and pharmacological testing (1972:200–201). Bertero's sample of local firms was limited to only 5 of the largest local companies, but among these companies 4 claimed to have engaged in product development (1972:209).

These general results can be supported by some specific examples. Both Bertero (1972:210–211) and myself (1971:136) discovered the local company I called Laboratórios Grande and were impressed by the export business that it had built on the basis of its own locally developed biological products. I also highlighted a company I called Laboratórios Familial, which has succeeded in launching 50 new pharmaceutical and dietetic products based on its own research. Laboratórios Familial's work on barium for radiography of the bronchial tubes even "resulted in a research report of sufficient originality to be published in an American research periodical." Between 1963 and 1968, Laboratórios Familial tested 705 substances and managed to come up with 41 industrial products (Evans, 1971:135, 136). This is, of course, a tiny number by international standards. At the same time, this number of successes also suggests that the substances initially tested were of some known therapeutic value. The fact remains that Laboratórios Familial, like Laboratórios Grande, succeeded until the end of the sixties in maintaining a commercially rewarding research and development operation within Brazil.

To reinforce these Brazilian examples, there is a more spectacular, though admittedly unique, example from Mexico. Syntex S.A., set up in Mexico over twenty-five years ago to exploit locally available raw materials, was extremely successful (see Gereffi, 1978). Until the company was bought out by U.S. capital and its research operations moved to Palo Alto, the productivity of its Mexican research laboratories was impressive. Carl Djerassi, one of the directors of Syntex, wrote: "By 1959 more scientific publications in steroid chemistry had emanated from Syntex in Mexico than from any other academic or industrial organization in the world. . . . In a matter of ten years Mexico—a country in which no basic chemical research had been performed previously—had become one of the world centers in one specialized branch of chemistry" (1968:24–25).

An even more impressive comparative example is provided by the work of Jorge Katz on Argentina. Argentina is a better place to look at local innovative activity because denationalization has not occurred to the same degree. Local firms represent over 50 percent of total sales and nine of the top twenty-five firms are locally owned. Katz calculated that it took ten to fifteen thousand dollars to launch a new product on the Argentine market and that the most innovative firms each launched between twelve and fifteen products in the period 1960–1968. Major local firms were quite capable of maintaining a flow of new products by making investments in research and development of about 1 percent of their sales. It is on the basis of such new products, according to Katz, that local firms were able to increase their share of the market relative to international firms between 1962 and 1970 (Katz, 1974:110–114, 62).

Neither I nor Bertero nor Katz claims that more local product innovation in pharmaceuticals would make important differences to the health of the population. Whether Brazil's most popular cough syrup in the future is locally developed (like BROMIL) or a multinational import (like VICKS) is of little significance to consumers' health. Samuel Pessoa's conclusion (1963:36) that the "fundamental cause of high rates of dissemination of parasite diseases is the pauperism of the Brazilian people" or Edmar Bacha's (1976:16) correlation between rising infant mortality rates and falling minimum wages are more to the point. Insofar as product innovation results mainly in the proliferation of sophisticated and expensive products (cf. Kucinski, 1975), then it can be considered, as Katz (1974:142) says, simply another example of "playing the oligopolistic game of product differentiation." It does not even seem extreme to conclude with Bertero (1972:214) that "most of the country's population is not served by a pharmaceutical industry structured and operated along a capitalist model."

What is being argued is that potentially profitable investments in local facilities for product innovation were avoided by multinationals to the detriment of local accumulation. In short, there would be a greater amount of local technologically innovative work in the Brazilian pharmaceutical industry if more of the larger firms were locally owned. In Bertero's (1972:214) words, "the situation of the pharmaceutical industry in Brazil today, basically controlled by multinational corporations, is one of self-perpetuating dependency, with no prospects for developing technology." While this judgment underestimates the degree to which the behavior of multinationals can be modified, it is certainly true that the tendency of multinationals to neglect or avoid investment in local facilities for product innovation presents an obstacle to the technological evolution of a dependent developing country.

The general lack of multinational investment in local research and development is confirmed by evidence outside the pharmaceutical industry. The strongest correlation in the INED study (see at note 2 above) is that between foreign ownership and lack of research and development. The INED result suggests that even partial local ownership is sufficient to induce interest in R & D. About 60 percent of all firms with at least 10 percent local ownership claimed to do research and development locally, the same as the proportion of firms with complete local ownership. Among firms with no local ownership, on the other hand, only a quarter claimed to do any R & D.

The INED study also reveals an interaction between paying royalties, doing research, and the degree of foreign ownership that is interesting. Among firms with some local ownership, paying royalties and doing research locally go together; three out of four of those paying royalties also do research. Among wholly foreign-owned firms, however, there is no such relationship. That is to say, the need for new technology (as expressed by willingness to pay royalties) is associated with attempts at local innovation as long as there is some local ownership, but not if the multinationals are completely in charge.

To look at the periphery and compare the R & D efforts of multinational firms to those of local firms is one way to evaluate the willingness of multinationals to decentralize innovative activities. The situation can also be viewed from the center, as it is in U.S. Tariff Commission's Report on Multinationals (1973:581–604). The commission reported that in 1966 multinationals committed only 6 percent of their total R & D expenditures outside the U.S., much less than the percentage of their sales accounted for by these markets. At the same time, according to the commission, multinationals "usually finance R & D costs by assessments against all affiliates." Affiliates' payments of royalties and fees alone were equivalent to 7.7 percent of multinationals' domestic R & D spending, a percentage larger than the share of R & D done overseas. The commission cautiously concludes that "there is a possibility that affiliates (at least in some industries) may contribute more to R & D in the United States than they take from it" (U.S. Tariff Commission, 1973:591, 593).

The research efforts of multinationals in Brazil can be compared with their efforts in the United States itself. Table 5 shows the R & D expenditures of U.S. multinational affiliates in Brazil as a percentage of their sales in Brazil in comparison with the R & D expenditures of American multinationals in the U.S. as a percentage of their U.S. sales. Overall, affiliates allocate about one-fifth the expenditures to R & D that their parents do. Industry by industry, with the exception of food, the story is the same. If multinationals allocated to R & D in Brazil the same proportion of local sales as they do in the United States, Brazilian expenditures would have been almost $150 million in 1972 instead of under $30 million.

Whether the comparison is between locally owned firms and foreign-owned or between multinationals' behavior in the center and their behavior in the periphery, whether the comparison is made within an industry or across the industrial spectrum, the conclusion is the same. Multinationals are reluctant to engage in technologically innovative activities in the periphery, even in the favorable investment climate of Brazil in the late sixties. With the transition to dependent development the multinationals were induced to decentralize the process of production, but the generation of knowledge is still kept at home.

. . .

NATIONALIST PRESSURE AND THE MULTINATIONAL RESPONSE

If there are differences between *correctness* born of the organizational frame of reference of the multinationals and *correctness* in terms of local accumulation, then shaping the behavior of the multinationals through

Table 5   RESEARCH AND DEVELOPMENT BY MULTINATIONALS: THE U.S. VERSUS BRAZIL

Industry	Brazil (1972)			U.S. (1970)		
	Sales of U.S. affiliated firms in Brazil	R & D expenditures	R & D as a percent of sales	U.S. multi-nationals' domestic sales	R & D expenditures	R & D as a percent of sales
Food	197	3.7	1.9%	14,300	176	1.2%
Paper	83	0.0	0.	7,500	87	1.2%
Chemicals	672	5.4	0.8%	28,100	1,556	5.5%
Rubber	243	0.0	0.	3,300	169	5.1%
Stone, Clay & Glass	70	0.6	0.8%	4,700	150	3.2%
Metals	85	0.3	0.4%	22,700	363	1.6%
Machinery	392	0.7	0.2%	20,600	984	4.8%
Electrical Machinery	347	3.7	1.1%	27,900	2,172	7.8%
Transportation Equipment	867	12.3	1.4%	55,200	2,790	5.1%
Instruments	25	0.0	0.	7,600	590	7.7%
All Manufacturing	3,056	27.0	0.9%	207,800	9,200	4.4%

Note: Individual industries will not add up to all manufacturing because "other" has been excluded. U.S. sales are rounded to nearest $100 million. Brazilian sales to nearest $1 million; U.S. R & D to nearest $1 million except total, which is to nearest $100 million, Brazilian R & D to nearest $100 thousand. All figures are in millions of dollars.

Sources: Newfarmer and Mueller, 1975:178; U.S. Tariff Commission, 1973:556, 733.

political pressure becomes a central element of successful dependent development. To the degree that *correctness* in local terms can be imposed without jeopardizing the commitment of the multinationals, prospects for local accumulation will be enhanced. The pharmaceutical industry in the seventies saw some interesting attempts at such shaping.

The foreign sector of the pharmaceutical industry was in a rather precarious political position in the 1960s. Before the military coup, some had advocated nationalization of the industry. In the series "Notebooks of the People," one of the volumes was entitled "Shall We Nationalize the Pharmaceutical Industry?" (Miranda, 1963). The pharmaceutical industry experienced price controls before they were generalized. In the early part of the decade, President Goulart formed a commission of inquiry to look into the situation of the industry. Many of the accusations against the foreign sector arose over the issue of denationalization. Critics like Colonel Mario Victor de Assis Pacheco (1962:28) inveighed against the misguided government policies that aided foreign capital while the local entrepreneur lived "without any privilege whatsoever." A favorite target of critics of the industry was the lack of local research. Pacheco wrote (1962:15): "If our technicians weren't pulled away, attracted by better salaries, better working conditions, and other advantages they would stay in our own laboratories, private or state owned, doing research, improving the quality of our production, and discovering new products, but this is exactly what the foreign trusts want to avoid and have succeeded in avoiding." Displeasure over the absence of local research and concern over the cost of importing basic pharmaceutical inputs combined to produce the elimination of patent protection in pharmaceuticals in 1969.

Those in the industry on the local level were well aware of their weak position. They responded with publications demonstrating the technological progressiveness of the industry and the extent to which it was harassed by government policies. Privately at least, some of the local managers were more candid. One of them, a Brazilian with long experience in the foreign-owned sector, related a conversation he had had with a military man in the government over the issue of abolishing patents. The manager reported that although the Colonel was "someone with whom it was possible to dialogue" it had not been possible to change his mind on the issue of patents because "logic was on his side." The manager tried to argue that no country without patent laws ever produced any new discoveries. The Colonel replied, "Do you think that anyone will discover anything even if we keep the patent laws?" The manager felt he couldn't refute the point.

At the same time as the Brazilian government made it harder for international drug companies to appropriate returns from discoveries made elsewhere, it undertook measures to stimulate research. It set up the National Fund for Scientific and Technical Development that would provide financing and technical assistance to enterprises establishing or expanding local R & D facilities and made local R & D expenditures tax deductible (*Business Latin America*, 1970:264). The attempt to combine sanctions and incentives was obvious. *Business Latin America* (1971:374) reported: "In not allowing royalty payment or patent protection the government has given for a reason the fact that companies actually perform little or no research in Brazil and are not discovering anything patentable. At the same time, the government has hinted that it might take a more lenient attitude of companies were to engage in R & D in Brazil."

Continued local discontent with the operations of the pharmaceutical industry manifested itself again in 1971 with the creation of the Central de Medicamentos (CEME, 1974; Bertero, 1972:243). The initial rationale for it was simply that it would complement the existing health insurance system and provide medicines for those too poor to buy them. Its functions soon expanded. By 1973, CEME was supporting research on basic pharmaceutical inputs and the government had published a decree amplifying the "Directive Plan for Medications" to include "studies for the implantation of a system which would oblige large pharmaceutical companies to apply a certain percentage of gross sales to local research projects" (Decreto No. 72.522, Art. 2, IV.d).

At the end of 1974, the head of the powerful Council on Industrial Development (which must approve any investment that is to benefit from fiscal incentives) made a speech that *Business Latin America* considered to contain "warning signals" for the drug industry. He spoke of past denationalization as *disquieting* and held it responsible for "making difficult local research and the adoption of new technological processes within the country." *Business Latin America* commented that it was "the first time that an official has linked foreign domination—particularly through acquisitions—with the frustration of Brazil in moving ahead with its prime goal of greater local R & D" (1975:26).

None of these pressures or accusations were particularly disturbing in themselves. But, as managers discovered in the seventies, the military government's support of *private enterprise* did not preclude the possibility of increased participation by the state in industry. In the pharmaceutical industry they spoke in 1974 of the possibility of CEME becoming a *Medibrás* on the order of Petrobrás. They did not consider this likely, but it was worrisome nonetheless.

Confronted with persistent nationalist pressures even after ten years of military government, multinational managers had to respond. No manager would want to risk being cut out of the Brazilian market; returns on equity among U.S. subsidiaries were running over 20 percent (Connor and Mueller, 1977:50). The need to reduce political risks, to strengthen the security of the whole Brazilian operation, became the justification for investing in local research facilities regardless of expected rates of return from those facilities. Managers found themselves exchanging one kind of uncertainty for another. Neither political factors nor research and development are easily controlled at a distance. Both are somewhat unpredictable; but between the two kinds of risk, local research and development is the less dangerous.

The Brazilian pharmaceutical industry in the early seventies provides a good illustration of the central role played by political pressure in pushing multinationals toward investment in local research facilities. The U.S. Tariff Commission's (1973:587) observation that "pressures and encouragement by host governments are often a deciding factor" in the decision to disperse research, and Wortzel's conclusion that in the pharmaceutical industry "by far the strongest motivation for setting up research facilities outside the U.S. comes from governments" (1971:10) could both serve as summaries of the Brazilian case.[4]

Given the generality of the pressure, the differential response among different firms was striking. A few responded strongly. Johnson and Johnson is the most often cited example. It started the Johnson and Johnson Research Institute in Brazil in 1970 (*Business Latin America,* 1971:374) and is reputed to have invested over 2 million dollars in the institute in the first two years of its operation (Kucinski, 1975:70). Johnson and Johnson was testing about 500 substances a month by 1974, not a large number by international standards, but far larger than any previous Brazilian operation. American Cyanamid, which has done work on veterinary products in Brazil for quite some time, may extend its work to products for human use. The Beecham group, a new entry into the Brazilian market, has reputedly undertaken to make Brazil one of the four countries in its worldwide operations in which research would be carried on.

Companies that engaged in research and development had reason to perceive the attendant risks differently from other firms. Their decisions were incremental, built on the previous existence of a certain level of R & D. Johnson and Johnson could cite products developed in Brazil as early as the fifties (*Business Latin America,* 1971:374). Beecham bought out a local company, Maurício Villela, one of the most respected research and development operations in Brazil. Having acquired it, Beecham would have had to make a decision to stop doing research in Brazil rather than take steps to *start* doing research. Given their delicate position in having just *denationalized* one of the largest, most prestigious locally owned drug companies, a commitment to local research obviously made sense.

The tendency toward incrementalism, or working on the basis of what exists, was evident in my discussions with drug company managers in the late sixties (Evans, 1971: 183-189). One company had started a research lab in Europe as a result of host government pressure and it had "just snowballed." Another had acquired a European firm with an ongoing research operation. "There was never a conscious decision to create a development unit there," the manager explained. "They just had the men so we had to give them something to do." Once established the European development unit "grew like Topsy."

Incrementalism is exactly what would be expected of a satisficing, risk-avoiding, information-short manager, and the importance of incrementalism in determining the differential response among firms is indicative of the way in which uncertainty magnifies interest-based resistance to decentralization. The ease with which some firms were able to overlook the economies of scale and inappropriate environment arguments also supports the idea that these arguments represent rationales rather than reasons for the centralization of R & D facilities. Predictably, those companies which already had some dispersed research units were unlikely to raise questions of the inappropriateness of the environment or economies of scale. They were more likely to praise the low costs or productivity of their overseas operations. Likewise, there were few complaints from Johnson and Johnson about the difficulties of engaging in research in Brazil.

It is not surprising that some firms responded to nationalist pressure to invest in local R & D nor that those who responded were firms which could do so on an incremental basis. What is surprising is that the response was not greater. Given the favorable economic climate for expanding operations in Brazil and the extreme political vulnerability of the industry, what is strange is that subsidiaries were not falling over each other in a rush to set up local R & D facilities. But they were not. Johnson and Johnson remained the exception rather than the rule. Furthermore, when ABIF, the local equivalent of the Pharmaceutical Manufacturers Association, made an attempt to improve the industry's image with respect to local research, the response was grudging at best.

At the end of 1970, ABIF created the Fundação ABIF, a general fund based on contributions from individual companies. Its purpose was to provide support for students and researchers in organic chemistry, pharmacology, and other areas related to pharmaceuticals. The connection between external political pressure and the organization of the Fundação ABIF was undisguised. In its fund raising letter for 1974, the Fundação ABIF pointed out to its member companies that the investment of an obligatory percentage of sales in research was envisaged in Decree No. 72.552 and suggested the Fundação ABIF as a potential way of investing those funds.

To one Brazilian, managing an American firm, it was incredible that some multinationals were apparently so obtuse as to miss the political connection. He claimed that it had been a terrible struggle to get the Fundação ABIF started. In his eyes the free advertising alone made it more than worthwhile and he could not understand why some multinationals were unwilling to contribute the few thousand dollars a year that the Fundação ABIF was asking for. It represented after all only a few tenths of 1 percent of their sales, much less than the obligatory contribution seemed likely to be. Most of the large firms did decide to contribute. By 1972 the Fundação ABIF was able to disburse almost $70,000 based on contributions from eighty-one companies. (Fundação ABIF, 1973:43, 67–68) with the largest contributions running between $5,000 and $10,000. But by 1974, there were rumors that several of the largest contributors wanted to withdraw.

The history of nationalist pressure and multinational response in the area of research and development suggests three conclusions. First, it is clear that a surprisingly large amount of political pressure may be required to produce modest changes in the behavior of multinationals, even in the most favorable context. At the same time, it would appear that even the modest successes are useful from the nationalist point of view in that they provide a base upon which future changes can be built incrementally. Finally, given the importance of incrementalism, it is clear that the success of nationalist pressure will vary not only by industry but also issue by issue and firm by firm. This last conclusion can be reinforced by a quick examination of another aspect of the pharmaceutical industry, the issue of backwards integration.

Pharmaceutical raw materials are an expensive item in Brazil's balance of payments. The government was willing to provide attractive fiscal benefits to those who would produce them locally, including "duty-free importation of manufacturing equipment, exemption of such equipment from the IPI and ICM indirect taxes, accelerated depreciation, and preferential treatment by government agencies in handling requests for import licenses and other formalities" (*Business Latin America,* 1975:26). Moreover, if no one is willing to produce a raw material locally, then there is the potential threat of duty-free, government-sponsored importation at the competitive international price rather than the parent-subsidiary price, which would wipe out the private, duty-paying competition.

If my 1974 interviews with multinational managers in pharmaceuticals are any indication, the campaign for local production of raw materials has been received enthusiastically. Since every project must be approved by the CDI (Council on Industrial Development) and the CDI is not likely to approve overcapacity, the chances of getting something close to a local monopoly are great. The fiscal incentives are sufficient to give the promise of good profits, and in addition to the threat of government importation there is always the threat that some competitor will take advantage of the incentives. The multinationals I spoke to were almost uniformly contemplating getting into the production of raw materials.[5]

Any firm that does not go along runs the risk of finding itself at a severe disadvantage. There are already some firms in Brazil that have been forced to buy their own patented exclusive active ingredients from third parties because a competitor set up local production and received tariff protection from the government. The situation parallels closely that which allowed the implantation of facilities for mixing and packaging in the early fifties. When Getúlio Vargas "virtually banned imports of finished packaged drugs by raising the duties and applying exchange restrictions" (U.S. Dept. of Commerce, 1967a:26), most multinationals realized that if they did not go into fabrication their competitors would.

Pressuring the multinationals into backward integration was easier than pressuring them into research and development because the latter put their profits more clearly in jeopardy. There were fewer uncertainties as to the consequences of the actions advocated. Research and development offered potential long-run gain, but a reduction in the bill for imported pharmaceutical inputs was clear-cut immediate gain. Moreover, the pressures of oligopolistic competition could more easily be brought into play. The gains of competitors could be linked explicitly to the failure to integrate backward in a particular product; and the loss of the market in that product could be attributed directly to a competitor. Refusal to grant fiscal incentives could, of course, have been used as a punishment for failure to make investments in R & D. But failure to engage in R & D does not open up any direct opportunities for competitors in the same way that failure to integrate backward does.

The contrast between research and development and the local production of raw materials suggests that nationalist pressure will be more effective insofar as the effects on local accumulation are concrete and unambiguous, and even more crucially, insofar as failure to comply can result directly in advantages to competitors. Nationalist pressure will succeed more often if it parallels the forces of oligopolistic competition. The implication of this last point is, of course, that nationalist pressure will be successful only if it refrains from trying to shape the process of accumulation in ways that deviate too much from the logic of profitability.

If it is difficult to push multinationals in the direction of investing in local product innovation, the difficulty of shaping the content of that innovation in directions other than those indicated by profitability is greater. Nationalist victories result in the expansion and diversification of the productive resources located in the periphery. The appropriateness of those productive resources to the satisfaction of needs is another question altogether. Illich's warning that the "ploughs of the rich may do more harm than their swords" remains completely outside the purview of bargaining between nationalists and multinationals. There is only one consolation for those taking Illich's point of view. If the nationalists win and innovative facilities are located in the periphery, then the population of the periphery may someday be able to shape the ends toward which those facilities are used. Without the prior nationalist victory there would be nothing to fight over.

The pharmaceutical industry illustrates the necessity of nationalist pressure, the possible gains that may result, and the limits of those gains. But, while pharmaceuticals shows neatly the divergence of *nationalist* and global rationalities, it provides only limited information on the strategies that may be used to bring the behavior of the multinationals more in line with the requirements of local accumulation. Denationalization has left the local bourgeoisie in pharmaceuticals marginalized. Consequently, there is no real question of alliance within the industry itself. Pharmaceuticals illustrate how the behavior of the multinationals can be modified even in an industry in which their control is essentially uncontested. But relative to other sectors, pharmaceuticals are a multinationals' preserve. . . . There are other sectors in which the question of joint control is meaningful and the alliances are more concrete.

· · ·

NOTES

1. The estimated rates of return are higher in the Senate Subcommittee sample. As mentioned earlier, Connor and Mueller estimate the rate of return on equity for 1972 at 16.1 percent. The U.S. Department of Commerce figures have been used here in order to provide a broader basis for comparison.
2. The INED study was done under the auspices of the Instituto Roberto Simonsen and the Federação das Indústrias do Estado de São Paulo in 1967. Some of the results are reported in Chiaverini (1968). The discussion here is based on my own analysis of the data, coded from the original questionnaires. I reanalyzed the data, checking for internal consistency and verifying the information on ownership against other sources. Chiaverini and the original INED report were only able to include two-way tables, but in my own analysis I was able to introduce controls and perform some simple multivariate analysis (see Evans, 1971:145–161).
3. Obviously there are major methodological problems with using self-report to evaluate a firm's investment in research and development. It might be argued that multinationals have higher standards for what they are willing to label "R & D" and therefore underreport their efforts relative to local firms. It was for this reason that I focused on whether or not firms could point to locally developed products when I did my analysis of the pharmaceutical industry.
4. One of the ironic aspects of the development of the pharmaceutical industry is that because political pressure fell more heavily on foreign than on locally owned firms and because of the effects of denationalization . . . local firms became less involved in research at the same time that foreign firms were becoming more involved.
5. An interesting sidelight on raw material production is that it may in fact have as great an effect on local technological innovation as the direct implantation of facilities for product innovation. One of the things that struck me in my 1969 interviews in the pharmaceutical industry was that companies which produced raw materials needed to engage in technologically innovative activity even if they didn't explicitly acknowledge it. The available examples were connected with the production of antibiotics. One of these companies (Evans, 1971:130) was engaged in irradiating its antibiotic-producing micro-organisms in order to obtain more productive mutants. The same company was developing diets for its organisms based on locally available foods. Another foreign company had worked out a way to save on raw materials (which were more costly in Brazil) by extending the length of the fermentation cycle used to produce penicillin.

   Moving backwards to the production of raw materials meant becoming interested in local technological innovation. The kind of research entailed in backwards integration is process-oriented rather than product-oriented as official R & D facilities would be, but the positive externalities are much the same. Both develop local skills and offer the possibility of making the industry more responsive to the local environment.

The Several Faces of the Multinational Corporation: Political Reaction and Policy Response

Robert T. Kudrle

With the acuity that goes with hindsight, I might better have entitled my 1971 volume *Everyone at Bay.*

Raymond Vernon (1981b)

The multinational corporation (MNC) exemplifies the era of transnationalism and the increasingly complex problems nearly all national governments face in devising effective, coherent international economic policies. The relative importance of the MNC has grown steadily over most of the postwar period. From 1960 until the late 1970s, annual foreign production of MNCs grew at over 10 percent, while world trade grew at 9.5 percent and world production at about 8 percent (Hawkins and Walter 1979, 161). Moreover, the enormous growth in world trade has taken place in large part under the aegis of the MNC. Over half of all U.S. exports are now accounted for by MNC activity (Vernon 1981, 24).

The growing interdependence of the world economy presents a threat to national sovereignty, and direct foreign investment (DFI) appears as perhaps the most palpable specific threat. The word *direct* implies control by a foreign-owned economic presence within a sovereign state, so that suspicion and conflict come almost automatically. The threat seems particularly formidable when the sizes of many of the firms are considered.

Robert Kudrle, "The Several Faces of the Multinational Corporation" in W. Ladd Hollist and F. Lamond Tullis, eds., *An International Political Economy,* Boulder, CO: Westview Press, 1985. Reprinted by permission.

Dozens of MNCs have sales greater than the GNPs of most members of the United Nations.

The focus of this chapter is a government policy toward the MNC. I look at how the MNC penetrates a country's national consciousness and generates political reaction and ultimately policy response. More specifically, I endeavor to explain why developed countries (DCs) and less developed countries (LDCs) have systematically different policy responses to MNC activities within their borders.

I begin with a general description of various kinds of political reactions and policy responses that receiving (host) countries generate toward MNCs, comparing and contrasting therein the experiences of DCs and LDCs.[1] Thereafter, from the interpretive vantage point of microeconomic public choice theory, I endeavor to shed light on the determinants of public policy toward MNC activity. A parallel discussion of the political impact on the sending (home) country and the implications of the interactions of the two sets of forces for international relations must await another forum.

INCOMING DIRECT FOREIGN INVESTMENT

I assume that the MNC presents several faces to politically conscious persons around the world. The reactions of these persons are mediated by political institutions that determine policies that governments actually pursue toward the MNC. A model of this policy process is presented later. Most writing on the MNC over the past quarter-century suggests that nearly all stimuli can be considered under three broad headings: the MNC as *extension of the home country,* the MNC as *rival,* and the MNC as *resource.* Broadly speaking, the first face stresses the general foreign influences brought by the firm, the second its claim on resources that might otherwise go to some domestic element, and the third its augmentation of the productive capacity of the host country's economy.

The MNC as Extension of the Home Country

Incoming Direct Foreign Investment (IDFI) can be seen as an extension of the home country (1) because the firm appears protected by its home government (protégé), (2) because it seems to act at the behest of the home government (agent), or (3) because it serves as a means whereby broad foreign influences are injected into the host country (conduit for alien influence).

Protégé The MNC generates politically relevant stimuli in the host country when the home country is seen to safeguard the MNC's interests. In the developed countries this face has not typically been prominent. The pre-World War II experience of more developed countries with IDFI generally was not dramatic. After the war, the U.S. government exercised influence to gain comparable treatment for its MNCs in European nations under the Treaty of Rome, but little in the way of further specific action on behalf of individual firms or the business community in a particular DC has been seen until recently. In 1982, the U.S. Congress considered legislation designed to counter pending measures before the EEC commission requiring MNCs to share their future plans with host governments and employees. Such exceptional behavior was widely regarded with dismay in Europe (Johnson 1983).

The less developed countries provide a sharp contrast. The large trading and producing companies of the colonial empires became despised symbols of hierarchy and privilege. In many popular versions of imperialism the principal purpose of political control was to help these enterprises develop and prosper. In many of the republics of Latin America the relation was experienced just as vividly. They saw their claims as sovereign states thwarted by the superior power of Europeans and North Americans who intervened militarily over many decades to assert the property rights and to protect the safety of home country citizens. Thus did the prerogatives of foreign capital become virtually defined as an offense to nationalism. The United States formally abandoned intervention claims for such purposes in 1933, but military action in Guatemala in 1954 and in the Dominican Republic in 1965, as well as CIA activity in Chile in 1971, were widely regarded as intended mainly to protect U.S. business there. (That this interference may have been incorrect is politically irrelevant. For a careful account of many interventions, see Krasner 1978). France appears willing to intervene for similar purposes in Black Africa.

LDCs also feel that the Hickenlooper and Gonzales amendments—which oblige the United States to withhold international assistance from states that have not paid adequate compensation in cases of nationalization of U.S.-owned industries—are a continuing affront to the general Third World doctrine that such disputes should not extend beyond the borders of the host country.

Agent   The MNC may also be perceived as an agent of the home country. In contrast to the image (and often the reality) in many LDCs, the United States has most often used MNCs in the industrialized countries to achieve broad goals of foreign and domestic policy rather than to assist in covert activities.

The U.S. government in the 1960s forbade overseas subsidiaries from selling to China and Cuba and obliged them to find non-U.S. finance in the farce of U.S. balance-of-payments problems. U.S. authorities also blocked mergers that were thought likely to affect adversely the U.S. domestic market (Behrman 1970; Leyton-Brown 1973). Changes in the international monetary system in the 1970s ended most conflicts arising from the balance of payments, however. The other two sources of conflict, also based on the extraterritorial claims of U.S. law, continue. By claiming that its laws extend to its MNCs operating abroad, the United States has aroused almost universal condemnation abroad from all parts of the political spectrum. Legislatures of many countries have attempted to assist their bureaucrats and courts in resisting the U.S. reach by passing specific legislation directing noncompliance.

In the LDCs the provocation stems less frequently from explicit claims of extraterritoriality and more often from evidence or rumor of spying and covert manipulation of the political system. The activities of the CIA in Latin America, sometimes working with U.S. business, and the claims of close ties between intelligence services of other countries and their MNCs have generated widespread suspicion and revulsion across a broad range of domestic politics (Sigmund 1980, ch. 2).

The potential threat to national security perceived from the connections of MNCs with their host governments has led both DCs and LDCs to block foreign firms from defense-related industries. France, largely because of her determination to maintain an independent foreign policy, has been particularly cautious in this area. Several Latin American governments in recent years have increased attention to such concerns. Dominguez suggests that limiting foreign participation in industries related to national defense is particularly likely where the military exercises strong political influence (1982a, 26, 33, and 59–60).

Conduit for Alien Influence   The apparent Americanization of the developed world, largely, or so it seemed, under the auspices of the MNC, stirred passion from the mid-1950s until perhaps the early 1970s. Servan-Schreiber stated the issues forcefully in *Le Défi Americain* of 1967. Except for Japan, most industrialized countries responded to the U.S. challenge by adapting more than resisting, as Servan-Schreiber recommended. His book was much less an attack on the United States or its MNCs than it was an indictment of the slowness of European public policy to respond to the challenges posed by the complex relations among technology, wealth, and especially power in the postwar world. His observations about Europe's educational system and social structure prompted policy responses, as did some of his suggestions for industrial policy. Governments became heavily involved in subsidized research, encouraged mergers, and increased their preferential purchasing from national firms (Moran 1976)—not merely European Community-based firms. The major states encouraged *national champions* in key industries.

Despite the pivotal role they seem to have played in provoking broad policy responses by other Western governments, the U.S.-based MNCs did not typically generate a large amount of political tensions toward specific firms or even the home government. The policy changes, even when they directly affected MNCs, did so in a way that left them a broad range of attractive, permissible activity.

An apparent threat to autonomy—and in some cases to security as well—was countered by disallowing or limiting foreign participation in

certain basic sectors of the economy in addition to defense-related industries. Some countries that have no restriction on the right of establishment
of foreign firms have used foreign exchange laws to monitor and perhaps
occasionally modify foreigners' plans (Britain and Italy). But some have
not (Germany, Switzerland, and the United States). Other countries have
employed direct screening. Norway and Sweden examine all incoming
investment but with little apparent deterrent effect, while France does so
with great thoroughness. In France, the rejection rate on proposed IDFI
ventures in the late 1970s was estimated to be much higher than elsewhere in Europe—at perhaps 5 percent. And where takeovers have been
proposed (even from elsewhere in the European Economic Community)
the French government has frequently tried to find a French buyer instead (Safarian 1978, 645–646). France presents yet another contrast to
most of the rest of Europe. Because the intimate role of the French
government in business decision-making is well known, the government
is likely to take much of the blame or credit for specific incursions by
foreign capital.

A third pattern of entry control is followed by Canada, Australia, and
Japan. Entry, expansion, and takeovers are monitored by a distinct entity.
In Canada, about half of all manufacturing output and 70 percent of oil
production were in foreign hands in 1970. Canada's Foreign Investment
Review Agency (FIRA), established in 1974, now requires *significant benefit* for the country from the proposed foreign-based activity. Its rejection
rate of 8 percent on new activity and 16 percent on takeovers in 1977 was
far higher than in Europe (Safarian 1978, 647). FIRA has been attacked
both by international business and from within the country because its
rationale for decisions is not public and is ultimately decided at the cabinet
level. The issue is kept constantly in the public eye by the greater enthusiasm for IDFI in poorer provinces. Regional differences in attempting to
attract IDFI may be less politically important in more centralized states
(Leyton-Brown 1980).

In Australia, where IDFI penetration is in many respects similar to
that in Canada, there is an additional emphasis on local participation, with
the required percentage varying by sector (*The Economist* 1980, 74; FIRA
1979). Among the Western developed countries, Canada and Australia are
unique, not simply because of their stringency, but because IDFI has long
been a major issue in their mass electoral politics, with a significant part
of the political leadership actively cultivating nationalist sentiment.

Japan presents the most restrictive case; foreign investment in more
than negligible amounts has been permitted only in recent years. Japan's
sense of uniqueness and vulnerability after an extremely unhappy series
of early contacts with Europeans on Japanese soil set an enduring pattern
of minimizing any permanent foreign presence, let alone one of substantial influence or control. In 1970 there were fewer than 25,100 residents
from Western countries in Japan (Henderson 1973, 16). Instead of allowing
substantial DFI, Japan increasingly broadened the scope of licensed tech-

nology (Shea 1980). Pressure from major home countries, particularly the United States, has led in recent years to a nominal lessening of restrictions but only minor changes in actual penetration.

Again, the conduit face of MNCs appears more dramatic and threatening in the less developed countries than elsewhere. In many LDCs, the MNC has virtually become the symbolic embodiment of the modern world in broad ranges of national life. Foreign business thus becomes a source of annoyance and frustration to those who must modify their behavior to work successfully as employees, customers, or suppliers. Those most wedded to the traditional society regard the MNC as a principal symbol of evil. There are many who welcome the modernization that the MNC symbolizes, but even most of these would prefer such change to take place under national auspices and control. One looks in vain for a strong defense of direct foreign influence from any part of the political spectrum in any country, rich or poor.

Foreign penetration leading ultimately to social decay features prominently in the *dependéncia* literature from Latin America. The comprehensiveness of the approach is captured by Sunkel:

> Foreign factors are seen not as external but as intrinsic to the system, with manifold and sometimes hidden or subtle political, financial, economic, technical, and cultural effects inside the underdeveloped country. These contribute significantly to shaping the nature and operation of the economy, society, and polity, a kind of "fifth column" as it were.[2]

For further discussion of *dependéncia* views, see Cardoso and Faletto (1979) and Caporaso and Zare (1981).

The threat to autonomy presented by the three dimensions of the MNC as extension of the home country take on different significance for most LDCs relative to DCs. In the developed world most people regard the challenges posed by MNCs as discrete and visible, but among the newly modernizing countries the fear of pervasive and largely invisible domination by MNCs has become widespread.

The MNC as Rival of Government

Although the MNC as conduit encompasses political phenomena generated by the MNC largely unintentionally, as a result of its pursuit of profit, the MNC as government rival encompasses certain intentional activities. The latter may be as minor as tax minimization within the apparent discretion of the law, or as major as deception and corruption, manipulation, and even system disruption.

In the developed countries direct rivalry between foreign firms and host-country governments has been far less of an issue than in the developing world. Although there are exceptions, foreign enterprises have generally operated within the realm of accepted law. Tax avoidance has seldom provided an important source of conflict (Vernon 1971, 139). Whenever such rivalry has become overt, however, the MNC has received condemnation in the media and in other public discourse. The opposition of the U.S. Chamber of Commerce in West Germany to certain elements of the co-determination legislation of the 1970s caused a furor in a country whose general hospitality toward DFI is very high. The lobbying action taken by the Chamber was, in essence, declared illegitimate by the West German chancellor (Bock 1980, 12).

The DCs have also experienced a vague uneasiness that the economic outlook of the MNC is somehow incongruent with that of the host state, or more specifically that a foreign firm can never be sufficiently subordinate to state power to be entirely satisfactory. The French adduce as evidence the ability of U.S. firms in the 1960s to obtain funds not controlled by the French government and hence to escape *le plan* (Kindleberger 1969, 81). Special competitive assets virtually define the MNC (Caves 1971); nonetheless, most evidence suggests that foreign and domestic firms now usually see and react to most economic situations quite similarly. However, some apprehension remains.

The history of rivalry between the MNC and host-country governments in the Third World is typically of a wholly different order from the situation elsewhere. Prior to World War II the overwhelming share of all direct investment in Third World countries was in natural resource extraction or public utilities. Even in the industrialized countries these two sectors have given rise to great policy difficulties because ownership often confers excess profits or rent. Excess profits of one kind or another thus frequently became a central focus of LDC government concern from the very earliest period. And yet, for extended periods, policymaking groups were frequently so inept, corrupt, or easily coopted that the host government gained little from the MNC relative to the host's potential. Foreign firms frequently manipulated not just specific decisions, but the broader political process. Goodsell's treatment (1974) of International Petroleum in Peru illustrates such activity.

The recent history of the rivalry between the MNC and developing country governments is recounted quite similarly in both the conventional and the radical literature (Bergsten, Horst, and Moran 1978, 369–395; Evans 1979b, 23–24). In the early postwar years, the broad security interests of the host countries, their lack of sophistication in dealing with the MNC, and the absence of alternative sources of foreign resources gave foreign—usually U.S.—firms the upper hand. U.S. MNCs established well over two-thirds of all new foreign-owned subsidiaries in LDCs between 1946 and 1959 (Bergsten, Horst, and Moran 1978, 370–371). Washington later reconsidered its security interests, excluding the protection of U.S. capital. MNCs could no longer count on strong support in disputes with host country governments.

Other developments also diminished with MNC power. Host governments developed much stronger skills and monitoring capacities during the 1960s and 1970s, a time when the emerging alternative of non-U.S.

MNCs provided additional leverage. In industries with large fixed investments and familiar technologies, including much of natural resource exploitation and public utilities, nationalization often became an irresistibly attractive option (Sigmund 1980, ch. 2). Where nationalization was rejected as an appropriate policy, governments learned that whatever bargain was initially struck, the rules could be continually changed on the foreign investor—up to the point at which the firm could no longer meet its out-of-pocket costs. This is Vernon's *obsolescing bargain* (Vernon 1971, 46–59).

In natural resources and elsewhere, the increasingly sophisticated policies of many Third World governments, including virtually all where large amounts of capital are invested, have focused on reducing the profitability of a broad range of foreign direct investments.[3] By the end of the 1970s, many countries had developed specialized agencies to act as sole national representatives to bargain directly with the MNCs for the best possible terms regardless of the type of activity.

Most recent case histories of the MNC in LDCs suggest few covert attempts to manipulate the political system (Leonard 1980). Corruption and attempts to evade profit-reducing regulations certainly continue, but now the MNCs sometimes assure that necessary payments are made indirectly (Biersteker 1980). Spectacular exceptions such as ITT's vendetta against the Allende government notwithstanding, contemporary practice by foreign firms appears in general to be politically cautious, a recognition both of the extent to which such activity is regarded as illegitimate and of the effectiveness of retribution.

Several factors beyond those already mentioned explain the sharp and systematic difference between DC and LDC practice on the stringency and specificity of controls on IDFI. First, there is typically little international competition in heavily protected LDC markets, and the MNC frequently fills a niche in the economy where there will also be little domestic competition. Second, the developing world has favored greater asymmetry of treatment between LDCs and DCs and sees no merit in the nondiscriminatory treatment of domestic and foreign business (Dominguez 1982a, 24ff). This position is bolstered by laws and social attitudes toward private property that are typically extremely flexible and often present no barrier to treating each case on its own apparent merits with no necessity for consistent application of general rules.

Finally, while nineteenth-century liberalism prevails less in nearly all countries, rich and poor, than it does in the United States, the history of all political factions in most developing countries reveals a particular willingness to use the state to any extent necessary to create the conditions for economic development. Even where the prevailing elite ideology has seen private enterprise as the principal engine of material advance, the state has been regarded as a crucial, positive actor (Bennett and Sharpe 1980).

A very broad notion of what constitutes infrastructural activity has characterized most poor countries; and, in most, the state also engages in a large amount of activity that is clearly substitutive for what could be done by the private sector (Duvall and Freeman 1983). Observers have identified at least three major rationales for the extension of state enterprise into the commercial sphere: First, there are occasions when domestic private firms appear to lack the capital or other requisites that the government deems necessary for national development; second, local private attempts to play such a role may have failed, with the state taking over; third, the state has often intervened to counteract *denationalization* of industry by MNCs (Bennett and Sharpe 1980, 179–180).

The third possible motive generates a variety of policies. Nationalization has already been mentioned. Compensation is typically paid, although it is often modest relative to the owners's valuation (Sigmund 1980, 36–37). Often the state becomes the operator of the enterprise. In other cases, the state moves into a promising new area to avoid entrance there by the MNC. Finally, increasing numbers of countries have laws prescribing the minimum amount of domestic ownership that foreign capital must employ in endeavors of various kinds. Mexico has a highly elaborated structure. There, the government may simply become the last resort investor when private firms do not come forward.

The MNC as Rival of Domestic Business

Rivalry for gain between domestic and foreign business has been a pervasive and significant political issue in the DCs. Particularly in the 1950s and 1960s, domestic firms in many countries felt deeply threatened both by the superior competitive potential of foreign firms (cost, design, and marketing advantages) and their relatively unrestrained exercise of that potential in what had often previously been an environment of mutual accommodation. This adverse but diffuse feeling generated little in the way of political product. Nevertheless, partly as a result of domestic business lobbying, sectors in addition to defense-related industries have been closed to foreign capital or meet resistance to foreign penetration from DC authorities. These include private utilities, transportation, and communications including the media, banking and finance, and to a widely varying extent, natural resources and land (Safarian 1978; Black et al. 1978).

The typical developing country entirely excludes foreign capital from at least as broad a range of activity as do most industrialized states. Moreover, several severely restrict operations in wholesale and retail trade (UN 1978, 40). In the early period of modern development, there were many firms whose activities complemented those of foreign firms and rather few that could have ambitions to duplicate them. But over time acquisition of skills and experience by indigenous firms typically shifted the balance quite radically and greatly increased elements wishing to displace foreign investment (Vernon 1971, 198–201; Dominguez 1982a). Several developments reflect this shift. Because of the absence of notions of nondiscriminatory treatment, locally-owned LDC business has lobbied for preferential government purchasing in a wide variety of industries (Dominguez 1982a, 40) and in some countries has successfully blocked MNCs from access to the local capital market (Fishlow 1982, 147). Such discrimination encourages the formation of joint ventures between local and foreign capital even where they are not mandated by law (Dominguez 1982a, 25).

Although the relative size of the state entrepreneurial sector varies widely, the growing strength of both the entrepreneurial bureaucracy and private business has accompanied more negative attitudes by both toward foreign business and, in some countries, has produced a more exclusionary policy (Frieden 1981, 429 and references).

The MNC as Rival of Labor

A third major rivalry is with organized labor, and in the DCs it takes several forms. One is the traditional quest for above-market wages, a goal that seems generally to have been achieved more fully in dealings with MNCs than with domestic firms. However, U.S. MNCs have typically been assertive about workplace organization and resistant to responsibility for the stability of employment. The greater paternalism of Japanese firms operating in the United States has generated tension.

In most DCs, labor has understandably tried to gain some package of high wages and increased employment as it stands firm against foreigners' preferences that threaten other goals. Vernon has observed that most European unions oppose the MNC because they feel that their bargaining power is threatened by its mobility and they see the welfare state threatened by decreased national autonomy. As a practical matter, however, national EEC unions must be concerned for jobs; they understand that presenting difficulties for foreign firms may simply drive these firms elsewhere (Vernon 1977, 113). Effective opposition to foreign capital awaits a Europe-wide labor organization, which shows little sign of developing. In the United States the AFL-CIO has shown little opposition to foreign investment in general but has criticized its frequent preference for location in right-to-work states. This position is consistent with U.S. labor's largely nonideological character.

Rivalry between the MNC and labor typically attains less importance in LDCs than in the DCs because industrial workers in LDCs usually have less power in both the political system and the workplace. Some successful industrializing countries, such as Singapore, Malaysia, Indonesia, and South Korea, have attracted foreign capital in part by promising and delivering a quiescent labor force (Navyor 1978, 77). Elsewhere, however, including Mexico, the government has sometimes encouraged nationalism in general and its own political base in particular by supporting organized labor in disputes with foreign capital (Bennett et al. 1978, 264).

The MNC as Resource

Despite the other manifestations, often negative, of foreign penetration, the major governments of the Western industrialized countries have generally regarded IDFI mainly as a means of increasing national material welfare by adding tangible resources. The Organization for European Economic Cooperation (OEEC) Council recommended the liberalization of capital movements in Europe in 1957 as part of the general restoration of normal economic activity; much liberalization was accomplished in the following few years. The successor Organization for Economic Cooperation and Development (OECD) incorporated these provisions and expanded cooperation on matters related to DFI (Aubrey 1967, 64–65), with the objective of non-discrimination between foreign and domestic capital. Elite surveys reveal that this policy has generally reflected informed opinion, and most economic analyses have confirmed the contribution of IDFI to national income through its capital, technology, management, and marketing innovations (Dunning 1957; Safarian 1973). Although administrative discretion may be used to discourage acquisition in some sectors to an extent that is not fully public, most countries continue to welcome investment in most sectors of the economy. They give special incentives— usually also available to domestic firms—for new operations in regions of high unemployment (Safarian 1978).

In Japan, management and marketing have been largely irrelevant to the country's unique social system, and Japan's high savings rate has greatly diminished the appeal of a foreign capital contribution. The only compelling MNC offering has been technology, much of which has become available through licensing. When Japan's general attitude toward foreign presence is combined with its actual economic needs, the tight restrictions on the MNC become easily understandable.

All of the negative political phenomena generated by the MNC in LDCs should not obscure the fact that most countries still actively recruit MNCs in many sectors of the economy and that this posture is consistent with informed opinion. For example, a substantial role for DFI is supported by a diverse set of groups in Latin America (Dominguez 1982a).

Foreign borrowing grew enormously in the 1970s, but it cannot completely replace DFI unless the other resources that equity brings are redundant or can be easily purchased separately. A richer set of international markets in management and technology coupled with increased domestic sophistication has certainly increased the second possibility. And yet a nearly universal demand for substantial MNC activity remains. In many fields the most attractive technology and expertise does not come in *unbundled* form; the advantages in foreign market access that are inherent in most manufacturing MNCs often cannot be duplicated except at a very high price (Vernon 1977, ch. 7). A rapid and premature jettisoning of the MNC—even in natural resource industries—has led some countries to economic disaster (Shafer 1983).

In 1975, OPEC accounted for 23 percent of all IDFI in LDCs; ten other countries hosted 41 percent (UN 1978, Table II-47). Much of the rest of the developing world, although maintaining a nominally complex set of requirements for entering investment, actively recruits DFI with various incentives but finds rather little interest.

POLITICS AND POLICY TOWARD IDFI: AN INTERPRETATION

From the foregoing description one can conclude that policies toward MNCs vary between developed and less developed countries. I now address in greater detail how these policies are made and why they differ. The interpretive scheme developed here draws heavily on economic theory. The relation between the two major types of economic goods and the faces of the MNC will first be established, to be followed by an outline of one public choice approach to the determination of policy. The interaction of the faces with a small set of policy determinants will then be used to illustrate the power of the public choice approach to explain (1) characteristics of MNC policy in both DCs and LDCs and (2) systematic differences between the two sets of countries.

A Public Choice Approach

Private goods such as apples or automobiles are exhaustible: If I eat the apple, you cannot eat it, too. Public goods, such as in the national defense, have the property that all citizens will be affected nonexhaustively; because you are protected, there is not therefore less protection left over for me. Typically, public goods also have the property that I cannot be excluded from experiencing the good once it is produced: I am *protected* whether I like it or not. Indeed, some public goods may not be regarded as *good* at all by many consumers. If I am a pacifist and you are not, defense expenditures may lower my welfare as they raise yours. But even where all consumers have a positive valuation, public goods are differently evaluated in a way that policy makers usually cannot measure accurately, so that the provision of the *right* amount of a costly public good must necessarily remain a largely unattained goal. The situation may be even murkier where policy making must trade off one public good for another.

The political impact of the MNC can be thought of in terms of public and private goods. Manifestations under the "extension of the home country" are largely issues involving public goods because they produce a directly experienced impact on fundamental values in the host country. As the discussion has suggested, the impacts of the MNC on autonomy and security have typically been perceived negatively. Some citizens have welcomed the modernization brought by the MNC.

Part of the rivalry with government is also a public good. If, as was frequently the case in earlier years, the MNC intentionally manipulated the very structure of host country governments for its own ends, this manipulation influenced the division of material profit between the MNC and the governments as it also generated other *products*—including damage to the psyches of local citizens. Such an outcome is also true of the lack of national economic control that the MNC has been alleged to bring in both rich and poor countries. Any sense of diminished autonomy (whatever the facts) can generate psychic costs.

Most of the MNC's present rivalry with LDC governments turns on the division of tangible resources, a private good. The rivalry with business and labor the world over is largely over such divisible private stakes as well. In all cases, the *game* is seen as essentially zero sum—one party's gain is necessarily another's loss.

The resource face of the MNC stresses augmentation of the productive potential of the host economy. There is at least implicit recognition that both parties may come out ahead in the exchange, or, if accommodation breaks down, both may lose. This emphasis on cooperative activity between economic agents in the production of private goods highlights perhaps the most fundamental idea of modern economics: bargaining that increases efficiency can improve the welfare of all parties.

Having established the economic character of the stakes involved in the MNC policy, the next step is to look at politics and policy. The analytic scheme employed here builds from one previously used by the author and Davis Bobrow (1982). It derives—in an eclectic fashion—from the application of microeconomic theory to political phenomena, an approach that has come to be known as *public choice* (Mueller 1979). Instead of beginning with the group or class as is usual in political science, microeconomics begins with the individual. Among other advantages, only such an approach can explain why some interests never organize, and why groups form and disintegrate. The inability of traditional pluralist political science to deal satisfactorily with these and other issues opened the door for the microeconomic approach. A pioneering discussion is Mancur Olson's *The Logic of Collective Action* (1965). The public choice approach treats the way in which individuals are stimulated by their environment on matters of potential political significance and how these stimuli interact with attitudes and interests to remain dormant or to lead individuals to act—to make, alter, or retain policy. In this approach the determinants of existing policy (including no policy at all) and all alternative policies can be interpreted under four headings: impact transparency, ideological consonance, the distribution of costs and benefits, and institutional context.[4]

Impact transparency, one central policy determinant, treats how clearly and completely the results of a policy are seen by all affected parties. Sometimes a policy impact is clear at the very outset, although it obviously can be differently evaluated by various members of a polity. Other policies may gain in general clarity over time or suggest certain results to some individuals and groups more clearly than to others. In such circumstances leadership may play a particularly important role by overcoming the information-gathering costs that plague individuals and minor groups. This leadership will typically try to link imperfectly understood policy ramifications either to ideological predispositions or material interests.

Another policy determinant, *ideological consonance,* gauges the extent to which the prevailing or an alternative policy better fits the value predisposition of the individual or group. This category concerns general value orientations, quite independently of specific interest. Nothing discovered in the study of national IDFI policies casts doubt on the fundamental national values of prosperity, autonomy, and security (Kudrle and Bobrow 1982).[5] Prosperity can be expected to include growth and employment. Autonomy means not only independence from foreign pressure and manipulation but also something close to a biological meaning: *organic independence.* Security implies sufficient military strength to discourage foreign adversaries. In the present instance, MNC activity can be seen to diminish or augment these three "goods" in various ways.

Where policymakers have no more immediate interests, in other words, where they are pursuing their conception of the *national interest,* these values can be expected to predominate. Citizens can be expected to share these values, but their link to specific policies will be based not only on the declarations of national leaders but also upon the views of the leaders of the other groups with which citizens are affiliated. The "untutored or experienced" sense of cause and effect as perceived by individual citizens will also come into play (and will, in turn, be affected by impact transparency).

A third consideration, the *distribution of perceived costs and benefits*—of *interests* as usually defined—provides the basis for much of the economic approach to the determinants of public policy. A concentration of perceived impact upon a small number of heavily affected actors is assumed to generate more response than a more diffuse impact of greater total magnitude. When the impact is very diffuse, no one party may expect a positive pay-off from efforts at organizing to take political action, and hence nothing is done. This may be called the collective action problem. (For the classic discussion, see Olson 1965, ch. 2).

A final policy determinant is *institutional context.* Issues related to IDFI arise in a context of preexisting organized groups and, more broadly, a specific institutional configuration of private and public power. These considerations seem to encompass approximately what Peter Katzenstein covers by the term *domestic structures* (Katzenstein 1976).

In sum, the first consideration deals with how clearly the impact of a policy is seen by various parties, the second with how the policy fits with fundamental values; the third with a policy's service of various interests, and the fourth with the institutional context in which the policy issue arises and is resolved.[6]

The usefulness of the approach just developed can be illustrated with reference to three key areas of policy toward the MNC: the pattern and extent of sectors in which IDFI activity is controlled in the DCs, the systematically greater exclusion in the South, and the role of state entrepreneurship in LDCs. One can further assess the value of the approach by applying it briefly to Robert Gilpin's (1975a) "Three Models of the Future" of MNCs and government policies.

Sectoral Protection in the North

The argument just presented suggests that economic policy will generally be skewed toward concentrated groups. Because consumers are far less concentrated than producers, the implication is that producers will typically have the upper hand in the formulation of economic policy (Downs 1957; Olson 1965). But among the DCs, this consideration alone would suggest a much higher level of domestic industry protection in both trade and investment than in fact prevails. Ideological consonance must be considered. Most DCs brought into the postwar world not only the desire for prosperity but also some strong presumptions about the general lines of policy that would serve to enhance it. Europeans have always had a more ambivalent attitude toward competition than have Americans, but the postwar period began with a commitment to increasing rather than diminishing the level of competition in most countries. Increased competition was widely regarded as one of the chief economic advantages of the Common Market, and those who drew up the Treaty of Rome fitted it with pro-competitive language that exceeded the national practice of all of the constituent states. Protectionism against foreigners per se would thus entail a transparent attempt to sell general inefficiency in the name of national autonomy. Where specific threats to security or autonomy could be claimed, of course, protectionist policy met with much less resistance. The private gain to local producers could be augmented with the public good of psychic gain for the community. A similar pattern is observed in most other DCs.

Defense industries provided the easiest case, and nearly every nation offers some protection to purely domestic producers in this sphere through preferential purchase. Other frequently reserved areas include private utilities, transportation, and communications. In most countries, these spheres are regarded as so fundamental to the national economy that they are partly nationalized; in all, they are heavily regulated. Nationalists have argued consistently that influence by foreigners would threaten both security and autonomy. Banking and finance constitute a part of an economy that has historically conjured up visions of manipulation and domination by foreign elements. And natural resource exploitation, with its aura of innate scarcity and the lurid history of MNC involvement in poorer countries, has generated a strong push for greater national control in Canada and Australia.

With the exception of some defense industries, most of the industries protected against IDFI involve output for which the relative international production efficiency is somewhat difficult to judge. In many cases services are produced for domestic consumption that are difficult to compare with those produced abroad. In natural resource exploitation, exploration and production conditions are highly specific to local circumstances. Thus, any inefficiencies in exploration or production that would result from confining these activities to nationally-owned companies would probably be very difficult to document. In all of these cases, the net cost of nationalism is therefore difficult to estimate; its impact transparency is low.[7]

In the media, protectionism seems to meet less resistance in proportion to the general fear of cultural imperialism, an assault on autonomy. Thus, Canada and Australia, high-income countries whose media might otherwise be far more an extension of the U.S. media than they are, have some of the most stringent controls.

The *national champion* strategy of the major European countries in the 1960s and 1970s presents a complex but powerful combination of national ambition and vested interest, an amalgam of reaction to the agent, conduit, and rival faces. The general objective was to make certain that some industries—frequently R & D intensive industries—were maintained independent of MNC domination. The basic claim held that a largely independent capacity to produce future prosperity was also an efficient strategy for such prosperity. Because legitimate doubts could be entertained, protectionist claims were typically most successful when combined with some national security objectives, e.g., relative independence in computer technology. Sometimes the *national champions* were developed in cooperation with MNCs, so they have not always represented exclusion, yet they do typify an important phenomenon: the combination of domestic capitalists (or sometimes state enterprises; see Freeman 1982b) and highly trained professionals to put the case for favoritism, resulting in higher earnings for both. The capitalists earn more because of the absence of competition, and the professionals earn more because they have the opportunity to duplicate—at least to some extent—a technology that is already known abroad. Most observers have been unimpressed by the economic efficiency of the *national champion* strategy; it thus appears that domestic capitalists and professionals gain at the expense of the rest of society.

While the protectionism just discussed promises higher income for domestic capitalists and some professionals, the reader will note that no such rewards generally accrue to agriculture or labor. Agriculture has succeeded in winning special subsidies for itself in most DCs, but this simply leaves a greater burden on labor. Such an indictment lies at the heart of the Breton-Johnson model of nationalism as an inequitable as well as inefficient component in policy toward production of material goods (Breton 1964; Johnson 1965). The two argue that only if there is some reason to believe that foreign-owned production would be relatively inefficient or if the working classes would benefit disproportionately from the public good that nationalism produces would this outcome be avoided. In fact, although there is little evidence that either condition holds, impact transparency is so low that the issue is seldom faced squarely, and most policy remains inertially determined. The situation is further confused by the frequent fusion of socialism with nationalism in politics. This consideration directs attention to the institutional context in which the policy is determined.

Both space and available information preclude a further investigation of the subject. But the general approach presented here might be useful in a detailed comparative study of restricted sectors across the developed states.

Exclusion in the South

The earlier discussion stresses how much more negative the extension and rival faces of DFI have been in most LDCs than in the industrialized world. Moreover, the two kinds of countries typically differ substantially in presumptions about how economic policy can best encourage prosperity. For most of the relatively advanced LDCs, particularly those in Latin America, open competitive markets either nationally or internationally are viewed with much suspicion. If such markets were sufficient—or even necessary—for national development, then why has satisfactory national development not taken place?

The nearly universal support for an activist state has generated a situation in most LDCs that provides a very different setting from richer countries. In particular, goods markets are not systematically disciplined by international competition, and domestic production often takes place with little if any competition. These two conditions frequently offer the possibility of high profits for local producers, whether MNCs or domestic firms. Hence the stakes for the substitution of domestic for foreign-owned production may fuel determined lobbying efforts. And where national firms can argue that their competence is sufficient, LDC governments will normally allow them to perform the activity (Dominguez 1982a). In doing so, the government can typically count on strong public support. The adequacy of subsequent performance may be quite difficult to judge. Competing foreign products are not available, and, where it can be discerned that domestic prices are high by international standards, assignment of responsibility to the producing firms as opposed to input suppliers or an overvalued exchange rate will frequently be difficult. Moreover, independent expertise to perform such evaluations is scarce in LDCs, and sponsors are not obvious.

A strong case can be made that the bias in favor of domestic capital and the professional classes at the expense of agriculture and labor is considerably greater in LDCs than in DCs. Among other political differences, business is not dominated by free trade forces as it is in many DCs.

Mancur Olson suggests that because developing societies are typically unstable, special interests based on small groups are particularly likely to prevail over interests requiring the organization of large groups; the formation and sustenance of the larger organizations is discouraged by an unstable society (Olson 1982). This small-group dominance will be most important where political power actively discourages large-group activity. Even during periods of general repression, small groups can frequently maintain some cohesion and hence capacity for quick collective action when the opportunity arises. Olson further argues that the entire policy of import substitution was pursued with such vigor largely because of the great advantage that numerically small urban interests had in communication. This resulted in high cohesion and effective lobbying. Import-substituting local firms would also be expected to be among the strongest purveyors of the ideology of economic nationalism. The greater ability of urban interests to bring down governments contributed to this result and also to governments's attempts to provide artificially low food prices at the expense of farmers and agricultural production (Bates 1981).

The public choice approach assumes that agents calculate their own or society's interest and act thereon. But they must have information. The distributional consequences of the policies toward the MNC and economic development in general have very low impact transparency and can hence be driven largely by general antipathy toward foreign capital and a *dirigiste* consensus about economic policy. The aggregate relative efficiency of such policies cannot, of course, remain hidden forever. If such policies produce apparently poor performance, they might be revised.[8] Rates of growth will inevitably be compared with the country's earlier performance or with countries that citizens or elites think are in some ways comparable. The possible existence of international reference groups lies beyond the scope of this paper, but, in general, the experience of LDCs in the 1970s does not provide unambiguous evidence that a restrictive and highly controlled regime toward IDFI is antithetical to aggregate advance. Brazil and Mexico, for example, experienced conspicuously high growth rates while maintaining among the world's most highly monitored MNC regimes.

Foreign dependence, against which nationalism is formally directed, and the diminution of which is widely held to be a pervasive and important national goal in LDCs (Sigmund 1980), seems by all definitions to be much broader than a simple reliance on IDFI. It is usually presented as containing two components: reliance on foreign capital and reliance on foreign technology (Freeman and Duvall 1983). A dependence on foreign capital can relate to at least three separate needs. First, there may be dependence on foreign savings to promote domestic capital formation in excess of what would otherwise be possible. Second, there may be a need for foreign exchange per se because of an inability to easily expand exports or diminish imports. Third, foreign *direct* investment brings resources in addition to capital.

Technological dependence too is innately ambiguous. The reliance on foreign sources of innovation is one sort, even though the embodiment of that technology in new goods may take place in the host country. Another is the dependence on foreign countries for capital goods. The prevailing literature gives little guidance about which kinds of dependence generate the strongest reaction among various groups. However, a public choice interpretation seems to fit such evidence as exists. If, as has been argued, ideological predisposition is most powerful when allied with the tangible interests of influential groups one would expect dependence on IDFI to be opposed far more strenuously than foreign debt. The opposition to IDFI engages the interest of domestic forces to replace foreign firms, whereas debt servicing is as diffuse and invisible a form of cost as can be imagined—unless calculations go awry and the country must turn to the International Monetary Fund for assistance.

One can also hypothesize that the lack of an autonomous innovative capacity will continue to receive less attention than the importation of capital goods. Import substitution will develop a relentlessly expanding constituency over time, but most of the potential beneficiaries of a drive to create an autonomous capacity are far weaker, more diffuse, and at least partially unconscious. Moreover, the value of such a capacity is difficult to measure and the results of its absence are far from transparent.

State Entrepreneurship

The public choice approach finds the desire to get the maximum out of the foreigner an obvious objective for governments that are otherwise unconstrained, and there are powerful motives for domestic business success fully to contest MNC activity. The expansion of state instead of private interests in many LDCs requires explanation, however. A plausible approach seems to be that, however modest its origins, the unfolding of state activity creates an ever more powerful interest group within the government and one of its key pillars of legitimacy and political support (Duvall and Freeman 1983).

Why does the state sector seem to be more on the offensive in many countries than the business classes that are also typically heavily represented in the ruling coalition? Why should salaried employees who only control the disposition of wealth be more assiduous and successful than those with an ownership stake? Why do local ownership requirements frequently go beyond anything that the private domestic sector seems able to supply?

In the first place, just as urban interests may often dominate rural sectors in LDCs because of the advantage physical proximity affords to overcoming the collective action problem, some combination of continuous interaction among leaders of government enterprise and the possibility for considerable logrolling in the budget process may lead to fewer resource constraints than the private sector faces. This possibility seems particularly likely where, as is frequently the case, the government provides a large amount of capital for both public and private sectors (Frieden 1981). Resource allocation from inside the bureaucracy may be manipulated in such a way that public enterprises gain precedence.

Second, although state entrepreneurship produces goods that are marketable, it intermittently or systematically embraces goals other than profit maximization, claiming to produce economic or political benefits that could not be expected from private firms (Choksi 1979). Indeed, some public enterprises have gained new functions in response to the political need to engage in uneconomic pricing (Bennett and Sharpe 1980, 185). Local purchasers of this output may be expected to support such state action (Dominguez 1982a, 22). These varied objectives are pursued in the context of general price distortion and weak competition. Moreover, the state sector frequently expands into producer goods industries in which any increased cost or reduced quality may not be transparent to the final purchaser.

The output of state enterprises may frequently involve monopolistic production—the value of which is extraordinarily difficult to judge—pursued by organizations attempting to maximize their size. These ingredients lead William Niskanen to a public choice model of bureaucracy in which output is likely to be much higher than would be the case if information were more clearly available to those bearing the costs, or their representatives (Niskanen 1971).[9] A detailed application of the Niskanen approach to state entrepreneurship could be rewarding.

Assessments differ about the direct influence of business classes on foreign economic decisionmaking in developing countries. In Mexico, for example, some have concluded that the direct connection is rather weak (Bennett et al. 1978, 262–263), but in Korea, ties have been claimed to be closer than in Japan (Frieden 1981, 427). A hypothesis suggested by this comparison is that those states in which the government is most isolated from domestic business will experience the most rapid growth of state entrepreneurship. A confirmation would provide some evidence for the superiority of the *empire building* over the *development need* explanation for the growth of the state sector.

The response to the growth of the state sector by local business has varied greatly, but in Brazil the rivalry has sometimes become a political issue of the same salience as the contest between either and the MNC. (For a formal discussion of this three-way rivalry, see Freeman 1982a.) In many countries, the government's control over finance, mass communication, or both may cause private business to moderate its overt competition with the state sector out of fear of retaliation.

Comparing the Public Choice Model to Gilpin's "Models of the Future"

In 1975 Robert Gilpin posited three *models of the future* for the MNC. He argued that the rapidly changing configuration of world economic and political power, and particularly the shrinking dominance of the United States, implied a future for the MNC that necessarily looked quite different from the recent past. Depending on the precise conditions, Gilpin argued that the future could be modeled by three contrasting scenarios: the *sovereignty at bay* model that foresaw increasing power for, and acceptance of, MNC activity in both rich and poor countries; the *mercantilist* model that forecast increasing and successful state resistance to the prerogatives of foreign investors, and the *dependéncia* model that saw a future of increasing inequality of wealth and power between rich and poor countries resulting from the international division of labor largely organized under the auspices of the MNC.

Consider the sovereignty at bay model that predicts a constant advance of the MNC in appeal and penetration. When the MNC is viewed from the perspective of public choice theory, the sovereignty at bay model is seen to greatly exaggerate several aspects of reality. First, it gives insufficient attention to the goals of autonomy and security (by comparison with prosperity) in the eyes of ordinary citizens. Perhaps more important, the model largely ignores the issues of impact transparency and concentrated versus diffuse interests that lie at the heart of much of the calculation of effective political power. The routes by which various economic policies retard or advance general prosperity are frequently subject to some dispute even by experts, and much of the public will necessarily be confused or divided about the appropriate course of policy. In this context, concentrated interests, whether predominantly oriented toward openness, as in the United States, or protection, as in most of the developing world, will gain dominant influence. Finally, the sovereignty at bay model pays insufficient attention to the ways in which the MNC can be channeled, rather than simply accepted or rejected.

Just as the sovereignty at bay model gives too much emphasis to the single goal of prosperity, with an excessive emphasis on clear perceptions of mutual gain, the mercantilist model places too much emphasis on the issues of security and autonomy. The mercantilist argument frequently implies that the admitted perils of economic interdependence can be overcome by subglobal arrangements based on physical proximity. What such lines of argument ignore is that the autonomy sacrificed in cooperative economic arrangements may purchase little in the way of increased prosperity. Economic theory predicts greatest gain from trade among economies that are most different from one another, a goal seldom achieved by regionalism.

More fundamentally for the present discussion, those seeing mercantilism as the wave of the future and largely as a shorthand for trade restrictions are frequently vague about just what mercantilist thinking implies for DFI. If the prediction is that both outgoing and incoming direct foreign investment will be subject to dramatically more stringent controls, then the model's predictions remain largely unrealized. In one regional arrangement, the Andean Pact, which envisioned severe restraints on IDFI, neither the pact nor its IDFI provisions have operated as originally intended. At the same time, the mercantilist model understates the extent to which extreme forms of national or regional economic protectionism of various kinds can be clearly seen by decisionmaking elites and informed publics as a threat to national prosperity.

Finally, the *dependéncia* model as presented by Gilpin minimizes the role of the MNC as resource and the mutuality of gain that can obtain between the MNC and the host country; it also vastly underestimates the power of even small and weak states to gain MNC adherence to a more restrictive participatory regime. Several LDCs have combined high growth rates, substantial use of IDFI, and an income distribution that compares favorably with some Western countries. Although most LDCs have not, the ineluctable linkage between international capital and quantitatively or qualitatively inadequate economic development becomes suspect. The single most misleading characteristic of the *dependéncia* model may be its identification of the home country's welfare with that of the MNC. This assumption masks the current serious debate within the DCs on whether LDC investment policies allow net welfare gains for the richer countries.

SUMMARY

Although necessarily brief, this presentation of a public choice approach to government policies toward the MNC clarifies sectoral protection and why the policies of DCs and LDCs toward MNCs differ substantially. I have also tried to illustrate briefly how this approach can throw light on the *models of the future* posited by Gilpin in 1975. Multinational corporations will continue to be targets of government policies, and better understanding of how those policies are made and why they differ will increase understanding of the transnational world we now experience.

NOTES

1. Regrettably, space does not permit an exploration of the Socialist world as host to MNCs.
2. Oswaldo Sunkel, "Big Business and 'Dependencia' " *Foreign Affairs* 50 (April 1972): 517–531.
3. Skills vary greatly among countries, and increased control is sometimes more nominal than real. For the Nigerian case, see Biersteker (1980).
4. In Kurdle and Bobrow (1982) the final consideration was "the initial political capacity of different groups and institutions." The earlier work concerned political developments within the United States; the broader focus employed here reflects comparative concerns. The category presented here includes the earlier phenomena.

5. The primacy of these values can be verified inductively. Similar fundamental values appear in Nye and Keohane (1971) and are cited with favor by Strange (1976b). The list could be made longer, perhaps to include the international assertion of national values and culture for nations such as the United States and France. The three desiderata will serve for present purposes.

6. The present paper deals with only a small part of the policy space for most countries, though IDFI has been a major issue in many developing countries. The public choice approach could be used to explain ideological change based on learning, a large-scale reconfiguration of political forces, and even institutional change over time. For a discussion of the ideological implications of narrowly economic concerns, see Stigler and Becker (1977). For a broader discussion of ideology that retains an economist's perspective, see North (1981, 45–58).

7. A protected sector in many countries that fits the public choice model only with difficulty is the control of agricultural land ownership, where protection (which limits demand) is apparently supported by the land owners who stand to lose by it. For some speculation about the situation in the United States, see Kudrle and Bobrow (1982, 366–367).

8. Voting is, of course, not the principal means of governmental change in the developing world, and governments are frequently able to operate with considerable autonomy from outside pressure for sustained periods. But governments and elites alike are committed to economic growth, and the failure to produce it undermines legitimacy.

9. In a pioneering article, Duvall and Freeman (1983) have modeled the preferences of the state techno-bureaucracy within the objective function of the ruling coalition. In so doing, the posit two arguments in the utility function of the bureaucracy: the tangible income accruing to the sector and the *psychic income* from a diminution of the foreign role in the economy. The second concept admits various formulations, but it should also be noted that the literature on bureaucracy suggests a tradeoff between *empire* and personal income (Niskanen 1971, 39). This observation implies that increasing remuneration in the upper strata of the public sector might sometimes be a cheaper strategy for a government attempting to maintain its coalition than increasing the revenue of the sector as a whole.

Knowledge-Intensive Production and the Changing Internationalization Strategies of Multinational Firms

Lynn Krieger Mytelka

Capitalism is clearly in transition. Some have described its changing nature as postindustrial (Bell 1973), emphasizing thereby that the share in national output and employment contributed by manufacturing activity has declined relative to that of the service sector. Others have designated *late capitalism* as that period in which all branches of the economy have become automated (Mandel 1978, 191). Still others, notably the French *école de la régulation,* characterize contemporary capitalism in terms of its unique articulation between a mode of capital accumulation, in which the rate of technological change is accelerating, and a mode of consumption in which mass consumption norms, national and international, are adjusted to the dramatic rise in productivity generated by the process of intensive capital accumulation (Aglietta 1976, 1982; Lipietz 1982).

Despite their ideological differences, each of these approaches focuses upon the extent to which knowledge inputs have become increasingly more salient in the contemporary process of capital accumulation and its attendant mode of consumption. If we include in knowledge not only research and development (R & D) but also design, engineering, advertising, marketing, and management, then present trends suggest that knowledge inputs may be displacing capital, land, and labor as the primary defining feature of the production process in advanced industrial capitalism. Much has been written, in this connection, about the growth of the service sector, particularly the expansion of engineering consultancy, data processing, banking, and advertising (Pastre 1979; Spero 1983; Stanback 1981). The impact of automation on the labor process and on employment has also come under careful scrutiny in the literature (Garson 1975; Noble 1979; Forester 1980; *Scientific American* 1982). Less well examined, however, is the way in which knowledge inputs are affecting the growth strategies of firms, the nature of corporate competition, and the internationalization of production.

In this chapter three new growth strategies of multinational firms are identified and their consequences for a changing international division of labor are examined. By way of introduction, section one analyzes the growing knowledge-intensity of competition, and its historical relationship to the process of concentration and internationalization. Sections two, three, and four then explore, through a number of specific illustrations, each of the three new growth strategies: (1) the decentralization and internalization of knowledge production via the creation of autonomous development units within the firm, the location of research and development laboratories in overseas subsidiaries, and the introduction of world product mandates, (2) the delocalization of knowledge production to universities and institutes, and (3) the pursuit of joint ventures in design and production of high-technology products. The final section summarizes the arguments, and speculates briefly upon the consequences of these changes for the international division of labor.

THE SALIENCE OF KNOWLEDGE INPUTS IN PRODUCTION

In the eighteenth and nineteenth centuries, contact between scientists and industry was neither systematic nor institutionalized. This changed with the growth of the chemical and electrical engineering industries in the latter half of the nineteenth and early-twentieth centuries (Landes 1979; Rosenberg 1972, 1982). Both product and process technologies, in these and newer industrial sectors, such as petrochemicals, electronics, and biotechnology were based largely upon scientific discoveries and theories. The high cost of research and development in these industries made it increasingly difficult for the individual investigator to commercialize new products and processes without entering into collaborative arrangements with a manufacturing firm. As cost and complexity were prompting researchers to seek access to the resources of large industrial firms—their sources of funds, laboratory facilities, and marketing networks—profitability considerations were inducing firms to create in-house professional research and development staffs (Freeman 1974). This was particularly true in the newer knowledge-based industries, in which innovation lay at the heart of the firm's profitability and in which control over the direction of research and ability to appropriate research results were thus crucial.

Within the multidivisional firms that began to emerge in the early part of this century, the integration of production also required increased knowledge inputs—this time in the form of centralized planning and administrative structures. The head office became the focus of these functions, as well as the center of research and development activities (Hymer 1975).

The growing importance of knowledge inputs in production is reflected in the large number of scientists and engineers engaged in research and development activities (table 1), and the magnitude of industrial research and development expenditures by firms in the advanced industrial capitalist countries (table 2). It is also evident in the accelerated increase in scientific and technical personnel and in R & D expenditures in Japan and Germany, two of the more technologically dynamic countries in the postwar years, as compared with the steady decline in these indicators experienced by the United Kingdom over the same period (Pavitt 1979, 1980; Walker 1980).

This change in the relationship of knowledge to production had immediate consequences for the nature of competition among knowledge-intensive firms and for the internationalization of production. First, in intermediate and capital goods industries, where economies of scale were important, the wedding of science and technology to industrial production either tended, as in the chemical and petrochemical industries (Freeman 1974) and more recently in semiconductors (Ernst 1981), to stimulate high levels of concentration or, as in the electrical industry, to encourage cartelization and patent-pooling (Lean, Ogur, and Rogers 1982; Newfarmer

Table 1   SCIENTISTS AND ENGINEERS ENGAGED IN R & D PER 10,000 LABOR FORCE POPULATION—SELECTED OECD COUNTRIES AND THE USSR: 1965–80

Country	1965	1968	1972	1975	1978	1979	1980
Canada	n.a.	n.a.	n.a.	22.4	23.0	23.2	24.0
France	21.0	26.4	28.1	29.3	n.a.	n.a.	n.a.
Germany (FR)	22.7	26.2	36.0	41.0	n.a.	n.a.	n.a.
Japan	24.6	31.2	38.1	47.9	49.4	n.a.	n.a.
UK	19.6	20.8	30.4	31.3	n.a.	n.a.	n.a.
US	64.1	66.9	58.2	56.4	58.3	59.2	60.4
USSR[a]	44.8	53.5	66.5	78.2	82.9	84.2	85.9

[a]lowest estimate

Sources: National Science Foundation (1981), *Science Indicators-1980:* Washington: National Science Board, NSB-81-1, Appendix Table 1.1, 208; Statistics Canada, *Annual Review of Science Statistics* (1977, 1981 editions).

Table 2 INDUSTRIAL R & D EXPENDITURES BY FIRMS IN SELECTED
OECD COUNTRIES FOR SELECTED YEARS: 1967–77

| Country | National currency in millions | |
	Business enterprise R & D (BERD)[a]	BERD as a % of the domestic product of industry
Canada		
1967	336	0.69
1971	468	0.70
1975	692	0.60
1977	841	0.60
France		
1967	6,292	1.42
1971	8,962	1.29
1975	15,617	1.37
1977	19,999	1.35
Germany (FR)		
1967	5,683	1.28
1971	10,521	1.54
1975	14,469	1.59
1977	15,717	1.64
Japan		
1967	378,969	0.84
1971	895,020	1.11
1975	1,684,846	1.19
1977	2,109,499	1.29
United Kingdom		
1967	605	2.00
1971	697	n.a.
1975	1,340	1.75
1977	n.a.	n.a.
United States[b]		
1967	16,385	2.49
1971	18,314	2.12
1975	24,164	1.98
1977	29,907	1.91

[a]Includes R & D performed in firms and funded by government.

[b]See also table 2.3, U.S. industry's expenditures for R & D in universities and nonprofit institutions.

Sources: National Science Foundation (1981), Appendix Table 1–9, 219; and Statistics Canada, Annual Review of Science, 1977 and 1981 editions.

1980). By limiting competition, each of these strategies served to reduce the risks in a knowledge-intensive industry where research results were not spread evenly over time yet sunken costs were high, and where firms were thus induced to guarantee their markets.

Second, in consumer-oriented knowledge-intensive industries, such as pharmaceuticals, risk reduction through concentration and cartelization was complemented by a systematic process of market segmentation through the establishment of brand-name loyalty via high advertising expenditures (Lall 1975). To a large extent, R & D expenditures in these industries were oriented to reflect this emphasis on product differentiation. Du Pont, where R & D expenditures in 1975 to 1977 averaged some $350 million annually, is a case in point. Their R & D expenditures were intended to

> generate product and process improvements and . . . [develop] new technology [but] new product introduction during the 1960s w[as] double [that] of the 1950s . . . during the first part of the 1970s, some two-thirds of R & D outlays supported modifications in existing product lines and processes. (Berhman and Fischer 1980, 144)

High research, development and advertising expenditures ultimately tended to create barriers to the entry of new firms in knowledge-intensive industries, although small firms might still survive in some of the newer industrial fields or in specialized niches, and some medium-sized firms might maintain themselves through state support in the form of procurement policies, R & D funding or export subsidization and (where this has proved inadequate) through nationalization (Boismenu and Ducantenzeiler 1983; Delion and Durupty 1982; Larue de Tournemine 1983; Steed 1982). Even then, the evolution of the computer and telecommunications industries, in the late 1970s and early 1980s, suggests that the process of concentration recorded above has continued to play itself out in successive new knowledge-intensive industries as firms in these industries moved beyond their initial innovative entry into second-and third-generation products (Duncan 1982; Roobeek 1984).

Third, the new relationship of knowledge to production also affected the foreign investment process. Whereas the search for new markets, market shares, and secure sources of raw materials at acceptable prices had traditionally impelled large firms to invest abroad, knowledge-intensive firms were initially motivated to internationalize operations in order to fully utilize the market power that their monopoly of technological knowledge and organizational skills made possible. Through the *internationalization of production,* such firms could cover the high costs of innovation from the widest range of sales possible, while *internalization of the market* reduced the risks of price fluctuations and guaranteed final sales (Hymer 1976; Kindleberger 1979; Caves 1982; Helleiner 1981).

American firms, as technological leaders in the immediate postwar period, and operating within the context of a high-income home market, were first to take advantage of knowledge as a unique asset in their growth and internationalization strategies (Hymer 1976; Vernon 1966). But firms in other advanced industrial capitalist countries soon followed suit. Thus a study of French multinational firms found that, whereas in 1971 "exploitation of a technological advantage" did not figure among the principal reasons French firms located abroad, in 1981 this was cited by thirty-seven percent of the firms and ranked as the third most important reason for overseas investment (Michalet et al. 1983, 89).

During the postwar period, the process of capital accumulation within the large, multinational firm thus came to be characterized by a dialectical interplay between profit maximization strategies that focused on product differentiation and/or labor specialization and risk minimization strategies, which emphasized increased planning and control over knowledge and labor inputs and over markets. Underlying the whole, however, was an accelerated rate of technological innovation and diffusion, which periodically raised the specter of overproduction. In the 1960s, new pressures for change in corporate structures emerged. Dynamic sectors spawned a host of new competitors, and where these did not spring up of their own accord, states intervened to support national champions in key high-technology industries. Simultaneously, traditional industries faced a dramatic rise in competition from low-wage countries.

. . .

THE DECENTRALIZATION AND INTERNATIONALIZATION OF KNOWLEDGE PRODUCTION

In the previous section, it has been argued that, during the nineteenth and twentieth centuries, control over the direction of research became central to the growth strategy of firms in knowledge-intensive industries. Initially, control and appropriation were ensured by bringing research and development activities within the confines of the firm and, wherever possible, patenting the results of such R & D activity. Where technical, financial, and economic know-how replace embodied technology as the primary source of a firm's technological advantage, and where product life cycles barely exceed the length of time required to secure patent protection, the ability to capture technological rents through patenting diminish and the importance of directly appropriating R & D results grows. These changes were reflected in the preference that firms in knowledge-intensive industries gave to direct foreign investment over licensing in their initial move abroad during the 1950s and 1960s. They were also a factor in the tendency of multinational firms to centralize R & D facilities in the parent firm (Britton and Gilmour 1978; Hymer 1976; Mytelka 1979; Vaitsos 1974). In the period 1967–1970, U.S. transnationals, for example, spent 97.4 percent of their total R & D expenditure in the United States, almost all of it in house (Michalet 1976, 164). As the costs and risks of knowledge production accelerated during the 1970s, however, large corporations began to decentralize, delocalize, and, in some instances, to internationalize research and development actitivies.

Decentralization of knowledge production has, thus far, taken three principal forms: the creation of autonomous development units within the firm, the decentralization of knowledge production to the firm's overseas research laboratories, or the quasi-merger of dispersed research units through the establishment of data networks and the grant of a world product mandate to selected foreign subsidiaries.

The decentralization of knowledge production to autonomous development units within the firm responds to the growing need for flexibility and speed in bringing new products to market, as well as to the firm's need

> on the one hand, to increase ways of maximizing return on technological innovation to make up for a shortened period of profit-making due to improved techniques. The technological advantage is inherently short-lived . . . (and) on the other hand, because of the existence of high-risk venture capital, to attempt to retain its engineers who might otherwise be tempted to profit from unused technologies available in the larger firm. This is why . . . Control Data has decided to make it easier for employees to start up new firms. It typically participates in these new companies through initial investment and maintenance of business ties. (Delapierre and Zimmermand 1984, 14)[1]

. . .

With this triple objective in mind, IBM has created thirty-five autonomous *special business units* within the firm. Xerox has set up a number of "strategic business units in which small engineering teams vie for the chance to take an idea from the concept stage to a feasibility model" (Dunk and Beinhorn 1984, 67). Hewlett-Packard has decentralized its R & D activities to sixty-six teams spread over fourteen of the United States (Dunk and Beinhorn 1984, 67).

Decentralization of knowledge production to the laboratories of foreign subsidiaries has also become more common in large multinational firms. Initially, overseas research laboratories were designed to modify products conceived in the firm's primary market, either to suit tastes in the new market of manufacture and sales or to match the design features or product quality of local competitors. Du Pont's paint laboratory in Belgium, for example, was established in 1962 once the local marketing group "realized that European customers would not readily accept the paint line used in the United States. Product adaptations were required, and some new products were needed . . . to match European types of paints and meet their qualities, which were fairly high. . . . The need for

Du Pont to develop European paint qualities resulted from Du Pont's not being a market leader in Europe; competitors set the product pattern, forcing its R & D to be reactive" (Behrman and Fischer 1980, 166–67).

Similarly, the research facility established by Wang laboratories in Taiwan, in 1981, and staffed with over 50 engineers, is part of a "plan to begin serving the Far East market with products that can handle input and output in the region's ideographic . . . languages. This requires developing hardware and software to modify the design of the original system" (*Data Networks* 1984, 32).

Most recently, however, this traditional function has given way, in a number of instances, to a new role for overseas research laboratories as suppliers of technology to parent firms. Ciba-Geigy, a large Swiss chemical company, now spends more than twenty-five percent of its annual R & D budget in the United States, much of it on the development of new technology. Germany's Bayer AG "is using its two U.S. acquisitions—Miles Laboratories and Cutter Laboratories—to beef up its R & D effort in biotechnology." Foxboro, an American electronics firm, used the engineers' facilities in its British facility to develop a new semiconductor control chip (*Data Networks,* 1984, 31–32). Similarly, Japanese, Korean, and Taiwanese firms have begun to take over American high-technology companies as a means of access to the knowledge resources such firms possess.

In the case of American multinational corporations, in a study of twenty-nine randomly selected overseas R & D laboratories representing several different industries and accounting for "about 10 percent of all overseas R & D spending by United States-based firms," Mansfield, Teece, and Romeo found that "about 47 percent of their 1979 R & D expenditures resulted in technologies that were transferred to the United States" (Romeo 1983, 5). This was particularly notable in the chemical industry, where 49 percent of the overseas R & D expenditures resulted in technologies transferred to the United States in 1979, up from 2 percent in 1965 and 22 percent in 1979 (Romeo 1983, 6). The "bulk of the transferred technologies" developed in these twenty-nine laboratories, moreover, "were new products, with product improvements a distant second" (Romeo 1983, 9), thus confirming the increasingly active role of selected overseas subsidiaries in new knowledge production.

The growth of data networks linking the geographically dispersed R & D facilities of a single corporation also reflects the need for flexibility and speed in the production of new knowledge, which the acceleration of technological change in knowledge-intensive industries has rendered essential to a firm's survival. Computer linkups of this sort, George Little of Foxboro pointed out, make "common resources available to widely distributed people" and they make "them available immediately" (*Data Networks* 1984, 31). Thus, Nixdorf Computers has linked its R & D centers in Europe and the United States; researchers at Bayer's pharmaceutical laboratories in Germany are electronically connected to their counterparts in Miles Laboratories, as are Digital Equipment Corporation (DEC) facilities in England and the United States.

THE INTRODUCTION OF WORLD PRODUCT MANDATES

A number of multinational firms have granted *world product mandates* (WPM) to selected overseas subsidiaries. Ideally, under the terms of a world product mandate, the local subsidiary is responsible for all aspects of research and development, including design and conceptualization, and for manufacturing and the international marketing of a particular product or set of operations (Atkinson 1985). As such, world product mandating is not simply "a new term for an old practice" and differs from earlier moves towards the decentralization of manufacturing divisions by such firms as General Electric, Westinghouse, or Philips (Rutenberg, 1981, 592). Despite the fact that corporate headquarters continue to control key personnel and capital appropriation decisions there is an important contrast to be made between "the typically centrally organized multinational . . . [and] the far more autonomous organization required by the existence of a world product mandate" (Poynter and Rugman 1982, 54), or by present modes of competition as was argued above.

Much as the development of the multidivisional firm stimulated greater efficiency by inducing competition among divisions, and the introduction of multiproduct marketing increased market shares by covering a larger number of market segments, world product mandating increases the flexibility, reduces the costs and spreads the risks of R & D. It taps local R & D resources, including host government funding for research and development, use of public sector procurement budgets, investment tax credits and export subsidies. This is of particular importance in those countries in which the grant of public funds to a foreign-owned firm can only be justified when that firm makes a significant contribution to the nation's R & D capabilities or its exports.

Given their unique combination of characteristics, world product mandates have come in for particular attention in Canada, where they are regarded as an innovative means to develop industrial R & D in a sector noted for its limited R & D activity and lagging manufactured exports (Britton and Gilmour 1978; Poynter and Rugman 1982; Science Council 1980). The Canadian government has thus actively funded firms that have received WPMs. For example, when it was granted a world product mandate to design and manufacture a new Cyber 170 computer, in the face of a dramatic rise in competition from low-wage countries, Control Data Canada received a significant portion of its funding for this project from the Canadian government's Enterprise Development Programme (*Finan-*

cial Post, 24 October 1981). Similarly, American Motors (AMC) (45 percent owned by Renault) is building an automobile plant in Canada that will have a WPM to produce a new series of intermediate-sized cars, the first of which is scheduled to roll off the assembly line in July 1987; the plant will be financed through a $121 million loan provided by the Ontario and Canadian Federal governments, to be paid back through a one percent royalty on sales over a 7.5 year period from the start of production. In addition, state participation was important in securing the support of a Canadian banking consortium (Nova Scotia, Canadian Imperial and Royal Bank), which is providing a $300 million loan. Of the total financing requirement only $343 million, in the form of equity, will come from AMC (*Globe and Mail,* 12 June 1984, B2).

The delocalization of knowledge production to university or inter-firm research centers fulfills three principal functions. First, it is a cost reduction strategy; second, like the decentralization and internationalization of knowledge production to overseas subsidiaries, the delocalization of knowledge production to universities also enable firms to capture knowledge resources from a wider range of sources than the parent firm alone; third, participation in research pools provides access to future technologies that an individual firm cannot afford to develop on its own, yet may require in order to survive in the context of the technologically based oligopolies discussed later. Data on the magnitude of industrial funding of research in universities and nonprofit institutions in the United States are provided in table 3.

Although company-funded research and development in universities, colleges and nonprofit institutions amounted to a mere 1.3 percent of total company-funded R & D in 1981, it was clearly on the rise; thus, whereas total corporation-funded research and development rose 113 percent in 1981 over 1967, United States industry's expenditures for R & D in universities and nonprofit institutions rose 281 percent during the same period. More recently in Britain, two major electronics groups have decided to finance chairs of molecular electronics and assist in the establishment of research laboratories at two universities, with the objective of ensuring a "more efficient technology transfer from university to industry" (*Financial Times,* 13 February 1983). In the United States over the next two years, supercomputer centers will be established at Cornell, Princeton, the University of California at San Diego, and the University of Illinois at a cost of $400 million, of which $200 million will come from firms such as IBM, Exxon, AT&T, and Lockheed (*International Herald Tribune,* 27 February 1985). In France, a number of *conventions générales de collaboration scientifique sur programme* have been signed between public corporations and the CNRS (*Le Courrier du CNRS,* September-November 1983).

In the United States, most corporate funds are currently complementing seed money provided by the U.S. government's National Science Foundation (NSF) which, since 1973, has facilitated the establishment of

Table 3   U.S. INDUSTRY'S EXPENDITURES FOR R & D
IN UNIVERSITIES AND NONPROFIT
INSTITUTIONS: 1960–81

Year	(Current U.S. $ millions)	
	Universities and colleges	Nonprofit institutions
1960	40	48
1963	41	55
1967	48	74
1972	74	101
1973	84	105
1974	96	115
1975	113	125
1976	123	135
1977	139	150
1978	170	165
1979 (prelim.)	194	180
1980 (est.)	225	220
1981 (est.)	240	225

Source: National Science Foundation (1981): Appendix Table 4.9,
285.

university/industry cooperative research centers. A number of such centers have now been established in several of the most dynamically changing and hence riskier high-technology sectors—in polymers at Case Western Reserve and MIT, in robotics at Carnegie-Mellon's Robotics and Integrated Manufacturing, in biotechnology at Washington University, in microelectronics at Stanford's Center for Integrated Systems, and at the Microelectronics Center of North Carolina (created by a consortium of universities):

> These centers investigate topics of interest to industry and promote technology transfer from lab to factory. In addition, corporate members receive access to center research and staff. . . . Martin Marietta brought researchers from MIT's Polymer Processing Center into its New Orleans Plant. Their mission: figure out how to process the special polymer used for thermal protection of the Space Shuttle's external tanks. Their . . . technique represents a potential cost savings of $25 million through the 1990s. (Ploch 1983)

Not only will the use of MIT staff save Martin Marietta money in the future, but it undoubtedly saved them considerable sums on the R & D that produced this cost-saving innovation. This is due to the fact that major overhead costs are borne not by the firm but by the university, yet "the main criterion for research is its industrial potential," and the main beneficiaries are the corporate members of the research center (Ploch 1983). The latter point is brought out clearly in the recently concluded agreement between Hoechst A. G. and the Massachusetts General Hospital to create a Department of Molecular Biology at the hospital. Massachusetts General Hospital is affiliated with the Harvard Medical School, and most members of the scientific staff of the new department are expected to hold faculty positions at Harvard. Their work will focus

> on somatic cell genetics, microbial genetics, virology, immunology, plant molecular biology, and eukaryotic cell gene regulation. MGM "agrees to do nothing" that might give any other entity a claim on work done by the department, staff members may consult only for nonprofit-making entities, and Hoechst gets exclusive world licenses—or the best possible licenses—for any commercially useful results. (Hancock 1983, I)

Although many U.S. university administrators see corporate financing as a boon, there is concern that academic research will be reoriented to serve short-term business interests. To the extent that such researchers "stop asking the tough questions, ones that will yield applications only twenty years from now, if ever, [and] skimp on their teaching duties [then] arrangements like this . . . constitute eating the seed corn?" (Hancock 1983, III-IV).

In addition to funding new university research facilities, U.S. corporate executives are actively seeking to rewrite antitrust legislation to facilitate greater interfirm collaboration in R & D. This is required, they argue, "in order to withstand the fierce competition from Japan, Germany, and other countries whose governments encourage and, indeed, organize cooperation within industries" (Dunk and Beinhorn 1984, 69).

In Japan, for example, MITI and the Agency for Industrial Science and Technology (AIST) have recently launched a series of long-term basic research programs in conjunction with private industry. One program, for which a budget of U.S. $75 million over the period 1979–1986 has been allocated, will focus on applied systems for measurement and control using a combination of fiber optics and electronics; the research will be undertaken by the association for the promotion of the *optoelectronic* industry, the collective laboratory for research in optoelectronics and fourteen private firms (CPE 1983b, 12–15). In the field of new materials and components, over the years 1981–1991, U.S. $104 million will be allocated for basic research to AIST's electrotechnical laboratory, in association with eleven private firms (CPE 1983b, 22–25).

Among U.S. firms, interfirm collaboration in basic research has begun through the establishment of such centers as the Semiconductor Research Corporation (SRC) and the Microelectronics and Computer Technology Corporation (MCTC). The former, with a projected budget of $30 million per year by 1986, was set up by the semiconductor equipment manufacturers' association to support basic semiconductor research in the United States. It brings together thirty-four firms, including IBM, Hewlett-Packard, Honeywell, Intel, Westinghouse, and Motorola (OECD 1984, 142); Erich Bloch, IBM's vice-president for research, is chairman of SRC's board. The board, with a budget of $50 million a year, is a joint venture among twelve high-technology companies. (Control Data, Honeywell, Motorola, Advanced Micro Devices, Harris, Digital Equipment Corporation, and National Semiconductor are members of both SRC and MCTC; major user companies, such as Martin Marietta Aerospace, RCA, and United Technologies, are also members of MCTC.) All patents and knowledge will belong to MCTC, and member companies will have first priority to license technology; member firms, moreover, will receive about 70 percent of all royalties, while MCTC itself will retain 30 percent (OECD 1984, 141). Intrafirm collaboration in nonstabilized, frontier technologies also occurs to the extent that no single firm can bear the costs of such research, and yet no firm can risk losing access to a new technology that membership in a R & D pool would provide. Thus Exxon, which is abandoning its efforts to enter the computer market, will nonetheless participate along with AT&T and Lockheed in a research center at Princeton University to develop supercomputers (*International Herald Tribune,* 27 February 1985).

Although earlier efforts to develop in-house R & D had been designed to ensure privileged access to new knowledge, the current move to delocalize research activities to universities and interfirm institutes in no way diminishes the private appropriation of research results by individual firms. This is due in large part to the growing distinction between *base* and *key* technologies. A base technology

> is common to most industry participants and to most products of a business. Though essential, it is no longer critical to competitiveness because it is so widely available. . . . To a particular electronic terminals manufacturer, for example, the base technologies were integrated circuits and keyboards, whereas the key technologies were applications engineering techniques: 8-bit microprocessor applications technology; and manufacturing process technology for high-volume assembly of complex equipment (Lorenz 1981).

In the electronics industry, where product cycles are excessively short, the microprocessor, which only a few years ago was a *key* technology, has already "become a 'base' technology: it is [so] widely available [that] . . . it has ceased on its own to provide many equipment manufacturers with a substantial competitive advantage" (*Financial Times,* 2 March 1984, 6).

By delocalizing *research* on base technolgies, firms liberate funds for investment in *development* activities that are more likely to enhance their competitive position. This shift in the composition of in-house R & D activities is further encouraged by the fact that research into base technologies in many of the most dynamic industries can generate a sufficiently large number of alternative development avenues, so as to make the private appropriation of development results for market advantage still possible.

By the end of the 1970s, both of these factors had led Japanese knowledge-intensive firms to significantly restructure their research and development activities. In the case of Nissan, for example,

> the various laboratories responsible for basic research (in the areas of engines, vehicle bodies, electronics, building materials) employ a total of 1,400 people. The technical headquarters, responsible for the product development, on the other hand, employs 3,700, even though it is not involved directly in production. (SEST 1984, 8)[2]

A similar reorganization was undertaken in the electronics industry by Toshiba, NEC, and Casio (SEST 1984, 9). In each of these cases, using the *tree* metaphor common to Japanese descriptions of their current business strategy, the objective was to combine a number of diverse technological capabilities (the roots) into a solid technological trunk which, in turn, would open up the possibility for a wide diversity of product applications corresponding to the multiple branches of a tree, any one of which could be eliminated as changing circumstances require.

Under these changing conditions, the ability to determine when a technology is no longer a key technology becomes central to the competitive advantage of knowledge-intensive firms. This increases both the level of uncertainty in investment decision making and enhances the importance of flexibility and risk-spreading in knowledge-production activities. To cope with these new needs, a move toward the delocalization and, in some instances, the internationalization of knowledge-production activities through the establishment of joint ventures with other firms has also taken place. This new strategy, by recreating a form of oligopoly transposed to a technological base, enhances the ability of the participating firms to influence the shape of future markets.

CONCLUSIONS

Underlying most views of the changing nature of capitalism is an implicit acknowledgement that knowledge inputs are becoming increasingly more important in the contemporary process of capital accumulation. While knowledge-intensity of production varies across industries, the consequences of the growing salience of knowledge inputs in production are being felt in all industrial sectors.

The changing relationship of knowledge to production has had numerous consequences for the nature of competition among firms and for their growth strategies. Initially, as production became more knowledge-intensive, control over the direction of research and ability to appropriate the results of that research stimulated the establishment of in-house research and development facilities. In knowledge-intensive industries, where research results are not spread evenly over time yet sunken costs are high, firms were also induced to guarantee their markets through concentration, cartelization, cross-investment, and market segmentation.

During the 1960s, the rise of new cost-efficient competitors, the declining profitability at home and the widening wage differentials between advanced industrial and Third World countries led large firms to delocalize labor-intensive segments of the production process and/or to form conglomerates in an effort to diversify. Both of these strategies proves short-lived as neither dealt directly with the effect that the growing knowledge-intensity of production was having on the global pattern of competition. Competition was increasingly knowledge-based; and, to the extent that it was, in the most dynamic industries product life cycles were shortening because the very nature of the products, their uses, and the manufacturing techniques required for their production differed substantially from one product generation to the next. Firms were thus required to simultaneously increase their flexibility of response to changing tastes, costs, and competitive conditions, and to position themselves so as to influence the shape of future, as yet indeterminant, markets. Not only did this raise the costs, but it substantially increased the risks and uncertainty of knowledge production.

Two broad strategies are being developed by firms to cope with the rising costs, risks, and uncertainty of knowledge production. The first deals with the process of knowledge production itself. It includes the decentralization of knowledge production to autonomous development units within the firm—to the firm's overseas research laboratories or through the use of world product mandates to selected foreign subsidiaries and the delocalization of knowledge production to university or interfirm research centers. The decentralization, delocalization, and internationalization of knowledge production increase a firm's flexibility of response. At the same time, they spread the costs and risks of response, along with the costs and risks of R & D, to universities and, through grants, subsidies, and state procurement policies, to host governments. The delocalization and internationalization of knowledge production, moreover, has the added advantage of enabling knowledge-intensive multinational firms to capture knowledge resources, frequently at lower cost, from as wide a range of sites as possible without inducing the migration of scientific and technical personnel, and without incurring the costs of reproducing such skilled manpower. Third World countries with a strong scientific and engineering base (e.g., Brazil, Argentina, India, Korea, and Taiwan) are excellent candidates for the decentralization and internationalization of knowledge production by the large multinational firms, which are forming the core of a global oligopoly in these industries (Hobday 1984; Kaplinsky 1984; Rada 1985; UNCTAD 1978).

Advanced industrial countries such as Canada, the United Kingdom, Belgium, and possibly France, whose firms are not at the technological frontier and/or whose domestic market cannot absorb the full range of product possibilities generated by the accelerated rate of technological change through political intervention can, nonetheless, negotiate to obtain world product mandates for products that complement the high-technology niches in which national firms can compete effectively.

The decentralization, delocalization, and internationalization of knowledge production improve a firm's global flexibility and introduce a new element of autonomy into the structure of the multinational corporation, but they do not imply a loss of control over the knowledge-generation process. Rather, such strategies extend this control to incorporate knowledge resources not hitherto directly appropriable by private firms. In so doing, they reduce still further the domain of petty knowledge production, much as petty commodity production in agriculture and artisanal manufacture in industry have largely disappeared under the pressures of expanding capitalism. The current move to delocalize research activities to universities and interfirm institutes, moreover, in no way diminishes the private appropriation of research results by individual firms. This, it was argued, is largely due to the distinction that has emerged between *base* and *key* technologies, and to the fact that joint research into base technologies capable of generating a broad range of development possibilities liberates funds for investment in development activities that are more likely to enhance the competitive position of the firm.

The second strategy attempts to cope with the increasing market risks and uncertainties to which the accelerated rate of technological change in knowledge-intensive industries has given rise. As in the past, a strategy that guarantees forward linking markets is ideally suited to this purpose. Joint ventures in design and development of new products and processes, by incorporating rivals in a technologically based oligopolistic market structure, do precisely this.

Interfirm collaboration through joint ventures in design and development, like the decentralization, delocalization, and internationalization of knowledge production discussed above, reduces the costs, risks; and uncertainty associated with rapid technological change. They do this primarily by structuring the market rather than by altering the cost structure of production. By bringing together nominal competitors in the design and development of new products and processes, they go beyond the joint venture and arm's-length technology swaps characteristic of earlier phases of product-based oligopolization. By so doing, they determine the very shape of the future markets at the same time as they raise profit levels for those firms able to appropriate the rents generated by the production of new knowledge within an oligopolistic market structure. . . . The development of a global telecommunications oligopoly, structured through a set of technologically based collaborative agreements among firms, was used to illustrate this hypothesis.

As knowledge-intensive industries are transformed into technologically based oligopolies, new barriers to entry are likely to be posed for latecomers, and the ability of small- and medium-sized enterprises to retain their independence diminishes. Indeed, the cherished notion of a *national* industry may be seriously out of date. The very logic of competition in knowledge-intensive industries suggests a gradual move from domestic concentration to international oligopolization and the survival of small and medium-sized firms seems predicated upon the establishment of technologically based collaboration agreement through which these *national* enterprises are progressively drawn into a global network of interfirm linkages, that, in the final analysis, structures their future development options.[3]

NOTES

1. Quotation appeared in French in the original article. Editor has provided English translation.
2. English translation provided by Editor.
3. The Centre d'études et de recherches sur l'entreprise multinationale (CEREM), Université de Paris-X, Nanterre, is examining the extent to which this process is currently structuring European knowledge-intensive industries.

Part
Five

AID FOR THE POOR

*T*he decade of the 1980s has seen a dramatic erosion of the once popular egalitarian principle that industrialized nations have an obligation to assist the world's poor in their efforts to promote economic growth, and eliminate gross economic inequality. It was determined by the Reagan administration that these two goals were mutually exclusive and that it was more important to promote growth, as a first-order priority, rather than equity. This central question has not lost its relevance simply because the dominant ideology has changed since the 1960s. The three articles in this section are intended to challenge the student who has been a consumer of supply-side economic theory for the past ten years. The positions taken by each of the authors, while markedly different, are all critical of the general approach taken by the United States and other industrialized nations in addressing the economic needs of the Third World.

Teresa Hayter assumes that capitalist industrialization and economic justice are inherently contradictory, and she provides substantial evidence to corroborate that belief. She focuses her attention on the activities of the World Bank, one of several institutions conceived and largely funded by American economic planners during the waning months of World War II. Created initially to be a multilateral Marshall Plan, since the 1960s the World Bank (also known as the International Bank for Reconstruction and Development or IBRD) has invested billions into large scale Third World development projects such as power plants, roadways, and deep-water ports. Hayter argues that these and other development projects have not only failed to bring about economic growth but have damaged the social and ecological fabric of these nations, and further subordinated the Third World to the economic interests of the First World.

During the 1970s, a lively debate was waged in the World Bank and other international institutions. It centered on the question, what should be the ordering principle of economic aid in the coming decade? The World Bank's staff, led by President Robert McNamara, emphasized a *basic needs* approach which funneled money into small scale, low-technology projects such as irrigation systems, basic sanitation programs, and rural health clinics. This approach contrasts with the "New International Economic Order" program advocated by the vast majority of Third World governments. This is an agenda for changing the distribution of power in the international system, as well as the distribution of wealth. Johan Galtung systematically compares these two approaches and offers his own alternative.

Sewell and Contee are speaking to a primarily American audience (especially an audience of policymakers) in their gentle, but firm, criticism of American foreign aid in the middle of the Reagan era. It is through this article that the student can most clearly see the contrast between liberal approaches to international relations and the realist approach of the American government at the time. Again, these three pieces bring to mind several questions: Is equity more important than efficiency? To what extent should the receiver of aid have a voice in the use of aid? What is the extent of the Western obligation to assist the poor worldwide? Is it politically wise to provide aid? How does one judge whether it is better to give aid to newly democratic Poland and Nicaragua, the poverty stricken nations of Bangladesh and Sudan, the environmentally important nation of Brazil, the strategic nation of Israel, or to the indebted nations of Argentina and the Philippines (which also have fledgling democratic governments)? Should the U.S. send aid in the form of concessional business loans to the Soviet Union? What criteria should government officials use to make these choices?

The Bank and Ideology

Teresa Hayter

A BASIC CODE OF CONDUCT

The Bank's view of what constitutes sound and desirable economic policies is still not as well known as it ought to be. For example, in 1982 the
British Labor Party published a report entitled *Development Cooperation.*
It contained some powerful criticisms of the IMF, including a case study
on Jamaica, which quotes complaints in internal IMF documents that the
government was abandoning "the basic tenets of the [IMF] program, viz,
reliance on the market mechanism and on the private sector to effect
recovery," and concluded that "the Fund was no longer playing neutral
finance or even political economy but straight politics."[1] In its section on
the World Bank, however, the Labor Party says it needs to decide whether
to make a substantial increase in its contribution to multilateral institutions. The report continues:

> Ten years ago, Teresa Hayter produced a damning report . . . which suggested
> that [the Bank's] contribution to the Third World was "negative." There was
> a good deal of evidence to support this claim—the Bank strongly encouraged
> "free enterprise" and especially the use of private foreign capital . . . Since
> then, however, the Bank has produced a much more radical approach to the
> problem of the poorest countries, and is now concerned to improve the posi-
> tion of the most disadvantaged section of the population through a policy of
> "redistribution with growth" . . .
>   In the light of these developments, IDA's claim for additional resources
> seems to be a strong one. The American commitment to the bank is now very
> suspect, so that its progressive initiatives will require the strongest support,
> both financial and intellectual, from other industrial countries if it is to be
> maintained. We should therefore make an appropriate contribution to its
> funding, and use our influence on its board of directors to support the progres-
> sive policies which it has been developing, and also encourage it to support
> forms of socialist organization where these can make a visible economic con-
> tribution to Third-World development.[2]

Teresa Hayter, "The Bank and Ideology" in Hayter, *Aid: Rhetoric and Reality,* London:
Pluto Press, 1985.

This is flying in the face of all the evidence of what the Bank is and can be expected to be, so long as the sources of its finance are what they are. There are some basic tenets of Bank philosophy which have been consistent throughout its history and undented in its last ten years. These are: support for reliance on market forces and the private sector; encouragement to foreign private investment and good treatment of existing foreign investments; support for the principles of free trade and comparative advantage; aversion to the use of controls on prices, imports and movements of capital; aversion to subsidies and support for the principle of *full cost recovery* on the projects it finances and public investments in general; support for financial stabilization policies to be achieved by austerity programs of the IMF variety, including overall reductions in demand and devaluation; and the requirement that debts be serviced and repaid.

A Bank official, writing in 1968 to say that "a major revision" to my draft would be necessary, identified "a sort of code of conduct" demanded by the Bank, to which he thought it was "difficult to take exception," including: "measures conducive to a larger flow of private capital and public funds"; "not . . . too much inflation"; "full-cost pricing of projects to which [the Bank] lends"; "not . . . large and rapidly growing administrative expenditures"; "not . . . administrative controls over production and prices"; "a financial plan for [public investment programs] which does not call for too much suppliers credit financing or too much printing of money"; and "service payments on . . . external debt."[3] The list remains valid. Requirements concerning the alleviation of poverty or the distribution of income were not, and still are not, part of this basic code, except in relation to projects, and then only formally and with dubious effect (see below).

An attempt to summarize the Bank's concerns is also made in the U.S. Treasury Report which says:

> While it is difficult to summarize the wide variety of policy reform urged upon developing countries by the World Bank, a review, such as that submitted for the record in 1981 at the request of the Subcommittee on Foreign Operations of the House Committee on Appropriations, of the individual country reports prepared by the Bank staff reveals that the advice is generally along neoclassical economic lines. On the external side, the reports emphasize the need for open international trading systems, realistic exchange rates, and the use of world market prices to reflect real opportunity costs. On the internal side, there is an emphasis on appropriate resource allocation (i.e., in accordance with true costs and benefits), realistic pricing policies, cost-recovery, and the maintenance of sensible fiscal and monetary policies.[4]

The priority attached by the Bank to the repayment of debt has been described . . . as has its attachment to the supposed virtues of foreign private investment. But perhaps the clearest demonstration of the true nature of the Bank is to be derived from the fact that it differs so little from the IMF in the basic policies it supports.

THE WORLD BANK AND THE IMF

The Bank's cooperation with the Fund has recently become more intense, and somewhat more institutionalized. But it is not new. The two institutions originally shared a building in Washington. When this building became too small for them, the IMF built a new one across the road, and the Bank subsequently built another one next to it. They have always cooperated closely and shared information; and "since 1963, however effective or ineffective staff cooperation may have been, relations at the top have been close and amicable."[5]

With the formalization of the Bank's attempts to exercise leverage in Structural Adjustment Lending, the Bank's relationship with the Fund has become even closer. The Bank is aware that this may be thought to imply an incursion into IMF territory and is anxious to ensure that the policies demanded by each of them do not conflict. In its 1982 *Annual Report* the Bank says that a recent staff report had noted that "experience over the past two years had shown that the Bank's structural adjustment lending operations and the IMF programs were, in practice, both complementary and mutually reinforcing." A 1980 unpublished staff report to the Boards of Governors of the Bank and the Fund says:

> Since lending for structural adjustment would normally address macro-economic policy issues related to the balance of payments, the need to consult the IMF is readily apparent . . . Fund staff have cooperated closely in processing program loans. In several cases a Bank staff member joined the Fund consultation or review team (e.g., Turkey, Jamaica, and Guyana). In other instances, the Bank's program loan appraisal mission overlapped with the Fund's consultation or review mission in the field (e.g., Sudan and Zambia). It is normal practice for the Bank and the Fund staff to consult each other closely in Washington and share information and views. *The Bank usually regards the success of the short-term economic stabilization or recovery program (on which the IMF standby arrangements are based) as important for the fulfillment of a government's medium-term investment or development program.* For its part, the IMF relies on the Bank's judgments on the appropriateness of a country's medium-term investment program which provides a context for stabilization measures and is particularly relevant to Extended Fund Facility (EFF) programs (emphasis added).[6]

This cooperation has continued, and it is now usual for a member of the Bank's staff to be attached to Fund missions with the formal purpose of pronouncing on the government's investment program, its *appropriateness,* and how it can best be cut. Similarly, the Bank is supposed to consult with the Fund before it makes recommendations and demands in fields which are clearly recognized to be in the competence of the Fund. This applies particularly to devaluation, a measure beloved of both institutions. Mason and Asher say:

> Although this understanding has been violated on a number of occasions, with a resulting protest from the managing director of the Fund, these violations are exceptional. Discussions of exchange rate policy in the Bank's country reports are cleared with the Fund, and in general there is a pooling of views of Bank and Fund staff members on aspects of exchange rate policy of interest to both organizations. It is understood that the actual negotiation of changes in exchange rates is a prerogative of the Fund and must be conducted in strict confidence.[7]

This did not prevent the Bank, in the late 1960s, claiming devaluation in India as its major achievement in the field of *leverage.*

Bank and Fund officials are unwilling to talk about cases where there have been conflicts between them. De Larosière, asked after one of his press conferences at the 1983 Annual Meetings whether the Bank had been critical of the severity of IMF programs, said he had always found the Bank "very cooperative."[8] What is fairly certain is that there are no consistent ideological differences between the two institutions. Both are committed to the usual list of orthodox neoclassical desiderata: reliance on market mechanisms and the price mechanism, no controls, and especially import liberalization (see below).

On perhaps the most important question that might arise between them, that of the relationship between short-term financial stabilization and long-term growth, the potential differences have been simply resolved by the convenient fact that the Bank shares with the IMF the view that short-term stabilization is an essential prerequisite to long-term growth. Indeed in 1959 a Bank official wrote that the "Bank might be even more interested than the Fund in a diligent search for stabilization measures outside the field of investment if only to minimize the cutback that might be necessary in the size of the investment program."[9] Mason and Asher categorically endorse this: "Indeed the Bank has generally accepted the Fund proposition that stabilization is a necessary though not sufficient condition for growth." They are moreover critical of it. Whereas the Fund, they say, is supposed to be concerned with short-term matters, the Bank

> has no such defense . . . If the Bank and the Fund have not moved further away from relatively short-term considerations, it may be the result of an overemphasis on stabilization as a necessary, though not sufficient, condition of growth—to the neglect of the equally important proposition that, in many situations, growth is a necessary, though not sufficient, condition for effective stabilization.[10]

The Bank's concern with public investment, or the *supply side,* is usually *within* ceilings imposed by the Fund, possibly after discussions with the Bank. Officials are unable, or possibly unwilling, to supply specific evidence that these ceilings are contested by the Bank, even though they may at times feel that their own projects are threatened by them. They have responded in part to this latter problem by what the Bank calls its Special Action Program under which the Bank is willing, as a temporary measure, to provide a higher proportion of the projects' costs itself.

To the extent that there are differences between the two institutions, the differences are probably random: they depend on the personalities of individual mission chiefs and directors of departments, rather than on any systematic differences in institutional ideology. There may well be cases where World Bank officials take a *softer* view than that of their IMF counterparts, especially outside the notoriously reactionary Latin American and Caribbean departments of the Bank.[11] Tanzania was said to be such a case, although Bank officials were unwilling, or unable, to supply any evidence that this was so,[12] and the Bank's position on Tanzania has clearly hardened. . . . Elsewhere, the reverse may equally be true. A senior Bank official, answering questions in 1981 about the nature of conditionality in Structural Adjustment Lending, said that it was often linked to (more quantifiable) agreement with the Fund. Where the government had an agreement with the Fund, he said, there was no need for the Bank to make its own separate agreements covering the same ground. But it would offer comments: sometimes the Fund was "less stringent"; the Fund was "a little bit too easy-going these days"; its Managing Director had "an expansionist approach."[13] According to another source,[14] the Bank's staff "viewed with dismay" the relaxation of the Fund's attitude on devaluation in the late seventies and early eighties; but of course the Fund's attitude has since hardened.

An IMF official tells the story of being invited to a meeting with Bank country economists. He embarked on a defense of the thesis that IMF standby programs are not damaging to growth. He was told that the Bank was much more worried that the Fund was giving countries too much leeway and was thus "pulling the rug from under their feet." Other IMF officials have said that there have been "some cases where we have given countries more leash—and *vice versa,*" and other cases where the World Bank has insisted that the IMF insist on devaluation, and "then done something messy themselves and made us look foolish." Bolivia, Ghana, and Senegal were cited, in 1981, as cases where "Bank/Fund coordination was falling apart." In another case, that of Guyana, the problem was simply that the Bank "changed its mind" about the advisability of financing a project on political grounds: the project was located in a disputed border area and somehow neither the Bank nor the Fund had realized that this was so. But the Fund lamented that its "whole program had been based on the assumption of the Bank's program and a lot of assurances from the Bank that it would be heavily involved, and it all came to nought after a couple of months."[15]

THE BANK AND FREE TRADE

Within its overall advocacy of market forces, the Bank is and always has been an advocate of the benefits of free trade. In this its enthusiasm at least equals the institutionalized enthusiasm of the IMF. Together with the IMF, it insists on overall limitations in demand and on devaluation, which discourage imports by an across-the-board increase in their prices, rather than selective import controls or tariff increases, as the means of controlling balance of payments deficits. One of the earliest major examples of the use of *leverage* by the Bank was in India in 1966, where it was involved in pushing for both devaluation and import liberalization.[16] The Bank is systematically enthusiastic about programs of import liberalization, welcoming them when, as in Chile, they occur, and is itself sometimes largely responsible for their introduction, as in the Philippines, and in Peru.

In the case of Peru, the World Bank hired a Peruvian economist, Roberto Abusada, who had been on a "major" Bank mission to Argentina in 1978 directed by his friend Enrique Lerdau of the Bank's Latin American and Caribbean department, to do preparatory work for the Bank's 1979 program loan to Peru; import liberalization was part of the conditionality for this loan. Then, under the terms of the program loan, he was hired by the government of Peru, with his salary paid from Washington, (which meant, he said, that he received in 1½ days the equivalent of his previous salary from the Universidad Catolica). He worked in the Ministry of Industry on further proposals for import liberalization and wrote a report on the Peruvian manufacturing sector, arguing for the removal of protection and other controls.[17] But he had difficulty in persuading the military government to adopt the proposals. When Belaúnde took office in 1980, however, and hired his economic team from Washington and Wall Street, Abusada was made Vice-Minister in charge of Trade in the Ministry of Economy and Finance. He was able to write out decrees embodying a program of substantial tariff reductions which were immediately put into effect, without any attempt to get them passed by Congress. It was "practically the program that the Peruvian government had asked the World Bank technical assistants to shape up."[18]

Free trade, and its accompanying theory of *comparative advantage,* clearly favors established producers and manufacturers. The theories were developed by British economists in the nineteenth century at the time of British industrial ascendancy, challenged by its now industrialized competitors such as the United States and Germany, and reasserted by the United States when it had achieved industrial supremacy for itself after the Second World War. The theory of comparative advantage does not take account of possible changes over time. The World Bank has been opposed to the setting up of major new industrial capacity in the Third World, on the grounds that the products in question can be more cheaply obtained from abroad, and no doubt also on the grounds that they would compete with established industries in the West. (It would be interesting to know whether its reports on Japan in the 1950s contained advice against Japan embarking on the motor-car industry, and the usual solemn invocations on the economic unsoundness of the required protective measures.) Its reports on South Korea in the 1970s did advise the South Koreans not to "go into heavy industry," i.e., make ships.[19] In Pakistan in the 1950s, "The Bank opposed investment in heavy industry and initially even discouraged the establishment of jute-processing mills."[20] Every country that contemplated manufacturing steel must have been advised not to do so by the World Bank.

Even of Brazil, a NIC (Newly Industrializing Country) with a potentially vast internal market, the Bank's 1983 *World Development Report* says with some skepticism:

> Since the mid-1970s the government has expanded its share of industry and played a bigger role in the choice of new investment. It has promoted a new wave of import substitution in the few activities where this remained possible. Some sectors (such as steel) may have been overexpanded, and many of the new industries (such as sophisticated machine tools and computers) have complex and rapidly evolving technology; being capital goods, their cost and quality will affect the whole economy. Whether these new activities will become internationally competitive remains to be seen.[21]

In the Bank's own projects, the question arises as to which inputs are to be procured locally and which from abroad. As Mason and Asher put it:

> The IBRD has two interests of central importance to be served by this choice: (a) to minimize the cost of the project by procuring inputs from lowest-cost sources, and (b) to encourage the development of borrowing countries by assisting their industries in producing inputs for Bank projects.[22]

The Bank has plumped heavily for the former. The Bank is, in its statutes, debarred from financing local costs, "except in exceptional circumstances." Although it has interpreted this rather widely to enable it to finance projects with unavoidably low import content, such as its rural development projects, it has insisted that wherever possible, the parts of its projects to be financed by itself must be open to international competitive bidding. In its early lending to industrialized countries, the Bank naturally found that local suppliers were often able to submit the most competitive bids, and it was nevertheless willing to finance them. It wondered whether this was *fair* in view of the fact that local bidders benefited from various forms of protection, but decided there was nothing it could do about it.[23] However, as it began to lend more to underdeveloped countries, and as these countries increased their industrial capability, the Bank decided that their industries benefited from protective barriers that were too high. The Bank, according to Mason and Asher,

> recognized that industrialization was difficult without some degree of protection of industrial "infants." However, it wanted to make sure that the infants

it encouraged by its procurement policies had some reasonable chance of
growing into industries that would eventually be capable of standing on their
own feet. After much discussion in the Bank's staff and board of directors, it
was decided in 1962 that local producers should be entitled to a maximum
level of protection of 15 percent in bidding on Bank projects. Henceforth
either the existing tariff rate or 15 percent, whichever was lower, would be
accepted.[24]

Rather curiously, Bank officials nowadays produce this 15 percent *preference* accorded to local suppliers as evidence of the Bank's willingness to
promote local industry, failing to mention that this preference is a substitute for, not an addition to, tariffs. It is nevertheless clear that the *preference* was introduced as a means of reducing, rather than increasing, the
protection accorded to industries in the Third World, and there are many
complaints that it is far too low and effectively excludes local bidders.
Attempts by the governments of Third World countries to get the level
of preference raised to 25 percent, still quite a low level of protection,
were defeated explicitly on the grounds that it would limit the opportunities of the major powers for export. Mason and Asher say that:

> the Bank continued to lend for local procurement in developed countries
> without any extensive enquiry into the question of tariff protection. The
> problem of the degree of preference to be permitted a domestic supplier
> apparently was raised only in connection with loans to less developed member
> countries.[25]

If borrowing governments want to reserve certain parts of projects to local
suppliers, they will not be financed by the Bank. The situation provides
an inducement to governments to open up a larger portion of projects to
international competitive bidding than they might otherwise do.[26] Moreover, even though the Bank has been willing to finance a substantial
amount of local costs especially in Africa and other "low income" countries
in cases where there is clearly no question of materials and skills being
provided from abroad, it has been known to manipulate project design so
as to facilitate *competition* from foreign suppliers, for example by insisting
that a road project should be put out to tender not in the usual small
sections suitable for local contractors, but as a lump, suitable for foreign
bidding.[27]

But while the Bank has been opposed to import-substituting manufacturing and the protection that it requires at least in its early stages, it has
become an advocate of exports of low-technology manufactured products
destined for Western markets and taking advantage of the Third World's
comparative advantage in the possession of cheap labor. During the 1970s
the Bank took from other economists and itself espoused and developed
a theory that programs of import liberalization can lead to growth in
exports, including manufactured exports. It has been a consistent advocate
of the greater integration of all Third World economies into the capitalist
world economy and of greater *openness* to and reliance on international

trade. In particular the work of Bela Balassa, a professor at Johns Hopkins University and a consultant at the World Bank who has more than a dozen publications listed in the 1983 World Bank *Catalogue,* has been "immensely influential," according to a Bank official.[28] Rejecting the *pessimistic* theses of Prebisch, the first Secretary-General of UNCTAD, and others on the externally imposed difficulties for developing countries in increasing their exports, his major thesis is that:

> the export performance of a number of developing countries was adversely affected *by their own policies:* the bias against exports in countries pursuing import substitution policies led to a loss in their world shares in primary exports and forestalled the emergence of manufactured exports (emphasis added).[29]

The Bank has persisted in its advocacy of import liberalization, export promotion, and an increase in countries' dependence on trade in the face of developing countries' drastic loss of markets and export revenues resulting from depression and protectionism in the industrialized countries. In fact the emphasis it attaches to such policies has been reinforced by the appointment of Anne Krueger as vice president in charge of economics and research, in succession to Hollis Chenery, who directed much of the Bank's research on basic needs and income distribution in the 1970s. Krueger is said by her staff to have "right-wing instincts." Her academic specialization is the economics of trade and she is very much an advocate of free trade. She is said to be mainly interested in using the Bank's research capabilities, which have themselves been reduced by about a third, to prove the thesis that developing countries can be turned into export platforms, exporting labor-intensive manufactured products and other *non-traditional* products such as fruits and flowers to the West, as well as their more traditional raw materials and primary products. The Bank's *Report on the World Bank Research Program,* published for restricted distribution in March 1983, under the heading "The evolution of the present program and emerging priorities," lists "international trade and finance" as the first of four subjects for new research.

Krueger gave one of the two press conferences by Bank officials at the 1983 annual meetings (the other was on co-financing); its subject was "Trade and Protectionism." A briefing issued to the press argues that, although "recovery is under way," it might be put at risk by protectionism. It then puts forward the Bank's credo on developing countries:

> Developing countries have an important stake in an open and expanding trading system . . . Outward-oriented strategies are characterized by the maintenance of realistic exchange rates, the provision of similar incentives for domestic and export production and the relative tolerance of import competition (= good). In contrast, inward-oriented development strategies are typically characterized by extensive protection against imports that extends well beyond infant industries; a bias in incentives in favor of import substitution and against exports; wide variation in degrees of import protection across

industries; and greater reliance on administered allocative mechanisms than on relative prices (= bad) . . .

[The outward-looking] countries have generally fared better in terms of growth of output, income and employment, and have also been able to adjust more rapidly to external shocks.[30]

At her press conference, Krueger recommended that developing countries should join the GATT and submit themselves to its rules.

While it might perhaps be true that developing countries' interests would be better served by a genuinely open and expanding trading system, the fact is that such a system does not exist. While the Bank does advocate less protectionism by the industrialized countries, it has no power whatsoever to achieve this objective. Its financial clout is of course effective only in the Third World. But to advocate import liberalization and an attempt to rely on increasing exports in the absence of expanding markets in the industrialized countries seems to have mainly theological value, as far as the peoples of the Third World are concerned. For them, it can be desperately disruptive, with the *long term gains,* on which the Bank explicitly relies, nowhere in sight. In the short term, both the exporters of industrialized countries and Third World elites, for whom the luxuries of the West suddenly become available, do nicely. Thus one Bank official, recognizing that the import liberalization in Peru was bound to lead to an influx of Mercedes, etc., because of *repressed demand,* said "if we took a moral position, we wouldn't be lending to any of these countries."[31]

What Bank statements and publications usually fail to mention is that the *outward-looking countries* that are supposed to have "fared better" are most of them virtually city-states: Hong Kong, Singapore, even Taiwan have small internal markets; South Korea is possibly the only one of them that is both of fair size and not in acute balance of payments and debt crisis. It is in any case doubtful whether South Korea should be counted as a showcase for liberalization, the price mechanism, and the free market, since its government pursued a highly interventionist policy, and promoted heavy industry against the advice of the World Bank. The idea that these countries' experiences as export platforms for the West could be replicated throughout the Third World seems far-fetched, even supposing there was a new sustained recovery in the West. China, following a policy of somewhat greater outward-orientation, as recommended, incidentally, in the World Bank's report on China, is already threatening to swallow up what markets there are for cheap textiles produced in the Third World.[32] Would the West tolerate the extra millions in the dole queues [unemployment lines] that would be the result of an export drive from India, Pakistan, and Indonesia similar to that of South Korea and Singapore?

Sometimes it seems unclear whether the Bank really believes that concentration on labor-intensive manufactured exports is a feasible policy for all countries, or whether it simply believes that developing countries should "stick to what they are best at": the export of primary commodities

and raw materials. In Peru, Abusada was said by one of his fellow economists to have believed initially that the import liberalization program
which he successfully promoted would lead to labor-intensive manufactured exports, and that incentives should be provided for such exports.[33]
"Taiwanisemos" (Let us Taiwanise), he is said to have said. But Abusada's
1981 report, written while he was working for the Bank, and on which the
Belaúnde government's liberalization measures were based (see above),
argues instead that "an appropriate basis for an effective long-term strategy of industrial development of Peru is to exploit the country's comparative advantage," and claims that, "in the past Peru has not followed this
principle, but rather has provided strong support to industry at the cost
of other sectors and, within the industrial sector, has promoted capital
intensive forms of manufacturing. Both aspects of the past strategy are not
in accordance with the country's resource endowments, which are mainly
abundant skilled labor and natural resources, including minerals, agricultural, and fishery products." Because, says the report, the exports of traditional products and oil will be high, "there should be no need to promote
non-traditional exports at any cost . . . and a balanced reduction of both
import protection and export incentives can be implemented as the key
industrial policy instrument to promote efficient industrial development."
Moreover, the report recognizes that, "for a substantial part of export
products, where Peru could utilize its comparative advantage of abundant
and well-trained labor (mainly garments, footwear, consumer durables),
Peruvian exporters will be latecomers on highly competitive markets.
. . . Trade restricting measures . . . by the industrial countries . . . provide
additional obstacles. Thus, while manufactured exports will play a major
role in the long-term industrial development of Peru, it appears improbable that the example of export-led high industrial growth set particularly
by East-Asian countries under favorable world economic conditions prevailing during the 1960s and early 1970s can be repeated."

Nevertheless, the report claims that: "If the trade policy suggested in
this report is implemented in successive steps, the manufacturing sector
will be thoroughly restructured toward higher labor intensity and increased export orientation."[34] Interviewed in 1982, Abusada waxed enthusiastic about the "immense variety of new things, fruits, flowers," that
Peru could export: Colombia, he said, exported more than $100 million of
such products and Peru had a better climate.[35] But the increase in Peru's
exports of agricultural products had led, he admitted, to some diminution
of production for local consumption. It could in fact be argued that at a
time of shrinking world markets it is suicidal for developing countries to
increase their dependence on trade, and that India, for example, has
actually fared "relatively well" during the recession precisely because the
dependence of its industries on external trade, as opposed to its internal
market, is relatively low, and because its moves towards import liberalization, much welcomed by the World Bank and the IMF, have been minor
compared to those of the Latin American countries.

While import liberalization may well fail to produce the desired rapid expansion of exports, it usually has a devastating effect on existing import-substituting industries. This is clearly partly intended by the Bank, which argues that such industries are inefficient and wasteful, and that they produce monopoly profits for local businesses. Thus, in the Philippines, the Bank complained of "heavily protected and inefficient manufacturing industries, controlled by politically well-connected Filipinos, which were gradually increasing in importance despite their inefficiency and the existing [sic] of some foreign competition."[36] Similar complaints were made by the Bank about import-substituting manufacturers in Peru and India. There is of course much truth in these attacks on Third World business elites; sometimes high profits are made from screwing together imported components, in Peru in particular. But there are ways of dealing with them other than by destroying their industries through import competition; for example they could be taxed, or nationalized, and perhaps induced to carry out more of the manufacturing process internally. There is also the possibility that this concern about "inefficiency" and excessive profits is a cloak for other fears. For example a panel of representatives of U.S. government and business at Georgetown University's Center for Strategic and International Studies said in 1971:

> As Filipino enterprises have grown and moved into new activities, Filipinos and American businessmen have become competitive and the former . . . have taken political action to minimize the threat of American competition. As the most influential political group motivated to limit access to Philippine resources and markets, they have provided a respectable nucleus around which diverse nationalist elements have coalesced. . . .[37]

The import liberalization policy itself has the effect of driving such people well and truly into the nationalist camp; it may even cause them to form alliances with the left. In the Philippines it has brought them out onto the streets. In Peru business interests affected by the liberalization program were vocal in their opposition to it, expressed partly through an extremely critical national daily newspaper, *El Observador.* But of course the people who suffer most from the destruction of import-substituting industries are not the business elite, who are likely to switch to making fat profits as importers, but workers and the owners of small workshops who lose their jobs. It is not, for example, clear why it is in the interest of the people of the Philippines that small, typically very labor-intensive manufacturers of leather shoes should be put out of business by liberalized imports of plastic shoes from Taiwan. In the Philippines, the Bank itself estimated that roughly 100,000 people in "inefficient" garment and textile firms, or 46 percent of the workforce in those industries and about 5 percent of total employment, would lose their jobs. As in other cases,[38] the Bank seemed little concerned about what might happen to them: "Reabsorbing those who may be displaced in the process—and who would be best placed and qualified to compete for new jobs—is a minor task in comparison to solving the fundamental employment problem."[39]

The Bank, in its advocacy of export-orientated industrialization, does claim as one of its virtues that it is labor-intensive. One of the Bank's criticisms of import-substituting industry is that it has been excessively capital-intensive (because *overvalued exchange rates* and *excessive wages* have created a bias in favor of imports of capital equipment). The induce-ment being offered to the multinational companies which make use of the Export Processing Zones proliferating, partly at the urging of the World Bank, throughout Asia and Latin America, is cheap labor. The Bank is a consistent advocate of lower wages on the hoary right-wing argument that workers are "pricing themselves out of jobs." It shows little sign of concern at the methods by which low wages are achieved: suppression of trade unions and other extreme forms of repression which are common in the Third World. The conditions of super-exploitation that exist in these ex-port processing zones are well known: extremely low wages, and extreme exhaustion of the workers, the majority of whom are young women consid-ered to be both *dexterous* and docile and who are habitually got rid of when they are worn out with overwork. While these activities may add to the number of people who are employed, government policies of *wage restraint* also add to the number of people who need work, to the extent that they make wages too low to support families. It is not uncommon for wages to have declined by 25 to 30 percent during the seventies in coun-tries under IMF/World Bank supervision.

Another benefit of export-orientated industrialization for its propo-nents is that it avoids the classic Keynesian dilemma: high wages increase costs, but if wages are cut too much, industry loses its markets. The mar-kets for the export platform industries are abroad, so wages can be cut with impunity. This is one reason why left-wing opponents of the policy in the Third World, while recognizing the limitations of import-substituting in-dustry, particularly since it is currently largely based on the limited inter-nal markets for luxury consumption provided by Third World elites, advo-cate a radical redistribution of income and an enlargement of internal markets as a way forward from the industrial stagnation experienced by some import-substituting economies. The export-orientated industries are usually enclaves, with few connections with the rest of the economy, and dependent on imported inputs, so that their foreign exchange benefits, like those of the import-substituting industries before them, are often illusory. They are also often merely the labor-intensive part of some total manufacturing process, the more skilled and technologically advanced components of which are performed in the industrialized countries.

The policy of export-orientated industrialization appears to have been on the whole acceptable even to liberals within the Bank, on the grounds presumably that some industrialization is better than none. In the case of the Philippines, and possibly elsewhere, one confidential Bank document does recognize that "in a fiercely competitive and fickle international market, Philippine handicrafts will be in fashion today, and tomorrow [sic]. The bread and butter and the basis of a modern manufacturing sector will always be at home."[40] There was apparently some debate within the World Bank and even between the World Bank and the Bank-orientated Filipino *technocrats* (although they all agreed that protection on imported consumer goods should be reduced) on whether there should not be some encouragement for import-substitution in intermediate and capital goods industries. The Filipinos proposed a range of such industries, attempting to justify them on the grounds that part of their production would be for export and that some of them would be 100 percent foreign-owned. But even these projects were effectively torpedoed by the Bank, and the export-oriented free traders appear to have won the day.

The Bank's wholesale espousal of the export-orientated industrialization strategy has coincided, fortuitously or not, with the outward drive of multinational companies in search of new sources of cheap labor and ways of getting round the high wages and strong trade union organization that exist in the advanced capitalist countries: what the first Brandt Report delicately described as "in a sense a new frontier, with fewer of the special economic difficulties and social and political constraints operating in the North."[41] The same kind of point is sometimes made about the Bank's prescriptions for agriculture, which include the expanded use of fertilizers, improved seeds, and other inputs available from the currently powerful and expanding agribusiness firms. The extent to which the Bank acts directly in the interests and at the behest of multinational firms is debatable. But what is clear is that its emphasis on making use of the abundant reserves of cheap labor that exist in the Third World does not run counter to the interests of multinationals based in the North, and has also been of benefit to Northern consumers of cheap textiles and cheap electronic goods.

In addition, while the concentration on manufacturing for export is justified on *free trade* arguments, there is some sophistry in this, as in most such apparently technical arguments. The export processing zones offer a number of inducements which are in fact the result of large-scale government intervention. First, and most importantly, a workforce which is as cheap and docile as government repression can achieve. But there are also very substantial tax concessions and other incentives; very expensive provision of infrastructure facilities such as power and water; and notional charges for land, in which the Bank's principles of market determination of prices and "full cost recovery," so zealously pursued when the poor are having to pay, go by the board.

All this is justified on the grounds that countries have to earn foreign exchange somehow. But calculations which offset the increases in foreign exchange earnings against the increases in imported inputs, repatriated profits, and the cost of infrastructure, tend to come up with a negative sum. The result—continuing balance of payments crisis through dependence on imported inputs—is not necessarily different from the effects of import-substituting industry. And there are, as always, ways of dealing with balance of payments crises, such as income redistribution, different priorities for consumption, greater self-reliance, refusal to pay extortionate interest rates to the banks, which would fall less heavily on the backs of the poor and, incidentally, be of less benefit to the multinational companies and banks of the North.

Except in a very few East Asian cases, the policies of the World Bank and the IMF have failed to achieve even the limited objective of resolving balance of payments crises. The fact that they might have been rather more successful if there had been no capitalist recession in the North does not excuse the renewed vigor with which the policies are currently being pursued in countries throughout the world.

MARKETS, THE PRICE MECHANISM, AND PRIVATIZATION

The underlying rationale for many of the Bank's favored policies is that the *market* should be allowed to work. Thus much of the argument for import liberalization is based on the supposed gains in efficiency that are to be achieved through the introduction of competition. The Bank now harps greatly on the need for *efficient pricing policies* and the need to avoid *price distortions.* Removing subsidies and price controls has for the Bank the double advantage that it supposedly reduces such *distortions* and cuts down government expenditures.

The second subject listed in 1983 as an "emerging priority" for Bank research was "Issues in the area of government intervention," and the main issue seems to be "pricing policies."[42] Like the IMF, the World Bank has put a good deal of emphasis on the need to raise the prices of goods and services such as food, petrol, public transport, and so on. Governments habitually subsidize services and the prices of some essential goods in order to protect consumers, many of whom may be poor. But the Bank is committed to the concept of *full cost recovery,* for its own projects in particular, although it does not always achieve it. Many of the Bank's most bitter battles with government officials are on the question of whether it is desirable to cover the costs of, for example, a water supply project by charging for the water. Its arguments for financial autonomy for public sector institutions include the argument that they should finance themselves by charging higher rates, and that this will provide an inducement towards greater efficiency.

The Bank appears to be somewhat more willing than it has been to recognize that there may be equity considerations involved. Often its arguments have some weight: for example the Bank argued that the West Bengal government (Communist Party-Marxist) should raise the fares on public transport because the massive subsidies on fares were a misallocation of scarce resources; many of the government's own supporters are inclined to agree. Bank officials will also argue that, for example, there is no reason why the mainly better-off users of telephones should not pay the full costs of the telephone service. The Bank's document on research says that it will evaluate

> the costs and benefits of institutional and policy reforms, particularly pricing policies, under competing objectives like economic efficiency, redistribution, and poverty alleviation, increasing fiscal revenues, as well as such non-economic objectives as maintaining political support. . . . Work in this area has become increasingly important as the result of many countries experiencing a decline in external and fiscal resources which has increased pressure [from the World Bank?] for a rationalization of pricing policies and other interventions such as quantitative restrictions of various kinds, particularly those which involve large subsidies.[43]

One of the Bank's major prescriptions for agriculture is that the prices paid to producers should be raised. The Bank sometimes argues that this will redress the pro-urban bias in income distribution. But it remains unclear whether the Bank pays adequate attention to the fact that many of the producers are likely to be rich landlords and that many of the consumers are not only the urban poor, but also the rural landless and near-landless, who often constitute a majority of the rural labor force.[44] Attempts to raise the prices of food have been the major factor in what have become known, since the popular protests that took place in Egypt in 1977 when the government attempted to increase the price of bread, as "IMF riots." They could be described as "IMF/World Bank riots," for the World Bank is fully behind the policies that cause them. In January 1984 the Tunisian government's attempt to double the prices of basic foodstuffs was met with such strong popular resistance that the army was brought in, a number of people died, and the government retracted the measures. A week or two later, similar price rises were similarly retracted in Morocco after popular protests. A World Bank official spoke of "necessary rationalizations in food grains subsidies in North Africa."[45] And in Morocco the increases were "prompted by austerity measures demanded of the government by the International Monetary Fund," according to the *Financial Times* of January 24, 1984. Yet subsidizing the prices of the basic food consumed by the poor is one certain way of helping them, especially in countries where there is much unemployment and landlessness. Opposition to such subsidies is to a great extent inspired by ideology. The Bank's predilections clearly lie in the direction of the neo-classical principles of full-cost recovery and market pricing, together with the view that those who can pay, should pay, rather than the principle of free provision of services to all.

The Bank's 1983 *World Development Report,* in a chapter entitled "Pricing for Efficiency," produced a remarkably imaginative negative correlation between growth rates and *'price distortions'* in a pretty picture with five different colors and shadings thereof and a box which states that: "The regression equation relating growth to the composite distortion index shows that price distortions can explain about one-third of the variation in growth performance."[46] There is a good deal more besides on "weights" and "the relative importance of different distortions in the total mix" and "the exchange rate distortion being the most significant" which all tends to go to show that the Chicago-trained Third World Bank official who said the whole exercise was "simplistic" and "analytically incorrect," was right.[47] The report also claimed that there was "virtually no correlation" between price distortions and equity: "the distortion index explains hardly 3 percent of the variation in equity, when the latter is measured by the proportion of income going to the bottom 40 percent of the population." In other words, the Bank feels that governments which alleviate hardship through, for example, a free rice ration, as the government of Sri Lanka did before the World Bank and the IMF got to work on it, or through indexing wages to the rate of inflation, don't *really* help the poor.

. . .

NOTES

1. *Development Co-operation,* The Labour Party 1982, p. 28.
2. *Ibid.,* pp. 31–32.
3. T. Hayter, *Aid as Imperialism,* Penguin 1971.
4. *United States Participation in the Multilateral Development Banks in the 1980s,* Dept. of Treasury, Washington, D.C. 1980.
5. Edward Mason & Robert Asher, *The World Bank Since Bretton Woods,* Brookings, Washington, D.C. 1973.
6. Memorandum to the Executive Directors, "Lending for 'Structural Adjustment," p. 4, Annex A to *Program Lending for Structural Adjustment,* Joint Ministerial Committee of the Boards of Governors of the Bank and the Fund, 2 April 1980.
7. Mason and Asher, *op. cit.,* p. 555.
8. Interview with Teresa Hayter, September 1983.
9. Quoted in Mason and Asher, *op. cit.,* p. 550.
10. Mason and Asher, *op. cit.,* p. 557.
11. See also Mason and Asher, *op. cit.,* p. 552.
12. Interviews with Teresa Hayter in Washington, September 1983.
13. Interviewed by Teresa Hayter, May 1981.
14. Tony Killick, ed., *The Quest for Economic Stabilization—The IMF and the Third World,* Heinemann, 1984.
15. Interviews with Teresa Hayter, May 1981 and September 1983.
16. For a full account, see Mason and Asher, *op. cit.,* p. 285, and Chapter 13.
17. *Peru: Development and Policy Issues of the Manufacturing Sector,* World Bank/United Nations Industrial Development Organisation, January 1981.
18. Interviews with Teresa Hayter, February 1982.
19. Comment by a Bank official to Teresa Hayter, September 1983.
20. Mason and Asher, *op. cit.,* p. 668.
21. The World Bank, *World Development Report 1983,* Box 7.4, p. 69.
22. Mason and Asher, *op. cit.,* p. 245.

23. See Mason and Asher, *op. cit.*, p. 245, footnote 23.
24. *Ibid.*, p. 246.
25. *Ibid.*, pp. 276–277.
26. Interview with Colombian official by Teresa Hayter, 1982.
27. Interview in New Delhi by Teresa Hayter, January 1983.
28. Interview with Teresa Hayter, May 1981.
29. Bela Balassa, "The 'New Protectionism' and the international economy," World Bank Reprint Series: Number Seventy, reprinted from *Journal of World Trade Law,* Vol. 12, No. 5 (1978).
30. "Trade and protectionism," Background Paper, World Bank, September 29 1983. See also the World Bank's *1981 World Development Report* and *1983 World Development Report,* Chapter 6.
31. Interview with Teresa Hayter, February 1982.
32. "China textile sales talks deadlocked in Brussels," *Financial Times,* 29 November 1983.
33. Interview with Javier Iguiñez by Teresa Hayter, February 1982.
34. *Peru: Development and Policy Issues of the Manufacturing Sector, op. cit.,* pp. 71 and 85–86.
35. Interview with Teresa Hayter, February 1982.
36. World Bank, "Political and administrative bases for economic policy in the Philippines," Memo from William Asher, Washington D.C., November 6, 1980, p. 3, quoted in *Development Debacle, op. cit.,* p. 137.
37. Quoted in *Development Debacle, op. cit.,* p. 137.
38. See, for example, Hayter, *Aid as Imperialism, op. cit.,* p. 160, fn. 8.
39. World Bank, "Report and Recommendations of the President of the IBRD to the Executive Directors on a Proposed Structural Adjustment Loan to the Republic of the Philippines," Report No. P-2872-PH, Washington D.C., August 21, 1980, p. 31, quoted in *Development Debacle, op. cit.,* p. 170.
40. World Bank, "Random thoughts on rural development," Memo from David Steel to Michael Gould, Washington D.C., September 1, 1977, quoted in *Development Debacle,* op. cit., p. 148.
41. Brandt Commission, *North-South, op. cit.,* p. 67.
42. *Report on the World Bank Research Program,* grey cover, March 1983, p. 14.
43. *Ibid.*
44. See Lappe et al., Table 1, p. 73.
45. Paper presented to a Seminar at Cornell University, April 1984.
46. *World Bank Development Report 1983,* pp. 62–63.
47. Interview with Teresa Hayter in Washington, September 1983.

The New International Economic Order and the Basic Needs Approach

Johan Galtung

The article explores, without claiming to do so in depth, the important political conflict that is shaping up between two "Grand Designs" in development theory and practice: the New International Economic Order (NIEO) and the Basic Needs (BN) approach, each of which has to be studied in relation to the other. It analyzes the two aspects of the debate—the *issues* and the *parties*—which are common to all conflict situations, and then goes on to examine if and how far the two theories are compatible, mutually contradictory, or conflicting.

INTRODUCTION: THE UNIVERSE OF DISCOURSE

First, a few words by way of definition. The New International Economic Order (NIEO) stands for a new way of ordering the international economic system so as to bring about, first, improved terms of trade between the present-day center and periphery countries (in other words, the First World and the Third World countries); secondly, more control by the periphery over the world economic cycles that pass through them (the controls to include nationalization of natural resources, soil, processing facilities, distribution machinery, financial institutions, etc.); and, thirdly, increased and improved trade between the periphery countries themselves.

To be sure, there are other ways of listing the issue areas of NIEO.[1]

Johan Galtung, "The New International Economic Order and the Basic Needs," in Galtung, *The North-South Debate: Technology, Basic Human Needs, and the New International Economic Order,* WOMP Working Paper #12 (1985), World Policy Institute.

But the three characteristics listed above are related directly to the world structure,[2] and they bring into sharp focus the specific changes sought to be made in that structure.

Very crucial in the evaluation of NIEO at the international level—which is the level at which it is intended to work—is the relative weight assigned to the first and the remaining two components. If the first predominates, the present structure may get frozen, though possibly at a higher level so far as the income of the periphery countries is concerned. This is already visible in the petroleum-exporting countries, which may be said to be the first to strike out for NIEO (without consensus, it is true, but after years of negotiation and discussion). There is now in these countries more money at the disposal of those who usually dispose; how exactly it is disposed of is instructive (on luxury consumer goods, capital goods for industrialization, and sophisticated weapons).[3]

If, however, the other two components predominate, the present world structure might be changed, the industrial capacities of the Third World countries might increase, and the center-periphery trade might decrease (in relative terms) while that between the Third World countries increases. According to the World Bank, the increase in manufacturing production in 1961–1965 was 8.7% in the developing countries and 6.2% in the industrialized countries; in 1966–1973, the corresponding figures were 9.0% and 6.2%; and in 1974–1975 the increase was 4.5% in developing countries and −4.7% in industrialized countries.[4] In the sphere of trade, however, the expectation that it would increase between the Third World countries has not been borne out; "the most rapid rate of growth in trade has been between the industrialized countries."[5]

The NIEO deals essentially with the relations between industrialized and developing countries at the global level (because, among other reasons, it is articulated in the UN between states or blocs of states). It is thus a *macro* approach to the problem of development. The BN approach, on the other hand, is a *micro* approach. It goes down to the level of the individual human being and, therefore, sees development in terms of the fulfilment of basic needs at the individual level. Some, like this author,[6] argue that that is the only level at which basic needs have to be met, if one has in mind basic *human* needs, not such abstractions as, for example, "urban needs" (for sewage), "historical needs" (collectivization of the means of production), "national needs" (for military defense or for a national language)—all of which are, at most, merely the necessary condition for meeting basic *human* needs.

It needs to be emphasized that the BN approach is meaningful only if it is accompanied by a list of needs. The list that comes out of the Programme of Action adopted at the 1976 ILO World Employment Conference, which divided needs into "minimum requirements of a family for private consumption" (adequate food, shelter, clothing, household equipment, furniture) and "essential services for the community at large" (safe drinking water, sanitation, public transport and health, educational and cultural facilities), is open to criticism on three counts: that it draws too rigid a line between private and public; that it allocates satisfiers (they are not needs) to these areas; and that it neglects non-material needs.

But however perfect the list, it must have a rider: *the first priority must always be given to those most in need.*[7]

In other words, BN approach would set priorities in production and distribution. It would give the first priority to the production of what is essential to meet human needs, and in such a way that it goes to meet the needs of the most needy. It would give a much lower priority to production of goods for other than human needs, for non-basic needs, and for the needs of those less in need (obvious examples of which are national airlines, cars, food too expensive to be within reach of the masses).

It should be emphasized, though, that *lower priority* does not mean that these goods will never be produced, but only that they may be produced *later,* even *much later.* There is nothing in the BN approach that strictly limits the concerns of a society to the satisfaction of basic needs—and certainly not at the lowest level. The BN approach does not call for asceticism or puritanism; all that it insists on is a certain order of priorities: first meet the basic needs of those most in need (assuming that the others have already had their basic needs met), and then, *and only then,* go about satisfying other needs if they are felt. The basic theoretical and empirical question in connection with the BN approach has to do with the ordering of these pursuits in terms of time. The assumption is that the pursuit of non-basic needs will stand in the way of meeting basic needs.

NIEO VERSUS BN APPROACH: THE ISSUES, THE PARTIES

There are at least two aspects of any conflict formation: the *issues* and the *parties.* On the subject of the relation between NIEO and the BN approach, on the level of issues the questions to be asked are: Is it theoretically possible to implement both the NIEO and BN approaches at the same time and at the same place (compatibility)? Or do they in some ways exclude each other simply because one comes in the way of the other (contradiction or conflict)? At the level of the parties, the set of questions is different: What kind of actors (individuals, groups, and classes of individuals; states, groups, and classes of states) favor one or the other? How do these actors relate to each other on other issues? How will this spill over into the relationship between the NIEO and BN approaches?

In discussing the issues, we shall first present the BN critique of NIEO and then the NIEO critique of BN.

BN CRITIQUE OF NIEO

We shall begin with a relatively abstract analysis detached from the concrete realities of today. It cannot be denied that the two approaches can be compatible, but under certain conditions. In the NIEO there is a *potential* for more economic surplus to accumulate in the Third World countries. But the far more important question is whether it is used to meet the basic needs of those most in need. Economic surplus, it is well known, can be used in several ways, depending on where in the society it is generated, who decides how it will be disposed of, and what kind of decision is made. To take it for granted that it will necessarily be used to meet basic needs is extremely naive.[8] A more realistic understanding is that most people in control of the economy will tend to use it for what *they* see as the pressing needs—be they "national needs," non-basic needs, or the needs of those less in need.[9]

In the *most optimistic model* imaginable, a society is so organized that much of the economic surplus remains at the level where it was generated. This can occur when, for instance, farmers are in control of land and workers of factories to the point where they can decide what to produce, how to distribute the produce, and how to dispose of the surplus. Under these conditions, it seems reasonable to assume that the hungry masses in the rural areas will prefer to produce food that can be eaten on the spot by themselves and their families. Lappè and Collins rightly observe:

> Hungry people can and will feed themselves if they are allowed to do so. If people are not feeding themselves, you can be sure powerful obstacles are in the way . . . the most fundamental constraint to food self-reliance is that the majority of the people are not themselves in control of the production process and, therefore, more and more frequently do not even participate.[10]

Similarly, workers will prefer to produce things that can be used for meeting basic needs, particularly in connection with farming, thus relating their activities to those of the farmers, guaranteeing to both themselves and the farmers at least a minimum in the way of food, clothing, and shelter (shelter being a typical item for farmer-worker direct cooperation).[11]

It may be argued that this does not take care of medical services and schooling, so one would add to the model the idea that the surplus generated on, or siphoned into, the top of society will trickle down in the form of free and easily accessible facilities in these two fields.

In contrast to this, the *most pessimistic model* is a society so organized that the surplus generated at the bottom not only "trickles up" but is pumped upwards through the powerful mechanism of elite ownership (private or state) into the centers of control located in the country's capital or in the world economic centers.[12] As to the economic surplus entering the top layer, the elites keep it for themselves, using it for purposes different from those of the BN approach. Evidently, whereas in the former case one might envisage a convergence between the living conditions of the elites and the masses, in the latter case a divergence will be unavoidable.[13]

To one who thinks that the pessimistic model gives a more realistic picture of a majority of Third World countries today, the NIEO and BN approaches will appear to be, in fact, contradictory. It may be argued, however, that NIEO has not created this situation in the Third World; indeed, it is to correct this situation that NIEO has been proposed. NIEO is an *inter*-national arrangement, and all that needs to be done is to complement it with corresponding *intra*-national measures to make the picture conform to the "optimistic" model.

But to proceed with the argument. NIEO cannot but affect the international situation. For one thing, NIEO may stimulate international trade. (We say *may*, not *will* advisedly; for no one can say what course the total volume of world trade would take.[14]) This will cause an increasing proportion of the economic factors of Third World countries to be steered in the direction of producing exportable goods. This means that a higher priority will be given to the use of, for instance, soil for the production of commodities for export than to its use for the production of food for direct consumption; coffee rather than black beans, to use the oft-quoted Brazilian example. It also means that an increasing production of the economic cycle in the country will pass through a narrow and easily controlled gate: the major import-export facilities (ports, airports, border crossing-points) and banking facilities as well as other financial instruments.

Since these points can be controlled by a small number of people, themselves controlled by private and state leadership, this will result in increasingly centralized control of the entire economic machinery. As a contrast to this, imagine a country based on a high level of local self-reliance, production for consumption mainly on the spot, exchange between these units when there is surplus production, low level of external trade, even low level of monetization of the economic cycle—an economy obviously much more difficult to control centrally. Now, which of the two types of countries would be able to move easily to satisfy the basic needs of those most in need?

Again, the answer will, to a large extent, depend on the kind of decision the elites take. If past experience is any guide, the outlook is not very bright. The elites might decide to convert much of the net earned income into means of control of possible external (and even more so, internal) enemies—in other words, the police and the army. For a very good reason, too; for the gap between expectations raised by NIEO and the continuation of the sad reality concerning basic needs may be intolerable for certain segments of the population, which might then try all means within its power to change the regime.

This is as far as one can carry the argument based on informed doubt about NIEO at present. This argument is perhaps inspired by empirical information about the Third World countries that were the first to benefit from increased income due to the increased prices for their commodities.[15] In short, the conclusion would be something like this: No doubt there are great possibilities of compatibility between the NIEO and BN approaches, but there are possibilities also of contradiction, depending on the international structure. In a brilliant analysis of this structure, Samir Amin observes:

> The incredible resistance of the developed world to this reduction [of the inequality of the international division of labor] is evidence that the center, despite so many misleading speeches, cannot do without the pillage of the Third World. If that pillage were to stop, the center would be forced to adjust to a new, less equal international division of labor. Then, and only then, could one begin to speak of a genuine world order, and not merely of new terms of the unequal international division of labor.[16]

THE NIEO CRITIQUE OF BN APPROACH

The Third World arguments against the BN approach, heard in conferences where the two "Grand Designs" are discussed, can be summed up in six propositions:[17]

1. *The BN approach is an effort to sidetrack the NIEO issue.* The real issue is international economic justice, and to throw in the BN approach is an effort to widen the agenda—possibly to insinuate into the essentially political discussion a *condition prealable:* No NIEO concessions to be given before BN policies are adopted. Since the First World is skeptical of the Third World ability to implement such policies, this amounts to postponing NIEO concessions or conventions indefinitely.

It is hardly relevant in this connection to argue, for instance, that the BN approach dates back to 1972 while the NIEO cannot claim to go farther back than the Sixth Special Session of the UN in 1974, and that therefore BN approach cannot be said to be an afterthought pregnant with ulterior motives. The reason why this is beside the point is that neither approach can be said to have a definite birth-date. Both are, rather, names of trends that have been operating in the world for a long time. NIEO can be traced back to UNCTAD I (Geneva, 1964), and the genesis of BN approach can be traced to social welfare policies pursued in welfare states and rooted in the compassion for the lowest and the most underprivileged and unfortunate found in many religions. The question is not whether some key points on the socio-political trajectories of these two approaches can be neatly ordered in time; the question is how the two approaches are used politically. NIEO is seen as a codification of a kind of *inter*-national social justice, whereas the BN approach is concerned with *intra*-national social justice (inside Third World countries). If the BN approach had taken within its purview and made it applicable to the whole world, with the focus on non-material needs as sharp as it is on material needs, so that the shortcomings in the First World showed up as clearly as those in the Third World,[18] then NIEO and BN approaches might be seen as two independent issues. The way the BN approach has been launched, and applied predominantly *only* to the Third World, the Third World has every reason to regard it as a ploy for side-tracking the world economic issue raised by NIEO.

2. *The BN approach is a new way of legitimizing external intervention.* Most Third World countries are former colonies; large parts of the Third World still are neo-colonies. Colonialism is gone, and neo-colonialism will also go.[19] So now comes the BN approach to legitimize intervention when military-political formulas will cease to work and direct economic investment will be threatened. Basic needs, like basic rights, attach to *individuals* in Western thinking,[20] which means that it is only at the individual level that their satisfaction can be monitored. The Third World posits against this the primacy of basic *national* needs and *national* rights as codified in the Charter of Economic Rights and Duties of States. National needs and rights are claimed, satisfied, or left unsatisfied in the international context. The Third World insistence that it is up to the Third World countries to decide, severally or collectively, how best to use this basic national right intranationally is clearly an anti-interventionist position. It does not say, "We shall continue to exploit our masses, and it is none of your business." It only says, "Whatever we do inside our countries is none of your business." In the light of past history, the First World's disavowal of interventionist intentions does not carry conviction, nor does its protestation that the BN approach will not have any unintended consequences. For it is clear that a BN clause added to a NIEO agreement might mean that a number of NIEO components (for example, a decrease in debt burdens, an increase in ODA) would be made conditional on the implementation of BN policies. This implies that implementation (necessarily at the individual level) inside Third World nations would be monitored by some international agency. One can easily imagine an international bureaucracy set up to supervise such agreements. However the agency might be staffed, the cycles of reporting and decisionmaking would have to pass through the First World centers to make sense of monitoring. On this reasoning, the First World can be suspected of supporting the BN approach precisely because other historically familiar handles of intervention are slipping.

3. *The BN approach is an instrument to enlarge the First World's market in the Third World.* The First World fears that NIEO will increase, perhaps greatly, the Third World competitive capability in the world market. The Third World supply of goods may increasingly be sufficient to meet

Third World demand, thereby closing *de facto* the Third World market to First World exports. (The *de facto* closure could be also made *de jure* before or after, or independently of, the *de facto* closure.) Some way will, therefore, have to be found to so relate the growth of Third World supply to the growth of Third World demand that a substantial portion of demand was still left unsatisfied.

This can be done in several ways. For instance, the revolution of rising expectations (increasing the middle-class demand for goods) is one, population control (reducing the number of those with needs but without effective demand) is another, and the BN approach may be a third. Indeed, the BN approach may, in fact, succeed in doing what population control largely failed to do. If one hears less about the population explosion today than one did some years ago, it may be because the First World has realized that the explosion is not all that bad: after all, the teeming millions are *potential* customers! All that need be done to convert them into *actual* customers is to bring them to a certain economic level so that, with their increased purchasing power, they can express their needs in terms of effective demand. And this is where the BN approach comes in. Instead of aiming at raising the expectations of the middle class, why not aim at raising the purchasing power of the vast Third World proletariat—in the countryside and in the city slums, living on the fringe of the money economy (as distinguished from self-supporting farmers, nomads, and other groups that live outside this economy), in numbers much more promising than the middle classes ever were.[21]

It is not difficult to visualize the implications of this type of reasoning. The BN approach would provide what is needed for the satisfaction of basic needs from the market. For the rest, schooling provided free; medical services, likewise free; meals, free or highly subsidized (in canteens, maybe). The list could be extended to cover basic clothing and basic housing. From single individuals the gains may be next to nothing, but from a country as a whole they could be something to be satisfied with. It is the First World that would be contracted to build the infrastructure for all these services, presumably to be provided by the state. The payments would be made from out of the increased assets resulting from the NIEO—a neat way of recycling NIEO-dollars via the BN formula.

There is also the possibility of marketing what is needed to meet basic needs; international agribusiness, construction business, textile business, and pharmaceuticals are already in the field. (The field of school materials, however, does not seem, as yet, to be so effectively transnationalized, educational videocassettes being a possible exception.) For all this to become a large-scale business at the level of those more, if not most, in need, two things have to happen: prices have to be lowered and the purchasing power of those at the bottom has to be raised. As the former can be, at least potentially, a function of the latter, a beginning might be made with efforts to raise purchasing power. One way of doing this is through higher guaranteed minimum wages and full employment—in

other words, the kind of approach that ILO advocates. And where is the
money for this to come from? Why, from the income accruing to the Third
World countries from a more just international economic order and from
big transnational corporations catering to the people most in need, who
will now be knocking at the doors of the market in the language the
market understands: coins, later on bills, and then, maybe, checks.

Whether it is the market device (for some of the basic needs) or the
non-market device (for other needs), or a combination of both, that may
be used, it will prepare the ground for a *planetary bargain:* "We give you
the NIEO, you give us the right to compete with you in your own market
for the satisfaction of basic needs." Needless to say, this extremely limited
perspective on basic needs (confined to material needs) totally disregards
the issue of identity; the urge to be master of one's own situation; to be
a subject, and not merely an object. As to freedom, the proponents of this
new strategy for the First World penetration into the Third World via the
BN formula would claim that the monetized approach offers more freedom of choice than is possible when basic needs are satisfied through
deliveries in kind.[22] They would further argue that a person should not
only be given a choice in consumer goods, several brands of food, several
types of clothes, but also enabled to decide his/her own trade-off formula
between food and clothes, given a minimum income.[23] One can very well
imagine transnational corporations making *basic-needs packages,* containing food, textiles, drugs, and some educational material in proportions to
be decided by the customer, given the price range of the package. If that
formula, or some other similar formula, works, there might be room for
an accelerating population explosion.[24]

4. *The BN approach is intended to slow down the growth of Third World
economies.* Generally speaking, there are two approaches to most problems that concern the Third World today: one aims at strengthening the
weaker states/countries, and the other aims at strengthening the weakest
individuals in those territorial units. This is very clearly seen in the choice
of technologies. On the one hand, there are the capital-intensive, labor-
extensive, research-intensive, and administration-intensive technologies
that might eventually make it possible for Third World countries to play
the First World game according to rules made by the First World. On the
other hand, there are the capital-extensive, labor-intensive, research-ex-
tensive, and administration-extensive technologies that are much more
relevant for the satisfaction of the basic needs of those most in need.[25] The
first approach is, for obvious reasons, the approach of the national elites;
the second approach is, for equally obvious reasons, the approach of the
less privileged groups, when, that is to say, left to themselves—such as the
groups building China's people's communes in the beginning of the life-
cycle of that institution.[26]

The first approach, which is highly capital-absorbing, may also be
capital-generating. The second approach does not generate capital but

other values, human values: restoration/strengthening of nature's ecological balance, autonomy, creativity, participation, etc. The two approaches
cannot mix well because the two are mutually inconsonant. The extent to
which local self-reliant communities can be incorporated in a national
economic structure (i.e., one that uses capital-intensive technology and
produces for exchange rather than for use) without being *perverted* is
strictly limited. Conversely, the extent to which self-reliant local communities (i.e., those that use capital-extensive technology and produce for use
rather than for exchange) can go their own way without weakening the
national purpose (i.e., the capability of participating on an equal footing
in the international game as defined by the First World) is strictly limited.
The *self-reliant basic needs approach* redefines the national purpose. It
involves rearrangement, not in the allocation of capital, but in the allocation of human and social energy, creativity, mobilization, etc.

The case of China is very instructive. A China in which the 70,000
communes, with their production for use rather than for exchange, dominate does not constitute much of a threat to the First World in terms of
economic competition in the world market, although it makes it extremely difficult for the First World to penetrate economically into the
Chinese market. A China that changes over to an economy dominated by
capital- and research-intensive technology—making use of a labor force of
about 600 million—may, in the first run, cause some satisfaction in First
World capitals (if only because it ceases to be a threat as an alternative
model of development), but, in the second run, may cause considerable
anxiety (because of its economic power). Such an apprehension has already
been expressed: "Every aspect of world economics and politics will be
transformed if these educated new Chinese in the 1990s attain a level of
productivity even approximately in accord with their ability, and hell
knows if they don't."[27] There is no doubt that, under certain conditions,
a systematically pursued BN approach, whether or not based on local
self-reliance as a major ingredient, may make the Third World less of a
threat to First World economic hegemony.

The case of Germany and Japan, where the Western "allied" powers
followed different tactics is equally instructive. After some time the "allies" realized that it was important that both be integrated into the military machine of the West, not only to benefit from their military tradition
and experience, but also to reduce their economic competitive strength
in the world market by forcing them to divert much more of their production factors in the military direction, including buying military wares from
the West. (It should be noted that the military production and marketing
system is protectionist; it is not an open world market but a market where
one is expected to trade within an alliance, or at least not far outside it,
the protection mechanisms being legitimized through concepts of security and secrecy.) This policy, however, failed to put an efficient brake on
German and Japanese economic growth in the 1950s; for the integration
of a country into a highly capital-intensive and research-intensive military

machine tends to push the economic growth of the country along the same line, possibly after a time-lag for some years. If a country chooses the self-reliant path of development, it does not neglect its security, but relies for it, not on capital-intensive conventional army, but on guerrilla (possibly non-military) defense of a highly localized nature.[28]

5. *The BN approach is an effort to reduce technical assistance.* The capital component of BN approach—particularly if it is based on self-reliance, mobilizing local forces and resources, building on local traditions—is relatively minor. External technical assistance is, to a large extent, ruled out as antithetical to self-reliance. Just as the First World might like to push the BN expenses in general on to the Third World leadership, it might also like to rid itself of obligations of technical assistance, thereby improving its own competitive capability. One cannot miss the hint in UK's position:

> Since our experience, and that of other donors who are trying to direct more aid towards the poor, suggests that there is a risk that at least initially rates of disbursement may fall, we will need to continue to finance other projects which are economically sound and to which developing countries attach priority if we are to disperse the UK aid program as fully and effectively as possible.[29]

However this may be, it is clear that a systematic change in the BN direction would raise a number of questions in connection with any kind of project in a Third World country. These questions have, to some extent, been raised by the World Bank recently. But the relationship between the various BN approaches, on the one hand, and the quantum of ODA, on the other, is not yet quite clear.

6. *The BN approach is a weapon of defense against the poor.* The BN approach springs less from compassion for the poor than from fear of the poor. The poor are seen as a vast amorphous mass of people increasingly conscious and envious of what the First World has and desirous of getting it anyhow. It is the image of the "hordes" knocking on the doors of Western affluence.[30] The more contemporary, political version of the same image—the communist subversion.

Together with this image comes the hypothesis that the danger is roughly proportionate to the poverty of the "hordes," implying that a reduction in their number means a reduction of the danger. One way of reducing the number of the poor is through *nature's regulatory devices* (earthquakes, tidal waves, floods, etc.), another is through genocide, yet another is through population control,[31] and, finally, the more "positive" approach: reducing the number of the poor by making them less poor through the BN approach.

The point simply is that the BN approach is a mystification of clear global power politics. It aims at reducing the political power of the Third World through the elimination of a major power element used, sometimes discriminately and sometimes indiscriminately, during the last generation or so: the threat of communist subversion ("if more aid is not given, it cannot be ensured that the forces of subversion will be contained").

It may be noted parenthetically that the proposition that subversive "aggression is proportionate to poverty" has not been proven. The historical experience is that very poor people tend to be apathetic because, among other reasons, of lack of resources, and that it is only when they manage, in one way or another, to move out of poverty that they can begin to think of revolution.[32] Nonetheless, it is generally believed that the proposition cannot be dismissed as one out of touch with reality. From the beginning, First World technical assistance has been urged and justified on the ground that it prevents conflicts from escalating and eventually becoming a threat to First World countries themselves. Hesitant parliaments have used this argument in defense of technical assistance. This idiom has been found to be more convincing and effective than the humanitarian idiom—or even the developmental idiom for that matter. Technical assistance without doubt plays a part in foreign commercial policy, as a way (through tied aid) of steering the flow of orders from the periphery to the center and as a way of creating goodwill in the wake of which general trade treaties might be more easily forged. Technical assistance is also used as an instrument in foreign-power policy, for shaping alliances to cope with present and future conflicts. The BN approach is a variation on this—only more refined, more directly aimed at the exact point inside societies from which a conflict is likely to emanate. Whether the assumption is right or wrong is not important. What is important is that it is *believed* to be correct by a sufficient number of decisionmakers in the First World.

Having examined the issues in the debate between the NIEO and BN advocates, we may now look at the *parties* involved in the debate.

NIEO-BN Debate: the Parties

It is clear that the polarization is between the First World and the Third World, with the Second (Socialist) World sitting, generally speaking, on the fence. To put it differently, there is a contradiction between the center (the capitalist world) and the periphery (the developing part of the world). This contradiction was brought about by historical circumstances but is still being built into the world structure. The Third World—or, to be more precise, the Third World elites—calls for NIEO; the First World (both elites and masses) is far from enthusiastic and tends to say, with a former U.S. secretary of state, that "the present world system has served us well" (us may also be written U.S.). It looks for arguments against a redistribution of the world income. One such argument is the BN approach: "What is the good of NIEO? It will only enrich the Third World elites. Look at the way they treat their own people".[33] This type of argument is most articulated in the Protestant northern fringe of the First World, perhaps by upper middle class intellectuals with an oversensitive conscience, who show far more concern for economic development oriented to the needs of those most in need (unlike their hardened compeers far less worried about the plight of the masses) than for their own disproportionate share of the world income. Naturally, they seize upon any argument they can find against NIEO. This process has already started, the World Bank having been among the first to articulate some kind of BN approach.[34]

That the Third World would hit back was only to be expected. But one hopes that this would make for an honest searching debate on the fundamental issues involved. The quality and validity of an argument lie in the eye of the beholder. To the Third World, the need for NIEO (in sum, a fairer distribution of the global wealth) is, not only conceptually but also in terms of basic norms of social justice, too obvious to need pleading. Similarly, to BN advocates nothing can be more sound or more reasonable in human terms than the uplift of those most in need. They would concede, of course, that the criteria and methods were open to discussion, but not the fundamental goal of the elimination of poverty. Both parties tend to view the opposition of the other as a subterfuge for pure self-serving. One can predict that the First World would dismiss the Third World argument in favor of NIEO as a disingenuous plea for ensuring privileges to Third World elites; and the Third World would regard the First World argument in favor of BN as a justification, equally disingenuous, of preserving the First World privileges at the international level.

We are now set to examine whether the NIEO and BN approaches are compatible or conflicting and in what sense and to what extent. But before we engage ourselves in that exercise, it may be useful to take stock of what has been said so far.

On the plane of issues, the six arguments brought up against the BN approach all converge to make the point that the BN approach is more than meets the eye, that it is not what it is dressed up to look like, and that there are other things behind and underneath. These are probings into the motivation of the BN approach. Understandably, for NIEO affects the interests in the old international economic order and is used to define parties and actors in a conflict of interests. The arguments against NIEO are directed against NIEO as it has been presented. The arguments against the BN approach seem to have been generated by the arguments against NIEO—in other words, third generation arguments. It is possible that if a consistent BN approach had been presented first (i.e., if the World Employment Conference of 1976 had been held before the Sixth Special Session of the UN General Assembly on 1 May 1974), then the nature and order of arguments would have been different. On the plane of parties, what is noteworthy is that although the issues are *debated* by different political actors, all essentially refer to the same actor—the Third World, the assumption (fallacious, as will become clear later) being that the Third World is debatable but the First World is not.

CONCLUSION: NIEO AND BN CONTRADICTORY OR COMPATIBLE?

The answer depends on whether NIEO is interpreted in a shallow sense (i.e., without involving intranational transformation) or in a deeper sense (i.e., requiring at least some measures of intranational transformation). It depends, too, on whether BN is interpreted in a shallow sense (i.e., with non-material needs kept out) or in a deeper sense (requiring the inclusion of non-material needs). Finer distinctions could admittedly be made, but these are sufficient to summarize the foregoing discussion as under:

		NIEO without intranational transformation	NIEO with intranational transformation
BN	without non-material needs	A : Compatibility	C : Compatibility
BN	with non-material needs	B : Contradiction	D : Compatibility

To spell out the table:

A: *Compatibility,* in the sense that the satisfaction of basic needs is managerially possible. It depends on the manner of "recycling NIEO-dollars for basic needs," from the top down, with or without First World participation.

B: *Contradiction,* the most important non-material needs in this connection are autonomy, being subject rather than object, having a major say in one's own sitaution as opposed to being a client/consumer. This applies also to the rich countries that have been the beneficiaries of the old international economic order.[35]

C: *Compatibility,* in the sense that the surplus generated locally will, to a large extent, remain at the bottom, and the surplus generated at, or entering, the top will trickle down. The combination is a *soul-less* one; it is economistic, not taking non-material concerns into consideration.

D: *Compatibility,* in an optimal combination. There is a transformation of the intranational order that permits a richer perspective of basic needs to come into play.

This raises the question of where the total world system is heading. As seen from the point of view of the way the United Nations' machinery is processing the two concepts of NIEO and BN, it seems to be heading towards the combination A. The UN being an intergovernmental machinery,[36] it will have a tendency to focus on inter- rather than intra-national transformation (although the situation is not very clear-cut). It would be easy to obtain a majority for *inter*-national transformation[37] when the majority of member-countries are victims of the old international economic order that dominates the world. This can then be combined with a majority against mandatory *intra*-national transformations, except for minor matters, under the general formula of non-intervention in national sovereignty—assuming that there is sufficient solidarity among the victims of the old international economic order.

At the same time, the UN machinery will probably continue to concentrate on the shallow interpretation of basic needs (i.e., without including non-material needs). There could be another possibility, though: the UN concern with human rights may lead to a broadening of the concept, through the basic-needs concern of such organizations as the ILO and the UNICEF.[38] But one must reckon with the pervasive influence of the hierarchy principle: *first,* material needs and *then* non-material needs. It is easier to obtain a consensus on material than on non-material needs. Around this formulation various types of ideologies (liberalism and Marxism,[39] for instance) can be brought together, bridges can be built between East and West, North and South. To achieve a consensus, the temptation to strip the concepts of BN and NIEO of its richness must be great. The deeper interpretation of the concepts are just too painful! This dénouement is bound to disappoint those to whom both NIEO and BN have much richer connotations. The rhetoric to be heard will doubtless be that of D (see table), the reality will be akin to A. But is it possible to move from A towards D to make the reality correspond better to the rhetoric?

One approach is obvious: never to give in to the shallow interpretations of NIEO and BN, always insisting that NIEO is meaningful only with intra-national transformations and BN only with the inclusion of non-material needs. The nature of the transformation and the non-material needs will be open to discussion, of course. It is obvious that the interpretations will vary according to the concrete situation in time and place; but one must guard oneself against being duped by these obvious considerations into facile compromises with the shallow interpretation of either. For the most likely outcome of compromises can only be that even material needs will be left unsatisfied, and even if satisfied they will be satisfied in a managerial, even corporate, fashion.

But neither should one succumb to the polarization that now seems to be crystallizing, with the Third World elites standing for a shallow NIEO interpretation and the First World for a shallow BN interpretation. One way of reorienting this debate would be to insist on symmetry: both parties must see the broad interpretations of NIEO and of BN as applicable to *all parts of the world.* There are some obvious transformations that will have to take place in the First World if NIEO is to be really implemented, such as more emphasis on agriculture again; probably much more emphasis on local energy production; more emphasis on local, national, subregional, and regional self-reliance; even self-sufficiency in some fields. There will probably have to be an orientation towards other lifestyles, more compatible with the objective situation brought about by NIEO. As for BN, both parties could use the full spectrum of basic human needs—such as security needs, welfare needs, identity needs, freedom needs[40]—and discuss the situation both in their own and in other countries. This would certainly widen the agenda; but care must be taken to keep in check the propensity to score points, as against the adversary in a conflict ("*You* have to undertake basic internal structural reform," "What about the mental illness rates in *your* country?"). This, however, puts no bar on self-criticism and criticism by others in an effort to improve the social order everywhere.

Then there is another, much more action-oriented approach. The basic formula that may transcend the present contradiction between the New International Economic Order and the Basic Needs approach is probably *self-reliance*. Self-reliance here is understood to mean a three-pronged approach: regional self-reliance, national self-reliance, *and* local self-reliance.[41] Self-reliance would mean raising the level of self-sufficiency and cooperation with others. Thus, regional self-reliance in the Third World, for example (the region being the Third World as a whole, the continental subdivisions, the subcontinental possibilities), would mean not only a much higher level of Third World production for its own consumption, but also a change in the pattern of exchange with the *developed* parts of the world towards more equity. The old pattern of exporting commodities in return for manufactured goods and services—even with the terms of trade not only stable but also improved—would gradually recede into the background in favor of trade of commodities against commodities, manufactures against manufactures, services against services (intrasector trade). In other words, regional self-reliance at this level would pick up the aspects of NIEO that are more oriented towards South-South trade and increased control by the South of economic structures in general, deemphasize the terms-of-trade approach in relation to the North, and go in for truly equitable North-South trade.

However, even with all this there would be no guarantee against the stronger countries in the South exploiting the weaker ones. Hence *national* self-reliance as a safeguard against such aggrandizement. The reasoning can be extended: national self-reliance provides no guarantee against national elites exploiting their own masses, hence local self-reliance as a similar protective shield. (This shield is admittedly less strong, since there is much less of institutional protection for local units than for national units. For one thing, they do not have secure and/or defendable borders. For another, they do not have armies—often not even distinct identities that would motivate any kind of defense.[42]) But the character of local self-reliance would be the same: increased local self-sufficiency, combined with horizontal exchange with other units at the same level (in a future world, not necessarily only other units in the same country).[43]

If the local unit is to carry the burden of self-reliance alone, it is doubtful whether it would be able to create a sustainable material base in most parts of the world. The national unit as an equalizer that could level out the sharp differences in economic geography in space and in the annual cycles (not only in agriculture, but also in the distribution of natural calamities) is crucial. But self-reliance at the national level alone, as experience has clearly shown, is not enough to achieve a more just, a more equitable international economic order as envisaged in the NIEO designs. Hence the need for self-reliance at the regional, national, and local levels at the same time, the rationale being that the regional level is best suited for the NIEO approach and the local level for the BN approach, on both material and non-material dimensions. The national level entity will have to be reorganized both upwards and downwards; it will have to integrate with other units at the same level for collective solidarity action and restructure itself so that local level units are given a chance to unfold themselves.[44]

Admittedly, this is an abstract formula, and this is not the place to develop all the details to give it flesh. But it should be made clear how apparent contradictions can be resolved. In the present world, short both on strong regional machineries (with the exception of the OPEC cartel action) and on structural transformations that would vest more autonomy at the local level, not only in political but also in economic and socio-cultural affairs, the NIEO and BN approaches may become more contradictory than they would be in a world differently organized. Hence, the task is to understand these relations better, not to feel that one must be against one or the other or both because of the very real issues involved and the equally real conflict polarizations.

For, regardless of the strong arguments that can be raised against these approaches seen in isolation and divorced from the broader political and historical context, there are extremely strong forces behind both. Seen in a UN perspective, it may be said that they both represent a third phase in United Nations development strategies. The first phase was *the import substitution phase* (developing countries have to produce themselves rather than import from developed countries), a phase motivated, among other things, by the perceived deteriorating terms of trade, with the United Nations Economic Commission for Latin America (CEPAL) providing the theoretical underpinnings. The second phase, partly growing out of frustration with the first one (manufactured goods produced in developing countries tended to become even more expensive) can be characterized as *the commodity export phase,* motivated by the "need" to earn foreign currency. This phase was, of course, more popular with the First World countries as it promoted their interest in exactly this type of trade. But there two basic problems: on the one hand, it became increasingly clear that somehow the developing countries were cheated in the bargain, that world resources were distributed highly asymmetrically in favor of the developed countries by this kind of arrangement (a polite way of saying that there was exploitation at work); and, on the other hand, it became equally clear that the masses in general were the losers. (For reasons mentioned in the introduction the internal gaps widened and misery increased.) The responses to these two problems, in a sense created by the same structure and the same process, were, in our view, the New International Economic Order and the Basic Needs approach. And this heralds the beginning of the third phase.[45]

The two approaches must be recognized for what they are: political movements, created and crystallized by particular historical situations. One can be against them or in favor of them, but one must recognize that they simply *are,* they *exist,* they *unfold* themselves like tidal waves. The political task is to help steer this tremendous political energy in directions that serve true human and social development, to deepen them and to find ways of resolving the contradictions between them.[46]

NOTES

1. In the joint UNITAR/CEESTEM (Centro de Estudios Economicos y sociates del tercer mundo, Mexico) Project 33, NIEO issue areas are divided into five categories: development financing, international trade, industrialization and technology, food and natural resources, institutional and organizational policies, and social issues.

   A content analysis of the original resolution of 1 May, 1974, of the UN General Assembly (Resolution 3201-S-VI at the Sixth Special Session), quoted by Roy Prieswerk in his 'Le novel ordre economique international, est-il nouveun?,' *Etudes Internationales,* Quebec, 1977, pp. 648–659, shows a predominance of associative relations and concepts relative to dissociative concepts. The former (such as cooperation, interdependence) occur 79 times, and the latter (such as sovereignty, self-determination) occur 19 times.

2. For further elaboration, see Johan Galtung, *Self-Reliance and Global Interdependence* (Ottawa: Canadian International Development Agency, 1978).

3. For one account of how petro-dollars are spent, see "Venezuela Begins to Question Spending," IHT, 5–6 August 1978, p. 5.

4. Quoted from Torkild Kirstensen, "Global Aspects of the Present Economic Crisis," SID North-South Roundtable.

5. *Business Week,* 24 July 1978, p. 70.

6. See Johan Galtung, "The Basic Needs Approaches," Paper for the GPID/IIUG Workshop on Needs, Berlin, May 1978.

7. "Unto this last" of the Bible, later used by John Ruskin as the title of his famous book which had a profound influence on Mohandas K. Gandhi.

8. The typical argument of Third World elites, heard in so many conferences, runs somewhat like this: The development agencies come and insist that funds, instead of being used for real development, should be spent on the uplift of the rural poor. But we have suffered for generations and can suffer for one or

two generations more if necessary. One answer to this is that he (it is rarely a she) who talks in this vein hardly suffers much; the suffering is left to countless small people planting rice with their feet in mud and water under a scorching sun and exposed to diseases—and producing a surplus.

9. For further elaborations, see Galtung (f.n. 2), ch. 2, "Poor Countries vs. Rich, Poor People vs. Rich: Whom Will NIEO Benefit?"

10. Frances Moore Lappe and Joseph Collins, *Food First* (New York, 1977) and *Diet for a Small Planet* (Ballantine Books, 1975), revised ed.

11. China has made use of this kind of emphasis for many years, exchanging these satisfiers between agricultural and industrial actors.

12. We are thinking of, for instance, trade surplus (knowing that this is "surplus" in another sense of the word) and the surplus generated by people high up in the tertiary sector in the form of patent fees, honoraria, bribes of some magnitude, etc.

13. The economic growth of a country as a whole, combined with an account of the disposal of surpluses, gives much information about the total situation. Thus, if economic growth is high, it *may* compensate for the divergence between elites and masses, giving a slight uplift to the poor. Conversely, if economic growth is very low, a convergence between the elite and masses may offer little comfort to the latter. Basic here, however, are less primitive conceptions of "economic growth" than those embedded in GNP-type concepts, more in the direction of basic needs satisfiers in physical terms.

14. *Business Week* (f.n. 5) talks in terms of "the intensifying competition for the lower-growing world trade pie [leading] to an alarming rise in protectionism that is slowing [down] world trade (p. 70)."

15. There is hardly any difference between petro-dollars and NIEO-dollars in general; the economics of recycling should be about the same, given stabilities in intra- and inter-national structures.

16. Samir Amin, "Self-Reliance and the New International Economic Order," *Monthly Review,* July-August 1977, pp. 1–21.

17. In the paper, "Basic Needs: the British Position," circulated at the SID North-South Roundtable in Rome, 18–20 May 1978, three of these arguments are summed up in a passage (brought to my notice after this article was written): "First, a number of them [developing countries] see the espousal of basic needs by the developed countries as a tactic designed to divert attention away from other North-South dialogue issues, such as commodity reform and debt, to which they attach great importance. Second, some developing countries object to the interference in sensitive domestic, political and economic issues which they believe the basic needs approach implies, and which conflicts with the demands in various North-South dialogue for an automatic transfer of aid without conditions. Third, some countries object to 'basic needs' as an anti-growth strategy." And the paper adds: "Our minister tends to share this view."

18. For one very tentative summary of some of these shortcomings, see Johan Galtung and Monica Wemegah, "Overdevelopment and Alternative Ways of Life in Rich Countries," a paper based on a workshop on this theme for the GPID Project of the UN University, and presented at the SID North-South Roundtable, Rome 18–20 May 1978.

19. The end of neo-colonialism means the end of the present form of economic penetration into the South by the North, based on transnational corporations. The accumulation through transfer of a sufficient amount of capital goods to

the South (which may be soon) will be followed by nationalization. Because of massive transfer of technology, however, the westernization of the South will continue unabated—may be even accelerated under local administration.

20. See Johan Galtung and Anders Wirak, "On the Relationship between Basic Needs and Basic Rights," UNESCO, 19–23 June 1978.

21. The poor may be well worth investing in, as can be seen by examining the products for sale in the poorest sections of the poor countries.

22. If the monetized approach implies a market under non-monopolistic conditions, then there will tend to be several brands of the same product, e.g., in medicine. For the sake of differentiation, trade marks then become essential. For one analysis of this process, see Peter O'Brien, "The International Trademark System and the Developing Countries," in IDEA, The Journal of Law and Technology, 1978, pp. 89–122.

23. The diversity in clothing among the lower 10% in capitalist countries, in contrast to such countries as the Soviet Union and China (and in these countries, not only the lower 10%), is a good example. For the top elites, there will always be a wide choice (that is the age-old prerogative of the elite!).

24. It can be predicted that the interest in population control will decline if Western economic penetration continues.

25. See Johan Galtung, *Development, Environment and Technology* (Geneva: UNCTAD, 1978), particularly the beginning of ch. 2.

26. With the change of leadership and the shift in policies, particularly the emphasis on more capital-intensive technology, one relatively safe prediction is that the people's communes will be abolished in favor of big state farms.

27. Norman Macrae et al., "Three People's China," *The Economist,* 31 December 1977.

28. See Johan Galtung, "Military Formations and Social Formations: A Structural Analysis," *Papers* (Chair in Conflict and Peace Research, University of Oslo), No. 60.

29. An understandable position, but it smacks of too much money in search of capital-intensive projects to fill the quota (particularly towards the end of the budget year), whether it helps people or not. It is sad to see a serious document referring to "developing countries" attaching priorities when, in fact, it is certain that it is special groups in these countries that set the priorities. It would be less misleading to say "delegates from developing countries."

30. The "barbarians" of the Greeks and the Romans. The image has a long history in western thinking. The "hordes" are usually yellow (not only of Attilla the Hun), the Turks, the communists, and now the Third World—all out to get "our" riches!

31. Historically, the rejection of Indira Gandhi in 1977 election in India may be seen as the first conscious rejection of this method of reducing the number of the poor.

32. See Johan Galtung, "A Structural Theory of Revolutions," in *Essays in Peace Research,* Vol. III (Copenhagen: Ejlers, 1978), pp. 268–314.

33. This constitutes the basis for a red-black alliance in the North between those highly critical of many "developmentalist regimes" in the South (because of the sharpness of class contradictions) and those who want the continuation of the *status quo* in both intra- and inter-national structures.

34. In the paper cited in f.n. 17, it is stated that "The ILO is the multilateral agency which has been most heavily engaged on basic needs since drawing up the

Declaration of Principles and Programme of Action for the World Employment Conference. The Phrase 'basic needs' was largely its invention." The last
statement is incorrect. The ILO Conference was held in 1976, whereas Mac-
Namara's speech in which this phrase occurs had been made in 1972.

35. The *welfare state* in the rich countries shows that basic material needs can be
satisfied within the framework of a top-heavy society, while needs for identity
and freedom in a broad sense cannot. Hence the great paradox: as somatic
health improves (judging by the indicator of longevity), mental health seems
to deteriorate.

36. As an intergovernmental machinery, the UN is capable of articulating issues
between governments, but it is very poor at articulating intra-national issues—
the latter are overshadowed, and even mystified, by the former. In consequence, it will tend to focus on the shallow interpretations of both NIEO and
BN.

37. A major transformation, too, considering that it is connected with regulating
the whole flow of surplus inside societies.

38. The location of these in Geneva would facilitate this. The WHO could also be
brought into the picture, particularly its Office of Mental Health.

39. See Johan Galtung and Anders Wirak, *Human Needs, Human Rights and the
Theory of Development* (UNESCO, Division of Social Sciences, 1977).

40. For a tentative definition of these four need-areas, see Johan Galtung, "The
Basic Needs Approach," prepared for the GPID-IIUG Workshop on Needs,
Berlin West, May 1978.

41. See Johan Galtung, Roy Preiswerk, Peter O'Brien (eds.), *Self-Reliance* (St.
Saphorin: Georgy, 1978).

42. This may be the reason why the most promising of these entities have an
ethnic identity. In the case of a multinational state the liberation struggle
becomes a struggle for national as well as local self-reliance.

43. The *Sarvodaya* movement in Sri Lanka has contacts with villages in 16 countries of the world.

44. At this point some new formulas, building on the old concepts of federalist
thought, will have to be found.

45. Andre Gunder Frank, in an interview to *Dritter Welt*, November 1976, suggests that we are now in the exports substitution phase, meaning by this that
some Third World countries produce for the world market cheap consumer
goods—cheap because of the combination of cheap labor with high labor-
productivity. This corresponds well with Dale Jorgenson's thesis that since
1973 the productivity of capital has been reduced relative to labor, benefiting
countries with cheap but well-trained labor (but not necessarily benefiting
those workers, which U.S. economists tend to forget). But this hardly reflects
the UN policy.

46. For some suggestions, see P. Streeten, "Basic Needs and the NIEO: Must there
be a conflict?", Report World Bank, March–April 1978, p. 3.

U.S. Foreign Aid in the 1980s: Reordering Priorities

John W. Sewell
Christine E. Contee

The last four years have been a time of considerable ferment in the U.S. aid program. Four major Executive Branch commissions have been appointed to examine various aspects of U.S. aid. Three major regional initiatives have been proposed. U.S. contributions to multilateral institutions have been a topic of considerable debate. And a new set of policy guidelines for U.S. development assistance has been superimposed over the existing aid legislation. Yet none of the recent initiatives or discussions has succeeded in creating a coherent set of foreign aid objectives capable of generating legislative and public support.

U.S. foreign aid[1] has always been used to achieve a broad range of often conflicting goals: meeting the emergency needs of the world's poorest people, satisfying U.S. strategic and political interests, fostering long-term development in the Third World, and expanding U.S. commerce. The multiplicity of goals has been the price paid for political support of the total aid program. There is no agreement between Congress and the Executive Branch—and certainly not a broad public consensus—on the overall purpose of the program, or even on the preferred pattern of development that the United States should support. In recent years, contradictory pulls on the U.S. aid program have led to frequent political stalemate, with the repeated failure of Congress and the Administration to agree on programs and with *ad hoc* funding of aid through the use of continuing resolutions instead of new legislation.

Current trends in the U.S. aid program raise serious questions about the continued feasibility of addressing such a wide range of divergent

John Sewell and Christine Contee, "U.S. Foreign Aid in the 1980s: Reordering Priorities," in Sewell et al., eds., *U.S. Foreign Policy and the Third World: Agenda 1985.*

interests in one program. The primary goal of U.S. development assistance has been defined by Congress as the alleviation of the worst aspects of poverty affecting the world's poor majority. The Reagan Administration's policies have generally downplayed this objective. A strong security thrust now characterizes the aid program, and there have been significant shifts in both program philosophy and implementation. Bilateral economic aid has become increasingly oriented toward short-term security and political interests while both poverty alleviation and longer-run political or economic interests receive greatly reduced priority.[2] Although these changes have, in effect, contributed some measure of coherence to the program, inasmuch as they all point to a greater effort to achieve perceived U.S. strategic and political aims in the developing countries, they are detrimental to other objectives of the program, and they have generated considerable controversy among the traditional aid constituencies.

The enormous increase in security aid designed to meet U.S. short-term strategic and political concerns is making it increasingly difficult to combine these programs in the same legislation with programs designed to improve human well-being and to further U.S. commercial interests; different countries demand priority for one or the other of these objectives, and budgetary stringency forces competition for resources between them.

The premise of this chapter is that it is nevertheless possible to reconcile these objectives and the tools to achieve them provided that debate on current and future aid policies takes into account the changes that have taken place in U.S.-Third World relations. First, in the last three decades, developing countries have emerged as important participants in the international economy, particularly in terms of trade and finance. Today these countries are major markets for U.S. exports, important suppliers of an increasingly sophisticated range of relatively low-cost goods, major customers (and profit centers) for U.S. banks, and the locus of a considerable amount of American private investment. Renewed growth in the developing countries is, moreover, one requirement for a full, sustained U.S. recovery.[3] Second, perceptions of a "Soviet threat" to the United States tend to be exaggerated in many areas of the developing world. Although instability and civil strife in the Third World sometimes offer the Soviet Union the opportunity to increase its influence, they are frequently due to indigenous causes and may be an inevitable part of the development process. This is particularly true given the current economic recession in the Third World, which makes it increasingly difficult for leaders to meet the needs and demands of their people. Finally, where the threat is real, U.S. military programs often are only one possible policy response among many. In contrast to the Soviet Union, which concentrates its assistance programs on military aid, the United States, like other industrialized countries, offers the Third World a great deal in trade and investment as well as development assistance. The real strengths of the United States lie in its economic power, in the desire of developing countries to attract American investment, finance, and technology; and in its democratic traditions.

This chapter analyzes U.S. aid policies over the last four years and makes some recommendations for policy change. The discussion focuses on bilateral development assistance, the Economic Support Fund (ESF), and U.S. support of the multilateral development banks.[4] Military assistance is here of concern only to the extent that it forces budgetary trade-offs within the total aid program.

THE CURRENT PROGRAM

The Reagan Administration entered office in 1981 with strong views both on the changes needed in American foreign policy to restore U.S. primacy and ensure American security and on the set of economic policies needed to lower inflation and restore economic growth. As reflected in the Administration's prescriptions for development cooperation with the Third World, these views have resulted in policies that represent a marked shift from U.S. aid programs developed over the last decade under both Democratic and Republican leadership.

Security Assistance

The centerpiece of the Reagan Administration's foreign policy is the restoration of U.S. global power vis-à-vis the Soviet Union. This emphasis on a single, over-arching theme has had a detrimental effect on U.S. development cooperation,[5] overshadowing the country's interest in fostering equitable economic and social development. In the 1970s, it was widely believed that equitable development was in the long-term U.S. interest, not only on humanitarian or commercial grounds, but because inequity and poverty contributed to political instability and regional tensions. Now the overriding concern is Soviet intervention or influence, which is perceived to be the major cause of Third World unrest. The East-West emphasis of U.S. foreign policy has also relegated other American interests in Third World development—such as trade and financial linkages—to a distant second place.

The priority accorded to security is apparent in the emphasis given to particular programs, regions, and countries. Military aid is favored over economic aid. Within the bilateral program, security-oriented economic aid is preferred over development assistance. And bilateral programs are considered more useful than multilateral contributions. Assistance is also heavily concentrated in countries where U.S. political and strategic interests are perceived to be threatened by the Soviet Union or its proxies (Table 1).

Total U.S. foreign aid grew from $10,600 million to $19,200 million between 1981 and 1985 (Table 2). But this increase was not evenly shared among programs. Assistance related to security concerns grew from 55

Table 1   CHANGES IN THE REGIONAL EMPHASIS OF U.S. BILATERAL AID
(\$ Millions Current)

Region	Development assistance[a]			Security assistance[b]		
	1977–1980 average	1983	Percentage change	1977–1980 average	1983	Percentage change
Sub-Saharan Africa	397.0	518.4	+31%	137.8	402.9	+ 192%
Middle East and N. Africa[c]	117.3	141.5	+21	602.9	1,147.1	+ 90
Israel and Egypt	193.0	255.1	+32	3685.4	4,561.9	+ 2.4
East Asia	395.2	237.3	−40	364.1	422.5	+ 16
South Asia	527.5	559.4	+ 6	1.0	461.3	+4,603
South America	151.0	194.7	+29	34.5	10.2	− 70
Central America[d]	232.5	417.8	+80	21.7	639.1	+2,845
Other	56.8	38.0	−33	450.5	827.1	+ 84

[a]Development assistance includes bilateral development assistance, P.L. 480, and other bilateral development programs.

[b]Security assistance includes all military assistance programs and the Economic Support Fund. Inter-regional programs are excluded.

[c]Excludes Israel and Egypt.

[d]Includes Central America, the Caribbean, and Mexico.

Source: Agency for International Development, U.S. Overseas Loans and Grants, various issues.

Table 2   THE FOREIGN AID BALANCE,[a] 1981–85
           ($ Millions Current and Percentages)

Account	FY1981	FY1982	FY1983	FY1984	FY1985
		($ millions and percentages)			
Security assistance					
Amount	5,800	7,200	8,500	9,000	12,900
Percentage of total assistance	54.7%	58.5%	62.0%	61.6%	67.2%
Military[b]	3,700	4,300	5,500	5,600	9,100
Economic Support Fund	2,100	2,900	3,000	3,400	3,800
Development assistance					
Amount	4,800	5,100	5,200	5,600	6,300
Percentage of total assistance	45.3%	41.5%	38.0%	38.4%	32.8%
Multilateral	1,300	1,500	1,800	1,600	1,900
Bilateral	2,300	2,600	2,400	2,500	2,900
P.L. 480 (Food for Peace)	1,200	1,000	1,000	1,400	1,500
Total foreign aid					
	10,600	12,300	13,700	14,600	19,200

[a]Budget authority. Figures for FY1981–FY1984 are actual; figures for FY1985 are estimates.

[b]Includes MAP, PKO, IMET, anti-terrorism assistance, and on- and off-budget FMS.

Sources: Agency for International Development, "Summary Tables: FY1985" (Washington, D.C.: A.I.D., 1984; Executive Office of the President, Budget of the United States Government (Washington, D.C.: Office of Management and Budget, various issues).

percent of total aid in FY1981 to 67 percent in FY1985, while the share of development assistance in total aid dropped from 45 percent to 33 percent. As reflected in the budget submitted to Congress in February 1985, the Administration apparently plans to continue this security-oriented trend.[6] If this budget is approved, security assistance will comprise 72 percent of total U.S. aid by FY1988.

From FY1981 to FY1985, the Economic Support Fund alone grew by $1,700 million. Although the Foreign Assistance Act requires that the ESF be used in a manner that is consistent with development "to the maximum extent feasible," it is first and foremost a tool to address U.S. strategic and political objectives.

The rapid growth in ESF levels is due largely to the increased emphasis on security and political issues. This trend began with the Camp David accords and was spurred by the Soviet invasion of Afghanistan and by the Iranian revolution. Most recently, ESF has been used in attempts to bolster stability in Central America, the Caribbean, and Southern Africa, and to ensure access to the Indian Ocean and the Persian Gulf region.

Beyond the ideological bent of U.S. policy makers, the growth in ESF also is a result of the harsh international economic environment of the late 1970s and the 1980s. The ESF program provides both direct cash transfers to developing-country agencies and financing of U.S. exports to developing countries through the Commodity Import Program. Thus ESF is one of the two major bilateral aid tools (Food for Peace, or P.L. 480, is the other) through which the United States provides balance-of-payments support to developing countries.

The resurgence of perceived security interests in the Third World, coupled with the balance-of-payments problems of developing countries, has also led to an increase in the number of countries receiving ESF. In FY1981, twenty-one countries received ESF funds; by FY1985, thirty-nine states will participate in the program.[7]

What does this growth in ESF mean for the aid program? Some effects of the expansion seem positive. First, while most ESF is allocated to the more advanced developing countries, the expansion of the total aid *pie* is incrementally advantageous to some of the poorer countries. In FY1985, some $259 million in ESF was allocated to countries with per capita incomes below $419.[8] And about 40 percent of ESF (25 per cent if funds earmarked for Israel are included)[9] is used to finance projects, some of which are largely indistinguishable from development assistance projects in design and implementation. Thus the growth in ESF has expanded the resources available for development-oriented projects (although it is important to note that development assistance itself has actually declined slightly in real terms since 1981).

Some A.I.D. missions actually prefer working with ESF because it is easier to use than development assistance. Over the years, a variety of implementation regulations have been applied to development assistance; ESF, in contrast, is relatively free of such restrictions. Finally, some observers claim that ESF "protects" development assistance. Without a separate fund for politically oriented aid, it is argued, support for high aid levels would not be forthcoming and scarce development assistance would be further diverted from long-term development projects to meet short-term U.S. political objectives.

Despite these possibly positive aspects, using ESF in lieu of development assistance presents some serious problems. The first of these is country allocation of the funds. The $259 million allocated to low-income countries in FY1985 represents only 7 percent of ESF. In contrast, five middle-income countries are slated to receive 59 percent of that year's ESF: Oman (per capita GNP, $6,090), Spain (per capita GNP, $5,430), Israel (per capita GNP, $5,090), Turkey (per capita GNP, $1,370), and Egypt (per capita GNP, $690).[10] Since all these countries are of strategic interest to the United States, it is perhaps understandable that they receive the bulk of economic security aid; yet since ESF now accounts for 45 percent of total bilateral economic assistance—which comprises ESF, development assistance, and Food for Peace—the result is to shift the whole program away from the poorer countries and toward the more advanced nations of the Third World (Table 3). This concentration of aid is not a new development. But it remains an issue of concern to those who, in keeping with the Foreign Assistance Act, view the improvement of the well-being of the majority in the poorest countries as the major objective of both development and the aid program.

The second problem posed by emphasizing ESF relates to how monies are spent. In many cases, the level of annual funding is determined at the political level, and the recipient country may come to expect a certain level of funding each year. There are no criteria for phasing out ESF recipients. And because ESF is generally offered in return for the political *quid pro quo,* projects using these funds are often designed to be immediately visible and quickly disbursable. In Egypt, many problems have arisen as A.I.D. has tried to spend enormous sums of money each year in project form. In the Philippines, almost 65 percent of ESF allotted under the base-rights agreement is spent around the bases, often on projects that can be completed rapidly and that are easily identifiable as U.S. supported.[11] Omani officials chose to have their ESF funds expended on projects because they wanted to provide tangible evidence of the U.S.-Omani relationship.[12] These types of projects are not necessarily designed or implemented in any relation to the needs of the poor.[13]

Approximately 60 percent of ESF (75 percent if Israel is included) is delivered through cash transfers or the Commodity Import Program.[14] This kind of assistance also does not necessarily benefit the poor. While ESF cannot be used for military purposes, it does free up domestic resources, possibly for military use. Cash transfers and CIP may also be used to import goods—whether luxury items or industrial equipment—that do not directly or even indirectly benefit the poor.

In addition, most of this type of ESF funding is, at least in theory, meant to foster a policy dialogue between the United States and the recipient country and to support policy reforms. As will be discussed below, A.I.D. has neither the scale of financial resources nor the number of appropriately trained personnel necessary to carry out policy dialogues, and these problems are exacerbated when ESF funding is the available tool. First, the political objectives of ESF funding prevent A.I.D. from pressing too hard for development objectives for fear that this might cause political friction. (For example, a General Accounting Office study of the aid program in Jamaica concluded that the United States had not pressed for policy reforms in some instances "because Jamaican resistance was strong and for political reasons the State Department did not want to require the reforms even though they would enhance development."[15] This problem also appears to have arisen in Egypt, where the attempt to

Table 3   U.S. BILATERAL AID, BY INCOME GROUP AND REGION,[a] FY1983

	Countries in category	Countries receiving aid[b]	Total aid ($ millions)	Aid per capita[c] ($)
Low-Income Countries	40	36	1,171.6	.50
Africa	27	27	344.2	1.55
Asia	12	8	781.2	.37
Latin America	1	1	46.2	7.35
Lower-Middle-Income Countries	40	24	2,182.7	4.05
Africa[d]	16	14	1,494.2	6.50
Asia	7	4	272.2	1.00
Latin America	11	4	414.7	13.94
Oceania	5	2	1.6	.28
Europe	1	0	0	0
Upper-Middle-Income Countries	39	24	982.5	1.61
Africa	7	4	28.1	.45
Asia	10	3	73.1	.55
Latin America	18	15	575.3	1.72
Oceania	1	0	0	0
Europe	3	2	306.0	3.81
High-Income Countries	23	5	816.7	11.65
Africa	3	1	1.5	.29
Asia[e]	9	2	800.1	34.36
Latin America	6	1	.1	.01
Oceania	2	0	0	0
Europe	3	1	15.0	.63
Total	142	89	5,153.5	1.45

[a]Developing countries, regions, and income group as defined by ODC plus Israel (see Statistical Annexes, Table E-1).

[b]Aid includes bilateral development assistance, P.L.-480, and the Economic Support Fund. Regional bilateral programs are not included.

[c]Indicates U.S. aid per capita for all countries in column 1.

[d]If Egypt is excluded, lower middle-income Africa receives $2.65 aid per capita

[e]Includes Israel.

Source: Agency for International Development, *U.S. Overseas Loans & Grants,* July 1, 1945–September 30, 1983 (Washington, D.C.: 1984).

shoehorn large amounts of money each year into development projects has led to growing U.S.-Egyptian political friction.) Moreover, because country allocations are made on political grounds, funds cannot be switched by A.I.D. from one country to another where policy change may be more promising—although occasionally A.I.D. can hold back funds to encourage policy change (as was done with programs in Kenya and Zaire). Paradoxically, it is precisely in those countries where U.S. aid looms large that the ability to promote policy change is limited simply because the overriding goal is political or strategic rather than economic.

Unfortunately there have been few solid assessments of whether these programs even meet their purported strategic and political goals.[16] (This contrasts sharply with development aid programs, which have been exhaustively evaluated by A.I.D., by Congress, and by outside specialists.) Judgments of results are relatively clear where security aid is direct compensation for base rights or some other facility (although observers question, for example, whether the price paid for base rights in the Philippines is not inflated); they are far less clear when the desired policy outcome is less concrete.

The United States will continue to have a range of foreign policy interests in the developing world, including security interests, that require financial support of particular countries and regimes. That being said, however, the current foreign aid program's emphasis on security and short-term political purposes at the expense of longer-term economic and development purposes raises serious questions about the balance of objectives.

The United States should be far more selective in providing financial support for particular regimes on political grounds. Even where such support is essential, it should not be considered a substitute for financing longer-term economic and development efforts. And in all cases, the political goals must be more clearly defined. Where ESF is used to compensate for U.S. military facilities, for example, it would be better to transfer these programs to the defense budget, where priorities among programs can be decided on the basis of their contribution to national security.

Setting aside security-related funds for a limited number of clearly justified country programs might also remove some of the ambiguities in the current program that serve to undercut the expected political and development returns. As already noted, the attempt to impose development performance criteria on funds allocated for political ends can make the political relationship more difficult. Conversely, the existence of American political goals often makes economic and development aims a secondary priority for the United States in some countries. It is probably wiser to establish a political aid program limited to a few carefully selected countries. Some aid observers may be disturbed by the idea of losing whatever development benefits security assistance does provide; however, the trade-off between political and developmental impact is not an issue that can be avoided.

Using political aid more selectively might also make funds available for non-project development assistance. Currently most development assistance is provided in the form of projects. Yet both project and non-project lending is needed, depending on particular country circumstances. Moreover, the need for non-project assistance will grow as developing countries work their way out of the current debt crisis. Especially in smaller countries, even small amounts of balance-of-payments support can be very beneficial. A development program that has the authority to provide both project and non-project funds to countries on the basis of their particular development situation would be far preferable to one that continues to rely heavily on a tool that is allocated largely on the basis of political aims.

BILATERAL DEVELOPMENT ASSISTANCE AND THE "FOUR PILLARS"

While the overall security orientation of the program is largely a result of the Administration's ideological proclivities, the currently preferred strategy for approaching economic development is in part a reaction to perceived shortcomings of development assistance in the 1970s. In the late 1960s and early 1970s, U.S. foreign aid was the target of heavy criticism by both the public and policy makers. The program was closely associated with U.S. involvement in the Vietnam war and thus became equated with American military intervention in the Third World. At the same time, those concerned about the impact of U.S. aid on human well-being in developing countries began to attack the program as ineffective. In the 1950s and 1960s, it was widely believed that the benefits of economic growth would automatically, if gradually, flow to the majority of the people, and development efforts therefore focused on stimulating growth. With a few exceptions, however, this theory, later labeled *trickle-down,* proved to be wrong—at least within any politically relevant timeframe; growth in many countries was impressive, but its impact on the poor majority was often marginal.

Faced with growing opposition to the foreign aid program, Congress rewrote the U.S. aid legislation. The Foreign Assistance Act of 1973 established the current goals for U.S. bilateral development assistance: a) alleviation of the worst physical manifestations of poverty among the world's poor majority; b) promotion of conditions enabling developing countries to achieve self-sustaining economic growth with an equitable distribution of benefits; c) encouragement of development processes in which individual civil and economic rights are respected and enhanced; and d) integration of the developing countries into an open and equitable international system. This "New Directions" focus called for targeted, long-term development assistance, primarily through projects carried out at the local level, to improve the lot of the poor majority.

The emphasis on poverty-oriented development resulted in a host of important changes aimed at enabling poor people within developing countries to meet at least the basic requirements for human life and dignity through a combination of economic growth and programs designed to deliver social services by direct means. More effort was directed toward the agricultural sector, the linchpin of most developing economies as well as the sector in which the poor are concentrated. In many countries, programs in health and education produced dramatic results. In the course of the 1970s, however, the international donor community came to realize that—just as economic growth alone would not alleviate poverty in many instances—local-level projects could not be self-sustaining in the midst of economic recession and in the absence of strong indigenous institutions and recipient-country economic policies conducive to growth and efficiency.

The Reagan Administration did not seek to change the basic legislation governing U.S. bilateral aid programs. Instead, it added an overlay to the existing programs in an effort to correct perceived problems. Described by A.I.D. Administrator M. Peter McPherson as program instruments, the new *four pillars* include (1) policy dialogue, (2) private sector initiatives, (3) technology transfer, and (4) institution-building. Unfortunately, it is difficult to analyze the full budgetary impact of these four instruments on A.I.D.'s activities, since the agency does not keep track of projects or expenditures by these categories.

Two of the policy instruments—institution-building and technology transfer—are relatively non-controversial programs that usefully reemphasize A.I.D. activities of the 1960s. A.I.D.'s institution-building focus responds to the need for strong, efficient, indigenous institutions and managers to plan and implement self-sustaining development programs. A.I.D. policy has stressed the need to upgrade a variety of local institutions, such as schools, voluntary organizations, agricultural extension services, cooperatives, agricultural research centers, training institutes, and health care delivery systems. The emphasis on technology transfer strives to foster "an indigenous capacity to adapt, create, and apply a continuing stream of usable technologies."[17] A.I.D. currently spends approximately $250 million a year on research activities. Agricultural research is heavily concentrated on pest and disease control, techniques of cultivation, and the development of hybrid crop varieties; in the health field, A.I.D. is currently placing a great deal of emphasis on developing a malaria vaccine and on expanding the use of oral rehydration therapy—a simple and inexpensive technology that could dramatically reduce infant mortality in the developing world. The United States has a long-standing comparative advantage in research and technology, and several of A.I.D.'s activities show promise of having a major impact on the world's poorest people.

The other two instruments are more controversial and warrant closer examination. The emphasis on *policy dialogue* is based on the generally accepted view that the domestic economic policies of developing countries are the prime determinant of development progress; in the absence of good policies, economic growth and efforts to improve human well-being cannot be fostered efficiently. In the words of A.I.D.'s FY1985 presentation to Congress, "policy dialogue with recipient governments can initiate needed reforms, and our assistance can smooth the path of such reforms in some countries."[18] Emphasis on policy dialogue is not new to A.I.D.; prior to the New Directions legislation, the agency was involved in program lending for *sectoral* policy reforms. Neither is the current emphasis on policy dialogue unique to the U.S. aid program. Most major bilateral and multilateral donors are urging similar changes in response to the lessons of the 1970s.

It is far from clear, however, that A.I.D. can play a useful role in *macro-economic* policy reform. The amount of U.S. aid to most countries is no longer significant enough to make recipient governments change established macro-economic policies, particularly if such changes involve significant economic or political costs. For example, in 1970 the United States provided approximately 54 percent of India's total official development assistance; in 1980, only 11 percent of India's aid came from the United States. Aid that carries with it conditions considered too onerous can be rejected without too high a cost.

It is almost impossible to separate the instruments of ESF funding and macro-economic policy dialogue, since ESF is one of A.I.D.'s key tools for attempting to facilitate and encourage policy change. Yet, as indicated earlier, it is difficult if not impossible for A.I.D. to press hard for reforms when a recipient country knows that, for political reasons, the United States is highly unlikely to exercise the ultimate condition of assistance withdrawal. In addition, aid funds that are not obligated in the year they are appropriated must be returned to the U.S. Treasury. The fact that recipient countries are well aware of this need to commit funds further weakens A.I.D.'s leverage.

Nor is A.I.D. well equipped to participate in discussions of macro-economic reforms—either in Washington or in its field missions. Although its large and experienced field organization does provide an opportunity rare among bilateral donors for closer dialogue on program and sectoral policy matters with the developing countries (having focused during the 1970s on project and key sectoral aid), the agency is insufficiently staffed with economists to provide the data and analyses for sophisticated macro-economic policy discussions. More economists are being recruited by A.I.D., but such staffing changes take time.

This is not to argue that A.I.D. has no role to play in urging policy reform. First, policy dialogue has had some useful effects with respect to micro-economic or sectoral policy reforms. For example, A.I.D. has successfully worked in Senegal to change policies toward user fees in health-care projects, lowering the recurrent costs of primary health care. In Bangladesh, the agency played a significant role in the phased elimination of fertilizer subsidies and the privatization of the marketing system—reforms that have resulted in record fertilizer distribution. Such reforms are also important building blocks in the direction of encouraging broader, macro-economic changes. Second, A.I.D.'s policy dialogue efforts have had an influence on the general discussion of development strategies and have therefore reinforced the messages being conveyed by the World Bank and the International Monetary Fund.[19] Coordination by the United States, the world's single largest bilateral donor, with multilateral organizations and other donors on the policy matters of specific countries is crucial. However, the multilateral agencies are better suited than A.I.D. to take the lead in macro-economic dialogue, and A.I.D. would do better to work where possible on micro-economic or sectoral reforms.

The emphasis on private-sector initiatives, like that on policy dialogue, is not a new element in U.S. aid programs; all legislation since the program's inception has sought to involve the private sector. While A.I.D.'s private-sector efforts diminished during the 1970s, due to the emphasis on projects targeted directly at the poor, the agency's focus on small farmers remained a constant theme throughout the 1970s.

The philosophy behind the re-emergence of interest in the private sector was perhaps best expressed by President Reagan himself when he stated, in an October 1981 speech in Philadelphia, that "free people build free markets that ignite dynamic development for everyone." The President's faith in the "magic of the marketplace" gave rise to great concern about two issues: Is the emphasis on growth through the private sector a return to the *trickle down* theory of the 1950s and 1960s? And to what extent is A.I.D.'s program to be devoted to promoting American commercial interests?

The emphasis on economic growth was—and, given recent global economic conditions continues to be—necessary. In the aftermath of the oil price increase of 1979, growth dropped precipitously in almost all developing countries. Adverse economic conditions presented major problems to donor and recipient countries attempting to implement poverty-oriented projects in the late 1970s and early 1980s. Developing countries were unable to maintain completed projects (such as roads or water and sewage systems), to meet recurrent costs in schools and health care, or to provide counterpart funding requirements for new projects. As a result, many donors, national and international, have begun to focus on projects that generate both local and foreign currency quickly. However, the experience of the 1960s demonstrated that economic growth does not necessarily assure, as the President has said, "development for everyone." Nor is it entirely clear that the private sector in developing countries can single-handedly generate equitable growth. Shortages of capital and human resources, as well as market imperfections, often require the public sector to play a more active role.[20] The key issue is the proper mix of the two.

Still, there is not necessarily a conflict between poverty-oriented development and projects focusing on the indigenous private sector. Private enterprises often can help meet basic needs in ways that overextended public sectors cannot. For example, much of the private sector in developing countries consists of small-scale farmers or entrepreneurs who are themselves part of the poor majority. One area in which A.I.D. has appar-

ently experienced considerable success is in creating or expanding intermediate financial institutions; the programs that make credit available to
previously excluded groups can inject much-needed capital into small-
scale farms and private enterprises. In the family planning field, to cite
another type of example, A.I.D. efforts to foster private marketing of
contraceptives in Bangladesh have widened their distribution and stabilized their prices.

To direct and focus the private-sector initiative, A.I.D. created the
Bureau for Private Enterprise (PRE). While the PRE budget has grown
from $7.5 million to $30.0 million in the last four years, it still receives only
about 1 percent of A.I.D.'s budget. The impact of the initiative extends
beyond the PRE, however. In addition, A.I.D.'s regional bureaus pro-
grammed $200 million in 1984 for private-sector projects.

One aspect of the private-sector initiative that differs from past A.I.D.
experiences is the current attempt to evaluate ways in which private
sector involvement can be useful in all kinds of development projects. An
A.I.D. policy paper on health assistance[21] illustrates how emphasis on the
private sector can be integrated into the functional accounts: Health care
practitioners, such as midwives and pharmacists, can be supported by
fostering private distribution channels for drugs and medicines, by encouraging local drug manufacturers to produce generic drugs (which cost
less than imported ones), and by instituting private contributions and user
fees for health services.

It is not yet possible to determine who the ultimate beneficiaries of the
private-sector projects will be. The projects are limited in number and are
only in the early stages of implementation. It is important to recognize,
however, that this approach carries with it the danger that project beneficiaries may turn out to be largely the better-off segments of populations
in developing countries. This could happen if private-sector targeting
were to divert resources away from necessary public-sector projects such
as health care, rural roads, or primary schools. Similarly, the desire to focus
on the commercial private sector—to stimulate jobs and exports—may
result in a neglect of the non-commercial private sector. As described by
A.I.D., the private sector initiative does not seem to run counter to the
main purposes of the U.S. bilateral assistance program's mandate. But
those concerned with ensuring the use of U.S. aid for fulfilling the legislative mandate need to monitor trends within the program.

It should also be noted that the private-sector initiative and the emphasis on policy dialogue are integrally related. The agency's policy paper
on private enterprise development states that "the primary emphasis of
A.I.D.'s efforts to promote private enterprise development will be to encourage policy reform and to improve the ways markets function."[22] A
good deal of effort has been focused on the importance of agricultural
pricing, the devaluation of foreign exchange, the creation of credit institutions, the removal of food subsidies, and a reevaluation of private investment regulations. Although much of this emphasis on greater reliance on

market forces is useful, it raises once again the issue of A.I.D.'s role in macro-economic policy reform.

A second major concern about the renewed stress on private-sector initiatives is that it may focus on the promotion of U.S. commercial interests in the Third World rather than on development needs. Perhaps the most disturbing development in this area is the recent appearance in the U.S. aid program of mixed credits—so called because concessional assistance is mixed with commercial financing to lower the overall interest rate for U.S. exports. The increased use of such mixed credits by European and Japanese competitors in recent years has spurred American business to pressure the U.S. government to follow suit. In 1983, Congress passed the Trade and Development Enhancement Act, which requires A.I.D. to draw on funds allocated for the Commodity Import Program to finance mixed credits under certain conditions and in cooperation with the Export-Import Bank. The first U.S. mixed credit—beyond an experimental program in Egypt—was recently approved.[23]

The United States has traditionally opposed mixed credits because they distort trade by encouraging countries to purchase goods they would not choose without the concessional element. A.I.D. Administrator McPherson has fought hard against mixed credits on the grounds that they divert scarce development aid and use it for the commercial purpose of stimulating exports. The introduction of mixed credits into the program could also have a negative effect on the ability of A.I.D. to undertake its stated aim of policy dialogue. Like economic support (ESF) funds, mixed credits obfuscate the objectives of aid; in this case, the purchase of American goods becomes the requirement for receiving assistance. The Administration maintains that the use of mixed credits is a defensive measure and that the United States will resort to them no longer than other industrial-country governments. But even a defensive program will require a considerable amount of money. The United Kingdom, for example, has estimated that, over the next two to three years, its mixed credits program could cost $1 billion.[24] From what sources can such amounts be drawn in the United States? Although there is considerable support within the business community and in Congress to place the administration of mixed credits (should their volume increase further) under the jurisdiction of the Export-Import Bank, the 1983 Act clearly expresses a willingness to use aid for commercial purposes.

U.S. Multilateral Assistance

The Reagan Administration entered office suspicious of multilateral institutions. Many political appointees, particularly in the Department of the Treasury, believed that the multilateral development banks tend to favor government solutions to development problems over reliance on market forces or the private sector. This belief persists, despite the findings of a 1981 Treasury Department study that few projects undertaken by multilateral institutions could be seen as displacing the private sector and that, in most instances, the multilaterals have been strong proponents of market-oriented development.[25]

The Administration's emphasis on security also caused it to cast a baleful eye on multilateral organizations. Conservatives, arguing that the World Bank has grown too powerful and does not sufficiently promote U.S. political interests, point to the number of times that U.S. votes against proposed World Bank projects have been overridden in recent years.[26] This type of criticism entirely overlooks the fact that the de-politicization of aid is one of the strongpoints of institutions like the World Bank. As the above-mentioned 1981 Treasury Department study concluded, "U.S. bilateral and multilateral aid have different comparative advantages. . . . multilateral assistance primarily serves long-term U.S. interests, can be very cost-effective, and promotes a stable international economic environment through the encouragement of market-oriented policies."[27]

The Reagan Administration's stance has softened toward some of these institutions. The importance of the International Monetary Fund to global financial stability became apparent to the Administration with the onset of the debt crisis in 1982, and it subsequently pressed for an increase in the IMF's resources (although the funds were approved in Congress only with considerable difficulty). The Administration has also favored general capital increases for some of the smaller multilateral institutions, such as the Inter-American Development Bank. It has, however, continued to oppose proposals for greater expansion of the World Bank's lending capacity.

The effects of the Administration's attitude have been most marked in the case of the World Bank's International Development Association (IDA), which provides long-term concessional loans to the poorest countries. The sixth *replenishment* (the three-year pledge of funds from Bank member governments) totaled $12 billion. Most major donor countries agreed that the seventh replenishment of IDA should provide resources at a level at least equal in real terms—and preferably somewhat higher—than that of the last replenishment. In a decision reportedly made by the President himself, however, the Administration agreed upon an annual U.S. contribution of $750 million a year, or $2.25 billion over three years. Under the complex formula governing contributions, this effectively held the total capitalization of IDA-VII at $9 billion, representing a 40 percent cut in real terms, since other industrial-country donors were unwilling to raise their contributions without a corresponding U.S. increase.

The Administration's opposition to increased resources for IDA-VII certainly is not in keeping with its expressed objective of assisting the poorer countries. A lower level for IDA effectively means a loss of some $3 billion in development resources for the world's low-income countries. Diminished support for IDA, and for the multilateral development institutions in general, is also inconsistent with the Administration's current concern with policy change and increasing the role of the private sector.

The multilateral institutions, particularly the World Bank, have played a central role in advising and assisting developing-country governments through the process of changing policies to give greater emphasis to efficiency and growth. Over the last two decades, these institutions have emerged as the preeminent development institutions, outweighing individual bilateral programs in terms of resources and influence on developing-country policies. Their "clout" stems not only from their available funds, but also from the caliber of their staffs and the widespread perceptions that multilateral institutions are much less politically motivated than bilateral agencies.

In many countries, A.I.D. has worked closely with the World Bank to support policy changes. Current U.S. policy, however, has sought to diminish the Bank's role and influence. The result has been to limit the utility of an institution that has a major impact on, and provides support for policy changes by, developing countries. The seriousness attached by the Administration to policy changes is therefore undercut by the greater priority awarded to accomplishing such changes bilaterally rather than multilaterally.

Multilateral organizations also have a crucial role to play in improving coordination among the growing number of bilateral and multilateral donors. Three decades ago the United States was practically the only major provider of development assistance; the other OECD countries were not yet in the business, and the multilateral development institutions were very small. Today, some forty official donors (not counting the programs of the centrally planned economies) are active in the developing world: seventeen OECD-country bilateral agencies; ten Arab or OPEC development funds; several OPEC and other governments; and the multilateral aid agencies. In addition, there are some 150 private voluntary organizations in the United States alone. Yet at the moment, very little operational coordination is taking place among either donors or recipients, and no serious attempts are being made to simplify and standardize donor procedures. The importance of these issues is rapidly increasing, particularly in relation to the Sub-Saharan countries, where the number of donors often overwhelms seriously understaffed governments.[28]

A PROGRAM FOR THE FUTURE

If the developing countries as a group are to regain long-term economic and social progress, two conditions must be met: The countries themselves must choose internal economic policies that will support their own goals for growth with equity, and their efforts must be supported by industrial countries. This support will have to include forms different from those of the past in trade, finance, and technology; foreign aid, however, will continue to be an important component, and its uses and levels in the future must be rigorously reassessed by the Executive Branch and by Congress.

Reaffirming the Mandate

The current mandate of the U.S. aid program—"to help the poor majority of people within developing countries to participate in a process of equitable growth"—must be reaffirmed. The sum effect of the Reagan Administration's aid policies, regardless of their intent, has been to undermine this goal. The country allocation of aid funds has been dominated by security concerns. The heavy focus on aid to the middle-income countries continues. And support for multilateral development institutions, particularly for the World Bank, has diminished considerably. These trends are especially disturbing in light of the recent global recession, which has forced most developing-country governments to adopt painful austerity policies; the impact of these policies, in turn, is an overall decline in the standard of living, with particularly grave effects on the poorer groups within those countries.[29]

The emphasis of U.S. aid must now begin to shift from the middle-income countries to where the need is greatest: to the low-income countries—and particularly to Sub-Saharan Africa. The dire condition of these countries is the greatest development challenge of our time. Long-term development prospects in these countries are not necessarily bleak, provided that both recipients and donors can reshape their policies; whatever approaches are tried, however, concessional assistance will continue to be necessary for investment in training and infrastructure-building—which are essential to the success of both official and private-sector initiated development programs.

To a certain extent, the book is still open on the impact of A.I.D.'s current four-pillar approach to development and poverty alleviation. Any policy innovation takes at least two years to permeate the bureaucracy and foster change in program planning and implementation. Thus the Administration's policy changes are only now beginning to be translated into actual projects within developing countries. (The same lag was evidenced in the implementation of the 1973 New Directions changes in the foreign aid program.) But there is a danger that the effort to tap the development potential of the private sector will lead to neglect of the poorest segments of the population or of necessary public-sector programs, and that overestimation of A.I.D.'s capacity to influence and support policy reform will result in marginal long-term improvements.

The obvious need for economic growth and efficiency—even more crucial now, given the particularly adverse economic conditions facing most developing countries—must be reconciled with the longstanding goal of enabling the world's poor majority to obtain at least the most basic physical essentials. Economic growth, market forces, and private enterprise are not necessarily antithetical to the address of poverty. But the development goals of the 1970s, which emphasized meeting basic human needs, urgently need to be reaffirmed. It is also important to learn from the experience of the last decade, instead of dismissing it as the international equivalent of supposedly failed domestic welfare programs. The key issue is to meld the two, and that task remains to be done.

U.S. Support for the Multilateral Development Banks

The international financial institutions—particularly the World Bank and the International Monetary Fund—all have a crucial role to play in responding to the needs of the developing countries. They are essential providers of capital for the middle-income countries, of concessional resources for the poorer countries, and of much-needed advice on overall policy changes and specific sector programs to promote efficient growth and meet human needs. All current assessments, whether conducted by the U.S. government or by outside sources, give these institutions high marks for their programs and for their alignment with U.S. interests. The low priority they currently receive in U.S. policy needs to be reversed.

Program Lending Through Development Assistance

Aid programs also could be made far more effective if development assistance were more readily available in *program* rather than *project* form. Merging a portion of the economic support (ESF) fund with the development assistance account for program lending would give A.I.D. decision makers increased flexibility and resources. They would be able to choose a mix of program and project assistance that meets the needs of a particular developing country, rather than having to rely largely on ESF—allocated primarily on security grounds—to provide balance-of-payments support. Such a program would take full advantage of A.I.D.'s considerable experience, its large and knowledgeable staff, and its useful sectoral expertise on issues such as population growth and intermediate credit. In addition, it would provide additional financial and technical resources to allow A.I.D. to work more closely with the multilateral institutions to support policy reforms.

What Can the United States Afford?

Pressures to cut federal expenditures in the United States will be a fact of life in the years ahead. With a projected budget deficit of over $200 billion and a defense budget seemingly immune to all but minor cuts, locating resources to support development becomes politically very difficult. Therefore the key issue for those concerned about the U.S. foreign aid program is how to allocate very scarce resources—among programs, institutions, and countries—to make their use more congruent with the fundamental foreign policy objectives of the United States. At the same time, it should be recalled that foreign aid is such a relatively small fraction of the federal budget (less than 2 percent in FY1985) that overall resource constraints are not a credible justification of the program's low level. If the political will existed, the aid budget could be raised significantly without doing any real violence to the deficit. The issue is not how much foreign aid the United States can afford, but how important it perceives it to be to U.S. and global interests.

The budget submitted to Congress in January 1985 shows expenditures in the foreign aid program rising from $14 billion in FY1984 to $18.7 billion in FY1985, and then declining to $14.4 billion by FY1988 (Table 4). However, neither the increases nor the subsequent declines are shared equally across programs; 69 percent of the FY1985 allocations are devoted to international security assistance. The budget indicates both security

Table 4   FOREIGN AID BUDGET AUTHORITY, FY1984–FY1988
          ($ Millions)

Foreign aid	1984[a]	1985[b]	1986[b]	1987[b]	1988[b]
International security assistance					
Foreign military sales credit:					
On-budget under current law	1,315	4,940	5,655	5,779	5,901
Off-budget under current law	3,503	3,147	1,311	524	262
Military assistance	712	805	949	970	991
Economic Support Fund	3,389	3,841	2,824	2,883	2,941
Other:					
Existing law	110	214	108	110	112
Proposed legislation				145	278
Offsetting receipts	−86	−93	−99	−105	−161
Subtotal, international security					
assistance	8,943	12,854	10,748	10,306	10,324
Foreign economic and financial					
assistance					
Multilateral development banks	1,324	1,548	1,348	1,348	375
International organizations	315	359	196	200	204
Agency for International					
Development	2,013	2,286	2,113	2,133	2,171
Public Law 480 (food aid)	1,377	1,540	1,307	1,296	1,286
Peace Corps	117	128	125	128	132
Refugee assistance	336	350	338	340	334
Compact of Free Association					
(Micronesia)			209	146	148
Other	80	95	96	99	101
Offsetting receipts	−493	−459	−479	−604	−660
Subtotal, Foreign economic and					
financial assistance	5,069	5,847	5,343	5,085	4,093
Total, Foreign Aid	14,012	18,701	16,091	15,391	14,418

[a]Actual.

[b]Estimate.

Source: Executive Office of the President, *Budget of the United States Government: FY1986* (Washington, D.C.: Office of Management and Budget, 1985), pp. 5–18.

and economic assistance shrinking over the next three years, but with security aid declining 20 percent (according to a budget which does not include any economic support funds for Israel after FY1988) while economic assistance drops 30 percent. By FY1985, security assistance is to total 72 percent of foreign aid funds.

Thus the important question is whether the priorities assigned to various programs grouped under the rubric of *foreign aid* match U.S. interests in the Third World. In FY1985, for instance, some $7.5 billion of a $18.7-billion total in foreign aid will go for military assistance, rental of military bases, or transfers to countries with annual per capita incomes of $2,500 or more. In many cases these expenditures are justified on the ground that they add to U.S. military security, with little effort devoted to assessing their returns to either U.S. strategic or political interests. Policymakers need to seriously consider whether some portion of the amounts to be spent on security programs would not yield greater returns for the United States if they were instead expended on programs fostering long-term economic development. The budget as presented shows no U.S. contributions to the International Development Association, the Asian Development Fund, the African Development Bank, or the African Development Fund after existing commitments are fulfilled in FY1987.

The federal budget also indicates that in FY1985 the United States will receive some $550 million in repayments from past foreign economic and military assistance and sales. Until the mid-1970s, these funds were reprogrammed for development purposes (with congressional approval), but now they are returned directly to the U.S. Treasury. In a period of scarce development assistance resources, restoring these repayments to A.I.D. is logical; the funds available were originally appropriated for development and their repayment should be used to continue to support the program. The funds available for reprogramming could total over $820 million in FY1988—an amount that could, for example, raise the U.S. contribution to IDA-VII to an adequate level.

The United States can afford to increase its support for the long-term development of the Third World—a goal that is very much in its own interest. Moreover, based on the projections cited, the United States can afford a considerable *increase* in development support without materially affecting current budget levels. The real challenge is to reorder priorities to harmonize expenditures on foreign aid with the long-term interests of the United States and with Third World development.

NOTES

1. The term "foreign aid" is used here as it is in the federal budget. It includes, therefore, not only traditional bilateral and multilateral programs but also international security assistance and military aid, on one hand, and refugee and Peace Corps programs on the other. This definition was chosen because

it includes a range of policy instruments and choices available to U.S. decision makers concerned about relations with the developing countries. The data used here should not be confused with that issued by the OECD. For the OECD definition of "official development assistance," see the Glossary of this volume.

2. Ironically, this conclusion is echoed by the Heritage Foundation's recent report, *Mandate for Leadership II,* which suggested, "If AID is to continue as a separate agency, its statutory authority, objectives, and focus should be changed to reflect the fact that much of its work is really security-related." Stuart M. Butler, Michael Sanera, and W. Bruce Weinrod, eds., *Mandate for Leadership II* (Washington, D.C.: 1985), p. 372.

3. A study by the Organisation for Economic Co-operation and Development concluded that the forty richest developing countries had added as much to the increment in gross world product in the 1970s as did the United States or Japan and West Germany combined. *World Economic Interdependence and the Evolving North-South Relationship* (Paris: OECD, 1983).

4. The P.L. 480 Program, popularly known as "Food for Peace," is not analyzed here; the problem and potential of using food aid either for political or development purposes is a complicated subject distinct from other U.S. aid programs and beyond the scope of this chapter. P.L. 480 is, however, included in the tables of this chapter.

5. John P. Lewis, "Can We Escape the Path of Mutual Injury?" in John P. Lewis and Valeriana Kallab, eds., *U.S. Foreign Policy and the Third World: Agenda 1983* (New York: Praeger, for the Overseas Development Council, 1983), pp. 20–21.

6. See Table 4.

7. Another factor contributing to the dispersion of ESF was a 1981 change in aid legislation that had previously prohibited the use of development assistance and ESF in the same countries.

8. A.I.D., Section 653(a) Report, *Program Allocations FY1985,* mimeographed, November 1984. Includes $200 million for Pakistan.

9. 1979–1983 average.

10. A.I.D., *Program Allocations,* op. cit.

11. General Accounting Office, *Economic Support Funds in the Philippines* (Washington, D.C.: GAO, January 27, 1984) p. 6.

12. General Accounting Office, *Political and Economic Factors Influencing Economic Support Funds Programs* (Washington, D.C.: April 18, 1983), p. 30.

13. For instance, one study estimates that in 1982, 19 cents out of each ESF dollar were spent on a project that fulfilled the current legislative mandate; in 1985, only 7 cents of every dollar will be used on these kinds of projects. Roy Prosterman, *The Quality of Foreign Aid,* RDI Monograph on Foreign Aid and Development No. 1 (Seattle: Rural Development Institute, 1984), p. 4.

14. 1979–1983 average.

15. General Accounting Office, *AID's Assistance to Jamaica* (Washington, D.C.: GAO, April 19, 1983) p. 8.

16. The Carlucci Commission, for example, simply worked from the premise that these programs were effective, but did not evaluate them. A recent examination of security assistance programs undertaken by the Center for Strategic and International Studies showed that in many cases their relationship to American *military security* is at best tenuous. The study concluded that secu-

rity assistance "cannot be defended primarily on military grounds. . . . both the Congress and many within the Executive Branch tend to perceive the security assistance programs as meeting U.S. *international political objectives* [emphases added]." (Franklin D. Kramer, "The Government's Approach to Security Assistance Decisions," in Ernest Graves and Steven A. Hildreth, eds., *U.S. Security Assistance: The Political Process* (Lexington, Mass.: Lexington Books, 1985), p. 123.

17. A.I.D., *Congressional Presentation FY1985* (Washington, D.C.: 1985), p. 5.
18. A.I.D., *Congressional Presentation, FY1985* (Washington, D.C.: 1985), p. 4.
19. Congress, however, has reservations about the link with the IMF. Last year, an amendment attached to the appropriations resolution stated that U.S. aid should not be linked to IMF requirements for economic reform.
20. For a full discussion of this point, see Chapter 1 of this volume.
21. A.I.D. Policy Paper, *Health Assistance* (Washington, D.C.: December 1982), pp. 9–10.
22. A.I.D. Policy Paper, *Private Enterprise Development* (Washington, D.C.: 1982).
23. The government of Botswana rejected the U.S. offer of $4.2 million to finance the purchase of General Electric locomotives when it discovered that the funds would not be additional, but would come out of A.I.D. funds already allocated to the country; Botswana instead accepted a Canadian offer that did represent additional aid.
24. Nicholas D. Kristof, "Foreign Aid by U.S. is Tied to Exports," *New York Times,* November 24, 1984.
25. U.S. Department of the Treasury, *United States Participation in the Multilateral Development Banks in the 1980s* (Washington, D.C.: 1982), pp. 161–162.
26. *Mandate for Leadership II,* op. cit., p. 374.
27. U.S. Department of the Treasury, *United States Participation,* op. cit. p. 42.
28. John P. Lewis, "Development Assistance in the 1980s," in Roger Hansen, ed., *U.S. Foreign Policy and the Third World: Agenda 1982* (New York: Praeger, for the Overseas Development Council, 1982), pp. 119–121.
29. Unfortunately, no overall data or analysis is available to assess the impact of these changes on human well-being or on the incidence of poverty within developing countries. Some examination of this issue has been undertaken. See, for example, "The Impact of World Recession on Children," *World Development,* Special Issue, March 1984.

Part
Six

POLITICAL
ECONOMY OF
SECURITY

Until very recently, students of international political economy
have largely ignored the issues of national and international security—
despite the primacy of security in foreign policies of contemporary nation-states. In the editors' opinion, the long-standing neglect of security
issues among the IPE community has its roots in the origins of the
field. IPE, as an area of inquiry, was born of the general dissatisfaction
among many students of international relations in the 1960s, with their
field's almost exclusive focus on state-actors and their presumed preoccupation with national security. As the scholars paid increasing attention to the growing phenomenon of international interdependence—
which was blurring the distinction between domestic and foreign
policy and placing non-security (i.e., economic, technological, social,
and environmental) issues on the national and international political
agendas alike—the state-centric paradigm proved woefully inadequate.
The resulting deemphasis of security affairs among IPE scholars has led
to an artificial division between *national security studies,* with its traditional ties to the field of international relations on the one hand, and
IPE on the other. Nor have national security studies acquired a secure
niche in the discipline of economics.*

The editors believe this state of affairs must be corrected, and this
correction requires the appreciation of insights from economics and
political science. Hence our inclusion of this section in this reader. The

---

*Helen V. Milner and David A. Baldwin, *The Political Economy of National Security: An
Annotated Bibliography,* Boulder, CO: Westview Press, 1990, p. xi.

new focus raises a host of important research and policy questions. For example, what is the causal relationship between the economic health of a nation and its ability to sustain political and security commitments abroad? Should economic policymakers be as involved in questions of alliances, defense spending, and arms control as defense policymakers? If so, what new institutional arrangements can facilitate this participation? Are there fundamental differences between economic and military security, and are they compatible? Especially in the context of both the ending of the Cold War and questions about how to spend the still hypothetical peace dividend of savings in defense spending, and the Iraqi oil grab of mid-1990, one is hard-pressed to separate economics and security.

Bruce Russett address the perennial question—conventionally termed the *guns vs. butter debate*—of whether there is a necessary trade-off relationship between a nation's resource commitment to national security and its spending on socioeconomic welfare. His quantitative analysis leads Russett to conclude that there is no systematic and uniform relationship.

Russett's conclusion challenges the oft-asserted argument that commitment of money and other resources to national defense diminishes opportunities for improving the socioeconomic well-being of a nation. This argument is articulated by Seymour Melman. Melman cites selective examples and data to support his contention that drastic increases in defense spending under the Reagan administration have directly and negatively affected the performance of the United States economy and the nation's socioeconomic well-being. Melman's findings tend to support the commonly held view today that many U.S. allies, most notably Japan, have benefitted disproportionately from the United States' willingness to bear the bulk of western defense costs.

Stephen Gill and David Law examine the economic, political, and social forces promoting or limiting military expenditures and the spread of the military-industrial complex around the world. More precisely, they address two questions: How far, and why, are arms production and military spending a systematic feature of the global economy? What are the relationships between these systemic features and the propensity to war and peace in the postwar world? The authors' conclusions tend to support Melman's argument. However, they also point out that the exact nature of causal relationships surrounding military-industrial production are more complex than may be implied by the characterization of the continuing debate as one of *guns vs. butter.* Gill and Law agree that military expenditures in the United States and the Soviet Union have contributed in an important way to their current economic difficulties. They add that the trade-off between military and civilian spending may be even more constraining in developing countries, where overall resources are sorely limited.

Defense Expenditures and National Well-being

Bruce Russett

GUNS OR BUTTER: WHAT KINDS OF TRADE-OFFS?

Most people believe there is some trade-off between guns and butter. If a nation increases the resources it devotes to military activities without increasing total product, civilian sectors of the economy must pay by foregoing benefits they would otherwise receive. This assessment is part of the conventional wisdom, but it has little specific content. It does not, for example, tell us what kind of trade-offs to expect; that is, what particular parts of the economy or social system will suffer the greatest impact. Will the costs be borne disproportionately by individuals or business, rich or poor, young or old, ethnic majority or minority? Will the decrease in nonmilitary spending affect mostly current consumption, or by discouraging capital investment, will it primarily affect future generations who will have to produce their GNP with a smaller-than-otherwise industrial plant? Or will the sharpest cuts come at the expense of social investment, causing future generations to be less healthy or less well educated than they would have been without the preceding military effort?

Conventional wisdom often emphasizes the trade-off between military spending and capital investment and attributes the undoubted economic success of postwar Japan and West Germany to their ability to shift their defense burdens largely onto the United States and therefore to devote their own resources to building modern, highly productive industry. This view, complete with detailed examination of industrial investment and productivity, has advocates on both the left and right, including Seymour Melman (1974) and Arthur Burns (1971). According to Burns, Chairman of the Council of Economic Advisers under President Eisenhower, "The real cost of the defense sector consists, therefore, not only of

Bruce Russett, "Defense Expenditures and National Well-being," *American Political Science Review* Vol. 76, No. 4. (December 1982), pp. 767–777. Reprinted with permission of the American Political Science Association.

the civilian goods and services that are currently foregone on its account; it includes also an element of growth that could have been achieved through larger investment in human or business capital." By this line of argument, whatever its desirable stimulative effects in a particular short-term condition of slack, the burden of American military spending is over the long term directly responsible for the decline of American productivity relative to Japanese and European competitors. Military spending would be particularly corrosive, because it attracts to ultimately unproductive uses the funds and workers in high technology industry which could otherwise constitute America's most promising export sectors (Thurow 1981).

Systematic evidence for this argument, though fragmentary, tends to support it. For example, in multivariate analyses of fifteen industrialized economies from 1960 to 1970, Smith (1977) and Smith and Smith (1980) report significant negative relationships between military expenditure and investment and the rate of growth in GNP. Benoit (1973) found a slight negative relationship for an earlier period, as did Szymanski (1973) for 1950 to 1968. In time-series examinations, Russett (1970, ch. 5 and 6) found a stronger trade-off between defense and fixed investment than between defense and personal consumption in the United States, France, and the United Kingdom, but not in Canada. Of course the precise trade-off between military spending and specific kinds of civilian expenditure (private consumption, investment, or government civil spending) is a matter for political decision, not some automatically dictated exchange. Different politicians or parties will have different preferences under different circumstances, although it is often tempting to preserve current consumption as much as possible to minimize current political protest, even at the expense of investment and thus long-term consumption.[1] A full investigation of the degree and circumstances of various trade-offs would require a complex model of the determinants of investment, only one of which is military spending. That is a difficult task even for professional economists and is surely beyond our ability here.

A very different view proposes that military spending undergirds modern industrial capitalist economies. According to this line of reasoning, if it were not for the prop provided by military spending, industrial capitalism would quickly collapse into underconsumption. To absorb "surplus capital" the government must increase its spending and taxing. *Welfare state* spending is opposed by conservatives because it is thought to damage work incentives in the labor market and to compete unfairly with private enterprise. Thus expanded public spending for civil purposes is not acceptable, but military spending is acceptable, precisely because it does not compete with any private vested interests (Baran and Sweezy 1968, especially chs. 6 and 7). With the short-term slack appearing in the economy, Arthur Burns was described as giving that precedence over his qualms, concluding that "unless some decisive governmental action were taken, and taken soon, we were heading for another dip, which would hit its low point just before the elections. . . . He urgently recommended that two steps be taken immediately: by loosening up credit and, where justifiable, increasing spending for national security" (Nixon 1962). Former Defense Secretary Schlesinger once made the counter-cyclical value of military spending explicit in testimony to Congress (*The New York Times* 1974).

The view of military spending as an essential prop to an "underconsuming" economy finds mixed support in the available evidence. Certainly the expansion of defense spending as war clouds gathered in 1940 and 1941 helped to pull the American economy out of the Great Depression, although economic recovery was already well under way. Until the major wartime exertions, expanded defense production could merely take up slack, without any significant trade-offs at all. In an analysis of year-to-year military spending changes in the postwar United States, Nincic and Cusack (1979, p. 108) found that "Military spending cut back at an expected rate of $2 billion per annum *after on-year presidential elections and expanded at a similar rate in the two years prior to those elections,*" suggesting deliberate utilization of defense increases as part of a "political business cycle." On the other hand, Smith (1977), despite sympathies for neo-Marxist interpretations, found no evidence to support the underconsumptionist hypothesis when examining data on all Organization for European Cooperation and Development countries, and concluded rather that military spending is pursued, even at direct economic cost, for its strategic value in securing the capitalist international system.

We can, however, focus with a little more promise on certain kinds of trade-offs within the government sector. Peacock and Wiseman (1961) found a consistent tendency for a *displacement effect* resulting from United Kingdom participation in wars. Typically the government sector expanded greatly to carry the new military burden, and then, at the end of the war, failed to contract proportionately. Thus after each war the government sector became permanently enlarged. Taxes legitimated by the war effort could be, in part, maintained, and some of the revenues freed from war devoted to public spending for civilian welfare, especially health and education. Stein (1980) reports a similar effect from United States twentieth-century participation in war, except for the Vietnam experience. According to this evidence, a trade-off occurs between military spending and government health and education spending, at least with the downturn of the former. The effect of military spending expansion need not simply be symmetrical to the effect of military contractions.

Yet the more one looks, the more complex and confusing the picture that seems to emerge. Russett (1969, 1970) found evidence of reasonably strong negative relations between military spending and government spending on health and education for the United States, France, and the United Kingdom, as did Lee (1972) for the United States. However, the data are limited in time (basically the 1940s through the 1960s), and the relationship virtually disappeared in Russett's analysis of the United Kingdom data for the whole period from 1890 to 1966. Moreover these results are largely based on simple bivariate regressions without controls for spurious relationships. Caputo (1975) analyzed data for the United States, United Kingdom, Sweden, and Australia, and was surprised to find largely positive relations between military spending and health and education expenditures. But Caputo's computations were for the absolute values of expenditures, over time in rapidly growing economies, so his (spurious) positive results should have been less than astonishing. Kennedy (1974) seems to have made the same error.

Finally, it matters very much just which spending series one looks at. Wilensky (1975, ch. 4) found a negative relationship between military and welfare spending in sixteen industrialized countries, but since heavy military spending often generates employment under conditions of economic slack, it operates to reduce unemployment and some other welfare payments, and the finding should not be generalized to other kinds of social programs. Whereas Russett found a strong negative bivariate relationship between military and *all* government spending on education and health in the United States, he showed rather weak relationships within the federal budget—the trade-offs were usually much stronger between defense spending and health and education expenditures at the state and local level. Although incomplete, this evidence suggests that federal budgeteers (bureaucrats or legislators or both) were likely to try to maintain all expenditures at the central level and to force the difficult choices downward by preempting tax revenues or cutting various kinds of assistance to state and local governmental units. This result is corroborated by the best study to date of the military-health trade-off. With the use of a somewhat larger data base (1929–1974) than Russett's, Peroff and Podolak-Warren (1979), like Russett, found a significant trade-off between military and total federal health appropriation requests, but none at all at the federal level when they looked either at federal allocations or at final federal expenditures. In the course of the full budgetary process, this trade-off effectively disappeared.

In light of contemporary controversies over the burdens of national defense, it is important to achieve some sophisticated long-term perspective. The data must apply to countries and periods where there is substantial variation in the relevant variables and where the levels of military spending are often high enough to force hard, deliberate political choice (i.e., trade-offs). The analysis is best restricted to industrialized capitalist states, since both domestic and international constraints are likely to be very different for communist systems and less-developed countries. The models must be complex and multivariate so as to identify the effects of a variety of other influences that might be related to both military and social spending, and thus if uncontrolled would suggest spurious relations. Here I shall investigate trade-offs between United States military spending and federal spending on health and education. My data cover federal outlays including transfers to lower government levels—the end-product

—reported in the *Historical Statistics of the United States* (U.S. Bureau of the Census 1975) and individual volumes of the *Statistical Abstract of the United States* (U.S. Bureau of the Census, various years). Fully comparable data solely at the state and local level simply do not seem to be available, and in any case it makes sense to look first for trade-offs within the same budget (federal). By choosing health and education we pick civil spending that is not simply consumption or current "butter," but which is a form of social investment. Trade-offs there would have major consequences for the long-term growth and well-being of the nation.

MODELLING THE DETERMINANTS OF FEDERAL CIVIL EXPENDITURES

My first model tries to explain changes in federal spending for education as a result of changes in military spending and other variables. Note at the outset that I am concerned with changes, not levels of spending. My assumption is that trade-offs occur at the margin, and hence respond to increments or decrements rather than total budgets. Even so, I must specify the kind of change. The absolute increase or decrease, presumably in constant dollars, is not the same as a rate of change. With the former, a regression weights analysis in favor of those years when the absolute changes up or down are very great. This is especially a problem in a growing economy (even when the data are in constant dollars), and the result is to weight recent years, with larger absolute changes, more heavily than earlier ones. Problems of autocorrelation are typically more serious with absolute change data as well. Thus, although I refer briefly to absolute changes, I usually use the rates of change, producing a more equal weighting. Such a procedure also has different theoretical assumptions, namely that the effects of different amounts of change depend in part on the size of the base from which they originate at each changepoint (Russett 1971).

My basic hypothesis of a trade-off between education and military spending is in the form:

$$\frac{E_t - E_{t-1}}{E_{t-1}} = a - b\,\frac{M_t - M_{t-1}}{M_{t-1}} + e$$

It is possible, of course, that other kinds of trade-offs operate within the federal budget. For example, under pressure of increased military spending the real crunch might occur, say, between health and education: education might substantially hold its position, but at the expense of some other federal civil spending programs. I hypothesize that this is not the case; rather, the major civil spending programs will be positively related, but to check it, I add two other major federal budget categories of interest as b_2 health and b_3 housing.[2]

I began, as indicated, with data on the yearly changes in federal outlays by different major budgetary categories. To avoid distortion by the widely varying effects of inflation, data are deflated by the appropriate price index where possible. For housing and health expenditures I used the Housing Price Index and the Health Price Index. No such long-term index was available for military or education expenditures, so for those I simply used the Federal Government Purchases Deflator. Since defense and education typically make up more than 40 percent of federal purchases, this is not an unreasonable measure. (Data on prices are from *Economic Report of the President, 1981.*)

Next I recognize that the effects are likely to be different in different international political circumstances. In particular the trade-offs may be different in wartime, and that difference may vary with the intensity of conflict. To control for the presence and intensity of war I introduce a new variable, battle deaths; that is, total number of deaths of U.S. military personnel in combat. For peacetime years this figure is of course very low (but not necessarily nil; e.g., there were some combat deaths among U.S. advisers in Indochina even in the early 1960s), but the figures are much higher for the three intensive American military efforts of the period, and especially for the years of World War II (1942–1945) and the Korean War (1950–1953). It effectively serves as a control for wartime experience, although I did perform some analyses that excluded entirely the World War II years from the data.[3]

Next, the effects will vary under different economic conditions. A military buildup occurring at a time of substantial excess economic capacity, e.g., early World War II, will not force the same painful trade-offs that may be faced in a period of already nearly full utilization, such as Vietnam. To control for this variation, I introduced three new variables: GNP growth rate in constant dollars, an index of increase in productivity in the economy, and the index of capacity utilization, both as reported by the *Economic Report of the President, 1981.* I hypothesized that spending on education would be cut sharply under military pressures when economic growth or productivity growth was essentially stagnant, or when the economy's productive capacity was already at nearly full utilization. An alternative index for the latter purpose might have been the level of (un)employment, but I decided to omit this index because it would have been rather collinear with capacity utilization except in the 1970s, and in those recent years the constraint on economic growth has been more one of highly utilized physical capacity than the (consistently high) level of human unemployment.[4]

Yet another determinant, partly economic, partly political, may be the level of federal tax revenues. The Vietnam War experience suggests it may matter greatly how military expenditures are financed. Most peacetime military buildups have been financed largely by tax increases, World War II and the Korean War were financed by a combination of taxes and deficit financing, with inflation partly held in check by wage and price controls, and the Vietnam War was funded primarily by deficit financing and subsequent inflation. Trade-offs between education and military spending should be minimized in years when tax revenues increase sharply, thus limiting the pressures for trade-offs to preserve some semblance of a balanced budget.

In addition to various constraints on the supply of funds for education, of course, there are also demand pressures. The most important of these concern changes in the size of the population to be educated, which we measure variously by the total population under age 18 and the total school enrollment.[5]

Finally, decisions about expenditure trade-offs occur in a political system where different actors subscribe to different political ideologies. According to the usual understanding, liberals or Democrats or both are more likely to value and hence to try to preserve social spending even in the face of military increases; conservatives or Republicans or both are more likely to wish to restrain such programs, and thus to be especially willing to make the trade-offs when military spending goes up. On the military downswing, however, the pattern is likely to be reversed. Liberals and Democrats conversely will choose to take advantage of defense cuts to promote social programs; conservatives and Republicans will prefer to return the money saved from military activities in the form of tax cuts and will not favor increasing social programs. A full test of this hypothesis would be very difficult, and if it required a coding of major political actors' ideologies might even risk falling into the trap of a tautology. We can, however, at least control for the party of the president, and thus include a dummy variable for a Republican president and hypothesize a negative sign for its coefficient.

A typical equation, therefore, is as follows in constant dollars:

$$\%\Delta\text{Education} = a - b_1\%\Delta\text{Military} + b_2\%\Delta\text{Health}$$
$$+ b_3\%\Delta\text{Housing} + b_4\%\Delta\text{Productivity} - b_5\text{Capacity} + b_6\%\Delta\text{GNP}$$
$$+ b_7\%\Delta\text{Taxes} + b_8\%\Delta\text{Population under 18} + b_9\%\Delta\text{Enrollment}$$
$$- b_{10}\text{Battle Deaths} - b_{11}\text{Republican} + e.$$

As noted, productivity and capacity were often omitted. Also, these relationships apply in a political system subject to substantial delays for information gathering, assessment, negotiation, recommendation, and implementation. To allow for that I usually lagged all but the expenditure variables and taxes one year behind the government outlays. I experimented with simultaneous relationships and a longer lag but found the one-year period to show the strongest effects.

A similar procedure was used for estimating the impact of military spending and other variables on health expenditures. Most of the independent variables are the same. Education of course moves to the right-hand side to replace health. Population under 18, or its equivalent, is replaced as a demand variable by population 65 or over, on the grounds that the greatest need for health care is typically among the aged. In addition, we know that the introduction of Medicare in 1966 changed the system by building in a higher level of fixed obligations for health spending, and thus I add a dummy variable for years when Medicare was in effect.

Some of these data, notably on production and capacity utilization, are not available for the full time-span covered by our expenditure data and so had to be employed in equations with slightly fewer years. Also, as noted, I computed some of the equations using absolute changes and others using percentage rates of change for the fiscal variables. Budgetary data were reported for fiscal years, whereas other variables typically were available only for calendar years; we reconciled this by assigning the appropriate portions (usually half) of each fiscal year to a calendar year; i.e., 1970 data were constructed from data for half of fiscal year 1970 and half of fiscal 1971.

RESULTS

First we should look at the bivariate relations between military spending on the one hand, and health and education on the other. Table 1 shows that military spending tended most often to move in the same direction as health or education. The military and major civil spending categories rose together (in current dollars) 21 of the 39 years; they fell together only three times for health and four times for education. Basically, however, health and education were going up in almost all of these years (33 or 34 of 39), regardless of what was happening with the military—hardly what the idea of a trade-off would lead us to expect. Figure 1 is a scattergram representing the percentage of change in each of the three major expenditure categories on the vertical axis and time on the horizontal axis. A careful perusal of Figure 1 supports this interpretation; the only very large reductions in health or education spending during this whole period coincided with very large cuts in military spending immediately after World War II. In this instance, the *permissive trade-off* did not hold. Notably,

Table 1   NUMBER OF YEARS WHEN VARIOUS COMBINATIONS OF MILITARY AND SOCIAL SPENDING CHANGES OCCURRED

Military	Education		Health	
	Increase	Decrease	Increase	Decrease
Increase	21	2	21	2
Decrease	12	4	13	3

Note: Chi square = 1.93 for education and .85 for health, neither of which is statistically significant. N = 39.

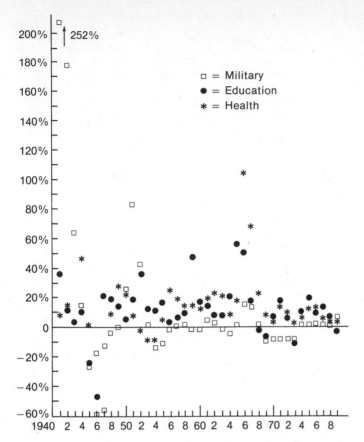

Figure 1 Percentage Change in Federal Spending Categories, 1940–1979.

most of the few years in which military spending was cut and health and education rose occurred during Republican administrations—Eisenhower and Nixon-Ford.

These results of course only show bivariate relationships between military and civil spending, and the comments about Republican presidents do not take into account other variables that may compound the relationships. It is important also to control for the World War II outliers, with a dummy variable or by removing those years or both. Therefore we turn now to Table 2, which displays some ordinary least squares (OLS) equations to explain percentage changes in federal education outlays. In the first version (with 9 independent variables, for the full 1941–1979 period), we see positive relationships between education spending and the other two major civilian public expenditure categories: health and housing. They are not subject to substantial trade-offs among themselves. Less

Table 2   EXPLAINING PERCENTAGE CHANGE IN FEDERAL EDUCATION OUTLAYS

	1941–1979		1947–1979	
	Full equation	Reduced equation	Full equation	Reduced equation
Constant	1.06[a] (.040)	1.42[a] (.44)	.097[b] (.048)	.102[b] (.057)
%ΔHousing	.013[a] (.005)		.014[a] (.004)	
%ΔHealth	.204[b] (.114)		.179[b] (.102)	
%ΔMilitary	.178[b] (.100)	.120 (.111)	.086 (.190)	−.030 (.227)
%ΔTaxes	−.175 (.218)	−.167 (.242)	.508 (.562)	.684 (.681)
%ΔPopulation under 18$_{t-1}$	1.42 (1.22)	2.02 (1.30)		
%ΔEnrollment$_{t-1}$	1.55 (1.23)	2.07 (1.31)	.982 (.919)	1.69 (1.08)
Republican$_{t-1}$	−.028 (.047)	−.063 (.051)	−.185 (.415)	−.045 (.049)
%ΔGNP$_{t-1}$	−.005 (.007)	−.003 (.007)	−.001 (.007)	−.001 (.008)
Battle deaths$_{t-1}$	−.000002[b] (.0000009)	−.000003[a] (.000001)		
$\bar{R}^2 =$	.50	.35	.35	.04
$D - W =$	1.75	1.52	1.62	1.35

[a]Statistically significant at the .01 level with a one-tailed test.

[b]Statistically significant at the .05 level.

Note: For each independent variable the top entry is the regression coefficient (b) and in parentheses below it is its standard error. The coefficient of determination ($\bar{R}^2$) is adjusted as appropriate to small samples. D–W is the Durbin-Watson statistic, a standard measure of autocorrelation.

expected may be the significant positive relation between education and military spending, at least as this model is constructed. That relationship, however, is deceptive, since it indicates a positive relationship after we have controlled for the stronger positive relationships between education and health and housing. In the model used in the second column, removing health and housing from the equation, the relationship with military remains positive, but not significant.

It is clear from the strength of the battle-deaths variable in the first two columns that wartime (especially big wars) experience is different from peacetime. The experience of war years is substantively important, these years should not simply be dismissed as outliers; nevertheless it is necessary also to reestimate the equation omitting the World War II years from the sample. In so doing we are able to remove battle deaths from the equation, since its primary purpose was to control for World War II, and also remove population under 18, which proved nonsignificant. The last two columns show these results. We again observe an initially positive (but nonsignificant) coefficient for military, which this time turns to a trivially negative coefficient when housing and health are removed from the equation in the last column. But in no column do we discover the anticipated significant negative coefficient for military, or anything approaching it. In the period in question, therefore, we find no evidence that rates of increase in military spending reflect trade-offs with educational expenditures. Although we can never be entirely confident that further analysis may not reverse negative findings like this, we believe it is quite robust. Various other runs, with simultaneous relationships or other lag structures, with variants of our *demand* variables and without nonsignificant variables, made little difference in the key coefficients. Whereas one should always wonder whether the equation is misspecified, it is not obvious to me that I have, for example, left out a variable importantly associated with both military and the dependent variable in a way that would seriously distort the results.

One other aspect of Table 2 is worth comment before proceeding: Note the nonsignificant relationship between education and the dummy for Republican president. Although the sign is always negative, the coefficient is trivially small. Republican presidents have not—whether by choice or by ineffectiveness—previously had notable effects in bringing federal educational spending below the levels that would have obtained under Democratic incumbencies.

Table 3 repeats the exercise for federal health outlays, with similar results. In the full period with all variables, the coefficient for military is, as anticipated, negative (at the .05 level), but this relationship turns much weaker in the second column, when the confounding effects of housing and education are removed and several nonsignificant variables are also dropped. Under these circumstances, however, the demand variable of an aging population becomes very important, as does the presumed *permissive* effect of rapid growth in federal tax revenue. When, as with education, we take the World War II years out of the sample, the coefficient for military spending turns positive, if not significantly so. In overview, the evidence is preponderantly against any systematic trade-off between military spending and our civilian outlay category, health. And again, there is little evidence of more effective opposition to health spending by previous Republican presidents; the coefficients are negative as expected, but trivial.

Although I prefer the rate-of-change model to one concerned with absolute changes because it is closer to my theory and less subject to distortion by overweighting the effects of recent years in a growing econ-

Table 3 EXPLAINING PERCENTAGE CHANGE IN FEDERAL HEALTH OUTLAYS

	1941–1979		1947–1979	
	Full equation	Reduced equation	Full equation	Reduced equation
Constant	.250 (.248)	.489[b] (.138)	.496 (.309)	.707[c] (.294)
%ΔHousing	−.007 (.008)		−.008 (.008)	
%ΔEducation	.566[b] (.223)		.644[c] (.319)	
%ΔMilitary	−.175[b] (.099)	−.074 (.093)	.384 (.371)	.503 (.378)
%ΔTaxes	.522 (.311)	.623[c] (.274)	−.395 (.999)	−.036 (1.02)
%ΔPopulation over 65$_{t-1}$	.803 (.802)	[a]14.67[b] (5.23)	−16.2 (9.89)	−19.8[c] (9.82)
Republican$_{t-1}$	−.050 (.069)		−.020 (−.075)	−.029 (.078)
%ΔGNP$_{t-1}$	.010 (.010)		−.001 (.014)	−.007 (.013)
Battle deaths$_{t-1}$	.0000005 (.000001)	[a].000001 (.000001)		
Medicare$_{t-1}$	.026 (.100)		−.127 (.112)	−.058 (.107)
$\bar{R}^2 =$	.27	.26	.17	.10
$D - W =$	1.30	1.17	1.19	1.23

[a]Not lagged.

[b]Statistically significant at the .01 level with a one-tailed test.

[c]Statistically significant at the .05 level.

Note: See Table 2 for identification of the statistics.

omy, I may briefly discuss the results of some equations using absolute changes. Despite introducing substantial changes in some parts of the results, the above basic conclusions are left intact. In the entire period from 1941 to 1979, once again the military coefficients are if anything positive, not negative. The party of the president remains unimportant. (Remember, by this procedure the more recent years, those during and after the Vietnam War, are heavily weighted. The war was financed largely by inflation rather than tax increases or severe cuts in the Great Society programs—i.e., no trade-offs at that level—and at the end of the war there was little distribution of the cut in military expenses in the form of increased social spending.)

CURRENT TRADE-OFFS

By some standards the results of this exercise have been disappointing. We did not produce powerful explanatory equations for the several categories of federal civil spending, but that was not really the purpose. Neither did we find systematic or powerful trade-off effects between that spending and military expenditure. Testing for those effects *was* the purpose.

The failure to find such relationships should not be generalized to other kinds of civil expenditures. For example, trade-offs between military spending and private investment, or between military spending and spending on civil functions by all levels of government combined, have not been considered here. What evidence exists suggests that systematic trade-offs have occurred, but that evidence is dated and ambiguous. Proper testing of hypotheses about these trade-offs will be a demanding task, either to obtain adequate data or to devise good theoretical specifications.

It is possible that with the use of other theoretical perspectives and thus other model specifications, others may find relationships in these data. More sophisticated analysis may help, but simply "massaging" this data set is not likely to be enough. The absence of a relationship between federal military and social spending appears to be quite robust.[6] Doubtless there are some times and political circumstances when major trade-offs can be avoided by picking up slack in a depressed economy. Other times trade-offs do occur, deliberately or inadvertently. Sometimes federal civil spending may be kept largely intact by imposing tax increases, or by permitting the hidden and unsystematic *tax* implied by deficit financing and inflation. The point is that I could find no regular pattern of trade-offs in the data for the last four decades of American history.[7] Different combinations of political will and environment have resulted in different patterns of choice.

Federal spending for education began to rise substantially immediately after World War II, at first partly because of the GI Bill of Rights. But other programs were expanded or initiated shortly thereafter, and federal educational spending increased in real dollars in every year from 1947 through 1968. Federal spending for health was slower to hit the upward track but even more persistent once it got well started; in every year from 1955 through 1979 it rose in real dollars.

One remarkable fact about this growth in federal education and health spending is that it continued through several major periods of military buildup. Expenditures for education rose throughout the cold war rearmament and Korean War, and during all but two of the Vietnam War years. Federal spending for health continued to rise throughout the Vietnam period. Even during the four costly World War II years from 1941 through 1944, these civilian federal programs continued to expand. Sacrifices surely were imposed, but they were largely sacrifices imposed on current consumption, not on the kind of long-run social investment required to build a healthier and better-educated population. Indeed, the problems of ignorance, ill-health, and malnutrition among many potential draftees during World War II helped to convince even the most defense-minded legislators and officials that the federal government had to take remedial action.

A second remarkable fact is that support for increased federal health and education programs was reasonably nonpartisan. Federal spending for education, e.g., the National Defense Education Act, went up sharply during the Eisenhower years and continued to rise during all but one year of the Nixon and Ford administrations. Federal health expenditures passed unscathed through the Nixon and Ford years. When these Republican presidents felt compelled to raise defense readiness, they kept the increases within limits and accepted the taxes necessary to maintain social programs.

The current Republican president [Reagan], sensing widespread public support for military expenditures (Russett and DeLuca 1981), has imposed trade-offs between military and federal civil spending. These trade-offs were not deterministically ordained by long-standing patterns of political choice.[8] Decisions to increase military spending, and simultaneously to slash federal support for education and health, were deliberately taken and imposed. Arguably the changes do not even represent trade-offs in the conventional sense, since the dominant philosophy advocates greater military spending and reduced social spending quite independently. If a SALT III treaty imposing a 50 percent cut in the arms budget were signed tomorrow, would social spending rebound?

The magnitude of current budget shifts is shown in Table 4, both for the proposals of the Reagan administration and the actual outlays for fiscal 1982. In the proposals we see an 8.0 percent increase ($12.7 billion) in

Table 4   RECENT FEDERAL OUTLAYS
           ($ Billion)[a]

	FY 1981	FY 1982 Reagan proposals	FY 1982 outlays
Education, training, and social services	31.8	23.3	23.8
Health	74.6	66.1	65.7
National defense	159.2	170.0	166.4

[a]The 1982 figures were reduced by 9 percent to approximate the effects of inflation. Outlays are as reported for the first 8 months of the fiscal year, plus 50 percent.

Sources: Clark (1981), p. 445; Executive Office of the President, O.M.B. (1981), pp. 32 ff., and *Treasury Bulletin,* July 1982, p. 9.

military spending, and decreases in education and health of 26.1 and 10.5 respectively. In the outlays the amounts are a 4.5 percent ($7.2 billion) increase for the military, and cuts of 25.2 and 11.9 percent for education and health.[9] None of the other variables in our model can account for these shifts. There is no shooting war, and the other variables are neither very volatile nor, in our equations, very powerful anyway. Most important, the data show that it is not merely the presence of a Republican in the White House which made the difference; the *Reagan* presidency *is* different.

NOTES

1. In his time-series analysis Pryor (1968, pp. 122–125) found a substitution effect between military spending and investment for only a few western industrial countries, but the time span was short (1950–62), the military levels low in the majority of countries, and the variation in military spending often not great enough to force significant trade-offs.
2. The classifications are the standard ones reported in the *Statistical Abstract of the U.S.* Military does not include veterans' benefits. Education includes education, employment training, social services and research, and general education aid. Health includes health care services, research, education and training of health care workforce, and consumer and occupational health and safety.
3. Earlier analyses have indicated that the coefficients usually are not significantly different in wartime from those in peacetime (Russett 1971, pp. 44–46; Lee 1972, p. 68), except when the subsamples used are so small as to be virtually meaningless (Hollenhorst and Ault 1971).
4. Because productivity and capacity data were available only for the post-World War II years, and when used they proved not significant and did not affect the coefficients of interest, in fact I do not usually report equations using them.
5. Alternative demand measures, such as the proportion of the population under 18, were sometimes substituted but with no notable effect on the other variables. The total population in the age group appears to capture our theoretical concept most precisely. Obviously there is substantial collinearity between school enrollment and population under 18, as there was between our measures of capacity/productivity. If we were seeking an elegant model specification of the cases of educational spending, this would be cause for concern. But since the purpose here is rather to be sure that important control variables (correlated in the equation with both military spending and the error term) are not omitted, and thus that the coefficient military spending is consistent and unbiased, it is better to include them.
6. Autocorrelation does not appear to be a serious problem with the majority of these equations, as indicated by the Durbin-Watson statistics for them. Where it is a problem, its effects are to exaggerate the apparent significance of the coefficients. Since we did not find many high coefficients for the variables that interested us, that is hardly a problem, and thus there is no cause to move to more sophisticated statistical analysis than OLS. Similarly, the relatively low power of the equations and the interesting variables suggests it would not yet

be profitable to move to a complex system of simultaneous equations, despite the undoubted interdependence of these variables.

7. The language of these sentences, appropriate to the 1980s, implies a concern only with trade-offs that may occur when military spending rises, not with the possible beneficiaries when spending decreases. In fact, as noted in Table 1, trade-offs actually occurred in only 14 or 15 of the 39 years under study and usually occurred when military spending went down. We should not assume one is merely the opposite of the other. Experience with reductions in military spending is relatively limited, occurring in just 16 of the 39 years in our sample. Table 1 suggests there is some trade-off in these years, and in principle we might analyze years with military upswings in separate equations from those with downswings. However, the samples—especially for years with military downswings—would be very small for adequate multivariate analysis, and the technical problems of analyzing yearly data for years that were often not adjacent would be formidable.

8. For a good analytical discussion on this theme see Ravenal (1978), ch. 7.

9. These changes are adjusted to be in constant dollars to indicate the real trade-offs accurately.

REFERENCES

Baran, P. A., and Sweezy, P. M. 1968. *Monopoly Capital: An Essay on the American Economy and Social Order.* Harmondsworth: Pelican.

Benoit, E. 1973. *Defense and Economic Growth in Developing Countries.* Lexington, Mass.: D.C. Heath.

Burns, A. F. 1971. The Defense Sector and the American Economy. In *The War Economy of the United States,* ed. Seymour Melman. New York: St. Martin's Press.

Caputo, D. 1975. New Perspectives on the Public Policy Implications of Defense and Welfare Expenditures in Four Modern Democracies, 1950–1970. *Policy Sciences* 6:423–446.

Clark, T. 1981. The Reagan Budget Round Two, *National Journal* March 14:445–448.

Economic Report of the President. 1981. Washington: U.S. Government Printing Office.

Executive Office of the President, O.M.B. 1981. *Special Analyses: Budget of the United States Government,* Fiscal Year 1982. Washington: U.S. Government Printing Office.

Hollenhorst, J., and Ault, G. 1971. An Alternative Answer to Who Pays for Defense. *American Political Science Review* 3: 760–763.

Kennedy, G. 1974. *The Military in the Third World.* London: Duckworth.

Lee, J. R. L. 1972. Changing National Priorities of the United States. In *Military Force and American Society,* ed. B. Russett and A. Stepan. New York: Harper and Row.

Melman, S. 1974. *The Permanent War Economy: American Capitalism in Decline.* New York: Simon and Schuster.

The New York Times. 1974. Military Budget Spurs Economy. January 27.

Nincic, M., and Cusack, T. 1979. The Political Economy of U.S. Military Spending. *Journal of Peace Research* 16:101–115.

Nixon, R. M. 1962. *Six Crises.* New York: Doubleday.

Peacock, A. T., and Wiseman, J. 1961. *The Growth of Public Expenditures in the United Kingdom,* Princeton, N.J.: Princeton University Press.

Peroff, K., and Podolak-Warren, M. 1979. Does Spending on Defense Cut Spending on Health? *British Journal of Political Science* 9:21–39.

Pryor, F. L. 1968. *Public Expenditures in Communist and Capitalist Nations.* Homewood, Ill.: Irwin.

Ravenal, E. C. 1978. *Never Again: Learning From America's Foreign Policy Failures.* Philadelphia: Temple University Press.

Russett, B. 1969. Who Pays for Defense? *American Political Science Review* 63: 412–426.

——1970. *What Price Vigilance? The Burdens of National Defense.* New Haven, Conn.: Yale University Press.

——1971. Some Decisions in the Regression Analysis of Time-Series Data. In *Mathematical Applications in Political Science,* V, ed. J. Herndon and J. Bernd. Charlottesville: University of Virginia Press.

Russett, B., and DeLuca, D. R. 1981. "Don't Tread on Me": American Opinion and Foreign Policy in the Eighties. *Political Science Quarterly* 96:381–400.

Smith, D., and Smith, R. 1980. *Military Expenditure, Resources and Development.* London: Birkbeck College Discussion Paper No. 87.

Smith, R. P. 1977. Military Expenditures and Capitalism, *Cambridge Journal of Economics* 1:61–76.

Stein, A. A. 1980. *The Nation at War.* Baltimore: Johns Hopkins University Press.

Szymanski, A. 1973. Military Spending and Economic Stagnation. *American Journal of Sociology* 79:1–14.

Thurow, L. 1981. How to Wreck the Economy. *New York Review of Books,* May 14.

U.S. Bureau of the Census, 1975. *Historical Statistics of the United States: Colonial Times to 1970.* Washington: U.S. Government Printing Office.

——(various years). *Statistical Abstract of the United States.* Washington: U.S. Government Printing Office.

Wilensky, H. 1965. *The Welfare State and Equality.* Berkeley and Los Angeles: University of California Press.

Limits of Military Power
Economic and Other

Seymour Melman

After 1945, a dream that was comforting to the nationalist temper suffused American life. The core components of this political-economic dream were three linked ideas: that the United States is endowed with indefinitely large resources; that this country can produce guns and butter on a sustained basis; and that thereby the United States could field the military power required to impose the political will of the U.S. government wherever and whenever desired.

This dream was supported by reassurances from American economists across the spectrum from right to left. *U.S. News and World Report* wrote in 1950, "Business won't go to pot so long as war is a threat; so long as every alarm can step up spending, lending for defense at home and aid abroad; cold war is almost a guarantee against a bad depression."[1] In the liberal center, Jerome Wiesner, a science adviser to Presidents Kennedy and Johnson, judged that "the armaments industry has provided a sort of automatic stabilizer for the whole economy."[2] And on the left, Herbert Gintis, professor of economics and a contributor to the *Review of Radical Political Economics,* noted in an evaluation of American Keynesianism, "the military industrial complex has eliminated the specter of secular stagnation."[3] A consensus of this breadth and depth is rather unusual. What are the theoretical foundations of this consensus? And second, what has been the reality against the implied prospect coming from the consensus?

The theoretical underpinnings of these reassurances include conventional wisdom about an "economic good" and the United States as a post-industrial society. An economic good is usually defined by the presence of a price, and so independently of function, purpose, or effect. Thus the presence of money values defines an economic good, and thereby the

Seymour Melman, "Limits of Military Power," *International Security,* Vol. 11, No. 1 (Summer 1986), pp. 72–86. Reprinted with permission of Seymour Melman.

well-being of an economy, as its growth is defined by the sum of money-valued goods and services.There are possible alternative criteria since, after all, that conception of an economic good comes neither on tablets from Sinai nor sprung from the earth. The price-based conception of an economic good is entirely man-made and is indeed quite serviceable, if one is primarily interested in the problems of money exchange, of money flow, of income distribution and the variability thereof.

However, if one is interested in gauging the ability of a community to produce the goods and services that constitute consumption, ordinarily understood, then an economic good must be seen in a different light. Serviceability for consumption and for further production are then the criteria of choice. The meaning of consumption is well defined by the list of goods and services used by the Bureau of Labor Statistics for calculating the consumer price index. It is the price of everything you buy from cradle to grave that constitutes the level of living. This differentiation has important bearing on the appreciation of military economy.

Whatever else you can do with a nuclear-powered submarine, an undisputed technological masterwork, you cannot eat it, wear it, live in it, or ride in it, and there is nothing you can produce with it. I underscore that the choice in the appreciation of what is an economic good derives from the problems one wishes to address, and lies at the core of what it is you choose to observe and try to measure. The choice of problems does not derive from some natural or divine phenomenon.

I am interested in this essay in the capacity of an economy to provide a level of living and to produce means of production for that purpose.

There is a second underpinning of the conventional wisdom on military economy. I judge it axiomatic that a community must produce in order to live. There is no theory or body of experience from which to infer that the main goods useful for consumption or further production will be provided to any community from the outside over an indefinite period. But there is an alternative orientation: that making money is what counts, not making goods. In fact, that idea is at the core of an institution that has grown massively in importance in American society—the schools of business from coast to coast. In turn, that orientation is strongly supported by theories about the United States as a post-industrial society. That brave prospect was formulated in the late 1950s and the essential point was the following. The production of work-a-day goods can be left to less advanced societies. The U.S. will focus on the knowledge industry, high-tech products, and management skills. And the U.S. will produce such goods and high-tech knowledge and will trade those, together with managerial and financial skills and services, for ordinary things like clothing, shoes, and furniture and for low-technology devices.

That perspective has collided with reality. By 1979, a committee of Congress reported that the ten most important imports by value—to Japan from the United States—were soybeans, corn, saw logs, coking coal, wheat, cotton, turbo jet airplanes (the only manufactured item), rawhide and skins of bovine animals, waste, and scrap metal for smelting (other than alloy steel). Meanwhile, the *post-industrial society* was importing from Japan, again by value: passenger cars, iron and steel plates, radio receivers, motorcycles, audio and video tape players and recorders, iron and steel pipes, still cameras and parts, nails, other fasteners, TV receivers, office machines, metal-cutting machine tools, calculating machines, trucks, microphones, speakers, iron and steel angles. (By 1983 Japan supplied somewhat more than half of the computer-controlled machine tools bought in the U.S.) To all of this a committee of Congress then observed: "A comparison of our leading exports to Japan versus our imports from her is devastating. The data seem to indicate that, aircraft excluded, we are a developing nation supplying a more advanced nation. We are Japan's plantation, haulers of wood and growers of crops in exchange for high technology value-added products."[4]

At the same time that these widely held perspectives were taking root, there was a rising malaise in the U.S. about military power. There was a growing appreciation that military power is not without limits. It is not possible to kill a person more than once. So piling up what is called overkill is not sensible on military grounds, though quite serviceable for safeguarding managerial power and profits. Second, it is appreciated that guerrilla forces cannot be overcome by superior equipment and numbers if the guerrillas are ready to die, if they have popular support, and if the enemy cannot differentiate them from ordinary people. Hence the U.S. defeat in Vietnam. Third, these limits cannot be overcome or bypassed by suboptimization, by a process of improving weaponry and military institutions, component by component. And fourth, we endured in October 1962 a near miss in nuclear war.

Was the Cuban missile crisis triggered by a set of U.S. military successes: outproducing the Soviets in aircraft; outproducing them in missiles; outproducing them in warheads; outmaneuvering them decisively in military intelligence, as the diary of Colonel Penkofsky testifies? Were the Soviets forced into a position (which they recognized a few months before October 1962) as leaving them without a nuclear deterrent capability, vulnerable to a U.S. first strike, because of the overwhelming advantage of the U.S. in warheads, delivery systems, and military intelligence? Hence, was the effort to put missiles in Cuba a desperate last-ditch effort to acquire a credible nuclear deterrent capability while the U.S. dominated the scene? There were 1,200 intercontinental bombers on the U.S. side, none on the Soviet side; more than 100 ICBMs on the U.S. side, 4 to 6 on the Soviet side. But discussion of such issues has not been at the center of attention in the public press or in American universities. Indeed, the question—why did the Soviets make that desperate move in Cuba—is addressed indecisively in the considerable literature that has been produced on the Cuban missile crisis. Obviously, if the queries that I put have substance, that yields an embarrassment for the idea of military power without limits. In the nuclear age, does military success yield failure? That is an interesting question and deserves to be examined.

While military force acquired limits of these sorts in conventional understanding, military economy was seen as fitting very nicely with other parts of conventional wisdom. At the same time, however, the effects of military economy were not anticipated as our economists celebrated economic growth as measured by the GNP. What happened with respect to military economy? First, what developed at the level of the firms or what the economists call the microeconomy? Second, what were the associated and consequent developments for the system as a whole, at the macro level?

A network of enterprises was brought into being of unprecedented quality. They no longer minimized production cost to maximize profit. They maximized cost, paralleling that with maximization of subsidy from the federal government. So we have the remarkable evidence of a 12-cent hexagon wrench, measuring about 4 inches in length, being modified with a hole drilled on one end to which a wooden handle is to be fastened; a name is to be engraved; a serial number is to be engraved; and a set-screw is to be provided so the handle will stay in place. For doing the research, development, and engineering design and to cover the manufacturing and administrative overheads, in addition to the cost of buying the hex-wrench, a firm billed the Air Force $9,609 per unit.

Furthermore, this did not represent greed or infamy, or even accounting manipulation. It was all accomplished by following the ordinary rules and regulations of the Department of Defense. All that appeared in a Hearing of a Committee on Governmental Affairs of the U.S. Senate on November 2, 1983. There is a B-1 bomber, the first four copies of which had a price that exceeded its equivalent weight in gold.[5]

But the existence of an economy that ordinarily operates in this fashion has not been known to students in our schools, or to the general public. Economics courses in high school and college use textbooks that do not include instruction on the existence of an economy with such characteristics.

The network of firms operating in this fashion was reorganized during the Kennedy Administration when Robert McNamara was in charge of the Pentagon. McNamara did what is completely understandable: he installed in the Department of Defense the system of central office organization and control that he had completed installing in the Ford Motor Company. That included a central administrative office, the type of head office that is at the peak of General Electric, General Motors, Westinghouse, Du Pont, and other large multidivision, multiplant firms. The central office formulates policy, presents policy to managers of subordinate units, and polices their compliance with policy. When appropriately set up, with all accompanying detail, it is possible for one central office, in the case of the Pentagon, to dominate policy affairs and police compliance in 37,000 prime contracting firms. Those firms relate to that central office as the Chevrolet division relates to the central office of General Motors. In the case of the Pentagon, this is done with a further invention: a pyramid of subcentral offices to cover the fourteen regions of the country, and there are even suboffices in certain of the very important districts.

A further feature of this microeconomy is the availability of finance capital. From 1951 to the present day, the yearly budget of the Department of Defense has exceeded the net profits of all U.S. corporations. No other single management commands a finance capital fund of this size.

But consider capital now, not in the financial sense, but in the sense of production resources. In an ordinary industrial enterprise, we understand capital to be composed of fixed and working capital. The fixed capital is the money-valued land, buildings, and machinery, and the working capital is the money-value assigned to all the other resources required to set the enterprise in productive motion. A modern military budget is a capital fund. When it is used, it sets in motion precisely those classes of resources. The magnitude of those capital resources is best understood when we view the military budget as a capital fund in relation to civilian capital.

A civilian capital category recognized in the national income accounts is the Gross Domestic Fixed Capital Formation, which counts the money value of new civilian capital items put in place in a given year. Conceptually, then, the military budget is a measure of fixed and working capital, which can be inputs for producing capital outputs. (This contrasts with the conventional measure of military budget as a percent of the GNP, which is now about 6.5 percent. Americans have been trained not to concern themselves about such a small slice of the GNP pie.)

Comparative international data are available for 1979, as collected and reported in United Nations statistical volumes. (I gave details on that in my last book, *Profits Without Production.* [6]) In the U.S., for every $100 of new civilian capital formation in 1979, the military were given $33 in their budget. (This is a ratio of 33 to every 100, not 33 out of 100.) In the United Kingdom that ratio was 32, in France 26, in West Germany 20, in Japan 3.7. The contrast of both Japan and Germany with the U.S. is dramatic and goes far to explain the modernity of their industrial systems and the quality of their products as against the deterioration of civilian plant and equipment in the U.S.

Of course we are interested in the Soviet Union, but no data of comparable categories are recorded. I prepared an estimate: in the USSR the 1979 military to civilian capital ratio was 66, which is certainly a large figure, signaling industrial distress. I have responded to the voiced dismay of Soviet colleagues by saying I will accept a corrected figure based on official data.

There is more. For what is important for us now is to understand not only how we got to where we are, but what the future portends in terms of present patterns already in motion.

There is a further characteristic of the military microeconomy: the lavish use of research and development resources and of engineering and scientific talent. By 1977 for every 10,000 persons in the labor force, Japan had 50 engineers and scientists engaged in civilian work. In Germany, it was 40 engineers and scientists in civilian work per 10,000 of the labor force, and in the U.S. it was 38. A third to a half of the greater number of engineers and scientists in the U.S. were working for the military.

The consequences of all this for the costs of the means of production have been dramatic. In an early work on industrial productivity,[7] I defined the regular pattern by which the mechanization of work in the U.S. was spurred by the ordinary pattern of production cost-minimizing. Increases in the wages of industrial labor were largely offset by internal enterprise economies. Thereby, the products of industry rose in price to a lesser degree than the wages of labor. Thus the wages of industrial labor in the United States from 1939 to 1947 rose 95 percent while the prices of machine tools increased 39 percent. That was a powerful incentive for further mechanization of industrial work. Machine tools are the master tools of modern industry. They are the lathes, drills, milling machines, and the like, which are used in every industrial system and which have the unique quality of being usable to replicate their own shape. Therefore, we should give particular attention to the percent changes of 1971–1978 in the average hourly earnings of industrial workers as compared to the percent change in the prices of machine tools.

In Japan, industrial wages increased 177 percent in that period, largely offset by enterprise economies and efficiencies, so that prices of machine tools rose 51 percent, a clear reflection of pervasive production cost-minimizing. This was a persuasive invitation to buy and use new productive equipment, and that is exactly what happened. That pattern was characteristic of industry in the United States before 1965. In West Germany, wages rose 72 percent, while machine tool prices rose 59 percent, a smaller differential, but still in the classic direction, denoting a cost-minimizing effort. But in the U.S. where wages also rose 72 percent, there was an 85 percent increase in the prices of machine tools, denoting a cost-maximizing economy. Following the presentation of these data in *Profits Without Production* and their link to military economy, I wrote: "These data mark the end of a way of industrial life in the U.S."[8] The "end" was the termination of production cost-minimizing as a pervasive pattern in U.S. industry. The industrial productivity engine broke down.

The consequences were dramatic and perfectly sensible. U.S. firms proceeded to buy fewer machine tools, kept the old ones, and patched them up. By 1978, U.S. industry had the oldest stock of metalworking machinery of any industrialized country.

Consider the meaning of this development in the much-discussed U.S. automobile industry and its newly acquired inability to produce competitively vs. Japan and Germany. A large periodical and monographic literature has featured discussions on the high wages of U.S. labor. Never once in those learned discussions was the reader informed that while 69 percent of machine tools used in U.S. industry in 1978 were 10 years old and older, in the auto industry 76 percent were of that vintage. In other words, by

1978 three-fourths of the production equipment in the U.S. auto industry was fully depreciated junk. Hence, on that count alone, there should be no surprise at the appearance of a cost disadvantage.

Such conditions are characteristic accompaniments of a major military economy independently of variation in social structure, language, history, culture, or geography. In *Pravda* on July 14, 1984, an article by academician Aganbegyan noted that in the Soviet Union the average rate of replacement of industrial machinery and equipment has been 3 percent per year, a disastrously slow rate.[9] That average must include the priority position that is accorded to military-related industry, as well as the lesser priorities assigned to civilian industrial establishments. Even if one makes allowance for the enlargement of the total stock of equipment by net additions to industrial plant, a 3 percent replacement rate denotes an aging stock and hence diminishing rate of productivity improvement. That is precisely what has taken place, by all reports, in the Soviet economy.

If this can be the consequence for the largest industrial nations in the world, what can you expect as the effect of military economies on lesser countries, endowed with fewer resources, with less accumulation of capital goods, or striving to carry out elemental economic development?

All this is amplified by the scale of the military economy. In the U.S., there are 37,000 prime contractor firms, over 100,000 subcontractors, 3 million persons employed in industry and the allied laboratories, 1 million direct civilian employees of the Department of Defense, and 2 million in the uniformed armed forces. The largest centrally administered management office in the world controls the largest aggregation of industrial facilities under one management, controls the largest labor force under one management, and controls the largest grouping of engineers and scientists under one management.

On a macro level, the consequences of these developments are somber. From 1960 to 1983, the manufacturing industries of the United States show the lowest average annual rate of increase in productivity of any industrialized country in the world. The relation between militarization and economic growth, however measured, was defined in a statistical study by Albert Szymanski that appeared in the *American Journal of Sociology.*[10] With data from all the major industrial countries in the world, it emerged that there was negative correlation between the intensity of military economy and various parameters of economic growth. There was positive correlation between military expenditure and immediate effect on employment. This is a perfectly plausible set of results in light of the known micro features of a military economy.

The consequences for the U.S. industrial system as a whole have been a new set of problems never recognized before as part of American economy and society. During the Great Depression, the worst of them all, it was understood that the economic problem was, at its core, a problem of market demand for consumer goods, for capital goods. The problem was:

how do you get market demand going? Keynes and those who interpreted his theory and proposed government policy addressed themselves to that problem. At no time during the Great Depression was there a whisper that the competence of the U.S. industrial system for production might be defective. There were no grounds for such discussion.

We are now in a completely different scene. The central problem of American industrial economy is not market demand. The central problem is the inability to produce competently, and that is revealed by the degree to which U.S. markets are being supplied by production taking place outside the United States. The following are some data on the percentage of U.S. consumption that was served by production abroad, 1979–80: automobiles, 27 percent; machine tools, 25 percent (it is now up to 42 percent, and for computer-controlled machine tools, half and more); steel mill products, 15 percent; black and white TV sets, 87 percent; hand calculators, 47 percent; microwave ranges and ovens, 22 percent; integrated microcircuits, 34 percent; X-ray and other irradiation equipment, 24 percent; motion picture cameras, 74 percent; sewing machines, 51 percent (it is now beyond that, because the last factory producing household sewing machines in New Jersey has been closed); office-type recorders and dictation machines, 100 percent (you cannot buy one made in the U.S.A. at any price); radios, 100 percent; bicycles, 22 percent; apparel, 20 percent (much higher by 1985).[11]

Every one of these statistics denotes a parallel reduction in U.S. employment in the industries indicated. But in much of conventional wisdom, we are told that high-tech will save us. I therefore call your attention to the March 11, 1985 issue of *Business Week* announcing "America's High-Tech Crisis." The crisis is in two parts: first, the firms of Silicon Valley find themselves pressed to the wall, unable to compete. Why they are not able to compete has two roots. The first lies in the fact that they attempted to operate without long-term investing and with only short-term expenditure. Instead of doing what their Japanese counterparts did, which was to design and build new sets of production equipment that produce standardized products reliably and at high quality, the American firms chose to set up shacks abroad in low-labor-cost areas and hire the locals to do manual manipulation that resulted in products that, finally, cost more than those produced by mechanized means and that also had dramatically higher failure rates than the chips produced by machine methods.

A second type of crisis is reflected here. Go to the back of the boxes of your IBM PC and here is what you will find: the cathode ray tube box comes from Korea or Taiwan. The keyboard is made in Japan. In the lower box, the floppy disk drives are made in Singapore (they will soon be made in Hong Kong), the semiconductors are made in Japan, and the power supply is made in Japan. The printer too is from Japan. The case and final assembly—and of course the billing—come from the U.S.A. Out of $860 manufacturing costs, $625 represented work done overseas.

This is a strategy that is just splendid for the finances of IBM, but terrible for the young people in Poughkeepsie and other IBM locations, because there is not much prospect for productive livelihood for them in this industrial style. IBM has announced plans for setting up a new factory to make the PC—in Mexico.

Once upon a time, before 1965, it was altogether ordinary for American manufacturing firms to pay the highest wage in the world. It was also ordinary that they tried (and usually succeeded) to offset that wage by mechanization of work and competent organization of work. This used to be called "Yankee Know How." And the whole thing went to smash. By 1980 the U.S. ranked 8th among countries of the world with respect to average industrial wages and was obviously no longer endowed with a microeconomy oriented to production cost-minimizing by offsetting increases in wages and other costs.

This pattern is now recognized even by the American Electronics Association—a senior trade association of the industry—which set forth a position paper, "Strategies for Innovation: High-Technology Industries and International Competitiveness."[12] They wrote: "We cannot allocate 70 percent of federally funded R&D to defense and severely limit U.S. high-technology exports even in West-West trade without paying a very significant price in terms of competitive position. We cannot siphon off a disproportionate share of our skills and technical resources to military application and still stay ahead of Japan in commercial markets."

This noncompetitiveness across the industrial spectrum has generated new standards of acceptable unemployment. That is to say, 4 percent unemployment was once acceptable. But we are experiencing a rising level of unemployment, in consequence of the durable (structural) unemployment induced by the avalanche of factory closings. So we now have more than 7 percent unemployed, in excess of 8 ½ million officially registered. At least another million and a half are not recognized in the formal categories (no longer registering), adding up to 10 million unemployed.

A war economy is also an inflation machine. The combination of unemployment on a large scale and inflation is given the name *stagflation.* But inflation is of two sorts. There is the old domestic price inflation that prevailed from 1965 to 1980, finally reaching double digit levels. It is said to be an achievement of the present administration that from 1980 on that kind of price inflation was diminished, until it averaged about 4 percent by 1985.

Does that mean that inflation was stopped? It was not. It was relocated in a way that is important for understanding the present condition of the U.S. economy and the consequences of a permanent war economy.

The state managers of the U.S., confronted with problems of paying for their military budgets ($2,001 billion 1945–1980; $2,089 billion 1981–1988), have found it necessary (or preferable) to borrow. As they borrowed, dominating the money markets and interest-rate setting, persons abroad found it inviting to lend to the U.S. Treasury. But they first had to buy dollars with their own currency. Under the Reagan Administration, the annual increases in holdings of federal debt securities by foreigners moved up from $6.9 billion (1980–1981) to $26.6 billion (1983–1984). The classic pattern of supply in relation to demand went into operation. The price of the local currency relative to the dollar fell, and the price of the dollar rose. From 1980 to 1985, there was a 75 percent increase in the price of the dollar compared with 15 other currencies. In order to hold their relative price position in the U.S. market, American producers had to reduce their costs and prices by about 75 percent. But there is no set of engineering and management devices for such cost/price reduction. Therefore U.S. manufacturing, agricultural, and extractive enterprises were subjected to drastic, and often fatal, competitive pressures from foreign firms—in American domestic as well as foreign markets.

The currency is the master commodity of an economy. The U.S. currency is being utilized as an administrative device for a particular mode of policy-handling by the government of the United States. Alternatively, a government might choose policies to stabilize, to safeguard the currency as a crucial instrumentality for economic exchange, both domestic and external. That is not the U.S. government's policy. The currency is being used as a manipulative commodity.

The consequence of the dollar price increase is more powerful than the older-fashioned domestic price increase, because a 75 percent increase in the price of the U.S. dollar meant that all commodities valued in dollar terms reflected that kind of relative price change with other currencies. Imports increased sharply. That is not a durable condition. There is no theory or body of experience from which to expect that foreigners will hold more and more dollars, indefinitely, as if they were gold bricks. When the price of the dollar declines, as it must, then the prices of imported goods will rise accordingly.

The designation of the inflated price of the dollar as *strong* is comparable to a physician announcing that the patient with a body temperature of 106° has a strong fever. The designation *strong dollar* does, however, shield the populace from unhappy speculations about what the state managers are doing to the U.S. means of exchange.

Observing the ways by which inflation mechanisms can be moved about, I judge that stagflation is a durable feature of a permanent military economy.

In the twelfth chapter of *Profits Without Production,* I detailed the catastrophic erosion of competence in the infrastructure as a production support system of the United States. I recorded that *U.S. News and World Report* had judged in 1982 that, with an outlay of $2,500 billion, it should be possible to repair the worst of the deterioration. What is the prospect for being able to do that repair (with planned military budgets of $2,089 billion 1981–1988), let alone address the renewal of industrial facilities?

For that we have to understand the social costs of the military economy. There are at least the following five components:

1) The money value of the budgets as voted year to year,

2) The value of the economically useful goods whose production is forgone because of the use of these resources for the military purpose.

3) When capital is used for making new means of production, there is characteristically modification and improvement in the means of production. That yields what economists call a marginal or incremental productivity of capital effect. But that marginal productivity of capital effect is lost as capital-type resources are used for military purposes. For no production-capable entity emerges from a military-producing factory. Therefore, there is a permanent loss to the economy of that productiveness.

4) New knowledge about how to carry on production for life-serving purposes is forgone because it has not been researched. If a third to half of our R&D engineers and scientists are functioning on behalf of the military, then there cannot be the equivalent activity on behalf of new production technology for civilian purposes.

5) Finally, as a consequence of the long operation of the military economy, we are left with a large engineering and scientific population with a trained incapacity for civilian work. The methods that are required for a cost-maximizing and a subsidy-maximizing economy are economically lethal if applied to a firm that must function in a civilian market.

The military budgets already expended and planned after 1980 checkmate the possible renewal of civilian economy, both in industrial plants and infrastructure.

Nevertheless, something has been achieved. The United States government has established an array of war-making institutions in the hands of state and private managers with unmatched capital resources, and a normal managerial imperative to maintain and to enlarge their decision power. These institutions, in their normal operation, may therefore be expected to strive to maintain and to enlarge the resources at their disposal, quite apart from the military limits of military power. Thus, apart from President Reagan and his Secretary of Defense, no one has proposed that the "Star Wars," or Strategic Defense Initiative, can really produce a perfect shield against nuclear warheads: that idea is absurd. Nuclear warheads can be delivered in the back of a truck, in a packing case, in a suitcase, and we now know that the U.S. armed forces possess a 58-pound nuclear *backpack* competent to release destructive power of up to 300 tons of TNT equivalent. The idea that nuclear warheads in desperate hands can only be delivered at 6,000 miles an hour is preposterous. Nuclear devices can be put in place by slow motion.

We have bred a military form of state capitalism in the United States. Even under *best-case* conditions of no major war, all of this has the consequence of limiting resources for the rest of the economy as the military part is granted continuous first call on the nation's capital resources. There is no longer a *long-term* that is separable from the array of *short-term* capital grants, for the long term is now. Thus, the 1986 budget of the federal government moves $32 billion of expenditures from civilian items to military items. It is infeasible, for proximate financial and other reasons, to pretend that a guns-butter trade-off can be deferred to a timeless long term.

In a series of trade-off analyses, I found that 450 meals for Grand Central homeless men and women cost $435. That is equal to the cost of one 155 mm high explosive shell. The proposed 1986 cuts in guaranteed student loans and campus-based student financial aid, $2.3 billion, equals the 1986 M1 Abrams tank budget. The administration-proposed 1986 cuts in veterans medical care and housing, $336 million, is the price of 236 Phoenix air-to-air missiles. The cost of one F-16 antenna pulley-puller tool, one antenna clamp alignment tool, one antenna puller height gauge, and one antenna hexagon wrench equals $42,087, the estimated cost of reconditioning a moderate-income, 5-room apartment.[13] By means of such trade-offs, increased hunger and homelessness have been made federal policy. Instead of enjoying guns and butter, we are suffering a national blight of street begging, homelessness, and hunger, unseen since the Great Depression.

American industries are crumbling and factories are closing like a row of tumbling dominoes. During the spring 1985 semester, I took a class to visit some machine tool factories in Connecticut. Where 10,000 people once worked, there were 150. Where 2,000 once worked, there were 125. In one firm, more than half the goods being sold are made in Japan, including the proud label on the front of the machine—the U.S. firm's name. In order to plan ahead, one management was attempting to negotiate some production of machine tools in China. In other words, to use the Chinese wage rate to undercut the Japanese wage.

For more than a century, from 1865 to 1975, it was possible, by means of internal efficiencies, to offset the American wage. There are no internal enterprise efficiencies to offset the new, inflated price of the dollar, grown 75 percent in four years. Cost-minimizing with a target of 75 percent reduction is simply out of reach. The state management has set in motion a process that is highly destructive to U.S. industrial competence.

If we pay close attention to the ratio of military to civilian use of capital, then—extrapolating the trends of the last years—by 1988 that ratio for the United States will be about 87 to 100. In the course of attaining that level, there will be a military-use concentration of capital so great that it will become physically infeasible to carry out any serious reconstruction of U.S. industry and infrastructure.

In all this, I am not implying that military economy is the sole causal factor. There has been a major alteration in civilian industrial management, correlating with the characteristics of military economy: great skill in making money, less attention to making goods. But the crucial point that emerges from this analysis is that no reindustrialization of the United States is feasible without a major conversion of the resources now being used up in military economy to civilian use. That defines the importance that I attach to a proposed law, H.R. 229 (introduced by Congressman Ted Weiss, Democrat of New York), comprising a detailed plan for how to carry out advance planning for moving from military to civilian economy. In 1974, I wrote in the preface to *The Permanent War Economy:*

> Traditional economic competence of every sort is being eroded by the state capitalist directorate that elevates inefficiency to a national purpose, that disables the market system, that destroys the value of the currency, and that diminishes the decision power of all institutions other than its own. Industrial productivity, the foundation of every nation's economic growth, is being eroded by the relentlessly predatory effects of military economy.[14]

That was the process ten years ago. The same mechanisms are operative in 1985. The economic factor is central to a new policy orientation that would confront the limits of military power and initiate a process of reversing the arms race and converting from military to civilian economy as the cutting edge of that process.

NOTES

1. *U.S. News and World Report,* May 19, 1950.
2. *U.S. News and World Report,* February 3, 1964.
3. H. Gintis, "American Keynesianism and the War Machine," in D. Mermelstein, *Economics—Mainstream Readings and Radical Critiques* (New York: Random House, 1970), p. 233.
4. U.S. Congress, House, Subcommittee on Trade of the Committee on Ways and Means, *United States-Japan Trade Report,* September 5, 1980, p. 5.
5. Based upon data provided by Rockwell International and the U.S. Air Force, including the estimated weight of the aircraft, unfueled, and full program costs of the B-1 program up to the time of cancellation by President Carter.
6. United Nations, *Yearbook of National Accounts Statistics, 1979.* Also the 1980 and 1981 volumes. U.S. estimate for 1988 in Seymour Melman, *Profits Without Production* (New York: Alfred A. Knopf, 1983), p. 263.
7. Seymour Melman, *Dynamic Factors in Industrial Productivity* (Oxford: Basil Blackwell; New York: John Wiley, 1956).
8. Melman, *Profits Without Production,* p. 174.
9. A. Aganbegyan, "Routes of Technical Progress: Spread Our Wings," *Pravda,* July 14, 1984.
10. A. Szymanski, "Military Spending and Economic Stagnation," *American Journal of Sociology,* July 1971; and comments July 1974.
11. Melman, *Profits Without Production,* p. 200.
12. American Electronics Association, "Strategies for Innovation, High Technology Industries, and International Competitiveness," a position paper, 1984.
13. Seymour Melman, "The Butter That's Traded Off for Guns" (Op-Ed), *The New York Times,* April 22, 1985.
14. Seymour Melman, *The Permanent War Economy* (New York: Simon and Schuster, 1974; rev. ed., 1985).

Military-Industrial Rivalry in the Global Political Economy

Stephen Gill
David Law

In this reading we examine the logic of military-industrial rivalry and the way it affects state policies and arms production. In particular, we analyze the economic, political, and social forces making for the rise of, and limits to, growing military expenditure and the spread of military-industrial complexes. The purpose of this is to begin to suggest answers to two related questions. The first is how far, and why, are arms production and military spending a systematic feature of the global political economy? The second is, what are the relationships between these systemic features and the propensity to war and peace in the post-war world?

"CATCH-UP LOGIC" AND REALIST-MERCANTILISM

As has been noted, the oldest political economy approach, realist-mercantilism, has long paid particular attention to the relationship between economic and military strength. . . . In this section we focus on the implications of this perspective.

Some of the ideas of early Mercantilists (for example the concept of inter-state rivalry) have been taken up by modern Mercantilists such as Gautam Sen.[1] Sen has stressed how concern with national security has made industrialization as much a military as an economic imperative. Strategic industries have been central to the industrial strategies and

Stephen Gill and David Law, "Military-Industrial Rivalry in the Global Political Economy," in Gill and Law, *The Global Political Economy: Perspectives, Problems, and Policies,* Baltimore, MD: Johns Hopkins University Press, 1988.

import-substitution programs of many countries. Subsidies and trade barriers have been justified on the grounds of defense requirements. Mercantilist policies are needed to *catch up* with other states: otherwise national independence may be compromised or even lost. Further, as Theda Skocpol has argued, national cohesion and political stability may break down as a state fails to *catch up*, or *keep up* with its powerful neighbors and rivals. Social revolution is made either more likely, or at least more possible. For example, Japan and Germany were able to *catch up* in the late-nineteenth and early-twentieth centuries, whereas Manchu China and Romanov Russia were not. Conservative reforms brought rapid industrialization in the former two countries, whereas in the latter two, the pace of industrialization was slower, and the state was unable to cope with external challenges. As a result social revolution occurred, sweeping away the old order.[2] Later, the Bolsheviks were able to mobilize and industrialize the U.S.S.R., and to build a large military apparatus whereas little industrialization took place in China, leaving the country vulnerable to further invasion and occupation by Japan in the 1930s. Only with the coming to power of the communists in 1949 was an effective central state created, in contrast with nationalist China, enabling sufficient internal and external autonomy to promote industrialization.

This *catch-up* logic, which helps to promote a pattern of military-industrial development, is consistent with the writings of Alexander Gerschenkron.[3] In his study of the contrast between Britain's "early" and other states' "late" industrialization, in the nineteenth century, it is argued that later developers seem to require more direct state intervention because of the large capital needed to produce on an efficient scale. (Capital markets are often very underdeveloped in backward or less-developed countries.) Further, the state may be able to take a more long-term and strategic view, than may private enterprise. Thus the state will tend to mobilize funds and create or organize larger productive units which have greater economies of scale.[4] If states wish to avoid dependence on foreign capital (which may be seen as necessary for reasons of national security), they thus have no alternative but to introduce more state enterprises, across a range of *strategic industries*.

The above logic of military-industrial rivalry explains and predicts a systematic tendency for arms and related industries to be more highly protected than most others. In less-developed countries, this usually means that the agricultural sector is discriminated against, so as to favor manufacturing industry. Only in already-industrialized countries can farmers hope to gain *strategic* status for agriculture. Another implication of military-industrial rivalry is that in developing countries there will be pressures which lead to the expansion of the public sector, perhaps even relative to, or at the expense of, the private sector. Such a pattern of military-industrial development is usually associated with the growth of nationalist interests (for both capital and labor) and ideologies which together may set limits to the power of transnational capital (see the previous chapter on the role of the public sector as a potential limit to the power of capital). In effect, vested interests may "wrap themselves in the flag." If they are highly influential, they may come to form part of an historic bloc in which there is a hegemonic fit between the material capabilities of certain industries, nationalist and statist ideas, and elements of the state apparatus, as well as quasi-state institutions in the civil society (e.g., veterans' associations, reservists). The hegemonic concepts within this type of bloc are those of national security and territorial sovereignty. From this point of view, national self-reliance and self-sufficiency are of the essence.

A good example of what can be termed a military-industrial historic bloc was in inter-war Japan, where the military gradually came to dominate domestic politics, and there was a shift from the earlier leading role for light industries such as textiles (before 1914), to an emphasis on heavy industries, such as iron, steel, and chemicals. The reasons for the triumph of militarism in Japan are to be found in a combination of internal and external factors. Japanese feudal traditions, through their stress on martial prowess, honor, and loyalty to leaders were conducive to a militarist mentality and set of priorities. The Great Depression and the closing of foreign markets in the 1930s undermined the export-oriented growth (based on light industries) which prevailed up to World War I. A second example is India, since independence in 1947, where the growth of a large and dominant state sector has increasingly gone with attempts to build up arms production, especially since its humiliation in the war with China in 1962. India has turned to the Soviet Union for some of its military technology, as a means of gaining more self-sufficiency in military production in the longer term. Thus MIG fighter aircraft are produced in India. A third example is Israel, which has fostered a special military and industrial relationship with the U.S.A., for similar reasons to those of India. Partly because of its small home market, Israel, to generate the necessary economies of scale, unlike India, has gone on to export a substantial proportion of its arms output.

Such military-industrial interests and ideas are to be found in most countries. However, their relative influence and political weight varies considerably. The hegemonic position they attained in inter-war Japan is an extreme case. In some countries military-industrial complexes have emerged, but they have been countervailed by other political forces.

THE LEVEL AND DETERMINANTS OF MILITARY EXPENDITURES

World military expenditure is on a vast scale and grew substantially during the 1970s. Growth has continued in the industrialized countries in the 1980s but since 1982 there has been some decline in military expenditures in less-developed countries.

Table 1 WORLD MILITARY EXPENDITURE, 1975–1984 (Selected Years)
(In $ Billions at 1980 Prices and Exchange Rates)

	1975	1981	1982	1983	1984	World share percent
IMEs	257,534	290,278	307,827	324,230	348,697	53.7
NMEs	171,972	185,448	189,757	191,671	196,133	30.2
MOECs	33,352	45,143	48,598	44,874	44,988	6.9
RoW	43,452	54,238	61,862	60,018	57,419	8.8
World Total	507,480	576,860	609,900	622,800	649,070	100.0

Notes: Industrial Market Economies = IMEs; Non-Market Economies = NMEs; Major Oil-Exporting Countries = MOECs; Rest of the World = Row.

Source: R. Luckman, "Disarmament and Development—the International Context," IDS Bulletin (October 1985), Vol. 16, No. 4, p. 3.

The factors influencing these high levels of military expenditure, both globally and for individual countries are complex and difficult to unravel, particularly in a short chapter such as this. Some of the factors relate to the internal structure of national political economies, whereas others relate to the structure of the global political economy. Still others relate to economic factors such as changes in the level of technology. However, the internal and external factors are linked. Above all, security interdependence between countries means that decisions concerning the military expenditure of one country cannot be made independently of assessments of trends in other countries. In addition, decision-making is complicated by alliance networks. Let us now consider some of the explanations in the literature for the scale of military expenditures.

One explanation of the factors affecting military expenditures would use the public choice approach. Here the various factors would be considered in terms of political demand and supply. *Demand* factors would include the perceived threats to the nation and a desire for security; a desire for national power and international status; the size of national income and wealth, especially as they affect the availability of resources for defense; the (opportunity) cost of defense equipment relative to the price of other goods and services; and the scope for free-riding on allies, thus transferring defense costs to other states. *Supply* factors might include the price and profitability of arms production; the nature and influence of political institutions; and the alternative uses of funds for politicians and bureaucrats. The *supply* factors concern the willingness and ability of governments to supply what is often seen as the "public good" of defense.

In the case of Japan there has been a post-1945 consensus, promoted by the powerful Japanese bureaucracy, in favor of spending a very low percentage of gross national product on defense, at least when compared to most other major countries. Until the mid-1980s, this was less than 1 percent, whereas in the United States and Britain it has usually exceeded 5 percent of GNP. This relatively low (although in absolute terms quite high) level of military expenditures in postwar Japan, in contrast to the inter-war militarist period, can be explained with reference to some of the factors noted above. First, the Japanese leaders were concerned with postwar political rehabilitation, particularly as their war-time endeavors were widely condemned in other Asian countries. In addition, the United States had defeated and occupied Japan, and had written what came to be known as the "Peace Constitution," which forbade the production of nu-clear weapons, and restricted the functions of the Japanese military to a narrow definition of "self defense." The U.S.A. stationed its own military forces in Japan, and consistently provided what the Japanese call the "nuclear umbrella" to protect Japan from China and the Soviet Union. Given the devastated condition of the Japanese economy in the aftermath of World War II, any attempt at high military expenditure would have resulted in even more malnutrition than occurred anyway. In this context, Japanese companies initially concentrated on the needs of economic re-construction, and later began to see greater profitability and export oppor-tunities in industries other than those concerned with arms production. In effect they have opted for peace, and victory in economic (notably trade) "war." A concept of economic security is at the heart of the new postwar outlook of Japanese leaders, premissed on being friendly with suppliers of raw materials, hosts to Japanese direct investment, and consumers of Japanese goods—in contrast to the imperialism of the Asian Co-prosperity Sphere of the 1930s. In consequence, the dominant business interests in postwar Japan have become those in consumer goods industries and in agriculture. This strategy has made Japan the world's second largest capi-talist economy. Despite their recent wealth, and the ability to carry a heavier defense burden, there is a strong temptation to go on free-riding on American military power.

It should be noted that in the application of the public choice ap-proach the demand and supply sides may not be independent of each other. In the above case there are very strong links between the Japanese bureaucratic leaders and the business elite, which arise because of com-mon social background, education (at the University of Tokyo), and out-look. Some of those who are *producers* on the supply side, are also active *voters* and *consumers* on the demand side. Where the public sector is large (its employees are also voters) this point may be of major consequence because politicians may be able to get sufficient popularity without either compromising their own preferences or coming into conflict with the bureaucracy. This is another way of explaining a mercantilist historic bloc. The existence of such a bloc, and indeed of military-industrial complexes, is one of the various factors influencing military expenditure.

One shortcoming of the analysis above is that it avoids explicit atten-tion to the interaction between states. Liberal theorists often resort to game theory to fill this gap, as in models of bilateral arms races, which are seen as involving zero-sum games, and perhaps the Prisoners' Dilemma (assuming little or no communication between states). More generally, higher expenditure in one country can lead to higher expenditure in other countries as others seek to catch up with the first country, or seek new allies to offset a decline in their relative military positions. Ratchet effects are likely in any arms race, with ever more arms needed to offset those of potential aggressors. Under certain types of international political conditions, any specific increase in demand for armaments in one country, perhaps due to pressure from vested interests, might trigger off a chain of similar demands in other countries. Military actions by one country might, of course, also produce such consequences, as others perceive their military interests as more threatened than before. Such pessimistic predictions are avoidable if models of arms expenditure are based on the Coordination Game. Concessions by any state in arms negotiations may be made contingent on concessions by the other side(s), with strict monitoring and verification. Parties might, in a practical sense, come to see arms reductions as mutually beneficial, in that apart from avoiding risks of an accidental war (for example through the launching of computer-controlled missiles), this would lead to a reduction in military expenditures, releasing resources for other purposes. In such a context, vested military-industrial interests would seek to hinder and block progress in arms reduction negotiations.

Game theory helps to illuminate some of the dynamics affecting the level of military expenditures. However, the *game* at the international level involves many players, with different types of communication between them: in some cases communication (for example between allies) is relatively easy, in many others (between ideological enemies, and rivals), it is difficult or nonexistent. This problem is compounded by the structure of the inter-state system, and in particular by the number of states within it.

The most militarily-intensive zones tend to be on, or close to frontiers. In a large empire or state, there is likely to be a vast, largely demilitarized area (although it may be heavily policed). If instead of such large empires there are many small states, often all parts of the country may be close to a frontier. In other words, there may be economies of scale in defending particular territories. During the heyday of the Roman Empire, approximately 300,000 troops patrolled a periphery which stretched from Scotland to Egypt, and from Morocco to Romania. At the heart of the Empire, in the Mediterranean zone, apart from the powerful Praetorian Guard in Rome, there were virtually no troops. Pressure on one frontier was often relieved by transferring troops from another frontier which was going through a peaceful phase. Hence the breakup of a large empire is likely to raise the level of military expenditures.

Further, a rise in the number of states disproportionately increases the potential number of military (and diplomatic) interactions. This can be represented diagrammatically, as in Figure 1, below.

Figure 1 (i) shows the bilateral interaction of two states, in what is a single relationship. Adding a third state results in three relationships (Figure 1 (ii)). For each state added, the number of interactions increases arithmetically, in a progressive series. Thus the number of potential interactions in a world of many states is massive, although not all of these would be significant in military terms. Nonetheless, a rise in the number of states is, other things being equal, likely to promote an increase in levels of militarization. The interaction effects of arms races have more scope, the greater number of states.

Recent historical evidence supports this theoretical argument. Decolonization, which greatly increased the number of states, has been followed by many wars in the Third World, and by regional arm races (as in the Persian Gulf and the Horn of Africa). These developments have been accompanied by higher growth rates for military expenditure in the Third World, as compared to the developed countries. This is one reason why the proportion of global military expenditures attributable to the superpowers has fallen dramatically since 1950 despite massively escalating costs of weaponry. The U.S.A., for example, accounted for approximately 50 percent of global military expenditures in 1950, a percentage

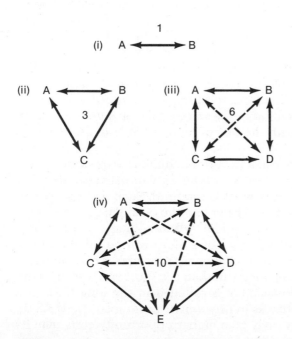

Figure 1 State Proliferation and Interaction Patterns.

which fell to about 23 percent in 1980, a level thought by Western experts to be similar to that of the Soviet Union.[5]

THE COSTS AND BENEFITS OF MILITARY EXPENDITURES

The opportunity costs of military expenditures depend on many factors, such as the degree of spare capacity and labor, the import-intensity of military expenditures, the alternative uses of capital and labor which have to be switched to military expenditures, i.e., whether higher military expenditure is at the expense of consumption, investment, exports, and/or research and development. These opportunity costs will vary according to the type of military expenditures, for example how capital- and skill-intensive it is. In the case of certain types of weapons development, there may also be significant social costs, such as the resources devoted to protecting weapons installations, as well as the potentially massive cost resulting from accidents (such as from nuclear or chemical weapons). Another type of cost is more subtle and long-term, in that a large military expenditure might have political and social repercussions in terms of the distribution of political power resources, and dominant ways of seeing and interpreting the world: for example with regard to the loss of political freedoms in the face of pressing "national security" problems. Such effects occur not just within particular societies, but also between them because of the dynamics of inter-state rivalry. This raises the issue of whether such effects are reversible, and if so under what conditions. Are there political "ratchet effects" when military expenditure rises? The points made above refer primarily to increases in military expenditure under *peace-time* conditions. However, the costs of military expenditure take on a new and more terrible dimension in war, with the loss of human life and also environmental damage.

Under conditions of spare capacity a rise in military expenditure may have little or no economic opportunity costs for a given state assuming that domestic firms are able to supply what is required. Such was the case in Germany in the 1930s. Indeed, for Hitler and the Nazi Party, there were political advantages since unemployment fell as military expenditures increased. Where little spare capacity exists there will be significant opportunity costs and the likelihood of inflationary pressures. These opportunity costs may be greater in the long run than the short run insofar as the stock of capital, skills, and knowledge is reduced in the long term as a result of more short-term cutbacks in *investment* programs. The U.S.S.R., as a fully-employed economy, may face higher opportunity costs than its Western rivals in increasing military expenditures.[6]

There are national variations in the pattern and extent of arms production and the relationship between such production and that in other industries: some countries are much more self-sufficient than others. The import-intensity of military expenditure tends to be higher in the Third World, where a severe shortage of foreign exchange is common, relative to what is needed for economic development. Thus regional arms races and wars may adversely affect development: for example that between Iran and Iraq in the 1980s. A growing number of less-developed countries have developed their own arms industries and some even export, as well as import arms, such as Brazil. This development reflects not only a concern for security of arms supply and the conservation of foreign exchange: it can be part of a wider import-substitution industrialization strategy, that is a part of *catch-up mercantilism.* For such a strategy to be successful, there must a correct *mix,* and sufficient quantity of resources, such as trained personnel across a number of sectors. The shortage of skilled people in less-developed countries means that the opportunity cost of skill-intensive military expenditure (for example, pilots and engineers) is greater than that for unskilled, labor-intensive military expenditures (as with conscript infantry). Indeed, skill shortages can, while military spending rises rapidly, result in a crisis of absorptive capacity, as happened under the Shah of Iran in the 1970s, so adversely affecting both the pace of industrialization and political stability.[7]

There are proponents of military expenditure who claim there are significant "spin offs"—economic and political—from military expenditures. Such economic arguments focus on technology and the way in which high military expenditures (based upon a *national* procurement policy) may contribute to the nurture of infant industries, and/or help maintain a nation's lead in high technology industries. Also, if the leading industries in a particular country are also the *strategic industries,* they may be boosted by strong military demand in addition to civilian demand, so obtaining scale economies and thus accelerating economic growth, for example in aerospace, high-speed computing, and telecommunications systems.

The political arguments focus upon the degree to which high military expenditure helps to maintain the dominance of one state relative to others with correspondingly lower levels of military expenditures. For example, only countries with high technology industries geared to military production can give and use military aid as a means of political influence. Conversely, only by the development of such military-industrial power resources can such influence be resisted. *Thus catch-up mercantilism* and *keep ahead mercantilism* are two sides of the same coin. They both reflect a response to the structural condition of military-industrial rivalry. Military strength, in some historical circumstances, has been used to gain economic advantages, such as trading opportunities, investment rights, access to land, and better terms of trade. This has taken various forms, resulting in, for example, unequal treaties, puppet regimes, and colonial conquest. Today, the scope for obtaining economic advantage from military actions may be less than it was, given the spread of weaponry and the wider acceptance of international norms of national sovereignty and self-determination. However, economic advantages may still be obtained by military aid in the form of training, advisors as well as subsidized weapons. An example is the granting of favorable fishing rights to the great powers by less-developed countries in exchange for military aid.

The problems of *keep ahead mercantilism* are to do with both maintaining the range and quality of military-industrial innovation and preventing its diffusion to rival states while seeking access to the technology of other rivals (and also allies). The increased complexity of modern technologies, including the development of new industries and products (such as satellites, space shuttles, optical lasers, biotechnology) means that the investment requirements, both in terms of physical and human capital, are greater than they once were. The costs of maintaining American military dominance are significantly greater than they were for Britain in the nineteenth century. In the *pax britannica* naval power was crucial, whereas today land, sea, air, and space power are needed: this is indicative of the ever expanding range of technologies and industries which arc now central for military-industrial rivalry. Moreover, the rate of change within these contemporary industries is faster than for sea power in the nineteenth century.

THE POLITICAL ECONOMY OF ARMS

Technology of many types is diffusing faster than ever before. It is not always easy to separate civil and military technology, but even when this can be done technology is still likely to diffuse because of the structural force of international economic competition. To be competitive in many high-technology industries the realization of scale economies is necessary, and if the home market is not large enough, exports are vital in order to generate the revenue to finance further research and development. Thus there is a contradiction between the structural dynamics of the inter-state system and those of international economic competition: for national security reasons states may wish to monopolize particular military-industrial technologies but the economics of technological innovation drive them to policies which facilitate diffusion. The spread dynamics noted here also interact with the quest by particular states (notably the superpowers) to maintain influence over other important states in part by supplying them with up-to-date weapons systems. The arms trade is a mechanism for the diffusion of armaments even where more fundamental technological capabilities are successfully withheld.

During the 1970s and 1980s there was a spectacular growth in the arms trade, much faster in the 1970s than the growth in world trade as a whole. Much of the arms supplied went to the oil-rich Middle Eastern states, fueling a regional arms race between, on the one hand, Israel and the "militant" Arab states, and, on the other hand, between Gulf states such as Iran and Iraq. The major suppliers were the U.S.A. and the U.S.S.R., followed by France and the U.K. Iraq was an example of a country which imported civilian nuclear technology, with a view to developing nuclear weapons— a venture which proved unsuccessful due to preemptive Israeli bombing. On the one hand, the West and Japan feared political upheaval in, and danger to, oil supplies from the Middle East; on the other, certain Western interests profited from arms sales to the region (as did the U.S.S.R.).

The case of the Gulf conflicts of the 1980s illustrated simultaneously the ease with which Western arms could be sold, as well as the growing difficulty for the U.S.A. to use its own force to intervene in the region. Although the U.S.A. created a Rapid Deployment Force (Central Command) its usefulness in the Middle East was doubtful, given the proximity of the U.S.S.R., the large stock of weaponry in the region, the strength of nationalism, fundamentalism, and anti-Americanism, and domestic constraints on the American use of force. The latter were, of course, tested by both American intervention in Lebanon and also by the 1986 bombing of Tripoli. What seemed acceptable to the American public was intervention without American casualties. It should also be noted that the U.S.A., U.S.S.R., France, Britain, and Israel had a financial interest in the continuation of the Iran-Iraq War during the 1980s, in their role as weapons suppliers. The U.S.A., the U.S.S.R., as well as other states, also had a military interest in a stalemate since then neither Iran nor Iraq could pose a serious threat to surrounding nations. These common interests were thus crucial to explaining the long duration of the war. Moreover, on the evidence of the 1970s and early 1980s, high arms sales to the Middle East have been associated with high oil prices. In this connection, it should be noted that the U.S. took an ambiguous position on the oil price rises in 1973–1974. American Secretary of State Kissinger was keen to see that the Shah had more money to buy U.S. arms, so as to be the "regional policeman" envisaged in the Nixon (Guam) Doctrine. This occurred at a time when the U.S. government's military and space spending was in decline as a percentage of GNP, so that the American arms industry needed a big rise in foreign demand. Analysis of this example suggests that evaluation of the size and scope of the U.S. military-industrial complex needs to consider arms sales and foreign policy as well as U.S. domestic military spending. In 1986 the U.S. found itself drawn into supplying arms to Iran in order to get the release of hostages. France faced similar dilemmas, yet neither country wanted an Iranian victory in the Iran-Iraq War. Ironically, the weapons of the Middle Eastern groups that have taken Westerners hostage have been supplied, in part by (private) international arms dealers.

The contemporary spread dynamics of military-industrial rivalry both contribute to, and in some ways undermine, a global military hierarchy, for example through nuclear proliferation and the massive arms trade. This is in contrast to the clear and rather easily defined military hierarchy of the nineteenth century. This argument thus sheds some doubt on the argument that there is now a relatively clear-cut *New International Military Order.*[8] This may possibly be true for nuclear weapons, but even here the situation seems to be changing, and possibly becoming more unstable. However, the spread of arms production in the Third World is limited by the size of a country's GNP and resources, due to economies of scale and the burdens that high military spending can place on a country's economy. Israel, perhaps the most successful small country in the production of arms, was forced to cancel its Lavi fighter program in 1987 due to soaring research costs and the unwillingness of the United States to increase its subsidies. Neuman concludes that the "inherent constraints of size and infrastructure will create a hierarchically structured world arms trade and production system as the military industries of states grow."[9] The position of countries in the hierarchy will also depend on cultural and political factors that affect the mobilization of resources and their scientific use.

THE NATURE AND SIGNIFICANCE OF MILITARY-INDUSTRIAL COMPLEXES

The notion of a *complex* implies something more permanent than a temporary, tactical coming together of different interests for the purpose of pushing for increased military expenditures. It implies a shared framework of thought, overlapping and interpenetrating institutions, and a congruence between these social forces. It also implies a congruence between the *means of production* and the *means of destruction.* If there is such a complex within a society, there is the possibility that military expenditures may grow in a way that is not just a function of inter-state rivalries and what some would see as basic security needs (which are often highly debatable). The very perception of these security needs is something that members of the complex have a vested interest in influencing and exaggerating. Arms producers have an interest in making more profits. Military bureaucrats have an interest in expanding their budget and prestige. "Security intellectuals" have an interest in both promoting the indispensability of their expertise, as well as their ways of seeing and interpreting the problems of war and peace. Most fundamentally, the armed services have an interest in obtaining better and larger amounts of weapons, better pay and conditions, and as much status as possible within the society. At the heart of this complex is the concept of *national security.*

In the American case it is embodied in the creation of such institutions as the U.S.A.'s National Security Council, where the National Security Assistant (a position variously held in recent decades by Henry Kissinger, Zbigniew Brzezinski, and Admiral Poindexter) has privileged access to the President as Commander-in-Chief and head of state on a daily basis. The task of the NSC is to coordinate the activities of a wide range of U.S. institutions concerned with foreign policy: the Pentagon, the State Department, the Central Intelligence Agency, and the various intelligence and defense activities of other government departments. The NSC also takes account of international economic aspects of security. Such institutionalization, which takes various forms in different countries, has been a significant ingredient in the emergence of military-industrial complexes.

Institutionalization has been carried to remarkable lengths in the Soviet Union. Here its extensiveness involves the way that the economy is organized, primarily to provide the military with the best in terms of skills, technology, materials, and finished products. It is almost as if the U.S.S.R. were organized as a single military-industrial complex. National security is the number one priority for the Soviet state and its citizens. This has served to legitimate the Soviet military-industrial complex. Its power also rests on a strong consensus within the Communist Party that the military should play an important role within the Soviet state, although under Party control. However, in the mid-1980s the head of the KGB (secret police and intelligence) but not the Defense Minister had full membership of the Politbureau, in contrast to the Brezhnev era, which implied Soviet attempts to restructure its economic priorities.[10] In sum, in the 1980s a new Soviet consensus on the need for economic reforms developed, albeit less so on their precise nature. The influence of the military appeared to have weakened in this process, particularly since the coming to power of Secretary Gorbachev in 1985. In America, the interests of the military-industrial complex have been more partisan, and, as such, have often faced fierce public criticism in Congress.

In the U.S.S.R. the very national and party-led nature of the military-industrial complex facilitates consideration of long-term national security interests. For both countries, arms control agreements and reduced spending on nuclear weapons can be seen as necessary for the economic growth of high-technology industries, which underpin military strength and spending in the long term. By contrast, in the U.S. "short-term rationality" may sometimes prevail given the business cycle, the strength of interest groups linked to the military-industrial complex, and electoral pressures on politicians. However, long-term planning and continuity are striking in the U.S. as well as the U.S.S.R. Thus although there are structural similarities between the two superpowers' military-industrial complexes, large differences in economic organization, balance of political forces, political culture, and military tradition distinguish one from the other.

THE SCALE OF AMERICAN AND SOVIET MILITARY-INDUSTRIAL COMPLEXES

The following figures suggest the scale of the military-industrial complexes of the U.S.A. and the U.S.S.R. One recent estimate of their military expenditures (which can only be indicative because of the difficulties of gaining precise information and establishing comparability of data) stated that together they accounted for around 50 percent of total world military spending, and they held 96 percent of the world's strategic nuclear forces.[11] American defense outlays in 1984 were $273.4 billion, and rose to approximately $300 billion in 1985, which meant a rise to approximately 7.55 percent of GNP. The projected figure for fiscal year 1986 was $302.6 billion, and expenditures requested by the Reagan administration for 1986–88 would, if they had been fully appropriated by the Congress, have totaled over $1 trillion. Soviet expenditures are impossible to compare but supported total armed forces of 5.15 million people as opposed to the U.S.A.'s 2.13 million. Western estimates of Soviet expenditures vary widely, ranging between 10 and 20 percent of GDP. Western experts say Soviet expenditures almost rival those of the U.S.A. in absolute terms although the U.S.A. generally pays much higher prices and wages than the USSR, and gets less "bang" per dollar than the Soviets have got per rouble. This seems to have increasingly been the case since the late 1960s as weapons have become more sophisticated and as Western prices have risen fairly rapidly.[12] These outlays compare with the entire 1983 GDP of the following countries, in $U.S. billions: Greece ($37.69 billion); Mozambique (in 1981, est. $2.9 billion); Cuba ($15.44 billion, including heavy subsidies of Soviet aid); Australia ($155.7 billion); and oil-rich Saudi Arabia ($153 billion in 1982 and $120 billion in 1983).[13]

Another facet of this debate is the degree to which the influence of the military-industrial complex has an inertial effect on military expenditures within the economy, that is when a war ends is military expenditure slow to come down? Soviet military expenditure seems to be a fairly steady proportion of net material product (which equals gross domestic product, GDP, less services). In the U.S.A. military expenditure has shown some tendency to fall in the aftermath of wars, especially World War II, but also the Korean and Vietnam wars. Although the Pentagon continues to be the largest single purchaser of goods and services, its share has declined as the overall economy has grown:

> While the military budget stayed the same, the . . . [GNP] . . . has almost tripled in real terms during the past three decades. As a result, the military's share of the GNP dropped from an average of 10% during the 1950s to an average of 6% during the 1970s. . . . The military's share of government spending has also fallen, but by a smaller amount. Of the goods and services directly purchased by the federal government during the 1970s, the military consumed 70%. . . . In the 1950s, the Pentagon's share averaged 85%. The military's portion stayed so high because much of the growth in civilian government spending has been in transfer payments, which are not direct government purchases.[14]

Most of these transfer payments concern pensions for veterans and war widows. These payments contribute substantially to the inertia of military expenditure. However, during the 1970s, in the post-Vietnam period, there was a significant fall in military expenditure, at the same time as expenditures for National Aeronautical and Space Agency (NASA) and other defense-related activities were also falling. Thus it would seem that the military-industrial complex in America cannot always hold its own in the face of other interests, whereas in the Soviet Union, at least until the mid-1980s, there has been less sign that the military has had to give ground in relative terms to more *civilian* production. On the other hand, the forces of the American military-industrial complex, embodied, for example, in the activities of the influential Committee on the Present Danger, have staged a substantial comeback since 1977–1978. Their arguments concern the degree to which consistently high levels of military expenditure in the U.S.S.R. have eroded the security of the U.S.A., and made the West more and more vulnerable to Soviet interventions in the Third World. This has helped to create a coalition of forces which have promoted an increase in the proportion of U.S. GNP devoted to military expenditure, which exceeded 7 percent in 1986. Although this is lower than the heights of the 1950s, it still represents a 25 percent proportionate increase on the previous decade. Given that the U.S. was in recession in the early 1980s the timing of this change fits in with one aspect of neo-Marxist theories of military expenditures, that is the promotion of counter-cyclical government spending, via what is called *military Keynesianism.*

However, the inertial power of the military-industrial complex in the United States, and of the military in the Soviet Union, reached a testing time in the latter half of the 1980s. Following the November 1985 Geneva summit between President Reagan and Secretary Gorbachev, the first meeting between American and Soviet leaders since 1979, progress in arms negotiations took place against a highly favorable background. The U.S.S.R. was keen to slow down the growth in military spending for economic reasons. Some American politicians were concerned about the high budget deficit, itself partly caused by the substantial rise in military expenditures. President Reagan was concerned about his place in history, and diverting attention away from the Irangate scandal of 1986–1987. With two well-established leaders in a hurry (for overlapping although different reasons), an agreement on medium-range weapons was reached in late 1987, with the promise of more to come. In addition, the U.S. Congress was bent on cutting back on Reagan's pet program, the SDI.

THE ECONOMIC AND POLITICAL IMPACT OF MILITARY-INDUSTRIAL COMPLEXES

An earlier American President, Dwight D. Eisenhower, who was the former General and Commander of U.S. forces in Europe during World War II, warned, in his farewell address in 1960 against the dangers to liberal democracy which were created by the development of the military-industrial complex. (The latter term was in fact coined by Eisenhower.) More generally, these dangers can also be said to arise from the role of the state in military-industrial rivalry. Eisenhower warned that, unless subjected to consistent scrutiny and democratic accountability, the military-industrial complex, through a variety of means, could subvert the democratic process and threaten civil liberties. Others have suggested that what has emerged in the United States since 1945, is a "state within a state," with secretive budgets and illegal activities rampant. These forces serve to undermine American constitutional guarantees and the separation of powers within the system.[15] In most countries, intelligence services and the armed forces are allowed a greater degree of secrecy than any other part of the state apparatus: all in the name of *national security*. As a result, scope for public criticism of the security complex is severely limited. Those defending these forms of secrecy argue that there is a necessary tradeoff between democratic accountability and national security, even though there is some evidence of abuse, corruption, inefficiency, and incompetence in the security services. Given the veil of secrecy, what evidence there is of democratic abuses and inefficiency has to be viewed as the tip of an indeterminate iceberg.

With respect to the relation between military expenditures and economic performance, management scientist Seymour Melman has argued that the relative decline of the American economic and industrial system since 1945 was the consequence of "the permanent war economy," in which the military fashioned a "Pentagon capitalism" based upon permanent mobilization for war.[16] The effects of this on the American economy have been predatory: they have eroded productivity, maximized waste, and created a relatively parasitic group of producers who are not subjected to the pressures of market competition and who are able to inflate the prices of the goods they supply to the military because of inefficient procurement and *logrolling*. The long-term effect of this has been to deplete the *civilian* parts of the American economy of capital and technology, contributing to an erosion in the U.S.A.'s technological lead. This has also, according to Melman, produced a military form of state capitalism. In addition, others, including the former Chairman of the Senate Foreign Relations Committee, Senator J. William Fulbright, have highlighted the use of propaganda by the Pentagon to sustain an ideological climate of anti-communism and an atmosphere of permanent crisis and insecurity. This is a technique for justifying military definitions of, and solutions to, the problems of world politics.[17]

The recent attempt by De Grasse to assess the impact of the military-industrial complex on American economic performance, adds weight to Melman's arguments. He does not rule out a favorable short-term impact, that is where there is considerable spare capacity, as in the late 1930s, and early 1980s. With respect to long-term effects, he argues that military expenditures have had little impact upon U.S. unemployment levels, which have been significantly higher than in most Western capitalist countries until the 1980s. Military expenditures create fewer jobs than other government expenditures, and are concentrated in more highly skilled occupations, which have the lowest unemployment levels. Second, high levels of military expenditures have contributed to the relatively lower levels of investment and productivity growth than in the U.S.A.'s main competitors, have skewed research and development priorities, and have tended to generate innovations with few commercial applications. Moreover, the nature of many military contracts is such as to "feather bed" the suppliers, who charge often exorbitant prices for their products because they incur unnecessarily high costs, such as perks for managers. Many military producers have not been subjected to competition, especially from foreign producers.

The Reagan administration's military buildup (1980–1986) was the largest in peacetime American history, only slightly smaller than that in the Vietnam War, and fueled the already spiralling budget deficits which contributed to the international debt crisis of the 1980s. These may threaten the long-term stability of the American economy, despite the favorable short-term effects. De Grasse estimates that 48.6 percent of Federal expenditures were spent on the U.S. military in 1981. In 1986, the Pentagon was expected to use 59.2 percent of the government's funds, while welfare and other social expenditures were being curbed.[18] Such economic burdens are much more severe for the U.S.S.R. with its smaller GNP and more monopolistic and bureaucratic economy. The U.S. can find it tempting to raise military spending so as to put pressure on the Soviet economy, even though this has adverse long-term effects on the American economy.

In terms of economic opportunity costs, Japan has been able to benefit from standing outside of such military-industrial rivalry and approach the U.S. level of GNP per head.[19] If and when the Japanese will aspire to be a military superpower is one of the great unknowns of international relations. Despite the Peace Constitution there are still elements in Japanese culture which support such aspirations: for example in the writings of the neo-nationalist poet Yukio Mishima, and the war memories and nationalist loyalties of men like the mid-1980s Prime Minister Nakasone. To date, most postwar Japanese leaders have been content to compete in economic rather than military terms. This might change if higher unemployment and barriers to export-led growth increase substantially since this would reduce the opportunity cost of higher military expenditure. (Signs of this possibility emerged with the rapid appreciation of the yen during 1986–87.) While this is speculative, it is indicative of how wider developments in the global political economy might affect spending on arms.

The reformist tendencies of Gorbachev can be related to Mancur Olson's notion of encrustation, whereby vested interests, including those of bureaucracies, build up over time, unless checked by radical change and/or defeat in war.[20] The Stalinist state was successful in industrialization, especially in arms-related industries. Its centralized planning was suitable to a certain stage of catch-up mercantilism, but perhaps less so to a higher stage. While this problem for the U.S.S.R. reflects the more complex economy and technologies of the post-Stalin period, it can also be seen in terms of the bureaucratic consolidation of the Soviet state apparatuses: they, like Brezhnev, grew old together. Olson's stress on organizations and interests can, following Robert Cox's analysis of social forces, be extended to include ideas. In the case of the U.S.S.R., ideas about the virtues of centralized planning and the dangers of allowing markets and private enterprise much scope have been hegemonic (in a Gramscian sense) for decades. Under Gorbachev they are being cautiously challenged, more timidly than in China where there has been less time for encrustation since the communist victory in the revolution of 1949.

The pressures on states to reform their institutions come from economic as well as military competition. This is especially the case in the more integrated global political economy that has emerged since 1950. States compete not just for markets and foreign exchange, but for capital, skilled labor, and access to new technology. For capitalist countries schemes like the Strategic Defence Initiative may result in "brain drains" from other nations to the United States. High military spending may require high tax rates which may deter the inflow of capital and labor. Insofar as high military expenditures (and government spending more generally) causes slow growth, it worsens what we have called "the business climate".

The pressures on the U.S.S.R. to moderate the growth of its military spending can be linked to a growing sense of economic failure compared to Japan and some of the newly industrializing countries. This is even more true for China. Further, improved global communications exert some pressure on communist governments to raise living standards, because of increased awareness of higher consumption in other countries.

Given the evidence on the economic burdens of defense, there is reason to think that there may be a conflict between developing a leading high-technology economy, as a basis for having a large arms industry and the maintenance of such an economy once a high defense burden is taken on. America's lead over other countries, both in technology and GNP per capita were built up in the first half of the twentieth century, at a time when (up to 1941) its industries were overwhelmingly geared to civilian rather than military production. After World War II, the years of American globalism were associated with the rise of the military-industrial complex, and from the early 1970s there was a near stagnation in the growth of American productivity and real wages in most sectors.

CONCLUSIONS

While realist theory is very important in explaining military spending and the spread of arms production, economic, cultural, and ideological factors need to be considered too. In particular, the effects of technological change, economies of scale, and a more integrated world economy on military-industrial rivalry need to be considered. When countries are competing for mobile capital and labor, military spending can exert both positive and negative effects on growth rates. These need more research and analysis. At the ideological level there is a tension between the spread of nationalist ideas which go with a mercantilist stress on strategic industries and the spread of liberal economic ideas which cast doubt on the efficiency of monopolistic state enterprises and the effectiveness of an inward-looking import substitution strategy of development. Similarly, there may be tensions between the spread of some aspects of militarism and consumerism. Above all, there is a tension between the attempts of states to gain a military technology gap and the economic pressures to sell both weapons and arms technology. This tension is especially marked for the smaller arms-exporting countries, including France and Britain, as illustrated by the proposed sale in 1978 of the Chieftain tank to the Shah of Iran before even the British army had it.

Still other tensions beset military expenditures. Even for the superpowers, arms spending has caused economic problems through impairing long-term growth rates and so perhaps weakening their positions as hegemons within their respective blocs. More immediate and tragic are the pressures of military-industrial rivalry on poor less-developed countries which can ill afford military expenditure. For some of their people it may be a matter of life and death—even if the arms are never used. All too often they are, not only in wars against rivals, but also in suppressing their own people—the latter use of weapons being in marked contrast to the situation in developed countries. It would be ironic if some disarmament proved easier to achieve between the superpowers than between countries in the Third World. However, such an outcome would also be logical in that the pressures of military-industrial rivalry are greatest on less-developed countries trying to establish their national identity, and to catch up economically.

NOTES

1. Gautam Sen, *The Military Origins of Industrialisation and International Trade Rivalry* (London: Pinter, 1984).
2. Theda Skocpol, *States and Social Revolutions* (Cambridge: Cambridge University Press, 1979).
3. Alexander Gerschenkron, *Economic Backwardness in Historical Perspective* (Cambridge, Mass.: Harvard University Press, 1962).
4. See S. Deger and S. Sen, "Military Expenditure Spin-Off and Economic Development," *Journal of Development Economics* (1983), Vol. 13, pp. 67–83. See also Robin Luckham, "Militarism and International Economic Dependence," in M. Graham et al. (eds), *Disarmament and World Development* (London: Pergamon, 1986), 2nd edition, pp. 43–65; Mary Kaldor and Aisborn Eide, *The*

World Military Order: The Impact of Military Technology on the Third World (London: Macmillan, 1979); M. Brozka, *Arms Production in the Third World* (London: Taylor and Francis, 1986); S. Deger, *Military Expenditures in Third World Countries: The Economic Effects* (London: Routledge and Kegan Paul, 1986).

5. Nobuhiko Ushiba et al., *Sharing International Responsibilities* (New York Trilateral Commission, 1981), p. 5; Fred Halliday, *The Making of the Second Cold War* (London: New Left Books, 1986), 2nd edition, p. 57. Halliday uses statistics from the Stockholm Peace Research Institute (SIPRI). These are generally regarded as the most reliable of the Western independent estimates.

6. Gautem Sen, "The Economics of U.S. Defence: The Military Industrial Complex and Neo-Marxist Economic Theories Reconsidered," *Millenium* (1986), Vol. 15, pp. 179–195.

7. See Kamran Mofid, *Iran: Oil Revenues, Development Planning, and Industrialisation—From Monarchy to Islamic Republic* (Wisbech, Cambridgeshire: Menas Press, 1987).

8. Jan Oberg, "The New International Military Order: A Threat to Human Security," in Aisborn Eide and Marek Thee, *Problems of Contemporary Militarism* (London: Croom Helm, 1980), pp. 47–74.

9. Stephanie G. Neuman, "International Stratification and Third World Military Industries," *International Organisation* (1984), Vol. 38, pp. 167–197.

10. C. Gluckham, "New Directions for Soviet Foreign Policy," *Radio Liberty Research Bulletin,* Supplement, February 1986.

11. Marek Thee, "Militarisation in the U.S. and the Soviet Union," *Alternatives* (1984), Vol. 10, p. 95.

12. U.S. figures are taken from Robert W. De Grasse Jr, *Military Expansion, Economic Decline* (New York, M. E. Sharpe/Council on Economic Priorities, New York, 1983), p. 20; and The International Institute for Strategic Studies (IISS), *The Military Balance 1984–85* (IISS, London, 1984), pp. 4, 15–16.

13. IISS, op. cit.

14. De Grasse, op. cit., p. 8.

15. Alan Wolfe, *The Limits of Legitimacy* (New York: Free Press, 1977).

16. Seymour Melman, *Pentagon Capitalism: The Political Economy of War* (New York: McGraw-Hill, 1970).

17. J. William Fulbright, *The Pentagon Propaganda Machine* (New York: Vintage Books, 1971); C. Wright Mills, *The Power Elite* (Oxford: Oxford University Press, 1956); Adam Yarmolinsky, *The Military Establishment: Its Impact on American Society* (New York: Harper and Row, 1971).

18. De Grasse, op. cit.

19. *The Economist,* 25 October 1986, p. 15.

20. Mancur Olson, *The Logic of Collective Action* (Cambridge, Mass: Harvard University Press, 1965).

Part
Seven

SOUTHERN CHOICES

This section should be read in conjunction with Part Five, since both address the question: What futures are available to the "South" in the North-South relationship? Although the Western media pay very little attention to what takes place in the Third World, IPE scholars are careful, as a rule, to take a global perspective and analyze international and even transnational structures with an emphasis on how the Third World fits in. The editors feel that a careful understanding of North-South issues is vital to the student of IPE.

Each of these articles focus on the emergence of a Third World coalition during the 1960s and 1970s. When large numbers of former colonies achieved independence in the 1960s, they became aware of their unique and pressing economic and political needs. The difficulty of bargaining with the West became quickly apparant to leaders in the Third World. Many began to coordinate their diplomacy until they eventually formed a fairly coherent negotiating position and strategy. This newly formed coalition was centered in the United Nations system, where their numbers gave Third World leaders an advantage when it came time to vote on resolutions. The high point of the Third World coalition came in the mid-1970s when it conceived and pressed for a New International Economic Order which would result in a distribution of wealth, opportunity, and influence. The success of OPEC (Organization of Petroleum Exporting Countries) and a sympathetic response from such Western leaders as Jimmy Carter and Willy Brandt gave the movement added momentum. Everything changed at the turn of the decade, however, when the explosion of the Debt Crisis, the second Oil Crisis, and the elections of Ronald Reagan, Margaret

Thatcher, and Helmut Kohl simultaneously eroded Third World solidarity and Western responsiveness.

Each of these selections addresses the specific question of how the Third World can alter the current economic balance of power in the world. All agree that the Third World is inherently disadvantaged when it comes to economic interactions. However, there is much disagreement over the appropriate form of Third World intervention. To begin, Robert Rothstein offers a brief overview of the most conciliatory of the Third World approaches—negotiation. Rothstein emphasizes that although the Third World has gone far in organizing a coherent and morally compelling agenda for change (the New International Economic Order), it has not made much progress in persuading the industrialized world to go along with it. In the years since this was written, in fact, the leverage of the NIEO coalition has been reduced to almost nothing. UNCTAD has become a virtual dead letter and the Third World is more divided on strategy and objectives than ever.

Edward Morse gives a specific example of how the Third World coalition has collapsed, with his focus on the all-important politics of oil. With the glut of oil production in the early 1980s, the central feature of OPEC's power—production control—was eliminated, and so was OPEC's influence. The organization has struggled for survival in an atmosphere of self-serving opportunism on the part of oil producers.

Finally, Stephen Krasner's rather biting commentary on the true nature of the NIEO agenda emphasizes the political element over the economic and moral ones. The NIEO was intended to be a vehicle for control, not a means of correcting injustice, according to Krasner. The problem (as also pointed out by Galtung in part Five), is that even if the NIEO were implemented, the poor in the Third World would not be its beneficiaries, contrary to the arguments of Third World elites.

Questions to ask yourself while reading these passages include: Does the Third World have any inherent right to a voice in global economic affairs? If so, what form should this take and who, within the Third World, should be the spokesperson? Are the goals of the Third World and the First World completely incompatible? What Third World goals would benefit the entire world, if achieved?

Global Bargaining: UNCTAD and the Quest For A New International Economic Order

Robert Rothstein

. . .

RULE MAKING: GUIDES FOR THE PERPLEXED

In a stable system rules presumably reflect common interests (and usually, but not always, common values), and they are implemented by institutions that function effectively and are perceived as legitimate. Rule making in the North-South context thus suffers a double burden: common interests are dominated by divisive interests, and the existing institutions are neither effective nor wholly legitimate. This sets sharp constraints to what we can reasonably expect from any venture into rule making, and it raises serious questions about what ends we can sensibly pursue.

Rules obviously cannot function in a vacuum. Consequently, what seems to be implied is an effort to limit the rule making enterprise to domains with a sufficiently strong sense of common interest where the institutional structure seems reasonably effective. The limitations would apply to the scope of the rules and to the range of state coverage. This immediately raises the question of adequacy: Are limited rules sufficient or are only global rules likely to be sufficient?

There appears to be a kind of systemic bias toward global rules and global solutions. Perhaps this reflects the literature on the *global village* and the shared consequences of environmental degradation that seems inevitably to lead to calls for *global compacts* or *planetary bargains* and other such ecumenical solutions to present difficulties. Interpretations of the Bretton Woods system established after World War II may have also contributed to the assumption that global rules were both necessary and possible, although in fact the *global* rules and institutions that were created were primarily the rules of the dominant subsystem of the international system. The very peripheral role of the developing countries (and the socialists) in that system has only led, however, to a demand for a differently structured global system, not a different kind of system altogether. The rationale for this has been essentially political, since the developing countries feel that movements away from the global focus reflect efforts by the developed countries to "divide and conquer." Nevertheless, whatever the justification, the tendency to seek global rules and global solutions is intensified. Finally, there is the apparently pragmatic argument that only a global focus can satisfy all the interests at play in the current system. Thus Hirsch and Doyle argue that

> although the diversity of interests itself would make such a negotiation difficult, the same diversity adds to the necessity for a comprehensive multilateral negotiation in preference to piecemeal and/or bilateral deals. . . . the scope of mutual agreement increases as the range of bargaining is widened.[1]

The objection to the global focus is not conceptual but practical. It may well be that a system based on a set of global rules would operate more effectively than a system based on more modest rules. It may also be that there are issues for which *only* global rules make sense, although I can think of no issue at the moment for which this is genuinely true.[2] And there may be some issues for which the negotiation of global rules suddenly becomes possible, perhaps as the result of a crisis or a conjunction of unusual circumstances. In the great majority of cases, however, I believe that the quest for global rules is bound to be futile: the clash of interests and values is too profound, the intellectual uncertainties are too great, the probability of "shocks" is too high, and the available institutions are not capable of the kind of quick and flexible reactions that are necessary in a very unsettled world. The pursuit of global rules may only deflect attention from the pursuit of less dramatic but more practicable alternatives.[3] Moreover, and not so parenthetically, global rules are likely to be loose, indicative, and qualified—characteristics that will not provide much protection against violation or much help in planning for poor and weak countries.

There is, of course, a problem with this argument. As I have already noted in the last chapter, the quest for comprehensive, global solutions has been attacked on many grounds: the increasing costs associated with increasing numbers and kinds of decisionmakers, the difficulties of dealing with complexity and uncertainty, and the loss of flexibility and responsiveness as the decisionmakers become more distant from the arena of concern. Nevertheless, simply shifting the locale or scope of decisionmaking to narrower or more functionally specific settings has its own costs, since drift, inertia, and the accumulation of problems may result. As with the earlier discussion of institutions, then, what we seem to need are rules that are set by those most directly affected by an issue, with some means to assure that such rules are not excessively self-interested or destructive of broader values and interests and that they do not preclude more general legitimization at some stage. Here we intersect with the earlier discussion of the difficulties of legitimizing decisions taken in narrower institutional settings: the rule-making process in particular areas or between particular groups of countries should also be sanctioned and approved by more general bodies. The difficulties are obviously enormous, but it should at least be noted that rules jointly agreed upon by those most directly affected may have more chance of being both acceptable and effective than rules imposed from above. In what follows we shall leave aside the legitimacy question and concentrate on the characteristics of the rules themselves.

We ask, then, whether it is possible to devise and implement a set of effective operational rules that fall somewhere between global rules that are desirable but impracticable and *realpolitik* rules that reflect only brute force (as with the "justifications" for attacking a few Middle Eastern oil producers) or a grudging effort to integrate the "new rich" into the old order.[4] There is no simple answer to this question, for even if such rules were judged to be necessary, the factors that impede the negotiation of global rules may still exert a strongly negative force. One needs only to recall that the effort to move negotiations out of large, public forums into smaller, relatively private forums has been undermined by the tendency of the smaller forums to continue the behavioral patterns that dominate in the larger. Perhaps we can attain a better perspective on this issue if we were to begin by asking what we seek (or can seek) from the operation of a set of rules and within what context they can be implemented.

The context within which rules are to be implemented could be dealt with by devising a series of models of possible alternative future international systems. This is not very useful, however, for model building in such circumstances tends to follow a very familiar pattern. Four alternatives are usually offered: one describes an increasingly centralized system dominated by a handful of the most powerful states; a second describes an increasingly decentralized system dominated by no one; a third describes a compromise between increasing regional centralization and global decentralization; and a fourth describes a system incrementally adapted from prevailing patterns. Since there is no clear way to indicate how to move (or not move) from the present (in which elements of all the models exist) to any of the first three models and since there is no way to guarantee that any of the first three models will be more stable or just (or less stable and just) than the present system, the outcome tends to be predetermined: incrementalism seems the only feasible alternative. Thus the point of going through an elaborate exercise to reach the conclusion that we must seek rules for the existing system or for minor adaptations of it seems of doubtful merit.

The most obvious deficiency of settling on a quest for rules within the existing context (beyond the fact that the context may be rapidly altered by unforeseen events) is that the developing countries are bound to find it inadequate. This does not mean that they have any clear idea of how to implement a new order but rather that they can impede efforts to improve the existing order by refusing to cooperate. What this implies, I believe, is that while we must seek rules for improved performance within the existing context those rules must also be tilted so that the developing countries can feel that, *faute de mieux*, they will at least receive an increasing share of the *joint* benefits and that more substantial movement is not being permanently foreclosed. This may make them amenable to taking less than they want and to accepting rules that do not reflect massive change for their benefit, especially if the alternative were correctly perceived not as a New International Economic Order but rather as an order in which the strong do what they want. Rules somewhat tilted for the benefit of the developing countries do not seem wildly improbable since the commitment to development has already been accepted (to an admittedly varying and uncertain degree) by the international community. But I believe such rules will be much easier to implement in a less than global context.

Efforts to establish operating rules for the international system before establishing an agreement such as this are unlikely to be successful. This is clear, for example, not only in reference to suggestions that the new rich be incorporated into the decisionmaking process but also in reference to suggestions for *managed incrementalism.*[5] Legitimacy is problematic in the first case and effectiveness in the second. As I have argued elsewhere, incrementalism without some effort to provide central guidance about direction and consistency is likely to work only in stable systems with substantial spare resources.[6] In any case, the developing countries will not accept operating rules that do not guarantee significant benefits. We need, therefore, to be clearer about the kind of rules that might be generally acceptable in a context where the conflict between efficiency and equity persists but in which there is some agreement to provide continued benefits to the developing countries. In what follows I shall be concerned only with the nature of acceptable rules in this context and not with detailed or specific rules.

An ordering principle needs to reflect a very wide degree of consensus. Neither efficiency nor equity qualifies, since the attempt to establish the dominance of either will only generate increased conflict. As I have argued in the last section, however, while a sensible compromise between the two seems conceptually justified, political factors sharply diminish the probability of agreement. Another alternative, as some analysts have argued, would emphasize the necessity of stability in a system that seems to be changing too rapidly for prevailing institutions or ideas; conversely, arguing from the same perception of rapid change, others have stressed the need for radically restructuring the existing system. But we are not in sufficient control of events to guarantee stability, and we are not sufficiently intelligent to know how to revolutionize the system or to know what promises to be revolutionary, equitable, and effective.

The exception seems likely to be the rule in the emerging international system. A continuing breakdown of the line between domestic and international economics and politics, increasing demands for special treatment by the developing countries, numerous efforts to protect domestic producers, more ad hoc and informal decisionmaking (in the midst of and partially as the result of a persistent quest for global solutions), and an increase in attempts to enhance national welfare, probably at the expense of the general welfare or a concern with the stability of the system itself—all of these developments are possible and some highly probable.[7] The result will be not only an extraordinarily complex system but also a system with great potential for conflict and disintegration into hostile fragments.

In these circumstances, the integrity of the decisional system—the heart of the political process—is likely to be under severe attack. The import of decisions will be very hard to calculate, legitimacy will be minimal and enforcement infrequent, and the commitment to maintain agreements in the face of temporary adversities will decline. The threat to the system of decision—that no one will take commitments seriously enough—is critically important, since whatever chance we have of working our way out of present difficulties will require a decisional process that produces intended effects and has earned the confidence of its actors. This suggests, I believe, that the ordering principle that might be most valuable in this and the emerging context is dependability.

Dependability might seem a trivial or irrelevant response to a very difficult and complex negotiating environment. In context, however, it may have some virtues that are not sufficiently appreciated. Dependability—keeping arrangements, fulfilling promises, honoring obligations—has occasionally been discussed as a principle of justice.[8] But in the present system it is clearly inadequate in that sense, for there is no prior agreement on the criteria by which to judge whether what one is being asked to be dependable about is just or wise. This deficiency could only be remedied in a very stable order reflecting widespread consensus on values and interests. Nevertheless, dependability may be a very valuable operating rule in a system dominated by uncertainty and fears of instability—provided it is properly understood.

To simply assert in the abstract that freely negotiated agreements must be honored, or that exceptions must be justified by resort to agreed procedures, or that sanctions must be available against deliberate and unjustified malfeasance is, of course, a venture into well-meant fantasy. Acceptance of any operating rule must rest on an implicit premise about the nature and purposes of the game itself. But under the present circumstances this requirement cannot be adequately satisfied, for there are obvious and profound disagreements about the viability of the game (the reform versus revolution debate) and about the ends sought (rapid growth, the reduction of poverty, closing the "gap," the primacy of the political or the economic, etc.).

The severity of these constraints might appear to justify the argument that negotiations are bound to be futile. Zartman, for example, has argued that agreement on *referents* or principles of justice are necessary before bargaining on details can proceed.[9] But this is a counsel of perfection: the absence of desired conditions limits what can be legitimately expected, but it does not (or should not) imply that beneficial outcomes are precluded. We *must* negotiate without agreed referents, for the consequences of not negotiating may well be worse than the consequences of negotiating, whatever the difficulties. Merely keeping the process going may be a minimal virtue, but it is a virtue nonetheless. One needs also to emphasize that the absence of common values and an agreed frame of reference has not always prevented successful negotiation—even in the midst of war and indeed in the North-South arena itself. So long as mutually perceived common interests are present, the possibility of agreement—although limited—is likely also to be present. What needs to be carefully specified are the enabling conditions that might facilitate such limited agreements. These conditions must attempt to work with and around each side's central fears and concerns, and they must help to concentrate attention on what can be negotiated—that is, on issues where mutual benefits (now and in the future) are salient and the metaphysics of disagreement can be bypassed.

Dependability would be easy to establish as an operating rule if an agreement on efficiency and equity (such as the one discussed in the preceding section) were feasible. Short of that, the implicit premise underlying the acceptance of dependability in the prevailing situation is a willingness not only to keep the negotiating process going but also to maintain at least the existing degree of openness. Threats to pull out, to proscribe discussion of certain issues, or to establish private decisionmaking channels that are indifferent to the question of system-wide legitimacy are unacceptable. Minimally, one seeks to establish the grounds for moving forward by agreeing not to move backward. The developing countries, fearful of losing place and leverage in the international system, are thus guaranteed an important right: a significant role in a continuing process and a process in which their concerns will not be shunted aside or treated as an addendum to the concerns of the rich. This does not guarantee outcomes but rather attention; as such, it is necessary but not sufficient (a point to which I will return shortly).

As I have already noted, the developing countries are also guaranteed the legitimization of a persisting *tilt* toward their interests, something considerably less than a radical redistribution of benefits but at least something consistently more than is implied by a mere commitment to efficiency. The tradeoff for the developing countries is clear: surrendering the notion that there can be no viable compromise short of acceptance of new and radical principles of order in exchange for acceptance of the notion that the wisest current tactic is to take the best offer available—so long as it does not foreclose greater change later. Dependability in this context has another virtue for the developing countries that could be very important: the developed countries would also have to make a greater effort to obey the principles they ostensibly support. That is, dependability is not a one-sided virtue, and the gains from diminishing the tendency of the rich to violate their own principles whenever it is convenient could be substantial. The developing countries have apparently already begun to see this more clearly, as indicated by their rising protest against *voluntary* export restraints, *orderly marketing arrangements, organized free trade,* and other such euphemisms for discrimination in favor of noncompetitive domestic industries. The key point is that effective rules either do not exist or are ambiguous in these cases, and as a result individual outcomes tend to be largely determined by the economic power of the different parties. These outcomes might be somewhat more favorable for the developing countries if dependability were widely accepted as an operating rule. The increased stability would also be beneficial in the sense that improved efforts to plan would be facilitated.

For the developed countries, commitment to a continuing relationship characterized by increasing degrees of dependability also offers a few potentially significant benefits. There is, for example, some virtue in *joint* recognition of the fact that what is at stake in a particular negotiation is not the constitution of a new order but a building block that involves mutual benefits and that may increase the possibility that the outlines of a new order will become more clear. But even more critically, this may encourage a decisional context in which the rhetoric of confrontation depreciates and in which the pattern of concerns begins to focus on practicalities, not principles. This may diminish the tendency to ignore questions of implementation or of the gap between the generalities of global policymaking and the practicalities of local decision making. And, finally, since two of the most salient fears of the developed countries are that demands will continuously escalate and that concessions will merely generate new demands, the increased probability that both sides will maintain agreements—that is, be dependable—may slow the process of demand formation, at least until the consequences of particular agreements become more clear.

I noted earlier that the developing countries will want more than a guarantee of concern; they will also seek more tangible benefits. These benefits must be substantial enough so that failure to achieve them is a strong disincentive to violations. Clearly, once again efficiency must be diluted by some degree of equity, but perhaps the costs are more bearable in this context because agreements themselves are more workable and because the two sides accept both rights and duties.

There are two reasons that I believe this argument points strongly away from a completely global focus. The complexities on the global level are too vast, the tradeoffs too uncertain, and the benefits too dispersed and contingent to provide enough developing countries with the sense that they will in fact receive enough compensation for altering present tactics. I believe we must begin with the more precise rules and the more easily perceived benefits that might emerge from narrower agreements and settings. And in the same sense a movement away from the quest for immediate global solutions is relatively more likely to engender a concern with implementation, to diminish the effects attendant upon maintaining unity among large numbers of very disparate states, and to encourage a spirit of compromise. It need hardly be added that the attempt to navigate through current difficulties with the aid of an operating rule like dependability can never be more than an imperfect approximation of the ideal, but successively more effective approximations seem more probable if ambitions and expectations were to be sensibly moderated.

I do not mean to imply that all global approaches are necessarily wrong but rather that the direction of effort should be upward from those directly concerned, not downward from general principles of order. Thus, even where a global focus seems built into the negotiating process (as with various codes of conduct for the transfer of technology or the control of restrictive business practices) such efforts should not seek to determine specific outcomes; what can be established on the most general level is only a better environment of decision or a more just boundary between the permissible and the impermissible. Agreements on access to resources or rules for the protection of investment that may seem to require global rules are only partial exceptions, for even here different rules or interpretations may be necessary for countries at different levels of development or for different industries. In any case, these rules would be good illustrations of dependability, for both sides are likely to benefit from consistent implementation.

There are three global subsystems for which different sets of rules seem appropriate:[10] developed country-developed country interactions, developed-developing country interactions, and developing-developing country interactions. Other subsystems obviously exist, and some are actually or potentially significant: for example, East-West and East-South interactions. But the three that I have noted are dominant, and they tend also to incorporate most of the characteristics that can be found in lesser subsystems. In what follows I shall comment briefly on each of these major subsystems.

The developed countries' relationship among themselves is beyond my immediate concerns. Nevertheless, since prosperity among the developed countries may provide the developing countries their largest gains and since the reduction of external shocks and the threat of protectionism are critical needs for poor, exposed, and inflexible economies, a very brief comment seems appropriate. The interplay of domestic and external factors suggests the importance of seeking joint optimization rules for developed-developed relations. What is implied are complementary domestic rules to facilitate adjustment to external changes: in trade for example, as Harry Johnson has argued, adjustment assistance to increase the speed with which a change can be absorbed and safeguards to control the speed of the change that has to be absorbed should go hand in hand.[11] At any rate, some direct effort to connect internal and external change is necessary to enhance dependability and predictability.[12]

For the relationship between the developed and the developing countries, different rules need to be applied to the advanced, semi-industrial countries and to the great majority of very poor countries. The richer developing countries should be treated as potential or emerging members of the bloc of developed countries. Preferential and exceptional treatment is still justified, but it needs to be carefully limited. Thus such rules should not be open-ended, but rather should contain specific time provisions. In addition, a form of reciprocity seems justified not only in requesting the steady dismantlement of the many tariff and nontariff barriers that these countries have established but also in assuring that they do not attempt to freeze trade patterns so that the poorer developing countries have great difficulty in expanding their own trade. The familiar injunction that shared goals and mutual interests should be emphasized in the negotiating process makes a good deal of sense in this context, provided that the need for exceptional if limited treatment were also recognized.

The poorer developing countries need an entirely different set of rules. Neither the demand for reciprocity nor the effort to set time or volume limits on exceptional treatment seems justified. Here the *first* goal should not be the quick integration of these countries into the international trading system but rather an effort to provide a decent standard of living for all the populace as rapidly as possible and only a gradual and piecemeal integration into the trading system. The rules need to be perceived as the basis for a social welfare system that will persist for many decades, not as transient exceptions to the rules of the trading system itself.

The developing countries have talked increasingly of improving ties among themselves—of *collective self-reliance.*[13] And while the potential for important mutual gains from cooperation surely exists, thus far only talk—or rhetoric—has resulted. It is true that the developed countries can do little to encourage more substantive outcomes since the impetus must come from the developing countries themselves, but it is equally true that the developed countries can do a great deal to discourage or harm such efforts, and therefore a self-denying ordinance seems necessary: no effort to undermine cooperation by offering special inducements to particular developing countries to stay within a "sphere of interest" is justified. The rules that the developing countries should establish among themselves should probably take the form of scaled down versions of rules in the larger trading system: wider exceptions, longer time periods, more generous safeguards. Two dangers need to be carefully watched: the gradual replacement of dominance by a few developed countries with dominance by a few developing countries; and the creation of a permanent pattern of protection that makes integration within the wider trading system increasingly doubtful. The aim should be to facilitate integration on fairer terms and not to prevent it.

In an environment of conflict and uncertainty, separate systems with different but interlocking sets of rules may be more realistic than the quest for global rules. The more specific rules may enhance dependability and reduce uncertainty, they may make the possibility of seeking shared goals more realistic, and they may make it easier to balance short-run imperatives against potential long-run needs. In particular, such rules may also be incorporated more effectively in binding agreements that would permit the weaker countries to apply an important degree of pressure if they were violated, and the emphasis on mutual interests should in itself lower the probability of violation. More specific rules may also provide more certainty about details (duration, precise content, increased information), a factor of some significance for the developing countries. In short, these are likely to be rules that respond more effectively to both the domestic and international bargaining weaknesses of the majority of the Third World.

One other potential virtue ought to be emphasized: as I have noted in an earlier chapter, the international decisionmaking system is very distant from the world it seeks to regulate. This seems an almost inevitable outcome of a global focus and of a negotiating system dominated by diplomats in quest of political and ideological "victories." The more differentiated focus that I have advocated does not guarantee that these deficiencies will be remedied, but it should at least increase the possibility that problem solving and negotiation can be moved somewhat closer to the individuals, the sectors, or the countries most significantly affected by a decision. More rapid evaluation of consequences and a more flexible system of response may ensue. To some extent, a differentiated focus may also reduce escalating pressures on the institutional system. The syndrome that has developed (in which weak and derivative institutions are handed problems that they cannot resolve—and then are blamed for the results) needs to be resisted. The rule of thumb should be that solutions are first sought at the lowest level that incorporates all those directly concerned, and global institutions should only be a last resort for problems that cannot be settled elsewhere.

An argument for a decisional setting that reflects the pattern of substantive interests on an issue does not imply indifference to wider concerns like equity and legitimacy. A narrower institutional setting may increase the probability that efficiency will receive its due; a more global institutional setting, conversely, may increase the probability that equity and legitimacy will receive their due, if at some potential cost to efficiency. The precise tradeoff in this familiar conflict of values cannot be established by any technical rule. But the key point is that there *is* a tradeoff involved,

not an either/or choice. In practical terms, the most pressing need is for
the articulation of an indicative or normative rule that might provide
some guidance—but not a blueprint—for where the tradeoff should be
made. Perhaps something akin to the economist's notion of external effects should be considered. An agreement negotiated only by those most
directly concerned could thus be considered legitimate only if it did not
generate negative external effects for states not party to the agreement.
From this perspective, global institutions would have something of a
watching brief for external effects—which is to say for a proper balance
between efficiency and equity. In the nature of the case, distinctions of this
kind are more easily stated than precisely specified, but even the effort to
articulate a rule that is widely acceptable may be important when the
alternative is ad hoc improvisation.

Dependability is a modest and essentially procedural goal in a world
where sharp conflicts of value and interest threaten to undermine the
possibility of achieving or even discovering the common interests that do
exist. The quest for such limited gains—for at least getting the most out
of a very difficult environment—may seem decidedly unheroic or insufficient, especially in comparison with *planetary bargains* or *global compacts.* Nevertheless, while such gains may not always help the right countries or groups and while they are surely insufficient, it remains difficult
to argue that no gains are better than some gains—unless one has a rather
naive faith in either the likelihood of revolution or revolution as a panacea.
Perhaps above all, dependability may help to create islands of stability and
(limited) progress that might provide the necessary base for more profound and enduring changes.

. . .

NOTES

1. Fred Hirsch and Michael W. Doyle, "Politicization in the World Economy:
   Necessary Conditions for an International Economic Order," in *Alternatives
   to Monetary Disorder,* Fred Hirsch, Michael Doyle, and Edward L. Morse
   (New York: McGraw-Hill, 1977), p. 64.
2. There is an element of "manner of speaking" in reference to the idea of *global*
   issues. In fact, even apparently obvious global issues like the Law of the Sea
   debate tend to have very little practical significance for some states and tend
   not to require nearly universal consensus to implement effective settlements.
   Surely the more that agree the better, but this is not to say that states with little
   at stake should be allowed to hinder progress. When I suggest that not every
   state needs to participate or be consulted on every issue, I definitely do not
   mean to exclude the weakest states—only those who are little affected (and
   many of the poorest *are* heavily affected and have both moral and practical
   rights to participate).
3. Radical spokesmen will reject my emphasis on rules that do not promise either

massive restructuring of the system or massive resource transfers. But I doubt that the real choice is between radical restructuring or reform of the status quo. Rather it is between reform rules and stabilization rules that at least keep open the possibility of steady but meaningful change (for the benefit of all) and continuation of the movement away from a system based on agreed rules. In short, for the developing countries the choice is between getting something (with a potential for getting more) and getting nothing (except for the lucky few, who may get a great deal). At the same time, I believe that there is utility in talking about the need for global rules—as a normative exercise and as a reminder of the limitations of lesser rules.

4. I do not mean to imply that there is any moral or political comparability between these very different efforts—the only comparability is in the probability that they will not succeed.

5. The term is from Ernst B. Haas, "Turbulent Fields and the Theory of Regional Integration," *International Organization* 30, no. 2 (Spring 1976): 195.

6. See Robert L. Rothstein, *Planning, Prediction, and Policymaking in Foreign Affairs* (Boston: Little, Brown, 1972), pp. 22–31.

7. Hirsch and Doyle, "Politicization in the World Economy," forecast a considerably looser international system in the 1980s and raise the question of how to keep the loosening under control—although they do not seem to provide an answer. At any rate, the same question is also important in the analysis that follows.

8. There is a very useful discussion in Paul Diesing, *Reason in Society—Four Types of Decisions and their Social Conditions* (Urbana: University of Illinois Press, 1962), pp. 166–167.

9. William Zartman, "Negotiations: Theory and Reality," *Journal of International Affairs* 29, no. 1 (Spring 1975): 71.

10. I note again two prior assumptions: the first, that there is general agreement that some *tilting* for the developing countries is justified; the second (already noted in Chapter 6), that efforts to legitimize in wider forums will be undertaken.

11. See Harry Johnson, *Technology and Economic Interdependence* (London: Macmillan, 1975), p. 158.

12. Another way of seeking to connect internal and external policy might be by a *fair weather* rule: a country agrees to reduce tariff and nontariff barriers when its balance of payments is favorable, but it is *not* permitted to increase them when the balance of payments is unfavorable (since another country will now be in surplus and thus have to reduce its barriers). All barriers would disappear in time. A rule that diminishes the possibility of withdrawing concessions in this way is an attractive stabilization mechanism—and increases dependability. I am not sure whether it is feasible, but it does seem that we should be seeking this kind of rule more intensively than we have.

13. See UNCTAD, *Economic Cooperation Among Developing Countries, Report of the Group of Experts* (Geneva: TD/B/AC.19/1), December 1975, which is a good place to begin examination of this issue.

After the Fall: The Politics of Oil

Edward L. Morse

The most startling surprise in the international economy during the 1980s has been the fulfillment of prophecies made five years ago—often voiced, seldom believed—that oil prices would decline significantly from their peak price of over $40 a barrel in 1980–1981. Prices have, in fact, fallen to less than $12 a barrel on the spot market this past winter.

There is almost universal agreement that, on the whole, lower oil prices are beneficial to the world economy. But very low prices will pose very big problems. A further dramatic decline in oil prices will have a revolutionary impact on world politics and the international economy of a magnitude tantamount to that of the oil price increases in 1973–1974 and 1979–1980.

An explanation of the events that will be triggered by an oil price collapse depends, first, on an understanding of the peculiar nature of the international oil trade, so unlike that of other commodities, and second, on a determination of exactly what happened this past winter. Then the conditions that would allow a free-fall in oil prices can be defined. The consequences of such a price drop, including the implications for Western energy security, will become evident. And appropriate policy responses can be discussed.

Whatever emerges in the coming months, it is clear that the oil sector, with its fundamental effects on international economic and political affairs, will never again be anything like what it was.

II

The international petroleum industry has always been somewhat special and different from other commodity sectors. Given its pervasive influence on industrial growth, and the record of government and industry

Edward Morse, "After the Fall: The Politics of Oil." Reprinted by permission of *Foreign Affairs*, Spring 1986, Vol. 64, No. 4. Copyright 1986 by the Council on Foreign Relations, Inc.

interventions over the decades, the oil sector has not generally functioned as a free transparent market in which price is determined by the interaction of many buyers and sellers. At most times in the past, rather, oil has been traded through a contrived mechanism to balance supply and demand. The market has also been a source of dynamic change since before the turn of the century, when oil was first produced in commercial quantities.

Throughout this period, beginning roughly in 1890, oil prices have experienced sharp cyclical change in a remarkably consistent pattern. The dollar price of oil in real terms has gone from trough to peak roughly every ten years, and then moved from peak to trough in the decade following. In the cycle that preceded the current phase, oil prices had reached a floor of less than $3 per barrel (in 1976 dollars) at the end of World War II, rising to a peak of about $4.25 in 1958. Throughout the 1960s, the real price of oil steadily declined, as low-cost Middle Eastern oil came on the market, and finally reached its trough at about $3.90 per barrel during 1969–1970.

The last cycle was the most volatile, with the peak reached by oil prices in 1981—about $12.50, in real price terms—representing a 225-percent increase over the previous decade. If the pattern continues, we will be in for a long price decline that will probably reach bottom in the early 1990s, when price levels will hover at a level, expressed in 1986 dollars, of $8 to $10 per barrel.

The twenty-year boom-and-bust pattern of the international oil market has shown another interesting pattern: each recent price trough has brought with it a reorganization of the petroleum industry, uniting governments and companies in actions to limit the damage of price declines and a contracting petroleum production cycle.

The first such extraordinary effort came with the price trough of 1932, when an oil glut developed in the United States. Oil companies and the governors of the various oil-producing states came together and agreed to impose production restraints. At various stages the Texas Railroad Commission and the U.S. federal government managed this *cartel*. In the period after World War II, the *Seven Sisters* (the major international oil companies), which had discovered and developed new supplies outside of traditional sources, especially in the Middle East, worked together informally to expand and contract production when market balancing was required. In the late 1950s, another price trough resulted in the creation of the Organization of Petroleum Exporting Countries (OPEC), which eventually developed strong mechanisms to control production levels and prices. OPEC had been formed in an effort to shift the burden of adjustment away from the oil producing members and back to the United States. Through the tumultuous 1970s, OPEC appeared to provide a successful mechanism for supporting prices via production restraints, but it was only in the early 1980s that the mechanism was actively tested. In early 1973 virtually no one imagined that an oil revolution was at hand, or that its impact would effect fundamental changes in the world's economy, the security of the West and the structure of the energy industry.

Today we can observe a similar set of revolutionary conditions, even though as recently as three years ago few foresaw that a price collapse could occur as rapidly as it has. This is because, until last year, the gradually accelerating decline in oil prices was both masked and tempered by the appreciation of the U.S. dollar. Oil is priced in dollars, so Europe and Japan appeared to be paying more for their oil in 1985 than in 1981, and most OPEC countries' earnings were modestly improved. Now, as the dollar has depreciated relative to other currencies, the consuming countries have gained the benefits of lower oil prices, just as the exporters have suffered.

III

Last fall, oil prices began to firm up on the spot market as the winter heating season approached; then, in January and February 1986, they tumbled by more than $15 in just a few weeks. Why did the oil market, which had been weakening for four years, suddenly appear to collapse out of control?

The answer can be found in decisions taken in Saudi Arabia in the summer and fall of 1985. The Saudis decided to flood a weak market, with the intention of pushing prices down rapidly. They made certain their oil would be sold by changing the method by which it was priced. Traditionally the Saudis, like other OPEC producers and non-OPEC producers such as Mexico, Britain, and Norway, had established official sales prices. The new approach—called *netback pricing*—assured refiners buying Saudi crudes of a profit on each barrel processed and sold as gasoline, diesel, fuel oil, and other petroleum products. Through this new pricing scheme, Saudi oil was valued by the market price of the products into which it was refined (e.g., gasoline, heating oil), less the costs of refining and transportation. Saudi production increased from a low level of 2.5 million barrels or less a day to a new targeted daily level of 4.3 million barrels or more. Why did the Saudi government change its traditional, conservative approach to selling crude oil?

Let us look at the context of the past half-decade. The 1980s began with a nervous and tight oil market. The revolution in Iran and the curtailment of Iranian production in 1979–1980 spurred an increase in the price of oil by more than two times, to $30 per barrel and above for oil sold under term contract and to more than $40 per barrel sold on a spot basis. These high prices, coming on top of the pricing revolution of 1973–1974, ushered in a world recession. They also served to accelerate the search for oil outside OPEC, to encourage energy-saving investments, and to make virtually all competitive fuels (e.g., nuclear power, natural gas, and coal) attractive alternatives to petroleum. Thus, demand for oil dropped, even as new oil supplies from non-OPEC sources were brought into production.

In order to protect the price of internationally traded oil, OPEC reached a series of internal agreements, first made in 1982–1983 and updated several times thereafter, to restrict its members' production to 18 million barrels per day (in contrast to the OPEC peak production level of

31 million barrels per day, reached in 1981), and to allocate that production among its members by quota. Some ten million barrels a day of production capacity had to be left untapped, or shut in, in order to balance supply and demand at a price in the range of $25 to $28 per barrel. Saudi Arabia, with by far the largest reserves in OPEC (and the world), assumed the role of swing producer, adjusting its production level up and down to balance supply with demand and to protect the price. OPEC's bet was that a revival in world economic activity would soon commence, bringing with it higher demand for oil and more robust OPEC production.

The bet was lost. Instead, OPEC saw its role in world oil trade diminish as new supplies outside OPEC came into the market. Through new investment, British and Norwegian production grew to new record levels in 1983, 1984, and 1985. India and Brazil, two of the largest developing countries, moved rapidly from being large importers toward achieving oil self-sufficiency. Other developing countries began to produce and export oil, and because of conservation, industrial restructuring, and fuel switching in the industrial countries, oil demand never rebounded as the OPEC strategists had expected.

The members of OPEC, the Saudis and other Persian Gulf states in particular, saw their plight worsening. OPEC's share of free-world oil production shrank from a high of 55 percent in 1973 to 30 percent in 1985, and the cartel was unable to market production at its targeted volume. Despite a widespread view that the lower-producing OPEC countries were "cheating" by producing at levels higher than their quotas, the remarkable feature of the oil market during 1981–85 was that OPEC held together so well. It did so essentially because Saudi Arabia was willing to be the swing producer and adjust its production downward to balance the market. The result was low Saudi production and Saudi oil income of $28 billion in 1985 as opposed to its peak income of $113 billion in 1981.

OPEC came to understand that it could not go on playing the role of market balancer and price supporter alone. But despite several efforts to gain the support of Britain and Norway, the North Sea producers refused to limit their production. Instead, in order to protect their market shares, Norway and Britain abandoned administered pricing in 1984 and let the market determined the price for their crude. By last summer, the Saudis recognized that the only way they could be assured a minimally acceptable income was to reduce prices and increase production, punishing the North Sea producers with lower income in hopes of gaining their future cooperation.

What are the chances of success for this new Saudi gamble? Is there any way OPEC and non-OPEC producers can together or separately regain control over the oil market and assure a higher minimum price? Should the Saudis again fail in their tactics, what would be the consequences—for them, for OPEC, for other oil producers, and for the world economy? The answers depend on certain fundamental changes that can now be discerned in the international oil industry.

IV

Successful oil market management depends on three basic conditions. The first is a limitation on the number of major participants in the market: the fewer the better. The second is the ability of the major players to take decisions to rationalize production, deciding where, for how long, and under what circumstances production is to be shut in. The third relates to the degree to which the petroleum industry is integrated, with networks of close ties between upstream activities (i.e., oil production) and down-stream activities (oil refining and marketing). The more integrated the industry, the more amenable the market will be to constructive management.

Bearing this in mind, it can be seen that the revolution of the 1970s in the petroleum sector was manifold. It involved not only the quadrupling of oil prices and the emergence of a powerful OPEC cartel, but it also involved a wave of nationalizations in the developing countries, including Kuwait, Venezuela, Iraq, Peru, and Saudi Arabia, of the oil-producing properties of the international oil companies. In the 1970s, nationalized firms accounted for nearly three-quarters of international production and included virtually all of the important oil exporters in the developing world.

Beyond the obvious transfer of equity interests, these nationalizations brought about fundamental and quite unintended changes in the structure of the oil market. They broke the linkages between the developing world's oil production and that of the industrialized countries, an essential connection if world production is to be rationalized. The nationalizations motivated the international oil companies to accelerate their search for oil in new frontier areas, including the North Sea and developing countries where governments permitted the companies to make reasonable profits. And finally, the nationalizations broke the tight coordination of production and refining, long considered a prerequisite to managing the petroleum economy by reducing price volatility.

The cumulative result of the developments of the 1970s is a paradoxical imbalance in the oil market, one that only invites pressures for substantially lower prices. For the past four years, supply and demand have been balanced only because the lowest-cost producers (the Middle East) have shut in their production. Meanwhile, the highest-cost producers have pumped oil at near maximum capacities and have had every incentive to expand production. This condition is exactly the opposite of what one would anticipate in a truly free market.

In a transparent and efficient marketplace, prices should decline toward the level of production expenses in the least-cost producing countries, and production capacity of higher-cost producers would be shut in until such time as demand warranted the production of higher-cost oil. In today's world, this would mean closing down production in the North Sea,

Alaska, and offshore North America, and the expanding of production in the Arabian peninsula. But the opposite has happened.

To further distort the classic model, new oil production is now anticipated from the North Sea, from new entrants to the ranks of oil producers and exporters such as Colombia and North Yemen, from steady increases in production elsewhere among importers in the developing world (Brazil and India), and from expected increases in Iraqi and perhaps Iranian production—once they are no longer at war—due to the completion of new pipeline outlets.

Non-OPEC production should rise by some 500,000 barrels a day in 1986, reaching nearly 28.8 million barrels, and by an additional similar amount in the following two or three years. With demand basically flat at 45.5 million barrels, even if prices fall, requirements for OPEC oil will average no more than 16.5 million barrels a day this year, some 700,000 barrels less than last year. This spring and summer, world oil demand is expected to drop to 44 million barrels a day; demand for OPEC oil should be no more than 15.6 million and perhaps as low as 14.5 million barrels— the lowest level since the oil price surge of 1973.

Furthermore, with the separation of production and refining operations, the volume of oil bought on the spot market rose in the late 1970s through the early 1980s from about five percent to perhaps 50 percent of all traded oil, creating enormous price volatility and, eventually, downward price pressure. Organized futures markets in petroleum products and crude oil came into existence in New York and London to compensate for the new volatility, providing opportunities not only for hedging, but also for speculation.

These structural circumstances bore down on the largest and most flexible of the producers, Saudi Arabia. By shutting in their production, Saudi Arabia and other OPEC countries have, in effect, subsidized the prices for the high-cost producers in the United States, Mexico, and the North Sea countries. Saudi Arabia has now demonstrated its frustration at the heavy revenue burdens incurred by subsidizing oil production outside of OPEC. Its new policy of higher production is thus partially punitive in nature, aimed at forcing non-OPEC exporters and other producers to share in the burden of balancing the market.

These new efforts will accelerate another structural change in the petroleum market and the petroleum industry: OPEC has, at least for the time being, lost its role as a key player in the political economy of oil.

The members of OPEC are basically interested in maximizing the rents to be gained from oil exploitation. They also, as a group, have wanted to make certain that the burdens of any market adjustments, introduced to compensate for changing conditions of supply, demand, and price, are pushed onto the oil-importing countries and the international oil companies. As of winter 1985–1986, this approach had failed.

Despite this common purpose, the members of OPEC differ significantly one from another. Some (e.g., Saudi Arabia and the smaller producers around the Arabian peninsula) are high-reserve, low-population countries, the remaining members have low reserves and a high population. From another perspective, the relationships within OPEC are based on the fact that one producer, Saudi Arabia, is so much more significant than the others.

In this respect, the bargaining relationships within OPEC look strikingly like those within NATO. OPEC and NATO both are comprised of like-minded governments, targeting a common external *"enemy,"* but also relating to one another through an array of asymmetrical relations: a large country at the *core* and many smaller and less influential countries around the *periphery.* Within NATO it is the interest of the U.S. government to maximize its own freedom in dealing with the Soviet Union and to assure that its allies undertake policies that do not undermine its bilateral relations with the U.S.S.R. Similarly, it is in the interests of the smaller NATO countries to restrain the United States, to make its behavior more regular and predictable, and to maximize their own freedom of action to pursue individual foreign policies *vis-à-vis* the countries of the Eastern bloc.

OPEC, too, is comprised of a large country at the core of the organization (Saudi Arabia) and smaller countries along the periphery. It has been the Saudi intention for the past decade to maintain a moderate international petroleum sector, one in which the life of petroleum as an important commodity in international trade is stretched out as long as possible. This has meant that although the Saudis do not want to see the price of oil fall precipitously, they have also not been eager to see the price increase dramatically. It has been the Saudi objective to maximize its own freedom and to constrain that of its OPEC partners. Similarly, it has been the goal of virtually all of Saudi Arabia's partners in OPEC to enlarge their own freedom to produce and price oil and to keep Saudi behavior predictable and constrained. That tension between Saudi Arabia and the other OPEC producers resulted in the stalemate that the Saudi decision to regain its market share broke open.

Given their large external financial reserves, their links to banks in the industrialized countries and their military links to the United States, the Saudis are torn between the Western industrialized countries and their OPEC partners. From this perspective, it can be concluded that Saudi Arabia's recent behavior reflects an understanding that a fundamental structural shift is required in the way the international petroleum sector is governed. The older ties among OPEC countries may become less relevant than the process of establishing new alignments among oil producers and consumers.

The upshot of all these circumstances is clear. A radical restructuring of the oil industry and the oil market is about to take place. That restructuring will require new approaches to the sensible management of the petroleum economy. What is required is a simplification in the number of major participants in the market, a mechanism to organize production in correlation with demand, and a reintegration between upstream and downstream petroleum operations. This restructuring will not take place without an intervening step: namely a radical collapse in oil prices sometime during the next 18 months, perhaps as early as this summer. Oil prices in the range of $8 to $10 per barrel cannot be dismissed.

V

What will be the consequences of such a price collapse? If Saudi Arabia's gamble to push the costs of adjustment onto non-OPEC producers fails, as the preceding analysis of structural changes in the petroleum sector implies it might, there is no logical stopping place for the price of oil above $8–$10 per barrel. Oil industry analysts agree that production capacity will not be restrained *for reasons of cost* unless the price falls below $8 per barrel. Furthermore, at various points between $10 and $20 per barrel, new investments in energy conservation cease. New capital expenditures by oil companies are also reduced, eventually almost to the point of elimination.

Absent political intervention, and given the extraordinary overhang of supply, with OPEC's production capacity still some ten million barrels per day higher than current production levels, this situation can continue for a long time. With oil prices dropping toward $10 per barrel, it should take at least five years before lack of investment in new supplies and increases in demand triggered by low prices begin to push prices upwards again—excluding, of course, the occurrence of a new supply disruption. Lack of new investment will result in dramatically decreasing production levels in certain parts of the world, probably most significantly in the United States. With oil priced at less than $16–$18 per barrel, new investments in the more costly techniques of secondary and tertiary recovery will cease. At less than $15 per barrel, stripper-well production, responsible for about one million barrels a day today, will be terminated. Overall, we can anticipate a decline in U.S. domestic production on the order of ten percent per annum.

In a relatively short period of time, therefore, Western economic security will begin to be threatened by a substantial decline in new energy investments. Given the steep rate of decline of some domestic reserves, the maintenance of American production at levels covering two-thirds of domestic consumption requires a constant effort to assure that new reserves are brought into commercial production. These reserves tend to be high cost and to require investments in secondary and tertiary recovery not needed elsewhere, particularly in the Middle East. Price uncertainty alone leads to the postponement of such investments. Very low prices preclude them.

The faster the decline to $10 a barrel and the longer it lasts, the more significant will be the implications for energy security and inflation in the 1990s. Without sustained efforts to seek out new sources of conventional oil supply, growing demand and diminishing surplus production capacity for petroleum could result in a price escalation in the 1990s not unlike that which the world experienced in the 1970s.

Beyond the economic effects are the political implications for Saudi Arabia and other Middle Eastern low-population oil producers. In the shorter term, a price decline will raise serious problems of political stability in all oil-exporting regimes. It would weaken the ability of the Saudi government to maintain the authority of the king *vis-à-vis* other members of the extended ruling family, given their sharp reductions in income. It would also affect their feelings toward the West in general, and the United States in particular, provoking a likely nationalistic response based on a belief that Western governments somehow engineered the price collapse in order to punish the Saudi regime (for reasons, for example, associated with America's ties to Israel). It would possibly further fuel Islamic fundamentalist nationalism in the Persian Gulf. In short, lower prices in a weakened Saudi regime could pose security dilemmas for America's strategic interests in the Arabian peninsula.

Over the longer run, especially if new exploration expenditures outside the Gulf are dramatically reduced, a price collapse would be a prelude to a reassertion of Saudi dominance in the international oil markets in the next decade, once the surplus production capacity of the world is drawn down. Such a development poses a dilemma for the West: this is true no matter whether one views the situation with the suspicion that heightened Middle Eastern control over the world's oil supplies will result in sharply higher prices and detrimental conditions for Western economic interests, or whether one believes that greater dependence on Saudi and Middle Eastern oil creates heightened vulnerabilities in fundamental Western economic and security interests. It is perhaps unwise to speculate on what type of Saudi regime will be in place in the 1990s when the United States and other Western countries will again be highly dependent on Middle Eastern supplies. It also matters less what the Saudis have been like in the past than what the implications are for Saudi behavior in the future. A new xenophobic Saudi leadership under circumstances of heightened Western dependence on Saudi oil might be dangerous indeed.

The concentration of extra production capacity that will be held by Middle Eastern countries in the 1990s could well make Western dependence much greater than it was in the 1970s. The "oil weapon" could return with a vengeance. In any event, the Saudi role as swing producer balancing the marketplace will be much more critical. Both the shorter- and longer-term consequences of a decline in oil prices therefore raise significant energy security questions.

Of special significance is the effect of lower prices on the oil exporting countries, especially those most heavily in debt, such as Mexico and Nigeria. Clearly, lower prices will result in lower revenues for virtually all of the oil exporting countries, whether they belong to OPEC or not (assuming OPEC production at its targeted level of 18 million barrels a day).

Petroleum Intelligence Weekly, in its January 13, 1986, issue, calculated that $20-per-barrel oil would result in total OPEC revenues of barely over $100 billion in comparison to total OPEC revenues last year of over $130 billion and, in 1980, of $280 billion. At $10 per barrel, revenues would drop to $50 billion, with demand levels still not increasing for a few years.

In such a scenario, the financial situation of virtually all indebted oil exporting countries would be jeopardized. Almost none would be able to service debt and also continue to import necessary consumer and capital goods. Political stability, already in question, would be in further danger, and bitterness among the OPEC countries toward one another and toward industrialized countries would be high.

A gentle decline in oil prices through December 1985 already brought nervousness to the international banking community and financial authorities in the United States and elsewhere before the latest price drop. A precipitous decline would create the fear of a tidal wave of bank failures, beginning with the regional banks of the southwestern United States and extending to the money-center banks as well, as the plight of debtors in the United States approaches in severity that of the developing countries.

The oil industry in the United States and elsewhere in the West will obviously be affected by a sharp drop in prices. So will the new crop of state-owned energy enterprises in the developing world. As oil prices fall toward $10 per barrel, the oil industry will bear an increasing share of the loss; governments will have to support a decreasing share because of the structure of most tax regimes. The oil companies' capital expenditures in new exploration investments will thus decline even more dramatically.

Each of the downward pricing spirals of the past century has resulted in a massive restructuring of the oil industry and in political efforts to put a floor under prices. The international petroleum industry has just adjusted to an extraordinary transformation during the last decade. Fifteen years ago, about 80 percent of the world's production of petroleum was dominated by the large international oil companies through their international activities. Now the oil industry has become both fragmented and decentralized.

The number of important producing companies, now including national oil companies as well as those owned by private shareholders, increased several fold. Today the national oil companies command an equal footing with the majors and independents as significant market participants. The international integration that once involved production abroad and refining in one's home country has been broken. And the number of parties participating in the international petroleum trade has increased from fewer than 20 to more than 100.

The future structure of the oil industry is by no means easy to foresee, but a radical rationalization seems inevitable. As a result of recent acquisitions and efforts to ward off corporate takeovers, the number of oil companies in the United States that have accumulated potentially dangerous levels of debt has increased. State-owned international oil companies, like

Kuwait Petroleum Company and Petrobras of Brazil, which have engaged in wide-ranging international exploration, could well be giants among the survivors in the next decade. They will be joined by such companies as Petróleos de Venezuela as it proceeds to acquire substantially larger downstream assets in the consuming countries of Europe and North America.

The petroleum industry that will emerge from this shakeout will be rationalized along lines involving an amalgam of state-owned and private enterprises with multiple joint ventures between them.

A precipitous price collapse would, in short, carry with it revolutionary consequences that now can only be partially discerned. What can be done to guard against the most dangerous consequences of a price collapse?

VI

Various political actions have been proposed to prevent a free-fall in oil prices to the $10 level or below. Any of them, to be effective, would require increasingly unlikely and delicate coordination between OPEC and non-OPEC countries, between producing and consuming countries, between governments and multinational companies, or among the consuming countries on their own. Failing such an unlikely coordinated political intervention, we can anticipate a radical price drop soon; prices should then hover at extraordinarily low levels for at least a half-decade. Moreover, with ample supplies and a reluctance on the part of companies to hold inventories due to market uncertainty, the oil consuming world will experience price volatility over an annual cycle in response to higher winter heating season demand for crude oil and overall lower summer demand.

In recent months a number of experienced observers of the oil industry have reminded us of the error of considering the international petroleum market to be like other commodity markets. Melvin A. Conant and Paul Frankel, for example, have been arguing for more than a year for a substantive dialogue between OPEC and non-OPEC producers and between producers and consumers. Walter J. Levy has frequently warned that the West ought not to be lulled into a false sense of security by the oil glut that emerged after 1981. These warnings have been unheeded so far. The imminence of a price collapse reminds us that such pronouncements stem from long experience and observation of the petroleum sector and of the fragile underlying political base that has supported international oil prices over the past few years.

Analysis of the international petroleum economy and its momentous political implications is a relatively easy first step. It is quite another matter to lay out policy proposals for addressing the worst ramifications of a price collapse. If a destabilizing price collapse is to be prevented, a new regime for managing the petroleum sector is required, a regime to provide mechanisms of coordination among producing and importing countries, among consuming countries, between private companies and government companies, and between companies and governments. With all these interests at stake, no simplified solution could satisfy them all.

Yet simplified responses are what come out of politics. Thus, proposals for the immediate imposition of barriers to the import of petroleum and petroleum products into the United States are already receiving attention in the U.S. Congress. Import barriers would protect prices for U.S.-based producers and, therefore, would also protect bank loans to the oil industry. This solution has also become increasingly attractive in the United States in light of the budget deficit. Tariff barriers would raise government revenues and protect producer interests within the United States by providing a de facto floor price for petroleum production.

This policy approach had an intellectual force in the recent past, when the oil market was tight and when conservation and fuel-switching were to be encouraged. Under past conditions, an import fee would also have served to recapture some of the "rents" of oil production that OPEC countries were receiving. In today's climate, however, a unilateral import fee would create more problems than it would solve. A *go it alone* policy by the United States would actually have pernicious ramifications for virtually all the oil exporting countries of the world. It would also create significant trade frictions with our most important industrial trading partners.

In a slack market, with a supply overhang, oil would be competitively poised to enter the U.S. market at the domestic U.S. price minus the tariff barrier price. World oil prices would thereby tend to be depressed even further in any competitive effort by foreign producers to gain access to the U.S. market. In short, what might work satisfactorily in a tight marketplace would be counterproductive in a slack market. A tariff would defeat any interests the U.S. government might have in trying to assist other producing and exporting countries, such as Mexico and some of the OPEC countries. And it would completely ignore the effects that significantly lower prices would have on Britain, Norway, and Canada.

It can be argued that there would be significant incentives to make an import tariff barrier multilateral by extending it well beyond the United States to include our industrial partners and Mexico as well. In all likelihood, a U.S. administration would probably seek to extend a tariff wall on a multilateral basis.

One system, in fact, is already in place through which the industrialized countries could collectively protect their gains in conservation, their future production base of petroleum and other conventional fuels, and their banking and trading system. It lies in the International Energy Agency (IEA), created in 1974 in the aftermath of the first oil shock, which includes nearly all of the 24 members of the Organization of Economic Cooperation and Development (OECD).

It should be recalled that the IEA, which is widely identified with its emergency oil-sharing arrangement, also has as a goal the promotion of petroleum resources within the IEA area. A mechanism instituted in 1974 to encourage "indigenous" IEA production was a floor under the price of oil; at that time the floor price was $7 a barrel. Political interests could now be refocused on a minimal floor price for oil on the order of $15 a barrel through the IEA mechanism.

In addition to protecting indigenous production and existing conservation gains, a tariff wall around the IEA to protect a minimum oil price would serve other interests as well. It would help resolve trade frictions among the industrialized countries with respect to petroleum products and petrochemicals, which are already heightened and which would be further exacerbated by a unilateral U.S. tariff. A multilateral oil tariff would serve financial interests by preventing panic and providing a rational basis for the settlement of at least a significant portion of oil-related debt. In all likelihood, it would be a condition of any U.S. administration's consent to such a scheme that it take in all of North America (including Mexico) and potentially much of the Western Hemisphere (i.e., Venezuela, Ecuador, and possibly Colombia) within the tariff wall.

The IEA solution would have a more cosmopolitan impact if Mexico were to be protected by the tariff wall. Placing an effective floor under Mexican oil prices through Mexico's incorporation in the network would, first and foremost, be of importance to the United States for bilateral foreign policy reasons. Beyond that, it would be of interest to the banking community. Mexico, Brazil, and Argentina together are the three largest debtor countries, responsible for nearly 30 percent of all outstanding developing-country debt. Argentina, being self-sufficient in oil, would have no need to require inclusion under the tariff wall's protection. Brazil, as a net oil importing country, would, on the whole, be better off with much lower oil prices so long as it was able to maintain adequate incentives for domestic exploration and production. Only Mexico, among the large debtor countries, could gain substantially from inclusion in this system.

An expanded IEA tariff wall would clearly provide one of the few viable options for dealing with a price collapse, as it would help serve many highly politicized interests and take advantage of an institutional framework that already exists.

In the long run, however, a solution based on the IEA and its mechanisms would be inadequate to the tasks ahead. It would, by providing special preferential arrangements for North Sea, U.S., and Mexican oil, polarize relationships between the IEA countries and the rest of the world, in particular OPEC countries and other indebted developing countries. It would permanently solve neither the difficulties inherent in the petroleum sector, nor those in the financial and trade arenas.

An IEA solution would exclude OPEC from any role other than that of marginal supplier, or balancer, of the international petroleum market. And it would probably not serve the interests of many governments and companies whose relationships with producer governments and national oil companies have become far more complex than was the case in 1974. It is tempting, therefore, to look at an alternative approach, which has been proposed at various times during the past ten years or so: a global oil compact involving all of the major oil exporting and importing countries.

Even if a global compact among all parties concerned could be achieved in the current context or in the aftermath of a price collapse, there is a significant residue of mistrust concerning how long such an agreement could last. No one has forgotten how difficult it was for the Saudis in the late 1970s and early 1980s to induce discipline among OPEC countries to prevent prices from escalating so rapidly and to such high levels as to ensure OECD conservation, decreased demand, and the substitution of other forms of energy for oil. Nor have they forgotten how rapidly recent OPEC production and pricing agreements have disintegrated.

Western governments would understandably refuse to be involved in an agreement that would shore up OPEC countries today, since the OPEC countries would be expected to be the first to break such an agreement once the demand/supply balance tightened again. An even greater set of political forces is reluctant to engage in any market intervention, given the recollections of how market interventions have worked in the past: they have given rise to corruption, they have been unmanageable, and they have created distortions in the economy at least as onerous as the management of those interventions themselves.

None of these policy options augers well for OPEC. Nor is there necessarily a convincing case that OPEC would be able to *organize itself* to deal with the problem. The protectionist wall that will probably emerge around the IEA is also more likely to lead individual OPEC countries to try to make their own side deals with the industrialized governments in order to gain market share. Their distrust of one another, the history of failure of sustained concerted action in OPEC during the past four years, and the need of the most severely indebted OPEC countries to maximize their revenues by expanding production would, in all likelihood, keep OPEC fragmented. The prospects are therefore exceedingly low for OPEC members to act together. So, the possibility of OPEC reaching a marketing agreement with the industrial countries is also low.

VII

The main weakness in any possible market rationalization program that the consuming or producing countries, acting separately, might take relates to the structure of the international petroleum market. A coherent line of action requires strong linkages among the major oil producers in the world. It also requires integrated linkages between upstream production activities and downstream refining and marketing operations. Neither of these linkages is strong under present conditions.

An international oil market with slack demand, such as today's, could be regulated through coordinated action by producers to shut in production and withhold excess supplies from the marketplace. Similarly, the integrated linkages between production and refining could enable the major international companies to shift their profits between production and refining activities, depending on the state of the marketplace.

In today's world, how might such a rationalization of the petroleum market and industry develop? What actions along these lines can we anticipate from the Saudis and other participants in the world oil market?

Let us take another look at the two elements that form the necessary conditions for a new rationalization of the petroleum market: coordinated production and reintegration of upstream and downstream activities.

Coordination of production on a worldwide basis has proved to be the most elusive of goals for OPEC since 1982. OPEC could not manage this on its own, as the marginal or balancing supplier to the world market. It failed in efforts to co-opt the non-OPEC exporters. And it was unable to induce cooperation from international oil companies, with whom it had severed its ties through the nationalizations of the 1970s. But a basis might well exist to crystallize a new form of production rationalization, with or without the erection of a protective wall by the IEA countries. The Saudis are one key to this issue; the other key is the condition of the marketplace today and the plight of many of the large producing companies.

Given the extraordinary indebtedness of some major oil companies, one can imagine that a precipitous collapse of oil prices might create conditions conducive to a deal between some of these companies and some of the principal producing governments, especially Saudi Arabia. Once prices collapse, some of these companies will be desperate to find ways to sell or finance their debt, as a matter of corporate survival. One can imagine a process through which an entity of the Saudi government, or of the governments of other oil exporting countries, would offer to purchase the non-OPEC reserves of these companies. For the oil exporting country, a choice would then exist; it could shut down these newly acquired reserves in order to increase the market share from its own domestic production; or it could shut down production at home and produce from the newly acquired reserves within the protected barrier.

A related possibility would be to arrange a swap of assets between the exporting countries and the production companies. Here the same companies would gain equity access to lower-cost oil in the Middle East, while the exporting countries would gain downstream refining and marketing assets in exchange. For the companies to be induced by such a swap offer, a "kicker" would need to be offered, via lower taxes or lower costs, to provide them with higher cash flow to service their debt. So long as some reserves would be shut in, an asset swap would have the same effect as a sales/purchase arrangement between strong national oil companies and weak international oil producing companies.

If this type of arrangement were worked out on a sufficiently large scale, the objective of rationalizing production could be achieved on a global basis. Nor would such an arrangement have to be tremendously extensive. As long as two million to four million barrels of oil production were thus managed, a basis could be provided for putting a floor under oil prices through production controls, thereby benefiting most of the parties involved.

To a substantial degree the market is already creating incentives to tie together the interests of producers with those of refiners. Many of the OPEC countries have moved into downstream activities, either by building refineries in their own countries, as is the case with Saudi Arabia, or, as Kuwait and Venezuela have done, by purchasing downstream operations within the consuming marketplaces in Europe and the United States.

Crises create strange partnerships. The circumstances of a price collapse could well do this not only with respect to rationalizing production, but also with respect to reintegrating upstream and downstream operations. With an impending price collapse, the high-reserve, low-population oil exporting countries would almost certainly take further steps to integrate themselves into the consuming marketplace. The national oil companies in the producing countries would thus be assured market access as the oil market becomes reintegrated. And the companies would gain new cash replenishment via partial sale of their downstream assets. And in a price collapse, downstream assets will have a much higher relative market value than will reserves.

The world has been abruptly reminded that the petroleum industry is cyclical and volatile. Its cycles are long term, but they involve enormous magnitudes of change in their impact on the petroleum industry itself, on oil end-users and on the macroeconomies of the world.

No commodity has been as politicized as oil. It is too fundamental to the operations of national economies for governments to allow free markets to operate without political guidance and administrative controls. Today's oil market is essentially out of control. The triumph by the marketplace over governmental intervention in the past half-decade has not brought with it the benefits of market transparency that market proponents once envisaged. It is beside the point that the reason these benefits have been so elusive is the record of politicization and interference by governments over past decades.

The question now is not whether a price collapse will create a new form of politically motivated intervention in the oil market by governments. The question, rather, is whether governments can take the necessary measures to reorient the petroleum sector in a manner compatible with all interests, guard their vested interests, and not create new impediments to market efficiency through which participants in the oil market will lose.

There are ways to build upon market tendencies to assure a rationalization of production and reintegration of the marketplace, without which the benefits of an efficient marketplace will escape producers and consumers alike. There are ways to achieve success and avoid failure. But the question is whether governments will be able to analyze the problems at hand, in a sufficiently detached and rational manner, and thereby avoid major errors and guard their interests, as well as the interests of most producers and consumers in the world market today.

Structural Conflict: The Third World Against Global Liberalism

Stephen Krasner

The nature and condition of the world economy has rarely been more deserving of investigation and analysis. The "great illusion" of indefinite economic well-being and stability, fostered during the later 1950s and 1960s, was shattered by a succession of shocks that assailed the global economy from the early 1970s onwards. By the mid-1980s the global economy had experienced a most distasteful cocktail of growing currency crises, accelerating inflation, shock oil price increases, the growing indebtedness of a number of *Less Developed Countries* (LDCs), induced recession, extensive unemployment, and widespread fears of a protectionist epidemic.

Responses to these awesome developments have, however, been extremely varied. Many have argued that they constitute a profound crisis that reflects fundamental, structural failings within the contemporary international economic system. However, the pronouncements of the governments of some of the leading *Advanced Industrial Countries* (AICs) have been such as to suggest that current problems might be overcome through perseverance with a set of relatively straightforward policies.

The responses of analysts of international economic matters have been equally mixed. Orthodox economists have sought solutions to contemporary problems within the mainstream of their chosen *discipline*. Many others, however, have seen the manifold disorders of the global economy as evidence of serious shortcomings, if not fundamental weaknesses, within widely accepted approaches to the analysis of economic life.

The issues, then, are whether the world faces fundamental problems and whether these confront orthodox views of economics with a profound challenge. If there are no pressing problems then further refinements of analysis remain of relatively marginal significance and of more academic than practical importance. However, if profound practical and intellectual challenges have arisen, then the exploration of alternative perspectives upon economic reality and approaches to economic policy becomes a matter of the greatest significance and urgency.

THE CONTEMPORARY "CRISIS"

Widespread currency crises characterized the late 1960s and early 1970s, reflecting both the widespread growth of inflationary pressures and the intensification of international economic competition. The immediate effects of these pressures manifested themselves in the international monetary system. The convertibility of the U.S. dollar into gold was suspended in August 1971 and the Bretton Woods system of fixed currency exchange rates finally collapsed in 1973. Such financial volatility was, however, but a weak foreshadow of what was soon to come in the international economy.

During 1973 and early 1974 the Organization of Petroleum Exporting Countries (OPEC) was able to impose spectacular increases in the price of crude oil: from some $2.50 a barrel in early 1973 to $11.50 a barrel in 1974. This price rise was accompanied by the general reduction of production and embargo of exports to the U.S.A. and the Netherlands. The rise was imposed by Middle Eastern oil producers in response to the Arab-Israeli war of late 1973.

There were three immediate and obvious effects of the oil crisis of 1973–1974. First, the Arab oil embargo crystallized concerns about the reliability of supplies of this vital energy source and prompted similar sensitivities towards other critical resources. Second, the oil-importing nations of the world were faced with a massively increased oil bill: an estimated additional bill of some $225 billion during the years 1974–1977 and lost some $600 billion's worth of economic production.[1] Third, but by no means least, a number of oil-exporting states found themselves in possession of huge sums of foreign currency which could not be spent immediately and which were placed on deposit in the international banking system. The second wave of substantial oil prices of 1979 merely repeated and intensified these effects.[2]

The oil *crises* of the mid- and late-1970s also had a number of more indirect, but no less significant, effects. Sensitivities about secure supplies stimulated the accelerated exploitation of alternative sources, such as the North Sea. The example of OPEC's success encouraged many Less Developed Countries (LDCs) to believe that similar achievements might be possible in respect of other basic commodities. This, furthermore, prompted hopes that *commodity power* might form the "South's" main weapon in a confrontation with the rich "North" over the structure and functioning of the international economic order. Such possibilities, in turn, merely reinforced the concerns of many in the North over the security of supplies of many important commodities and resources.

The oil price increases of the 1970s also intensified the inflationary tendencies which were already well established in many countries, including some of the leading AICs. Varied, but increasingly frenetic, official efforts to restore monetary stability soon materialized and contributed to the global recession of the early 1980s. The international banks, for their part, embarked upon a hectic search for "suitable" borrowers for the massive quantities of *petrodollars* that had been placed on deposit by the more financially replete of the oil-exporting nations. Such borrowers were discovered in the form of the more promising of the LDCs. Unfortunately, the counterinflationary (so-called *monetarist*) policies adopted by most of the AICs involved substantial domestic deflation and marked increases in interest rates. The effects of such policies were to induce recession, both domestic and global. Less Developed Countries were particularly hard hit by these developments, for the markets for their exports of basic commodities and their newer manufactured goods were substantially reduced at the precise time that they were seeking increased export earnings to repay their recently acquired debts.

The situation currently facing the world is thus one of serious unemployment within many AICs and LDCs, retarded global economic growth, and the massive indebtedness of many LDCs. The continuing danger of comprehensive default on payments of interest and capital by one or more of the major LDC debtors carries with it a profound threat to the stability, and even the survival, of the international banking system. With such a threat to the banking system of the Western world comes the additional danger of world economic dislocation on an awesome scale.

The threads connecting the dramatic developments of the 1970s and the crises of recession, indebtedness, and intensifying friction in the international trading system are thus complex but fairly clear. The central question for both practitioners and analysts, however, is whether the developments of the 1970s were an aberration within an essentially healthy system or, in contrast, symptoms of an inherently flawed world economic system. If the former, then many of the policy measures adopted by Northern governments during the early 1980s could be seen as no more than the bad-tasting, but essentially short-term, medicine necessary to secure a return to order, prosperity, and well-being. If, however, the problems were symptoms of deeper ailments, then budgetary restraint, deflation, wholesale "bloodletting" within public services, and widespread industrial dislocation and rationalization, might have been both misconceived and ultimately futile.

The intellectual difficulty encountered in attempting to answer such a basic question is that the answer is by no means self-presenting. The contemporary global system is a phenomenon of such complexity and dynamism that no theory or approach can be subject to simple and straightforward testing. Any specific event or development within such a complex whole can provide some support for any one of a number of quite different propositions or approaches. Indeed the very ascription of significance to any *fact* is possible only if it is located within a broader framework of ideas about reality.[3] Thus, the orthodox, *conservative* economist might see the recent economic policies of many of the AICs as merely the realism and discipline necessary to restore stability to a basically viable and vital economic system. The Marxist, in direct contrast, might view recent policy developments as no more than the desperate, predictable, and ultimately futile efforts to stave off the impending collapse of a fundamentally unsound, and even self-destructive, economic system. To the former, every sign of economic improvement is evidence of the soundness of economic orthodoxy:[4] to the latter, such "signs" mark no more than a temporary remission.

Empirical *facts* about the world of economic, political, and social affairs are thus interpretatively malleable and difficult, if not impossible, to prove or disprove in any simple manner. Acceptability remains, in large part, an essentially social and psychological matter. Established ideas thus appear "obvious" while the claims of less orthodox approaches arouse suspicion and unease. The exploration of alternative perspectives remains essential, however, both as a corrective to orthodoxies which, once enthroned, dull critical thought and as an insurance against the possibility, if not probability, that current difficulties will compound and overwhelm established perspective and policies. To be unaware of alternatives is to be unarmed in a world of constant change, complexity, and difficulty.

PERSPECTIVES UPON THE INTERNATIONAL POLITICAL ECONOMY

The condition of the contemporary international political economy is clearly in need of careful examination. The notion of an international *political economy,* rather than a simple *economy,* reflects a number of considerations. First, economics, both domestic and international, are a major policy concern of political authorities. Second, developments within the economic realm have a substantial impact upon almost all the other areas of policy which are of concern to governments. Third, but slightly more controversial, it can be argued that much of the structure and functioning of the contemporary international economic system is a direct product of the policies and actions of governments in the past and the present. In this last sense, then, a *political* economy is such, precisely because it is a creation of politics and will ever be so!

The three major perspectives upon the contemporary world political economy, the liberal, the Marxist, and the "Economic Realist," with its neo-mercantilist leanings, have developed in response to, and interaction with, one another.[5] These basic approaches have, themselves, generated many variants, each of which attracts committed adherents. The discussion in this book will concentrate upon idealized forms of the liberal and the Economic Realist approaches. The *Economic Realist* approach has been so titled for two reasons. The approach claims, firstly, to reflect and accommodate the complex set of *"realities"* exhibited by the empirical world. The approach, secondly, shares a basic identity of outlook with the "Realist" theory of international relations, as will be indicated subsequently.

Marxist interpretations will not be considered directly in this study, although the approach that is to be propounded is quite compatible with insights and ideas of a Marxist parentage. Indeed, it well may be that an effective analysis of the structure of the contemporary global political economy must incorporate such notions, irrespective of their origin.

THE MARXIST APPROACH

Marxist analysis of the contemporary global political economy constitutes a powerful and largely self-contained system of ideas and interpretations.[6] Its approach to current "realities" is systematically critical and, at many points, based upon an analysis of underlying forces and dynamics, many of which are not open to direct and immediate observation.[7] Prescriptively the bulk of prevailing arrangements and institutions are to be repudiated, overthrown, and replaced by a new global order based upon socialist (or even communist) principles. Analytically, and predictively, Marxism remains essentially deterministic. The majority of Marxist studies are also somewhat ambivalent in their attitudes towards ideas derived from non-Marxist sources. Many reject such ideas as reactionary rationalizations or obfuscations; a few are willing and able to use such ideas and analytical techniques as complement analysis, irrespective of their formal origin.

. . .

Practitioners and analysts alike are also faced with the problem that Marxist predictions of socialist transformations, both domestic and global, are necessarily atemporal. Prior to such transformations, which may be long awaited, relations within and between states will reflect non-socialist principles and practices. Indeed, in a world in which socialism has yet to achieve its final triumph, much of the international economic behavior of nominally socialist states shows little influence of socialist principles. While critical forms of neo-Marxism may be instructive with regard to such "anomolies," non-Marxist perspectives may have much to offer on prevailing behavioral "realities."

LIBERAL THEORY VERSUS ECONOMIC REALISM

The center of the intellectual and political stage within the societies of the rich, North-Western (structural rather than geographical) quadrant of the modern world is occupied by the liberal analysis of economics, and such influential derivatives as modern neoclassical economic theory. This approach offers a system of ideas and analytical techniques which, by appearing to be extremely rigorous, exerts considerable appeal. It is, however, a theoretical construction which, as will be shown later, has acquired its apparent virtues as a direct result of basic characteristics and assumptions which seriously distance it from the reality to which it is supposed to relate and even correspond.

The classical forerunner of modern liberal economics was, however, developed as a prescriptive program as well as a statement about the nature of contemporary reality. The prescriptive purpose of Adam Smith was to attack, and hopefully dismantle, the mercantilist economic doctrines that governments were supposedly pursuing at the time of writing *The Wealth of Nations.* This prescriptive-positive fusion has continued to characterize liberal economics, despite the pretensions and claims of many latter-day adherents, throughout its long evolution from classical into modern neoclassical forms.

As liberal economics has evolved through time, experience, and continued confrontation with competing approaches, so too has the mercantilist perspective. The reality of systematic mercantilism in the seventeenth and eighteenth centuries has been contested by some historians, who see it as no more than a *straw-man* invented by writers like Adam Smith for their own polemical purposes.[8] However, many of the policies and practices of the European states of those days did include features that warrant the title *mercantilist.*

The common purpose of mercantilist measures was to promote the strength and potential power of the state, and its ruler(s), against other communities with which conflicts of interest, and arms, might develop. Initially, classical mercantilism was seen to be primarily *bullionist;* policy being directed towards the accumulation of bullion, specie, and all other readily transportable forms of wealth that might be used for recruiting and sustaining armed forces. Later, classical mercantilism broadened its vision to include the promotion and protection of the society's general economic strength and capacity, and the establishment of a strategically advantageous balance of trade with other states.

The classical mercantilist view of the international system thus accords with that of the modern *Realist* school of international relations' analysis, pioneered by E. H. Carr[9] in Britain and Hans J. Morgenthau[10] in North America. Economic policy was to be based upon the certainty of conflict with other societies and the need to ensure that the state was optimally placed to sustain itself in, and through, such eventualities. Unfortunately, the practical implications of such a disposition could be extensive and, as Adam Smith emphasized, encourage governmental involvement in, and interference with, virtually every element of economic and social life. Personal freedom and economic vigor might be suppressed by such rampant mercantilism; possibilities which might best be prevented by the adoption of a liberal, free enterprise system in which the role of government would be minimal.

Modern Economic Realism perpetuates the concern of classical mercantilism with strategic security but is equally, if not primarily, motivated by a perceived need to promote the economic well-being and stability of the societies which governments serve. Extensive, and often intensive, governmental involvement in many areas of economics and society is a response to the chronic uncertainties of the modern economy, both domestic and global, and complexities of advanced industrial societies and the numerous demands that populations now place upon their rulers. General economic well-being has thus been added to the traditional quest for national security and international influence.

The issue between the liberal and the Economic Realist perspectives upon the global political economy has both empirical and prescriptive aspects. At one level, proponents of the two contrasting approaches to economic policy and behavior assert that theirs offers the best prospect of general stability and well-being. At another level, there is disagreement about the principles upon which the contemporary global economy actually operates.

The latter controversy is particularly interesting and directly germane to this discussion. It is often an explicit assertion, or an implicit assumption, of liberal writers that much of global economic progress of both the late-nineteenth century and the post-Second World War era was a direct function of the liberal trade system developed and sustained during those periods. Moreover, departures from liberal purity are viewed as economically and politically damaging aberrations. Protectionism is the outstanding departure from the path of economic purity, a perversion of national economic policy that is held to undermine economic efficiency, and well-being, and hence to stimulate political and military conflict between nation-states.[11]

Critics of the liberal position, in contrast, reject all these basic arguments. A truly liberal global order, it is contended, has never been more than a fantasy of liberal theory and ideology, and has certainly not constituted a necessary condition of economic progress. The periods of substantial economic progress in the past were actually characterized by conditions that significantly departed from those envisaged by, or enshrined in, liberal theory. Indeed, Economic Realists would argue that it is precisely those practical departures from the liberal prescription that produced the combination of stability and effective leadership within the system that was necessary for such impressive global economic advance.

This, it would be held, is precisely because the liberal approach rests upon a number of fundamental misconceptions and is quite misleading in the picture that it paints of present, and potential, realities.

The lines of battle between the liberal and the Economic Realist are thus clearly drawn. The liberal believes that economic progress, nationally and internationally, is dependent upon the maintenance of a *laissez-faire* domestic economy and international free trade. The Economist Realist believes, in contrast, that effective governmental influence, or even control, over the economy is essential for national economic progress and well-being, while international economic control and regulation are necessary conditions for long-term global stability and prosperity.

Beyond the central axes of dispute, the liberal and the Economic Realist approaches also differ substantially in the way in which they deal with many prominent features of the contemporary global economy. Liberal economic theory, and its neoclassical variant, has never been happy in dealing with monopolies and oligopolies. Much of the appeal of the liberal paradigm rests upon two claims: first, that it establishes that a true *laissez-faire* system ensures the maximum possible satisfaction of the economic wants and needs of the population; and, second, that it is capable of subjecting the realm of economic life to determinate analysis: a form of analysis that establishes what *must* be the ultimate outcome in any identifiable situation. Unfortunately, micro-economic theory demonstrates that monopolies will, by virtue of economic logic rather than mere greed or mendacity, charge more and produce less than would competitive suppliers.[12] The existence of monopolies thus necessitates a reduction of aggregate well-being and satisfaction for the community. Studies of oligopolies, moreover, demonstrate that their behavior is intrinsically indeterminate.[13] As any casual observer of the behavior of the oil companies recently in the United Kingdom will know, at times oligopolists engage one another in determined price-cutting competition, at others they lapse into a tacit and harmonious price-stabilizing cartel.

Monopolies and oligopolies, then, are phenomena with which liberal theory would really prefer not to have to deal. Individual economists may study them, but monopolies and oligopolies continue to confront the governing theoretical paradigm with fundamental problems that are both serious and consistently evaded. Thus the existence of monopolies and oligopolies are stated in conventional economics textbooks but their development is not explained. Again, their damaging welfare effects tend to be glossed over. Finally, the future prospects of monopolies and oligopolies are barely considered.

The evasive schizophrenia of liberal economics is accentuated when the phenomenon of the multinational, or transnational, corporation (MNC or TNC) is addressed. Many TNCs are worldwide oligopolists, in fact or in the making, which have profound, and by no means always benign, effects upon the societies within and between which they operate. Some liberal economists would, however, treat them as no more than ordinary competitive, free-market enterprises which, by virtue of size and breadth of operation, are able to maximize productive efficiency, put the world's productive resources to their optimal use and, hence, provide consumers with the widest range of goods and services at the lowest possible cost. Others, in contrast, express clear apprehensions about the behavior of such world-striding corporations and their structural impact upon the global system. However, when such critics of TNCs remain firmly within the liberal paradigm their work remains, of necessity, pragmatic and bereft of a systematic basis.

The Economic Realist, or neo-mercantilist, has no such difficulties with TNCs. Their emergence, nature, and behavioral characteristics are quite comprehensible. They are organizations that act precisely in accordance with the expectations of the Realist. In a complex and turbulent world, the TNC seeks size, strength, and influence in pursuit of the maximum attainable level of control over its environment. It is no more than another major actor within a formally *anarchical* global system: an actor that lacks some of the resources of a territorially based nation-state, but which is also free of many of its pressing responsibilities.

The liberal approach remains embarrassed by such common features of the contemporary international scene as the efforts of groups of states to establish control over the global economy, or some sector, and the existence, and activity, of TNCs. The Economic Realist encounters no such difficulty with such enduring aspects of reality.

The analytical strengths and weakness of the liberal and the Economic Realist schools thus differ in type and significance. The liberal approach offers a deductive system of argument and a variety of powerful analytical techniques that, in sum, appear both rigorous and intellectually attractive. In contrast, Economic Realism embraces a bare few fundamental assumptions and deductive arguments. It is, however, able to accommodate far more aspects of reality.

Power and influence are two outstanding features of reality that Economic Realism is better equipped to handle. Liberal economic theory is based upon the analysis of competitive markets in which, by definition, no consumer(s) or supplier(s) is able to influence market developments solely by its own actions. Power and influence are thus excluded, from the outset, in the basic construction of this theory of economics.

Economic Realism, in marked contrast, is founded upon the assumption that actors, be they firms, states, or coalitions, will seek power and influence within their environment and over those with whom they interact. Economic Realism does not exclude competitive markets in the way that the liberal approach denies power and influence. Indeed, perfect competition can be treated as a special case, while gradations of competitiveness can be defined, identified, and analyzed as they appear in the real world. The *analytical power* of Economic Realism is thus greater than that of neoclassicism, for it can accommodate the content and purview of the latter. The reverse is not true of the liberal approach, its analytical rigor notwithstanding.

Liberal theory is also, with one or two particular exceptions, consistently condemnatory of protectionist policies. However, the liberal argument has had a further and equally serious influence, for it has encouraged excessive concentration upon the more manifest protectionist measures and other overt forms of governmental intervention to support national exporters. This has encouraged a form of tunnel vision which has often inhibited a proper recognition of the wide range of policies available to governments that seek to enhance the economic performance of their communities and the economic strength of their states. The consequences of this perceptual disturbance are twofold: the analysis of contemporary reality is simplified to the point of serious distortion, while the prescriptions for policy, and policymakers, are ill founded and often misleading.

. . .

NOTES

1. D. Pirages, *Global Ecopolitics: The New Context for International Relations*, (Belmont, Cal.: Duxbury, 1978), pp. 124 and 125. See also H. Askari and J. T. Cummings, *Oil, OCED, and the Third World: A Vicious Triangle* (Austin, Texas: Center for Middle Eastern Studies, 1978), pp. 1–11; and Edith Penrose, "Oil and International Relations," *British Journal of International Studies*, Vol. 2 (1976), pp. 41–50.
2. J. E. Spero, *The Politics of International Economic Relations*, (London: George Allen and Unwin, 2nd ed., 1982), pp. 265–270.
3. See the discussions in the chapters by R.J. Barry Jones, John Maclean, and Richard Little, in Barry Buzan and R.J. Barry Jones, John Maclean and Richard Little, in Barry Buzan and R.J. Barry Jones (eds.), *Change and the Study of International Relations: The Evaded Dimension*, (London: Frances Pinter, 1981).
4. See, for instance, the eulogy to monetarism by Alan Walters in *The Economist*, 4 May 1985, pp. 19–23.
5. Not all writers in the field follow this classification. Many offer *structuralism* as an additional major perspective to the liberal and Marxist. See, for instance, D.H. Blake and R.S. Walters, *The Politics of Global Economic Relations*, (Englewood Cliffs, NJ: Prentice-Hall, 1976) and Spero *op. cit.* This *structuralism*, however, is not a theory of the same status, or implication, as the others with which it is arrayed. Economic Realism/neo-mercantilism lacks some of the theoretical rigor of the other approaches but can lay claim to equal historical and practical significance.
6. On which, see, M. Barratt Brown, *The Economics of Imperialism* (Harmondsworth: Penguin Books, 1975); R. Owen and Bob Sutcliffe (eds.), *Studies in the Theory of Imperialism*, (London: Longman, 1972); M. C. Howard and J. E. King, *The Political Economy of Marx* (Burnt Mill: Longman, 1975); and A. Gamble, "Critical Political Economy," in R.J. Barry Jones (ed.), *Perspectives on Political Economy: Alternatives to the Economics of Depression*, (London: Frances Pinter, 1983), pp. 64–89.
7. See John Maclean, "Marxist Epistemology, Explanations of 'Change' and the Study of International Relations," in Buzan and Jones *op. cit.*, pp. 46–67.

8. See D. C. Coleman, "Introduction," esp. p. 4, and "Eli Heckscher and the Idea of Mercantilism" esp. pp. 92–93, in D.C. Coleman (ed.), *Revision in Mercantilism* (London: Methuen, 1969).
9. E. H. Carr, *The Twenty Years' Crisis: An Introduction to the Study of International Relations,* (London: Macmillan, 2nd edn., 1946).
10. Hans J. Morgenthau, *Politics Among Nations: The Struggle for Power and Peace,* (New York: Alfred Knopf, 4th ed., 1967).
11. For a clear presentation, and critical discussion, of this view see Barry Buzan, "Economic Structure and International Security," *International Organization,* Vol. 38 (Autumn 1984), pp. 597–624.
12. See, for instance, R.G. Lipsey, *An Introduction to Positive Economics,* (London: Weidenfeld and Nicolson, 1st ed., 1963), Ch. 18.
13. See, for instance, Peter Kenyon, "Pricing," in A. S. Eichner (ed.), *A Guide to Post-Keynsian Economics,* (London: Macmillan, 1979), pp. 34–35; and Joan Robinson, "Imperfect Competition" Revisited," in Joan Robinson, *Contributions to Modern Economics,* (Oxford: Basil Blackwell, 1978), pp. 166–181.

Part
Eight

ORDER IN THE INTERNATIONAL ECONOMY

*O*rder (or *stability*) has long been an analytical preoccupation of many students of international relations. Most IPE scholars share the assumption that order is good and stability is desirable because they enhance the opportunities for and reduce the costs of the pursuit of economic well-being for all members of the international system. Some do not necessarily attach themselves to the normative notion of order and stability and instead search for a logic, desirable or not, in the comings and goings of order and stability through history. Robert Keohane and Joanne Gowa, whose works are introduced in Part Eight, are examples of the former group of IPE scholars, and Immanuel Wallerstein represents the latter group.

In the first selection below, Wallerstein presents his understanding of one important facet of an historical logic—i.e., the rise and fall of hegemonic powers in the evolution of what he calls the *capitalist world-economy* from the sixteenth century to the present. He observes that the capitalist world-system has experienced three periods of hegemony, or a "situation in which one power can largely impose its rules and its wishes . . . in the economic, political, military, diplomatic, and even cultural areas." The three instances are the United Provinces in the mid-seventeenth century, the United Kingdom in the mid-nineteenth century, and the United States in the mid-twentieth century. Wallerstein observes that the situation of hegemony is not only rare but unstable, and points out that none of the three hegemonic rules lasted very long.

The theory that a hegemonic period is unstable is not accepted by all IPE students. On the contrary, many have believed, and continue to believe, that hegemony is either a necessary, or at least a contributing factor for international stability. First introduced by Charles Kindleberger in 1973,[1] the notion that hegemonic rule is necessary for world stability has been developed into what is called *hegemonic stability theory.* Keohane summarizes this theory and critically evaluates it. He acknowledges that United States hegemony may have facilitated the stability of the postwar world but argues that hegemonic leadership, as a source of stability, is no longer necessary to sustain multilateral cooperation. The major capitalist powers of the world have learned it is in their national interest to cooperate through *international regimes,* or "sets of implicit or explicit principles, norms, rules, and decisionmaking procedures around which actors' expectations converge in a given issue-area."[2]

The debate between hegemonic stability theory and its critics is not over. This is made clear in the selection by Joanne Gowa, who exposes and explores the limits of the critics of hegemonic stability theory. Limiting her study to international trade, the author argues that a hegemon may prefer a less than optimal tariff because, contrary to the rationality argument, international trade agreements affect not merely gains of an economic nature but also the security of the contracting parties—for example, when increased efficiency in domestic resource allocation resulting from trade frees economic resources for military uses.

All of these authors present a coherent and convincing argument regarding the need for a hegemon. Your challenge, as a reader and student, is to compare the evidence and logic in each article. For example, how does one measure hegemony? Can you separate the term from the theory and the evidence from the term? To what extent do the authors agree on this question, and how do these conceptual and definitional problems affect their analysis? Does the time frame of analysis make a difference? What about the statistics employed? Which of these approaches is the most biased?

---

[1]Kindleberger, *The World in Depression, 1929–1939,* (Berkeley, CA: University of California Press, 1973.)

[2]This definition was proposed by Stephen Krasner in "Structural Causes and Regime Consequences: Regimes as Intervening Variables" in Krasner, ed., *International Regimes,* Ithaca: Cornell University Press, 1983, p. 2.

The Three Instances of Hegemony in the History of the Capitalist World-Economy

Immanuel Wallerstein

When one is dealing with a complex, continuously evolving, large-scale historical system, concepts that are used as shorthand descriptions for structural patterns are useful only to the degree that one clearly lays out their purpose, circumscribes their applicability, and specifies the theoretical framework they presuppose and advance.

Let me therefore state some premises which I shall not argue at this point. If you are not willing to regard these premises as plausible, you will not find the way I elaborate and use the concept of hegemony very useful. I assume that there exists a concrete singular historical system which I shall call the *capitalist world-economy,* whose temporal boundaries go from the long sixteenth century to the present. Its spatial boundaries originally included Europe (or most of it) plus Iberian America but they subsequently expanded to cover the entire globe. I assume this totality is a *system,* that is, that it has been relatively autonomous of external forces; or, to put it another way, that its patterns are explicable largely in terms of its internal dynamics. I assume that it is an *historical* system, that is, that it was born, has developed, and will one day cease to exist (through disintegration or fundamental transformation). I assume lastly that it is the dynamics of the system itself that explain its historically changing characteristics. Hence, insofar as it is a system, it has structures and these structures manifest themselves in cyclical rhythms, that is, mechanisms which reflect and ensure repetitious patterns. But insofar as this system is historical, no rhythmic movement ever returns the system to an equilibrium point but

Immanuel Wallerstein, *The Politics of the World Economy.* (Cambridge, UK, 1984), pp. 37–46. Reprinted with permission of Immanuel Wallerstein.

instead moves the system along various continua which may be called the secular trends of this system. These trends eventually must culminate in the impossibility of containing further reparations of the structured dislocations by restorative mechanisms. Hence the system undergoes what some call "bifurcating turbulence" and others the "transformation of quantity into quality."

To these methodological or metaphysical premises, I must add a few substantive ones about the operations of the capitalist world-economy. Its mode of production is capitalist; that is, it is predicated on the endless accumulation of capital. Its structure is that of an axial social division of labor exhibiting a core/periphery tension based on unequal exchange. The political superstructure of this system is that of a set of so-called sovereign states defined by and constrained by their membership in an interstate network or system. The operational guidelines of this interstate system include the so-called balance of power, a mechanism designed to ensure that no single state ever has the capacity to transform this interstate system into a single world-empire whose boundaries would match that of the axial division of labor. There have of course been repeated attempts throughout the history of the capitalist world-economy to transform it in the direction of a world-empire, but these attempts have all been frustrated. However, there have also been repeated and quite different attempts by given states to achieve hegemony in the interstate system, and these attempts have in fact succeeded on three occasions, if only for relatively brief periods.

The thrust of hegemony is quite different from the thrust to world-empire; indeed it is in many ways almost its opposite. I will therefore (1) spell out what I mean by hegemony, (2) describe the analogies in the three purported instances, (3) seek to decipher the roots of the thrust to hegemony and suggest why the thrust to hegemony has succeeded three times but never lasted too long, and (4) draw inferences about what we may expect in the proximate future. The point of doing all this is not to erect a Procrustean category into which to fit complex historical reality but to illuminate what I believe to be one of the central processes of the modern world-system.

I

Hegemony in the interstate system refers to that situation in which the ongoing rivalry between the so-called "great powers" is so unbalanced that one power is truly *primus inter pares;* that is, one power can largely impose its rules and its wishes (at the very least by effective veto power) in the economic, political, military, diplomatic, and even cultural arenas. The material base of such power lies in the ability of enterprises domiciled in that power to operate more efficiently in all three major economic arenas—agro-industrial production, commerce, and finance. The edge in efficiency of which we are speaking is one so great that these enterprises can not only outbid enterprises domiciled in other great powers in the world market in general, but quite specifically in very many instances within the home markets of the rival powers themselves.

I mean this to be a relatively restrictive definition. It is not enough for one power's enterprises simply to have a larger share of the world market than any other or simply to have the most powerful military forces or the largest political role. I mean hegemony only to refer to situations in which the edge is so significant that allied major powers are *de facto* client states and opposed major powers feel relatively frustrated and highly defensive *vis-à-vis* the hegemonic power. And yet while I want to restrict my definition to instances where the margin or power differential is really great, I do not mean to suggest that there is ever any moment when a hegemonic power is omnipotent and capable of doing anything it wants. Omnipotence does not exist within the interstate system.

Hegemony therefore is not a state of being but rather one end of a fluid continuum which describes the rivalry relations of great powers to each other. At one end of this continuum is an almost even balance, a situation in which many powers exist, all somewhat equal in strength, and with no clear or continuous groupings. This is rare and unstable. In the great middle of this continuum, many powers exist, grouped more or less into two camps, but with several neutral or swing elements, and with neither side (nor *a fortiori* any single state) being able to impose its will on others. This is the statistically normal situation of rivalry within the interstate system. And at the other end lies the situation of hegemony, also rare and unstable.

At this point, you may see what it is I am describing but may wonder why I am bothering to give it a name and thereby focus attention upon it. It is because I suspect hegemony is not the result of a random reshuffling of the cards but is a phenomenon that emerges in specifiable circumstances and plays a significant role in the historical development of the capitalist world-economy.

II

Using this restrictive definition, the only three instances of hegemony would be the United Provinces in the mid-seventeenth century, the United Kingdom in the mid-nineteenth, and the United States in the mid-twentieth. If one insists on dates, I would tentatively suggest as maximal bounding points 1620–1672, 1815–1873, 1945–1967. But of course, it would be a mistake to try to be too precise when our measuring instruments are both so complex and so crude.

I will suggest four areas in which it seems to me what happened in the three instances was analogous. To be sure, analogies are limited. And to be sure, since the capitalist world-economy is in my usage a single continuously evolving entity, it follows by definition that the overall structure was different at each of the three points in time. The differences were real, the outcome of the secular trends of the world-system. But the structural analogies were real as well, the reflection of the cyclical rhythms of this same system.

The first analogy has to do with the sequencing of achievement and loss of relative efficiencies in each of the three economic domains. What I believe occurred was that in each instance enterprises domiciled in the given power in question achieved their edge first in agro-industrial production, then in commerce, and then in finance.[1] I believe they lost their edge in this sequence as well (this process having begun but not yet having been completed in the third instance). Hegemony thus refers to that short interval in which there is *simultaneous* advantage in all three economic domains.

The second analogy has to do with the ideology and policy of the hegemonic power. Hegemonic powers during the period of their hegemony tended to be advocates of global *liberalism*. They came forward as defenders of the principle of the free flow of the factors of production (goods, capital, and labor) throughout the world-economy. They were hostile in general to mercantilist restrictions on trade, including the existence of overseas colonies for the stronger countries. They extended this liberalism to a generalized endorsement of liberal parliamentary institutions (and a concurrent distaste for political change by violent means), political restraints on the arbitrariness of bureaucratic power, and civil liberties (and a concurrent open door to political exiles). They tended to provide a high standard of living for their national working classes, high by world standards of the time.

None of this should be exaggerated. Hegemonic powers regularly made exceptions to their anti-mercantilism, when it was in their interest to do so. Hegemonic powers regularly were willing to interfere with political processes in other states to ensure their own advantage. Hegemonic

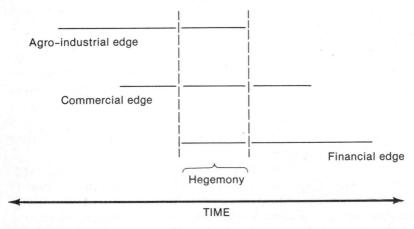

Figure 1 Economic Position of Hegemonic Power.

powers could be very repressive at home, if need be, to guarantee the national "consensus." The high working-class standard was steeply graded by internal ethnicity. Nevertheless, it is quite striking that liberalism as an ideology did flourish in these countries at precisely the moments of their hegemony, and to a significant extent only then and there.

The third analogy is in the pattern of global military power. Hegemonic powers were primarily sea (now sea/air) powers. In the long ascent to hegemony, they seemed very reluctant to develop their armies, discussing openly the potentially weakening drain on state revenues and manpower of becoming tied down in land wars. Yet each found finally that it had to develop a strong land army as well to face up to a major land-based rival which seemed to be trying to transform the world-economy into a world-empire.

In each case, the hegemony was secured by a thirty-year-long world war. By a world war, I shall mean (again somewhat restrictively) a land-based war that involves (not necessarily continuously) almost all the major military powers of the epoch in warfare that is very destructive of land and population. To each hegemony is attached one of these wars. World War Alpha was the Thirty Years' War from 1618 to 1648, where Dutch interests triumphed over Hapsburg in the world-economy. World War Beta was the Napoleonic Wars from 1792 to 1815, where British interests triumphed over French. World War Gamma was the long Euroasian wars from 1914 to 1945, where U.S. interests triumphed over German.

While limited wars have been a constant of the operations of the interstate system of the capitalist world-economy (there having been scarcely any year when there was not some war somewhere within the system), world wars have been by contrast a rarity. In fact their rarity and the fact that the number and timing seems to have correlated with the achievement of hegemonic status by one power brings us to the fourth analogy.

If we look to those very long cycles that Rondo Cameron has dubbed *logistics*, we can see that world wars and hegemony have been in fact related to them. There has been very little scholarly work done on these logistics. They have been most frequently discussed in the comparisons between the A–B sequences of 1100–1450 and 1450–1750. There are only a few discussions of the logistics that may exist after the latter point in time. But if we take the prime observation which has been used to define these logistics—secular inflation and deflation—the pattern seems in fact to have continued.

It therefore might be plausible to argue the existence of such (price) logistics up to today using the following dates: 1450–1730, with 1600–1650 as a flat peak; 1730–1897, with 1810–1817 as a peak; and 1897–?, with an as yet uncertain peak. If there are such logistics, it turns out that the world war and the (subsequent) hegemonic era are located somewhere around (just before and after) the peak of the logistic. That is to say, these processes seem to be the product of the long competitive expansion which seemed to have resulted in a particular concentration of economic and political power.

The outcome of each world war included a major restructuring of the interstate system (Westphalia; the Concert of Europe; the UN and Bretton Woods) in a form consonant with the need for relative stability of the now hegemonic power. Furthermore, once the hegemonic position was eroded economically (the loss of the efficiency edge in agroindustrial production), and therefore hegemonic decline set in, one consequence seemed to be the erosion of the alliance network which the hegemonic power had created patiently, and ultimately a serious reshuffling of alliances.

In the long period following the era of hegemony, two powers seemed eventually to emerge as the "contenders for the succession"—England and France after Dutch hegemony; the U.S. and Germany after British; and now Japan and western Europe after U.S. Furthermore, the eventual winner of the contending pair seemed to use as a conscious part of its strategy the gentle turning of the old hegemonic power into its "junior partner"—the English *vis-à-vis* the Dutch, the U.S. *vis-à-vis* Great Britain . . . and now?

III

Thus far I have been primarily descriptive. I realize that this description is vulnerable to technical criticism. My coding of the data may not agree with everyone else's. I think nonetheless that as an initial effort this coding is defensible and that I have therefore outlined a broad repetitive pattern in the functioning of the interstate question. The question now is how to interpret it. What is there in the functioning of a capitalist world-economy that gives rise to such a cyclical pattern in the interstate system?

I believe this pattern of the rise, temporary ascendancy, and fall of hegemonic powers in the interstate system is merely one aspect of the central role of the political machinery in the functioning of capitalism as a mode of production.

There are two myths about capitalism put forward by its central ideologues (and strangely largely accepted by its nineteenth-century critics). One is that it is defined by the free flow of the factors of production. The second is that it is defined by the non-interference of the political machinery in the "market." In fact, capitalism is defined by the *partially* free flow of the factors of production and by the *selective* interference of the political machinery in the "market." Hegemony is an instance of the latter.

What defines capitalism most fundamentally is the drive for the endless accumulation of capital. The interferences that are *selected* are those which advance this process of accumulation. There are however two problems about "interference." It has a cost, and therefore the benefit of any interference is only a benefit to the extent it exceeds this cost. Where the benefits are available without any "interference," this is obviously desirable, as it minimizes the "deduction." And secondly, interference is always in favor of one set of accumulators as against another set, and the latter will always seek to counter the former. These two considerations circumscribe the politics of hegemony in the interstate system.

The costs to a given entrepreneur of state "interference" are felt in two main ways. First, in financial terms, the state may levy direct taxes which affect the rate of profit by requiring the firm to make payments to the state, or indirect taxes, which may alter the rate of profit by affecting the competitivity of a product. Secondly, the state may enact rules which govern flows of capital, labor, or goods, or may set minimum and/or maximum prices. While direct taxes always represent a cost to the entrepreneur, calculations concerning indirect taxes and state regulations are more complex, since they represent costs both to the entrepreneur and to (some of) his competitors. The chief concern in terms of individual accumulation is not the absolute cost of these measures but the comparative cost. Costs, even if high, may be positively desirable from the standpoint of a given entrepreneur, if the state's actions involve still higher costs to some competitor. Absolute costs are of concern only if the loss to the entrepreneur is greater than the medium-run gain which is possible through greater competition brought about by such state actions. It follows that absolute cost is of greatest concern to those entrepreneurs who would do best in open-market competition in the absence of state interference.

In general, therefore, entrepreneurs are regularly seeking state interference in the market in multiple forms—subsidies, restraints of trade, tariffs (which are penalties for competitors of different nationality), guarantees, maxima for input prices and minima for output prices, etc. The intimidating effect of internal and external repression is also of direct economic benefit to entrepreneurs. To the extent that the ongoing process of competition and state interference leads to oligopolistic conditions within state boundaries, more and more attention is naturally paid to securing the same kind of oligopolistic conditions in the most important market, the world market.

The combination of the competitive thrust and constant state interference results in a continuing pressure towards the concentration of capital. The benefits of state interference inside and outside the state boundaries is cumulative. In political terms, this is reflected as expanding world power. The edge a rising power's economic enterprises have *vis-à-vis* those of a competitive rising power may be thin and therefore insecure. This is where the world wars come in. The thirty-year struggle may be very dramatic militarily and politically. But the profoundest effect may be economic. The winner's economic edge is expanded by the very process of the war itself, and the postwar interstate settlement is designed to encrust that greater edge and protect it against erosion.

A given state thus assumes its world "responsibilities" which are reflected in its diplomatic, military, political, ideological, and cultural stances. Everything conspires to reinforce the cooperative relationship of the entrepreneurial strata, the bureaucratic strata, and with some lag the working-class strata of the hegemonic power. This power may then be exercised in a "liberal" form—given the real diminution of political conflict within the state itself compared to earlier and later periods, and to the importance in the interstate arena of delegitimizing the efforts of other state machineries to act against the economic superiorities of the hegemonic power.

The problem is that global liberalism, which is rational and cost-effective, breeds its own demise. It makes it more difficult to retard the spread of technological expertise. Hence over time it is virtually inevitable that entrepreneurs coming along later will be able to enter the most profitable markets with the most advanced technologies and younger "plant," thus eating into the material base of the productivity edge of the hegemonic power.

Secondly, the internal political price of liberalism, needed to maintain uninterrupted production at a time of maximal global accumulation, is the creeping rise of real income of both the working strata and the cadres located in the hegemonic power. Over time, this must reduce the competitivity of the enterprises located in this state.

Once the clear productivity edge is lost, the structure cracks. As long as there is a hegemonic power, it can coordinate more or less the political responses of all states with core-like economic activities to all peripheral states, maximizing thereby the differentials of unequal exchange. But when hegemony is eroded, and especially when the world-economy is in a Kondratieff downturn, a scramble arises among the leading powers for the smaller pie, which undermines their collective ability to extract surplus via unequal exchange. The rate of unequal exchange thereby diminishes (but never to zero) and creates further incentive to a reshuffling of alliance systems.

In the period leading to the peak of a logistic, which leads towards the creation of the momentary era of hegemony, the governing parable is that of the tortoise and the hare. It is not the state that leaps ahead politically and especially militarily that wins the race, but the one that plods along improving inch by inch its long-term competitivity. This requires a firm but discrete and intelligent organization of the entrepreneurial effort by the state machinery. Wars may be left to others, until the climactic world war when the hegemonic power must at last invest its resources to clinch its victory. Thereupon comes "world responsibility" with its benefits but also its (growing) costs. Thus the hegemony is sweet but brief.

IV

The inferences for today are obvious. We are in the immediate post-hegemonic phase of this third logistic of the capitalist world-economy. The U.S. has lost its productive edge but not yet its commercial and financial superiorities; its military and political power edge is no longer so overwhelming. Its abilities to dictate to its allies (western Europe and Japan), intimidate its foes, and overwhelm the weak (compare the Dominican Republic in 1965 with El Salvador today [1983]) are vastly impaired. We are in the beginnings of a major reshuffling of alliances.[2] Yet, of course, we are only at the beginning of all this. Great Britain began to decline in 1873, but it was only in 1982 that it could be openly challenged by Argentina.

The major question is whether this third logistic will act itself out along the lines of the previous ones. The great difference is the degree to which the fact that the capitalist world-economy has entered into a structural crisis as an historical system will obliterate these cyclical processes. I do not believe it will obliterate them but rather that it will work itself out in part through them.[3]

We should not invest more in the concept of hegemony than is there. It is a way of organizing our perception of process, not an "essence" whose traits are to be described and whose eternal recurrences are to be demonstrated and then anticipated. A processual concept alerts us to the forces at play in the system and the likely nodes of conflict. It does not do more. But it also does not do less. The capitalist world-economy is not comprehensible unless we analyze clearly what are the political forms which it has engendered and how these forms relate to other realities. The interstate system is not some exogenous, God-given variable which mysteriously restrains and interacts with the capitalist drive for the endless accumulation of capital. It is its expression at the level of the political arena.

NOTES

1. I have described this in empirical detail for the first instance in Immanuel Wallerstein, *The Modern World-System, vol. II: Mercantilism and the Consolidation of the European World-Economy,* 1600–1750 (New York and London: Academic Press, 1980), ch. 2.
2. See I. Wallerstein, "North Atlanticism in Decline," *SAIS Review,* no. 4 (Summer 1982), pp. 21–26.
3. For a debate about this, see the "Conclusion" in S. Amin, G. Arrighi, A. G. Frank, and I. Wallerstein, *Dynamics of Global Crisis* (New York: Monthly Review Press, 1982).

Cooperation and International Regimes

Robert Keohane

Hegemonic leadership can help to create a pattern of order. Cooperation is not antithetical to hegemony; on the contrary, hegemony depends on a certain kind of asymmetrical cooperation, which successful hegemons support and maintain. . . . Contemporary international economic regimes were constructed under the aegis of the United States after World War II. In accounting for the creation of international regimes, hegemony often plays an important role, even a crucial one.

Yet the relevance of hegemonic cooperation for the future is questionable. The United States is less preponderant in material resources now than it was in the 1950s and early 1960s. Equally important, the United States is less willing than formerly to define its interests in terms complementary to those of Europe and Japan. The Europeans, in particular, are less inclined to defer to American initiatives, nor do they believe so strongly that they must do so in order to obtain essential military protection against the Soviet Union. Thus the subjective elements of American hegemony have been eroded as much as the tangible power resources upon which hegemonic systems rest. But neither the Europeans nor the Japanese are likely to have the capacity to become hegemonic powers themselves in the foreseeable future.[1]

This prospect raises the issue of cooperation "after hegemony". . . . It also leads back to a crucial tension between economics and politics: international coordination of policy seems highly beneficial in an interdependent world economy, but cooperation in world politics is particularly difficult. One way to relax this tension would be to deny the premise that international economic policy coordination is valuable by assuming that international markets will automatically yield optimal results (Corden, 1981). The decisive objection to this argument is that, in the absence of cooperation, governments will interfere in markets unilaterally in pursuit of what they regard as their own interests, whatever liberal economists may say. They will intervene in foreign exchange markets, impose various restrictions on imports, subsidize favored domestic industries, and set prices for commodities such as petroleum (Strange, 1979). Even if one accepted cooperation to maintain free markets, but no other form of policy coordination, the further objection could be raised that economic market failure would be likely to occur (Cooper, 1983, pp. 45–46). Suboptimal outcomes of transactions could result, for a variety of reasons including problems of collective action. It would take an ideological leap of faith to believe that free markets lead necessarily to optimal results.

Rejecting the illusion that cooperation is never valuable in the world political economy, we have to cope with the fact that it is very difficult to organize. One recourse would be to lapse into fatalism—acceptance of destructive economic conflict as a result of political fragmentation. Although this is a logically tenable position for those who believe in the theory of hegemonic stability, even its most powerful theoretical advocate shies away from its bleak normative implications (Gilpin, 1981). A fatalistic view is not taken here. Without ignoring the difficulties that beset attempts to coordinate policy in the absence of hegemony, this [reading] contends that nonhegemonic cooperation is possible, and that it can be facilitated by international regimes.

In making this argument, I will draw a distinction between the creation of international regimes and their maintenance. . . . When shared interests are sufficiently important and other key conditions are met, cooperation can emerge and regimes can be created without hegemony. Yet this does not imply that regimes can be created easily, much less that contemporary international economic regimes actually came about in this way. . . . I argue that international regimes are easier to maintain than to create, and that recognition of this fact is crucial to understanding why they are valued by governments. Regimes may be maintained, and may continue to foster cooperation, even under conditions that would not be sufficiently benign to bring about their creation. Cooperation is possible after hegemony not only because shared interests can lead to the creation of regimes, but also because the conditions for maintaining existing international regimes are less demanding than those required for creating them. Although hegemony helps to explain the creation of contemporary international regimes, the decline of hegemony does not necessarily lead symmetrically to their decay.

This reading analyzes the meaning of two key terms: *cooperation* and *international regimes*. It distinguishes cooperation from harmony as well as from discord, and it argues for the value of the concept of international regimes as a way of understanding both cooperation and discord. Together the concepts of cooperation and international regimes help us clarify what we want to explain: how do patterns of rule-guided policy coordination emerge, maintain themselves, and decay in world politics?

HARMONY, COOPERATION, AND DISCORD

Cooperation must be distinguished from harmony. Harmony refers to a situation in which actors' policies (pursued in their own self-interest without regard for others) *automatically* facilitate the attainment of others' goals. The classic example of harmony is the hypothetical competitive-market world of the classical economists, in which the Invisible Hand ensures that the pursuit of self-interest by each contributes to the interest of all. In this idealized, unreal world, no one's actions damage anyone else; there are no "negative externalities," in the economists' jargon. Where harmony reigns, cooperation is unnecessary. It may even be injurious, if it means that certain individuals conspire to exploit others. Adam Smith, for one, was very critical of guilds and other conspiracies against freedom of trade (1776/1976). Cooperation and harmony are by no means identical and ought not to be confused with one another.

Cooperation requires that the actions of separate individuals or organizations—which are not in pre-existent harmony—be brought into conformity with one another through a process of negotiation, which is often referred to as *policy coordination.* Charles E. Lindblom has defined policy coordination as follows (1965, p. 227):

> A set of decisions is coordinated if adjustments have been made in them, such that the adverse consequences of any one decision for other decisions are to a degree and in some frequency avoided, reduced, or counterbalanced or overweighed.

Cooperation occurs when actors adjust their behavior to the actual or anticipated preferences of others, through a process of policy coordination. To summarize more formally, *intergovernmental cooperation takes place when the policies actually followed by one government are regarded by its partners as facilitating realization of their own objectives, as the result of a process of policy coordination.*

With this definition in mind, we can differentiate among cooperation, harmony, and discord, as illustrated by figure 1. First, we ask whether actors' policies automatically facilitate the attainment of others' goals. If so, there is harmony: no adjustments need to take place. Yet harmony is rare in world politics. Rousseau sought to account for this rarity when he declared that even two countries guided by the General Will in their internal affairs would come into conflict if they had extensive contact with one another, since the General Will of each would not be general for both. Each would have a partial, self-interested perspective on their mutual interactions. Even for Adam Smith, efforts to ensure state security took precedence over measures to increase national prosperity. In defending the Navigation Acts, Smith declared: "As defense is of much more importance than opulence, the act of navigation is, perhaps, the wisest of all the commercial regulations of England" (1776/1976, p. 487). Waltz summarizes the point by saying that "in anarchy there is no automatic harmony" (1959, p. 182).

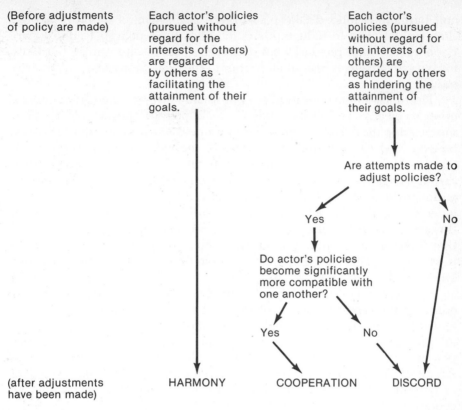

Figure 1 Harmony, Cooperation, and Discord.

Yet this insight tells us nothing definitive about the prospects for cooperation. For this we need to ask a further question about situations in which harmony does not exist. Are attempts made by actors (governmental or nongovernmental) to adjust their policies to each others' objectives? If no such attempts are made, the result is discord: a situation in which governments regard each others' policies as hindering the attainment of their goals, and hold each other responsible for these constraints.

Discord often leads to efforts to induce others to change their policies; when these attempts meet resistance, policy conflict results. Insofar as these attempts at policy adjustment succeed in making policies more compatible, however, cooperation ensues. The policy coordination that leads to cooperation need not involve bargaining or negotiation at all. What Lindblom calls "adaptive" as opposed to "manipulative" adjustment can take place: one country may shift its policy in the direction of another's preferences without regard for the effect of its action on the other state, defer to the other country, or partially shift its policy in order to avoid adverse consequences for its partner. Or nonbargained manipulation— such as one actor confronting another with a *fait accompli*—may occur (Lindblom, 1965, pp. 33–34 and ch. 4). Frequently, of course, negotiation and bargaining indeed take place, often accompanied by other actions that are designed to induce others to adjust their policies to one's own. Each government pursues what it perceives as its self-interest, but looks for bargains that can benefit all parties to the deal, though not necessarily equally.

Harmony and cooperation are not usually distinguished from one another so clearly. Yet, in the study of world politics, they should be. Harmony is apolitical. No communication is necessary, and no influence need be exercised. Cooperation, by contrast, is highly political: somehow, patterns of behavior must be altered. This change may be accomplished through negative as well as positive inducements. Indeed, studies of international crises, as well as game-theoretic experiments and simulations, have shown that under a variety of conditions, strategies that involve threats and punishments, as well as promises and rewards, are more effective in attaining cooperative outcomes than those that rely entirely on persuasion and the force of good example (Axelrod, 1981, 1984; Lebow, 1981; Snyder and Diesing, 1977).

Cooperation therefore does not imply an absence of conflict. On the contrary, it is typically mixed with conflict and reflects partially successful efforts to overcome conflict, real or potential. Cooperation takes place only in situations in which actors perceive that their policies are actually or potentially in conflict, not where there is harmony. Cooperation should not be viewed as the absence of conflict, but rather as a reaction to conflict or potential conflict. Without the specter of conflict, there is no need to cooperate.

The example of trade relations among friendly countries in a liberal international political economy may help to illustrate this crucial point. A naive observer, trained only to appreciate the overall welfare benefits of trade, might assume that trade relations would be harmonious: consumers in importing countries benefit from cheap foreign goods and increased competition, and producers can increasingly take advantage of the division of labor as their export markets expand. But harmony does not normally ensue. Discord on trade issues may prevail because governments do not even seek to reduce the adverse consequences of their own policies for others, but rather strive in certain respects to increase the severity of those effects. Mercantilist governments have sought in the twentieth century as well as the seventeenth to manipulate foreign trade, in conjunction with warfare, to damage each other economically and to gain productive resources themselves (Wilson, 1957; Hirschman, 1945/1980). Governments may desire "positional goods," such as high status (Hirsch, 1976), and may therefore resist even mutually beneficial cooperation if it helps others more than themselves. Yet even when neither power nor positional motivations are present, and when all participants would benefit in the aggregate from liberal trade, discord tends to predominate over harmony as the initial result of independent governmental action.

This occurs even under otherwise benign conditions because some groups or industries are forced to incur adjustment costs as changes in comparative advantage take place. Governments often respond to the ensuing demands for protection by attempting, more or less effectively, to cushion the burdens of adjustment for groups and industries that are politically influential at home. Yet unilateral measures to this effect almost always impose adjustment costs abroad, and discord continually threatens. Governments enter into international negotiations in order to reduce the conflict that would otherwise result. Even substantial potential common benefits do not create harmony when state power can be exercised on behalf of certain interests and against others. In world politics, harmony tends to vanish: attainment of the gains from pursuing complementary policies depends on cooperation.

Observers of world politics who take power and conflict seriously should be attracted to this way of defining cooperation, since my definition does not relegate cooperation to the mythological world of relations among equals in power. Hegemonic cooperation is not a contradiction in terms. Defining cooperation in contrast to harmony should, I hope, lead readers with a Realist orientation to take cooperation in world politics seriously rather than to dismiss it out of hand. To Marxists who also believe in hegemonic power theories, however, even this definition of cooperation may not seem to make it relevant to the contemporary world political economy. From this perspective, mutual policy adjustments cannot possibly resolve the contradictions besetting the system because they are attributable to capitalism rather than to problems of coordination among egoistic actors lacking common government. Attempts to resolve these contradictions through international cooperation will merely transfer issues to a deeper and even more intractable level. Thus it is not surprising that Marxian analyses of the international political economy have, with few exceptions, avoided sustained examinations of the conditions under which cooperation among major capitalist countries can take place. Marxists see it as more important to expose relationships of exploitation and conflict between major capitalist powers on the one hand and the masses of people in the periphery of world capitalism on the other. And, from a Leninist standpoint, to examine the conditions for international cooperation without first analyzing the contradictions of capitalism, and recognizing the irreconcilability of conflicts among capitalist countries, is a bourgeois error.

This is less an argument than a statement of faith. Since sustained international coordination of macroeconomic policies has never been tried, the statement that it would merely worsen the contradictions facing the system is speculative. In view of the lack of evidence for it, such a claim could even be considered rash. Indeed, one of the most perceptive Marxian writers of recent years, Stephen Hymer (1972), recognized explicitly that capitalists face problems of collective action and argued that they were seeking, with at least temporary prospects of success, to overcome them. As he recognized, any success in internationalizing capital could pose grave threats to socialist aspirations and, at the very least, would shift contradictions to new points of tension. Thus even were we to agree that the fundamental issue is posed by the contradictions of capitalism rather than the tensions inherent in a state system, it would be worthwhile to study the conditions under which cooperation is likely to occur.

INTERNATIONAL REGIMES AND COOPERATION

One way to study cooperation and discord would be to focus on particular actions as the units of analysis. This would require the systematic compilation of a data set composed of acts that could be regarded as comparable and coded according to the degree of cooperation that they reflect. Such a strategy has some attractive features. The problem with it, however, is that instances of cooperation and discord could all too easily be isolated from the context of beliefs and behavior within which they are embedded. This book does not view cooperation atomistically as a set of discrete, isolated acts, but rather seeks to understand patterns of cooperation in the world political economy. Accordingly, we need to examine actors' expectations about future patterns of interaction, their assumptions about the proper nature of economic arrangements, and the kinds of political activities they regard as legitimate. That is, we need to analyze cooperation within the context of international institutions, broadly defined . . . in terms of practices and expectations. Each act of cooperation or discord affects the beliefs, rules, and practices that form the context for future actions. Each act must therefore be interpreted as embedded within a chain of such acts and their successive cognitive and institutional residues.

This argument parallels Clifford Geertz's discussion of how anthropologists should use the concept of culture to interpret the societies they investigate. Geertz sees culture as the "webs of significance" that people have created for themselves. On their surface, they are enigmatical; the observer has to interpret them so that they make sense. Culture, for Geertz, "is a context, something within which [social events] can be intelligibly described" (1973, p. 14). It makes little sense to describe naturalistically what goes on at a Balinese cockfight unless one understands the meaning of the event for Balinese culture. There is not a world culture in the fullest sense, but even in world politics, human beings spin webs of significance. They develop implicit standards for behavior, some of which emphasize the principle of sovereignty and legitimize the pursuit of self-interest, while others rely on quite different principles. Any act of cooperation or apparent cooperation needs to be interpreted within the context of related actions, and of prevailing expectations and shared beliefs, before its meaning can be properly understood. Fragments of political behavior become comprehensible when viewed as part of a larger mosaic.

The concept of international regime not only enables us to describe patterns of cooperation; it also helps to account for both cooperation and discord. Although regimes themselves depend on conditions that are conducive to interstate agreements, they may also facilitate further efforts to coordinate policies. . . . To understand international cooperation, it is necessary to comprehend how institutions and rules not only reflect, but also affect, the facts of world politics.

Defining and Identifying Regimes

When John Ruggie introduced the concept of international regimes into the international politics literature in 1975, he defined a regime as "a set of mutual expectations, rules and regulations, plans, organizational energies and financial commitments, which have been accepted by a group of states" (p. 570). More recently, a collective definition, worked out at a conference on the subject, defined international regimes as "sets of implicit of explicit principles, norms, rules, and decision-making procedures around which actors' expectations converge in a given area of international relations. Principles are beliefs of facts, causation, and rectitude. Norms are standards of behavior defined in terms of rights and obligations. Rules are specific prescriptions or proscriptions for action. Decisionmaking procedures are prevailing practices for making and implementing collective choice" (Krasner, 1983, p. 2).

This definition provides a useful starting point for analysis, since it begins with the general conception of regimes as social institutions and explicates it further. The concept of norms, however, is ambiguous. It is important that we understand norms in this definition simply as standards of behavior defined in terms of rights and obligations. Another usage would distinguish norms from rules and principles by stipulating that participants in a social system regard norms, but not rules and principles, as morally binding regardless of considerations of narrowly defined self-interest. But to include norms, thus defined, in a definition of necessary regime characteristics would be to make the conception of regimes based strictly on self-interest a contradiction in terms. . . . I will maintain a definition of norms simply as standards of behavior, whether adopted on grounds of self-interest or otherwise. However, the possibility may be taken seriously that some regimes may contain norms and principles justified on the basis of values extending beyond self-interest, and regarded as obligatory on moral grounds by governments.

The principles of regimes define, in general, the purposes that their members are expected to pursue. For instance, the principles of the postwar trade and monetary regimes have emphasized the value of open, nondiscriminatory patterns of international economic transactions; the fundamental principle of the nonproliferation regime is that the spread of nuclear weapons is dangerous. Norms contain somewhat clearer injunctions to members about legitimate and illegitimate behavior, still defining responsibilities and obligations in relatively general terms. For instance, the norms of the General Agreement on Tariffs and Trade (GATT) do not require that members resort to free trade immediately, but incorporate injunctions to members to practice nondiscrimination and reciprocity and to move toward increased liberalization. Fundamental to the nonproliferation regime is the norm that members of the regime should not act in ways that facilitate nuclear proliferation.

The rules of a regime are difficult to distinguish from its norms; at the margin, they merge into one another. Rules are, however, more specific: they indicate in more detail the specific rights and obligations of members. Rules can be altered more easily than principles or norms, since there may be more than one set of rules that can attain a given set of purposes. Finally, at the same level of specificity as rules, but referring to procedures rather than substances, the decisionmaking procedures of regimes provide ways of implementing their principles and altering their rules.

An example from the field of international monetary relations may be helpful. The most important principle of the international balance-of-payments regime since the end of World War II has been that of liberalization of trade and payments. A key norm of the regime has been the injunction to states not to manipulate their exchange rates unilaterally for national advantage. Between 1958 and 1971 this norm was realized through pegged exchange rates and procedures for consultation in the event of change, supplemented with a variety of devices to help governments avoid exchange-rate changes through a combination of borrowing and internal adjustment. After 1973 governments have subscribed to the same norm, although it has been implemented more informally and probably less effectively under a system of floating exchange rates. Ruggie (1983b) has argued that the abstract principle of liberalization, subject to constraints imposed by the acceptance of the welfare state, has been maintained throughout the postwar period: *embedded liberalism* continues, reflecting a fundamental element of continuity in the international balance-of-payments regime. The norm of nonmanipulation has also been maintained, even though the specific rules of the 1958–1971 system having to do with adjustment have been swept away.

The concept of international regime is complex because it is defined in terms of four distinct components: principles, norms, rules, and decisionmaking procedures. It is tempting to select one of these levels of specificity—particularly, principles and norms or rules and procedures—as *the* defining characteristic of regimes (Krasner, 1983; Ruggie, 1983b). Such an approach, however, creates a false dichotomy between principles on the one hand and rules and procedures on the other. As we have noted, at the margin norms and rules cannot be sharply distinguished from each other. It is difficult if not impossible to tell the difference between an "implicit rule" of broad significance and a well-understood, relatively specific operating principle. Both rules and principles may affect expectations and even values. In a strong international regime, the linkages between principles and rules are likely to be tight. Indeed, it is precisely the linkages among principles, norms, and rules that give regimes their legitimacy. Since rules, norms, and principles are so closely intertwined, judgments about whether changes in rules constitute changes *of* regime or merely changes *within* regimes necessarily contain arbitrary elements.

Principles, norms, rules, and procedures all contain injunctions about behavior: they prescribe certain actions and proscribe others. They imply obligations, even though these obligations are not enforceable through a hierarchical legal system. It clarifies the definition of regime, therefore, to think of it in terms of injunctions of greater or lesser specificity. Some are far-reaching and extremely important. They may change only rarely. At the other extreme, injunctions may be merely technical matters of convenience that can be altered without great political or economic impact. In between are injunctions that are both specific enough that violations of them are in principle identifiable and that changes in them can be observed, and sufficiently significant that changes in them make a difference for the behavior of actors and the nature of the international political economy. It is these intermediate injunctions—politically consequential but specific enough that violations and changes can be identified—that I take as the essence of international regimes.[2]

A brief examination of international oil regimes, and their injunctions, may help us clarify this point. The pre-1939 international oil regime was dominated by a small number of international firms and contained explicit injunctions about where and under what conditions companies could produce oil, and where and how they should market it. The rules of the Red Line and Achnacarry or "As-Is" agreements of 1928 reflected an "anti-competitive ethos": that is, the basic principle that competition was destructive to the system and the norm that firms should not engage in it (Turner, 1978, p. 30). This principle and this norm both persisted after World War II, although an intergovernmental regime with explicit rules was not established, owing to the failure of the Anglo-American Petroleum Agreement. Injunctions against price-cutting were reflected more in the practices of companies than in formal rules. Yet expectations and practices of major actors were strongly affected by these injunctions, and in this sense the criteria for a regime—albeit a weak one—were met. As governments of producing countries became more assertive, however, and as formerly domestic independent companies entered international markets, these arrangements collapsed; after the mid-to-late 1960s, there was no regime for the issue-area as a whole, since no injunctions could be said to be accepted as obligatory by all influential actors. Rather, there was a "tug of war" (Hirschman, 1981) in which all sides resorted to self-help. The Organization of Petroleum Exporting Countries (OPEC) sought to create a producers' regime based on rules for prorationing oil production, and consumers established an emergency oil-sharing system in the new International Energy Agency to counteract the threat of selective embargoes.

If we were to have paid attention only to the principle of avoiding competition, we would have seen continuity: whatever the dominant actors, they have always sought to cartelize the industry one way or another. But to do so would be to miss the main point, which is that momentous changes have occurred. At the other extreme, we could have fixed our attention on very specific particular arrangements, such as the various joint ventures of the 1950s and 1960s or the specific provisions for controlling output tried by OPEC after 1973, in which case we would have observed a pattern of continual flux. The significance of the most important events—the demise of old cartel arrangements, the undermining of the international majors' positions in the 1960s, and the rise of producing governments to a position of influence in the 1970s—could have been missed. Only by focusing on the intermediate level of relatively specific but politically consequential injunctions, whether we call them rules, norms, or principles, does the concept of regime help us identify major changes that require explanation.

As our examples of money and oil suggest, we regard the scope of international regimes as corresponding, in general, to the boundaries of issue-areas, since governments establish regimes to deal with problems that they regard as so closely linked that they should be dealt with together. Issue-areas are best defined as sets of issues that are in fact dealt with in common negotiations and by the same, or closely coordinated, bureaucracies, as opposed to issues that are dealt with separately and in uncoordinated fashion. Since issue-areas depend on actors' perceptions and behavior rather than on inherent qualities of the subject matters, their boundaries change gradually over time. Fifty years ago, for instance, there was no oceans issue-area, since particular questions now grouped under that heading were dealt with separately; but there was an international monetary issue-area even then (Keohane and Nye, 1977, ch. 4). Twenty years ago trade in cotton textiles had an international regime of its own— the Long-Term Agreement on Cotton Textiles—and was treated separately from trade in synthetic fibers (Aggarwal, 1981). Issue-areas are defined and redefined by changing patterns of human intervention; so are international regimes.

Self-Help and International Regimes

The injunctions of international regimes rarely affect economic transactions directly: state institutions, rather than international organizations, impose tariffs and quotas, intervene in foreign exchange markets, and manipulate oil prices through taxes and subsidies. If we think about the impact of the principles, norms, rules, and decisionmaking procedures of regimes, it becomes clear that insofar as they have any effect at all, it must be exerted on national controls, and especially on the specific interstate agreements that affect the exercise of national controls (Aggarwall, 1981). International regimes must be distinguished from these specific agreements; . . . a major function of regimes is to facilitate the making of specific cooperative agreements among governments.

Superficially, it could seem that since international regimes affect national controls, the regimes are of superior importance—just as federal laws in the United States frequently override state and local legislation. Yet this would be a fundamentally misleading conclusion. In a well-ordered society, the units of action—individuals in classic liberal thought—live together within a framework of constitutional principles that define property rights, establish who may control the state, and specify the conditions under which subjects must obey governmental regulations. In the United States, these principles establish the supremacy of the federal government in a number of policy areas, though not in all. But world politics is decentralized rather than hierarchic: the prevailing principle of sovereignty means that states are subject to no superior government (Ruggie, 1983a). The resulting system is sometimes referred to as one of "self-help" (Waltz, 1979).

Sovereignty and self-help mean that the principles and rules of international regimes will necessarily be weaker than in domestic society. In a civil society, these rules "specify terms of exchange" within the framework of constitutional principles (North, 1981, p. 203). In world politics, the principles, norms, and rules of regimes are necessarily fragile because they risk coming into conflict with the principle of sovereignty and the associated norm of self-help. They may promote cooperation, but the fundamental basis of order on which they would rest in a well-ordered society does not exist. They drift around without being tied to the solid anchor of the state.

Yet even if the principles of sovereignty and self-help limit the degree of confidence to be placed in international agreements, they do not render cooperation impossible. Orthodox theory itself relies on mutual interests to explain forms of cooperation that are used by states as instruments of competition. According to balance-of-power theory, cooperative endeavors such as political-military alliances necessarily form in self-help systems (Waltz, 1979). Acts of cooperation are accounted for on the grounds that mutual interests are sufficient to enable states to overcome their suspicions of one another. But since even orthodox theory relies on mutual interests, its advocates are on weak ground in objecting to interpretations of system-wide cooperation along these lines. There is no logical or empirical reason why mutual interests in world politics should be limited to interests in combining forces against adversaries. As economists emphasize, there can also be mutual interests in securing efficiency gains from voluntary exchange or oligopolistic rewards from the creation and division of rents resulting from the control and manipulation of markets.

International regimes should not be interpreted as elements of a new international order "beyond the nation-state." They should be comprehended chiefly as arrangements motivated by self-interest: as components of systems in which sovereignty remains a constitutive principle. This means that, as Realists emphasize, they will be shaped largely by their most powerful members, pursuing their own interests. But regimes can also affect state interests, for the notion of self-interest is itself elastic and largely subjective. Perceptions of self-interest depend both on actors' expectations of the likely consequences that will follow from particular actions and on their fundamental values. Regimes can certainly affect expectations and may affect values as well. Far from being contradicted by the view that international behavior is shaped largely by power and interests, the concept of international regime is consistent both with the importance of differential power and with a sophisticated view of self-interest. Theories of regimes can incorporate Realist insights about the role of power and interest, while also indicating the inadequacy of theories that define interests so narrowly that they fail to take the role of institutions into account.

Regimes not only are consistent with self-interest but may under some conditions even be necessary to its effective pursuit. They facilitate the smooth operation of decentralized international political systems and therefore perform an important function for states. In a world political economy characterized by growing interdependence, they may become increasingly useful for governments that wish to solve common problems and pursue complementary purposes without subordinating themselves to hierarchical systems of control.

CONCLUSIONS

. . . International cooperation has been defined as a process through which policies actually followed by governments come to be regarded by their partners as facilitating realization of their own objectives, as the result of policy coordination. Cooperation involves mutual adjustment and can only arise from conflict or potential conflict. It must therefore be distinguished from harmony. Discord, which is the opposite of harmony, stimulates demands for policy adjustments, which can either lead to cooperation or to continued, perhaps intensified, discord.

Since international regimes reflect patterns of cooperation and discord over time, focusing on them leads us to examine long-term patterns of behavior, rather than treating acts of cooperation as isolated events. Regimes consist of injunctions at various levels of generality, ranging from principles to norms to highly specific rules and decisionmaking procedures. By investigating the evolution of the norms and rules of a regime over time, we can use the concept of international regime both to explore continuity and to investigate change in the world political economy.

From a theoretical standpoint, regimes can be viewed as intermediate factors, or "intervening variables," between fundamental characteristics of world politics such as the international distribution of power on the one hand and the behavior of states and nonstate actors such as multinational corporations on the other. The concept of international regime helps us account for cooperation and discord. To understand the impact of regimes, it is not necessary to posit idealism on the part of actors in world politics. On the contrary, the norms and rules of regimes can exert an effect on behavior even if they do not embody common ideals but are used by self-interested states and corporations engaging in a process of mutual adjustment.

NOTES

1. Historically, . . . hegemonies have usually arisen only after major wars. The two principal modern powers that could be considered hegemonic leaders—Britain after 1815 and the United States after 1945—both emerged victorious from world conflicts. I am assuming, in regarding hegemony as unlikely in the foreseeable future, that any world war would have such disastrous consequences that no country would emerge as hegemonic over a world economy resembling that of the present. For a discussion of the cycle of hegemony, see Gilpin (1981) and Modelski (1978 and 1982).
2. Some authors have defined *regime* as equivalent to the conventional concept of international system. For instance, Puchala and Hopkins (1983) claim that "a regime exists in every substantive issue-area in international relations where there is discernibly patterned behavior" (p. 63). To adopt this definition would be to make either "system" or "regime" a redundant term. At the opposite extreme, the concept of regime could be limited to situations with genuine normative content, in which governments followed regime rules *instead of* pursuing their own self-interests when the two conflicted. If this course were chosen, the concept of regime would be just another way of expressing ancient "idealist" sentiments in international relations. The category of regime would become virtually empty. This dichotomy poses a false choice between using "regime" as a new label for old patterns and defining regimes as utopias. Either strategy would make the term irrelevant.

Rational Hegemons, Excludable Goods, and Small Groups: An Epitaph for Hegemonic Stability Theory?

Joanne Gowa

The political correlates of a stable world market economy remain unclear. Early in the 1970s, a burst of scholarly interest in this subject produced what at the time appeared to be a compelling thesis: the world was safe from tariff wars and great depressions only if a single state or hegemonic power dominated the international political system. Defining international free trade as a public good, "hegemonic stability theory" concluded that its reliable supply depended upon a distribution of international power analogous to that within a privileged group.

In relatively short order, however, critics challenged three assumptions fundamental to hegemonic theory. They argued that: (1) rational hegemons, according to standard international trade theory, adopt an optimum tariff rather than free trade; (2) small groups, as public-good theory itself claims, are close substitutes for privileged groups; and (3) the provision of open international markets implies the supply of excludable rather than public goods. Thus, they concluded, hegemony is not necessary for, and indeed may be antithetical to, a stable world economy based on market exchange.

The potential power of these criticisms is considerable: a persuasive argument on their behalf would destroy the analytic foundations of a theory that is already the target of attack on empirical grounds.[1] In this paper I argue, however, that these attacks are not fatal to the theory: on economic grounds alone, a *nonmyopic* rational hegemon may reject an

---

Joanne Gowa, "Rational Hegemons, Excludable Goods, and Small Groups: An Epitaph for Hegemonic Stability Theory?" *World Politics* 41, No. 3 (April 1989). Copyright © 1989 Princeton University Press. Reprinted with permission of Princeton University Press.

optimum tariff; exclusion from a free-trade accord is itself a public good; and hegemons enjoy a clear advantage relative to small groups with respect to the supply of international public goods. Strategic interdependence, incomplete information, and barriers to "k" group formation are the core elements of the argument presented here.

I conclude that the most significant flaw in hegemonic theory is its neglect of the essence of the domain to which it applies: the politics of interstate trade in an anarchic world. Because the security externalities that inevitably accompany the removal of trade barriers can shift the balance of power among states, any analytic representation of international free trade must model these effects explicitly. In short, hegemonic stability theory must include security as an argument in the utility functions it assigns to states opening their borders to trade.

Several important limitations of this analysis should be stated at the outset. Because the public-good variant of hegemonic theory is cast at the systemic level, this paper also focuses exclusively on the incentives to trade freely that arise at the level of the international system. As a result, it does not consider the influence of domestic factors on the pursuit of these incentives: neither the organization of domestic exchange via hierarchies instead of markets nor the role of special interest groups, for example, is considered.[2]

The argument also assumes as given the conditions under which standard international trade theory applies, and the paper contains only illustrative rather than systematic empirical referents.[3] These restrictions are appropriate in view of the essay's objectives: (1) to demonstrate that the assumptions about rational hegemons, public goods, and privileged groups actually allow hegemonic stability theory to represent analytically several critically important barriers to free trade among states, and (2) to make clear that any theory of international trade in an anarchic world must explicitly model its security externalities.

After a brief explanation of hegemonic stability theory, a careful review of the arguments of its most persuasive critics is presented. The paper concludes with the suggestion that hegemonic theory is problematic largely because it neglects the political consequences of agreements to trade freely.

HEGEMONIC STABILITY THEORY

In 1973, Charles P. Kindleberger laid the foundations of what Robert O. Keohane, almost a decade later, labeled "hegemonic stability" theory.[4] The term is also frequently applied to the arguments of both Robert G. Gilpin and Stephen D. Krasner, although Kindleberger's emphasis is on the stability of the international system, and Gilpin's and Krasner's is on the self-interest of the dominant state.[5] Common to all three, however, is the claim that, because a stable system of international free trade involves the supply of a public good, it has a political prerequisite: the existence of a hegemonic power. As Kindleberger puts it, "for the world economy to be stabilized, there has to be a stabilizer, one stabilizer."[6]

The analytics of hegemonic theory are drawn from the literature on public goods. Unlike private goods (cookies or Big Macs), public goods (nuclear deterrence or clean air) are joint in supply and nonexcludable. That is, any individual's consumption of these goods does not preclude their consumption by others, and no individual can be excluded or prevented from consuming such goods whether or not he has paid for them.

As a consequence, Prisoner's Dilemma (PD) preferences characterize each member of a large group or of any short-lived group facing a public-good or collective-action problem. The corresponding payoff matrix is found in Figure 1. Confronting these payoffs, the dominant strategy of each player is to refuse (defect) rather than to contribute (cooperate) to the supply of the public good: DC > CC > DD > CD. A Pareto-inferior equilibrium outcome (DD) results: no one contributes, no public good is produced, and another—albeit unstable—outcome (CC) exists in which all would be better off.[7]

Kindleberger argues that, if states locked into an international free trade PD are to be able to escape their dilemma, a hegemon must exist. Because of its relative size in the international system, Kindleberger's hegemon is the equivalent of what public-good theory calls a *privileged group*: that is, a group "such that each of its members, or at least some one of them, has an incentive to see that the collective good is provided, even if he has to bear the full burden of providing it himself."[8]

Casual empiricism appears to confirm Kindleberger's argument. British hegemony in the nineteenth and U.S. hegemony in the mid-twentieth century coexisted with relatively open international markets. The inability of Britain and the unwillingness of the United States to lead coincided with the construction of "beggar-thy-neighbor" trading blocs in the interwar period.[9] The apparent decline in U.S. hegemony in recent decades and the simultaneous increase in trade barriers among the industrialized

	Column	
	Cooperate	Defect
Cooperate	2, 2	4, 1
Defect	1, 4	3, 3

Row

Note: Payoffs are ranked from 1 (best) to 4 (worst); Row's payoffs are listed first.

Figure 1

countries also appear to support Kindleberger's assertion. Whether a correlation between hegemony and free trade actually exists or represents a causal relationship has became extremely controversial.[10]

Much ink has also been spilled over three analytic issues: (1) Do rational hegemons have an interest in free trade? (2) Is free trade necessarily nonexcludable? and (3) Does a hegemon provide the only solution to whatever public-good problems exist? Although analyses of these issues appear to damage hegemonic theory irreparably, the critics have in fact chosen boomerangs as their weapons.

RATIONAL HEGEMONS AND FREE TRADE

Some observers contend that the attribution of free-trade preferences to a hegemon violates the principles of standard international trade theory.[11] According to the latter, they note, any state large enough to influence its terms of trade—the relative price of its exports on world markets—will maximize its real income by imposing an optimum tariff: that is, a tax on trade set at the point that maximizes the net gain which accrues from the resulting improved terms and reduced volume of trade. Thus, they suggest, only an irrational hegemon would conform to the behavioral prescriptions of hegemonic theory.[12]

Flawed premises undercut the power of this argument. It implicitly assumes that the hegemon's influence over its terms of trade is the most efficient source of leverage available to it. More importantly, the argument ignores strategic variables that can affect a hegemon's choice of tariff levels. As a result, it effectively violates the logic of game-theoretic models of price setting by domestic monopolists, thereby inflating the costs an economic hegemon incurs when it abandons its trade barriers for political reasons.

The possession of power in the trade-theory sense, for example, necessarily implies the use of a tariff only if the hegemon cannot find a more efficient way to redistribute income from its trading partners to itself. Because other states lose more than the hegemon gains, a tariff "is an inferior way to redistribute income between countries."[13] In its *own* long-run interest in enhancing its revenue base, therefore, the dominant state has an incentive to pursue either of two potentially Pareto-superior alternatives to trade barriers: bribes or taxes.[14]

In practice, the transaction costs associated with both alternatives are likely to exceed the deadweight loss produced by a tariff. In the case of small states engaged in a collective effort to bribe the hegemon to adopt free trade, a public-good problem arises: each small state that is potentially a party to such bribery has an incentive to let the others assume its costs. Free riding can be prevented only in the unlikely event that the hegemon can cheaply discriminate among the exports of a large number of small countries.

Designing, implementing, and enforcing a system to tax other states is likely to be prohibitively costly to the hegemon. Although the international equivalent of a lump-sum tax may leave small states better off than would an optimum tariff, these states may recognize that they would be even better off as free riders: the hegemon's threat to sanction tax evaders may not be credible to them. The situation of the hegemon is analogous to that of the incumbent firm in the chain-store paradox: it confronts a tradeoff between the short-term costs to it if it punishes defiance and the longer-term costs to its reputation if it does not do so.[15] In any case, unilateral imposition of an optimum tariff is likely to be less costly to the hegemon than the theoretically Pareto-superior alternative of taxation.

Despite the dearth of alternative means to redistribute income in its favor, a clear-thinking, nonmyopic hegemon may still reject the optimum tariff recommended to it by standard trade theory. Its interest in doing so would be the preservation of its monopoly power. Thus, it would act on the same logic that motivates a domestic monopolist to set prices below their short-run maximizing levels: the incumbent firm thereby attempts to deter entry into its markets. By "limit" pricing, the monopolist seeks to signal potential entrants that its costs of production are lower than they are in reality.[16] Its ability to sacrifice short-run gains in order to earn higher long-run returns depends on the existence of costs to entry as well as asymmetric information about the monopolist's costs of production.[17]

A rational, nonmyopic hegemon may set its tariff at less than the short-run optimum level under analogous conditions—if, for example, it has some private information about the elasticity of global demand and supply curves, and if small countries organizing to exert countervailing power in world markets incur some costs in doing so.[18] A hegemon may indeed have private information about global markets because of its incentives to become informed about them; a small country, by contrast, has little incentive to acquire such information because it cannot influence its terms of trade. Significant transaction costs may be incurred in the process of forming customs unions because of the distributional effects both within and across the potential members that result from the setting of uniform external trade barriers.[19]

The trading practices of both Britain and the United States suggest that the analogy to limit pricing is of more than just analytic interest. Mid-nineteenth century Britain, according to one observer, maintained its tariffs at less than optimum levels in order to fix its "monopoly of manufactures on the rest of the world for a few more decades than its natural term."[20] The logic of limit pricing apparently impressed itself on the United States when it attempted, in the 1930 Smoot-Hawley tariff, to turn the terms of trade in its favor. This effort provoked the construction of trading blocs abroad,[21] and apparently induced the United States to try to lower global barriers to trade after the war.[22]

In short, because an attempt to exploit its power in the short run may undermine that power over time, a nonmyopic, rational hegemon may reject an optimum tariff. Although the limit-pricing argument does not support an inference that free trade—the international analogue of competitive prices at the domestic level—will prevail, it does suggest that unilateral restrictions on the use of an optimum tariff can be in the strictly economic self-interest of a far-sighted, clear-thinking hegemon.

Because the limit-pricing analogue suggests that it may be cheaper to forgo an optimum tariff than standard trade theory implies, it also suggests that the incidence of decisions to do so for political reasons may be higher than would otherwise be expected. Thus, for example, the introduction of long-term elasticities into empirical estimates of the welfare losses incurred by Britain as a consequence of its unilateral adoption of free trade in the mid-nineteenth century suggests that the magnitude of these losses was "extremely small."[23] Although Britain's repeal of the Corn Laws is conventionally attributed to domestic politics, the British case nevertheless suggests that a hegemon does not need very strong political incentives to adopt free trade: the economic losses it incurs by doing so may be insignificant.

In sum, even the exclusively economic self-interest of a rational hegemon may not persuade it to adopt the optimum tariff of standard trade theory. Its preferences will depend on the relative costs of bribery, taxation, and tariffs, and on its ability to deter entry through the strategic use of its monopoly power. It is certainly possible that, under some circumstances, a hegemon will choose an optimum tariff as conventionally defined. Under different circumstances, however—even in situations in which political factors do not influence its choice—it may not do so.

FREE TRADE AND PUBLIC GOODS

The public-good premise of hegemonic theory has also become controversial. Arguing that the "benefits of free trade are largely excludable," John A. C. Conybeare asserts, for example, that "countries may, individually or collectively, penalize a country that attempts to impose a nationally advantageous tariff at the expense of the international community."[24] Thus, Conybeare contends that free trade is not a public good because it fails to fulfill the nonexcludability attribute of such goods.

Arguing that free trade is, instead, a Prisoners' Dilemma, Conybeare notes that an optimum tariff maximizes the gains of a large state. If all states employ tariffs, however, the outcome is inferior to a free-trade truce, as it reduces the volume but does not change the terms of trade.[25] The mutually preferred outcome of free trade is difficult to achieve because it is not a stable or Nash equilibrium of the one-shot game: each state has an incentive to deviate to an optimum tariff if others adhere to free trade. Thus, Conybeare observes, trade theory effectively assigns PD preferences to large states (where C represents free trade and D an optimum tariff).

Conybeare is correct: free trade *is* excludable, and his argument is an important modification of hegemonic theory. But implicit in this argument is an assumption that each state benefits from sanctioning would-be free riders. If, however, the policing of a cooperative agreement is costly, enforcement itself becomes a public good.[26] As Michael Laver observes, costly exclusion "simply replaces one collective action problem with another, the problem of raising exclusion costs."[27]

Whenever defection is either ambiguous or easily concealed, sanctioning is likely to be costly.[28] Ambiguity threatens to make punishment appear as provocation, thus initiating a feud that will not eliminate the alleged offense, but will impose costs on the would-be enforcer. Ambiguity is virtually indigenous to PDs because incentives to conceal cheating are strong; as George Stigler observes of industrial cartels, "the detection of secret price-cheating will of course be as difficult as interested people can make it."[29]

Informational asymmetries pervade trade agreements, arising from the varied sources of ambiguity inherent in them. Among these sources are: the need to translate international agreements into domestic law; the difficulty of determining if conditions of breach have occurred; the inability to specify illegal behavior precisely; and the possibility of currency manipulation as a substitute for overt action on trade.[30] Would-be free riders may also conceal cheating by shipping their exports through third countries.

Thus—as is true of many PDs—monitoring, assessing, and punishing attempts to cheat are crucial but costly aspects of international trade agreements. As a result, it becomes individually rational but collectively suboptimal for states to free ride on the enforcement efforts of others: whenever incomplete information exists, exclusion of deviants from a trade agreement itself becomes a public good.[31]

In short, while technically excludable, free trade nonetheless presents public-good problems under realistic assumptions about the costs of sanctions. Even if the public-good problems that may inhere in other regimes ancillary to the trade regime are set aside, therefore, open international markets do involve the supply of a public good. Although, as the next section demonstrates, a variety of game-theoretic solutions to enforcement problems exist that do not require the presence of either a privileged *or* a small group, their relevance in the context of international politics is considerably less than is their abstract analytic appeal.

PRIVILEGED AND SMALL GROUPS

Following Thomas C. Schelling, small-group critics of hegemonic theory contend that even large-number systems can successfully resolve collective action problems if there exists a k or subgroup of actors who would profit by doing so even if they alone absorbed its costs.[32] Small-group theory, however, does not satisfactorily confront two issues that are critical to the ability of a group of states to substitute for a hegemon: the theory addresses neither the origins nor the enforcement mechanisms of the group adequately. Although game-theoretic solutions to both problems exist, their assumptions provide a poor fit to the situation of states that are engaged in trade in an anarchic political structure.

Origins

The origin of small groups is typically approached as an empirical rather than as an analytic issue: the legacy of hegemony explains the creation of k groups.[33] In some respects, the neglect of k-group genesis is unimpeachable: proponents of small-group theory themselves readily acknowledge that they do not systematically address the issue,[34] and no theory of international cooperation should be indicted simply because it cannot explain completely the evolution of inter-state cooperation.

The reliance on hegemony, however, remains troubling for several reasons. First, it implies that the international system evolves peacefully from a hegemonic to a nonhegemonic structure, despite evidence that such power transitions can be potent sources of war.[35] Second, its recourse to history leaves small-group theory mute before a problem that is central to the field of international political economy: because the great powers are always few in number, the theory cannot explain why wide variations exist in the capacity of different systems to support market exchange among their constituent states.

The role attributed to history also dismantles axiomatically a formidable barrier to entry that a small group would otherwise confront: the need to agree on the cooperative equilibrium it will thereafter enforce. The literature on oligopolistic supergames has been strongly criticized for its silence on this aspect of collusion:[36] this criticism applies *a fortiori* to discussions of free-trade k groups.[37] If neither oligopolies nor would-be international k groups can reach agreement on what is to be enforced, it is, as James Friedman observes in the industrial context, "cold comfort to know that the firms, should they ever find themselves at the equilibrium, would never seek to deviate from it."[38]

Agreement on any single equilibrium is problematic because different equilibria imply different distributions of the net benefits of cooperation.[39] Although several game-theoretic solutions to this problem exist, no single solution currently commands general acceptance.[40] Moreover, insofar as they assume that the utility functions of all players are common knowledge, these solutions tend to assume away rather than confront directly what R. Duncan Luce and Howard Raiffa refer to as the "real" bargaining problem: the existence of strategic incentives to conceal preferences.[41]

Apart from abstract game-theoretic solutions, several solutions exist that are arguably more feasible. As is true of firms attempting to form cartels, states can readily agree to maximize their joint profits or gains from trade either if the distribution of profits that results will benefit all equally, or if side-payments are possible. It is unlikely that collusion on the joint maximum will lead to a symmetrical distribution of benefits. This will occur within an industrial cartel only in the highly improbable event that all firms are "absolutely" identical to each other.[42] In the context of international trade, it will occur only if reciprocal demand curves are identical in the negotiating countries—an equally improbable event.

The joint maximum theoretically retains its appeal if side-payments are possible. Side-payments redistribute the net benefits of cooperation among the relevant actors precisely in order "to equalize any inequities arising from their cooperation."[43] Significant impediments to their use exist, however: utility must be transferable; the contracting parties must agree on a redistributive mechanism;[44] and, most importantly, recipients must accept the potential threat that inheres in their reliance on what is, in effect, the extension of subsidies to them from others. Oliver Williamson's assessment of the risks to subsidized firms applies to states as well:

> Firms which are authorized to expand relatively as a result of the agreement will be powerfully situated to demand a renegotiated settlement at a later date. Wary of such opportunism, firms for which retrenchment is indicated will decline from the outset to accept a full-blown profit-pooling arrangement.[45]

If neither natural nor induced symmetry of profit distribution renders the joint maximum a workable point of agreement, the "intrinsic magnetism of particular outcomes" may yet single out one from among the set of Pareto-optimal points.[46] The "egalitarian nature" of the Swiss tariff-reduction proposal at the Tokyo Round negotiations, for example, reportedly led to its general acceptance.[47] Yet this example only serves to illustrate how difficult it may be for a unique focal point to emerge: behind agreement on equity as the standard for the Tokyo Round formula stood the relatively equal power of the four principal parties to that negotiation, a long history of tariff cuts and a relatively low level of tariffs among them, and no discernible security ramifications to the accord.

In the absence of any of these facilitating conditions, would-be international k groups may face insuperable obstacles to organization. Moreover, if the play of the game violates the "heroic" assumption of supergame analysis that the payoff matrix does not change over time,[48] this problem will arise not only at the initial but at *every* stage of the iterated game in which change occurs. The international context poses particularly difficult problems in this respect, as any distribution of the gains from trade can affect not only the economic but also the military balance of power among participating states. In the international system, therefore, small groups are poor substitutes for privileged groups.

Enforcement

Despite their emphasis on enforcement, small-group advocates have not yet addressed adequately the deterrence and punishment of cheating.

The discussion that follows focuses on the three hostages to good behavior in any single regime that are prominent in the small-group literature: linkage to existing regimes and, through reputation, to future regimes, and the breakdown of the regime in which the defection occurs.[49]

What is not explained, however, is why exclusion from other existing regimes is a credible threat: the literature does not specify either the excludable goods they supply or the cooperators' interests in punishing those who free ride on a *different* regime. As both theoretical and empirical analyses suggest, linkage may as easily torpedo as reinforce cooperation in any specific issue area: the interests of states in linking cooperation on one to cooperation on other issues can as easily diverge as converge.[50] Analytically, then, there is no reason to assume that linkages stabilize cooperation.

Analogously, in order to attribute significant explanatory weight to reputation, small-group advocates must show that: (1) extrapolations from past to future behavior are reliable because the interests of states are the same in both the past and the present situations, *and* (2) informational asymmetries exist between the contracting parties.[51] Theoretical and empirical work on strategic deterrence, however, suggests that state interests and behavior vary widely across time and place.[52] As a consequence, states tend to discount the past heavily as a predictor of the behavior of other states in later situations.

In addition, the regime context suggests that informational asymmetries will be rare: regimes are created specifically to correct the "market for lemons" problem.[53] Because regimes supply information to states about the behavior of others, they do not provide opportunities for states to develop a reputation for honesty. As Robert H. Frank observes,

> if people act rationally, . . . we [cannot] discover that someone is honest by observing what he does in situations where the detection of cheating is not *unlikely.* . . . These are situations in which we frequently discover how a person has acted. For precisely this reason, however, it will not be rational to cheat in these cases. To observe that someone does not cheat would tell us only that he is prudent, not honest. . . . The kinds of actions that are likely to be observed are just not very good tests of whether a person is honest.[54]

That states understand the logic of Frank's argument is nicely illustrated by Lord Salisbury's comment about Prussian intentions. He noted "that they should have been pacific when they were weak is not unnatural, but if we wish to know the character of their disposition when left to itself, we must ask what they were when they were strong."[55]

In the abstract, at least, it may not matter much that these two hostages do not adequately secure cooperation. Sufficient power to deter free riding inheres in the one mechanism to which the existing literature generally gives relatively short shrift: each state's recognition that, "because regimes are difficult to construct, it may be rational to obey their rules if the alternative is their breakdown. . . ."[56] Endowed with additional structure, this recognition alone renders the cooperative a Nash or self-enforcing equilibrium. If each state realizes that its attempt to free ride will lead to the collapse of the regime, it has no incentive to defect, and the problem of enforcement does not arise. A critical omission in existing analyses, however, is how such a self-destruct mechanism might be built into a regime.[57]

A credible threat that the response to any attempt to free ride will be the collapse of the entire regime creates just such a self-destruct mechanism. Existing work on tacit collusion among oligopolists relies on precisely this threat in order to stabilize cooperation: all firms agree to revert to the Cournot or noncooperative equilibrium for some period if *any* firm attempts to free ride.[58] The threat is credible because it is in every firm's interest to execute it provided all others do so: by definition, if one firm believes that all other firms will, after any deviation, begin to produce their Cournot outputs, that firm cannot do better than do so itself.[59] Thus, no firm has an interest in deviating from the collusive equilibrium: sanctions need never be implemented.

In effect, this solution generalizes the two-person Tit-for-Tat solution to the n- person game, with analogous restrictions on the discount rate relative to the payoffs, and on the information available to each player about the others.[60] Unlike the two-person game, however, the n-person situation confronts the nondefecting players with the temptation to respond to any defection in either of two ways that return short-term profits higher than those of the noncooperative equilibrium: to offer the defector a second chance or to recontract among themselves in order to maximize their profits in light of the defection. The fact, however, that both alternatives tend to unleash a chain of defections strengthens incentives to execute the original threat.[61] Thus, this solution is a self-enforcing agreement that sustains cooperation without the need for linkage to other PDs or to reputations.

The relevance of this solution in the context of international politics is considerably smaller than is its abstract analytic appeal, however. Its application requires agreement among the contracting states that a deviation has occurred; it also requires a consensus on the response. Yet, not only the economic but also the political interests of states influence their judgments on these issues: incentives to perceive and sanction a deviation can vary widely as the identity of the alleged deviant varies. Kindleberger observes that free riding can result when "the police are politically opposed to a rule . . . or to its application in a given case . . .": he points out that the United Nations and the League of Nations before it demonstrate that attempts to protect the international collective good are highly vulnerable to the tendency of states to interpret any alleged threat to that good in a highly self-interested fashion.[62] Thus, in enforcing a cooperative equilibrium, any small group of states encounters political problems that do not confront hegemonic states.

CONCLUSION

Although critics of hegemonic stability theory have not destroyed its analytic foundations, they have achieved several less ambitious objectives. They have, for example, argued persuasively that a hegemonic preference for free trade cannot be assumed: a more discriminating analysis is essential to establish the conditions under which a rational hegemon will, in its *own* interests, act benevolently rather than coercively toward others. In addition, the critics have forced a rigorous examination of the assumed public character of free trade. Moreover, they have successfully challenged the assumption that international public goods can, under *all* conditions, be provided only by a privileged group.

They have not, however, deprived hegemonic stability theory of its analytic base: hegemons can reject the prescriptions of standard trade theory; whenever asymmetrical information prevails, open international markets do present public-good problems; and privileged groups enjoy a stronger advantage than small-group advocates acknowledge.

More importantly, its critics have not challenged the public-good variant of hegemonic theory at its point of maximum vulnerability. Focusing exclusively on the real income gains that accrue to a state which opens its borders to trade, the theory analyzes economic exchange in a political vacuum. Yet, national power is engaged in free-trade agreements because such agreements inevitably produce security externalities: the removal of trade barriers affects not only the real income but also the security of the contracting states.[63]

The security externalities of trade arise from its inevitable jointness in production: the source of gains from trade is the increased efficiency with which domestic resources can be employed, and this increase in efficiency itself frees economic resources for military uses.[64] Thus, trade enhances the potential military power of any country that engages in it.[65] In doing so, free trade can disrupt the preexisting balance of power among the contracting states.[66]

Thus, the most durable barrier to open international markets may not be the trade preferences of a rational hegemon, the effectively public character of free trade, or the inability of small groups to substitute easily for privileged groups. Instead, it may be the anarchic international system that makes two facts common knowledge among states: (1) each seeks to exploit the wealth of others to enhance its own power, and (2) trade is instrumental to this end.[67] The structure of international politics, in short, may lead a state to prefer the status quo ante because it fears that any change may benefit others more than itself.[68]

In a first-best world, of course, these fears would not paralyze states. A two-step process would neutralize them: states would first maximize their absolute gains from trade, and would then adjust their defense strategies to compensate for any changes in the balance of power that occur as trade barriers fall. In a more realistic, less than first-best world, however, the time lag that intervenes between these two steps may open a window of vulnerability that can allow one state to threaten the existence of another.

As a consequence, states may prefer the conservative course. Open markets thus become victims of the primacy of security concerns in an anarchic international political structure. The failure of hegemonic stability theory to acknowledge this barrier to trade constitutes the theory's most profound flaw. Progress toward a more powerful theory of the political economy of international trade must begin with an explicit recognition of the influential role played by security concerns in the determination of national trade policies.

NOTES

1. Timothy James McKeown, "The Rise and Decline of the Open Trading Regime of the Nineteenth Century," Ph.D. diss., Stanford University, 1982; McKeown, "Hegemonic Stability Theory and 19th-Century Tariff Levels in Europe," *International Organization* 37 (Winter 1983), 73–91; John A. C. Conybeare, "Tariff Protection in Developed and Developing Countries," *International Organization* 37 (Summer 1983), 441–468.
2. John Gerard Ruggie, "International Regimes, Transactions, and Change: Embedded Liberalism in the Postwar Economic Order," *International Organization* 36 (Spring 1982), 379–415; Jeff Frieden, "Sectoral Conflict and U.S. Foreign Economic Policy," *International Organization* 42 (Winter 1988), 59–90.
3. Wilfred Ethier, *Modern International Economics* (New York: W. W. Norton, 1983).
4. Kindleberger, *The World in Depression, 1929–1939* (Berkeley: University of California Press, 1973); Keohane, "The Theory of Hegemonic Stability and Changes in International Regimes, 1967–1977," in Ole Holsti, ed., *Change in the International System* (Boulder, CO: Westview Press, 1980), 132.
5. Gilpin, *U.S. Power and the Multinational Corporation* (New York: Basic Books, 1975); Gilpin, *The Political Economy of International Relations* (Princeton: Princeton University Press, 1987); Krasner, "State Power and the Structure of International Trade," *World Politics* 28 (April 1976), 317–347.
6. Kindleberger (fn. 4), 305.
7. A Pareto-superior equilibrium is one in which at least one individual would be better off and no individual would be worse off than at the existing outcome.
8. Mancur Olson, *The Logic of Collective Action* (Cambridge: Harvard University Press, 1971), 50.
9. Kindleberger (fn. 4), 28.
10. For examples of the large literature that violently and sometimes persuasively objects to every historical interpretation in this paragraph, see McKeown (fn. 1); Kenneth A. Oye, "The Sterling-Dollar-Franc Triangle: Monetary Diplomacy 1929–1937," *World Politics* 38 (October 1985), 173–199; and Bruce Russett, "The Mysterious Case of Vanishing Hegemony," *International Organization* 39 (Spring 1985), 207–232.

11. John A. C. Conybeare, "Public Goods, Prisoners' Dilemmas and the International Political Economy," *International Studies Quarterly* 28 (March 1984), 5–22.

12. This argument is intended to apply only to single-minded hegemons. Critics acknowledge that hegemons which pursue political as well as economic goals may prefer free trade for political reasons. See, for example, *ibid.*

13. Richard E. Caves and Ronald W. Jones, *World Trade and Payments: An Introduction* (Boston: Little, Brown, 1973), 244.

14. For a brief discussion of bribery as an alternative to tariff retaliation in the context of two states of equal size, see Conybeare (fn. 11), 14–15.

15. For a formal analysis of the chain-store paradox, see David M. Kreps and Robert Wilson, "Reputation and Imperfect Information," *Journal of Economic Theory* 27 (August 1982), 253–279.

16. Paul Milgrom and John Roberts, "Limit Pricing and Entry Under Incomplete Information: An Equilibrium Analysis," *Econometrica* 50 (March 1982), 443–459.

17. Since potential entrants are aware of the incentives of established firms to engage in limit pricing, the established firm's strategy may not work. See *ibid.*

18. In his most recent work, Conybeare notes that heavy export taxes may induce substitution that, in turn, dictates the use of lighter taxes in the interest of maximizing long-run profits. Conybeare dismisses this argument unpersuasively: he maintains that "long-term elasticity ... arguments merely assert that the hegemon is not really a hegemon." See John A. C. Conybeare, *Trade Wars: The Theory and Practice of International Commercial Rivalry* (New York: Columbia University Press, 1987), 72.

19. John McMillan, *Game Theory in International Economics* (New York: Harwood Academic Publishers, 1986), 67.

20. William Cunningham, cited in Donald N. McCloskey, "Magnanimous Albion: Free Trade and British National Income, 1841–1881," *Explorations in Economic History* 17 (July 1980), 303–320, at 304; but see also fn. 23 below.

21. For an analysis that suggests that the Great Depression would have led to the same outcome even without this provocation by the United States, see Barry Eichengreen, "The Political Economy of the Smoot-Hawley Tariff," NBER Working Paper No. 2001, 1986 (cited in Jagdish Bhagwati, *Protectionism* [Cambridge, MIT Press, 1988], 22).

22. The present analysis seems to suggest that the American encouragement of what became the European Economic Community was illogical. Even without introducing security factors, however, the U.S. action can be interpreted as taking control of, rather than waiting for, the inevitable: in promoting the formation of the EEC when it did, the United States had an opportunity to exert significant leverage over the direction of the union. Thus, it could successfully demand, for example, that the EEC treat foreign direct investment as it did national investment, thus ensuring that U.S. firms would be able to circumvent EEC tariffs, albeit at some cost to those firms. See Gilpin (fn. 5).

23. Donald McCloskey has argued that Britain lost "at most" 4 percent of national income when it chose free trade rather than an optimum tariff (fn. 20, p. 305). Bhagwati notes that McCloskey's analysis relies on "intuition"; he observes that Douglas Irwin has

estimated British foreign trade elasticities for that period and calculated the welfare loss of unilateral tariff reduction at about 0.5 percent of national

income in the very short run. As Irwin points out, though, longer-run elasticities imply an extremely small welfare loss, and if foreign tariff reductions are factored in (resulting from Britain's demonstration effect promoting free trade) Irwin finds that Britain was made better off.
Irwin, "Welfare Effects of British Free Trade: Debate and Evidence from the 1840s," presented to Mid-West International Economics Meetings, Ann Arbor, Michigan, 1987, cited in Bhagwati (fn. 21), 29–30.

24. Conybeare (fn. 11), 6.

25. This assumes that states possess similar degrees of market power. If they do not, it is possible for one state to be better off, even after the cycle has been completed, than if it had pursued free trade. See H. G. Johnson, "Optimum Tariffs and Retaliation," *Review of Economic Studies* 21 (No. 55, 1953–54), 142–153.

26. Robert Alexrod and Robert O. Keohane, "Achieving Cooperation under Anarchy: Strategies and Institutions," *World Politics* 38 (October 1985), 226–254.

27. Laver, "Political Solutions to the Collective Action Problem," *Political Studies* 28 (June 1980), 195–209, at 200.

28. Kenneth A. Oye, "Explaining Cooperation under Anarchy: Strategies and Institutions," *World Politics* 38 (October 1985), 1–24, at 15.

29. Stigler, "A Theory of Oligopoly," *Journal of Political Economy* 72 (February 1964), 44–61, at 47.

30. Beth V. Yarbrough and Robert M. Yarbrough, "Cooperation in the Liberalization of International Trade: After Hegemony, What?" *International Organization* 41 (Winter 1987), 1–26, at 7–9.

31. Thus, the supply of information assumes a central role in recent analyses of international regimes. See, for example, Robert O. Keohane, *After Hegemony: Cooperation and Discord in the World Political Economy* (Princeton: Princeton University Press, 1984), 259; Russett (fn. 10), 222.

32. Schelling, "Hockey Helmets, Daylight Savings, and Other Binary Choices," in Schelling, ed., *Micromotives and Macrobehavior* (New York: W. W. Norton, 1978), 211–244.

33. Keohane (fn. 31), 6; Duncan Snidal, "The Limits of Hegemonic Stability Theory," *International Organization* 39 (Autumn 1985), 579–614, at 603; cf. Stephan Haggard and Beth A. Simmons, "Theories of International Regimes," *International Organization* 41 (Summer 1987), 491–517, at 506.

34. Keohane's book (fn. 31) is titled, after all, *AFTER Hegemony* (emphasis added).

35. See, for example, A.F.K. Organski and Jacek Kugler, *The War Ledger* (Chicago: University of Chicago Press, 1980).

36. Carl Shapiro, "Theories of Oligopoly Behavior," *Discussion Papers in Economics,* No. 126 (Princeton University: Woodrow Wilson School, March 1987), 56–58 (cited by permission).

37. Snidal, however, provides a good discussion of the distributional problems that small groups encounter with respect to collective action generally. See Snidal (fn. 33), 604–612.

38. Friedman, *Oligopoly and the Theory of Games* (Amsterdam: North-Holland, 1977), 15.

39. R. Duncan Luce and Howard Raiffa, *Games and Decisions: Introduction and Critical Survey* (New York: John Wiley & Sons, 1958), 121.

40. James W. Friedman, *Game Theory with Applications to Economics* (New York: Oxford University Press, 1986), 170.
41. Luce and Raiffa (fn. 39), 134.
42. Friedman (fn. 38), 28.
43. Luce and Raiffa (fn. 39), 180; see also Snidal (fn. 33), 605.
44. Oran R. Young, "Introduction," in Young, ed., *Bargaining: Formal Theories of Negotiation* (Urbana: University of Illinois Press, 1975), 32, n. 40.
45. Williamson, *Markets and Hierarchies: Analysis and Antitrust Implications, A Study in the Economics of Internal Organization* (New York: Free Press, 1975), 224.
46. Thomas C. Schelling, cited in David A. Baldwin, "Politics, Exchange, and Cooperation," paper prepared for delivery to the 28th Annual Convention of ·the International Studies Association, Washington, DC, 1987, p. 30.
47. Kenneth S. Chan, "The International Negotiating Game: Some Evidence from the Tokyo Round," *Review of Economics and Statistics* 67 (August 1985), 456–464, at 463.
48. Michael D. McGinnis, "Issue Linkage and the Evolution of International Cooperation," *Journal of Conflict Resolution* 30 (March 1986), 141–170, at 164.
49. Keohane (fn. 31), 100, 104–105.
50. For discussion, see James K. Sebenius, "Negotiation Arithmetic: Adding and Subtracting Issues and Parties," *International Organization* 37 (Spring 1983), 281–316; Robert D. Tollison and Thomas D. Willett, "An Economic Theory of Mutually Advantageous Issue Linkages," *International Organization* 33 (Autumn 1979), 425–449; Kenneth A. Oye, "The Domain of Choice: International Constraints and the Carter Administration," in Kenneth A. Oye, Donald Rothchild, and Robert J. Lieber, eds., *Eagle Entangled: U.S. Foreign Policy in a Complex World* (New York: Longman, 1979), 3–33.
51. It is this combination that motivates the role of reputations in such games as the chain-store paradox and formal analyses of cooperation in finite PDs. See Kreps and Wilson (fn. 15); also David M. Kreps, Paul Milgrom, John Roberts, and Robert Wilson, "Rational Cooperation in the Finitely Repeated Prisoners' Dilemma," *Journal of Economic Theory* 27 (August 1982) 245–252.
52. Richard Ned Lebow, "Conclusion," in Robert Jervis, Richard Ned Lebow, and Janice Gross Stein, eds., *Psychology and Deterrence* (Baltimore: The Johns Hopkins University Press, 1985), 303–332.
53. Moreover, any government known to put stock in past behavior invites others to cheat it. L. G. Telser observes:
    The accumulation of a fund of goodwill of a buyer toward a seller that depends on past experience stands as a ready temptation to the seller to cheat the buyers and convert their goodwill into ready cash. It is the prospect of the loss of future gain that deters and the existence of past goodwill that invites cheating. Therefore, rational behavior by the parties to an agreement requires that the probability of continuing their relation does not depend on their past experience with each other.
    See Telser, "A Theory of Self-enforcing Agreements," *Journal of Business* 53 (January 1980), 27–44, at 36.
54. Frank, *Passions Within Reason: The Strategic Role of the Emotions* (New York: W. W. Norton, 1988), 74–75; emphasis in original.
55. Lord Salisbury, "The Terms of Peace," in *The Quarterly Review* 129 (October 1870), 540–556, at 546.

56. Keohane (fn. 31), 100. One article that *does* briefly discuss this solution is Beth V. Yarbrough and Robert M. Yarbrough, "Reciprocity, Bilateralism, and Economic 'Hostages': Selfenforcing Agreements in International Trade," *International Studies Quarterly* 30 (March 1986), 7–22.

57. Snidal (fn. 33), 610–611.

58. See Jonathan Bendor and Dilip Mookherjee, "Institutional Structure and the Logic of Collective Action," *American Political Science Review* 81 (March 1987), 129–154.

59. James W. Friedman, *Oligopoly Theory* (New York: Cambridge University Press, 1983), 131.

60. For a discussion of these limits, see Friedman, *ibid.*, 133; also Bendor and Mookherjee (fn. 58), 133–134.

61. Friedman (fn. 59), 133–134.

62. Kindleberger, "Systems of International Economic Organization," in David P. Calleo, ed., *Money and the Coming World Order* (New York: New York University Press, 1976), 24–26, quotation at 24.

63. More generally, an external economy "is said to be emitted when an activity undertaken by an individual or firm yields benefits to other individuals or firms in addition to the benefits accruing to the emitting party." External diseconomies inflict injury rather than confer benefits. See Robin W. Boadway and David E. Wildasin, *Public Sector Economics*, 2nd ed. (Boston: Little, Brown, 1984), 60.

64. William A. Root, "Trade Controls that Work," *Foreign Policy* 56 (Fall 1984), 61–80.

65. David A. Baldwin, *Economic Statecraft* (Princeton: Princeton University Press, 1984).

66. McKeown (fn. 1), 225.

67. As Baldwin observes, trade "is by far the most [cost-] effective . . . way for one country to acquire the goods or services of another." Baldwin (fn. 65), 116.

68. In theory, it is possible for states negotiating with each other to conclude an agreement that improves the absolute welfare of each while it preserves the pre-existing balance of power between them. The prerequisites of such an agreement are formidable, however: the utility functions of the states must be common knowledge, and the contracting states must agree on a utility scale that will determine both the status quo ante and the division of benefits from cooperation. (Anatol Rapoport, *Fights, Games, and Debates* [Ann Arbor: University of Michigan Press, 1974], chap. II.) In practice, it seems unlikely that these conditions will be fulfilled.

Part
Nine

U.S. HEGEMONY IN THE WORLD ECONOMY

As the essays in Part Eight have demonstrated, the role of great powers in the establishment and maintenance of international order and stability is one of the main interests of IPE analysis. The current theoretical and policy discussions on this point are of particular importance in view of the ongoing debate over the fate of the postwar United States hegemony.

Once an unchallenged military power with a monopoly over nuclear weapons, the United States is now in strategic parity with its rival, the Soviet Union. Once an unequaled economic superpower representing two-fifths of the world's production, the United States has lost ground to its competitors in Japan and in Western Europe (although it retains the number one position in most areas). The U.S. global trade balance turned from a surplus of $2.2 billion in 1975 to a deficit of $148 billion in 1985; the U.S. federal budget deficit increased from a mere $2.8 billion in 1970 to $221.2 billion in 1986, with the accumulated debt amounting to over $2 trillion and steadily rising. The United States turned from the world's largest creditor nation (by far) to the leading debtor nation in one decade. In the opinion of many observers, these economic woes have seriously undercut the credibility of U.S. world leadership. Many today assert that the time has come for the United States to share world leadership with other rising economic powers, namely Japan and the European Community (EC). Among the IPE community, however, no consensus has emerged regarding the nature, extent, and cause of U.S. decline and whether it is irreversible.

The Introduction to Paul Kennedy's best-selling *The Rise and Fall of the Great Powers* is reprinted here to illustrate the currently popu-

468   PART NINE/U.S. HEGEMONY IN THE WORLD ECONOMY

lar argument that great powers have a tendency to fall. Kennedy gives
an overview of his book, which covers some five hundred years in six
hundred pages, by emphasizing the patterns he noticed: First, political
power tends to gravitate in regions of highest economic production
over time. Specifically, economic and political fortunes tend to go together, although the political zenith and nadir tend to lag behind the
economic. Also of significance was the general correlation between economic and military success, insofar as major coalition wars are concerned. Finally, as a nation declines economically in relative terms, it
tends to spend greater resources on political (read military) objectives—to its eventual demise. Kennedy spends the last two chapters of
the book relating these general historical trends to the current situation of the United States and concludes that the nation has passed its
economic prime and shows all the symptoms of a declining great
power. The reader is encouraged to read the entire book for a better
appreciation of these dynamics and these arguments.

Kennedy's thesis is challenged by Samuel Huntington and Joseph
Nye, Jr. Huntington asserts that the declinists' argument ignores the
fact that America's current economic difficulties are a direct result of
policy choices that the Reagan Administration made and, as such, are
correctable through appropriate policy measures. Huntington maintains that the U.S. share of world production has remained at about 25
percent since the late 1960s, and that the fact that the United States
produces twice as much as any other individual country qualifies the
nation as a hegemonic power. He adds that needed increases in the
nation's savings can be secured not by cutting its defense spending but
by reducing private consumption. Finally, Huntington argues that the
competition, mobility, and diversity which characterize American society give this nation an advantage over other countries which he claims
depend on a single source of power.

Nye echoes many of Huntington's assertions and adds an argument
against policies of national retrenchment—a return to an isolationist
America. He asserts that the United States has not experienced an absolute decline, and that the relative decline it has experienced is in
large part an artifact of the extraordinary baseline of the 1950s, when
the United States was an overwhelmingly large economic and military
power in comparison to war-ravaged Europe and Japan. He sees no
military power challenging the United States. Nor does he see the
overcommitments abroad that Kennedy warns about. Nye concludes
that cooperative partnership with economic competitors such as Japan
and security allies such as NATO members will assure U.S. leadership
in the multipolar and interdependent world.

Clearly the debate over U.S. leadership is not over. The student
will do well to contemplate the following: What is the relationship between economic power and political influence? Are there limits to
each in relation to the other? Are the 1940s and 1950s an historical ab-

erration and a misleading baseline? Is there evidence of a genuine American economic and political decline regardless? Is a great power's rise and decline a result of deliberate, if misguided, national policy, or the consequence of global forces which lie beyond the reach of any nation's control? Is the United States prepared to share global leadership with other nations?

Introduction to The Rise and Fall of the Great Powers

Paul Kennedy

This is a book about national and international power in the "modern"—that is, post-Renaissance—period. It seeks to trace and to explain how the various Great Powers have risen and fallen, relative to each other, over the five centuries since the formation of the "new monarchies" of western Europe and the beginnings of the transoceanic, global system of states. Inevitably, it concerns itself a great deal with wars, especially those major, drawn-out conflicts fought by coalitions of Great Powers which had such an impact upon the international order; but it is not strictly a book about military history. It also concerns itself with tracing the changes which have occurred in the global economic balances since 1500; and yet it is not, at least directly, a work of economic history. What it concentrates upon is the *interaction* between economics and strategy, as each of the leading states in the international system strove to enhance its wealth and its power, to become (or to remain) both rich and strong.

The "military conflict" referred to in the book's subtitle is therefore always examined in the context of "economic change." The triumph of any one Great Power in this period, or the collapse of another, has usually been the consequence of lengthy fighting by its armed forces; but it has also been the consequence of the more or less efficient utilization of the state's productive economic resources in wartime, and, further in the background, of the way in which that state's economy had been rising or falling, *relative* to the other leading nations, in the decades preceding the actual conflict. For that reason, how a Great Power's position steadily alters in peacetime is as important to this study as how it fights in wartime.

The argument being offered here will receive much more elaborate analysis in the text itself, but can be summarized very briefly:

The relative strengths of the leading nations in world affairs never remain constant, principally because of the uneven rate of growth among different societies and of the technological and organizational break-throughs which bring a greater advantage to one society than to another. For example, the coming of the long-range gunned sailing ship and the rise of the Atlantic trades after 1500 was not *uniformly* beneficial to all the states of Europe—it boosted some much more than others. In the same way, the later development of steam power and of the coal and metal resources upon which it relied massively increased the relative power of certain nations, and thereby decreased the relative power of others. Once their productive capacity was enhanced, countries would normally find it easier to sustain the burdens of paying for large-scale armaments in peace-time and of maintaining and supplying large armies and fleets in wartime. It sounds crudely mercantilistic to express it this way, but wealth is usually needed to underpin military power, and military power is usually needed to acquire and protect wealth. If, however, too large a proportion of the state's resources is diverted from wealth creation and allocated instead to military purposes, then that is likely to lead to a weakening of national power over the longer term. In the same way, if a state overextends itself strategically—by, say, the conquest of extensive territories or the waging of costly wars—it runs the risk that the potential benefits from external expansion may be outweighed by the great expense of it all—a dilemma which becomes acute if the nation concerned has entered a period of relative economic decline. The history of the rise and later fall of the leading countries in the Great Power system since the advance of western Europe in the sixteenth century—that is, of nations such as Spain, the Netherlands, France, the British Empire, and currently the United States—shows a very significant correlation *over the longer term* between productive and revenue-raising capacities on the one hand and military strength on the other.

The story of "the rise and fall of the Great Powers" which is presented in these chapters may be briefly summarized here. The first chapter sets the scene for all that follows by examining the world around 1500 and by analyzing the strengths and weaknesses of each of the "power centers" of that time—Ming China; the Ottoman Empire and its Muslim offshoot in India, the Mogul Empire; Muscovy; Tokugawa Japan; and the cluster of states in west-central Europe. At the beginning of the sixteenth century it was by no means apparent that the last-named region was destined to rise above all the rest. But however imposing and organized some of those oriental empires appeared by comparison with Europe, they all suffered from the consequences of having a centralized authority which insisted upon a uniformity of belief and practice, not only in official state religion but also in such areas as commercial activities and weapons development. The lack of any such supreme authority in Europe and the warlike rival-ries among its various kingdoms and city-states stimulated a constant search for military improvements, which interacted fruitfully with the newer technological and commercial advances that were also being thrown up in this competitive, entrepreneurial environment. Possessing fewer obstacles to change, European societies entered into a constantly upward spiral of economic growth and enhanced military effectiveness which, over time, was to carry them ahead of all other regions of the globe.

While this dynamic of technological change and military competitiveness drove Europe forward in its usual jostling, pluralistic way, there still remained the possibility that one of the contending states might acquire sufficient resources to surpass the others, and then to dominate the continent. For about 150 years after 1500, a dynastic-religious bloc under the Spanish and Austrian Habsburgs seemed to threaten to do just that, and the efforts of the other major European states to check this "Habsburg bid for mastery" occupy the whole of Chapter 2. As is done throughout this book, the strengths and weaknesses of each of the leading Powers are analyzed *relatively,* and in the light of the broader economic and technological changes affecting western society as a whole, in order that the reader can understand better the outcome of the many wars of this period. The chief theme of this chapter is that despite the great resources possessed by the Habsburg monarchs, they steadily overextended themselves in the course of repeated conflicts and became militarily top-heavy for their weakening economic base. If the other European Great Powers also suffered immensely in these prolonged wars, they managed—though narrowly—to maintain the balance between their material resources and their military power better than their Habsburg enemies.

The Great Power struggles which took place between 1660 and 1815, and are covered in Chapter 3, cannot be so easily summarized as a contest between one large bloc and its many rivals. It was in this complicated period that while certain former Great Powers like Spain and the Netherlands were falling into the second rank, there steadily emerged five major states (France, Britain, Russia, Austria, and Prussia) which came to dominate the diplomacy and warfare of eighteenth-century Europe, and to engage in a series of lengthy coalition wars punctuated by swiftly changing alliances. This was an age in which France, first under Louis XIV and then later under Napoleon, came closer to controlling Europe than at any time before or since; but its endeavors were always held in check, in the last resort at least, by a combination of the other Great Powers. Since the cost of standing armies and national fleets had become horrendously great by the early eighteenth century, a country which could create an advanced system of banking and credit (as Britain did) enjoyed many advantages over financially backward rivals. But the factor of geographical position was also of great importance in deciding the fate of the Powers in their many, and frequently changing, contests—which helps to explain why the two "flank" nations of Russia and Britain had become much more important by 1815. Both retained the capacity to intervene in the struggles of west-central Europe while being geographically sheltered from them; and both expanded into the *extra-*European world as the eighteenth century unfolded, even as they were ensuring that the continental balance of power was upheld. Finally, by the later decades of the century, the Industrial Revolution was under way in Britain, which was to give that state an enhanced capacity both to colonize overseas and to frustrate the Napoleonic bid for European mastery.

For an entire century after 1815, by contrast, there was a remarkable absence of lengthy coalition wars. A strategic equilibrium existed, supported by all of the leading Powers in the Concert of Europe, so that no single nation was either able or willing to make a bid for dominance. The prime concerns of government in these post-1815 decades were with domestic instability and (in the case of Russia and the United States) with further expansion across their continental landmasses. This relatively stable international scene allowed the British Empire to rise to its zenith as a global power, in naval and colonial and commercial terms, and also interacted favorably with its virtual monopoly of steam-driven industrial production. By the second half of the nineteenth century, however, industrialization was spreading to certain other regions, and was beginning to tilt the international power balances away from the older leading nations and toward those countries with both the resources and organization to exploit the newer means of production and technology. Already, the few major conflicts of this era—the Crimean War to some degree but more especially the American Civil War and the Franco-Prussian War—were bringing defeat upon those societies which failed to modernize their military systems, and which lacked the broad-based industrial infrastructure to support the vast armies and much more expensive and complicated weaponry now transforming the nature of war.

As the twentieth century approached, therefore, the pace of technological change and uneven growth rates made the international system much more unstable and complex than it had been fifty years earlier. This was manifested in the frantic post-1880 jostling by the Great Powers for additional colonial territories in Africa, Asia, and the Pacific, partly for gain, partly out of a fear of being eclipsed. It also manifested itself in the increasing number of arms races, both on land and at sea, and in the creation of fixed military alliances, even in peacetime, as the various governments sought out partners for a possible future war. Behind the frequent colonial quarrels and international crises of the pre-1914 period, however, the decade-by-decade indices of economic power were pointing to even more fundamental shifts in the global balances—indeed, to the eclipse of what had been, for over three centuries, essentially a *Eurocentric* world system. Despite their best efforts, traditional European Great Powers like France and Austria-Hungary, and a recently united one like Italy, were falling out of the race. By contrast, the enormous, continent-wide states of the United States and Russia were moving to the forefront, and this despite the inefficiencies of the czarist state. Among the western European nations only Germany, possibly, had the muscle to force its way into the select league of the future world Powers. Japan, on the other hand, was intent upon being dominant in East Asia, but not farther afield. Inevitably, then, all these changes posed considerable, and ultimately insuperable, problems for a British Empire which now found it much more difficult to defend its global interests than it had a half-century earlier.

Although the major development of the fifty years after 1900 can thus be seen as the coming of a bipolar world, with its consequent crisis for the "middle" Powers, this metamorphosis of the entire system was by no means a smooth one. On the contrary, the grinding, bloody mass battles of the First World War, by placing a premium upon industrial organization and national efficiency, gave imperial Germany certain advantages over the swiftly modernizing but still backward czarist Russia. Within a few months of Germany's victory on the eastern front, however, it found itself facing defeat in the west, while its allies were similarly collapsing in the Italian, Balkan, and Near Eastern theaters of the war. Because of the late addition of American military and especially economic aid, the western alliance finally had the resources to prevail over its rival coalition. But it had been an exhausting struggle for all the original belligerents. Austria-Hungary was gone, Russia in revolution, Germany defeated; yet France, Italy, and even Britain itself had also suffered heavily in their victory. The only exceptions were Japan, which further augmented its position in the Pacific; and, of course, the United States, which by 1918 was indisputably the strongest Power in the world.

The swift post-1919 American withdrawal from foreign engagements, and the parallel Russian isolationism under the Bolshevik regime, left an international system which was more out of joint with the fundamental economic realities than perhaps at any time in the five centuries covered in this book. Britain and France, although weakened, were still at the center of the diplomatic stage, but by the 1930s their position was being challenged by the militarized, revisionist states of Italy, Japan, and Germany—the last intent upon a much more deliberate bid for European hegemony than even in 1914. In the background, however, the United States remained by far the mightiest manufacturing nation in the world, and Stalin's Russia was quickly transforming itself into an industrial superpower. Consequently, the dilemma for the *revisionist* "middle" Powers was that they had to expand soon if they were not to be overshadowed by the two continental giants. The dilemma for the status quo middle Powers was that in fighting off the German and Japanese challenges, they would most likely weaken themselves as well. The Second World War, for all its ups and downs, essentially confirmed those apprehensions of decline. Despite spectacular early victories, the Axis nations could not in the end succeed against an imbalance of productive resources which was far greater than that of the 1914–1918 war. What they did achieve was the eclipse of France and the irretrievable weakening of Britain—before they themselves were overwhelmed by superior force. By 1943, the bipolar world forecast decades earlier had finally arrived, and the military balance had once again caught up with the global distribution of economic resources.

The last two chapters of this book examine the years in which a bipolar world did indeed seem to exist, economically, militarily, and ideologically—and was reflected at the political level by the many crises of the Cold War. The position of the United States and the USSR as Powers in a class of their own also appeared to be reinforced by the arrival of nuclear weapons and long-distance delivery systems, which suggested that the strategic as well as the diplomatic landscape was now entirely different from that of 1900, let alone 1800.

And yet the process of rise and fall among the Great Powers—of differentials in growth rates and technological change, leading to shifts in the global economic balances, which in turn gradually impinge upon the political and military balances—had not ceased. Militarily, the United States and the U.S.S.R. stayed in the forefront as the 1960s gave way to the 1970s and 1980s. Indeed, because they both interpreted international problems in bipolar, and often Manichean, terms, their rivalry has driven them into an ever-escalating arms race which no other Powers feel capable of matching. Over the same few decades, however, the global productive balances have been altering faster than ever before. The Third World's share of total manufacturing output and GNP, depressed to an all-time low in the decade after 1945, has steadily expanded since that time. Europe has recovered from its wartime batterings and, in the form of the European Economic Community, has become the world's largest trading unit. The People's Republic of China is leaping forward at an impressive rate. Japan's postwar economic growth has been so phenomenal that, according to some measures, it recently overtook Russia in total GNP. By contrast, both the American and Russian growth rates have become more sluggish, and their shares of global production and wealth have shrunk dramatically since the 1960s. Leaving aside all the smaller nations, therefore, it is plain that there already exists a *multi*polar world once more, if one measures the economic indices alone. Given this book's concern with the interaction between strategy and economics, it seemed appropriate to offer a final (if necessarily speculative) chapter to explore the present disjuncture between the military balances and the productive balances among the Great Powers; and to point to the problems and opportunities facing today's five large politico-economic "power centers"—China, Japan, the EEC, the Soviet Union, and the United States itself—as they grapple with the age-old task of relating national means to national ends. The history of the rise and fall of the Great Powers has in no way come to a full stop.

Since the scope of this book is so large, it is clear that it will be read by different people for different purposes. Some readers will find here what they had hoped for: a broad and yet reasonably detailed survey of Great Power politics over the past five centuries, of the way in which the relative position of each of the leading states has been affected by economic and technological change, and of the constant interaction between strategy and economics, both in periods of peace and in the tests of war. By definition, it does not deal with *small* Powers, nor (usually) with small, bilateral wars. By definition also, the book is heavily Eurocentric, especially in its middle chapters. But that is only natural with such a topic.

To other readers, perhaps especially those political scientists who are now so interested in drawing general rules about "world systems" or the recurrent pattern of wars, this study may offer less than what they desire. To avoid misunderstanding, it ought to be made clear at this point that the book is not dealing with, for example, the theory that major (or "systemic") wars can be related to Kondratieff cycles of economic upturn and downturn. In addition, it is not centrally concerned with general theories about the *causes* of war, and whether they are likely to be brought about by "rising" or "falling" Great Powers. It is also not a book about theories of empire, and about how imperial control is effected (as is dealt with in Michael Doyle's recent book *Empires*), or whether empires contribute to national strength. Finally, it does not propose any general theory about which sorts of society and social/governmental organizations are the most efficient in extracting resources in time of war.

On the other hand, there obviously is a wealth of material in this book for those scholars who wish to make such generalizations (and one of the reasons why there is such an extensive array of notes is to indicate more detailed sources for those readers interested in, say, the financing of wars). But the problem which historians—as opposed to political scientists—have in grappling with general theories is that the evidence of the past is almost always too varied to allow for "hard" scientific conclusions. Thus, while it is true that some wars (e.g., 1939) can be linked to decisionmakers' fears about shifts taking place in the overall power balances, that would not be so useful in explaining the struggles which began in 1776 (American Revolutionary War) or 1792 (French Revolutionary) or 1854 (Crimean War). In the same way, while one could point to Austria-Hungary in 1914 as a good example of a "falling" Great Power helping to trigger off a major war, that still leaves the theorist to deal with the equally critical roles played then by those "rising" Great Powers Germany and Russia. Similarly, any general theory about whether empires pay, or whether imperial control is affected by a measurable "power-distance" ratio, is likely—from the conflicting evidence available—to produce the banal answer sometimes yes, sometimes no.

Nevertheless, if one sets aside *a priori* theories and simply looks at the historical record of "the rise and fall of the Great Powers" over the past five hundred years, it is clear that some generally valid conclusions can be drawn—while admitting all the time that there may be individual exceptions. For example, there is detectable a causal relationship between the shifts which have occurred over time in the general economic and productive balances and the position occupied by individual Powers in the international system. The move in trade flows from the Mediterranean to the Atlantic and northwestern Europe from the sixteenth century onward, or the redstribution in the shares of world manufacturing ouput away from western Europe in the decades after 1890, are good examples here. In both cases, the economic shifts heralded the rise of new Great Powers which would one day have a decisive impact upon the military/territorial order. This is why the move in the global productive balances toward the "Pacific rim" which has taken place over the past few decades cannot be of interest merely to economists alone.

Similarly, the historical record suggests that there is a very clear connection *in the long run* between an individual Great Power's economic rise and fall and its growth and decline as an important military power (or world empire). This, too, is hardly surprising, since it flows from two related facts. The first is that economic resources are necessary to support a large-scale military establishment. The second is that, so far as the international system is concerned, both wealth and power are always *relative* and should be seen as such. Three hundred years ago, the German mercantilist writer von Hornigk observed that

> whether a nation be today mighty and rich or not depends not on the abundance or security of its power and riches, but principally on whether its neighbors possess more or less of it.

In the chapters which follow, this observation will be borne out time and again. The Netherlands in the mid-eighteenth century was richer in *absolute* terms than a hundred years earlier, but by that stage was much less of a Great Power because neighbors like France and Britain had "more . . . of it" (that is, more power and riches). The France of 1914 was, absolutely, more powerful than that of 1850—but this was little consolation when France was being eclipsed by a much stronger Germany. Britain today has far greater wealth, and its armed forces possess far more powerful weapons, than in its mid-Victorian prime; that avails it little when its share of world product has shrunk from about 25 percent to about 3 percent. If a nation has "more . . . of it," things are fine; if "less of it," there are problems.

This does not mean, however, that a nation's relative economic and military power will rise and fall *in parallel.* Most of the historical examples covered here suggest that there is a noticeable "lag time" between the trajectory of a state's relative economic strength and the trajectory of its military/territorial influence. Once again, the reason for this is not difficult to grasp. An economically expanding Power—Britain in the 1860s, the United States in the 1890s, Japan today—may well prefer to become rich rather than to spend heavily on armaments. A half-century later, priorities may well have altered. The earlier economic expansion has brought with it overseas obligations (dependence upon foreign markets and raw materials, military alliances, perhaps bases and colonies). Other, rival Powers are now economically expanding at a faster rate, and wish in their turn to extend their influence abroad. The world has become a more competitive place, and market shares are being eroded. Pessimistic observers talk of decline; patriotic statesmen call for "renewal."

In these more troubled circumstances, the Great Power is likely to find itself spending much *more* on defense than it did two generations earlier, and yet still discover that the world is a less secure environment—simply because other Powers have grown faster, and are becoming stronger. Imperial Spain spent much more on its army in the troubled 1630s and 1640s than it did in the 1580s, when the Castilian economy was healthier. Edwardian Britain's defense expenditures were far greater in 1910 than they were at, say, the time of Palmerston's death in 1865, when the British economy was relatively at its peak; but which Britons by the later date felt more secure? The same problem, it will be argued below, appears to be facing both the United States and the U.S.S.R. today. Great Powers in relative decline instinctively respond by spending more on "security," and thereby divert potential resources from "investment" and compound their long-term dilemma.

Another general conclusion which can be drawn from the five-hundred-year record presented here is that there is a very strong correlation between the eventual outcome of the *major coalition wars* for European or global mastery, and the amount of productive resources mobilized by each side. This was true of the struggles waged against the Spanish-Austrian Habsburgs; of the great eighteenth-century contests like the War of Spanish Succession, the Seven Years War, and the Napoleonic War; and of the two world wars of this century. A lengthy, grinding war eventually turns into a test of the relative capacities of each coalition. Whether one side has "more . . . of it" or "less of it" becomes increasingly significant as the struggle lengthens.

One can make these generalizations, however, without falling into the trap of crude economic determinism. Despite this book's abiding interest in tracing the "larger tendencies" in world affairs over the past five centuries, it is *not* arguing that economics determines every event, or is the sole reason for the success and failure of each nation. There simply is too much evidence pointing to other things: geography, military organization, national morale, the alliance system, and many other factors can all affect the relative power of the members of the states system. In the eighteenth century, for example, the United Provinces were the richest parts of Europe, and Russia the poorest—yet the Dutch fell, and the Russians rose. Individual folly (like Hitler's) and extremely high battlefield competence (whether of the Spanish regiments in the sixteenth century or of the German infantry in this century) also go a long way to explain individual victories and defeats. What does seem incontestable, however, is that in a long drawn-out Great Power (and usually coalition) war, victory has repeatedly gone to the side with the more flourishing productive base—or, as the Spanish captains used to say, to him who has the last *escudo*. Much of what follows will confirm that cynical but essentially correct judgment. And it is precisely because the power position of the leading nations has closely paralleled their relative economic position over the past five centuries that it seems worthwhile asking what the implications of today's economic and technological trends might be for the current balance of power.

This does not deny that men make their own history, but they do make it within a historical circumstance which can restrict (as well as open up) possibilities.

An early model for the present book was the 1833 essay of the famous Prussian historian Leopold von Ranke upon *die grossen Mächte* ("the great powers"), in which he surveyed the ups and downs of the international power balances since the decline of Spain, and tried to show why certain countries had risen to prominence and then fallen away. Ranke concluded his essay with an analysis of his contemporary world, and what was happening in it following the defeat of the French bid for supremacy in the Napoleonic War. In examining the "prospects" of each of the Great Powers, he, too, was tempted from the historian's profession into the uncertain world of speculating upon the future.

To write an essay upon "the Great Powers" is one thing; to tell the story in book form is quite another. My original intention was to produce a brief, "essayistic" book, presuming that the readers knew (however vaguely) the background details about the changing growth rates, or the particular geostrategical problems facing this or that Great Power. As I began sending out the early chapters of this book for comments, or giving trial-run talks about some of its themes, it became increasingly clear to me that that was a false presumption: what most readers and listeners wanted was *more* detail, *more* coverage of the background, simply because there was no study available which told the story of the shifts that occurred in the economic and strategical power balances. Precisely because neither economic historians nor military historians had entered this field, the story itself had simply suffered from neglect. If the abundant detail in both the text and notes which follow has any justification, it is to fill that critical gap in the history of the rise and fall of the Great Powers.

The U.S.—Decline or Renewal?

Samuel P. Huntington

In 1988 the United States reached the zenith of its fifth wave of declinism since the 1950s. The roots of this phenomenon lie in the political economy literature of the early 1980s that analyzed the fading American economic hegemony and attempted to identify the consequences of its disappearance. These themes were picked up in more popular and policy-oriented writings, and the combination of the budget and trade deficits plus the October 1987 stock market crash produced the environment for the spectacular success of Paul Kennedy's scholarly historical analysis in early 1988. Decline has been on everyone's mind, and the arguments of the declinists have stimulated lively public debate.[1]

Although predominantly of a liberal-leftist hue, declinist writings reflect varying political philosophies and make many different claims. In general, however, they offer three core propositions.

First, the United States is declining economically compared to other market economy countries, most notably Japan but also Europe and the newly industrializing countries. The declinists focus on economic performance and on scientific, technological, and educational factors presumably related to economic performance.

Second, economic power is the central element of a nation's strength, and hence a decline in economic power eventually affects the other dimensions of national power.

Third, the relative economic decline of the United States is caused primarily by its spending too much for military purposes, which in turn is the result, in Kennedy's phrase, of "imperial overstretch," of attempting to maintain commitments abroad that the country can no longer afford.

In this respect, the problems the United States confronts are similar to those of previous imperial or hegemonic powers such as Britain, France, and Spain.

Declinist literature sets forth images of a nation winding down economically, living beyond its means, losing its competitive edge to more dynamic peoples, sagging under the burdens of empire, and suffering from a variety of intensifying social, economic, and political ills. It follows that American leadership must recognize and acquiesce in these conditions and accept the "need to 'manage' affairs so that the *relative* erosion of the United States' position takes place slowly and smoothly, and is not accelerated by policies which bring merely short-term advantage but longer-term disadvantage."[2]

Before one accepts the policy conclusions of the declinists, however, their basic propositions should be critically examined. Does their argument hold water? Is the United States fundamentally a nation in decline? Or is it a nation in the midst of renewal?

The declinists point to many urgent if transitory American problems and other serious if long-standing American weaknesses. Overall, however, their argument fails; it is seriously weak on both the extent and cause of decline. The image of renewal is far closer to the American truth than the image of decadence purveyed by the declinists.

II

With some exceptions, declinist writings do not elaborate testable propositions involving independent and dependent variables. With a rather broad brush, they tend to paint an impressionistic picture of economic decline, mixing references to economic trends and performance (economic growth, productivity), educational data (test scores, length of school year), fiscal matters (deficits), science and technology (R&D expenditures, output of engineers), international trade and capital flows, savings and investment, and other matters. In general, however, they point to three bodies of evidence to support their argument for decline:

- first, mounting U.S. trade and fiscal deficits which, to date, the U.S. political system has shown no signs of being able to correct;
- second, continuing and even accelerating declines in U.S. shares of global economic power and in U.S. rates of growth in key areas of economic performance;
- third, sustained systemic weaknesses, including research and development practices, primary and secondary education, production of scientists and engineers, and most seriously, savings and investment patterns.

Each body of evidence requires separate examination.

Deficits

Escalating current account and budgetary deficits have been the most important changes affecting the U.S. position in the world in the 1980s. They furnish dramatic immediacy to the declinist argument. In a few short years the United States was transformed from the principal creditor nation in the world to its largest debtor. The current account balance, which had a surplus of $6.9 billion in 1981 and a small deficit of $8.7 billion in 1982, plunged to deficits of almost $140 billion in 1986 and about $160 billion in 1987. In 1981 the United States had a net credit in its international investment position of $141 billion; by 1987 it was a net debtor to the tune of $400 billion. Assets in the United States owned by foreigners roughly doubled between 1982 and 1986 to $1.3 trillion.

Coincidental with this growth of U.S. international deficits and a major cause of them was the burgeoning of the U.S. budget deficit. The annual deficit had fluctuated in the vicinity of $50 billion to $75 billion in the Ford and Carter Administrations. In 1982 it began to increase rapidly, reaching a peak of $221 billion in FY 1986. It dropped back to $150 billion in FY 1987 and was modestly higher at about $155 billion in FY 1988.

Declinists see these deficits as evidence of fundamental weaknesses in the American economic position. They correctly point out that the massive influx of foreign funds has largely gone not for investment but for private consumption and governmental spending for defense. Such borrowing will not generate revenues with which it can be liquidated. The United States is living in a style it cannot afford and is imbued with an "eat, drink, and be merry" psychology. Ominous precedents are called to mind. Peter G. Peterson argues:

> To find the proper historical parallel for the United States in the 1980s . . . we must look to those rare historical occasions when an economy's large size, its world-class currency, and its open capital markets have allowed it to borrow immense sums primarily for the purpose of consumption and without regard to productive return. The illustrations of lumbering, deficit-hobbled, low-growth economies that come most easily to mind are Spain's in the late sixteenth century, France's in the 1780s, and Britain's in the 1920s.[3]

In similar fashion, Paul Kennedy warns that "the only other example which comes to mind of a Great Power so increasing its indebtedness in *peacetime* is France in the 1780s, where the fiscal crisis contributed to the domestic political crisis."[4]

Several points must be made to disentangle the valid from the invalid elements of these declinist arguments.

First, trade and budget deficits were not a major problem before 1982. They then mushroomed. This development may in some small measure flow from underlying weaknesses in productivity, savings, and investment, but it cannot primarily result from such causes. If the deficits did come from these causes, they would have developed slowly rather than rapidly and very probably would have manifested themselves before the advent of the Reagan Administration. Instead, the deficits are overwhelmingly the result of the economic policies of the Reagan Administration: reduction in tax rates, expansion of defense spending, a strong dollar. These policies were premised on the assumption that domestic governmental spending could be curtailed and that lower tax rates would stimulate investment, growth, and revenues. These assumptions did not prove to be valid, and the policies that were based on them produced the surging deficits. A different administration with different fiscal and economic policies would have produced different results. The deficits stem from the weaknesses, not of the American economy, but of Reagan economics. Produced quickly by one set of policies, they can be reversed almost as quickly by another set of policies.

Second, that reversal has begun and is likely to intensify. The reversal results partly from changes in policy by the Reagan Administration, partly from policies adopted by other governments and partly from the workings of the international economy, which naturally generates equilibrating tendencies. President Bush will probably move to reinforce U.S. policies designed to reduce the deficits. Through tight controls on spending, promotion of economic growth, "revenue enhancements," and, at some point, new taxes (luxury taxes, gasoline taxes, and a general value-added tax are most frequently mentioned), the budget deficit is likely to be brought down to a sustainable level at which it does not pose a threat to long-term economic growth. As it is, the deficit in 1988 is only about half of what it was in 1983 as a percent of gross national product (3.1 percent versus 6.3 percent).

The trade deficit began to decrease with the rapid expansion of American exports in 1988. Its further reduction will be facilitated by budget deficit reduction, increases in manufacturing productivity (which rose significantly in the 1980s), ceilings on the exchange rate of the dollar, and pressure which the U.S. government will—and must—apply under the new trade law to open up foreign markets. Cutting the trade deficit will be further enhanced, of course, to the extent that oil prices do not increase, American wage levels remain below those of the principal U.S. competitors, the developing countries' debt problem is contained, and foreign economies grow at healthy rates. The trade deficit, some analysts predict, will become a trade surplus in the coming decade.[5]

Third, both the deficits and the processes of curing them impose significant costs on the American economy. The substantial increase—absolute and net—in American foreign indebtedness means that a larger portion of U.S. GNP will be paid to foreigners in debt service. These funds will not be available for either personal consumption or savings and domestic investment. The future American standard of living will be less than it would have been otherwise.

The declinists are absolutely right to highlight this development as the principal long-term effect of the Reagan spending spree. Correction of the trade balance will impose costs not only on the United States but also on those other countries that have become *addicted* to the U.S. market. Some of these costs are already visible in Japan, which is struggling to de-emphasize exports (39 percent of which went to the United States in 1987) and stimulate internal demand. In addition, reduction of the trade deficit might conceivably require a recession in the United States, which in turn would at least temporarily exacerbate the budget deficit.

In the coming years both deficits will probably be reduced to sustainable and nonmalign proportions. Their effects, however, will be around for some while to come. But it is a mistake to view them as open sores that will continue to bleed away American strength. They are wounds that will heal, although their scars will remain.

Declining Shares

This argument has been put most explicitly by Paul Kennedy. "The U.S.A.'s share of total GNP," he says, "of world manufacturing output, and of many other indices of national efficiency has steadily declined." The United States has suffered "relative industrial decline, as measured against world production, not only in older manufactures such as textiles, iron, and steel, shipbuilding, and basic chemicals, but also—although it is far less easy to judge the final outcome of this level of industrial-technological combat—in global shares of robotics, aerospace, automobiles, machine tools, and computers." American agriculture has also declined. The decline in the U.S. share of world GNP was "natural" after 1945, but it "has declined much more quickly than it should have over the last few years" and the decline has become "precipitous."[6]

These propositions need serious qualification. Various estimates exist of global and national gross products for various times. All have to be used with caution. Virtually all, however, show a common pattern.

The United States produced 40 to 45 percent of the gross world product in the late 1940s and early 1950s. That share declined rapidly, reaching the vicinity of 20 to 25 percent of gross world product by the late 1960s. That is roughly where it has remained.

It certainly has not declined more rapidly in the past two decades than it did during the previous two decades. Figures of the U.S. Council on Competitiveness (whose mission is to voice alarm about declining U.S. competitiveness) and from other sources show, for instance, that:

- between 1970 and 1987 the U.S. share of the gross world product varied between 22 and 25 percent and most recently was 23 percent;
- the U.S. share of world exports was 12 percent in 1970 and ten percent in 1987, and varied between nine and 14 percent in the years between;

- the U.S. share of the exports of the seven economic summit countries was 24 percent in 1970 and 23 percent in 1987, varying between 20 and 25 percent in the intervening years;
- in 1965 the United States accounted for 27.5 percent of world exports of technology-intensive products; this dropped to a low of 22.9 percent in 1980 and was back at 25.2 percent in 1984.[7]

Overall, the United States accounts for 22 to 25 percent of the major forms of global economic activity and has done so fairly consistently for twenty years or more. The declinists are clearly right in saying that this is much less than the U.S. shares according to the same indices during the decade after World War II. A situation in which one country accounted for up to 50 percent of the global economic action was clearly a temporary product of the war. The ending of that imbalance was a major and successful goal of U.S. policy. The shift from 40–45 percent of global economic activity to 20–25 percent had generally occurred by the late 1960s. It is an increasingly remote historical event. For about a quarter-century U.S. shares in global economic activity have fluctuated within a relatively narrow range.

During the 1980s U.S. economic performance improved markedly compared to that of other leading countries. Between 1965 and 1980 the United States ranked 15th out of 19 industrialized market economies in terms of economic growth; between 1980 and 1986 the United States ranked third out of 19. The most notable decline in gross domestic product growth rate was that of Japan: its average annual growth rate between 1980 and 1986 was 58.7 percent of what it had been between 1965 and 1980. In contrast, the U.S. average annual growth rate in 1980–1986 was 110.7 percent of what it had been in 1965—1980.[8] During the past five years (1983—1987) the U.S. and Japanese economies grew at almost the same rate, with the United States leading in three of these years. In all five years U.S. growth exceeded that of the European Community. The biggest economy has been getting bigger, absolutely and relatively. Declinist arguments that the United States has suffered precipitous decline in recent years and that the locus of economic production is shifting dramatically to Japan are simply not supported by the facts.

The decline in Japanese economic growth manifest in Table 1 was to be expected: no country will grow indefinitely at ten percent or more per year. As the Japanese economy has matured its growth rate has approximated that which may currently be considered normal for complex modern economies. In similar fashion, just as Japan has lost its edge in growth, so also has the United States lost its lead in productivity. In 1970 productivity in U.S. manufacturing was more than twice that of Japan. By 1986 the gap between the two had almost disappeared. There is little reason why the Japanese economy as a whole should grow much faster than the U.S. economy and there is little reason why an individual U.S. worker should be significantly more productive than a Japanese worker. On such indices

Table 1   AVERAGE ANNUAL GROWTH RATES OF REAL GNP

	United States	Japan	European Community
1961–1965	4.6	12.4	4.9
1966–1970	3.0	11.0	4.6
1971–1975	2.2	4.3	2.9
1976–1980	3.4	5.0	3.0
1981–1985	2.6	4.0	1.5
1986–1987	2.9	3.1	2.5
1983–1987	3.8	3.8	2.3

Source: Annual Report of the Council of Economic Advisers, in *Economic Report of the President,* Washington: U.S. Government Printing Office, 1988. Based on Table B-111, p. 374.

of economic performance, one should expect long-term convergence among countries at similar levels of economic development and with economies of comparable complexity.

Convergence in economic performance reinforces stability in the distribution of economic activity. The argument can be made that the GNP pattern that has emerged in the past two decades is, in some sense, the historically "normal" pattern, roughly approximating the distribution that existed before World War II. The world of the 1970s was, as Thorold Masefield put it, "a world restored—with the U.S. still preeminent if not predominant."[9]

Apart from the rapid growth of some developing countries, this pattern is unlikely to change drastically in the future. According to one estimate, for instance, the United States had 44.1 percent of the gross product of a total of 15 major countries in 1950, 31.6 percent of this total in 1980, and will have a projected 29.2 percent of the total in 2010. In that year, according to this estimate, the U.S. GNP of $7,859 billion (in 1986 dollars) will still be twice that of China ($3,791 billion), Japan ($3,714 billion), and the Soviet Union ($2,873 billion).[10]

In short, if "hegemony" means having 40 percent or more of world economic activity (a percentage Britain never remotely approximated during its hegemonic years), American hegemony disappeared long ago. If hegemony means producing 20 to 25 percent of the world product and twice as much as any other individual country, American hegemony looks quite secure.

Systemic Failures

A third set of phenomena cited by declinists consists of what might be termed systemic failures. These involve the sustained inability of America's society and its economy to function either at the levels of comparable societies or at levels presumed necessary to sustain the American role in the world. Since systemic characteristics have, by definition, been present for a long period of time, their contributions to American decline presumably stem from their cumulative impact. Among other deficiencies, declinists point to the poor quality of American primary and secondary education (manifested, for instance, in the low scores of American students in comparative tests of mathematics and reading skills), the small numbers of scientists and engineers produced in the United States (particularly compared to the high production of lawyers), and the complexity and inefficiency of American governmental policymaking processes. The most heavily emphasized systemic weakness, however, concerns low savings and investment rates.

Americans clearly save less than most other people. During the 1970s and 1980s U.S. gross savings as a proportion of GDP varied between 14.8 and 19.1 percent. During this period Japanese savings varied between 27.1 percent and 32.9 percent of GDP. In 1970 the Japanese savings rate was more than twice that of the United States (32.9 versus 16.1 percent); in 1987 it was almost twice the U.S. rate (28.2 versus 14.8 percent). Throughout these years U.S. savings lagged behind those of the other major industrialized democracies.

Similar differences existed in the relation of personal savings to disposable personal income. During the 1960s and 1970s the U.S. rate averaged about six percent; those of Germany and Japan averaged 14 percent and 20 percent respectively. In the 1980s the already low U.S. savings rate dropped even further, reaching 3.7 percent of disposable income in 1987. In 1987 net national savings were only 2.2 percent of GNP, compared to an average of eight percent between 1949 and 1981.

As one might expect, similar patterns across countries exist with respect to investment. Between 1965 and 1984 U.S. gross fixed capital formation varied between 17 percent and 19.8 percent of GNP. That for Japan varied between 27.8 percent and 35.5 percent of GNP. The OECD average, less the United States, varied between 21.6 and 26 percent.[11] Other measures of investment yield comparable results: the U.S. rates tend to be slightly more than half those of Japan and perhaps 75 percent of those of the other major industrialized democracies.

The significance of these differences in savings and investment can be debated, and mitigating factors may explain and compensate for some low U.S. rates. In addition, the poor U.S. performance seems not to have noticeably affected U.S. economic growth as yet. Nonetheless, clearly the declinists are right in highlighting savings and investment as long-term systemic weaknesses that require correction if economic growth is to be maintained.

Many, although not all, declinists go wrong, however, when they identify the reasons for poor U.S. performance. They argue that overexpenditure for military purposes crowds out investment for economic growth and hence leads to economic decline. Decline flows from imperialism and militarism.

This argument has little to support it, especially as applied to the United States. Kennedy's historical examples themselves suggest that the burden of empire usually becomes onerous when it amounts to ten percent or more of the society's product. Defense, however, takes only six to seven percent of American GNP. The declinists' thesis is clearly more relevant to the Soviet Union, which apparently (Soviet officials themselves claim they do not know for sure) spends 17 to 18 percent or more of its GNP for military purposes. Is this, however, a cause of Soviet decline? Its military sector is widely held to be the most technically efficient sector of the Soviet economy, and it is the only sector that is able to compete internationally. More generally, there is little comparative evidence to suggest that military expenditures are necessarily a drag on economic development. Some analysts, indeed, have argued that defense spending stimulates economic growth. One does not necessarily have to buy that argument in order to reject its opposite.

In fact, of course, how much a country invests is influenced by, but not determined by, how much it spends on defense. The Soviet Union spends close to three times as much of its GNP on defense as does the United States. It also invests more of its GNP than does the United States. This occurs at the expense of Soviet consumption. In theory, a country can allocate its resources as it wishes among consumption, defense, and investment. In fact, countries make different choices, and the countries with the three largest economies in the world do exactly that. It is difficult to get comparable figures for the Soviet Union and market economy countries, and the portions of government spending which are in fact investment do not always show up in national accounts. Nonetheless, a rough prototypical allocation of GNP for the three largest economies might be as follows:

- U.S. consumption (private and public) at about 78 percent of its GNP, Japan's at 67 percent, and the Soviet Union's 56 percent;
- U.S. defense spending at about seven percent of its GNP, Japan's about one percent, and the Soviet Union's 18 percent;
- U.S. investment at roughly 17 percent of GNP, Japan's at about 30 percent of its GNP, and the Soviets' about 26 percent.

In short, the Soviets arm, the United States consumes, Japan invests.

At present, efforts are being made in each of these countries to alter these patterns. General Secretary Mikhail Gorbachev apparently is attempting to limit Soviet military spending in order to increase consumption and investment. Japan is expanding its defense effort and is beginning to attempt to increase consumption. In the United States it is widely recognized that defense cannot be allowed to rise and investment should be expanded at the expense of consumption. How successful any of these efforts will be remains open to question.

In some measure, allocations to investment, defense, and consumption are a product of government policies and can be changed by changing those policies. Almost 75 percent of the U.S. federal government's revenues come from taxes on income, including interest on savings. By contrast, the Japanese government gets only 40 percent of its revenues from income taxes and until recently did not tax interest on 70 percent of Japanese personal savings. Changes in tax codes can affect the investment/consumption balance in both countries. Yet tax codes also reflect national values and culture. Much evidence exists that levels of arms expenditures have deep roots in national cultures, religion, and history and do not necessarily reflect only external threats.[12] Investment and consumption patterns are undoubtedly shaped by similar causes.

In any event, even if half the resources the United States uses for defense were shifted to investment, the American investment ratio would still lag behind the ratios of Japan and the Soviet Union. If the United States is to increase its investment ratio significantly, that increase will have to come primarily from the 75 percent or more of the GNP devoted to consumption, not from the less than seven percent committed to defense. If the United States falters economically, it will not be because U.S. soldiers, sailors, and airmen stand guard on the Elbe, the Strait of Hormuz, and the 38th parallel; it will be because U.S. men, women, and children overindulge themselves in the comforts of the good life. Consumerism, not militarism, is the threat to American strength. The declinists have it wrong; Montesquieu got it right: "Republics end with luxury; monarchies with poverty."[13]

III

The predominant view among declinists points to external expansion rather than internal stagnation as the principal cause of the decline of nations. This argument runs counter to a tradition of political thought going back to Plato and Aristotle which focuses on the internal ability of a society to renew itself. According to modern formulations of this view, a society declines when bureaucratic stagnation, monopoly, caste, hierarchy, social rigidity, organizational obesity, and arteriosclerosis make innovation and adaptation difficult or impossible. As societies age, these characteristics tend to become more predominant.

In his sophisticated theoretical analysis which departs from the declinist mainstream, Mancur Olson argues this point persuasively, explaining the decline of nations by the development of vested interests or "distributional coalitions" that reduce economic efficiency and constrain economic growth.[14] Societies whose social, economic, and political structures are substantially destroyed through war, revolution, or other upheaval grow rapidly. Over time, however, distributional coalitions develop and economic dynamism wanes. Although Olson does not discuss it in his book, the prototypical contemporary case of an economy grinding to a halt because of the constrictions imposed by distributional coalitions, is, of course, the Soviet Union under Brezhnev.

Successful societies, in contrast, are those that find ways short of their own destruction to sustain the dynamism of their youth. The structure of such societies will presumably encourage competition, mobility, fluidity, pluralism, and openness—all qualities that prevent a society from becoming mired in a network of collusive deals in which everyone benefits to everyone's disadvantage.

Viewed from this perspective, the United States is less likely to decline than any other major country. It is distinguished by the openness of its economy, society, and politics. Its engines of renewal are competition, mobility, and immigration.

Competition and opposition to monopoly, both public and private, are hallmarks of American society. The United States led the way in the modern world in attempting to institutionalize antitrust and antimonopoly practices in business. Government bureaucracy in the United States is weaker and more divided against itself than bureaucracies in most other countries. State-owned enterprises are rare. New companies are created—and go bankrupt—on a scale unknown in European societies. Small, new companies have been responsible for the bulk of the twenty million new jobs created in the past decade.

Labor unions have never been strong and are declining. American universities, it has been argued, are the best in the world because of the intense competition among them for faculty, students, and money.[15] Secondary education, it might be noted, is, in contrast, overwhelmingly a public monopoly and is inferior as a result; widely considered proposals for improving it are to introduce competition among schools for students and state support.

In comparison to other societies, individual mobility, both horizontal and vertical, is extremely high. Far more rapidly than elsewhere, American workers shift from job to job, up and down the income scale, in and out of the poverty brackets. People move from region to region at about three times the rate they do in European countries. With the notable exception of race, ascriptive obstacles to upward mobility have been relatively minimal compared to other societies.

The continuing flow of immigrants into American society reflects the opportunities it offers and contributes to its renewal. Historically, first- and second-generation immigrants have been a dynamic force in American society. Under the Immigration Act of 1965, about 600,000 legal immigrants enter the United States each year. Thousands more enter illegally. These newcomers renew the pools of cheap labor, entrepreneurial skill, intellectual talent, and driving ambition to succeed. Thirty-six of the 114 American citizens who won Nobel prizes in science and medicine between 1945 and 1984 were born elsewhere. In the 1940s and 1950s American scientific and intellectual life was tremendously enriched by Jewish refugees from Hitler and the children of East European Jewish immigrants before World War II. Today Asian-Americans sweep the intellectual honors. (About two percent of the total population, they make up 14 percent of the 1988 freshman class at Harvard.) In the coming decades, immigration also means that the American population will continue to grow, unlike those of many European countries and will remain relatively young, unlike that of Japan.

IV

The ultimate test of a great power is its ability to renew its power. The competition, mobility, and immigration characteristic of American society enable the United States to meet this test to a far greater extent than any other great power, past or present. They are the central sources of American strength. They are supplemented by three aspects of the American position in international affairs.

First, in comparison to other major countries, American strength is peculiarly multidimensional. Mao Zedong reportedly said that power grows out of the barrel of a gun; the declinists see power coming out of a belching smokestack. In fact, power comes in various forms and international influence can stem from very different sources. The Soviet Union, it has often been said, is a one-dimensional superpower, its international position resting almost exclusively on its military might. Whatever influence Saudi Arabia has in international affairs flows from its oil reserves. Japan's influence has come first from its manufacturing performance and then from its control of financial resources.

Countries dependent upon a single source of power, however, are highly vulnerable to degradation of the particular type of power in which they specialize. OPEC's power drops with falling oil prices; Japanese power is challenged by the rise of Taiwan, Korea, Singapore, and Thailand; Soviet power is reduced by the Reagan defense buildup. In addition, countries dependent on a single source can exercise influence only in arenas where that type of power is relevant. The Soviet Union does not cut much of a figure in international finance and Japan does not sway the military balance in the Middle East. Countries can, of course, attempt to transform one type of power into another, and economic power is more fungible than others. There are, however, very real limits to the extent to which conversion is possible, and it can be a very costly process.

In contrast to other countries, the United States ranks extraordinarily high in almost all the major sources of national power: population size and education, natural resources, economic development, social cohesion, political stability, military strength, ideological appeal, diplomatic alliances, technological achievement. It is, consequently, able to sustain reverses in any one arena while maintaining its overall influence stemming from other sources. At present, no country can mount a multidimensional challenge to the United States, and with one conceivable exception no country seems likely to be able to do so in the relevant future.

Second, U.S. influence also flows from its structural position in world politics. The United States benefits from being geographically distant from most major areas of world conflict, from having a past relatively free of overseas imperialism, from espousing an economic and political philosophy that is antistatist and, hence, less likely to be threatening to other peoples, from being involved in a historically uniquely diversified network of alliances, and from having a sense, stronger in the past than more recently, of identification with universal international institutions.

These factors pull the United States into a leadership role in dealing with international problems and disputes. They help create a demand for the American presence overseas. Slogans of "U.S. go home!" may command headlines, but in many regions the underlying fear is that the United States might just do that. Neither Germans, French, Dutch, nor (some say) the Soviets are eager for the United States to pull out of Europe. Many Filipinos act as if they wished the bases removed from their country, and some may actually want that to happen, but many others worry deeply that an American withdrawal from Southeast Asia would leave them to the tender mercies of the Soviets and the Japanese. Long before diplomatic relations existed between Washington and Beijing, China supported the American presence in Japan and Korea.

In similar fashion, the United States is called upon to play a leading role in the resolution of regional conflicts (Middle East, southern Africa), to balance and mediate between regional rivals (Greece, Turkey), and to assist other powers (Britain) or international institutions (the United Nations) in resolving other conflicts (Zimbabwe, Iran-Iraq). American involvement in a region generally tends to stabilize the status quo and to protect weaker powers from the regional leviathans. The exception to this pattern is the one region—Central America and the Caribbean—where the United States itself is the preponderant local power.

Finally, no alternative hegemonic power, with one possible exception, seems likely to emerge in the coming century. A short while ago, of course, it was widely thought that the Soviet Union would perform that role. Mr. Khrushchev talked confidently about the U.S.S.R. overtaking the United States economically and the grandchildren of Western capitalists playing under red flags.

These seem not just forlorn but bizarre hopes. The Soviet Union still has the resources, size, and military strength of a superpower, but it has lost out economically, ideologically, and diplomatically. Conceivably, the Gorbachev reforms could start a process that would put the Soviet Union back into competition to become the number-one actor on the world stage, but at the moment the success of his efforts is in doubt and the impact of the reforms, if they are successful, will not necessarily enhance Soviet power.

Currently, the popular choice—and the choice of the declinists—for the country that will supersede the United States is, of course, Japan. "The American Century is over," a former U.S. official has said. "The big development in the latter part of the century is the emergence of Japan as a major superpower."[16] With all due respect to Clyde Prestowitz, this proposition will not hold up. Japan has neither the size, natural resources, military strength, diplomatic affiliates, nor, most important, the ideological appeal to be a twentieth-century superpower.

In a world of instant communication, widespread literacy and social mobilization, a superpower has to stand for an idea with appeal beyond its borders. In recent history the United States and the Soviet Union have done this. Today the message of the Soviet Union is tattered and apparently rejected, in part by its own leadership. The appeal of the American message of political democracy and economic liberalism has never been stronger. Conceivably, Japan could also develop a message to the world, but that would require fundamental changes in Japanese culture and society.

In addition, most characteristics of a society impart both strength and weakness. American individualism, mobility, and competition encourage innovation but weaken cooperation, institutional loyalty, and commitment to broader community goals. The American constitutional system, well designed to minimize government and maximize liberty, is ill designed to produce sustained and coordinated action to deal with serious long-term problems. In Japan corporatism, hierarchy, consensus, and the close business-government relation spur its export drive. At the same time, however, such a social structure combined with a mature economy could be peculiarly prone to collusion, corruption, and stagnation. In a worst-case scenario—improbable but not inconceivable—Japan could face a Brezhnevian era in its future. Even without that development, Mr. Prestowitz's prediction as to which century belongs to which country is likely to be less accurate than that of Seizaburo Sato: "The twentieth century was the American century. The twenty-first century will be the American century."[17]

The most probable challenge to this prediction could come from a united European Community. The European Community, if it were to become politically cohesive, would have the population, resources, economic wealth, technology, and actual and potential military strength to be the preeminent power of the 21st century. Japan, the United States, and the Soviet Union have specialized respectively in investment, consumption, and arms. Europe balances all three. It invests less of its GNP than Japan but more than the United States and possibly more than the Soviet Union. It consumes less of its GNP than the United States but more than Japan and the Soviet Union. It arms less than the United States and the Soviet Union but more than Japan.

It is also quite possible to conceive of a European ideological appeal comparable to the American one. Throughout the world, people line up at the doors of American consulates seeking immigration visas. In Brussels, countries line up at the door of the Community seeking admission. A federation of democratic, wealthy, socially diverse, mixed-economy societies would be a powerful force on the world scene. If the next century is not the American century it is most likely to be the European century. The baton of world leadership that passed westward across the Atlantic in the early twentieth century could move back eastward a hundred years later.

V

Current declinism is, as noted, the fifth such wave since the 1950s. The first occurred in 1957 and 1958 as a result of Soviet missile launches and the Sputnik. The Gaither Commission, advising the president, and other groups warned that the United States was falling seriously behind the Soviet Union in science, technology, and future military capability. The Soviet Union was said to have a growth rate 50 percent higher than that of the United States, to be spending probably twice as much as the United States on armaments, and to be well on its way to establishing an unchallengeable lead in missiles while U.S. strategic forces were increasingly vulnerable. The Soviets were producing many thousands of scientists and engineers while American education was lagging.

A second declinist surge came at the end of the 1960s. President Nixon and his national security adviser took the lead in announcing the end of the bipolar world. The United States and the Soviet Union were losing their primacy and a "pentagon of power" was coming into existence. These predictions were quickly supplemented by academic warnings that the military power in which the United States and the Soviet Union excelled was rapidly losing its usefulness and that economic power, the hallmark of Europe and Japan, would ensure the emergence of the latter as at least the equals of the two previous superpowers.

A third declinist scare followed immediately thereafter, triggered, of course, by the OPEC oil embargo of 1973 and the dramatic increase in oil prices. The West and increasingly the United States were highly dependent on Persian gulf oil; whoever controlled oil controlled the economic life of the West and hence had the means to be the dominant influence, economically and politically, throughout the world. Saudi Arabia was seen as the new superpower as the huge flow of funds into Arab hands was recycled in U.S. bonds, factories, and real estate.

In the latter 1970s the Soviet Union again became the focus of fear in a fourth declinist surge. The U.S. defeat in Vietnam, Watergate, the expansion of Soviet power in Angola, Mozambique, Yemen, Ethiopia, Nicaragua, and eventually Afghanistan, and the continued development of Soviet nuclear forces that rendered U.S. strategic forces increasingly vulnerable, all generated the feeling that the Soviet Union was supplanting the United States as the world's number-one power. Feelings of decline and malaise, reinforced by another oil price hike and inflation, generated the political currents that brought Ronald Reagan to power in 1981.

These earlier decline scares were triggered by Sputniks and missiles, pressure on the dollar, oil embargoes and price hikes, SS-18s and Angola. The fifth wave has been largely triggered by budget and trade deficits and the seeming competitive and financial threat from Japan. It thus bears certain resemblances to the second wave of the late 1960s and early 1970s, and familiar themes are repeated. In 1972 President Nixon predicted the emergence of "an even balance" among "a strong, healthy United States, Europe, Soviet Union, China, Japan." In 1988 Professor Kennedy argues that we are "moving very swiftly" into a "multipolar world" with five centers of economic and military power: "the U.S., the Soviet Union, China, Japan, and the EEC."[18] It remains to be seen whether his prediction will be realized any more rapidly than President Nixon's.

The declinist waves often, not always, come at the end of American administrations. There is a certain *fin d'administration* air to them which leads one to suspect that people want to believe in decline at that moment. In this respect, they may be better indications of American psychology than of American power. Indeed, many developments that might otherwise be interpreted as evidence of strength or progress are pointed to by declinists as symptoms of decline. Current declinists, for instance, make much of the disappearance of American manufacturing industry. Fifteen years earlier, however, a substantial group of social theorists, including Daniel Bell and Zbigniew Brzezinski, articulated a widely accepted thesis that the relative decline of manufacturing industry was a sign of progress from industrial to post-industrial or technetronic society, and the United States was leading the world in that direction.[19] Decline, in short, may be in the eye of the beholder.

The prevention of decline, however, requires that it be there. In all its phases declinism has predicted the imminent shrinkage of American power. In all its phases that prediction has become central to preventing that shrinkage. Declinism is a theory that has to be believed to be invalidated. Given the openness of its politics and the competitiveness of its economy, the United States is unlikely to decline so long as its public is periodically convinced that it is about to decline.

The declinists play an indispensable role in preventing what they are predicting. Contrary to Professor Kennedy, the more Americans worry about the health of their society, the healthier they are.[20] The current wave will serve a useful historical function if it encourages the new president and Congress to take prompt and effective actions on the deficits and to inaugurate longer-term policies designed to promote saving and investment.

"If Sparta and Rome perished," asked Rousseau, "what State can hope to endure forever?"[21] The obvious answer is "no state" and that may be the right answer. The United States is not immortal and American preeminence is not inevitable. Yet, some states endure for extraordinary lengths of time, and little reason exists to assume that recent prophecies of American decline are more accurate than earlier ones. Every reason exists, however, to encourage belief in such prophecies in order to disprove them. Happily, the self-renewing genius of American politics does exactly that.

NOTES

1. Apart from the more academic international political economy literature, declinist works that have been widely discussed in policy debates and the general media include: Walter Russell Mead, *Mortal Splendor*, Boston: Houghton Mifflin, 1987; David P. Calleo, *Beyond American Hegemony*, New York: Basic Books, 1987; and, of course, Paul Kennedy, *The Rise and Fall of the Great Powers: Economic Change and Military Conflict from 1500 to 2000*, New York: Random House, 1987. In discussing declinist ideas, I will rely primarily on Kennedy's writings and statements, since they have had the greatest impact on public debate in the United States.
2. Kennedy, *op. cit.*, p. 534.
3. Peter G. Peterson, "The Morning After," *The Atlantic*, October 1987, p. 49.
4. Kennedy, *op. cit.*, p. 527.
5. Martin Feldstein, "Correcting the Trade Deficit," *Foreign Affairs*, Spring 1987, pp. 795ff.; James R. Schlesinger, "Domestic Policies and International Capital Flows," in Martin Feldstein, ed., *The United States in the World Economy*, Chicago: University of Chicago Press, 1988, pp. 652–653.
6. Kennedy, *op. cit.*, p. 525; Kennedy, "Does America Need Perestroika?" *New Perspectives Quarterly*, Spring 1988, p. 6; and his written submission to the House of Representatives, Committee on Foreign Affairs, Defense and International Affairs Task Force, June 21, 1988, p. 2.
7. Council on Competitiveness, *Competitiveness Index: Trends, Background Data, and Methodology*, Washington, D.C., 1988; Rachel McCulloch, *The Challenge to U.S. Leadership in High Technology Industries (Can the United States Maintain Its Lead? Should It Try?)*, Cambridge, Mass.: National Bureau of Economic Research, Working Paper No. 2513, February 1988, Table 2.
8. The World Bank, *World Development Report 1988*, New York: Oxford University Press, 1988, Table 2, pp. 224–225.
9. Thorold Masefield, "Co-prosperity and Co-security—Managing the Developed World," *International Affairs*, Winter 1989; Charles Wolf, "America's 'Decline': Illusion and Reality," *The Wall Street Journal*, May 12, 1988, p. 22.
10. Future Security Environment Working Group, *The Future Security Environment: Report to the Commission on Integrated Long-Term Strategy*, Washington, Department of Defense, August 1988, Chapter 1.
11. See Annual Report of the Council of Economic Advisers, in *Economic Report of the President*, Washington: U.S. Government Printing Office, 1988, p. 100; Jeffrey A. Frankel, "International Capital Flows and Domestic Economic Policies," in Feldstein, ed., *United States in the World Economy, op. cit.*, pp. 606–614.
12. See James L. Payne, *Why Nations Arm*, London: Basil Blackwell, 1990.
13. Baron de Montesquieu, *The Spirit of the Laws*, New York: Hafner, 1949, Vol. 1, Book VII, p. 98.
14. Mancur Olson, *The Rise and Decline of Nations*, New Haven: Yale University Press, 1982, especially Chapters 3 and 4.
15. See Henry Rosovsky, "Highest Education," *The New Republic*, July 13 and 20, 1987, pp. 13–14.
16. Clyde Prestowitz, *Time*, July 4, 1988, p. 28.

17. Seizaburo Sato, *The Economist,* Aug. 13–19, 1988, p. 30.
18. Richard Nixon, *Time,* Jan. 3, 1972; Kennedy, *New Perspectives Quarterly, op. cit.*
19. See Daniel Bell, *The Coming of Post-Industrial Society,* New York: Basic Books, 1973; and Zbigniew Brzezinski, *Between Two Ages: America's Role in the Technetronic Era,* New York: Viking Press, 1970.
20. Kennedy, *Rise and Fall, op. cit.,* pp. 529–530. One of Kennedy's most perceptive critics, Richard N. Haass, makes a similar argument, "The Use (and Mainly Misuse) of History," *Orbis,* Summer 1988, p. 419: "There is a real risk that predictions of decline could become self-fulfilling."
21. Jean-Jacques Rousseau, *The Social Contract,* London: J. M. Dent, 1947, Book III, Chap. XI, p. 73.

Understanding U.S. Strength

Joseph S. Nye, Jr.

Many Americans see the end of the Reagan administration as the end of an era. The popular press reports regularly on the decline of American power. The historian Paul Kennedy's 1988 book *The Rise and Fall of the Great Powers* became an unexpected best seller. Foreign-policy experts quote Walter Lippmann about the need to adjust the country's commitments to fit the country's strength. Public opinion polls reveal increased anxiety over economic security, and congressional resolutions press the allies to relieve the United States of some of its defense burdens.

American concern about decline is nothing new. As Arthur Schlesinger, Jr., pointed out in his book *The Cycles of American History* (1986), such anxieties have arisen from time to time since the earliest days of the Republic. History also suggests that concern among countries about their rise and fall can produce political instability. For centuries historians and political scientists have drawn lessons from Thucydides' conclusion that not merely the rise of Athenian power, but also the fear it created in Sparta, led to the Peloponnesian War, which was so fatal for ancient Greece. At the beginning of this century Great Britain was concerned about the rise of Germany, which in turn worried about the expansion of Russia. The resulting anxieties contributed to the start of World War I.

As the end of the Reagan administration and the end of the century approach, it is important to develop an accurate understanding of America's world position. Clearly, major changes in American power have taken place since the 1950s. Depending on the base year chosen, the United States then represented one-third to two-fifths of world product and world military expenditure, whereas today it is responsible for a little more than one-fifth of both measures. But the notion of American decline confuses different times and causes. There has been a relative decline since the 1950s but less decline in America's share of world product if the 1930s or

Joseph S. Nye, Jr., "Understanding U.S. Strength," *Foreign Policy*, 72 (Fall 1988): 105–129. Professor Nye's arguments are further elaborated in his 1990 work *Bound to Lead: The Changing Nature of American Power*, published by Basic Books.

the late 1960s is taken as the baseline. From a longer perspective, the century that began in the 1870s, when the United States became the world's largest economy, may be the first of several to come.

Moreover, the decline of America's position from the artificial high of the 1950s could have several causes. One is an absolute decline stemming from society's loss of cohesion and inventiveness generally. A second cause might be the external rise of a new economic and military power that surpasses the previous great power. A third cause combines both internal and external factors: The efforts to stave off a rising power might sap the internal strength of an older power.

None of these theories fits the United States well. It has not experienced an absolute decline, and relative decline is in large part an artifact of the extraordinary baseline of the 1950s. The United States is not being challenged by a rising military power. Nor are external commitments sapping America's internal strength. And, with certain domestic reforms, the United States will be better placed than most societies to adapt to the new dimensions of power in the information age.

Although the United States must adjust to a new era of multipolarity and interdependence in world politics, Americans should not understate U.S. strength. Misleading historical analogies and false anxieties might prompt Americans to adopt policies of retrenchment that, ironically, could produce the results they are supposed to forestall.

The theme of American decline ran like a dark thread through the 1980 presidential election. Images from the 1970s, such as gas-ration queues, Soviet troops in Afghanistan, and revolutionaries in Iran burning American flags, brought about fears in the early 1980s that reflected real problems. But these problems were exaggerated. One fear was expressed in the self-limiting inclinations on foreign affairs after the Vietnam War. U.S. foreign policy long has been characterized by cycles of inward- and outward-oriented attitudes. Thus it is not surprising that the reaction against the U.S. involvement in Vietnam limited the use of American power in other areas, such as Angola in 1975.

Similarly, the military dimensions of the U.S.-Soviet balance shifted during the 1960s and early 1970s. The Soviet Union had established rough strategic nuclear parity and an improved ability to support conventional and proxy forces far from its homeland. But many Americans overreacted in believing that these changes indicated Soviet superiority. They failed to discern the stagnation that clearly has constrained Soviet power in the 1980s.

Also in the 1970s, the United States grew dependent on imports for nearly one-half of its oil consumption. However, the degree of disruption was partly the result of inept domestic policies that controlled oil prices and failed to develop an adequate strategic petroleum reserve. The ensuing economic slowdown was typical of all of the big capitalist economies.

Two other changes in the American world position have deeper roots. One is that power in the global economy increasingly has spread among other countries, particularly U.S. allies. This was in large part the result of postwar American policy. Rather than seeking hegemony over its allies, the United States opted to stimulate their economic revival and create a strategic partnership in balancing Soviet power.

To the extent that the United States has had a grand strategy for foreign policy over the past 40 years, it has been to promote economic prosperity and political stability in Western Europe and Japan and a close alliance with them. As George Kennan, then a U.S. diplomat, pointed out after World War II, only a few areas in the world have the industrial and technological creativity to affect the global balance of power deeply: the United States, the Soviet Union, Western Europe, and Japan. Of these, Europe and Japan are close geographically to the Soviet Union. That they are close to America politically is profoundly important. The diffusion of economic growth was a deliberate U.S. foreign-policy goal and a wise one.

The other long-term cause of America's changed global position is the increased complexity of international interdependence, which has reduced the potential for any country to exercise decisive influence over the whole system. Complexity derives from more actors, more issues, greater interactions, and less hierarchy in international politics. The role of military force has changed in subtle ways. Force remains the most effective form of power in some situations: Witness U.S. actions against Grenada and Libya. But in general, force has become more costly for great powers to apply effectively, as the Americans found in Vietnam and the Soviets discovered in Afghanistan.

The Soviet experience in Afghanistan illustrates that the increased costliness of force does not constrain only democracies. But modern technologies, including cheap and reliable means of destroying planes and ships, may ease the way for both lesser states involved in regional rivalries and terrorist groups to employ force. The net effect of these changes eats away the international hierarchy traditionally based on military power. Other power resources, such as economic vitality, diplomatic skill, attractive cultural values, and a society attuned to an open flow of information, all become more important.

This erosion of international hierarchy is sometimes portrayed as the decline of America, as though the causes lie with its own internal processes. But with more than one-fifth of world military expenditures and global economic product, the United States still is the most powerful state in the world and will very likely remain that way far into the future. To understand what has happened, the distinction must be made between influence over other countries and influence over outcomes in the international system as a whole. The United States still carries more leverage than other countries. However, it has less leverage than in the past because the heightened complexity of interdependence makes extracting the outcomes it prefers more difficult. In addition, all of the major powers have less power than in the past over nationalistically awakened populations.

Thus the task of reversing the decline of American power that the Reagan administration accepted in 1981 was both easier and more difficult than it thought. It was easier because some of the causes of apparent decline reflected the particular conditions of the 1970s and had been exaggerated in public debate. It was harder because some of the factors in America's changing global position reflected not decline in the United States but historical trends in world politics. Trying to reverse those deeper external causes—incipient multipolarity and the increased complexity of interdependence—is like trying to turn back the tide. The American position of the 1950s cannot be recaptured. The relevant question is how a broader range of power resources can be used to meet American goals in this changed world.

By and large, the Reagan administration coped well with the short-term, self-inflicted causes of the relative decline of U.S. power in the 1970s. Despite the wasteful manner in which some of it was spent, the unprecedented real increase in the defense budget over the first 5 years of the Reagan presidency sent a strong signal both to the allies and to the U.S.S.R. Ronald Reagan's "get tough" attitude reinforced the message. Since perceptions of what the Soviets call the "correlation of forces" are influenced heavily by psychological factors, these actions went a long way toward reversing the effects of the inward orientation that followed the Vietnam War. Reagan in effect relaxed some of the "Vietnam syndrome" constraints on American foreign policy.

Reagan restored confidence in the institution of the presidency by following Dwight Eisenhower's example and realizing its monarchical potential. Alas, unlike Eisenhower, he was inattentive to the prime ministerial aspects of the job, and the Iran-*contra* scandal subsequently squandered many of the beneficial aspects of his public posture. If Reagan had quit after his first term, he could have been remembered widely as the man who restored American power and confidence after the pessimistic 1970s.

The larger question, however, is how well the Reagan administration responded to the longer-term trends in the diffusion of economic growth among the allies, to the emergence of multipolar dimensions in the non-military aspects of world politics, and to the increasing complexity of interdependence that complicates the application of American power. In these areas the Reagan record has been less satisfying. Michael Howard, an astute British observer, argues that 1987 "saw relations between the governments of the United States and its European allies reach a nadir" because of the inept handling of the nuclear guarantee at the superpower summit meeting in Reykjavík, Iceland, the Iran-*contra* affair, and the budget deficit. The Princeton University political scientist Robert Gilpin argued in the Summer 1987 issue of *Daedalus* that "the Reagan years have masked the profound developments that have occurred and the challenges they have posed. The United States has been living on borrowed time—and borrowed money—for much of the last decade; this has enabled the United States to postpone the inevitable and painful adjustments to the new realities in global diplomatic, economic, and strategic relationships."

BACK TO THE CENTER

In 1981 the new administration reflected the diversity of a victorious coalition. It included traditional internationalist Republicans, disaffected neoconservative Democrats, and unilateralists descended in part from the old isolationist wing of the Republican party. They agreed on an increased defense budget, a greater willingness to use force, hostility toward the Soviet Union, and a diminished role for arms control. Initially the Reagan coalition downgraded the role of international institutions and global issues such as human rights and nonproliferation.

In retrospect, two things are particularly striking about this 1981 world view. First, it differs considerably from Reagan administration policies in 1988. In some ways there is a greater difference between the views at the beginning and the end of the Reagan era than there is between Reagan and the Democratic opposition in 1988. Conservatives such as Howard Phillips ended up calling Reagan "a useful idiot for Soviet propaganda"; neoconservatives such as Irving Kristol complained that Reagan's "most dismaying performance has been in foreign affairs"; and the *Wall Street Journal* predicted that "the U.S. will lapse into a position of strategic inferiority, as the result of trends started in the last year of the Reagan Administration."

The second striking thing about the 1981 approach was its deviation from traditional Republican views of containment. In surveying postwar strategies of containment, the historian John Lewis Gaddis noted that the Democrats (Harry Truman, John Kennedy, and Lyndon Johnson) were fiscal liberals willing to tax and spend. They tended to take a broader view of containment because they were optimistic about the means of U.S. power. Republican fiscal conservatives (Eisenhower, Richard Nixon, and Gerald Ford) were more reluctant to tax and spend and thus chose more selective goals and methods of containment.[1] Not only did Reagan take an expansive view of containment, but his supply-side fiscal unorthodoxy broke the postwar partisan pattern. On security issues, he spent like a Democrat but taxed like a Republican. Reagan was drawn back toward the mainstream of postwar American foreign policy, but he refused to raise taxes to finance his strategy. Both points are important in judging Reagan's legacy for America's global position.

The most dramatic changes came in Reagan's rhetoric and policies toward the Soviet Union. Some explain the new approach as a response to changes in the Soviet Union that Reagan brought about. Talking and acting tough had helped bring the Soviets to the bargaining table. Reagan's defense build-up and the successful deployment of the intermediate-range nuclear missiles in 1983 certainly contributed to the Soviet view that their 1970s estimation of a favorable correlation of forces no longer held in the 1980s.

Yet there is a danger that Americans might learn lessons from the recent U.S.-Soviet relationship that are too simple. Economic problems in the Soviet Union and the client socialist countries, as well as a series of dying leaders, helped to persuade the Soviets that the correlation of forces had turned against them. The changes in Soviet policy under Mikhail Gorbachev have come in response not only to American pressure, but also to structurally rooted internal Soviet problems that would have existed whether or not Reagan came to power or Jimmy Carter had been re-elected.

Moreover, that Reagan began to soften his rhetoric in 1984, an election year, suggests that changes in the Soviet Union were not the only cause of the new U.S. policy. As an astute politician faced with growing congressional resistance to his nuclear modernization program, Reagan made adjustments.

By making the adjustments in 1984, Reagan deprived his Democratic opponent of a major campaign issue, the charge that he was the only postwar president not to meet with his Soviet counterpart. Now Reagan has taken part in more U.S.-Soviet summits than any other postwar leader. As the political scientist Samuel Huntington wrote: "By talking like Ronald Reagan, in short, Ronald Reagan may end up acting the way Jimmy Carter wanted to act but could not. Moderation, especially in practice, may be the child of extremism, particularly in rhetoric."[2] Although the causation is more complex than officials like to admit, Reagan has left U.S.-Soviet relations in better shape than he found them. In the management of the basic East-West balance, Reagan, so heavily criticized in his first term, deserves credit for these improvements.

Reagan's modification of the traditional Republican strategy of containment, however, has had less happy consequences. The so-called Reagan Doctrine of rolling back Soviet advances in the Third World has had mixed success. In one case, providing arms to the anticommunist rebels in Afghanistan, Reagan enjoyed broad popular and congressional support, and the policy scored an impressive success. But other cases have been more controversial at home and less successful abroad. Support for the anti-Sandinista *contra* forces in Nicaragua proved to be a major source of contention; Reagan failed to couple diplomacy with force, and administration efforts to bypass congressional restraints severely damaged Reagan's presidency.

Even greater damage was done, however, by abandoning the traditional Republican approach to financing security policy. The Reagan administration succeeded in shifting resources into defense with a 50 percent increase in real terms over the first 5 years. The share of gross national product (GNP) devoted to defense rose from slightly more than 5.2 percent to 6.3 percent. But Reagan failed to provide additional financing for this increase. Instead, the national debt rose by almost $1 trillion. In a sense, the tax reductions of 1981 gave away the revenue base that could have financed much of the increase in defense spending. As Senator Bill Bradley (D-New Jersey) wrote in the Spring 1988 issue of *New Perspectives Quarterly:* "In 1981, the government was defunded. This was a decision . . . that was taken by a small group of ideologues whose real objective was to eliminate government from many areas of American life. They chose to accomplish this goal by causing a crisis—the enormous deficits—which they assumed would force massive cuts in social programs." Although the deficits put congressional Democrats on the defensive, they did not force major social cuts.

The administration turned to financing its deficits through foreign borrowing, and to attract foreign funds it raised interest rates. Not only did the United States become the world's largest debtor country but also the influx of capital pushed up the value of the dollar, encouraging imports and discouraging exports. That, in turn, contributed to massive trade deficits, the erosion of the U.S. manufacturing sector, and rising domestic protectionist pressures. Federal spending's share of GNP rose from 20.5 percent in 1979 to 23.8 percent in 1986; the increase was financed by borrowing an average of 3.4 percent of GNP each year. This borrowing from other countries and against America's future will have to be serviced. In the future Americans will have to cut consumption and increase savings to defray the Reagan debt. The adjustment may be painful, but it is well within the capacity of the American economy over the next decade.

The twin deficits have created an uneasiness about the economic future. But some observers read more into America's economic problems at the end of the Reagan era. The analyst David Calleo, writing in the Spring 1988 *New Perspectives Quarterly,* believes that "thanks to economic strain and mismanagement, relative decline has begun to turn absolute." A particularly popular theory of imperial overstretch. In his formulation, economic change shifts productive capabilities and interests among countries. Growing countries project military power to protect their interests, but eventually the cost of projecting military power saps their strength. Then they are replaced by another rising economic power.

Kennedy's history is impressive and certainly correct about the importance of the economic foundations of power. But his theory of imperial overstretch does not fit the American case. In Kennedy's words, "The difficulties experienced by contemporary societies which are militarily top-heavy merely repeat those which, in their time, affected Philip II's Spain, Nicholas II's Russia and Hitler's Germany."[3] But the United States is nothing like Philip II's empire, where, as Kennedy shows, three-fourths of all government expenditures were "devoted to war or to debt repayments for previous wars." In the United States today, approximately 29 percent of the federal budget is spent on defense and veterans' benefits.

Even after Reagan's build-up, the current U.S. defense outlay is about 6 percent of GNP and is lower than those of the Eisenhower and Kennedy administrations, which spent about 10 percent. Those who wish to rescue the theory of imperial overstretch sometimes argue that the net burden today is greater because the United States has a lower share of world product than it had previously. They liken the United States to an aging man carrying a pack up a hill. He has become less able to carry the burden. But the facts still do not fit the theory. The ratio between the defense share of U.S. national product and the American share of world product has changed little since the 1950s.

Alternatively, theorists of imperial overstretch sometimes simply assume that defense spending is bad for the economy. They cite Japan's spending a bit more than 1 percent of its GNP on defense and its higher economic growth rate than the United States. Such simple correlations are misleading. South Korea and the People's Republic of China (PRC) spend a much higher proportion of their GNP on defense than Japan does; yet they have higher economic growth rates than Japan. Moreover, it is difficult to find careful and balanced economic studies that show that defense spending has a negative net impact on the economy. The myriad effects of defense spending are very complex, and the net effect is difficult to sort out.[4]

Cutting defense expenditures and withdrawing from global commitments might do little to solve U.S. economic problems, but it very likely would exacerbate America's international situation. Providing for the defense of other countries is a source of American influence and regional stability. It affects the way Western Europe and Japan respond to U.S. interests in the economic as well as the military and political arenas. For example, defense ties with the United States helped persuade Japan to rely on an American plane rather than developing a new fighter aircraft by itself. Further, Japanese business and government leaders appear to see no substitute for U.S. global leadership.

The Persian Gulf offers another example of the problems with backing away from foreign commitments. Although the United States receives only 7 percent of its oil from the gulf while Japan receives nearly 60 percent, a loss of gulf oil would severely damage the U.S. economy. The interdependence of world oil markets would spread a price rise equally for all oil imports regardless of source. The United States is in the gulf to defend its own as well as its allies' interests. America's influence there rests in part on the defense it provides for conservative oil-producing states. Power in the gulf does not come only out of the barrel of a gun, but neither does it come only from a barrel of oil.

Curtailing international commitments would leave the United States less able to influence other governments in areas such as cooperating against terrorism, slowing the rate of nuclear proliferation, restricting arms supplies, and managing regional balances. Pulling out of defense commitments would add to America's vulnerability rather than restore its strength.

Another fashionable analogy is drawn between the United States at the end of the twentieth century and Great Britain at the end of the nineteenth century. Those who question the theory of decline are likened to the conservatives of Edwardian England who did not want to face change.

Yet important differences exist between the British and American positions. Britain was a small island country governing a vast territorial empire and was heavily dependent on trade. Imports represented 25 percent of British GNP in 1914. The comparable U.S. figure in 1985 was 10 percent. Moreover, America already has allies that include the most significant countries in the world economy. The challenge is not to seek new allies but to maintain relations with those America already has. Cutting back on defense commitments to those allies would reduce U.S. influence with them over the broad agenda of common interests, as well as benefit the Soviet adversary in the East-West military balance.

Most important, Britain faced rising contenders in Germany, the United States, and Russia. The nearest of those contenders, Germany, not only had surpassed Britain in economic strength but also was en route to becoming militarily dominant on the European continent and a threat to Britain's supremacy. America's external situation today is very different. Its principal military adversary, the Soviet Union, is the power suffering from imperial overstretch. Not only does the U.S.S.R. dominate an unstable East European empire, but also its economy has suffered a serious deceleration of the growth rates that previously allowed Soviet expansionism. In addition, Soviet defense is estimated to be at least 15 percent of GNP, and some estimates place the costs of defense and empire generally at more than 20 percent of GNP—some three times higher than the relative burden on the U.S. economy.

It is not surprising, then, that Gorbachev seeks a period of external calm in order to concentrate on restructuring the Soviet economy. His task is monumental and may not be accomplished at all. Even over the long run it may prove impossible without major internal political changes. The proper analogy would be if Emperor William II's Germany, rather than passing Britain in economic and military strength, had been declining and searching for a breathing spell from its military buildup.

When the other major world powers indentified by Kennan some four decades ago are studied, it is difficult to say that any of them are overtaking the United States in both military and economic power. Western Europe has the skilled population and GNP but not the political unity to play a powerful defense or political role in the world. Despite the plan to reduce barriers within the Common Market by 1992, few observers predict that European integration will progress soon to a single government or a single security policy. In short, Western Europe lacks the necessary cohesion to play a great-power role.

Similarly, the PRC is a potential rival of the United States over a much longer term. Chinese economic growth has maintained the high annual rate of nearly 9 percent for much of the 1980s, and Beijing, of course, possesses a growing force of nuclear weapons. But the PRC remains a country whose human and technological infrastructure is developed to an extent far below that of the United States or even the Soviet Union. And in any case, the prospect is slight that the PRC will become an equal contender on a global scale in the next half century.

THE JAPANESE CHALLENGE

Thus the question of external challenge from rising powers boils down to the American relationship with Japan. Although Japan's economy is roughly one-half the size of America's, it has kept its political cohesion and its ability to grow consistently through the fat years of the 1960s, the lean years of the 1970s, and the mixed years of the 1980s. In addition, Japan has taken the lead from the United States in certain areas of high technology and has challenged the United States in markets long dominated by the Americans.

An increasing number of Americans believe that Japanese economic strength is a greater national challenge than Soviet military power. But economic competition is not a zero-sum game where one country's gain is its competitor's loss. Japan has chosen the strategy of a trading state rather than of a military power. In this role Japanese growth not only challenges the United States but also benefits it through greater choice for American consumers and competition that keeps American industry on its toes. For example, the rise of Japanese competition has had both a useful and a painful effect on the American automobile industry. Of course, the competition should be fair; governmental help and hard bargaining will be necessary to prevent the erosion of certain strategic industries, such as semiconductors. But such a government role should not expand into broad protectionism.

Is it inevitable that Japan will develop military power commensurate with its economic power? Not necessarily. Military posture does not always closely follow economic power. It took 70 years from the time America became the world's foremost economic power to fully project its military strength and become a dominant factor in the global military balance.

An American strategy that forced Japan to spend more of its GNP on defense or closed U.S. markets might push Japanese nationalism into full-blown independence from the United States. A tolerable situation could become a true threat. Spending 1 percent of its GNP on defense has allowed Japan to develop a military capability on the scale of the major West European countries. Those who would press Japan to triple its defense spending should realize that the probable consequences include frightening the PRC, South Korea, and the Southeast Asian countries into increasing their defense expenditures and perhaps pressuring the United States to increase its military spending in the area.

The balance of power in East Asia illustrates the complexity of the situation America now faces. Twenty years ago the United States squandered lives, resources, and prestige in a futile effort to contain communism in Southeast Asia. The prevailing image was the domino theory. A more realistic metaphor would have been the game checkers. As the West should have learned from the Yugoslavian experience, the nationalism of one communist country can be used to check another. The current pattern of relations among communist states in East Asia follows the realist adage that "the enemy of my enemy is my friend." If the Soviet Union is colored red, the PRC black, Vietnam red, and Cambodia black, the pattern of the larger Asian game outside Indochina is not dominoes at all. Thus despite the American defeat in Vietnam and Vietnam's occupation of Cambodia, East Asia is an area of relative tranquility where American security interests are well protected.

In fact, the American position is unique in the East Asian balance. Only the United States is both an economic and a military superpower. As a result the United States has more influence in the area than any other country. Both the PRC and Japan want the United States involved in diplomatic events. The U.S. naval presence and alliances are an important source of American strength. East Asia is a balance of asymmetries in economic and military strength, with the United States best placed to moderate among them. A sensible U.S. strategy for Asia must build upon a complex view of power that includes military and economic dimensions and uses America's unique diplomatic position.

The economic dimensions of power require another look at the sources of American strength. In his article in the Summer 1987 issue of *Daedalus,* Gilpin says that

> the economic crisis of the American System is a consequence of the long-term relative decline of the American economy and, more immediately, the policies of the Reagan Administration. . . . At the same time that the United States has assumed the largest portion of the burden of financing the American System and of confronting the growth of Soviet power, the American people have demanded both an ever-rising standard of living and improved government services.

The issue of American competitiveness in the international economy has touched a raw nerve. It is noted often that America's share of global exports of manufactured products declined from 21.3 percent in 1957 to 13.9 percent in 1983. Part of that decline resulted from the ill-conceived fiscal policies described above; but part had deeper roots. The American economy has a much lower rate of saving than do those of its major industrial competitors, leaving fewer resources for investment. While the American economy has been more successful in creating jobs in the 1980s than those of the West European states, most have come in the service sector where measured rates of productivity growth are lower than in manufacturing. Annual U.S. gains in productivity have averaged 1.4 percent in the 1980s, down from 2.7 percent between 1947 and 1968.

The United States will need to invest more in human resources, particularly in education. American test scores in mathematics and the sciences compare poorly with those of other industrial countries. The United States does not produce enough engineers to meet its needs. Fully one-fifth of American engineers are foreign or foreign-born. America's global share of new patents has been declining as Japan's has been rising.

These problems are serious, but they are not irremediable if Americans develop an effective political consensus. Americans should be cautious about overinterpreting such problems as symptomatic of long-term declines in the work ethic or American management. Rather than a diminishment of the work ethic, a large part of the export problem was the overvaluation of the dollar. With a fall in the value of the dollar, exports began to increase. Other changes reflect the evolving nature of the international economy. For example, the evolution of manufacturing by transnational corporations demonstrates their ability to shift production from place to place in the global market. Such transnational flows create problems, but they can also offer rewards for the national economy. While domestic manufacturing matters, it would be a mistake to use indexes of manufacturing exports as the sole criterion for judging America's economic role in the world.

Throughout the centuries statesmen and other observers have made mistakes in perceiving the metric of economic power. For example, in the seventeenth century, mercantilist theorists who focused on Spain's reserves of gold bullion would not have understood the rise of France with its stronger administrative and commercial structure, or later, Britain with its conditions favorable to political stability and the industrial revolution. At the turn of the century, when the historian Brooks Adams used the control of metals and minerals as the predictive index of future military and economic power, he was led to expect the ascendancy of Russia and China. But as the Harvard University social scientist Daniel Bell has pointed out, the core of postindustrial societies lies in the professional and technical services, and in that realm the United States and Japan are the two leading countries.

In Bell's ordering, the first technological revolution came 200 years ago with the application of steam power to transportation and factory machine production. The second technological revolution arrived a century ago with the spread of electricity and chemistry that allowed the production of synthetics and plastics. The third technological revolution, underway today, is joining computers and telecommunications to produce such technologies as television imagery, voice telephone, digital computer data, and facsimile. These technologies in turn offer a single though differentiated system of services from interlinked computers and electronic mail to information storage and retrieval. This revolution is changing the notion of markets from geographic places to global networks.[5] So the United States remains at the forefront of new sources of economic power, even though it shares that position with Japan. The United States should exploit its competitive advantage in information-based production processes, an advantage that is directly related to the openness, decentralization, and democracy of the American system. This is precisely where the communist societies are at their weakest. As Gorbachev realizes, a closed system could prevent the Soviet Union from remaining a first-rate global power in the information age.

The principal danger at the conclusion of the Reagan era is that misunderstood causes and nationalistic impulses will lead to inappropriate responses. A *Newsweek* poll published on February 22, 1988, showed economic nationalism rising in the United States, with one-half of the respondents favoring trade barriers to reduce the flow of foreign products into the country. In fact, protectionism in America is on the rise; the percentage of U.S. imports that are protected rose from 8 percent in 1975 to 21 percent in 1985.[6] But inward-turning and protectionist responses would cut the United States off from the open flow of goods, talents, and information that are sources of its strength; they allow the United States to draw upon global resources in its periodic surges of self-renewal. For example, while Americans are properly concerned that the American education system does not yield enough engineers, the other side of the coin is that few societies remain so open that they are able to cope with a shortage of talent by importing and absorbing it. The openness of American society, as manifested in the success of new immigrants, is a great source of strength not shared by the Soviet Union or Japan.

At a more general level, the economist Mancur Olson, in his study *The Rise and Decline of Nations* (1982), found that falling productivity and growth are linked to declining domestic competition. Advanced societies face the danger of domestic sclerosis as interest groups use government to protect their privileges and thereby curb national competitiveness. The best remedy for such institutional and group sclerosis is maintaining an open attitude to international competition and talents.

Seen in this perspective, the appropriate U.S. strategy is not to withdraw from international commitments in the illusory hope of protecting America from interdependence or arresting the change in its relative power position. On the contrary, such measures would contribute to, rather than arrest, the relative decline of American power because the sources of that change are mainly outside the United States. Instead, Americans must face the fact that they have to transfer resources from consumption to investment. At home, they need to invest in new technologies, infrastructure, and human resources. Abroad, they need to invest in defense, aid, and institutions that afford leverage with the international system on the many issues in which the United States is heavily interdependent.

Recent polls suggest that Americans are increasingly concerned about international economic security. The next decade may see a considerable shift in the foreign-policy agenda, particularly if a Soviet preoccupation with domestic matters leads to a period of quiescence in East-West relations. Still, Americans must remember that the balance of military power will remain crucial so long as there are great powers. Domestically, America must rebuild the economic foundation of its power by reasserting a balanced fiscal policy; providing incentives for saving; investing in education, research, and development; and using government judiciously to smooth the process of adjustment. If America is to compete in a global information economy, it cannot afford its current waste of human resources. Enhancing its competitive position will also require hard bargaining to develop international cooperation, as well as stronger support for international economic institutions. Similarly, the United States must strengthen the structure of the postwar alliances whereby two of the five major centers of global power are allied with America rather than the Soviet Union. This will require a better sharing of alliance burdens, for Western Europe and Japan can do more. But the United States should avoid escalating friction and pullbacks over burden sharing that could rupture the alliances and thus diminish U.S. power.

Such a strategy will also require a strong conventional and naval presence along with a backdrop of credible nuclear deterrence. Certainly domestic reforms are needed to reduce wasteful military expenditure. At the same time, the United States can explore opportunities created by internal Soviet problems for reducing the level of armament at which the balance of power is maintained. Although arms control has not saved money in the past, it may in the future if U.S.-Soviet relations continue to improve. Finally, in a world where transnational communications are the basis for economic and social strength, the United States needs to be forthright in asserting its values of openness and human rights, for American influence rests not only on military and economic might but also on values. The attractiveness and global spread of American culture in the information age is a subtle yet important source of influence that few other countries possess.

A GAIN FOR BOTH SIDES

Of the two major sources of long-term change in America's position in the world, the emergence of multipolarity is less difficult to deal with than the increased complexity of interdependence. America will remain a preponderant power in a multipolar structure if it wisely maintains its alliance relationships. No other state is likely to surpass the United States in both economic and military power in the next few decades unless America follows foolish policies. As the United States struggles with Japan over how to distribute the mutual gains of interdependence in trade and investment, Americans must remember that both sides can, in fact, gain. Japan should be encouraged to accelerate the internal economic expansion suggested in the report of its own Advisory Group on Economic Structural Adjustment for International Harmony, also known as the Maekawa report. It can be asked to play a larger role—in return for a larger voice—in maintaining international institutions. Japan should be pressed not to increase military expenditures but to boost assistance to strategically important developing countries such as the Philippines and to help relieve the enormous burden of Third World debt. Japan will soon replace the United States as the largest aid donor in the world.

Similarly, in America's struggle with its European allies over defense burden sharing, Americans have to avoid the use of tendentious measurements of percentages of GNP because they fail to reveal major European contributions—60 percent of NATO's active forces (partly by draft) and 80 percent of alliance force reserves. The size of American defense budgets reflects broader defense interests than West Europeans have. It is in part the price of being the preponderant global power. Moreover, unilaterally withdrawing U.S. troops from Europe would not save money unless the army's overall size were cut. Over the coming decade adjustments will be made in the NATO alliance, but they should come through consensus among the allies and arms control with the East, not from unilateral measures. Otherwise the Soviets would simply receive a gift.

It will be crucial not to let the politics of petulance blind the United States to its long-term interest. After all, the U.S. involvement in European defense is not a matter of charity. It is a matter of self-interest in maintaining a global balance of power and stability in a region that has led the way into two world wars. Even in a period of reduced Soviet threat, the American presence remains a stabilizing force in Europe. Gradually, with further European integration, including enhanced defense cooperation, the American presence may become less central. But the U.S. interest in European stability will continue.

In the coming years the greater problem for the United States and other countries will be the complexity of interdependence and the difficulty of maintaining world order in the face of such issues as the spread of technology for nuclear-armed ballistic missiles and biochemical warfare, the rise of fundamentalist religious and nationalist movements, terrorism, environmental pollution, and the maintenance of the international economic and financial system. The United States will be the leading state in an era when, in contrast to the 1800s or the 1950s, the conditions for economic hegemony no longer obtain. As a great power, America will not be helpless, but it will face considerable frustration in trying to move others toward sharing the burdens of leadership. Leadership by unilateral example will be important, but the United States will have to coordinate its positions with those of other states more closely than it did in the extraordinary period immediately following World War II. In that sense, the problem will not be solely the challenge that the growing multipolarity of major states will pose for American power, but also what might be called entropy, or the notion that the major states will not be able to maintain order as easily as in the past.

It is safe to predict that some places in the Third World will always be experiencing turmoil. Communication advances and social modernization stir populations from old patterns and lead to strong pressures on weak political institutions. The best approach will be to have nationalism work for, rather than against, America. Nationalism is the most effective counter to Soviet expansionism even though nationalist regimes are sometimes anti-American as well. The United States is bound to be confronted with governments that refer to themselves as Latin American Marxists, African socialists, and Asian communists. With some exceptions, the United States can be relaxed about the domestic social changes that such regimes proclaim so long as those changes do not ally them with the Soviet opponent in ways that alter the world balance of power or contribute to the problems of disorder, terrorism, and proliferation. The dividing line between what is domestic and what is international can never be absolute, and America cannot be indifferent to gross violations of human rights abroad. Nonetheless, the broad distinction can help the United States to thread its way through social complexity and Third World change without backing itself into a corner that benefits the U.S.S.R.

The capacity of major powers to control affairs is further constrained by the increase in the number of foreign-policy issues that has accompanied growing economic and social interdependence. As a great power with a stake in world order, the United States has a strong interest in developing and supporting international regimes—sets of rules and institutions that govern areas of interdependence. Such regimes vary greatly in their scope and membership. They deal with everything from monetary issues, international trade, and management of natural resources to cooperation against terrorism, control of armaments, environmental pollution, and the management of particular geographic areas.

Orderly processes allow the pursuit of multiple national interests in a way that reduces their mutual interference, the cost of tradeoffs, and the degree of risk. Thus even an imperfect nonproliferation regime reduces some uncertainties and insecurities. The treaties and institutions that govern international nuclear energy are not perfect, but they do create a presumption against proliferation that slows the spread of nuclear weaponry and thus enables the United States to cope better with potential destabilizing effects. Certainly it does not follow that all international regimes are in the U.S. interest. Some may be beyond repair. For one, the United Nations Educational, Scientific and Cultural Organization may be too politicized to serve American interests in scientific and educational cooperation. In some cases the United States may want to establish smaller groups with higher standards. Some trading partners may be willing to agree to a greater reduction of nontariff barriers than could be agreed upon by all members of the General Agreement on Tariffs and Trade. Sorting out U.S. interests as they relate to each international organization certainly will require more attention in the future.

Importantly, the dichotomy between unilateral and multilateral action is not as sharp as it first appears. That may seem paradoxical, but unilateral action can play an important role in building up international regimes. Exercising leadership often calls for someone to go first. Nonetheless, the unilateral action should not prevent others from joining in, and the action should be consistent with the long-term goals the United States has for international organizations.

A special form of unilateral action, of course, is the use of military force. Judiciously used, or threatened, military force can play a critical role in maintaining international order. For example, the knowledge that great powers can, at least in principle, assert their right of passage through contested waters is certainly a useful background to American bargaining over the law of the sea. Indiscriminate use of force, however, can prove too costly in relation to the particular interests pursued. Trying to seize oil fields as a response to an oil crisis could bring about an economic crisis. In some cases, such as environmental pollution and international monetary issues, force is largely irrelevant, and diplomatic hints of force may generate resentment that interferes with American objectives. A key consideration is always the coupling of force with legitimacy. If a military action is regarded broadly as justifiable at home and abroad, the cost of employing force can be reduced. In contrast to its rhetoric, the Reagan administration's practice was more cautious in the direct use of American force and thus kept the costs within manageable bounds.

In sum, Americans are right to be concerned about the changing position of the United States in world politics. But portraying the problem as American decline is misleading. For it directs attention away from the real causes, which lie in long-term changes in world politics, and suggests remedies that would weaken rather than strengthen American standing. Withdrawal from international commitments would reduce U.S. influence without necessarily strengthening the domestic economy.

Although the next decade will require Americans to cope with Reagan's debts, there is no reason why the world's wealthiest country cannot pay for both its international commitments and its domestic investments. Americans can afford both social security and international security. The ultimate irony of the Reagan legacy would be if Americans perceived the short-term problems he has bequeathed as indicators of long-term decline and responded by cutting themselves off from the sources of their international influence. In short, it is important not to mistake the short-term problems arising from the Reagan period's borrowed prosperity for a symptom of long-term American decline. The latter need not be the case unless Americans react inappropriately to global changes and inflict the wounds upon themselves.

NOTES

1. John Lewis Gaddis, "Containment and the Logic of Strategy," *National Interest,* no. 10 (Winter 1987–1988): 27–38. *See also* Gaddis, *Strategies of Containment* (New York: Oxford University Press, 1982).
2. Samuel P. Huntington, "Renewed Hostility," in *The Making of America's Soviet Policy,* ed. Joseph S. Nye, Jr. (New Haven: Yale University Press, 1984), 289.
3. Paul Kennedy, *The Rise and Fall of the Great Powers: Economic Change and Military Conflict from 1500 to 2000* (New York: Random House, 1987), 444.
4. See Gordon Adams and David Gold, *Defense Spending and the Economy: Does the Defense Dollar Make a Difference?* (Washington, D.C.: Defense Budget Project, 1987).
5. See Daniel Bell, "The World and the United States in 2013," *Daedalus,* Summer 1987, 1–31.
6. Alan Murray, "As Free-Trade Bastion, U.S. Isn't Half as Pure as Many People Think," *Wall Street Journal* 1 November 1985, 1.

Index